W9-CDX-492

LEARNING AND MEMORY

AN INTEGRATED APPROACH

LEARNING AND MEMORY

AN INTEGRATED APPROACH

John R. Anderson

Carnegie Mellon University

JOHN WILEY & SONS, INC.

New York • Chichester • Brisbane • Toronto • Singapore

ACQUISITIONS EDITOR   Karen Dubno
MARKETING MANAGER   Catherine Faduska
PRODUCTION EDITOR   Deborah Herbert
MANUFACTURING MANAGER   Susan Stetzer
PHOTO RESEARCHER   Hilary Newman
ILLUSTRATION   Jaime Perea

This book was set in 10/12 ITC Palatino Light by V&M Graphics, Inc. and
printed and bound by Courier Stoughton. The cover was printed by the Lehigh Press.

Recognizing the importance of preserving what has been written, it is a
policy of John Wiley & Sons, Inc. to have books of enduring value published
in the United States printed on acid-free paper, and we exert our best
efforts to that end.

Library of Congress Cataloging-in-Publication Data
Anderson, John R. (John Robert), 1947-
    Learning and memory : an integrated approach / John R. Anderson.,
      p.   cm.
    Includes bibliographical reference and index.
    ISBN 0-471-58685-4
    1. Learning, Psychology of.   2. Memory.   3. Conditioned response.
  I. Title.

BF318.A53   1994
153.1—dc20
                                         94-14189
                                         CIP

Printed in the United States of America

10 9 8 7 6 5 4 3 2 1

Preface

Research on learning and memory has been part of psychology since it began as a science in the 1800s. At the height of the behaviorist era, around 1950, learning was perceived as the key issue in psychology. Behaviorists believed that understanding any aspect of human behavior depended on understanding how that behavior was acquired. Learning was pushed somewhat from center stage by the cognitive movement in the 1960s. Cognitive psychology emphasized understanding the functioning of the mature cognitive system rather than understanding the learning that led to the system. The cognitive movement also marked a major schism in the field. Traditional learning research continued on animals, while research on human memory became a major part of cognitive psychology. These two research traditions have evolved as almost completely separate disciplines.

Research on animal learning and research on human memory must address many of the same issues. For this reason their continued development independent of one another is not satisfactory. Many colleges recognize the relationship between the two areas by offering a Learning and Memory course rather than separate courses for learning and memory. The scientific community is also starting to recognize that pursuing independent paths is not desirable. Animal learning research has become more and more cognitive over the decades, and animal learning theory is no longer cast in such stark behaviorist terms that it is incompatible with the cognitive perspective. Also researchers on animal learning have profitably borrowed methods and theory from human memory research. On the other side, research on human memory is turning more and more to issues concerning the neural basis of memory, which inevitably require the use of animal models. Cognitive psychology has become increasingly interested in the adaptive function of human memory, which again brings in the biological perspective. Finally, cognitive psychologists are beginning to recognize the centrality of learning to the understanding of memory. In the last few years, the two areas of research have come closer together.

This textbook on learning and memory examines the current state of the traditional learning and cognitive fields, and identifies the exciting opportunities for the synthesis of ideas. Learning and memory are brought together in one textbook because of my firm belief that one cannot properly describe research in either field without describing research in the other. Ideally, there should be only one field to describe. However, research and theory still tend to divide into that concerned with animal learning and that concerned with human memory.

In addition to reviewing the behavioral research and theory in the various areas, the discussion of this book emphasizes several themes. Two of these themes contribute to the integration of research on animal learning and human memory. One theme, that of understanding the neural basis of learning and memory, is presented throughout the text at appropriate places. This accurately reflects the current state of learning and memory research, and the excitement about new advances in understanding the neural basis of learning and memory.

The second major theme is appreciating the adaptive character of learning and memory. Learning and memory are processes that arise in all species as solutions to the problem of adapting to the changing structure of the environment. This functional view of the system is stressed throughout the book, and it is emphasized how different mechanisms can achieve the same function.

This book has been, in part, an effort to gain a perspective on my own intellectual history. I entered psychology in the 1960s, interested in animal learning. I joined the cognitive movement and spent years doing research on human memory. Dissatisfied with the rather narrow perspective this research gave on issues, I gradually shifted to research on cognitive skills and educational applications. As part of this experience I have come to appreciate that human learning and memory are part of an adaptation of the human to the environment. These adaptational interests brought me back to the research on animal learning that I had left more than 20 years earlier. I found that there were many new and deep analyses in that field and that many were quite compatible with the issues that I was dealing with in my own research. Although this is a textbook and not a monograph, these perspectives clearly color the story that I tell in these chapters.

Plan of the Book

Chapter 1 reviews the history of learning and memory research. It explains ideas and paradigms that have dominated the field and why they became prominent. It also reviews some of the ideas that have failed. These past efforts have set the stage for current research, enabling rather dramatic progress toward an understanding of human learning and memory.

The rest of the book describes the modern understanding of learning and memory. Chapters 2 through 4 are principally devoted to research on animal learning: Chapter 2 addresses classical conditioning, Chapter 3 describes instrumental conditioning, and Chapter 4 discusses issues of reinforcement.

Although there have been some useful human studies in these areas, animal research is the basis for most current progress. This section of the book reflects this fact, while also noting applications of this research to humans. The principal contribution of this research to human learning is probably the establishment of a better context in which to understand human learning and memory.

The remainder of the book focuses on human learning and memory, although there are many instances where the later chapters turn to animal research for perspectives. Chapters 5 through 8 review the rather sophisticated understanding of the nature of memory that has evolved over the past four decades. Chapter 5 examines how information is processed and stored in temporary memories when it is initially received. Chapter 6 investigates how a permanent record of this information is built up in long-term memory. Chapter 7 explores how information is maintained over potentially long periods of time and what underlies forgetting. Chapter 8 looks at the different ways in which information can be retrieved when it is needed.

The final three chapters examine issues of learning and memory in a larger context. Chapter 9 reviews the learning phenomena that arise when potentially complex skills are acquired, such as learning how to use a word processor. This topic contrasts with most of the research described earlier in the book, which is concerned with learning simple facts and behaviors more tractable for experimental study. Chapter 10 focuses on issues of inductive learning, how people discover things about the structure of their environment. This chapter returns to some issues of the early conditioning chapters, but it employs the perspective of the human situation. The final chapter is concerned with the major application of research on learning and memory to education, bringing together many of the ideas discussed in the preceding. chapters.

This book incorporates a number of features to help achieve instructional and learning goals. The terminology of the field can be a bit overwhelming. I have tried to minimize unnecessary jargon, but part of the educational mission of this book is to introduce the student to the important concepts. Each important new term is highlighted in the text and explained. These definitions are brought together in a glossary at the end of the book. I have also concluded each section of every chapter with a summary statement that identifies the main point of the section. This provides students with a way to check their understanding of the sections and to quickly identify the content of a chapter. To assist the instructor, Michael Toglin of SUNY at Cortland has prepared an Instructor's Manual that includes chapter outlines, teaching tips, media resources, and a test bank.

Acknowledgments

Writing this book has afforded me the enjoyable experience of reflecting on the intellectual structure of our field. Such reflection is best not done in isolation, and I appreciate the efforts of others to help set an appropriate context for me.

Preface

The undergraduates in my learning and memory class have provided an important part of that context. It has been a major challenge to understand how to communicate this field to the next generation in a way that is meaningful to them. However, it has been an enjoyable challenge, and I have been much helped by their feedback. For another student's perspective, I turned to my son Jay, who read the book with me. He has been a stern critic and a great help.

My experience with Wiley has been exceptional. From the outset, my editor, Karen Dubno, has been closely involved in the project. She organized an outstanding set of reviews and has provided helpful feedback. The following reviewers provided insightful comments about the book and about their teaching experiences. They have been very helpful in trying to achieve the twin goals of accurately reflecting the intellectual character of the field and communicating that character to an undergraduate audience: Victor Agruso, Drury College; Robert Allen, Lafayette College; John Anson, Stephen F. Austin State University; William Baum, University of New Hampshire; Steven Coleman, Cleveland State University; Robert Crowder, Yale University; Ellen Gagné, Catholic University; Peter Graf, University of British Columbia; James Grau, Texas A & M University; Robert Green, Case Western Reserve University; Mike Grelle, Central Missouri State University; Douglas Hintzman, University of Oregon; David Hogan, Northern Kentucky University; John Jahnke, Miami University; Douglas Mandra, Francis Marion University; Philip Marshall, Texas Tech University; Ralph Miller, SUNY-Binghamton; Tom Moye, Coe College; Mitch Rabinowitz, Fordham University; Ken Salzwedel, University of Wisconsin-Whitewater; Michael Scavio, California State University-Fullerton; Richard Schmidt, UCLA; Robert Schneider, Metropolitan State College; Steven Sloman, Brown University; John Staddon, Duke University; Edward Wasserman, University of Iowa; Fred Whitford, Montana State University. I particularly thank Steven Coleman, who read the book in its entirety and whom I came to regard as the best indicator of whether I was succeeding or not. Lael Schooler also went through this book in its entirety with me. We had many enjoyable conversations in my office as we reflected on where the field is going. Anne Boynton-Trigg was terrific as a developmental editor, keeping me on task for every topic from the Rescorla–Wagner theory to attitudes about mathematics education. I can truly say that in 25 years I have never had as good an editorial experience. There still may be flaws in my ideas and my exposition, but it is surely not for lack of ample and judicious feedback. Finally, I thank my secretary, Helen Borek, who once again kept up with the endless revisions while keeping track of all the aspects of my professional life.

Pittsburgh, PA

JOHN R. ANDERSON

Contents

7 RETENTION OF MEMORIES 232

Contents

1

Perspectives on Learning and Memory

Learning and Adaptation

Learning is a crucial activity in a human culture. The very existence of a culture depends on the ability of new members to learn sets of skills, norms of behavior, facts, beliefs, and so on. People create educational institutions devoted to learning and invest a substantial fraction of their resources in them. They spend a large proportion of their lives not doing, but rather learning to do. Humans are exceptional in how plastic they are behaviorally; they can learn to live in the world of the Stone Age tribes in New Guinea and in the weightless world of an astronaut orbiting the earth. Of course, humans have no monopoly on learning. Primitive creatures are capable of some degree of learning, as are certain computer programs today. However, the human capacity for learning is unmatched by that of any other living or artificial thing.

Survival of a species requires that its members behave in a way that is adapted to their environment. Behavior can become adapted to the environment in two ways. Through evolution, pressures from the environment select behavioral traits that are optimal in that environment and these traits can be passed from generation to generation as part of the innate genetic endowment of the species. For example, human beings are born with a sucking reflex that becomes activated when the infant's mouth is placed near its mother's nipple. Through learning, the second mode of adaptation, the organism adjusts its behavior to reflect what it has learned about its environment. Because adaptation through innate behaviors enables the organism to enter its environment immediately ready to act, it is preferable to adaptation through acquired behaviors, which entails a dangerous learning period during which the organism does not know how to act.

Why, then, would any behavior be acquired through learning rather than innately specified? Some environments are not stable or predictable enough to enable behaviors to be shaped through an evolutionary process. When the environment changes, the behaviors that served one generation will not serve the next. For example, honeybees must learn new routes to food every year and humans must adapt to technological revolutions every generation. The advent of the automobile, for instance, required that humans learn a set of behaviors not anticipated in their evolutionary history. Species' behaviors are shaped by learning to the extent that their environments are complex and changing. The more variable the environment, the more plastic the behavior must be.

Species can be placed on a dimension of behavioral plasticity. For some species most behaviors are innately specified; others are capable of learning a great many new behaviors. The creature with the greater learning capability is not necessarily at the advantage in terms of its ability to survive. As an example of three creatures on this continuum of behavioral plasticity, consider the cockroach, the rat, and the human. The cockroach is capable of learning only the simplest things, such as avoiding a dangerous area; the rat can learn a lot more about the nature of its environment and for this reason has been one of the favorite laboratory animals for studies of learning; the human is proportionately still more plastic. Despite their vastly different learning abilities, all three creatures inhabit modern cities and one has not proved notably more successful than the others in terms of the survival of its species. Within the city, they occupy different niches that afford great variability in the range of behaviors. Cockroaches live mainly within walls and survive using basic instincts, such as fleeing light and seeking tight, crowded places, that have served them for 320 million years (and that serve them well in modern apartments). The behavior of rats is richer. Rats are capable of exploiting the knowledge they acquire about their environment, such as various paths between locations and where food is to be found. The behavior of humans is even more complex, particularly considering the human potential for using a wide variety of artifacts, from light switches to pesticides. It is the potential complexity of the behavior that creates the demand for learning.

An especially important dimension of complexity in the human environment is produced by the artifacts or tools created by humans themselves. City dwellers (and to a large extent rural dwellers) live in an environment almost totally of their own fashioning and one that is far different from the environments of just 100 years ago. A common belief is that the human capacity for complex learning is responsible for tool use, but archaeological evidence suggests the reverse. Small-brained human predecessors started using tools. Only after tool use was well established did brain size increase in our evolutionary ancestors. Tool use created a more complex environment that required greater learning capacity. Once learning capacity increased, tools became even more complex, creating a snowball effect: more complex environments demanded more learning, which created more complex environments, and so on. The snowball has in some sense spun out of control in modern society—technology has created an environment of great dangers (drugs, environmental hazards, nuclear weapons, etc.), which we have not learned to manage and which we have had no time to adjust to through evolution.

Learning is the mechanism by which organisms can adapt to a changing and nonpredictable environment.

Behaviorist and Cognitive Approaches

The title of this book is *Learning and Memory*. The subsequent section offers definitions of these two terms. Although related in their meanings, the two words have referred to separate lines of research in psychology. *Learning* has been associated with behaviorist approaches to psychology, and *memory* has been associated with cognitive approaches to psychology.

Behaviorism is an approach to psychology that started in the United States at the beginning of the twentieth century. Behaviorists wanted to develop theories about the behavior of an organism with no reference to what might be happening in the mind of the organism. They held that speaking about things happening in the minds of lower organisms, such as rats, was unscientific and thought only a little better of attributing minds to humans. Behaviorism dominated American psychology for the first half of this century. Some of the key ideas of behaviorism will be reviewed in a later section of this chapter that discusses some of behaviorism's most important practitioners.

Learning was central to the behaviorists' conception. They thought that most human and animal behavior could be understood as the result of basic learning mechanisms operating on the experiences provided by the environment. Much of the behaviorist research on learning took place with nonhuman animals for a number of reasons:

- Behaviorism arose at the turn of the century when there was still great excitement about the new ideas surrounding evolution. Darwin had argued that humans were continuous with other animals; it was believed that the laws of learning that held for animals would hold for humans.
- Animals might allow researchers to study learning in a purer form, not contaminated by culture and language.
- Experiments performed on animals were subject to fewer ethical constraints than those performed on humans.

A major theoretical shift in psychology began in the 1950s based, in part, on the belief that the behaviorists had created too simple a picture of human cognition. **Cognitivism** was the position that complex mental processes played an important role in shaping human behavior, and much of

---

the field shifted to studying these mental processes. Cognitive research has come to occupy a greater and greater proportion of psychology since the 1950s, and a correspondingly smaller proportion has been occupied by purely behavioral research. Cognitive psychologists studied learning, but they did so in the guise of so-called memory experiments on human subjects. A typical experiment might involve having subjects study a section from a textbook such as this and later testing the subjects to see what they could recall.

This history has resulted in two traditions for studying learning. The behaviorally oriented tradition focuses on animal learning; the cognitively oriented tradition focuses on human learning. Much of the research on human learning has been conducted under the title of human memory, hence the pairing of *learning* and *memory* in the title of this book. The separation of these two traditions is fundamentally artificial and has begun to break down. Much current research on animal learning has a strong cognitive orientation, and there has been a resurgence of more behavioristic learning theories in research on human memory.

This book covers the research from both traditions, but takes note of the syntheses occurring in the field today. The emphasis throughout is on the significance of research results for understanding human learning and memory. The basic purpose of this chapter is to describe the traditional approaches to studying learning and memory and so set the stage for the remaining chapters, which are concerned with what these approaches have revealed. Before proceeding we must turn to the thorny issue of defining the terms *learning* and *memory*.

For historical reasons research on learning has been divided into behaviorally oriented studies of animal learning and cognitively oriented studies of human memory.

Definitions of Learning and Memory

Most people feel they have a good sense of what is meant by the terms *learning* and *memory*. However, it can be frustratingly difficult to specify the precise meaning of these terms. The following is the most commonly offered definition of **learning**:

Learning is the process by which relatively permanent changes occur in behavioral potential as a result of experience.

Let us review the key terms in this definition.

Process. Learning typically refers to the *process* of change. In contrast, memory typically refers to the *product* of the change.

Relatively permanent. The qualification that change is relatively permanent is designed to exclude certain transient changes that do not seem like learning. Fatigue is a simple example of what learning theorists want to exclude. A person who performs a task repetitively may become tired, resulting in a change in performance. With rest, the individual returns to the original performance level.

Behavioral. For learning to be significant for psychologists, whether they are behaviorists or not, there has to be some external manifestation of the learning in the behavior of the individual. If a person learns something, but it does not affect the person's behavior because it is kept secret, how is a psychologist to know that it was learned? Psychologists cannot see into the minds of their subjects; they can only observe behavior and make inferences from their observations.

Potential. Not everything we learn has an impact on our behavior. An individual may learn another person's name but never have occasion to use it. Thus, psychologists do not demand a spontaneous change in behavior, only a change in the *potential* for behavior. The psychologist must devise a behavioral test to tap this potential and show that learning has taken place. For instance, to determine whether a pet has learned a trick it is often necessary to offer that pet a reward. Psychologists make a distinction between learning and performance, where the former refers to some underlying change and the latter refers to a behavioral manifestation of that change.

Experience. Behavioral potentials change for reasons other than learning. As we age our bodies develop and our potential for behavior changes, but we would not want to consider physical growth learning. Similarly, a serious injury might substantially change a person's potential for behavior, but we would not want to consider breaking an arm learning. The term *experience* is intended to separate those behavioral changes that are the concern of the learning theorist from those that are not.

Now let us consider a definition of the term **memory**.

Memory is the relatively permanent record of the experience that underlies learning.

This definition of memory depends on the definition of learning. However, it contains an element that is not included in the definition of learning, the term **record**. Use of this term implies the theoretical proposal that there is some mental change that embodies the learning experience. This mental change is the creation of a memory record. Learning theorists have not always agreed that learning requires the creation of memory records. John Watson, the founder of the behaviorist school of learning, argued that there was no such thing as memory and that people just learned ways of behaving. Behaviorists preferred theories that were couched only in behavioral terms and distrusted references to mentalistic constructs such as a memory record. The reluctance to discuss such memory constructs has largely disappeared, however, because researchers are beginning to understand the neural changes that embody the memory records. When it is possible to speak of some precise neural change rather than some vague mental change, the behaviorists' distrust of memory constructs begins to evaporate. A portion of this book is concerned with the neural basis of memory.

Learning refers to the process of adaptation of behavior to experience, and memory refers to the permanent records that underlie this adaptation.

History of Research on Learning and Memory

Psychology as a scientific field is only a little over 100 years old. From the beginning, learning has been an important area of research. One of the reasons for the early interest in learning was Charles Darwin's theory of evolution. The publication of his *Origin of the Species* in 1859 captured the imagination of the intellectual world with its emphasis on how natural selection had changed species so that they were better adapted to their environment. Learning theorists saw their research as the obvious extension of Darwin's. Whereas Darwin was concerned with adaptation across generations of a species, learning theorists were concerned with the ongoing adaptation of an individual member of a species within its lifetime. Understanding the relationship between species-general adaptation and individual learning is a current research topic.

Three research enterprises begun at the turn of the twentieth century influenced much of the subsequent history of research on learning and memory. One was a series of studies undertaken by the German psychologist Hermann Ebbinghaus, who used himself as his sole subject. The second was a series of studies conducted by a Russian physiologist, Ivan Pavlov, on conditioning in dogs. The third was a series of studies directed by an American psychologist, Edward Thorndike, on trial-and-error learning in cats. Pavlov and Thorndike helped inspire the American behaviorist movement, which dominated research on learning in the first half of the twentieth century. Ebbinghaus started a tradition of research that, after the cognitive revolution in the 1950s and 1960s, became the dominant paradigm for the study of human memory. The history of research on learning in the United States is really a history of the research traditions started by these three individuals and how these traditions interacted with the intellectual mood of American psychology.

The research of these three pioneers and of other influential psychologists is presented next. The purpose of this historical review is twofold. First, it introduces the methodologies that are part of current research practice. Second, it sets the background against which current research and theory can be appreciated, in particular, by showing that a number of ideas about learning and memory were considered before the field settled on the current conceptions.

Research on learning and memory was started by Ebbinghaus, Pavlov, and Thorndike at the turn of the twentieth century.

Hermann Ebbinghaus (1850–1909)

Ebbinghaus performed the first rigorous studies of human memory and published his treatise *Über das Gedächtnis* ("Concerning Memory") in 1885. Ebbinghaus used himself as his sole subject. He taught himself series of nonsense syllables consisting of consonant–vowel–consonant trigrams, such as DAX, BUP, and LOC. He thought nonsense syllables were better experimental material because they had no prior learned associations. In one experiment, Ebbinghaus learned lists of 13 syllables to the point of being able to repeat the lists twice in order without error. He then looked at his ability to recall these lists at various delays. He measured the amount of time he needed to relearn the lists to the same criterion of two perfect recitations. In one case it took 1156 sec to learn the list initially and only 467 sec to relearn the list. He was interested in how much easier it was to relearn the list. In this example, he had saved 1156 − 467 = 689 sec. Ebbinghaus expressed this savings as a percentage of the original learning: 689 ÷ 1156 = 64.3 percent. Figure 1.1 displays these measures of retention as a function of the delay with relearning in what is referred to as a **retention curve**. Initial forgetting is rapid, but the rate of forgetting slows down dramatically over time. The function in Figure 1.1 is said to have **negative acceleration** because of the rapid decrease in the rate of forgetting. Chapter 7 discusses retention curves in detail.

In another experiment Ebbinghaus relearned the lists of nonsense syllables each day for 6 days. Figure 1.2 shows the number of trials needed to relearn the lists each day. As shown, the number of trials decreased over time, reflecting improved learning of the lists.[1] The plot in Figure 1.2 is referred to as a **learning curve**. Like the retention curve in Figure 1.1, it is negatively

[1]Smaller numbers imply better performance in Figure 1.2, which uses a dependent measure of trials to relearn; larger numbers imply better performance in Figure 1.1, which uses a dependent measure of percentage of time savings.

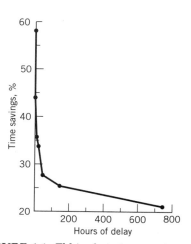

FIGURE 1.1. Ebbinghaus's retention function showing the percentage of time saved as a function of delay. Ebbinghaus used delays from 20 min. to 31 days.

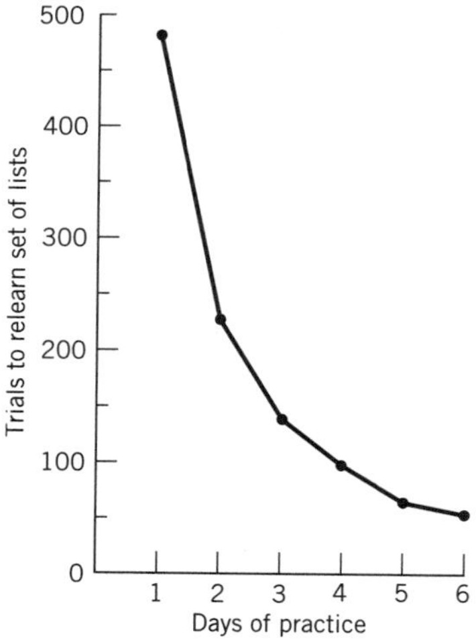

FIGURE 1.2. Ebbinghaus's practice data, showing the total number of trials needed to master a set of lists as a function of the number of days of practice.

accelerated, with smaller gains each day. The shape of learning curves is discussed in more detail in Chapter 6.

Ebbinghaus's primary contributions were methodological and empirical. He showed how human memory could be rigorously studied, and he identified some important empirical relationships, such as the retention and learning curves, which have stood the test of time. Ebbinghaus's theoretical explanations for the phenomena did not have much influence on the learning research that followed.[2] However, he did sow the seeds of a tradition of research on human memory that eventually became more prominent than the learning research on animals.

> *Ebbinghaus established experimental methodologies for studying memory phenomena, such as the retention curve and the learning curve.*

[2]Ebbinghaus's theory of remote associations was an exception. It was the dominant theory of serial list learning until the modern era, when it was replaced by the chunking hypothesis (see Chapter 6). A series of papers discussing Ebbinghaus's contributions was published in 1985 in the *Journal of Experimental Psychology* on the 100th anniversary of his treatise.

Ivan Petrovich Pavlov (1849–1936)

Pavlov's landmark discovery of the conditioned reflex was an accidental by-product of his Nobel Prize–winning study of the physiology of digestion. As part of his research, he put meat powder in a dog's mouth and measured salivation. He discovered that after a few sessions precise measurement was impossible, because the dogs salivated as soon as the experimenters came into the room. Pavlov began to experiment with this phenomenon, which is known as **classical conditioning**.

Figure 1.3 illustrates classical conditioning in Pavlov's experimental situation. The basic methodology starts with a biologically significant **uncondi-**

FIGURE 1.3. Experimental procedure in classical conditioning. (*a*) CS is paired with US that evokes a UR; (*b*) as a result the CS acquires the ability to evoke the CR; (*c*) the CS can continue to evoke the CR for some time after the US is removed, but will eventually extinguish.

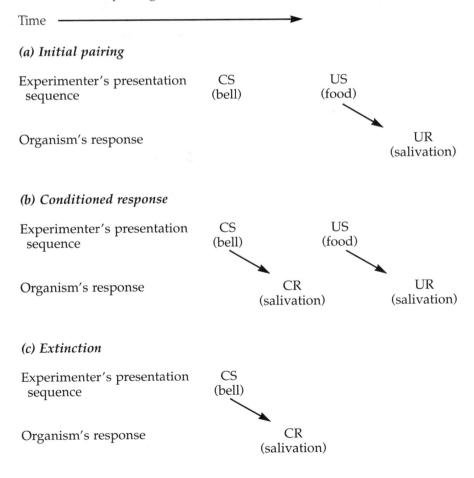

Pavlov observing the conditioning of a dog.

tioned stimulus (US), which reflexively evokes some **unconditioned response (UR)**. For instance, food is a US and salivation is a UR. The US is paired with a neutral **conditioned stimulus (CS)**, such as a bell. After a number of such pairings, the CS acquires the ability to evoke the response by itself. When the response occurs to the CS it is called a **conditioned response (CR)**.

Although Pavlov's original research involved food and salivation, a variety of USs and URs have been used to develop CRs. A frequently used paradigm with humans involves conditioning an eye blink (UR), which occurs in response to a puff of air to the eye (US). A light or tone repeatedly paired with the puff of air acquires the ability to evoke an eye blink in the absence of the original US. Eyelid conditioning is also a frequent paradigm with nonhumans.

A classical conditioning paradigm that has received considerable research focus in the last few decades involves the **conditioned emotional response (CER)**. When an animal, such as a rat, is presented with an aversive stimulus, for example, a mild shock, it responds in a characteristic way. Its heart rate accelerates, its blood pressure elevates, and it releases certain hormones. It also tends to freeze and halt whatever response it has been performing. Parts of this response pattern can be conditioned to a CS, such as a tone. To measure the CER researchers train an animal to perform some task, such as pressing a lever for food; the degree to which the animal freezes and so reduces its rate of lever pressing when the CS is presented is taken as a measure of the strength of the CER.

Chapter 2 discusses contemporary research and issues involving the classical conditioning paradigm, but some of the basic phenomena established by Pavlov (1927) are worth noting here.

1. *Acquisition.* The magnitude of the conditioned response can be measured as a function of the number of pairings between the US and the CS. The CR does not suddenly appear in full strength. Figure 1.4 illustrates that the strength of the CR gradually increases with repetition. This is referred to as the process of **acquisition**. The typical **conditioning curve** obtained during acquisition shows a little increase at first, then a larger increase, until some asymptotic level is reached at which the rate of increase levels off. The pattern of initial slow conditioning, then rapid, and then slow again is often summarized in the term **S-shaped curves**. Chapter 6 compares the conditioning functions (or curves) obtained in classical conditioning with learning curves, such as those obtained by Ebbinghaus (Figure 1.2). They are similar but not the same in that the conditioning function often starts off with rather slow change, whereas the learning curve almost always shows its most rapid change at first.

2. *Extinction.* What happens when the US is no longer paired with the CS? Figure 1.4 shows that the magnitude of the conditioned response gradually decreases with the number of trials in which no US occurs. This is referred to as the process of **extinction**. The extinction function for conditioning has a similarity to the retention or forgetting function for memory (e.g., Figure 1.1). However, as with the relationship between the acquisition functions for mem-

FIGURE 1.4. Acquisition and extinction of a conditioned response. (After Pavlov, 1927). *Source:* From *Introduction to psychology*, Eighth Edition, by Rita L. Atkinson, Richard C. Atkinson, and Ernest R. Hilgard. Copyright © 1983 by Harcourt Brace & Company, reproduced by permission of the publisher.

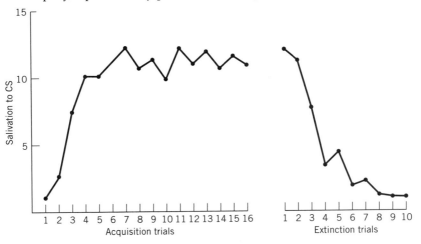

ory and conditioning, there are differences. The most important is a methodological difference between the experiments that produce the two functions. A forgetting function is obtained by waiting, without presenting a stimulus; but extinction requires presentation of the CS without the US.

3. *Spontaneous recovery.* Some time (e.g., a day) after a series of extinction trials, the CS can be presented again. The magnitude of the CR often shows some recovery. This *spontaneous recovery* is one difference between forgetting and extinction, because there is seldom, if ever, any spontaneous recovery from forgetting.

4. *Temporal ordering.* Conditioning is strongest when the CS precedes the US and often fails to occur if the US precedes the CS. For instance, eyelid conditioning is unsuccessful if the CS (tone) follows the US (puff of air). Depending on the response, the optimal interval between the CS and the US can vary from .5 sec to 30 sec or more. The order dependency of conditioning is not found in the results from a typical memory experiment. In a memory experiment a subject might have to learn to say one word like *dog* in response to another word like *cream*. The subject's learning of this fact does not depend on the order in which the two words are studied.

Pavlov speculated about the neural basis of classical conditioning. He proposed that neural excitation flowed from an earlier and weaker center in the brain to a later and stronger center; that neural excitation in the brain center aroused by the conditioned stimulus flowed to the brain center aroused by the unconditioned stimulus. The CS excitation evoked the response when it arrived at the US center. Pavlov embellished this physiological proposal with many speculative ideas that found little subsequent support. Several alternative theoretical analyses have been offered over the years. Although disagreeing with Pavlov on many details, researchers have tended to regard classical conditioning as a direct reflection of automatic neural processes of association. Thought to reflect automatic learning, classical conditioning has been a favorite paradigm in studies trying to understand the neural basis of learning, as shown in Chapter 2. Classical conditioning has also gained popularity in such physiological research because it can be displayed in primitive organisms, which are often easier subjects for physiological study. For example, Chapter 2 includes a discussion of conditioning in the sea slug, whose nervous system is much easier to study than that of mammals.

Despite the tendency to see classical conditioning as reflexive and automatic, Chapter 2 shows that modern understanding of the phenomenon often views it in a more cognitive and less reflexive light. Even today, however, classical conditioning is often regarded as the paradigm of choice for the study of simple and basic learning processes.

Pavlov discovered that when a neutral stimulus (CS) is paired with a biologically significant stimulus (US), the CS acquires the ability to evoke responses associated with the US.

Edward L. Thorndike (1874–1949)

Thorndike studied a rather different learning situation than did Pavlov. His original research was reported in 1898. Figure 1.5 illustrates Thorndike's experimental apparatus, called a puzzle box. He placed a hungry cat in such a box with some food outside. If the cat hit an unlatching device (e.g., a loop of wire) the door would fall open, and the cat could escape and eat the food. Cats were given repeated trials at this task, and Thorndike was interested in how quickly they learned to get out of the puzzle box. Thorndike's observation was that cats would at first behave more or less randomly, moving about the box, clawing at it, mewing, and so on, until they happened to hit the unlatching device by chance. He referred to this as trial-and-error learning. Over trials the random behavior gradually diminished as the cats headed for the unlatching device sooner and hence were able to leave the box sooner. Figure 1.6 shows typical learning curves relating number of trials to time to get out of the box.

Arguments continue as to whether Thorndike's cats gradually learned (over a series of trials) to get out of the box or whether they suddenly caught on and learned on a single trial. Thorndike chose to see gradualness in these learning curves and proposed that the correct response of hitting the unlatching device was gradually strengthened to the stimulus situation of being in the puzzle box, so that it came to dominate the other random responses. He thought that this strengthening process was automatic and that it did not require any cognitive activity on the part of the cats.

FIGURE 1.5. One of the four puzzle boxes used by Thorndike in his doctoral thesis.

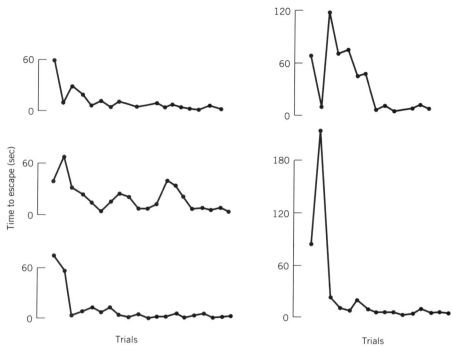

FIGURE 1.6. Learning curves for five cats in Thorndike's puzzle boxes. *Source:* From *Psychological Monographs, Volume 2* (Whole No. 8). by E. L. Thorndike. Animal intelligence: An experimental study of the associative processes in animals. Copyright © 1898 by The Macmillan Company. In the Public Domain.

The kind of learning process Thorndike studied is referred to as **instrumental conditioning**, in contrast with Pavlov's classical conditioning. In both cases a response is learned to a stimulus situation. In classical conditioning the stimulus is the CS and the response is the CR. In Thorndike's puzzle boxes, the stimulus is the puzzle box and the response is the appropriate unlatching action. Both kinds of learning show the phenomena of practice, extinction, and spontaneous recovery. In instrumental conditioning the response is performed to obtain the **reinforcer** of escape and food. The reinforcer (food, escape) may be seen as analogous to the US in classical conditioning in that it is the biologically significant stimulus. However, the US precedes the response in classical conditioning, whereas in instrumental conditioning obtaining the reinforcer is conditional on the response. Some people view instrumental conditioning as a more volitional kind of learning, but many view it, as did Thorndike, as every bit as automatic as classical conditioning.

Thorndike remained an active researcher and theoretician throughout his life. He was especially interested in applications of learning theory to education and is associated with a number of principles of learning. The following three principles are particularly important and identify issues that remain fundamental today.

1. *Law of effect.* Thorndike believed that the reinforcer was critical to learning. As he originally formulated his **law of effect**, reinforcers, such as food, strengthened stimulus–response connections (or associations), and punishments, such as shock, weakened them. Later evidence convinced Thorndike that punishment was relatively ineffective in weakening responses, but he maintained his belief that reinforcement was absolutely critical to learning.[3] The position that reinforcement was necessary to learning, common to a number of learning theories of his time, provoked numerous attempts at experimental disproof. The most notable research efforts were the latent learning experiments, discussed later in this chapter in the section on Edward Tolman's work.

2. *Law of exercise.* Thorndike originally proposed that repeated practice of a stimulus–response association strengthened it. He later retracted this statement and argued that pure exercise did not have a benefit and that only rewarded exercise produced learning. He pointed to experiments such as that of Trowbridge and Cason (1932) in which subjects practiced drawing 4-in. lines without any feedback and failed to improve in accuracy. However, in many situations unreinforced practice does appear to lead to improvement, for example, rehearsing material for a test. Indeed, as discussed in Chapter 6, practice seems to be a fundamental variable in learning and memory.

3. *Principle of belongingness.* In 1933, Thorndike accepted the notion that some things are easier to associate than others because they belong together. This was a concession to the Gestalt psychologists of the time who argued that it is easier to associate things if they are perceived as belonging together. Thorndike accepted the principle of belongingness with some reluctance, because it seemed to involve a cognitive component in the mechanical process of forming an association. This idea of belongingness has played a large role in modern theories of learning and memory. Animals have certain biological predispositions to associate things; for instance, as indicated in Chapter 2, rats are especially prepared to associate taste with poisoning. Also, in the arena of human memory how material is organized affects what is easy to associate; for instance, as shown in Chapter 6, memory for a pair of words is greatly enhanced if they are imagined in an interactive visual image.

Thorndike and Pavlov provided much of the inspiration for the behaviorist movement that dominated American psychology in the first half of the twentieth century. They were thought to have shown that learning could be understood as the direct association of stimuli and responses without postulating intervening mental processes. This idea led to the belief that all behavior could be accounted for in terms of such **stimulus–response bonds**. John

---

[3]As discussed in Chapter 4, Thorndike's assessment of reinforcement and of the ineffectiveness of punishment was incorrect.

Watson, who is credited with founding the behaviorist movement in the 1910s, was greatly influenced by Thorndike and Pavlov. Watson argued that mental constructs such as decision making and memory were excess baggage and that all human behavior could be understood as the result of learned associations between stimuli and responses.

> *Thorndike thought that a stimulus–response bond would be formed whenever a reinforcement followed emission of the response in the presence of the stimulus.*

Clark L. Hull (1884–1952)

From roughly 1930 to 1970, American psychology was dominated by a series of grand learning theories. These theories came to overshadow the ideas of Thorndike and Watson, who were considered intellectually shallow by comparison. Certainly, the grandest of the grand was Hull's behavior theory, which was not only impressive in its own right but became the reference point for new theoretical ideas in the 20 years after his death. A group of learning theorists called neo-Hullians (e.g., Abram Amsel, Frank Logan, Neal Miller, O. H. Mowrer, Kenneth Spence, and Allan Wagner) tried to extend his theory in various ways.

The basic goal of Hull and the other theorists was to develop a systematic theory of classical and instrumental conditioning to explain all behavior—human and animal. The details of their theories are of historical interest only, but the concepts and issues that they defined remain important to research on learning. Hull's final theory (Hull, 1952a), involved many elaborate equations, but can be summarized by this one:

$$E = (H \times D \times K) - I$$

Each symbol in this equation reflects a critical construct in Hullian theory, and it is worthwhile going through them one at a time.

E—Reaction potential. The ultimate goal of the Hullian theory was to predict something called reaction potential, which determined the probability, speed, and force with which a behavior would be performed in response to a stimulus. The organism was viewed as having a set of potential responses, each with its own force or reaction potential, striving to become the actual behavior of the organism in that situation. So, in running a maze, a rat might have the potential responses of turning left, turning right, and stopping to scratch itself. To determine what response would actually occur would require knowledge of the controlling factors—the *H, D, K,* and *I* in Hull's equations.

H—Habit strength. A strength of association was built up between stimulus and response through past reinforced trials. Thus, Hull's theory embraced Thorndike's law of effect in positing that reinforcement was necessary for learning.

D—Drive. According to Hull, behavior was not simply a function of habit strength, as with Thorndike's law of effect. A rat satiated after many reinforcing experiences would no longer run the maze for food. Hull proposed that the drive state of the organism was an energizer for habits. If drive was zero, all the habit strength in the world would not produce behavior. Note that drive and habit strength multiply in this equation.

K—Incentive motivation. Habit strength and drive were still not enough for behavior. A rat trained to run a maze for food would soon stop running no matter how well it knew the path or how hungry it was if the food were removed. If the amount of food were decreased, the rat's performance would decline; if it was increased, performance would improve. Incentive motivation was taken as a measure of the amount and delay of reward. Note that incentive motivation also bears a multiplicative relationship to reaction potential.

I—Inhibition. Inhibition reflected both fatigue and the effect of extinction trials in which the reinforcer was no longer given. It referred to an active suppression of a behavior that might otherwise be expected to occur. The concept of inhibition originated with Pavlov and continues to play an important role in theories of learning. In Hull's equation it is subtracted from the effect of the other factors.

The fundamental issue with which Hull and other learning theorists struggled was how to relate learning and motivation. Learning was not enough for behavior; there had to be motivation. Hull, a behaviorist, could not allow for an organism to mentally consider and weigh its options before making a decision. The equation presented here was proposed to relate the various factors.

Hull aspired to a highly formal theory of learning. He proposed a set of basic postulates of learning and then attempted to derive predictions from the postulates. His effort and others like it were greeted with great enthusiasm in the field of psychology, as they were considered a sure sign that psychology had passed to the stage of being a true science. In retrospect, these efforts were incomplete and flawed as a logical exercise. Inconsistency and incompleteness became apparent with the development of computers capable of carrying through all the derivations and delivering specific predictions about behavior. Nonetheless, modern theories of learning and memory still show the influence of Hullian theories.

Hull tried to produce a formal theory that would predict behavior as a function of reinforcement history, drive, and incentive.

Edward C. Tolman (1886–1959)

Learning theories such as Hull's or Thorndike's were not without their critics. The most influential critic of the time was Edward Tolman. He came from within the behaviorist camp and so spoke a language that the others understood and did research that they could relate to. His major point was that behavior was best understood as a response to a goal. Two of his most famous demonstrations involved maze learning by rats, which was the popular experimental paradigm of the time.

The first demonstration involved **latent learning,** previously mentioned with respect to Thorndike's law of effect. The basic experiment by Tolman and Honzik (1930b) involved three groups of rats running a maze with 14 choice points. Rats were put in at one end of the maze and were retrieved when they got to the other end. All rats ran the maze once a day for 17 days. For one group food was always at the end of the maze. For another group food was never at the end of the maze. For a third group food was introduced on the 11th day. Figure 1.7 shows the performance of the rats in terms of how many wrong choices they made before reaching the end of the maze. The group given food on the 11th day dramatically improved its scores on the 12th day and even performed slightly better than the group that was reinforced all along. According to Tolman, the unreinforced rats were learning all the while. However, their learning was latent; only when a goal was introduced was the learning translated into performance. Thus, for Tolman, reinforcement was not necessary for learning but was necessary for performance.

A second demonstration (Tolman, Ritchie, & Kalish, 1946, 1947) attempted to show that what was learned was not a specific set of stimulus–response associations but rather a model of the environment on which the creature could choose to act. In the case of mazes, such a model was called a **cognitive map**; it included information about the spatial layout and not just specific routes. The existence of a cognitive map was demonstrated in experiments on place learning, another famous set of demonstrations by Tolman. Figure 1.8 shows the maze used in one of the experiments. The rat was put in S_1 or S_2 and food was available at F_1 or F_2. One group of rats always found food by turning to the right. Thus, if they started in S_1, they found food in F_1, whereas if they started in S_2, they found food in F_2. The other group of rats always found food in F_1, no matter where they started. This group had to alternate turning right or left depending on the starting point. Tolman et al. found that the rats in this second group, who were learning to go to a place, learned much faster than the rats in the first group, who were learning a constant

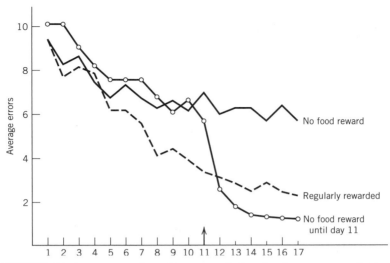

FIGURE 1.7. Average number of incorrect choices for three groups of rats who are running a maze. *Source:* From E. C. Tolman, and C. H. Honzik, *Introduction and removal of reward and maze performance in rats.* Copyright © 1930 by University of California Press. In the Public Domain.

response. Thus Tolman argued that specific responses are not learned, but rather the rat learns locations in a cognitive map.

Some researchers have replicated this result, but others have found that the response-learning rats do better. Restle (1957) suggested that rats could learn to respond to either cue (piece of information)—place or direction of turn. Which was easier depended on the relative saliency or prominence of the two cues.

FIGURE 1.8. Maze used to test the relative ease of learning either the response that brings reward or the place at which the reward is found. *Source:* From E. C. Tolman, B. F. Ritchie, and D. Kalish. *Studies in spatial learning II. Place learning versus response learning.* Copyright © 1946, In the Public Domain.

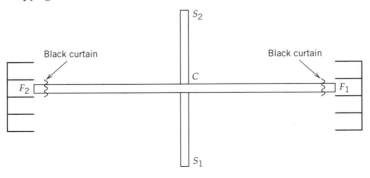

Tolman's greatest contribution was the demonstration that it is not behavior that is learned but rather knowledge that can be used to guide behavior. He proposed that organisms learned means–ends readinesses, or MERs. An MER was the expectation that certain actions would lead to certain results. For instance, rats in the maze experiments learned that going to a specific location would lead them to the goal box. These expectations remained passive until some goal energized them into action. The fundamental problem with Tolman's theory was that he never explained how goals energized these MERs. This problem led Guthrie (1952), another learning theorist of the time, to complain that Tolman left his rat in the maze buried in thought. A later section in this chapter describes how Newell and Simon's computer simulation theory of problem solving provided the bridge missing in Tolman's theory.

Tolman argued that animals learn means–ends readinesses independent of reinforcement and that reinforcers energize these means–ends readinesses.

B. F. Skinner (1904–1990)

B. F. Skinner was a behaviorist whose approach was as different from Tolman's as one could imagine. Skinner's influence lasted long beyond the heyday of behaviorism. Because of his popular books *Walden Two* (1948) and *Beyond Freedom and Dignity* (1971), he became synonymous with behaviorism in much of the popular culture. He is often called a radical behaviorist because he carried behaviorism to one of its extremes. Not only did Skinner lack tolerance for mentalistic constructs such as memory, but he also had little tolerance for many of the theoretical constructs that occupied other behaviorists. For instance, he criticized the concepts of drive and habit strength that were part of Hullian theory because they referred to internal states rather than to observable stimuli and responses.

Skinner made his major contributions to the study of instrumental conditioning or, as he preferred to call it, operant conditioning. He thought the idea of stimulus–response associations, a cornerstone of many behaviorist theories, was just theoretical fantasy. He noted that animals emitted responses in situations without any apparent stimuli controlling them. These responses were called free operants. Thus, a rat in a box might move around, scratch itself, press a lever, try to climb out, and so on. Learning changed the relative frequency of these various responses; if lever pressing was followed by food, it would come to be a more dominant response.

Skinner is famous for developing the **Skinner box** (so-called by others) for the study of rats. This soundproof box contains a lever that rats can press to deliver a pellet of food. The typical dependent measure was how often the rat pressed the lever. A similar device was developed for pigeons, in which

A rat pressing a bar in a skinner box

A pigeon pecking a key in an operant chamber.

they pecked at a key. Some important behavioral phenomena were discovered in these environments, and much of the data discussed in Chapters 3 and 4 came from use of these devices or variations of them.

Although Skinner denied a role for stimulus–response bonds, he had to allow external stimuli to have some role in controlling behavior. According to Skinner, external stimuli defined a situation in which operants (responses) would occur. Stimuli that determined which operants would occur were known as discriminative stimuli; that is, they served to discriminate one situation from another. To say that a stimulus defined the situation for a response but was not associated with it might seem to be a subtle distinction, but it typifies Skinner's approach. He was concerned with what the behavior of organisms would be in various stimulus situations and not with what internal mechanisms mediated the behavior.

Probably most typical of Skinner's research was his work on schedules of reinforcement (e.g., Ferster & Skinner, 1957), which is considered in some detail in Chapter 4. This work was concerned with how various contingencies between reinforcement and response affected the frequency with which the response was emitted. For instance, in an example of what is known as fixed-interval reinforcement, a rat might be given a pellet for its next response after 2 min had passed since its last pellet. Figure 1.9 illustrates a fixed-interval schedule in which a reinforcement is delivered every 2 min. Note that the total number of responses increases with the passage of time. The figure displays this information as a **cumulative response record**, which is a popular way of displaying data in Skinnerian research. It provides a record of the total number of responses that have been emitted at any point in time. The function increases at a rate that reflects the number of responses currently being made. As the time for another reinforcer approaches, the organism increases its rate of response; once the reinforcer is given, response rate slows down. This kind of function is referred to as a **scalloped function**. Skinner was not interested in why the organism behaved in this way; he was content with knowing what kind of behavior could be expected from many different organisms (including humans) given a fixed-interval schedule.

Figure 1.10 is a striking illustration of the generality of Skinnerian analysis. Weisberg and Waldrop (1972) plotted the number of bills passed by the U. S. Congress as a function of month. They argued that adjournment was a major reinforcement for congressional representatives; thus, there should be an increase in their behavior (bill passing) just before the reinforcer. Indeed, their behavior showed the same scalloped form as that of rats in a Skinner box. The exact same mechanisms could not be operating in Congress as in the rats, but Skinner was not interested in mechanisms—only in the generality of behavioral laws.

For Skinner, understanding was not found in an explanation of what was happening inside the organism. A person did not understand a behavior unless that person knew how to train an organism to perform the behavior. The emphasis was on understanding how behavior was controlled and how it could be changed. A lot of practical knowledge emerged from Skinner's laboratory and from those of his students about how to control behavior.

One important concept was that of response shaping; that is, an existing behavior could be shaped gradually into a desired form by suitable scheduling

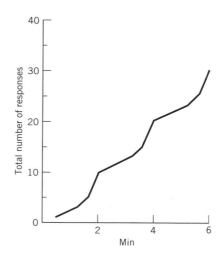

FIGURE 1.9. Hypothetical behavior of an organism under a fixed-interval reinforcement schedule in which it receives a reinforcement every 2 minutes.

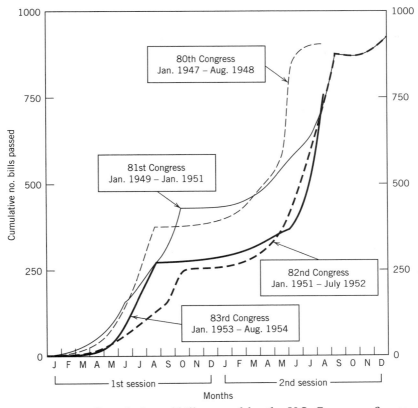

FIGURE 1.10. Cumulation of bills passed by the U.S. Congress. *Source:* From P. Weisberg and P. B. Waldrop. Fixed-interval work habits of congress. Copyright © 1972 by *Journal of Applied Behavior Analysis*. Reprinted by permission.

of reinforcement. For example, by selectively reinforcing the more forceful bar presses a rat could be trained to press a lever harder. First, presses exceeding low level of force would be rewarded; as the rat pressed harder, the criterion for reward would be raised. The rat's response would gradually move in the desired direction.

To the idea of response shaping was added the idea of response chaining. Skinner considered most complex behaviors to be a sequence of responses, each response setting the context for the next. A complex behavior could be taught by beginning with the first step and teaching each element of the chain until the whole sequence was completed. By combining response shaping and response chaining, truly amazing pieces of animal behavior were produced. For example, a pig was trained to go through a complete morning routine, including making breakfast, picking up dirty clothes, and vacuuming (Breland & Breland, 1951).

These demonstrations made an important point. Skinner concluded that all complex behavior, including human behavior, was just a matter of response shaping and chaining produced by appropriate schedules of reinforcement. Skinnerian principles have been applied to many domains, such as education and psychotherapy, where the goal is to shape appropriate human behavior. Part of the popularity of Skinner's work resulted from its practical successes, but controversy resulted as well because many people thought it ignored essential aspects of human personality and emotion, inappropriately trying to turn human beings into robots.

The major scientific problem with Skinner's approach, however, was its failure to extend to complex human cognition. This problem came to a head with the publication of *Verbal Behavior* (1957), in which Skinner tried to provide an analysis of language and language acquisition. The linguist Noam Chomsky (1959) published a highly influential critique of the work, arguing that the theory was incapable of accounting for the complexities of human language. Chomsky showed that Skinnerian principles could not explain the complex grammatical control humans exercise over their utterances and argued that many of Skinner's attempts at explanation were vague and metaphorical. Skinner never responded to the Chomsky critique, although others did (e.g., MacCorquodale, 1970), and he lived to see the cognitive approach supplant the behaviorist approach, partly because of the Chomsky critique. Skinner complained bitterly to the end that the criticisms were unjust and that cognitive psychology was full of fanciful mechanisms that failed to achieve the control of behavior that he took as the true measure of scientific understanding.

Skinner studied how reinforcement contingencies affected the distribution of responses in a situation.

The General Problem Solver (Newell & Simon, 1961)

About the time behaviorism was beginning to experience difficulties, a new method of theory construction based on computer simulation was gaining attention in psychology. The approach was introduced by Allen Newell and Herbert Simon, two collaborators at Carnegie Mellon University who were also leaders in the field of **artificial intelligence**, which is concerned with getting computers to behave intelligently. They incorporated many ideas from artificial intelligence into their theories of human cognition as well as incorporating ideas from their theories of human cognition into their work on artificial intelligence.

Newell and Simon brought a new definition of rigor into the field that changed the level of theorizing even among those who disagreed with them. They showed how it was possible to precisely determine the predictions of a theory without the reliance on loose verbal arguments that had formerly characterized psychological theory. Previous mathematical theories were either logically flawed, like Hull's, or very simple, like the theories described in an influential book by Atkinson, Bower, and Crothers (1965) on mathematical learning theory. Newell and Simon showed that **computer simulation** could use the powers of the computer to derive the predictions of complex scientific theories. Computer simulation techniques have had a profound effect on the character of theorizing in psychology. As in all fields of science, they have enabled exploration of complexities that formerly had to be ignored. Many modern theories discussed in this book depend on computer simulation techniques, including theories of animal conditioning, human memory, and the neural basis of learning.

Newell and Simon's use of the computer was more than mere simulation, however. Influenced by developments in artificial intelligence, they came to describe human cognition much as if it were a computer. The computer metaphor aspect of their theories remains controversial and its acceptance is difficult for most psychologists, who believe that the human brain is very different from a computer and that theories based on analogy to computers are likely to be misleading (e.g., Rumelhart & McClelland, 1986).

Newell and Simon's influence resulted in the development of a number of simulations of cognition and learning at Carnegie Mellon and elsewhere. However, their greatest contribution was not to the study of learning per se, but to problem solving. A difficulty in earlier theories of learning was determining the relationship between knowledge (what the organism learned from experience) and behavior. How did a creature's acquisition of new knowledge relate to behavior? As indicated, some behaviorists such as Thorndike and Hull, merged the two issues and argued that behavioral tendencies were learned—that there was no difference between knowledge and behavior. Tolman's major criticism was directed against this position, but he was unable to derive a coherent alternative. Newell and Simon in their theory of problem solving showed how knowledge could be decoupled from behavior and still result in behavior. Along the way, they showed that rigorous and precise theories of behavior could allow mentalistic constructs. More than anything else, this demonstration destroyed the prohibitions against mentalism that Watson had introduced to the field 50 years earlier. In eliminating these prohibitions, Newell and Simon established the basis for the cognitive revolution that has transformed all of psychology, including learning theory.

The centerpiece of Newell and Simon's work was the General Problem Solver, or GPS (Newell & Simon, 1972). GPS was a computer simulation that used a way of deploying knowledge in problem solving called **means–ends analysis**. The basic steps in applying means–ends analysis are the following:

1. Identify the major difference between the current situation and the goal; that is, focus on the end.

2. Select some action that is relevant to eliminating that difference; that is, select some means relevant to that end. Newell and Simon used the term **operator** to refer to the action or means. An operator is much like an operant in Skinner's theory.

3. If the operator can be applied, apply it. If not, make the goal to enable the operator and start over again at step 1; that is, make the means the new end.

Newell and Simon give the following everyday example of means–ends analysis:

> I want to take my son to nursery school. What's the difference between what I have and what I want? One of distance. What changes distance? My automobile. My automobile won't work. What is needed to make it work? A new battery. What has new batteries? An auto repair shop. I want the repair shop to put in a new battery; but the shop doesn't know I need one. What is the difficulty? One of communication. What allows communication? A telephone . . . and so on. (p. 416)

The critical feature that gives means–ends analysis its name is step 3, which allows the operator chosen in step 2 to become the goal. In the Newell and Simon example, the focus switches from the goal of getting the son to nursery school to the means, which is a functioning automobile. Thus the means becomes, temporarily, the end. This step, called **subgoaling**, can organize coherent behavior in response to a complex situation and represents a major advance over the response chaining concept of Skinner. Subgoaling is discussed more fully in Chapter 9, which considers problem solving in detail. There can be complex sequences of subgoals. In the example here, taking the child to nursery school has a functioning automobile as its subgoal, which has a battery as its subgoal, which has an automobile repair shop as its subgoal, which has a telephone as its subgoal.

GPS solved a great many problems that had proved impossible for other theories, including problems in algebra, calculus, and logic. Newell and Simon (1972) showed that their program was not only capable of solving complex problems in logic but that it went through the same steps undertaken by humans solving those problems. GPS realized a degree of intelligence unmatched by previous theories in psychology.

Although GPS was not specifically concerned with learning, it is fairly clear how to conceive of learning within the theory. Learning is involved in acquiring the operators on which this theory is based. Operators are like Tolman's MERs in that they encode potentially useful knowledge about the world. In Tolman's latent learning situation, the rats might learn that making a certain turn in a maze changes their position in the maze. However, in the absence of any goals, this knowledge remains dormant and latent. When they realize that food is in a certain location, they have a goal, getting to that food, and can treat their knowledge as operators relevant to that goal. Each turn in the maze can be treated as an operator that gets them closer or further away from the goal. Given this operator knowledge, GPS could plan a path through the maze to reach the goals. Thus, GPS offers a mechanism for making the transition from knowledge to behavior. This is what Tolman was unable to do.

It is questionable whether what a rat does corresponds to the means–ends method of problem solving, which, as seen in Chapter 9, is more appropriate for describing human (and perhaps primate) cognition. However, GPS has demonstrated that knowledge can be translated to behavior by problem-solving methods. Many problem-solving methods have been proposed in recent years. Chapter 9 discusses another method, difference reduction, which seems more appropriate for modeling lower organisms.

> *Newell and Simon showed that computer simulation could be used to model rigorously complex cognitive processes and that problem-solving methods could convert knowledge into behavior.*

A Model of Memory (Atkinson & Shiffrin, 1968)

Richard Atkinson and Richard Shiffrin published a theory of human memory in 1968 that captured the then current wisdom about the nature of human memory. Their work typifies much of the research of the modern era and influenced subsequent developments in the study of both animal learning and human learning. There had been growing evidence for two types of storage in human memory, short-term memory and long-term memory. **Short-term memory** was thought to be a temporary storage system that could hold a small amount of information. The classic example of short-term memory is remembering a telephone number just heard. Short-term memory was thought to have a capacity slightly more than seven digits—just enough to hold a phone number. Most people can remember a seven-digit phone number but experience difficulty when they have to add a three-digit area code. This storage is temporary; the phone number is quickly forgotten if the person is distracted. The way to maintain the information is to say it over and over again to oneself as it is held in short-term memory. This process of repeating the information to oneself is called **rehearsal**. **Long-term memory** was thought of as a more permanent repository of knowledge, without any apparent capacity limitations but hard to get knowledge into. It was generally thought that knowledge had to be rehearsed in short-term memory for a while in order for it to get into long-term memory.

These basic ideas about the distinction between short-term memory and long-term memory had existed for a number of years; Broadbent (1957) was one of the first to describe them. Atkinson and Shiffrin crystallized these ideas into a precise theory, expressed as both a mathematical model and a computer simulation model, and demonstrated that the theory could account for the results of various experiments current in the study of human memory.

Figure 1.11 illustrates the basic theory. Information comes into short-term memory from the environment through various perceptual processes. Short-term memory has several slots, often specified around four, in which it can hold these elements. The subject engages in a rehearsal process of reviewing or rehearsing the information held in short-term memory. Every time the information is rehearsed there is another chance for it to be transferred into long-term memory. Thus, increased rehearsal of information results in increased probability of long-term retention. Since there is only a limited number of slots in short-term memory for rehearsal, each time the subject decides to take in a new item for rehearsal, an old item is displaced and lost.

One of the paradigms in which this theory was studied was **free recall**, an experimental paradigm in which subjects are read a list of words at a fixed rate, for example, 2 sec per word, and then asked to recall the words in any order. This experiment results in what is called the **serial position curve**, illustrated in Figure 1.12*a* for a list of 20 words. This figure plots the probability of recalling a word, averaged over subjects and lists, as a function of the position of the word in the list that was read to the subjects (subjects are not constrained as to the order in which they recall these words). Note that recall is better at the beginning of the list and much better at the end of the list. The level of recall is relatively constant between the beginning and the end. The good performance at the beginning of the list is referred to as the **primacy effect**, and the good performance at the end of the list is referred to as the **recency effect**.

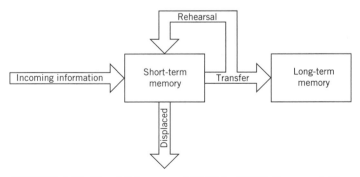

FIGURE 1.11. The Atkinson and Shiffrin (1968) theory relating short-term and long-term memory. Incoming items enter short-term memory and can be maintained there by rehearsal. As an item is rehearsed, information about it is transferred to long-term memory. Another item coming in can displace an existing item from short-term memory.

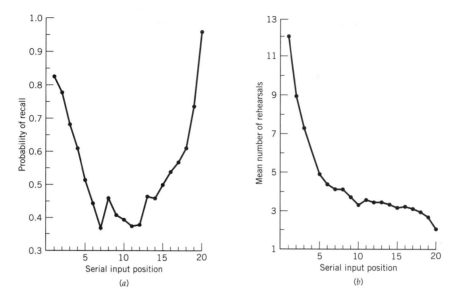

FIGURE 1.12. (*a*) The mean probability of recall as a function of its serial position in the input, and (*b*) the mean number of rehearsals of an item (From Rundus, 1971).

The Atkinson and Shiffrin theory accounts for the shape of this serial position curve. The theory assumes that subjects fill up their short-term buffer with words as they read the words and rehearse them. When the buffer is full and a new word is encountered, the subject chooses one word to delete in order to study the new word.

The recency effect is easiest to explain in the Atkinson and Shiffrin theory. The last few words are still likely to be in the short-term buffer and so have better recall. The last word is definitely still in the buffer. The next to last word is in the buffer unless it was deleted to accommodate the last. The decreasing recall farther from the end reflects the decreasing probability that the item is still in short-term memory.

According to Atkinson and Shiffrin's theory, the primacy effect occurs because the first words in a list have a higher probability of being stored in long-term memory. The words at the beginning of the list are at an advantage because initially they do not have to compete with other words for rehearsal in the short-term memory. Thus, they receive more rehearsals and are held longer before they are pushed out by an intervening word. Rundus (1971) asked subjects to rehearse out loud and was able to show that the probability of recalling a particular word could be predicted from the number of times it was rehearsed. As postulated by Atkinson and Shiffrin, the words at the beginning of a list received more rehearsals. Rundus's results are displayed in Figure 1.12b, which illustrates that the number of rehearsals is highest for the first word and then drops off quickly.

The research paradigms on which this theory was based were rather simple experiments like this free-recall experiment. They reflected a return to the kinds of experimental paradigms introduced by Ebbinghaus almost a century earlier. As more complex experiments were performed, the Atkinson and Shiffrin theory fell into disfavor. New evidence threw doubt on the distinction between short-term and long-term memory, and their theory of long-term memory ignored many important issues, such as the role of organization and retrieval conditions. As people began to look at memory in more realistic situations, these problems became more and more apparent. Much of the research that led to rejection of Atkinson and Shiffrin's theory is presented in Chapters 5 through 8. Chapter 5 specifically reviews some of the evidence against the theory.

The Atkinson and Shiffrin theory is of only historical interest now. Although few researchers believe in it, many current theories still show its influence, including a new theory developed by Shiffrin called SAM (Gillund & Shiffrin, 1984), which is discussed in Chapter 5. The theory's rejection by the field represents a triumph for modern psychology, indicating that psychology had moved beyond decades of indecisive, verbal arguments to precise statements that enabled theories to be tested and rejected. With such theoretical precision comes scientific progress.

Atkinson and Shiffrin's theory proposed that information was rehearsed in a limited-capacity short-term memory and was transferred to a high-capacity long-term memory.

Neural Basis of Learning and Memory

Since learning obviously takes place in the nervous system, it might have struck the reader as strange that there was almost no discussion of the neural basis of learning in the theories of learning and memory presented. Until recently, not enough was known about the nervous system to pursue the issue. However, rapid advances in our understanding of the nervous system and in the research techniques that enable this understanding have resulted in a surge of research in this area. This new research is one of the reasons for the recent rapprochement of the learning research focused on animals and the memory research focused on humans. It has become apparent to researchers in human memory that they can begin to understand the neural basis of memory, but to do this they have to rely to a large extent on research with nonhuman subjects.

Most chapters of this book discuss some of the relevant research on the neural basis of learning and memory. These discussions assume a basic familiarity with the nervous system. Therefore, this chapter concludes with a short review of the nervous system from the perspective of understanding research on learning and memory.

The Nervous System

The nervous system of higher organisms comprises a central nervous system, consisting of the spinal cord and brain, and a peripheral nervous system, consisting of sensory nerves, which carry information from receptors, and motor nerves, which send commands to the muscles. Almost all learning of any note takes place in the brain. Figure 1.13 shows the brains of several organisms. The human brain has a volume of about 1300 cc, which is very large, particularly in relation to the size of the human body. One difficulty in understanding the brain is that it is a three-dimensional structure; many important areas are hidden inside it. Figures 1.14 and 1.15 present two views of the brain: Figure 1.14 shows the outside, and Figure 1.15 shows the inside of the brain as if sliced in half.

FIGURE 1.13. Representative brains of different animals show how large the human brain is compared with those of other animals.

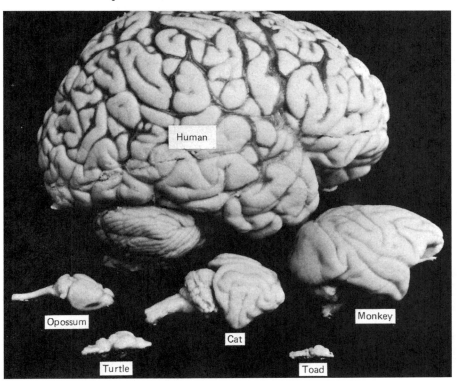

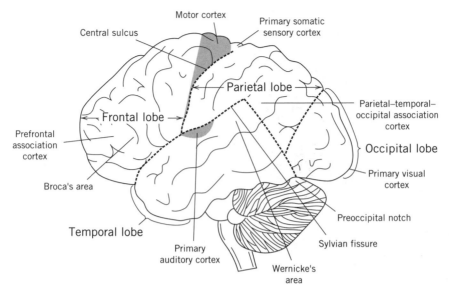

FIGURE 1.14. A side view of the cerebral cortex. *Source:* From E. R. Kandel, J. H. Schwartz, and T. M. Jessell. *Principles of neural science*. Third Edition. Reprinted by permission of the publisher. Copyright © 1991 by Appleton and Lange. Reprinted by permission.

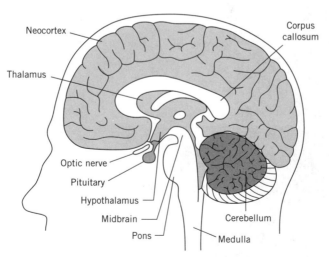

FIGURE 1.15. Major components of the brain. (From Keeton, 1980). *Source:* Reproduced from *Biological science*, Third Edition, by William T. Keeton, illustrated by Paula DiSanto Bensadoun, by permission of W. W. Norton & Company, Inc. Copyright © 1980, 1979, 1978, 1972, 1967 by W. W. Norton & Company, Inc.

The brain can be divided into the **cerebral cortex** and the subcortical areas. The cortex is thought to involve most of the higher cognitive functions. Its size increases dramatically with a rise up the phylogenetic scale. The human cortex can be thought of as a sheet about 1 meter square; to fit into the human skull, it has to be folded up, which accounts for the many folds that distinguish the human brain.

The cortex engulfs many of the lower brain structures, so that they are invisible from the outside. The lower parts of the brain tend to be found in more primitive species that have no or only a poorly developed cortex. Many of these lower areas support basic functions. For instance, the medulla controls breathing, swallowing, digestion, and heartbeat. The **cerebellum** is involved in motor movement and coordination, as discussed in Chapter 9. The **hypothalamus** regulates expression of basic drives, as discussed in Chapter 4. The limbic system refers to parts of the brain that are at the border between the cortex and these lower structures. The limbic system, and in particular the **hippocampus**, which borders the temporal lobe, is important in memory and is discussed in many chapters. The hippocampus is not shown in Figures 1.14 or 1.15 because it is neither a structure on the outside nor a structure at the center, but rather is between the temporal lobe of the cortex and the central structures.

The cortex itself can be divided by major folds into four regions, shown in Figure 1.14. The **occipital lobe** is mainly devoted to vision. The **temporal lobe** has the primary auditory areas and is also involved in the recognition of objects. The **parietal lobe** is involved with a number of higher-level sensory functions, including spatial processing. The **frontal lobe** can be divided into the motor cortex, which is involved with movement, and the **prefrontal cortex**. The prefrontal cortex is much larger in primates than in other animals, in apes (such as chimpanzees) than in other primates (such as monkeys), and in humans than in apes. It is thought to be important to planning and problem solving. Most areas of the cortex are thought to be capable of supporting various sorts of learning.

The brain consists of the cortex and various subcortical areas.

The Neuron

The most important cells in the nervous system from the point of view of information processing are the **neurons**. There are estimated to be some 100 billion neurons in the human brain. Neurons come in many shapes and sizes. Figure 1.16 shows some of the variations. Most neurons consist of some basic components, illustrated in Figure 1.17. Each neuron has a cell body with branches called **dendrites** emanating from it. Also typically emanating from the neuron is a long, thin extension called the **axon**. The axon reaches from one part of the nervous system to another part. Axons vary in length from a

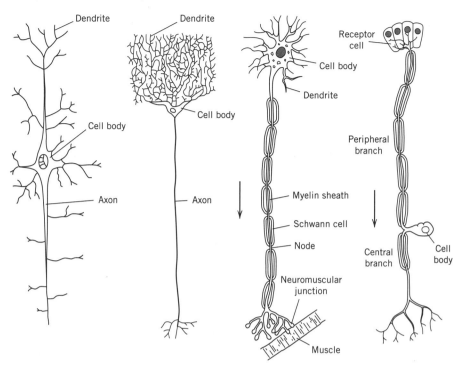

FIGURE 1.16. Some of the varieties of neurons. (From Keeton, 1980). *Source:* Reproduced from *Biological science*, Third Edition, by William T. Keeton, illustrated by Paula DiSanto Bensadoun, by permission of W. W. Norton & Company, Inc. Copyright © 1980, 1979, 1978, 1972, 1967 by W. W. Norton & Company, Inc.

few millimeters to a meter (the longest axons stretch from the brain to various locations in the spinal cord).

Axons contact other neurons by means of arborizations (tiny branches) at their ends. They typically contact the dendrites of other neurons. They do not actually touch; there is a gap of perhaps 10 to 50 nm (a nanometer is one-billionth of a meter). This point of near contact is called a **synapse**. In the mature adult one axon may synapse on a thousand or more other neurons and one neuron may received synapses from a thousand or more axons. Thus the nervous system is characterized by a great many interconnections among neurons.

The axon of one neuron communicates with another neuron by releasing chemicals called **neurotransmitters**. When the neurotransmitters reach the other neuron, they change the electrical potential at the membrane of the neuron where the axon synapses. The inside of the neuron is typically about 70 mV (millivolts) more negative than the outside. The difference results because the concentration of chemical substances on the inside differs from that on the outside of the membrane. Outside the neuron there is a concentration of positive sodium ions and negative chloride ions; inside there is a concentration of positive potassium ions and proteins with a negative charge. The distributions are not equal, and the inside is negatively charged compared with the outside. Depending on the nature of the neurotransmitter released by the axon, the potential difference can decrease or increase. Neurotransmitters that decrease the potential difference are called **excitatory**, and neurotransmitters that increase the difference are called **inhibitory**.

If there are enough excitatory inputs onto the cell body and dendrites of a neuron and the difference in electrical potential is reduced to about 50 mV, the membrane becomes suddenly permeable to sodium ions and they rush in, causing the inside to become more positive than the outside. This entire process may only take about 1 msec before it reverses and returns to normal. This sudden change is called an **action potential**. It begins at the axon hillock and travels down the axon. The rate at which an axon potential travels down an axon varies from .5 m/sec to 130 m/sec, depending on the character of the axon. For example, the more myelin (myelin is a natural insulation around the axon) the axon has the more rapidly the action potential moves down the axon. When this moving action potential, called the **nerve impulse**, reaches the ends of the axon, it causes the axon to release neurotransmitters, thus starting a new cycle of communication among neurons. The time for information to progress from the dendrite of one neuron through its axon to the dendrite of another neuron is roughly 10 msec.

It is thought that all information processing in the nervous system involves such passage of signals among neurons. As you read this page, neurons are sending signals from your eye to your brain. As you write, signals are sent from the brain to the muscles. Cognitive processing involves sending signals among neurons within the brain. At any one time, billions of neurons are active, sending signals to one another.

Neurons can be thought of as more or less active. Activity level refers both to the degree of reduction in the difference in membrane potential and to

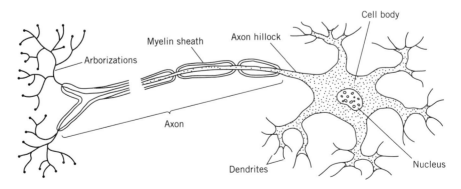

FIGURE 1.17. A schematic representation of a typical neuron. *Source:* From *The nerve impulse* by B. Katz. Copyright © 1952 by Scientific American, Inc. All rights reserved.

the rate at which nerve impulses are sent down neurons. The rate at which nerve impulses are generated along the axon is called the **rate of firing**; it is generally thought that the number of firings, not the temporal pattern of the firings, is important. Neurons can fire at the rate of 100/sec or more. Generally, the more active a neuron is, the stronger the message it is sending. For instance, the way in which a motor neuron tells a muscle to increase the force of its action is by increasing its rate of firing.

Learning involves a change in behavior and so must involve some change in the way neurons communicate. It is currently believed that changes in such communication involve changes in the synaptic connections among neurons. Learning takes place by making existing synaptic connections more effective. The axon may emit more of a neurotransmitter, or the cell membrane may become more responsive to the neurotransmitter. Recall that neurotransmitters have either excitatory influences, reducing the difference in membrane potential, or inhibitory influences, increasing the difference; inhibitory influences can be as important as excitatory influences. Many cells have spontaneous rates of firing, and learning can involve lowering these rates.

Neurons communicate with one another at synaptic connections where one neuron may inhibit or excite the neural activity of another neuron.

Neural Explanations and Information-Processing Explanations

It is impossible to study directly what is happening in 100 billion cells that are all crammed into the human skull and can only be seen through a microscope. However, scientists have found various ways of making inferences about what is happening at the neural level. In one method, studies look at mass actions in regions of cells; that is, they see what regions of the brain tend to be more active in particular tasks. For example, during a spatial reasoning task, areas of the brain that perform spatial reasoning are more active. In another method, scientists insert electrodes in lower animals to record what is happening in specific cells. They then infer from the patterns recorded in a hundred or so cells what is happening in the remaining neurons in that region. Another methodology used with lower organisms is selective removal of areas of the brain. For example, as described in Chapter 3, much has been learned about the role of the hippocampus in memory by studying organisms from which it has been removed. Humans who have suffered damage to specific regions of the brain from accidental injuries can also be studied. Finally, scientists can study the connections among neurons and how neurons interact with each other. From this information, they can devise computer simulation models of possible patterns of interaction among subsets of neurons.

Brain study is one of the most rapidly growing areas in psychology and has provided genuine insights about what may underlie different learning phenomena. However, we are still far from an adequate understanding of the neural basis of learning or memory. Thus the majority of this book is devoted to behavioral studies of learning and memory and the kinds of theories that such studies allow. These theories are often called information-processing theories, in that they talk about the processing of information in the abstract. For instance, in a discussion of how experience strengthens a piece of knowledge so that it is processed more rapidly and reliably, there may be no mention of the possible neural realizations of the knowledge or its strengthening. Theories cast in such terms have always been part of the field of learning and memory, although they were not called information-processing theories until the advent of the cognitive approach.

Neural and information-processing explanations offer two levels of description; both are necessary to an understanding of learning and memory. Information-processing theorists are interested in ideas about the neural realizations of their theories. Researchers on the neural basis of learning and memory look to information-processing theories to help them make sense of their data. Information about what is happening in a few neurons or in a particular region of the brain is not useful unless there is a bigger picture in which to place its interpretation. Thus research progress in learning and memory depends on advancing both the neural and the information-processing theories and understanding their interrelationships.

Information-processing theories try to understand the general changes brought about by learning, whereas neural theories try to understand how these changes are implemented in the brain.

Outline of the Book

This chapter has provided a basic review of the background needed to understand current research in learning and memory. The rest of this book presents what is currently known about learning and memory. The next three chapters are devoted largely to animal research, which has certain advantages over research on humans. The researcher can exercise more complete control over the learning history of a nonhuman—controlling its environment from birth and subjecting it to manipulations that would be unethical if the subject were human. Also, to the extent that the creature is simpler, the researcher may be able to look at a purer form of learning, without the complex cognitive processes and strategies of humans. Chapter 2 looks at classical conditioning, which provides a basic analysis of how associations are formed. Chapters 3 and 4 look at instrumental conditioning, which is concerned with how learning is used to achieve critical biological goals.

Four central questions should be kept in mind when reading these chapters on animal learning. First, to what degree is animal learning like human learning? There are some remarkable commonalities in the behavioral manifestations of learning. Second, what is actually happening in the animal during a learning experiment? The traditional view that simple learning processes are occurring has largely been replaced by the view that animals try to adapt to their environment. Third, what is happening in the nervous system to produce such learning? Here animal research is at a considerable advantage over human research because physiological experiments can be performed on animals that cannot be performed on humans. Finally, what is the relationship between learning and motivation? This question has been central to the psychology of learning.

Chapters 5 through 8 consider the current concept of memory, which is based largely on research with human subjects. Human research has two advantages over animal research. Humans can follow complex instructions and therefore yield richer data about the learning process; and the results obtained are closer to what we are presumably interested in, that is, human learning outside the laboratory. Chapters 5 through 8 present what is known about how knowledge is encoded, stored, maintained, and retrieved. Chapter 5 discusses sensory and working memories, which are systems for encoding information currently being processed. Chapter 6 discusses how information is originally encoded into long-term memory. Chapter 7 considers how information is retained, and Chapter 8 discusses how it is retrieved. Although most of the research presented is from humans, these chapters show that much of it extends to other animals. Thus, the principles of memory, although perhaps easier to study in humans, also apply to many species.

The last three chapters consider important extensions of the research on learning and memory. Chapter 9 considers skill learning, such as the learning involved in operating a computer system, and demonstrates that profound changes occur in a skill with extensive practice—something that is ignored in most traditional research on learning and memory. Chapter 10 reviews inductive learning, which is concerned with how we form inferences, such as what is or is not a dog, and with how children learn language. Issues of inductive learning are of great concern not only in psychology but in philosophy, linguistics, and artificial intelligence. The final chapter discusses the applications of research on learning and memory to the problems of education.

Further Readings

Several books recount the history of psychology, including Leahey (1992) and Wertheimer (1979). Boring (1950) remains a classic review of the early history of experimental psychology. Bower and Hilgard (1981) provide an excellent discussion of the major theories of learning. Kandel, Schwartz, and Jessell (1991) offer a thorough discussion of the nervous system and the neural basis of learning and behavior.

2

Classical Conditioning

Overview

This chapter discusses research on classical conditioning, which was introduced to the world by Pavlov. As presented in Chapter 1, the basic paradigm for demonstrating classical conditioning is one in which a conditioned stimulus (CS), such as a light, is followed by an unconditioned stimulus (US), such as food. The US evokes an unconditioned response (UR), for example, salivation. After a while the CS comes to evoke a conditioned response (CR). Although the conditioned response in this case is salivation, the CR is not always identical to the UR.

Conditioning of the Eye Blink in Humans

Most contemporary research on classical conditioning has been conducted on animals, but in the past a great deal of research was conducted on humans. Imagine what it would be like to be a subject in a procedure such as eyelid conditioning. In a typical eyelid-conditioning experiment, the subject is fitted with a padded headband containing a nozzle pointed toward the eye and a device for recording change in muscle activity in the eyelid. The US is a puff of air directed toward the outside of the cornea, and the CS is a light or tone. The US normally evokes a UR of an eye blink, and conditioning is concerned with how the CS comes to evoke a similar CR.

In one experiment (Moore & Gormezano, 1961), the interval between the CS and the US was 500 msec. Subjects were given 70 acquisition trials in which the CS was followed by the US and 20 extinction trials in which the CS was presented alone. Figure 2.1 shows the percentage of trials in which subjects emitted a CR in anticipation of the puff of air. As in the salivation data presented in Figure 1.4, these human subjects showed a rather standard conditioning curve, in which the probability of the CR increased, followed by a standard extinction curve, in which the probability of the CR decreased.

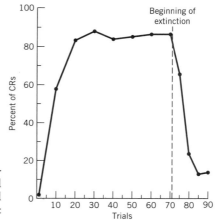

FIGURE 2.1. Probability of a conditioned eye blink during 10-trial blocks of acquisition and 5-trial blocks of extinction. (From Moore & Gormezano, 1961).

All the standard classical conditioning phenomena can be shown in human eyelid conditioning. For example, consider the effect of the intensity of the US. Prokasy, Grant, and Myers (1958) manipulated the intensity of the puff, using two intensities, 50 mm or 260 mm.[1] Subjects were given 40 acquisition trials and 20 extinction trials. Figure 2.2 shows that subjects given more intense US reached higher levels of conditioning. Once extinction set in, however, they reverted to the same levels.

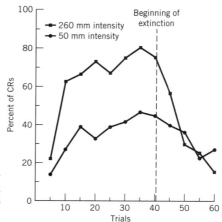

FIGURE 2.2. Percentage of conditioned eye blink during acquisition and extinction as a function of US intensity. (From Prokasy, et al., 1958).

[1]They measured the intensity of the air by the length of the fall of a column of mercury that produced the air puff.

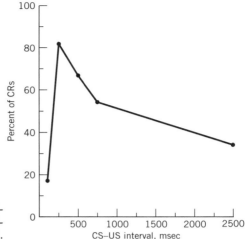

FIGURE 2.3. Percentage of conditioned eye blink as a function of CS-US interval. (From McAllister, 1953).

Another standard parameter of a classical conditioning experiment is the interval between the CS and the US. McAllister (1953) varied the time between a CS of a tone and the US of an air puff using intervals of 100, 250, 450, 700, and 2500 msec. Figure 2.3 shows the results in terms of percentage of conditioned responses after 20 conditioning trials. Nearly maximal conditioning was achieved in the intervals between 250 and 700 msec, which are typical values for optimal conditioning in most, but not all, conditioning paradigms.

> *The classical conditioning of the human eye blink demonstrates typical acquisition and extinction functions as well as typical effects of US intensity and CS–US intervals.*

Conditioning and Awareness

The conditioned eye blink is adaptive. By blinking in anticipation of the puff of air, the subjects are protecting themselves from an aversive stimulus. This phenomenon has raised the issue of whether human subjects are voluntarily choosing to blink to avoid the light. Human subjects report being aware of the CS–US relationship and blinking in response to the US (Grant, 1973). However, they tend to be unaware that they are blinking to the CS in anticipation of the US. It has been argued that certain eye-blink CRs look like eye blinks that subjects give when instructed to blink; in particular, that the eye closes more sharply, more rapidly, and stays closed longer when it is a voluntary response (Spence & Ross, 1959). There is considerable controversy over whether it is possible to discriminate between automatic and voluntary eye blinks (Gormezano, 1965; Ross, 1965).

At one time, classical conditioning was considered automatic and instrumental conditioning was considered voluntary. This viewpoint led to the argument that the purported voluntary eye blinks in a classical conditioning paradigm were really instances of covert instrumental conditioning in which the human was responding for the reward of avoiding the aversive puff of air. This distinction has not proved useful and is not pursued here. Whether voluntary or automatic, certain behavioral regularities tend to be associated with conditioning (for example, those reviewed in Figures 2.1 through 2.3, although, there may be subtle behavioral differences, such as in the shape of the CR). Research has focused on understanding these regularities. An important theme in modern research is that classical conditioning serves an adaptive function, whatever the awareness of the organism or the degree of voluntariness in responding.

Classical conditioning shows similar behavioral properties whether the subject is aware or not.

What This Chapter Will Cover

One of the striking features of classical conditioning is its ubiquity. Virtually all organisms can be conditioned. Dogs and humans have already been mentioned. This chapter reviews classical conditioning in organisms ranging from sea slugs to rabbits, as well as some of the enormous variety of stimuli that can be used for the CS and the US.

Classical conditioning is often considered the paradigm of choice for studying how associations are made. The similar properties it displays over a wide range of situations and organisms might lead to the conjecture that learning is taking place according to the same neural mechanisms in all these situations. Recent research on the neural basis of some instances of classical conditioning in certain organisms is discussed next. The research shows that different neural mechanisms underlie classical conditioning in different organisms and, indeed, different mechanisms underlie different types of conditioning in the same organism. Creatures have found various ways of forming associations in different situations. What is constant across these circumstances is the need to form associations. The constancy in the behavioral manifestations of classical conditioning reflects the constancy of this need.

After this review, the chapter will discuss the behavioral properties of classical conditioning. In particular, subsequent sections address the following questions:

What is associated?

What is the conditioned stimulus?

What is the conditioned response?

What is the nature of the association?

The answers are surprising in light of earlier views about classical conditioning. The Rescorla–Wagner theory, an elegant but simple theory that captures much of the complex structure of the data, is presented next. Finally, the chapter addresses applications of classical conditioning to important problems outside the laboratory.

At a behavioral level, a wide variety of organisms display similar classical conditioning phenomena when a neutral CS is followed by a US.

Neural Basis of Classical Conditioning

As reviewed in Chapter 1, Pavlov speculated, incorrectly, about what was happening in the nervous system to underlie classical conditioning. More recently, researchers have traced the neural basis of certain instances of classical conditioning in certain organisms. This research offers a glimpse of the neural mechanisms behind the behavioral phenomena, and may provide a sobering influence on overly simplistic or overly grandiose interpretations of classical conditioning.

As reviewed in Chapter 1, neural information processing takes place by transmission of signals among neurons, which are the individual cells that make up the nervous system. Neurons transmit signals from one part of the nervous system to another by sending electrical pulses along their axons. The axon of one neuron makes contact with the cell bodies of other neurons. The point of contact between the axon of one neuron and the cell body of another neuron is called the synapse, and communication is achieved by transmitter chemicals, called neurotransmitters, going from the axon of one neuron to the other neuron. These neurotransmitters can increase or decrease the electrical potential of the neuron. If enough electrical potential accumulates on its cell body, a neuron sends a signal down its axon. It is generally believed that learning involves changes in the effectiveness of synaptic connections among neurons, so that one neuron comes to produce greater changes in the electrical potential of another.

All learning, including classical conditioning, involves changes in the effectiveness of synaptic connections among neurons.

Simple Learning in *Aplysia* (Sea Slug)

Some of the most influential research on neural mechanisms has been done on invertebrates that have simple nervous systems with very large neurons. The simplicity of these nervous systems allows researchers to understand in detail how the systems work; the large neurons make studying what is happening to an individual neuron relatively easy.

One of the creatures that has received extensive study is the sea slug, Aplysia californica (see Figure 2.4). The gill and the siphon (a fleshy spout, surrounding and enveloping the gill, used to expel water) of **Aplysia** have withdrawal reflexes that can be evoked by touching the siphon (or other nearby parts, such as the mantle). This reflex is largely controlled by direct synaptic connections between the sensory neurons that are excited by the tactile stimulation and the motor neurons that control the reflex. Figure 2.5 shows the synaptic connections for the gill-withdrawal reflex. The sensory neuron from the siphon skin synapses directly onto the motor neuron for withdrawing the gill. Thus touching the siphon stimulates the sensory neuron, which stimulates the motor neuron, which in turn evokes the gill-withdrawal reflex.

The withdrawal reflex to tactile stimulation is not that strong and tends to weaken with repeated touching. The strength of the response can be enhanced by a classical conditioning procedure that pairs tactile stimulation to the siphon (CS) with shock to the tail (US). After five such pairings the tactile stimulation (CS) evokes a much stronger withdrawal reflex than is present without pairing with an US. Carew, Hawkins, and Kandel (1983) compared using a CS of tactile stimulation to the siphon with a CS of tactile stimulation to the mantle. If the siphon stimulus is paired with the US, it comes to evoke a stronger withdrawal reflex than that evoked by the mantle-stimulus; if the mantle stimulus is paired with the US it comes to evoke a stronger reflex than

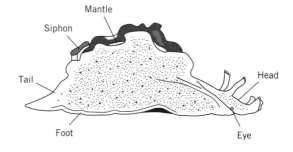

FIGURE 2.4. The aplysia. *Source:* From *Cellular basis of behavior* by Eric Kandel. Copyright © 1976 by W. H. Freeman and Company. Reprinted with permission.

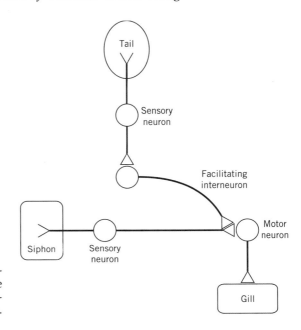

FIGURE 2.5. Neural connections underlying the conditioning of the gill-withdrawal reflex in *Aplysia*.

that evoked by the siphon stimulus. Thus *Aplysia* can learn to discriminate between the two locations.

The mechanism of conditioning appears to involve the facilitating interneurons shown in Figure 2.5. These are neurons onto which sensory neurons from the tail synapse. They, in turn, synapse on the axons of the sensory neurons from the siphon, providing an example of an **axoaxonic synapse**—a synapse on a synapse. The shock to the tail activates these interneurons, which operate on the synaptic connection between the sensory neurons from the siphon and the motor neurons. They change the synaptic connection by increasing the release of the neurotransmitter from the sensory neuron coming from the siphon. This process is referred to as **presynaptic facilitation**, because it enhances a process that is occurring on the axon side of the synapse.

Bailey and Chen (1983) studied the structural basis for these changes in neurotransmitter release. When there was conditioning, they found an increase in sites on the axon where neurotransmitter release occurs. A neurotransmitter called serotonin released by the facilitating interneurons starts a relatively long chemical chain reaction that results in more release sites at the synapse of the sensory neuron from the siphon. This presynaptic facilitation is maximal if the sensory neuron from the siphon is active just before the interneuron from the tail. If the sensory neuron from the siphon (CS) has just fired, the chemical chain reaction is enhanced, resulting in the exposure of release sites at the synapse between the sensory neuron and the motor neuron (Hawkins, Abrams, Carew, & Kandel, 1983). This dependency of presynaptic facilitation on recent activity from the siphon makes classical conditioning in

Aplysia dependent on CS–US intervals. Maximal conditioning occurs if the tactile stimulation (CS) takes place .5 sec. before the shock (US), and no conditioning occurs after as little as 2 sec. The axon from the siphon is only very briefly in the state that results in presynaptic facilitation.

Classical conditioning has been studied in another invertebrate, the nudibranch mollusk, Hermissenda crassiconis (Alkon, 1984). Classical conditioning in this animal also involves a change in neurotransmitter release, but the actual cellular mechanisms differ from those at work in *Aplysia*. These studies show that there is no single mechanism of learning at the cellular level.

Classical conditioning in Aplysia *is produced by enhancing the neurotransmitter release between the sensory neuron from the CS and the motor neuron producing the CR.*

Classical Conditioning of the Eye Blink in the Rabbit

Thompson (1986) has been engaged in a 15-year project with the goal of understanding the neural basis for a more complex example of classical conditioning, the conditioning of the eye blink in the rabbit. In the standard procedure the US is a puff of air to the eye, which produces a UR of an eye blink (Gormezano, Kehoe, & Marshall, 1983). The CS is a tone, which also comes to evoke an eye blink (CR), although at greater latency (the latency for the UR is about 20 msec from air puff to blink, whereas the latency for the CR is about 70 msec from tone to blink).

Figure 2.6 illustrates the complex circuitry that is relevant to understanding this instance of classical conditioning. Sensory neurons from the cornea synapse onto the fifth cranial nerve, from which neurons go to the sixth and seventh cranial nerves, from which motor neurons go to produce the eye blink. This circuit, which produces the UR, takes about 20 msec. A second, longer circuit goes from the fifth cranial nerve to an intermediate neuron, and from there to the cerebellum (a subcortical structure—see Figure 1.15). Among other neurons in the cerebellum, this path synapses onto cells in a structure called the interpositus. There is also a path of synapses going back from the interpositus to the eye blink, which produces a discrete electromyographic[2] component to the eye blink (UR) about 70 msec after the puff of air (US). The longer latency reflects the greater number of neurons along this path (at least six).

The longer US–UR circuit is of interest because it is involved in the conditioning. There is a circuit by which sensory neurons encoding the tone (CS)

---

[2]Electromyographic recordings measure electric activity associated with contraction of muscles.

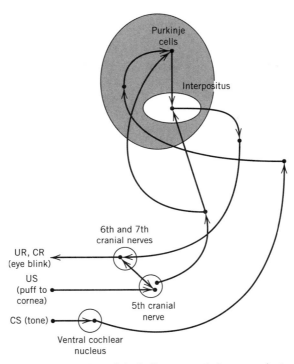

FIGURE 2.6. Simplified diagram of the neural circuitry responsible eye-blink conditioning.

synapse onto the ventral cochlear nucleus, and from there by intermediate neurons to Purkinje cells in the cerebellum. It is possible to produce conditioning by directly stimulating this CS circuit and omitting the tone. It is generally thought that the conditioning is taking place in the cerebellum, since lesions (selective removal of neural tissue) to the cerebellum eliminate eye-blink conditioning. Cells from the CS synapse by many paths onto the Purkinje cells, which are also reached by cells from the US. The Purkinje cells synapse onto the interpositus, which is part of both the CR and the UR paths. The logic by which the CS is thought to evoke the CR is somewhat complicated:

1. The Purkinje cells normally tend to inhibit the interpositus from evoking the response.
2. Learning involves developing inhibitory connections from the CS path to the Purkinje cells.

It is proposed that learning involves inhibiting the Purkinje cells, which normally inhibit the response, and so enabling the CR. (In effect, two neural negatives are combining to make a neural positive.) Electrodes put into the cerebellum to record from the Purkinje cells show reduced firing after conditioning, which is in line with this proposal. This situation is different and more complex than that of conditioning in *Aplysia*. The path of conditioning in *Aplysia* involves two neurons directly associated such that the sensory neuron turns on the motor neuron. In the rabbit, the path involves more than a half-dozen neurons and has the sensory stimulus turning off the cells that normally turn off the eye blink. Although not as thoroughly studied, other instances of mammalian classical conditioning appear equally or more complex and involve different neural structures from the spinal cord to the cortex and different neural circuitry and modifications (Thompson, Donegon, & Lavond, 1988). No single neural process underlies all classical conditioning.

Despite the diversity of neural realizations, classical conditioning presents a rather consistent picture at the behavioral level. These behavioral regularities are identified next.

> *Classical conditioning of the eye blink takes place in the cerebellum, where paths involving the CS, the US, and the CR meet, and it appears to involve learning to inhibit inhibiting connections.*

S–S or S–R Associations?

What is associated to what in classical conditioning? Figure 2.7 shows two possible answers to this question. The US starts out associated to the UR, but what is the CS associated to? Figure 2.7*a* illustrates the more obvious answer given the experimental description: from repeated pairings of CS and UR, the CS comes to evoke the UR. The CR then is just a version of the UR. This association is called a stimulus–response or **S–R association**. Another possibility is that the CS becomes associated to the US (Figure 2.7*b*). The organism behaves as if it expects the CS to be followed by the US; it emits the CR in anticipation of the US and perhaps as preparation for the US. This situation is called a stimulus–stimulus, or **S–S association.**

(a)

FIGURE 2.7. The two possibilities for association formation in classical conditioning: (*a*) the CS is associated to the UR, and (*b*) the CS is associated to the US.

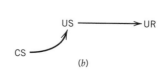

(b)

In reviewing conditioning in *Aplysia*, the choice between the S–S position and the S–R position may seem obvious. The sensory neuron encoding the CS from the siphon was directly connected to the motor neuron that produced the gill retraction, a clear victory for the S–R position. However, *Aplysia* has a nervous system very different from that of mammals. In the case of the circuitry underlying the eye blink in the rabbit, the issue is far from clear. The CS, US, and UR all met in the cerebellum, it could be argued that the CS and the US were associated at the Purkinje cells.

A peculiarity of the S–S position from a biological point of view is evident in the sentence, "The organism comes to behave *as if it expected* the CS would be followed by the US." Although human subjects may have conscious expectations, ascribing such conscious thoughts to animals, such as rabbits, is problematic. Hence, the words *as if* are used. Some rather simple associative mechanisms can produce behavior that mimics conscious deliberation. One example is provided by the Rescorla–Wagner theory, which will be reviewed later in this chapter.

Although the neural evidence is unclear, several behavioral paradigms provide evidence relevant to deciding between an S–S position and an S–R position. These include response prevention, US devaluation, sensory preconditioning, and second-order conditioning. Each of these paradigms is considered in the following subsections.

> *The two possibilities for the association are the S–R hypothesis that the CS becomes associated to the UR and the S–S hypothesis that the CS becomes associated to the US.*

Response-Prevention Paradigm

One way to test the S–R position is to block the response and see if associations can still be formed. This method is referred to as the **response-prevention paradigm.** For instance, Light and Gantt (1936) paired a CS of a buzzer with a US of shock to dogs' paws. This US normally produces a UR of leg lifting, which gets conditioned to the CS. However, they prevented this response by temporally damaging the spinal motor nerves that went to the affected legs. Thus, the dogs never had an opportunity to perform the response and so to form an association between CS and UR. The spinal nerves recovered, and within a couple of months the dogs had complete use of their limbs. Then when presented with the CS of a tone, they displayed the CR of leg lifting. More recent studies have shown similar conditioning when an animal was prevented from responding by use of drugs (Fitzgerald, Martin, & O'Brien, 1973) or by temporary paralysis with curare (Leaf, 1964). In all these experiments, there is a US but no UR to which the CS can become associated. The existence of conditioning supports the S–S position over the S–R position.

It could be argued that this interpretation of the S–R association is too peripheral. Even if these organisms were prevented from executing motor responses, their central nervous systems might well have been sending signals for the response, which were blocked from producing the response by the experimental interventions. It could thus be argued that the stimulus was associated directly to a representation of the response in the central nervous system. The other paradigms provide more definitive evidence in favor of the S–S position.

Weak evidence for the S–S position is that classical conditioning still occurs when the animal is prevented from making a response.

US Devaluation Paradigm

A different test of the S–S versus S–R alternatives involves devaluing the US after classical conditioning has taken place (e.g., Holland & Rescorla, 1975; Rescorla, 1973). For instance, a CS of light can be paired with a US of food for hungry rats. The CS comes to evoke a number of responses associated with the US of food, including increased activity (Holland & Rescorla, 1975); the rats can then be satiated. When the rats are no longer hungry, will the CS (the light) still evoke activity? If the CS were directly associated to the CR, it would still produce increased activity. On the other hand, if the CS had produced increased activity through anticipation of the US of food, and the US has lost its power to produce increased activity, the CS would lose its power to evoke activity. In fact, it loses its ability to evoke activity, implying that S–S associations were formed.

This type of test is referred to as a **devaluation paradigm**. The US is devalued. If the CS is directly associated to the CR, it will not be affected by the devaluation, but if it is associated to the US, it will be affected. As another example, consider the conditioned emotional response, or CER, behaviors, such as freezing, shown by animals such as rats to CSs in anticipation of aversive stimuli, such as shock (see Chapter 1). The shock US can be devalued by repeated administration (in the absence of the CS), which makes the rat less sensitive to it. When the CS is finally presented after such US devaluation, the rat shows a reduced CER. Generally, the response to the CS is reduced when the US is devalued, indicating that the CS was associated to the US.

If the US is devalued after conditioning, response to the CS is reduced, suggesting an S–S association.

Sensory Preconditioning Paradigm

Experiments using a **sensory preconditioning paradigm** (e.g., Rizley & Rescorla, 1972) also suggest that the CS and US become associated. A typical sensory preconditioning experiment (see Table 2.1) has two phases. In the first phase, one neutral stimulus, such as a light (CS_2), occurs just before another neutral stimulus, such as a tone (CS_1). In the second phase, CS_1 is paired with a US. For instance, the tone (CS_1) may precede a shock to the leg, which produces the UR of leg withdrawal. After a while, the tone acquires the ability to evoke leg withdrawal.

What happens if the other neutral stimulus, the light (CS_2), is then presented? If classical conditioning involves associating responses to stimuli, nothing will happen because the light was never paired with leg withdrawal. On the other hand, if stimuli are directly associated, the light (CS_2) will evoke the anticipation of the tone (CS_1), because of their pairing, and therefore the light, like the tone, will evoke the anticipation of the shock (US). Thus the animal will anticipate shock in response to light and withdraw its leg. This is exactly what happens. In general, sensory preconditioning experiments show that CS_2 evokes the CR even though it was never paired with the US and so never preceded the UR.

Sensory preconditioning shows that two neutral stimuli can be associated, consistent with the S–S position.

Second-Order Conditioning Paradigm

An alternative paradigm, the **second-order conditioning paradigm** (see Table 2.1), provides evidence for S–R associations. Holland and Rescorla (1975) performed an experiment with rats, in which a light (CS_1) was paired with a US

Table 2.1 *Three Paradigms and the Associations Formed to the CS*

Paradigm	Phase 1	Phase 2	CS_1 Association	CS_2 Association
Standard	—	CS_1–US	S–S (to US)	—
Sensory Preconditioning	CS_2–CS_1	CS_1–US	S–S (to US)	S–S (to CS_1)
Second-order conditioning	CS_1–US	CS_2–CS_1	S–S (to US)	S–R or S–S (to CR or CS_1)

of food. The CS comes to evoke a CR of increased activity. Then a second stimulus, a tone (CS_2), was paired with the first, the light (CS_1). Thus, as in the preconditioning experiment, there is a CS_2–CS_1 pairing and a CS_1–US pairing. However, in the second-order conditioning paradigm, the order is CS_1–US, then CS_2–CS_1. As in the preconditioning paradigm, the second-order CS_2 (in this example, the tone) acquires the ability to evoke the CR (in this example, increased activity). This phenomenon is not evidence for an S–S association, however. Since the first-order CS_1, the light, already evoked its own CRs, it could be that the CR is now being transferred to the second-order CS_2. In effect, CS_1 could be behaving like a US and the CR like its UR. Thus, there are two possibilities: the tone could be associated to light (S–S) or increased activity (S–R).

Holland and Rescorla used a devaluation paradigm to determine whether the associations were S–S or S–R. They devalued the US of food by satiating the rats. As noted earlier, US devaluation reduces the conditioned response to the first order CS_1, suggesting an S–S association between CS_1 and the US. However, it does not lead to reduced responding to the second-order CS_2, suggesting a direct association between CS_2 (tone) and the CR (activity). If the first-order association is extinguished by presenting light without food, the second-order association is not extinguished and the tone continues to produce increased activity (e.g., Amiro & Bitterman, 1980). Thus the surprising result from this and other second-order conditioning experiments seems to be that first-order associations are S–S and second-order associations are S–R. However, other second-order conditioning experiments (e.g., Rashotte, Griffin, & Sisk, 1977) have found evidence for S–S second-order associations.

In second-order conditioning experiments, second-order associations tend to be S–R, in contrast to first-order associations, which are S–S.

Conclusions

The current conception (e.g., Holland, 1985a) is that both stimulus and response aspects of subsequent events compete for association to the stimulus. Different paradigms produce S–S or S–R associations depending on whether the subsequent stimulus or response aspects are more salient or prominent. A preconditioning experiment provides evidence for S–S associations because no salient responses are associated to the neutral stimulus. A second-order conditioning experiment supports S–R associations because the first-order conditioning usually gives the CS_1 response characteristics that are more salient than its stimulus characteristics. First-order associations are more often S–S in character because the US is typically so salient. Table 2.1 attempts to summarize the results. There are three paradigms: standard, which involves one pairing, and the sensory preconditioning and second-order conditioning, which involve two pairings but differ in their ordering. S–S associations appear to be the rule except with respect to CS_2 associations in second-order conditioning.

Whether associations are S–S or S–R depends on whether the stimulus or response is more salient.

What Is the Conditioned Stimulus?

What exactly is the conditioned stimulus that gets associated in classical conditioning? If an organism forms an association to a tone of a particular pitch or frequency (for example, 1000 Hz), will the organism display the association to a slightly different pitch (1010 Hz), a very different pitch (4000 Hz), an entirely different sound (a dog barking), or a flash of light? Intuitively, it would seem that a slightly different stimulus, such as 1010 Hz, should elicit the association but that a very different one (the flash of light) should not.

Siegel, Hearst, George, and O'Neil (1968) conditioned the eyelid response in rabbits to tones of different frequencies. Different rabbits experienced tones with frequencies of 500, 1000, 2000, 3000, or 4000 Hz paired with a puff of air to the eye. They were then tested with a variety of stimuli at different frequencies. Figure 2.8 shows the **generalization gradients** obtained for each training stimulus. The amount of eyelid response to various sounds falls off as the sounds become more different from the original training stimulus. For instance, a rabbit trained with 1000 Hz, responded most often to a test of 1000 Hz, next most frequently to 500 or 2000 Hz, then to 3000 Hz, and least frequently to 4000 Hz.

Subjects can learn to restrict the range of stimuli to which they respond. This phenomenon is called **discrimination learning.** In one experiment with humans, Gynther (1957) trained an eye-blink response to a CS involving a dim light to the right. When initially tested with a dim light to the left, his subjects showed a strong tendency to respond. However, the US (puff of air to the eye) was never associated with the light to the left. After 100 discrimination trials (50 with each CS), subjects discriminated between the two stimuli and showed a much greater tendency to blink to the right light.

Experiments such as these show that classical conditioning can generalize to a range of stimuli and that this range of stimuli can change as the subject learns whether the CSs are or are not associated with the US. The phenomena of stimulus generalization and discrimination are discussed at greater length in the next chapter as they have received more attention in research on instrumental conditioning.

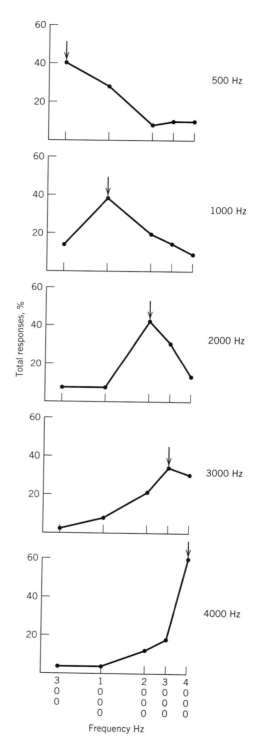

FIGURE 2.8. Mean percentage of total generalization test responses for groups trained at each CS value. (The arrow indicates the frequency of the training stimulus for each group.) *Source:* From S. Siegel, E. Hearst, N. George, and E. O'Neal. Generalization Gradients Obtained from Individual Subjects Following Classical Conditioning. *Journal of Experimental Psychology, Volume 78.* Copyright © 1968 by the American Psychological Association.Reprinted by permission.

54

Organisms naturally generalize a CR to a range of similar CSs, but they can be trained to change the range of CSs to which they emit the response.

What Is the Conditioned Response?

Two possibilities exist as to the nature of the CR in classical conditioning. The CR may be the UR. Perhaps the CS causes the organism to experience some internal image of the US, which then produces the same behavior for whatever reason it was produced by the US. The other view is that the CS is informational; it allows the organism to anticipate that the US will occur and thus to take appropriate action in anticipation of the US. In this view, the CR is a preparation for the US, not a response to it. It is noteworthy that the CRs that are conditioned are adaptive; that is, the CRs tend to prepare the organisms for the US. As noted earlier in this chapter, it is to the human's benefit to blink in anticipation of a puff of air. It is also to the dog's benefit to salivate if food is coming and to flex its leg in anticipation of shock. The original US–UR reflex is in the organism to begin with because it is adaptive. Thus the CS–CR connection tends to be adaptive also.

One kind of evidence for the preparatory character of the CR comes from cases in which the CR is not the same as the UR. A striking example concerns heart-rate changes in response to electric shock. The unconditioned response to electric shock is heart-rate acceleration; but in some organisms the conditioned response is heart-rate deceleration (Obrist, Sutterer, & Howard, 1972; Schneiderman, 1973). In anticipation of a shock, the organism relaxes, which may reduce the perceived magnitude of the pain. This relaxing reduces the heart rate. Similarly, some organisms, such as rats, tend to show increased activity in response to shock but freeze in response to a stimulus associated with shock (Rescorla, 1988b). Thus the behavioral responses to the CS can be quite the opposite of the responses to the US, but both can be viewed as adaptive responses. The shock is a noxious stimulus that requires escape, whereas the CS is treated as a warning that may require a different response. For example, in nature when an animal sees a predator (CS), freezing may help it avoid detection, but once the predator attacks (US), flight is the appropriate response.

A number of unconditioned responses involve a biphasic structure in which an initial response is followed by an opposing response. One of the most dramatic involves responses to narcotics, such as heroin. The initial response to heroin, a feeling of euphoria, is followed by a second, opponent response, which tends to counteract the initial response and produces unpleasant withdrawal symptoms. Another example of such an **opponent process** is skydiving (Epstein, 1967). The feelings of terror the skydiver has just before the dive are followed by an antagonistic response of pleasure when the dive is successful. Solomon and Corbit (1974) suggest that the antagonistic opponent response is caused by the body trying to avoid extreme arousal states, which are demanding of resources. In the case of heroin, the increased pain threshold it produces can also be dangerous.

Wagner (1981) proposed that in the case of such biphasic URs, the compensatory second response is conditioned to the CS because it is an appropriate response to blunt the effect of the US. On the other hand, when the UR is monophasic, like an eye blink, and does not involve an opponent process, the UR is conditioned because the UR is the appropriate response in anticipation of such a US.[3] Wagner called his theory **SOP**, for **sometimes opponent process**, because sometimes (i.e., in the case of biphasic responses) the conditioned response is the opponent process.

It has been suggested that the conditioning of the opponent process is responsible for drug tolerance (Siegel, 1983). With repeated use of a drug, the high becomes weaker and weaker; consequently, the addict needs to take more and more of the drug to produce the same high. It is claimed that the stimuli that accompany drug use (for example, a needle) serve as a CS that becomes conditioned to a second, opponent process. Thus, the conditioning of the opponent process is producing the drug tolerance. The CR evoked by these stimuli is the opponent process that negates the effect of the drug. There is evidence that much of the tolerance built up to drugs such as morphine can be removed by changing the stimuli that accompany their administration (for a review, see Siegel, 1983).

The CR (which is not always the same as the UR) is often an adaptive response in anticipation of the US.

Association: The Role of Contingency

An idea that extends back at least to Aristotle's writings on associations is that two things become associated when they occur together in time and space. This is the principle of **contiguity**. Some associative theories have claimed that contiguity of CS and US is sufficient for classical conditioning. Perhaps

---

[3]However, even in the case of the eye blink, Wagner distinguished two components and argued that only the second component becomes conditioned. His position is supported by Thompson's research on the circuitry underlying eye-blink conditioning reviewed earlier. This research showed that there were two components to the unconditioned eye blink, one with a latency of 20 msec and one with a latency of 70 msec.

the best evidence for contiguity is the strong influence that the CS–US interval can have on conditioning. For instance, Figure 2.3 showed that eye blink conditioning was maximal if the CS occurred very close in time to the US. However, as discussed later in this chapter, short intervals are not always necessary. In some situations conditioning can be obtained at delays of several hours.

An alternative view is that conditioning occurs only if there is a **contingency**; that is, the first stimulus predicts the occurrence of the second. In this view, mere co-occurrence of CS and US is not sufficient to form an association. For instance, when my two sons watch TV, they argue. However, my two sons argue a lot when they are involved in other activities. Thus, the mere co-occurrence of TV and arguments does not mean that there is a contingency (i.e., watching TV causes them to argue). The probability of arguments must be greater when the TV is on for there to be a contingency. Said symbolically, a predictive or contingent relationship requires

$$P(\text{argument} \mid TV) > P(\text{argument} \mid \overline{TV})$$

where $P(\text{argument} \mid TV)$ is the probability of an argument when the TV is on and $P(\text{argument} \mid \overline{TV})$ is the probability of an argument when the TV is not on.

Rescorla's Experiment

Rescorla (1968b) conducted an experiment to determine whether contiguity or contingency is essential in classical conditioning. He intermittently presented a 2-min tone while rats were pressing a bar. In different conditions, he presented shock during 10, 20, and 40 percent of these 2-min tone intervals. Rescorla was interested in the degree to which the rats would show a CER (freeze) and decrease their rate of bar pressing during a tone interval.

Rescorla also varied the probability of shock during the 2-min intervals when no tone was present, creating three separate conditions with 10 percent, 20 percent, or 40 percent probability of a shock during the no-tone intervals. Figure 2.9 shows the results for various combinations of probability of shock in the two types of intervals. The plot shows how much less the rats pressed the bar in the presence of a tone relative to how much they pressed in the absence of a tone. If they pressed P times in the presence of a tone and A times in the absence of a tone, the measure of suppression is the proportion $(A - P)/(A + P)$.[4] Since P and A are measured over the same periods of time, they should be equal if the rat is unaffected by the tone and the suppression rate should be zero. To the extent the animal is conditioned to the tone, P should be near zero, and the suppression rate should be near one, indicating that the animal is freezing in the presence of the tone.

[4]This is an algebraic transformation of the measure reported by Rescorla.

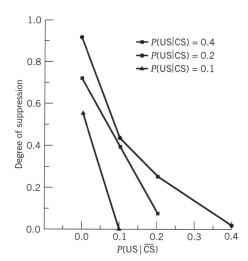

FIGURE 2.9. Dependence of conditioning on both $P(US \mid CS)$ (likelihood of the US during the CS interval) and $P(US \mid \overline{CS})$ (likelihood of the US in the absence of the CS). (Adapted from Rescorla, 1968.)

Consider the degree of conditioning displayed when the probability of a shock was .4 during a tone interval. The amount of conditioning is a function of the probability of a shock when no tone is present. When the probability of a shock in a no-tone interval was zero, the classical conditioning result of large response suppression occurred. The degree of suppression was near one, indicating that the rats almost never pressed the bar in the presence of the tone. However, as the probability of a shock in the no-tone interval increased to .4, the level of suppression decreased. When the probability of shock was the same in the presence or absence of a tone (i.e., both were .4), no conditioning occurred; the degree of response suppression was zero, implying that the rate of bar pressing was the same in both the presence and the absence of the tone. The other conditions in Figure 2.9 displayed similar results. The amount of conditioning is not a function of contiguity (frequency with which shock and tone co-occur) but rather of contingency (difference between probability of shock given tone and probability of shock given no tone).

Conditioning only occurs when presentation of the CS is associated with increased probability of the US.

Conditioned Inhibition

The previous paradigm demonstrated that organisms show conditioning when the probability of the US is greater in the presence of the CS. What if the probability is lower? In that case there is evidence that the organism acts as if it expects the US not to occur. This phenomenon is called **conditioned inhibition.**

The standard paradigm for demonstrating conditioned inhibition involves using two CSs: a CS+, which is positively associated to the US, and a CS−, which is negatively associated to the US. In an experiment by Zimmer-Hart and Rescorla (1974), when a clicker (CS+) was presented, a shock followed, but when both a clicker (CS+) and a flashing light (CS−) were presented, no shock occurred. (The CS− was never presented alone during this initial training.).The animal came to show conditioning of the CER to the CS+ alone but not to the combination of CS+ and CS−.

How does the animal treat the CS− in this paradigm? There are a number of ways to show that CS− leads to anticipation of no shock. One method, the summation test (originally devised by Pavlov), looks at what happens when the CS− is presented with another CS that has been associated with the US. So, for instance, Zimmer-Hart and Rescorla also conditioned a 1200 Hz tone to shock. When the tone and flashing light (CS−) were presented together, the CER was reduced. Thus, the CS− negates anticipation of the US to any CS. A second paradigm, the retardation paradigm, involves trying to condition the CS− to the US. It takes longer to condition the CS− than to condition a new CS, indicating that the animal has to overcome an association of CS− with the anticipation of no US.

An interesting manifestation of conditioned inhibition has been demonstrated by Wasserman, Franklin, and Hearst (1974), who trained pigeons to associate food with an experimental context (CS+). A light (CS−) signaled that there would not be food and so became a conditioned inhibitor. Pigeons actively withdrew from the light and went to the other side of their pen. Thus they engaged in a behavior that seemed to actively signal that they anticipated no reinforcement.

Organisms can be trained to negatively associate a CS with a US, and the CS then becomes a conditioned inhibitor for responding.

Associative Bias

This chapter has reviewed the evidence that organisms are sensitive to the statistical regularity between a CS and a US. However, there is also evidence that they are predisposed to associate certain CSs to certain USs independent of their statistical regularity. This preference for certain associations is referred to as **associative bias**, which is similar to Thorndike's concept of belongingness discussed in the first chapter.

Suppose you heard a loud noise that sounded like an explosion followed by the shaking of the ground. How likely would you be to think the explosion sound and the shaking of the ground were related? Suppose, on the other hand, you heard a bird's song followed by the shaking of the ground? How likely would you be to think that the bird sound and the shaking were related? Presumably, you would think the first pair are more probably related than the second pair. Certain pairs of stimuli are more likely to be related than are other pairs of stimuli, and organisms condition more readily with such pairs of stimuli.

In a well-known study, Garcia and Koelling (1966) used rats whose only access to water was from a water spout. While drinking the water, the rats were exposed to a compound CS consisting of a flavor component (a saccharine taste) and an audiovisual component (light flash and click). Different groups of rats then received either a shock or an injection of a drug that produced nausea. Garcia and Koelling tested the rats separately with saccharin-flavored water and with the audiovisual stimulus to see which had a greater impact on water intake. Rats that had received a shock later showed greater CER (i.e., reduced drinking) to the audiovisual stimulus, whereas rats that had received the injection showed greater CER to the flavor stimulus. Thus rats were more prepared to associate a CS of light with a US of shock and a CS of flavor with a US of poisoning. A great deal of subsequent research has focused on conditioned taste aversions of a distinctive taste (CS) with a poisoning (US). Rats (and many other organisms, including humans) learn such taste aversions after a single CS–US pairing and after intervals between the CS and US up to 24 hr (Etscorn & Stephens, 1973). It is unusual for conditioning to operate over such long time delays (e.g., see Figure 2.3). Organisms presumably have this unusually strong propensity to associate taste and poisoning because it is adaptive.

The associations that organisms are prepared to form are somewhat species specific. Wilcoxon, Dragoin, and Kral (1971) compared using the CS of water taste (sour) or water color (dark blue) in conditioning to a US of poisoning . They compared rats and quail and found that rats displayed greater aversion to taste and quail displayed greater aversion to color. This result makes sense when the two species are compared. Rats are nocturnal animals with an excellent sense of taste and smell but with poor vision; quail are daytime animals with excellent vision.

Organisms have a bias for associating stimuli that are likely to be related in their environment.

Conclusions About the Nature of the Association

Associations are formed in the classical conditioning paradigm when the appearance of the CS increases the probability that the US will occur. When this is not the case, associations are not formed even if there is a high degree of co-occurrence between the CS and the US. An organism is also sensitive to the likelihood of an association between the two stimuli (associative bias). The organism might be characterized as forming a statistical inference. Bayesian statistical models for inference about probabilistic relationships, consider not only the data but also prior beliefs about what relationships are likely. The fundamental relationship in Bayesian statistics is[5]

Posterior belief = Prior belief * Evidence

That is, the posterior, or final, belief in a hypothesis (e.g., that the CS predicts the US) is a product of the prior belief and the strength of the evidence for the hypothesis. Organisms in a conditioning experiment can be viewed as acting according to this statistical prescription. Posterior belief would map onto strength of conditioning between the CS and the US, prior belief onto a bias to associate the CS and the US, and evidence onto the degree of contingency between the CS and the US.

> *Classical conditioning may be viewed as forming associations that are well-founded inferences from a statistical perspective.*

Conditioning to Stimulus Combinations

The research just reviewed shows that organisms respond to the predictiveness of individual stimuli. This sensitivity to the predictive structure of the stimulus situation has been further documented by a number of lines of research studying conditioning when multiple stimuli are present as part of the CS.

Blocking

Experiments have shown that an association is not formed with one CS if another CS is more informative. In one experiment, Kamin (1968) contrasted two groups:

Control. The animals experienced eight trials in which a CS of noise and light was followed by shock.

---

[5]For those who prefer the odds formula in terms of probabilities:

$$\frac{P(H|E)}{P(\overline{H}|E)} = \frac{P(H)}{P(\overline{H})} * \frac{P(E|H)}{P(E|\overline{H})}$$

where $P(H|E)$ is the posterior probability of the hypothesis given the evidence; $P(\overline{H}|E)$ is $1 - P(H|E)$; $P(H)$ is the prior probability of the hypothesis; $P(\overline{H})$ is $1 - P(H)$, $P(E|H)$ is the conditional probability of the evidence given the hypothesis; and $P(E|\overline{H})$ is the conditional probability of the evidence given that the hypothesis is false.

Experimental. The animals received 16 trials in which just the noise was followed by the shock. Then, like the control condition, the animals received eight trials in which a CS of noise and light was followed by shock.

Kamin conducted separate tests to see if the CER could be evoked to noise or to light. He found that the CER had been conditioned to both noise and light in the control group but only to noise in the experimental group. Thus, for the experimental group, the CER was not conditioned to the light even though there were eight reliable pairings of light and shock, which normally would have produced conditioning. The noise had already been established as a reliable predictor of the shock, and the light added no more information; therefore, no association was formed. The tendency for one stimulus to overshadow another stimulus is called **blocking.**

In a variation of this paradigm, Kamin (1969) presented a more intense shock to the light–tone combination than to the tone alone. The animals were first given 16 trials of tone–shock pairings with a shock intensity of 1 mA (milliampere), followed by eight trials of tone and light followed by shock with an intensity of 4 mA. In this condition rats showed significant conditioning of the CER to the light. The light was now informative, because it signaled a more intense shock.

In another variation of this paradigm, Wagner (1969) trained three groups of rabbits in an eyelid-conditioning paradigm in which the US was a 4.5-mA shock to the area of the eye:

Group 1. Two hundred trials of light and tone followed by shock.

Group 2. Two hundred trials of light and tone followed by shock, intermixed with 200 trials of light followed by shock.

Group 3. Two hundred trials of light and tone followed by shock, intermixed with 200 trials of light followed by no shock.

In contrast to Group 1, which defines the reference condition, Group 2 showed little conditioning of the eyelid response to the tone. As in Kamin's studies, this result can be interpreted to mean that the light was the better predictor. On the other hand, Group 3 showed even greater conditioning of the tone to the eyelid response than did the reference Group 1. The rabbits in this group were getting evidence that the light was not a good predictor of shock and so came to treat the tone as the sole reliable predictor of shock.

When one CS is a more reliable predictor of a US than a second CS, that CS blocks conditioning of the other CS.

Configural Cues

In the experiments discussed thus far, separate stimuli developed separate associations to the US. However, it is possible to condition an organism to respond only if a particular configuration of stimuli are present. Organisms can be trained to respond when both stimuli A and B are present and not when just one is present. Although this result could mean that the AB combination is associated, it could also indicate that A and B are separately associated to the US but are too weakly associated to evoke the CR individually and are only strong enough to do so in combination. Whereas it is possible to explain this result in terms of separate associations, in some situations the only possible explanation is that a configuration of stimuli have become associated and not separate stimuli. For example, organisms can also be trained to respond when A is present, and when B is present, but not when AB is present (see Kehoe & Gormezano, 1980, for a review). If there is a positive strength association between A and the US and between B and the US, an even stronger association would be expected when both A and B are present. However, it appears that associations can be learned to cue combinations. In this case, the cues A + noB and noA + B become associated to the US, but the combination A + B does not. Another situation that shows configural associations involves four cues, A, B, C, and D. Organisms can be taught to associate A + B and C + D to the US but not A + C or B + D. Again, it is not possible to account for this result in terms of associations to the individual stimuli. Associations must be formed to the combinations. Such stimulus combinations are referred to as **configural cues.**

This phenomenon is quite different from blocking, where one cue (A) in a combination masks the other (B). In the typical blocking paradigm the organism comes to respond to A alone and to AB in combination, but not to B alone. In a typical configural conditioning experiment the organism comes to respond to A alone, to B alone, but not to AB (although as described earlier there are other ways to demonstrate configural conditioning). Configural conditioning also differs from a conditioned inhibition paradigm, where one cue negates the effect of the other and acquires the properties of a conditioned inhibitor (the organism learns to respond to A alone, but not to AB or to B alone). In a typical configural conditioning paradigm, both cues maintain positive effects, but only when presented alone.

Configural conditioning involves learning associations to combinations of stimuli that are different from the associations to the individual stimuli.

Conclusions

In some cases (blocking and conditioned inhibition) it seems that the response to the combination of stimuli can be predicted from the response to the individual stimuli, but in other cases (configural cues) it cannot. The next section reviews the Rescorla–Wagner theory, which accounts for the occasions in which the response to the stimulus combination can be understood in terms of the response to the individual stimuli.

The Rescorla–Wagner Theory

In 1972, Rescorla and Wagner proposed a theory that successfully predicts many phenomena of classical conditioning. Their theory shows how simple learning mechanisms can be sensitive to the contingency between the CS and the US and illustrates the principle that simple mechanisms can produce the highly adaptive statistical sensitivities documented in the previous section. Although the theory is 20 years old, it has gained renewed currency as a popular theory of neural learning.

The Rescorla–Wagner theory has three basic constructs. One construct is the strength of association, V, between CS and US that controls the amount of conditioning displayed. The second is the maximum level, λ, that this strength can reach, thought to be a function of the US such that stronger USs can maintain stronger associations. The third construct is the rate of learning, α, that determines how rapidly this limit can be reached. The fundamental assertion in the theory is that when a CS and a US are paired, the strength of their association increases proportionally to

the rate of learning, α, and

the difference between the maximum strength possible and the current strength, $(\lambda - V)$.

Cast as an equation this becomes

$$\Delta V = \alpha(\lambda - V)$$

where ΔV is the change in strength.

Consider the application of this theory to a simple situation in which the US and the CS are paired 20 times. Assume that the maximum strength of association, λ, is 100 and that the rate of learning, α, is .20. The initial strength of association is zero. After the first learning trial, the increase in the strength of association is

$$\Delta V = .20 \, (100 - 0) = 20$$

The strength of association is the sum of this increment plus the prior strength of 0: $20 + 0 = 20$. In the next trial, the same formula applies, except that the prior strength is now 20 instead of zero, and so the increment is

$$\Delta V = .20 \, (100 - 20) = 16$$

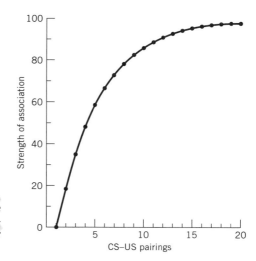

The total strength is this result plus prior strength: 16 + 20 = 36. This process can be continued, calculating for each trial the total amount of strength. Figure 2.10 shows the growth of strength over the first 20 trials; the growth looks like a typical conditioning function (e.g., see Figures 1.4 and 2.1).

> *The Rescorla–Wagner theory asserts that learning is proportional to the difference between the current strength of association and the maximum strength that the US will allow.*

Application to Compound Stimuli

The Rescorla–Wagner theory is similar to several mathematical theories developed to account for learning, and it is not surprising that it succeeds in accounting for the approximate form of the conditioning curve. The theory derives special interest from how it deals with compound cues such as those used in blocking experiments. Before considering blocking experiments, consider a simpler situation. Suppose that, two stimuli, A and B, are simultaneously presented as the CSs for the US. For example, the US might be food, A might be a tone, and B might be a light. The Rescorla–Wagner theory holds that the total strength of association between the compound cue and the US, which can be denoted V_{AB}, is the sum of the strengths of the individual associations of A and B to the US, which can be denoted V_A and V_B. That is,

$$V_{AB} = V_A + V_B$$

When A and B are paired with the US, they will grow in strength of association to the US as in the case where there is only one CS:

$$\Delta V_A = a(\lambda - V_{AB})$$

$$\Delta V_B = a(\lambda - V_{AB})$$

On the first trial, since there is no prior conditioning, these equations become (assuming $\alpha = .20$ and $\lambda = 100$):

$$\Delta V_A = .20(100 - 0) = 20$$

$$\Delta V_B = .20(100 - 0) = 20$$

Thus after the first trial, the individual stimuli have strengths of 20 and V_{AB} is the sum, or 40. On the next trial, the equations become

$$\Delta V_A = .20(100 - 40) = 12$$

$$\Delta V_B = .20(100 - 40) = 12$$

and the individual stimuli have strengths $20 + 12 = 32$. Figure 2.11 shows the growth in the strength of association to a single cue when the cue is part of a compound versus when it is alone. The cue strength of A can only reach 50, because it must share the strength of association with B. This example illustrates an important feature of the Rescorla–Wagner theory, that the various stimuli compete for association to the US, a situation often referred to as **competitive learning.**

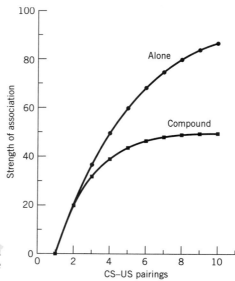

FIGURE 2.11. Comparison of growth in strength to cue alone versus cue in compound combination.

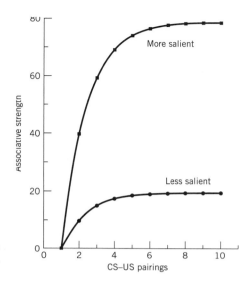

FIGURE 2.12. Growth in strength of association to a more versus a lesss salient stimulus.

In the preceding equations, α is the same for A and B. But Rescorla and Wagner allow for the possibility that the stimuli may vary in their salience and therefore one stimulus may have a more rapid learning rate. Suppose that the rate of learning for A is .4 and for B it is .1. Figure 2.12 plots the rate of strength accumulation for the two stimuli. As shown, A overshadows B and acquires most of the strength. When one stimulus is sufficiently less salient than another, it fails to be conditioned when presented in a compound cue, even though it can be conditioned when presented alone (e.g., Kamin, 1969).

When there are multiple CSs, the Rescorla–Wagner theory assumes that they will compete for the total associative strength.

Application to Blocking and Conditioned Inhibition

The Rescorla–Wagner theory can be applied to the phenomenon of blocking. Recall the original Kamin experiment in which rats were given an initial 16 trials pairing A with the US followed by eight trials pairing A and B with the US. The effect of the first 16 trials is that A has already acquired most of the available strength and nothing is left for B. That is, the effect of the conditioning is to set the strength of association to A to full value.

$$V_A = 100$$

The stimulus combination can only have the same strength. That is,

$$V_A + V_B = 100$$

which implies that the strength of association for B is zero:

$$V_B = 0$$

The Rescorla–Wagner theory also explains why B conditions if a stronger shock is used for the AB combination than for A alone. Rescorla and Wagner postulated that the value of λ was related to the intensity of the US. Thus, if a higher value is used for the shock, as in Kamin (1969), the value of λ is larger and strength is available to be conditioned to B. As noted earlier, B can be conditioned if the shock intensity is increased.

The Rescorla–Wagner theory can also predict the phenomenon of conditioned inhibition discussed earlier. In the paradigm, A (e.g., a clicker) is associated with the US (e.g., a shock) but AB (e.g., clicker plus flashing light) is not. The Rescorla–Wagner theory implies that the organism will learn strengths of association, V_A to the clicker and V_B to the light, such that

$$V_A = 100$$

$$V_A + V_B = 0$$

since A is always associated with shock but the AB combination never is. The only way these equations can hold is for $V_B = -100$. Thus, B has a negative strength of association that corresponds to the result of conditioned inhibition. Figure 2.13 shows the growth in strength to the positive CS+ (e.g., clicker) and the negative CS− (e.g., light) over trials, assuming that the trials presented to the organism alternate between A (CS+) and AB (CS+ and CS−). The learning curves go to +100 and −100.

The Rescorla–Wagner theory predicts blocking and conditioned inhibition because of its assumption that stimuli compete for association to the US.

Problems with the Rescorla–Wagner Theory

The Rescorla–Wagner theory explains a wide variety of experimental data, but there are some things it does not explain. A phenomenon that proves difficult for the theory concerns the effect of stimulus preexposure. If an organism is exposed to the CS a number of times before an experiment begins, and then is given CS–US pairings in the experiment, the rate of conditioning is impaired (Reiss & Wagner, 1972). The phenomenon of preexposure slowing conditioning to a stimulus is called **latent inhibition.** The organism has been exposed to a number of occurrences without anything happening and has a bias to

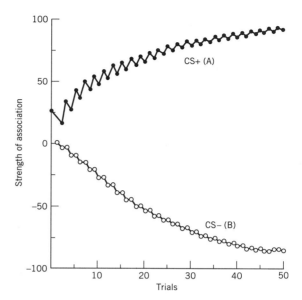

FIGURE 2.13. Growth in strength of association for the positive and negative CSs in a conditioned inhibition paradigm.

maintain a belief in CS ineffectiveness after the conditioning trials have begun. However, there is no place in the Rescorla–Wagner theory for such an effect. The CS–US strength starts out at zero, and with no US presentations in the preexposure trials, it stays at zero. Thus the Rescorla–Wagner theory predicts that conditioning should proceed as if there had been no preexposure trials. It has been suggested that the rate of learning, α, should reflect the salience of the CS and that the effect of CS preexposure should be to make it less salient. Wagner (1978) proposed an extension of the Rescorla–Wagner theory that includes, in effect, this assumption.

Other researchers (e.g., Mackintosh, 1975; Pearce & Hall, 1980) have extended the idea that stimuli change in terms of how effectively they can be associated. Mackintosh assumes that a CS that has proved more effective than another CS at predicting the US will result in faster learning. Pearce and Hall propose that CSs that are more surprising produce faster learning. Thus, the competition in these theories is among the learning rates associated with the CSs and not the strength of associations that can be maintained to a US. These theories can explain latent inhibition. Because the stimulus has a history of not being associated with any significant US, it comes to have a lower learning rate and so is harder to associate when the CS–US contingency is introduced.

One of the triumphs of the Rescorla–Wagner theory is its treatment of blocking in which the two stimuli combine independently. However, the research on configural cues indicates that the stimuli are not always independent and stimulus combinations can be conditioned. Such results can only be accomodated within the Rescorla-Wagner theory by introducing compound stimuli as CSs different from the individual stimuli. Thus, not only are A and B treated as stimuli that can be conditioned, but so is the compound AB. This idea was proposed by Spence in 1952, was suggested by Rescorla and Wagner, and has been actively developed by Gluck and Bower (1988) in an application of the Rescorla–Wagner theory to human learning. However, the predictive power of the Rescorla–Wagner theory is weakened by the introduction of compound stimuli because there is no basis for predicting whether the cues will be treated separately or configurally.

The data on associative bias also present problems for the Rescorla–Wagner theory because they indicate that learning is not just a function of the CS or the US, but depends on the interaction between the two. Some pairs belong together and are easier to associate; for example, rats are especially prepared to condition a US of poisoning to a CS of taste. The Rescorla–Wagner theory can accommodate this phenomenon by assuming that the learning rate, α, varies with the CS–US combination. As in the case of compound cues, however, such a maneuver weakens the theory because the theory offers no basis for knowing how to assign α's to CS–US combinations.

Organisms are more sensitive to the statistical relationships among stimuli than the Rescorla–Wagner theory can accommodate.

Neural Realization: The Delta Rule

The Rescorla–Wagner theory corresponds to a current idea about how learning may take place at the neural level, which has played a particularly important role in a theory of neural processing called **connectionism**. This theory stresses the importance of synaptic connections among neurons. Figure 2.14 illustrates a typical neural processing module according to connectionism, where neural activation comes in along a set of input neurons (at the bottom), each of which synapses onto a set of output neurons. Every input neuron is associated to every output neuron. The pattern of connections presents a more complex situation than that found in Aplysia (Figure 2.5), where one neuron (a motor neuron) becomes more active when another neuron (a sensory neuron) becomes active. The learning task for such a neural net is to set the strengths of associations among the neurons such that when a particular pattern of activation occurs on the input neurons, a desired pattern of activation occurs on the output neurons. There is a connectionist learning rule, called the **delta rule**, which is based on the Rescorla–Wagner equation, that explains how to do this neural learning.

Figure 2.15 illustrates an application of this modeling approach to a medical diagnosis problem studied by Gluck and Bower (1988). Their subjects studied records of fictitious patients who suffered from four symptoms (a

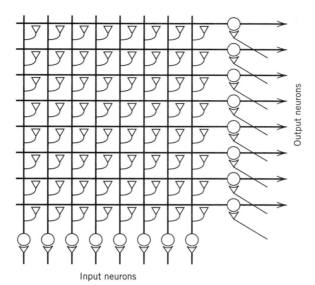

FIGURE 2.14. Schematic representation of a neural net, where input neurons come in (at the bottom) and synapse on output neurons (at the right). All input neurons have synaptic connections to all output neurons. *Source:* From W. Schneider. Connectionism. Is it paradigm shift for psychology? *Behavior Research Methods, Instruments & Computers, Volume 19*, pp. 73-83. Copyright © 1987. Reprinted by permission of Psychonomic Society, Inc.

bloody nose, stomach cramps, puffy eyes, and discolored gums) and made discriminative diagnoses as to which of two hypothetical diseases the patients had. In this case, the four symptoms are the inputs and the two diseases are the outputs. For each patient, the input neurons corresponding to that patient's symptoms would be active and the goal would be to have the output neuron corresponding to that patient's disease active. This problem can be mapped onto the Rescorla–Wagner theory by having the inputs correspond to CSs and the outputs to USs. Just as a rat is trying to predict shock in a particular stimulus situation, subjects are trying to predict a disease given certain symptoms. The delta rule treats the neural learning as if each input-to-output association is being learned as a separate CS–US association. In the case of Figure 2.15, there are $4 \times 2 = 8$ associations being learned.

In the context of neural modeling, the Rescorla–Wagner equation, or the delta rule, is taken as a rule for adjusting the strength of the synaptic connection between the input neuron i and an output neuron j. The delta rule is stated as

$$\Delta A_{ij} = \alpha A_i (T_j - A_j)$$

where ΔA_{ij} is the change in the strength of synaptic connections between input i and output j; A_i is the level of activation of input neuron i; A_j is the level of activation of output neuron j; and T_j is the target or desired activity of j. This equation should be compared with the Rescorla–Wagner equation, which states

$$\Delta V = \alpha(\lambda - V)$$

where ΔV corresponds to ΔA_{ij}; α corresponds to αA_i; λ corresponds to T_j; and V corresponds to A_j. As in the Rescorla–Wagner theory, learning is proportional to the difference $T_j - A_j$. According to the delta rule, learning is also proportional to A_i, the level of activation of the input neuron. Recall that one proposal for an extension of the Rescorla–Wagner theory was to make learning proportional to stimulus salience.

In the case of a network, as shown in Figures 2.14 and 2.15, where there are m possible inputs and n possible outputs, the system uses the delta rule to simultaneously learn some $m \bullet n$ synaptic connections. The behavior of the whole system can be complicated, but it still reproduces the basic competitive learning behavior of the original Rescorla–Wagner theory.

The actual Gluck and Bower experiment was quite complex. Subjects saw hundreds of patients reflecting different combinations of symptoms. Each combination had a different probability of each disease. Overall, one disease was much rarer than the other, and each symptom had a differential association with the disease. The subjects were supposed to learn from this experience how to predict a disease given a pattern of symptoms. Figure 2.15 illustrates the final strengths of association that were learned in accordance with the delta rule. These strengths of association did an excellent job of predicting subjects' classification behavior and how they rated each symptom as to whether it was diagnostic of the rare disease or the

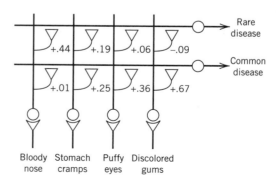

FIGURE 2.15. An adaptation of Figure 2.14 to the Gluck and Bower experiment in which subjects associate symptoms to diseases.

common disease.[6] As seen from the synaptic weights in Figure 2.15, a bloody nose was treated as more symptomatic of the rare disease (.44 strength versus .01 strength), whereas the other three symptoms were treated as more symptomatic of the common disease. In their ratings of the symptoms after the experiment, subjects agreed that only a bloody nose was predictive of the rare disease.

The delta rule has become an important construct in theories of neural learning. It has been used in a wide variety of models of neural processing and has been imported by computer science to build models of machine learning. As this example illustrates, it has also been used to predict complex human learning.

The Rescorla–Wagner theory corresponds to a popular theory of competitive learning among neural elements, called the delta rule.

Evaluation of the Rescorla–Wagner Theory

Probably the most significant contribution of the Rescorla–Wagner theory is that it shows how the buildup of simple associative strength can produce a complex pattern of learning in which predictive associations are formed and nonpredictive associations are not. The difficulties with the theory arise in situations in which the organism is more sensitive to contingencies in the environment than are the simple equations of the theory. These equations may not always capture what is happening, but they give an idea of the kinds of changes that might underlie conditioning. The next chapter applies the theory to instrumental conditioning, for which it offers an equally good model of learning.

Applications of Classical Conditioning Techniques

Classical conditioning techniques have been applied to a number of important phenomena outside the laboratory, including human behavior pathologies.

---

[6]Gluck and Bower's model actually has a single output, which varies from +1 to −1 depending on the probability of the rare disease. The model in Figure 2.15 is formally equivalent but more in keeping with the Rescorla–Wagner theory. In this model, each disease is predicted separately in a 0–1 scale and the maximum strength of association is 1. The Gluck and Bower values can be determined by subtracting the strength of the common disease from the strength of the rare disease.

Several of these applications make use of the fact that it is impossible to maintain antagonistic responses to the same stimulus; that is, conditioning one response to a stimulus will suppress another, and thus, an unwanted response to a stimulus can be eliminated by conditioning a competing response. This method of treatment is referred to as **counterconditioning.**

One application of counterconditioning is in the treatment of addictions to substances such as nicotine and alcohol. The idea is to condition negative reactions to the taste of alcohol or nicotine, formerly associated with pleasurable reactions. In one study (Raymond, 1964) an alcoholic was injected with a drug that induced vomiting after ingesting a drink. This taste-aversion conditioning successfully eliminated the subject's drinking habit. The technique often does not work, however (Nathan, 1976), because after the training, if the subject drinks without the drug, no negative reaction occurs; rather, the positive result reoccurs, leading to the extinction of the taste aversion.

A somewhat more successful application of the counterconditioning technique is in **desensitization** of phobias or fears. Wolpe (1982) developed a technique known as systematic desensitization. The patient is asked to order situations in terms of how much fear they arouse. Table 2.2 lists a series of situations identified by a patient terrified of exams, in order from the most frightening to the least frightening. The patient at first imagines the least fearful situation and is induced to relax. (Relaxation can be achieved by muscle tensing and then relaxing; sometimes drugs are used to enhance the relaxation response.) Gradually, over a series of sessions, the patient comes to relax while imagining more and more fearful situations. The patient is being conditioned to associate a relaxation response with the stimuli of a particular fear-inducing

Table 2.2 *Spatial–Temporal Hierarchy of Anxiety*

Level	Scene
1.	On the way to the university on the day of an examination.
2.	In the process of answering an examination paper.
3.	Standing before the unopened doors of the examination room.
4.	Awaiting the distribution of the examination papers.
5.	The examination paper lies face down before the student.
6.	The night before an examination.
7.	One day before an examination.
8.	Two days before an examination.
9.	Three days before an examination.
10.	Four days before an examination.
11.	A week before an examination.
12.	Two weeks before an examination.

Note: In the anxiety hierarchy, a higher level represents lower anxiety.

Source: From J.Wolpe, 1982. *The practice of behavior therapy* (3d ed.). Oxford: Pergamon. Reprinted by permission.

situation. Because relaxation is incompatible with the response of fear, this technique eventually blocks the fear response. The process of desensitization must be gradually built up, because it is initially impossible for the patient to relax while imagining the most fearful situations. Wolpe (1958) reported that 90 percent of his patients benefited from this desensitization process.

Another interesting application of classical conditioning involves food aversions. As noted earlier, taste stimuli preceding a poisoning become conditioned to the poisoning; as a consequence the organism comes to avoid that food. In some situations a conditioned food aversion can be a serious problem. For instance, cancer patients undergoing chemotherapy develop strong aversions to the foods they eat because chemotherapy produces nausea; thus they do not eat adequate food. One means of combating this problem is to schedule eating and chemotherapy so that food intake does not precede nausea. Another possibility for patients is to consume a bland diet, because nondistinctive stimuli do not appear to become conditioned as readily as distinctive stimuli. Yet another possibility is to have patients consume a very distinctive-tasting food before the onset of nausea so that the taste aversion will only be conditioned to that stimulus. For example, the problem of taste aversion with children was reduced if they received a distinctive-tasting "mapletoff" ice cream before chemotherapy (Bernstein, Webster, & Bernstein, 1982).

Classical conditioning techniques can be used
to replace harmful associations by beneficial associations.

Final Reflections on Classical Conditioning

Classical conditioning is a phenomenon defined by experimental procedures: the US is made contingent on the CS and, as a consequence, the CS acquires the capacity to elicit a CR. Early in the history of classical conditioning researchers tended to view the learning that was taking place as an unconscious and automatic consequence of the contiguity of CS and US. Classical conditioning was attractive in part because it was seen to embody pure and simple learning, uncontaminated by cognition on the part of the organism.

More recent research on classical conditioning has viewed the learning as much more cognitively involved, which is undoubtedly the case, at least some of the time in higher organisms, such as humans. However, classical conditioning also occurs in animals, such as *Aplysia*, that do not have central nervous systems, let alone a mammalian brain; hence it seems unlikely that all classical conditioning requires cognitive involvement.

As discussed at the beginning of the chapter, different processes in the nervous system underlie different instances of classical conditioning. Despite these many differences, there are strong behavioral similarities across most forms of conditioning: similar acquisition and extinction histories, spontaneous recovery, generalization, temporal parameters, relationships between the CR and the UR, and so on. The reason for the similarities lies in the fundamental adaptiveness of classical conditioning. Classical conditioning allows organisms to respond adaptively in anticipation of a biologically significant UR. The common functionality of classical conditioning across species underlies its common behavioral properties. An analogy can be drawn from the relationship between the eye of the mammal and the eye of the octopus. The two have independent evolutionary histories and are formed from different tissue, but they function almost identically. They function so similarly because both have to deal with the same problem of extracting information from light. Likewise, the reason classical conditioning is so similar across organisms in terms of its behavioral properties is that it serves the same function of allowing the organism to respond in anticipation of the US.

Thus there are generalities at a behavioral level in classical conditioning that may not be supported by generalities at a physiological level. In science diverse underlying processes often give rise to common higher-order generalities in the behavior of the system. For example, in economics industries producing different products display the same economic realities. Similarly, in biology different organisms display similar relationships. For instance, as reviewed in Chapter 4, rather different creatures follow rather similar principles of foraging for food.

This book identifies many generalities in learning that apply to diverse species. The study of learning and memory has traditionally been about identifying these generalities and understanding them. Much of psychology is devoted to understanding generalities at the behavioral level. However, it should not be concluded that all species learn the same way at the behavioral level. Species show different preferences for various CS–US combinations, reflecting differences in their biological makeup and in their environment. The closest thing to a universal claim that can be made about classical conditioning is that it tends to reflect an adaptive response by the organism to CS–US contingencies. Even this claim depends on carefully choosing the meaning of "adaptive." For instance, it is really not adaptive for chemotherapy patients to develop food aversions, although their tendency to form food aversions might be adaptive in other contexts, where it would lead them to avoid poisonous food.

The behavioral properties of classical conditioning reflect its adaptive character.

Further Readings

A number of texts are devoted to discussion of classical and instrumental conditioning, including books by Domjan (1993), Catania (1992), Mazur (1994), and Schwartz (1989). Rescorla (1988b) wrote a highly accessible article describing the changes that have occurred in the conception of classical conditioning in the last 25 years. Hearst (1988) provides a survey of research in classical and instrumental conditioning. Many books contain discussions by modern researchers, including those by Gormezano, Prokasy, and Thompson (1987) and Spear and Miller (1981). The September 1992 issue of *Scientific American* was devoted to the relationship between brain and mind and presented a number of relevant articles, such as one by Kandel and Hawkins on the biological basis of learning and another by Hinton explaining recent developments in connectionist theories of learning, among them a mechanism called "backprop," which is a popular extension of the delta rule. Thompson, Donegon and Lavond (1988) published a fairly exhaustive review of the psychobiology of learning. Bernstein and Borson (1986) reviewed research on learned food aversions. Journals that frequently publish research on classical conditioning include the *Journal of Experimental Psychology: Animal Behavior Processes; Behavioral Neuroscience; and Animal Learning and Behavior.*

3

Instrumental Conditioning

Overview

This chapter discusses research and theory on instrumental conditioning. In instrumental conditioning, an organism is reinforced if it makes a response (R) in a certain stimulus (S) situation. For instance, Thorndike's cats were reinforced by escape and food if they hit the correct knob in his puzzle box. Just as classical conditioning is associated with Pavlov, instrumental conditioning is sometimes associated with Thorndike, but the association is not as strong because its use and study did not really originate with Thorndike. In contrast with classical conditioning, the discovery of which came as something of a surprise, instrumental conditioning is what everybody means by learning. It has been used by teachers and parents since time immemorial, and there has never been any lack of speculation as to how it should be used. Thorndike was simply the first to propose a scientific theory of its operation.

Most of what happens in a classroom can be thought of as instrumental conditioning. Consider a child learning that the sum of 3 and 4 is 7. The stimulus can be thought of as "3 + 4," the response, "7," and the reinforcer, the teacher's approval. Or consider a student learning to read a word. The stimulus is the orthographic representation, the response is saying the word, and the reinforcement might be some sort of social approval. Similarly, parents' shaping of their children's behavior can be conceived of as instrumental conditioning, for example, parents rewarding children with money for cleaning their rooms.

Although these instances of human learning can be considered instrumental conditioning, they differ in an important way from the situation of Thorndike's cats. In the examples given here, humans are told the contingencies that are operative, whereas Thorndike's cats had to discover them. Humans do sometimes find themselves in instrumental conditioning situations in which they must discover the contingency. For instance, many students feel they have to discover by trial and error what kind of an essay will earn a high grade from a teacher.

This chapter focuses on instrumental conditioning in animals. The issues involved in instrumental conditioning in humans occupy center stage in the later chapters on memory, skill acquisition, and inductive learning. However, as shown later in this chapter, humans placed in the same instrumental conditioning paradigms as animals do produce similar behavior.

The typical instrumental conditioning experiment requires organisms to discover that a response in a stimulus situation produces a reinforcement.

Classical and Instrumental Conditioning Compared

Contrasting the procedure in classical conditioning with the procedure in instrumental conditioning helps define them both. In classical conditioning, the experimenter sets up a certain contingency such that if a particular stimulus condition occurs, another stimulus will occur. For instance, if a dog is in the experimental apparatus and a light flashes, the dog will be given food. In instrumental conditioning, the experimenter sets up a contingency such that if a particular stimulus condition occurs *and* if the organism emits a response, then a particular reinforcer will occur. For instance, if a rat is in a Skinner box and it presses a lever, a pellet will appear in the feeder. Thus the difference is that in instrumental conditioning, the reinforcer (which is like a US) is contingent on the conjunction of stimulus and response, whereas in classical conditioning it is only contingent on the stimulus. Thus in instrumental conditioning the organism can control whether the reinforcer occurs.

If the organism successfully learns in either situation, it comes to behave *as if* it had figured out the experimenter's contingency. In the case of classical conditioning, it comes to perform a response (the CR) in preparation for the US. In the case of instrumental conditioning, it comes to emit the response if it finds the reinforcer desirable. The fundamental learning is the same in both cases. The organism is learning to form an association between an antecedent configuration of elements (stimuli and, in instrumental conditioning, a response also) and a consequence that can be predicted from these antecedents. Thus both paradigms involve learning environmental contingencies. The difference between the two involves the role of the response. In classical conditioning the organism cannot control the resulting US, but its response can prepare for it. In instrumental conditioning the organism's response determines whether the resulting reinforcer will occur.

There has been much debate about whether the process of learning is the same in classical conditioning and instrumental conditioning. Classical conditioning has often been considered an automatic process, and instrumental conditioning a voluntary process. However, as noted in the previous chapter, specifying which behaviors are automatic and which are voluntary can be problematic. Interest has waned in this distinction, and attention has focused on the behavioral similarities between these two types of conditioning, with the implicit assumption that the two kinds of conditioning involve the same learning process. Among their common characteristics are that both kinds of conditioning show the same effects of practice, both extinguish in the same way when the contingency is eliminated, and both show spontaneous recovery. Both kinds of conditioning are hurt if a delay is placed in the contingency. Both paradigms result in successful conditioning only if there is a contingency among the elements (not just a contiguity). With respect to stimulus control, both show blocking effects, both can show configural learning, and both show similar generalization and discrimination processes. Also, both show effects of associative bias. Since classical and instrumental conditioning are so similar, this chapter essentially uses research on instrumental conditioning to expand further on the nature of conditioning in general.

Instrumental and classical conditioning share many similar behavioral properties.

What This Chapter Will Cover

The chapter focuses on the same four questions that organized much of the discussion in the previous chapter.

What is associated?

What is the conditioned stimulus?

What is the conditioned response?

What is the nature of the association?

After addressing these questions, this chapter considers the similarity between conditioning and causal inference and the evidence about the important role of a particular brain structure, the hippocampus, in conditioning.

What Is Associated?

Instrumental conditioning involves a stimulus followed by a response followed by a reinforcement. For instance, a dog might learn to respond to the stimulus "sit" with the response of sitting, and receive food as a reward. As in the case of classical conditioning, there are a number of possibilities for what is associated to what. One possibility is that the stimulus becomes associated to the response. In this case, the reinforcer would stamp in the association but would not be part of the association. This was the original idea of Thorndike and a number of the early learning theorists. However, nearly from the beginning there was evidence that organisms also develop specific expectations about the reinforcer. For instance, Tinklepaugh (1928) showed that monkeys registered disappointment when an expected reinforcer (slice of a banana) was replaced by a less valued reinforcer (lettuce). This result would seem to imply that the reinforcer is part of the association.

Colwill and Rescorla (1985a, 1985b, 1986, 1988) argued that organisms develop associations involving all three terms—the stimulus, the response, and the reinforcer. They showed that organisms can learn to expect specific reinforcers to specific responses. For instance, rats learned to associate different types of food pellets to two different responses (lever pressing and chain pulling). When fed with one kind of food pellet outside the experiment, they performed a predominance of responses that yielded the other kind of food pellet. Colwill and Rescorla argued that organisms develop expectations; that is, that if a certain response is emitted in the presence of a certain stimulus, it produces a certain reinforcer.

Colwill and Rescorla (1986) used a reinforcer devaluation paradigm to make a similar point. They trained rats to make two different responses— pushing a rod to the left and to the right. One response was always rewarded with food and the other with a sugar solution. Then one of the reinforcers was paired with an injection of lithium chloride to produce a taste aversion to that reinforcer. The rate of response associated with the devalued reinforcer decreased. This result would not occur if the association was just between stimulus (rod) and response (pushing left or right), but would occur if the association also involved the reinforcement.

> *In instrumental conditioning, organisms are learning a three-term contingency, that a response in a particular stimulus situation will be followed by a reinforcement.*

Associations Between Responses and Neutral Outcomes

Discussion thus far has reviewed evidence that organisms can learn associations between responses and reinforcing stimuli. What about associations between responses and neutral stimuli? Organisms can learn about associations between stimuli and other neutral stimuli in classical conditioning (see the discussion of sensory preconditioning and second-order conditioning). Can they similarly acquire such neutral associations in an instrumental conditioning paradigm? In one experiment by St. Claire-Smith and MacLaren

(1983), rats learned as part of their free exploration of a Skinner box that a lever press produced a noise. The experimental group was then trained on pairings of the noise with food without a lever present in the box, and the control group was trained on pairings of light and food. When the lever was reintroduced (but no food was given), rats in the experimental group pressed the bar more often than did the control rats who had not learned the noise–food pairing. As a result of their earlier free exploration, they appeared to have learned that lever pressing produced the noise. Putting this result together with the classical conditioning of noise and food, they acted as if they *inferred* that lever pressing might also produce food. Thus, it appears that organisms are capable of learning associations between a response and any stimulus that follows just as they are capable of learning associations between a CS and any stimulus that follows in a sensory preconditioning experiment. The resulting stimulus need not be reinforcing.

The ability to form associations between responses and neutral outcomes is critical to learning complex chains of responses, only the last of which involves reinforcement. Consider a rat learning to run a maze. It must learn a sequence of associations of the sort that making a turn in a certain direction in a certain part of the maze leads to another part of the maze. There is nothing inherently reinforcing about such turn–maze associations. Only the final turn becomes directly associated with food (even it may not be directly associated with food, but instead with a part of the maze that is associated with food). However, the rat has to learn all these associations in order to put them together to run the maze. The latent learning experiments showed that rats could learn all these neutral associations before they learned that there was food in part of the maze. When they learned where food was, they could recruit this neutral information to help them get to the food.

> *Organisms can learn that certain responses produce neutral outcomes and combine this information with other experiences to obtain reinforcement.*

Secondary Reinforcement

The previous section described a situation in which the rat first learned the association bar press–noise and then the association noise–food. This situation is similar to sensory preconditioning in classical conditioning in that the organism first learns a neutral association, then a biologically significant association, and then puts them together. Reversing the order of learning the associations results in the equivalent of second-order conditioning; the animal first learns the biologically significant association noise–food and then bar press–noise. The noise acquires the ability to reinforce the bar press for an animal trained with such a procedure, and the animal will press the bar just for the click without food (Skinner, 1938). The noise is said to be a **secondary reinforcer**, or a **conditioned reinforcer.**

The classic example of a secondary reinforcer is money for humans, which can be extremely reinforcing but has no biological function in and of itself; human beings have learned to associate money with more primary reinforcers. Examples of the many other such secondary reinforcers in human society include letter grades in courses and promises of favors. In an experiment Saltzman (1949) presented rats with food in a white goal box. Then he introduced them to a T-maze, where the rats had to choose between a path leading to a white box and a path leading to a black box. The rats learned to take the path that led to the white box even though the box did not contain any food. The white box had acquired the ability to reinforce behavior. With enough exposure to the white box in the maze without food, the rats extinguished and no longer chose that path. When the currency in a particular country deflates to the point where it is useless, people cease seeking the money, also.

The functions of secondary reinforcers such as money are clear in the human world (it turns out that chimps are also capable of treating coins and other tokens as money; Cowles, 1937; Wolfe, 1936). Secondary reinforcers are promises of primary reinforcement, and people know that they can be exchanged for primary reinforcers. It is not clear whether it is always appropriate to attribute such a cognitive explanation to secondary reinforcers in lower animals, but it does appear that secondary reinforcers are good at bridging delays in reinforcement for many species. For instance, if a 5-sec delay is inserted between pecking and reinforcement, a pigeon will not peck a key at a substantial rate. On the other hand, if a green light comes on immediately after the peck and the pigeon has seen the light paired with food, the pigeon will learn to peck rapidly at the key. The green light becomes a secondary reinforcer that enables the pigeon to bridge the delay in reinforcement (Staddon, 1983).

> *A secondary reinforcer is a previously neutral stimulus that has acquired the ability to reinforce behavior as a consequence of being paired with a primary reinforcer.*

What Is the Conditioned Stimulus?

As reviewed in the previous chapter some, but not all, variations on the original stimulus are effective in producing the response. The extension of the conditioned response to new stimuli is called **generalization** and the restriction of the conditioned response from other stimuli is called **discrimination.** The phenomena of stimulus generalization and stimulus discrimination occur in instrumental conditioning just as they do in classical conditioning, and they have been studied much more extensively in the domain of instrumental conditioning.

Generalization

In a prototypical study of stimulus generalization, Guttman and Kalish (1956) trained pigeons to peck at a key of a particular color (measured by wavelength). During 60-sec intervals the key was lit with a certain color and pecking produced a reinforcement of food. These intervals were separated by 10-sec intervals of total darkness during which the pigeons did not respond. Following the experiment, the key was illuminated at different wavelengths and the number of key pecks was recorded to test for generalization. Four conditions were defined by the wavelength of the original key, 530 nm (green) 550 nm (greenyellow), 580 nm (yellow), or 600 nm (yelloworange). After training, the pigeons were tested without reinforcement. Figure 3.1 shows, for each training condition, the number of responses for different test wavelengths. Pigeons showed maximal response when the test wavelength matched the wavelength on which they were trained. Their rate of responding decreased as the difference increased between training and test wavelength. These results do not simply reflect the ability to discriminate the study stimulus from the test stimulus, that is, that pigeons responded to a test color to the degree that they thought it was the study color; pigeons are capable of making much sharper discriminations than those illustrated in Figure 3.1. In some sense, pigeons were registering their "opinion" on whether this difference in wavelength was likely to be relevant to their reinforcement.

The curves in Figure 3.1 are often referred to as **generalization gradients.** Most generalization gradients are not as steep as those in Figure 3.1. Figure 3.2 from Jenkins and Harrison (1960) illustrates a generalization gradient from an experiment in which pigeons were trained to peck when a key was lit and a 1000 Hz tone was on and then were tested for tones that varied from 300 to 3500 Hz. The data are plotted in terms of percentage of all responses given to that tone.[1] The generalization gradient curve is nearly flat, showing very little decrease in response as the tone varied from the training stimulus of 1000 Hz. Pigeons were registering their "opinion" that the actual pitch of the tone was irrelevant to whether reinforcement would be delivered. The pigeons behaved as if the only critical feature was that the key was lit and that it did not matter whether there was a tone or not. In effect, they ignored the pitch of the tone.

Figure 3.1 shows a positive generalization gradient, but negative generalization gradients are possible, too. Terrace (1972) created a situation in which

---

[1]The original Jenkins and Harrison data included a no-tone condition, which is not shown.

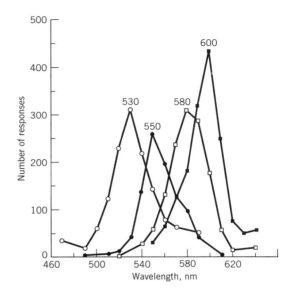

FIGURE 3.1. Pigeons are trained to peck at lights with wavelengths of 530, 550, 580, and 600 nm. The curves show the total responses to stimuli of similar wavelengths. These are cumulative responses for 6 min. (From Guttman & Kalish, 1956).

pigeons could receive reinforcement for pecking when the light was homogeneous white light and not when the light was a specific color (570 nm). They were then tested with lights of specific colors. Figure 3.3 shows their rate of responding as a function of wavelength. The minimum rate of responding occurred at the nonreinforced frequency; the rate gradually recovered as the wavelength moved away from this frequency.

Organisms have biological predispositions to treat certain dimensions and certain differences in these dimensions as important in defining the CS, while they ignore other dimensions and differences. However, as shown next, organisms can change their behavior if experience indicates that these other dimensions and differences are significant.

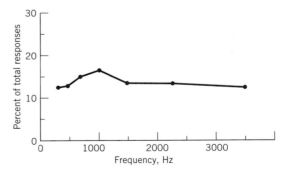

FIGURE 3.2. Rate of responding to tones of various frequencies for pigeons trained to respond to tones of 1000 Hz. (From Jenkins & Harrison, 1960).

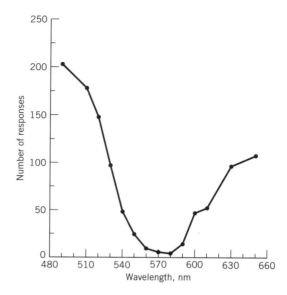

FIGURE 3.3. Gradients of inhibition for three pigeons following learning where only 570 nm was not reinforced.

Organisms generalize the CS, ignoring certain dimensions and certain differences in other dimensions.

Discrimination

What happens if the organism is exposed to multiple stimuli and learns that some are accompanied by reinforcement and others are not? The simplest possibility is an experiment in which the presence of a stimulus is associated with reinforcement and its absence is not. Jenkins and Harrison (1960) looked at what would happen in such a condition. The results when there was only a positive stimulus of 1000 Hz were displayed in Figure 3.2: pigeons pecked at the lighted key no matter what the frequency of the tone. Jenkins and Harrison compared this condition with a condition of differential training: when the key was lit and there was a 1000-Hz tone, the pigeons were reinforced for pecking the key; but when the key was lit and there was no tone, they were not reinforced for pecking the key. Figure 3.4 shows the results. There are strong generalization gradients around 1000 Hz. The effect of the discrimination training was to indicate that the tone was relevant.

This experiment compared the presence of a tone with the absence of a tone, in contrast with many other experiments in which different values of a stimulus were positive and negative. In another experiment by Jenkins and Harrison (1962), pigeons were first reinforced for pecking in the presence of a 1000-Hz tone and not in the absence of a tone, as described earlier. Then the pigeons were trained to respond to a 1000-Hz tone but not to a 950-Hz tone. Figure 3.5 compares the generalization gradients of a pigeon before and after

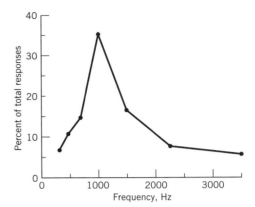

FIGURE 3.4. Generalization gradients following differential training with a 1000 Hz tone. Individual gradients are based on the means of three generalization tests.

learning that the 950-Hz tone was negative. The generalization gradient is much steeper after the animal was trained to discriminate between a 1000-Hz tone and a 950-Hz tone. This pigeon actually showed maximum response to a tone of 1050-Hz, which is away from the negative 950 Hz. To explain this phenomenon the next section considers a popular theory of discrimination learning.

Organisms can be trained to discriminate among stimulus values and to respond only to certain ones.

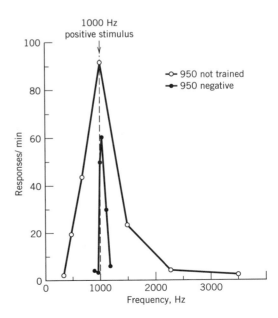

FIGURE 3.5. Generalization gradients obtained from a pigeon trained to respond to a 1000 Hz tone and then later trained to discriminate it from a 950 Hz tone. (From Jenkins & Harrison, 1962).

Spence's Theory of Discrimination Learning

Spence (1937), a learning theorist strongly influenced by Hull (see Chapter 1), developed a theory of how training on positive and negative stimuli combined to produce a net generalization gradient. Modern versions of his theory feature various technical differences that make them more sophisticated and accurate (e.g. Blough, 1975); however, Spence's theory is described here, since it contains the essential ideas and is the original proposal. We learned earlier that if an animal is reinforced for the response in the presence of a stimulus, it builds a positive generalization gradient (Figure 3.1) around the stimulus, and if an animal is not reinforced for the response in the presence of a stimulus, it builds a negative generalization gradient (Figure 3.3) around that stimulus. Spence's basic idea was that behavior in discrimination training is just a combination of these positive and negative generalization gradients. Figure 3.6 illustrates his analysis. Suppose a circle of 256 cm² is the positive stimulus and one of 160 cm² is the negative stimulus. Figure 3.6 illustrates the positive generalization gradient around 256 and the negative generalization gradient around 160. Subtracting one from the other produces the net generalization gradient. Note that the positive peak of this gradient has been shifted from 256 in a direction away from the negative stimulus. This is the prediction of a **peak shift**—the stimulus that evokes the most responding is not the positive training stimulus, but one shifted away from it and the negative stimulus. This prediction is somewhat counterintuitive, since the organism is responding more to a stimulus that it has not been trained on than to a stimulus it has been trained on. This prediction is typically confirmed in discrimination experiments of this sort. Figure 3.5 from Jenkins and Harrison (1962) is one example of this peak shift; the pigeon responded more to a 1050-Hz tone than to the 1000-Hz tone with which it had been trained.

> *Spence proposed that discrimination learning resulted from subtracting generalization gradients for nonreinforced stimuli from generalization gradients for reinforced stimuli.*

Relational Responding

Spence extended his theory to a simultaneous presentation procedure in which the organism must select between two stimuli. Suppose that an organism is trained to discriminate between stimuli of 160 cm² and 256 cm² given the generalization gradients illustrated in Figure 3.6 and is then given a choice between two stimuli of 256 and 409 cm². Because of the peak shift, the organism should select 409 rather than the original positive 256. A number of experiments supported this prediction of a preference for the stimulus shifted from the original.

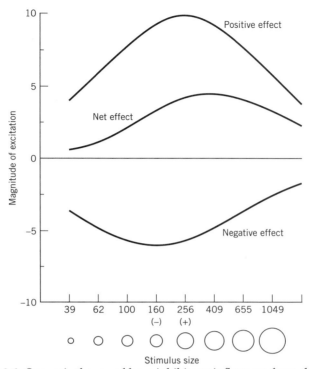

FIGURE 3.6. Spence's theory of how inhibitory influences from the negative stimulus subtracted from excitatory influences of the positive stimulus yield a net generalization gradient.

However, this result was explained in another way by Köhler (1955) and other Gestalt psychologists. He argued that the organism was responding to the relationship between the two training stimuli and had learned to select the larger. There has been a long history of controversy between relational accounts and accounts like that of Spence, which propose that the organism responds to the absolute value of the stimulus. It is fair to say this controversy has been settled with the conclusion that both are right. Under appropriate circumstances an organism can be trained to respond to a relationship between two stimuli, and under other circumstances it can be trained to respond to the absolute properties of the two stimuli.

An experiment by Lawrence and DeRivera (1954) provides an example of animals responding relationally. Figure 3.7 illustrates the stimuli used: cards of two shades of gray. In Figure 3.7 these shades are indicated by the numbers 1 through 7: 1 is white, 7 is black, and the other numbers denote the various shades between. The bottom half of the card was always 4 and the top half varied. When the top half was lighter (1 to 3), rats were trained to turn right; when it was darker (5 to 7) they were trained to turn left. The critical test

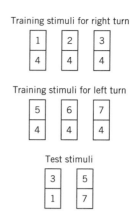

FIGURE 3.7. Stimuli used by Lawrence and DeRivera (1954). The numbers 1 through 7 denote shades of gray.

occurred after training. The rats were presented with a card with 3 on top and 1 on the bottom. Both 3 and 1 were associated with moving right, but the top was darker than the bottom and this relation was associated with turning left. The rats responded to the relational information and turned left. In contrast, when they were tested with a 5 on the top and 7 on the bottom, they went right, confirming again the relational theory.

The fact that organisms can encode and respond to either relational or absolute information raises an extremely troublesome problem in the discussion of what constitutes the conditioned stimulus. It is not immediately apparent how an organism will encode a particular stimulus. One organism may encode it one way (e.g., absolute size) and another a different way (relative size). Without knowing how the stimulus is encoded, it is not possible to know what patterns of generalization and discrimination will take place. Researchers and theorists typically assume what seems to be the obvious encoding. But what seems obvious to the experimenter may not seem obvious to the organism. Chapter 6 has more to say about how information is represented.

> *The Gestalt psychologists proposed that organisms responded to the relationship between stimulus values rather than to the absolute values.*

Errorless Discrimination Learning

It is sometimes possible to get organisms to form a discrimination between two stimuli without making any errors. Typically to train a discrimination such that pigeons peck at a key when it is red but not when it is green, many thousands of trials may have to be presented before the pigeon stops choosing the negative green key. So much training is necessary to fight the natural tendency of pigeons to peck at lighted objects in the context of food (see the forthcoming discussion of autoshaping). However, rather than presenting both positive and negative keys initially, Terrace (1963) first presented only the key in the positive red. The pigeon learned to peck at the key for food reward. The positive red was then alternated with a darkened key, which pigeons do not peck (reflecting their biological predisposition to peck only at lighted objects). Next a very dim green light was presented instead of the dark key. The animal continued to peck only when the key was red. Gradually the green light was increased in intensity, and the pigeon continued not to peck. Finally the pigeon was discriminating between a full intensity red light and a full intensity green light without making any errors. This phenomenon has been called **errorless discrimination learning**.

Terrace (1972) has used this idea of gradually fading in to teach a discrimination in another way. First, he established a discrimination between a positive red and a negative green key by the errorless discrimination procedure just described. Then he trained a discrimination between a key with a positive vertical bar and a key with a negative horizontal bar. The vertical bar was superimposed on the key when red, and the horizontal bar was superimposed on the key when green. Showing the dominance of color as a cue, the pigeons continued to peck at the red key with the vertical bar and not the green key with the horizontal bar. Gradually, the colors were faded out and the pigeons wound up pecking to vertical bars and not to horizontal bars without making errors.

Not all discriminations can be taught this way; success relies on species-specific traits, such as not pecking at a darkened bar and the dominance of color over shape. However, Terrace (1972) argued that when such discrimination learning is obtained, it displays properties that distinguish it from the results of the more traditional discrimination learning. In the traditional situation, the negative stimulus becomes aversive to the animal and may elicit negative responses. Many human beings, for example, display aggressive responses to red lights. Terrace found that pigeons trained to discriminate traditionally would flap their wings and peck at another key that removed the negative key. Terrace claimed that such aggressive and escape behaviors do not occur in the situation of errorless discrimination learning.

Rilling (1977) questioned Terrace's claim that such discrimination learning is qualitatively different from that produced by the normal procedure. He showed that errorless discrimination learning still produced aggressive behavior to the negative stimulus, although to a lesser degree. Whether Terrace's procedure produces qualitatively different behavior or not, it can be an effective means for teaching a discrimination. It also makes the point that there is nothing critical about errors in learning a discrimination. What is critical is that the organism comes to incorporate in one way or another the different contingencies that exist for responding in the presence of different stimuli.

*Near errorless discrimination learning can result when an
existing discrimination in the organism's behavioral repertoire
is gradually transformed into a new discrimination.*

Dimensional Learning

Thus far we have focused on patterns of generalization and discrimination along a single dimension. However, most stimuli have many dimensions. For instance, visual stimuli have color, size, shape, and position in space. In addition, there are various background contextual stimuli, such as the appearance of and possible sounds in the laboratory. How is the organism to identify which dimension or dimensions determine reinforcement? The last chapter described one theory of dimensional combination for classical conditioning, the Rescorla–Wagner theory. According to that theory, various dimensions or stimuli divided a total associative strength according to how reliably they were associated with the US. In effect, they competed for association to the US. A similar process seems to occur in instrumental conditioning in which stimuli compete for association to the reinforcer.

Blocking phenomena can also be shown in instrumental conditioning (Mackintosh, 1974). Blocking phenomena are when one stimulus or dimension becomes so strongly associated that it blocks out other dimensions. The blocking data are among the strongest data in support of the Rescorla–Wagner theory. As in classical conditioning, there is evidence that learning cannot be simply a matter of responding to individual dimensions because animals can be trained to respond to various combinations of dimensions but not to respond to the individual dimensions (Razran, 1971).

Instrumental conditioning paradigms have been used to explore a somewhat different kind of competition among dimensions. Organisms have limited encoding capacity and can only pay attention to so many dimensions at a time. With experience, they can change which dimensions they attend to. For instance, flat generalization gradients can be transformed into peaked generalization gradients by discrimination experiments that simply make the dimension relevant (contrast Figures 3.2 and 3.4).

Another kind of evidence for dimensional learning (sometimes called attentional learning) comes from experiments that involve learning multiple, successive discriminations. The basic paradigm is illustrated in Figure 3.8. A value on one dimension is reinforced (in the training example of Figure 3.8, this is red on the dimension color). After mastering this discrimination, the subject is transferred to a condition in which the opposite value on the dimension becomes positive (a reversal shift—in Figure 3.8, yellow is now positive) or another dimension is used (a nonreversal shift—in Figure 3.8, squares now become positive). Reversal shifts might appear more difficult because the organism must respond in the completely opposite way; on the other hand, nonreversal shifts might seem more difficult because the organism has to learn to pay attention to a new dimension. Most humans and higher apes find reversal shifts easier, whereas very young children and nonprimates find nonreversal shifts easier (Mackintosh, 1975).

Figure 3.8 also illustrates intradimensional shift, which requires the subject to learn to discriminate between new values (such as blue and green) on the previously relevant dimension. This situation is contrasted with learning new values on the other dimension (extradimensional shift). Intradimensional shifts are almost always easier than extradimensional shifts (e.g., Mackintosh & Little, 1969). The contrast between intradimensional and extradimensional shifts, unlike the contrast between reversal and nonreversal shifts, does not require that the organism respond to the same stimuli in different ways; hence, there are no competing responses to the stimuli from the original training.

Thus it appears that one thing that is learned is what dimensions are relevant. In the case of humans, this dimensional learning overwhelms any competing responses on that dimension and so humans find reversal shifts easier than nonreversal shifts. Lower organisms do not show such dramatic results, but still find intradimensional shifts easier than extradimensional shifts.

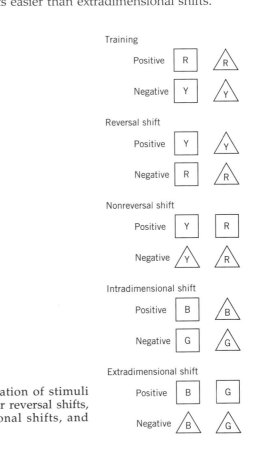

FIGURE 3.8. Schematic representation of stimuli and reinforcement contingencies for reversal shifts, nonreversal shifts, intradimensional shifts, and extradimensional shifts.

Organisms can learn which stimulus dimensions are relevant in discrimination learning.

Learning of Categories

Animals are not only capable of responding to single dimensions or simple combinations of dimensions; they are able to detect situations that correspond to what people consider categories. Figure 3.9 shows some of the stimuli shown to pigeons in a discrimination experiment by Herrnstein, Loveland, and Cable (1976). Some pigeons were trained to peck at instances of the category "tree." Pigeons were trained with some 700 slides of trees and nontrees. The only characteristic that the positive pictures had in common (and that discriminated them from the negative pictures) was that they involved a tree. The positive pictures could not be discriminated from the negative pictures on the basis of simple features; thus pigeons could only make this discrimination if they knew what a tree was. For humans, this is a relatively easy discrimination, because they possess the category of trees. It also turned out to be a fairly easy discrimination for pigeons. Pigeons not only were able to learn to make such discriminations, but they learned in fewer trials than needed in the simple one-dimensional problems described earlier. Moreover, after being trained to discriminate one set of pictures of trees from a set of pictures of nontrees, the pigeons were capable of generalizing this ability to new pictures that had not been used for training.

Wasserman, Kiedinger, and Bhatt (1988) demonstrated category learning by pigeons in a slightly different paradigm. Pigeons were trained to peck at four different keys according to the rules

Peck key 1 if the stimulus was one of 10 cat pictures.

Peck key 2 if the stimulus was one of a second set of 10 cat pictures.

Peck key 3 if the stimulus was one of 10 flower pictures.

Peck key 4 if the stimulus was one of a second set of 10 flower pictures.

Pigeons got quite good at discriminating keys 1 and 2 from 3 and 4, corresponding to the cat–flower distinction. However, they had great difficulty in distinguishing key 1 from 2 (the cat pictures) or key 3 from key 4 (the flower pictures). They found it difficult to learn discriminations within a category. Humans would show similar patterns, finding discriminations between categories easy and discriminations within categories hard.

Chapter 10 provides much more information on concept learning, focusing mainly on human learning of concepts. The experiment just described illustrates that lower animals as much as humans see the world in terms of categories and specific objects and not in terms of simple colors and shapes.

FIGURE 3.9. Four typical pictures used in the experiment by Herrnstein, Loveland, and Cable (1976). (Negative stimuli are on the left; positive on the right.)

Often the meaningful representation of the world is much more salient than the simple dimensional representation, and animals find it easier to learn discriminations when the discriminating factor is a salient category.

Animals easily learn to respond to complex dimensional combinations that define significant categories.

What Is the Conditioned Response?

The next question to address concerns the nature of the response. The traditional view was that a specific response was being learned. As early as the 1920s, however, problems began to be seen with that particular point of view. Muenzinger (1928) trained guinea pigs to press a bar and found that sometimes they pressed with one paw, sometimes with another, and sometimes even with their teeth! Macfarlane (1930) taught rats to swim through a maze for food and then found that they were capable of running the maze for food. Lashley (1924) taught monkeys to solve a manipulation problem with one hand and found they could generalize the solution to the other hand when the first was paralyzed. It seems that organisms come to some representation of the functional structure of their environment and select their responses appropriately. Thus what the guinea pigs in Muenzinger's experiment were learning was not that a particular response was associated with reinforcement, but rather that depression of the bar was associated with reinforcement. As in classical conditioning, the response is an adaptation of the organism to what it has learned about the environment.

Skinner (1938) recognized the nature of the response in his definition of an operant. Different responses that had identical effects in the environment (had identical reinforcement consequences) were defined to be instances of the same operant. Organisms can be trained to discriminate among responses that appear to have equivalent effects (e.g., use of the left hand versus the right hand) if the experimenter sets up reinforcement contingencies that differentiate them. However, they behave as if their default assumption is that actions that have equivalent effects on the world produce equivalent rewards—certainly a plausible default assumption.

Organisms tend not to discriminate among responses that are equivalent in their effect on the environment.

Maze Learning

Maze learning by rats provides some of the strongest evidence that the response is an adaptation by the organism to what it has learned about its environment. Rats are animals whose natural environments are much like mazes, and they are skillful at learning complex mazes, challenging humans in their ability. As noted in the discussion of Tolman in Chapter 1, rats' ability to navigate in mazes depends in part on their developing cognitive maps; they learn the locations of food and other objects in space and traverse the maze to get to those locations. However, there is also evidence that rats can learn the specific turns involved in navigating a maze.

More recent research has brought out some of the other ways in which rats cope with mazes. Research (e.g., Olton, 1978) has been conducted with a radial maze such as that shown in Figure 3.10; the rat is put in the center of the maze, and food is placed at the end of each of the eight arms. Rats on their first encounter with this maze tended to perform very well, visiting about 7 of the 8 arms in their first eight choices. The rats displayed an amazing ability to avoid revisiting these arms. How were they able to explore these mazes so efficiently? One might think that the rats had some systematic plan such as going through all the arms in a left-to-right order. However, this does not seem to be the answer because they did not display any specific order in visiting the arms. Rather, the evidence is that rats have good memories for locations and avoid repeating visits. This is an adaptive trait in their natural environment, where they

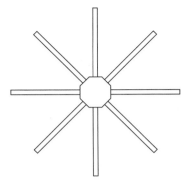

FIGURE 3.10. A top view of a radial maze. *Source:* From D. S. Olton and R. J. Samuelson. Remembrance of places passed. **Spatial memory in rats.** *Journal of Experimental Psychology. Animal Behavior Processes Volume 2.* Copyright © 1976 by the American Psychological Association. Reprinted by permission.

need to keep track of where they have been and consumed food. If they have depleted the food in a particular location, there is no point in repeating the trip.

Other research on rats has compared their ability to learn shift versus stay strategies in a T-maze (Haig, Rawlins, Olton, Mead, & Taylor, 1983). A T-maze (see Figure 3.11) is a simple maze in which a rat runs from a start box to a choice point, at which it must go in one of two directions. There are goal boxes to the left and to the right, and one of them contains food. Shift and stay strategies refer to two different principles experimenters have used for determining which goal box to place food in. The strategies differ in terms of where to look for food after the first trial. If the rat is being trained with a stay strategy, it finds food if it goes down the path that had food before. In a shift strategy, it finds food if it goes down the other path. Rats find it much easier to learn the shift strategy. This result is just the opposite of what would be predicted if rats were learning specific responses, but it is exactly what would

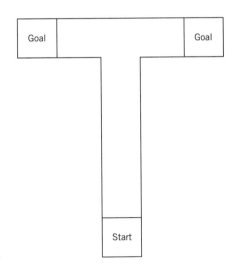

FIGURE 3.11. An example of a T-Maze.

be predicted from their foraging habits in the wild, where they need to avoid food locations that they have already depleted. Several other species also show this tendency to learn better with a shift strategy (e.g., Kamil, 1978). Interestingly, animals find shift strategies harder to learn when they are not allowed to deplete the food in the goal box (Haig et al., 1983); then they have a reason to return to the same part of the maze.

Rats navigate in various environments according to a cognitive map, which includes where significant objects like food are to be found.

Response Shaping and Instinctive Drift

Although organisms tend to select their responses to have specific effects on their environment, they can be trained to emit quite specific responses. Chapter 1 (under Skinner) discussed procedures for shaping responses by successive approximation. However, it turns out that an organism's instincts about appropriate responses can get in the way of such response shaping. Chapter 1 mentioned that a pig was trained to go through an elaborate set of procedures mimicking the morning routine of a human. Pigs are normally easy to train, but the trainers described a problem with what they termed **instinctive drift** (Breland & Breland, 1961). They wanted to train a pig to take a large wooden coin and place it in a piggy bank. The pig was able to learn this behavior quite well given food reinforcement, but after a few weeks, instead of putting the coin in the bank, it would repeatedly drop the coin, root it (dig or turn it up with its snout), and toss it up in the air. The pig became useless as a performer, and the Brelands had to train another pig, which soon developed the same problem. This behavior is part of the natural food-gathering behavior of pigs. They had come to regard the coins as a food and consequently began to behave toward the coins as they did toward food.

The Brelands reported a variation of this problem when they tried to train raccoons to place coins in a container. The raccoons began engaging in behaviors that corresponded to washing and cleaning the food. Although the intrusive behavior was different from that of the pigs, the behavior was part of the species-specific food-gathering behavior of raccoons. Thus organisms' instinctive response patterns can overwhelm responses carefully shaped by instrumental conditioning.

Attempts to shape behaviors in organisms may be frustrated by species-specific response patterns.

Autoshaping

The previous subsection described how conditioning efforts can be frustrated by organisms' biological predispositions toward appropriate response patterns. A somewhat different result can also happen: experimenters can train a behavior without trying. A well-known example, called **autoshaping**, was discovered by Brown and Jenkins in 1968 in their work with pigeons. At irregular intervals they illuminated a response key and then followed the key with food from a grain dispenser. Although the birds did not have to peck at the key to obtain the food, they all started to peck at the key. They wound up behaving as if there had been a contingency between pecking and food.

Considerable effort has been made to understand why the pigeons would peck at a key when it was unnecessary. One enlightening experiment was performed by Jenkins and Moore (1973). They deprived the pigeons of either water or food, and then used the autoshaping procedure of the illuminated key followed by the appropriate reinforcer. All the pigeons began pecking at the key; however, the way in which they pecked at the key differed depending on the reward. When a pigeon had been deprived of food and the reward was food, the pigeon pecked with an open beak and made other movements similar to those that pigeons make when they are eating. When the reward was water for a pigeon deprived of water, the bird pecked at the response key with a closed or nearly closed beak; again, this and other features of the pecking movement were like the movements that pigeons make when drinking.

These results can be interpreted as examples of classical conditioning. That is, the lit key is a CS that predicts the US of food or water, and the animal is giving a conditioned response of pecking to that CS. Although this

Pigeons pecking for water (top row) and for food (bottom row).

interpretation may be basically correct, it fails to capture the full complexity of autoshaping behavior. A good example of this complexity was observed by Timberlake and Grant (1975) in a study of autoshaping in rats. Two groups of rats received different CSs presented in advance of the delivery of a food pellet. For one group the CS was a block of wood; the rats came to gnaw at the wood. For the second group the CS was another rat; in this case the rats approached the other rat and engaged in various social behaviors, such as sniffing and grooming. Thus, depending on the CS, rather different behaviors were autoshaped. The difference makes sense if the eating behaviors of rats are considered. Rats usually eat in groups and display social behaviors to other rats while eating; they also gnaw at inanimate objects as part of their eating behavior. There is a complex species-specific pattern of eating behavior, and different aspects of it are selected by different stimuli.

Generally the lesson of the research on autoshaping and instinctive drift is that animals come to learning situations with strong patterns of instinctive behavior. These patterns may cause the organisms not to learn what the experimenter intended but rather something else. With respect to the issue of what the conditioned response is, this research shows that the organism is not just a bundle of simple muscle movements waiting to be conditioned to a stimulus. Rather, the responses are parts of existing behavioral systems and their conditioning cannot be understood unless these systems are understood. Timberlake (1983, 1984) has called this approach to understanding learning *behavior systems analysis*.

Autoshaping occurs when a stimulus evokes some species-specific behavior because of its association with a reinforcer.

Association: Contiguity or Contingency?

One issue in the case of classical conditioning is whether the learning is produced because the CS and the US are contiguous or because they are contingent. The corresponding issue in the case of instrumental conditioning is whether learning is produced because the response and the reinforcer are contiguous or because they are contingent. Again, contiguity is the requirement that the two occur in close temporal proximity; contingency is the further constraint of a predictive relationship between the two. For example, drinking a glass of water and feeling healthy may be contiguous, but this does not mean that drinking water produces a feeling of being healthy, because the person may usually feel healthy. For there to be a contingency, the probability of feeling healthy would have to be greater after drinking a glass of water than otherwise.

Experiments have varied the probability that the reinforcer would be delivered when the response was made versus when the response was not made—on the analogue of the Rescorla experiment discussed in Chapter 2. For instance, Hammond (1980) trained rats to press a bar for reinforcement in an experiment that involved four phases. Figure 3.12 illustrates the results in each phase.

> ***Phase 1.*** If the rats pressed the bar in any 1-sec interval, they had a chance of a reinforcer. Hammond shaped the rats to a point where they were receiving reinforcers after only 5 percent of these response-filled, 1-sec intervals. The rats were making about 3000 bar presses an hour.
>
> ***Phase 2.*** Hammond began giving reinforcements 5 percent of the time when 1 sec passed and no response had been made. He still gave a reward 5 percent of the time when a response was made, but the reward was no longer contingent on response—it was equally likely whether a response had been made or not. The rats' rate of responding dropped off rapidly until they were making virtually no responses. Thus even though the contiguity of response and reward was maintained, rats stopped responding because there was no longer a contingency.
>
> ***Phase 3.*** Hammond stopped giving reinforcers when the rats did not respond, and the response rate of the rats picked up.
>
> ***Phase 4.*** Hammond removed the contingency again, and the response rate went down again.

FIGURE 3.12. Responses per hour for rats when there is a contingency between pressing and reinforcement and when there is not. *Source:* From L. J. Hammond. *Journal of the Experimental Analysis of Behavior,* The effect of contingency upon the appetitive conditioning of free-operant behavior, 34, 297–304. Copyright © 1980 by the Society for the Experimental Analysis of Behavior, Inc. Reprinted by permission.

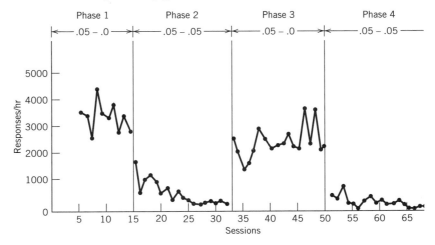

These animals were shown to be sensitive to the experimenter's contingencies just as animals were shown to be sensitive to CS–US contingency in classical conditioning.

Organisms display conditioning only when there is a contingency between response and reinforcement.

Partial Reinforcement

In the experiment described, Hammond used a **partial reinforcement schedule**, that is, only some of the responses were rewarded. It is sometimes hard to discern that the partial reinforcement rate for a response is greater than the background rate of reward. Suppose that the probability of getting a reward in 1 sec is 5 percent if an animal presses a bar, but 4 percent if the animal does not press the bar. The animal might fail to detect the contingency and not display conditioning.

When organisms are being maintained on partial reinforcement schedules, especially schedules with low rates of reinforcement, they also have a problem discriminating when extinction begins. It is easy to discriminate 0 percent reinforcement in extinction from 100 percent during conditioning, harder to discriminate 0 percent from 25 percent, and much more difficult to discriminate 0 percent from 1 percent. Organisms are found to take longer to extinguish after training on a partial reinforcement schedule, and their resistance to extinction increases as the reinforcement rate is lowered. This phenomenon is called the **partial reinforcement extinction effect**. It is a bit paradoxical because it implies that the less reinforcement received in the past, the slower the organism is to give up on an activity. This effect has interesting implications for molding the behavior of people. For instance, if parents want their children to be persistent in pursuing a goal in the face of adversity, it suggests that they should only occasionally reinforce their children's goal-seeking activities.

Partial reinforcement increases resistance to extinction because the conditions under which the animal learns are similar to the conditions of extinction. Basically, the animal learns to respond to the features that occur during extinction. Several researchers have proposed what these features might be. Capaldi (1967) suggested that during learning organisms come to associate sequences of nonreinforced responses with eventual reinforcement. Thus, in extinction, when the organism encounters a sequence of nonreinforced trials, it expects reinforcement. Amsel (1967) proposed that during initial training the organism becomes frustrated when it does not receive reinforcement and has associated its frustration with reinforcement. Thus, when frustrated in extinction, it also expects reinforcement. Both theories have in common the idea that the partially reinforced organism learns to associate reinforcement to the kinds of features encountered in extinction.

Conditioning is more difficult in partial reinforcement schedules but such schedules result in greater resistance to extinction.

Superstitious Learning

Some of Skinner's famous experiments (Skinner, 1948) on what has been called **superstitious learning** were thought to be evidence that contiguity was sufficient for learning and contingency was not necessary. Food was made available to pigeons from a feeder at fixed intervals (e.g., 15 sec for some, longer for others) irrespective of what they were doing. Although there was no contingency between behavior and reinforcement, pigeons in this situation developed highly routinized behaviors. One pigeon turned counterclockwise; another pigeon thrust its head into the upper corners of its cage. Skinner reasoned that these systematic behaviors appeared because of accidental contiguities between what the pigeon was doing and the delivery of food. For instance, when the food was delivered the pigeon might be hopping from one foot to the other. The contiguity between this response and the food would increase the pigeon's tendency to hop from one foot to the other and would thus increase the chance that the pigeon would be engaged in this behavior the next time the food was delivered, increasing the tendency for the behavior even more, and so on, until the pigeon would always be hopping from foot to foot. Thus, even though there was only accidental contiguity between behavior and reinforcement and there was no contingency, conditioning would occur. In effect, the pigeons developed the superstition that their behavior was necessary for the reinforcement. Skinner speculated that this might be the cause of superstitious behavior by humans, such as rain dances to produce rain; sometimes rain dances are followed by rain, but, presumably, they do not produce the rain.

Subsequent research and analysis have raised doubts about Skinner's interpretation of these experiments. Staddon and Simmelhag (1971) repeated the superstition experiment and replicated many of Skinner's results. However, they demonstrated that the situation was more complicated than Skinner realized. They noted that the pigeons' behavior could be divided into two categories. Immediately after receiving a reinforcement, pigeons displayed interim behaviors. There was a wide variety of such behaviors, including the sort Skinner reported. After a while, pigeons began to engage in terminal behaviors, pretty clearly in anticipation of the next feeding. This terminal phase always involved some variety of pecking.

Staddon and Simmelhag's results present serious difficulties to an attempt to explain superstitious behavior as learning by contiguity. First, there is no reason for two segments; second, there is no reason for all pigeons to peck in the terminal segment, which is contiguous with the reinforcement. Staddon and Simmelhag argued that terminal behaviors should be understood as examples of autoshaping, which is perhaps best thought of as a classical conditioning phenomenon.

Although each pigeon evolved systematic interim behaviors, these behaviors were not contiguous with reinforcement and thus whatever caused them was not learned by contiguity. Therefore, what was contiguous was not instrumentally conditioned, but was classically conditioned, and what might be instrumentally learned was not contiguous. Staddon (1983) suggested that these interim behaviors often served other functions, such as grooming or exercise.

According to this view, human behavior is often analogous to that of rats in these experiments. Many of us eat on rather fixed schedules. When food is not likely, we often engage in predictable interim behavior (e.g., studying or watching television). When food is likely, we engage in predictable terminal behavior in anticipation of the food (e.g., going to the kitchen and setting the table).

Given food at fixed intervals, organisms will first engage in interim behaviors when food is not likely and then in terminal behaviors when the time for food approaches.

Learned Helplessness

Perhaps the most dramatic evidence that organisms can be aware of the contingency (or lack thereof) between their behavior and reinforcement is found in the experiments on **learned helplessness**. In a prototypical experiment by Seligman and Maier (1967), dogs were given painful shocks at unpredictable intervals. A control group of dogs could avoid the shocks by pushing a panel, whereas the experimental group could do nothing to escape the shock. Thus one group of dogs learned a behavior that would eliminate shock, whereas the other did not. Both groups were then placed in the same escape avoidance condition: they could avoid the shock if they jumped over a barrier after hearing a tone. Dogs in the control group, which could control their shock in the first phase, readily learned to jump over the barrier. In contrast, the experimental dogs whined and yelped but made no attempt to escape the shock. After many trials the animals simply lay down and hardly moved at all. They had learned that nothing they could do would prevent shock—that there was no contingency between their behavior and receiving shock.

Maier, Jackson, and Tomie (1987) argued that learned helplessness is produced because the organism comes to pay less attention to its own behavior. Past behavior has been a poor predictor of whether it will receive shock, and so the organism continues to assume its behavior will have no effect in a situation where it could learn to escape shock. This situation is like latent inhibition in classical conditioning, where an organism comes to ignore a certain CS (see Chapter 2), or like dimensional learning in instrumental conditioning, where the organism comes to ignore a dimension (see earlier in this chapter).

Similar effects occur in many situations with many species, including humans. Some argue that this may be what is behind such phenomena as math phobia. After a long series of failures, people come to believe that nothing they do can help them learn math and so they stop trying. In one experiment, Hiroto and Seligman (1975) showed that humans subjected to a long series of unsolvable anagram problems failed to learn other easy-to-learn experimental tasks. Seligman (1975) also suggested that clinical depression may be a variety of learned helplessness; when people suffer a number of uncontrollable negative life events they may withdraw, thinking that they have no control over all aspects of their lives.

Seligman has suggested a number of measures, based on analogy to research with dogs, to deal with these clinical problems. If a helpless dog is forced to cross the barrier enough times with success, it will eventually cross on its own. By analogy, depressed patients might be helped by exposure to success experiences. Dogs can also be immunized by initial exposure to situations where they can escape from shock; they are then less likely to learn helplessness when later exposed to inescapable shock. By analogy, children should be given early success experiences in math to inoculate them against later math phobia.

Organisms that have repeatedly received unavoidable aversive stimuli come to ignore the relationship between their behavior and environmental outcomes.

Associative Bias

Although organisms may be capable of learning many response–reinforcer associations, they are biologically predisposed to learn certain associations, just as they are predisposed to learn certain stimulus–stimulus associations in classical conditioning (e.g., taste–poisoning discussed in Chapter 2). A pigeon can more readily learn to peck to receive food than to avoid shock (Hineline & Rachlin, 1969; MacPhail, 1968; Schwartz, 1973), but it can quite readily learn to flap its wings to escape shock (Bedford & Anger, 1968). These outcomes make sense because pecking is part of the pigeon's eating repertoire and wing flapping is part of its repertoire of escape behaviors.

Shettleworth (1975) did an interesting analysis of the effects of reinforcement on various behaviors of hamsters. She noted that they tended to engage in certain behaviors when hungry, such as standing on their hind legs (which she called open rear), scraping at walls (scrabbling), and digging in the ground. Other activities, such as washing their faces, scratching, and marking (pressing a scent gland), did not increase when they were hungry. Different hamsters were reinforced by food for each of these six behaviors. Figure 3.13 shows the results. Subjects learned to increase the eating behaviors but not the noneating behaviors in response to food reinforcement. Thus, organisms show associative biases in instrumental conditioning as in classical conditioning; in instrumental conditioning they are biased to certain response-reinforcer pairings.

Bolles (1970) argued that associative bias was a particularly important factor in the case of escape behavior. He argued that each species has **species-specific defense reactions**, which determine the difficulty of learning an escape behavior. For instance, rats find it easy to learn to flee to avoid a shock but hard to learn to press a bar to escape shock. The relative ease of these two responses is reversed if the reinforcer is food.

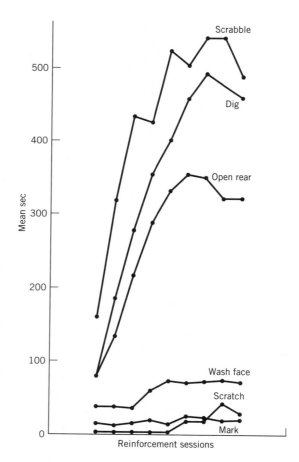

FIGURE 3.13. Mean time spent performing the reinforced response per 1200-sec session. *Source:* From S. J. Shettleworth. Reinforcement and the organization of behavior in golden hamsters. Hunger, environment, and food reinforcement. *Journal of Experimental Psychology. Animal Behavior Processes, Volume 104.* Copyright © 1975 by the American Psychological Association. Reprinted by permission.

Humans face difficulties in skill learning when the skills entail learning responses that are antagonistic to human predispositions. For example, in downhill skiing the skier leans forward to control speed and should lean forward more the steeper the hill. Most beginners have difficulty because of their natural tendency to lean backwards. As another example, when a car is skidding on an icy road the driver needs to turn into the skid and not slam on the brakes—drivers have great difficulty learning both responses.

Organisms are biologically prepared to learn certain response–outcome combinations.

Instrumental Conditioning and Causal Inference

This chapter has thus far focused on instrumental conditioning experiments from the animal's perspective. But human subjects can be placed in similar situations. Imagine what it would be like if you were put in a room to explore and discovered that sometimes when you flipped a switch on the wall, money came forth. If you thought you would be able to keep any money you found, you might find yourself flipping that switch as fast as a rat pushes a lever or pigeon pecks a key. Your performance could be plotted in cumulative response records, and we could speak of you as learning an association between the switch and money. To speak of it as an association, although accurate, would probably not fully express your mental state. You probably also would have formed the belief that flipping the switch *caused* the money to come forth. It is unclear to which other organisms such causal beliefs may be ascribed, but it is appropriate to ascribe them to humans.

Wasserman (1990) studied the development of causal beliefs of humans in instrumental conditioning paradigms and found that these causal beliefs develop much as associations do in lower organisms. Subjects were given a key, which they were encouraged to press. Sometimes when the subject pressed the key a light went on, and sometimes when the subject did not press the key the light went on. The light was like a reinforcer (or in this case more like a neutral stimulus) that followed the response. Wasserman varied the probability that the key press would be followed by the light. He broke the experiment into 1-sec intervals. If a subject pressed the key in the interval, the interval would end with a light flash with different probabilities in different experimental conditions. He used probabilities of 0.00, 0.25, 0.50, 0.75, and 1.00. These probabilities were referred to as $P(O|R)$ for probability of outcome given response. Wasserman also manipulated the probabilities that a 1-sec interval without a key press would result in a light. These probabilities were referred to as $P(O|-R)$, for probability of outcome given no response, and they similarly took on the same values of 0.00, 0.25, 0.50, 0.75, and 1.00. Wasserman looked at all combinations of $P(O|R)$ and $P(O|-R)$ for $5 \times 5 = 25$ conditions.

He asked subjects to rate the causal relationship between the press and light on a scale that varied from -100 (prevents light) to $+100$ (causes light). Figure 3.14 illustrates the results. As in the animal conditioning experiments, subjects' ratings of causal strength was a function of the difference between $P(O|R)$ and $P(O|-R)$. The particular level of causal strength for a value of $P(O|R)$ depended on the value of $P(O|-R)$. This is the same sort of relationship Rescorla illustrated in his experiment on classical conditioning (see Figure 2.9). Chapter 10 examines human causal inference further, but the research described here indicates that causal inference may be closely related to conditioning.

> *Human judgments of causality are affected by the same contingency variables that influence animal conditioning.*

Application of the Rescorla–Wagner Theory

Wasserman, Elek, Chatlosh, and Baker (1993) showed that the behavior of their human subjects could be predicted by the Rescorla–Wagner theory. First, let's consult how the Rescorla–Wagner theory would apply to instrumental conditioning in general. Recall that in classical conditioning this theory

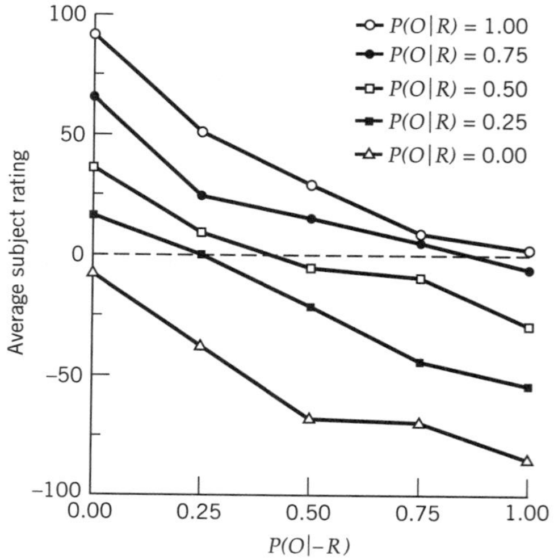

FIGURE 3.14. Causal inference as a function of the probability of a light given a key press and the probability given no key press. (Data from Wasserman et al., 1993).

assumes that the strength of association between the CS and the US changes according to the following equation:

$$\Delta V = \alpha(\lambda - V)$$

where α is the learning rate; λ is the maximum strength of association; and V is the sum of the existing associative strengths from the CSs presented on that trial. This theory can be mapped onto instrumental conditioning by letting the experimental context and the response be two cues (i.e., the CSs) that are associated to the reinforcement (i.e., the US). Then λ represents the strength of association that can be conditioned to the outcome or reinforcement. When the outcome occurs after a response, there are two cues for conditioning: the response and the stimuli of the experimental context. If the outcome occurs without the response, then only the contextual stimuli are present. This is a competitive learning situation in which the response and the context are competing for association to the reinforcement. This way of applying the Rescorla–Wagner theory to instrumental conditioning predicts many features of instrumental conditioning, just as it predicts the features of classical conditioning.

One outcome that the Rescorla–Wagner theory predicts is the subject's sensitivity to the difference in reinforcer rates in the presence versus the absence of the response. This sensitivity is seen in Hammond's experiment on bar pressing with rats (Figure 3.12) and in Wasserman's human analogue (Figure 3.14). Chapman and Robbins (1990) showed mathematically that, according to the Rescorla–Wagner theory, the competition between context and response results in a strength of association to the response that is proportional to the difference in reinforcement rates. Thus the process by which people form causal inferences corresponds closely to the predictions of an associative learning theory.

The Rescorla–Wagner theory can predict behavior in an instrumental conditioning paradigm by assuming competitive learning between context and response.

Interpretations

Two rather different conclusions might be made from this research on causal inference and the Rescorla–Wagner theory. One conclusion is that the simple associative learning processes of the Rescorla–Wagner theory are responsible for causal inference. As noted, Chapman and Robbins showed that the theory results in strengths of association between response and outcome that are exactly equal to the difference $P(O|R) - P(O|-R)$. The theory in no way explicitly estimates probabilities $P(O|R)$ and $P(O|-R)$, let alone takes their differences, but it nonetheless estimates this quantity, supporting the point made in the previous chapter that simple associative learning judgments can mimic sophisticated statistical inference.

A dramatically opposite conclusion can also be drawn. Subjects in these experiments were not in conditioning experiments; that is, they were not in situations in which experimental contingencies reinforced their responses. Rather, they were asked to make judgments of causal relatedness between response and outcome. The fact that their causal inferences were like conditioning suggests that causal inference, and not simple associative learning processes, underlies conditioning. That is, what organisms are learning in an instrumental conditioning experiment might be a causal model of the environment, and they act consciously according to it. As discussed in Chapter 10, this view is the appropriate interpretation of the human situation, and it may be the appropriate interpretation of the conditioning behavior of higher non-human organisms as well. Recently, Holyoak, Koh, and Nisbett (1989) showed that a great many conditioning phenomena in classical and instrumental conditioning can be explained by assuming that organisms learn causal rules to predict the structure of their environment.

A wide range of conditioning phenomena can be explained by assuming either simple associative learning or conscious cognitive judgment. To reiterate a theme of this book, this is not an either–or situation. Some instances of conditioning in some organisms may be due to associative processes and other instances of conditioning in other organisms may be due to development of causal models. There may be subtle differences between conditioning behavior produced by simple associative learning versus conscious inference, but by and large they look similar behaviorally because both reflect learning adaptations of the organism to the structure of its environment.

Conditioning phenomena can be explained by assuming either acquisition of simple associations or development of causal models.

The Hippocampus and Conditioning

The hippocampus (see Chapter 1) is a relatively small brain structure that has been strongly implicated in learning and memory. Chapters 7 and 8 discuss its role in human memory. This section considers its role in conditioning experiments with lower organisms.

Rats with lesions to the hippocampus perform poorly in a wide range of instrumental and classical conditioning paradigms. They show a particular deficit in tasks involving a substantial spatial component, such as maze learning. An example that illustrates the deficit involves the Morris water-escape task (Morris, 1981). Rats are placed in a circular pool of water and must swim to an escape platform. If they climb onto the escape platform the experimenter removes them from the pool; otherwise they are left to swim around. The water is murky, and so the rats are unable to see anything below the surface. In some conditions the escape platform is above the water's surface and the rats can see it, and in other conditions it is just below the surface and they cannot see it. In the original experiment Morris contrasted these four conditions:

1. *Cue + place.* The escape platform is always visible and always in the same location.
2. *Place.* The platform is submerged but always in the same location.
3. *Cue only.* The escape platform is always visible but in different locations on different trials.
4. *Place random.* The platform is submerged and in different locations.

Rats learned to swim quickly to the escape platform in all conditions but the last. Figure 3.15 shows the tracks taken by a rat in each group on the last four trials. Only the rats in the last group wandered much in the pool. This task is significant because it shows that rats are excellent in using a spatial representation to navigate through their environment. As Figure 3.15 illustrates,

FIGURE 3.15. A vertical view of the tracks taken by rats in each group. *Source:* From R. G. M. Morris. *Learning and Motivation, Volume 12.* Copyright © 1981 by Academic Press. Reprinted by permission.

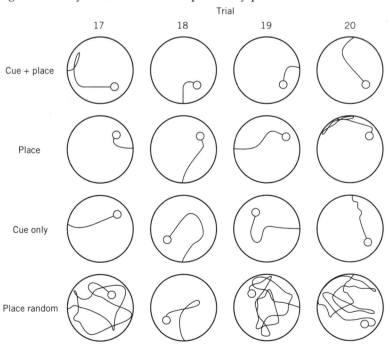

although rats in the place condition started from a different part of the pool on each trial, they knew where the submerged platform was and swam to it.

This experimental paradigm has become important for understanding the role of the hippocampus. Rats with hippocampal lesions perform poorly in the place condition—no better than normal rats perform in the place-random condition. In contrast, normal and lesioned rats behave similarly when the platform is visible (Morris, Garrud, Rawlins, & O'Keefe, 1982).

Results such as this have been used to argue that the hippocampus is significant in spatial learning. Many other kinds of learning are not impaired by hippocampal lesions. For instance, lesioned rats can still learn taste aversions and how to make simple visual discriminations.

Rats with hippocampal lesions perform poorly in many tasks that require spatial learning.

The Nature of the Hippocampal Deficit

The field has been struggling to characterize what kinds of learning are impaired by hippocampal damage. O'Keefe and Nadel (1978) proposed that the hippocampus, at least in the rat, is especially designed for learning spatial information. In effect, it encodes Tolman's spatial map (see Chapter 1). They reported that many neurons in the hippocampus only fire when the animal is in a certain location in space.

Olton, Becker, and Handelmann (1979) argued for a different interpretation of hippocampal deficits. Noting that many deficits occur in nonspatial tasks and that some spatial tasks fail to show a deficit, they argued that the deficit is a more general inability to hold information in working memory (a concept discussed at length in Chapter 5, "Transient Memories") over short periods of time. An example of the distinction to which they refer can be illustrated with respect to the radial maze (Figure 3.10). Olton et al. reported a study that used a 17-arm version of this maze in which 8 of the arms were baited with food and the other 9 were not. With experience with this maze normal rats learned two things:

1. Never to enter the 9 arms that were never baited with food.
2. To efficiently explore the baited arms to avoid repeat visits, as discussed with respect to Figure 3.10.

Rats with hippocampal lesions learned only 1 but not 2. Both sorts of information are spatial, but lesioned rats can learn one and not the other. In Olton's terms what they cannot do is rapidly update their working memory to avoid repeated visits (2). Given enough experience, though, they can learn permanent properties of their spatial environment (1).

Sutherland and Rudy (1991), taking a more traditional conditioning perspective, argued that the deficit is in the ability to form configural associations (see the discussion in the previous chapter of the distinction between associations to stimulus configurations versus stimulus elements). They argued that to solve the Morris water-escape task when the platform was submerged, the animal had to respond to a configuration of spatial cues, whereas when the platform was visible the animal could simply respond to the visible platform. They performed the following experiment, which showed that rats with hippocampal lesions had difficulty learning a nonspatial task that involved forming configural associations. Animals were rewarded with food for pressing a bar when a light alone or a tone alone appeared. However, they were not reinforced for responding when the light and tone were presented simultaneously. As discussed in Chapter 2, normal animals can perform this task, which requires learning associations to stimulus configurations of light + no tone and tone + no light. Rats with hippocampal lesions are unable to learn these associations, although they can learn to respond to the simple single stimuli. Thus this is a nonspatial task in which lesioned rats show a deficit.

> *There are many competing theories as to the kind of learning that the hippocampus supports.*

Long-Term Potentiation (LTP)

Another reason for the interest in the hippocampus is that it is one region of the brain where a particular type of neural learning has been displayed. When brief, high-frequency electrical stimulation is administered to some neural areas of the hippocampus, there is a long-term increase in the magnitude of the response of the cells to further stimulation (e.g., Bliss & Lomo, 1973). This change, called **long-term potentiation (LTP)**, occurs immediately and lasts for weeks. LTP involves increasing the synaptic connections among neurons. For LTP to take place, the presynaptic and postsynaptic neurons must be simultaneously active. Because it is a permanent change and depends on joint activation of two neurons, it is thought to be involved in at least some kinds of associative learning. Although LTP in the hippocampus has been studied most, it occurs in many other regions of the brain as well.

There has been a great deal of research on the physical basis for LTP in the hippocampus (for a review see Bliss & Lynch, 1988, or Swanson, Teyler, & Thompson, 1982). The LTP procedure results in structural changes in the dendrites onto which axons synapse. The dendrites grow new spines at points where the axons synapse, and existing receptors on the dendrites become rounder. The change in the shape of the receptors appears temporary, but the increase in the number of spines is more long lasting. In addition to these postsynaptic changes there are presynaptic changes involving an increase in the release of neurotransmitters. Recall that the neural basis of learning in *Aplysia* also involved an increase in the presynaptic release of neurotransmitters.

Considerable work has been done on the biochemistry that might underlie these changes in the spines. Certain receptors in the postsynaptic membrane on the dendrite (NMDA receptors) are normally blocked and only become unblocked if the postsynaptic cell has fired. If the presynaptic cell fires and sends a neurotransmitter to the postsynaptic membrane at the same time that the postsynaptic cell is firing, then these unblocked receptors can receive the neurotransmitter. It is thought that the unblocking of these NMDA receptors is the critical step in the production of LTP. This unblocking in turn enables calcium to enter into the postsynaptic neuron, resulting in an increase in both the receptors in the postsynaptic neuron and in the presynaptic release of the neurotransmitter. Kandel and Hawkins (1992) speculated that the postsynaptic influx of calcium may cause chemical messengers to be transmitted to the presynaptic axon, resulting in the increased release of neurotransmitter.

Simultaneous activity of presynaptic and postsynaptic cells in the hippocampus can produce a long-term facilitation of the synaptic connection.

Long-Term Potentiation and Hippocampal Learning

Much of the interest in LTP arises because LTP has been well documented in the hippocampus and hippocampal damage is known to produce learning deficits in a wide range of tasks. Thus it has been conjectured that, when intact animals learn these tasks, LTP is the neural process that underlies their learning. Recently there has been an effort to bolster this connection by showing that pharmacological interventions that interfere with LTP produce learning deficits similar to those produced by hippocampal lesions.

Morris, Anderson, Lynch, and Baudry (1986) examined the effects of blocking LTP by injecting a drug that prevents activation of NMDA receptors involved in LTP. They looked at the performance of injected rats in the Morris water tasks and found significant impairment, similar to that of lesioned rats. The same injected rats were not impaired in tasks such as visual discrimination, which are also not impaired by hippocampal lesions. Similar drug-induced learning deficits that mimic those of rats with hippocampal lesions have been reported by Staubli, Thibault, DiLorenzo, and Lynch (1989) and Robinson, Crooks, Stinkman, and Gallagher (1989).

Keith and Rudy (1990) wrote a recent review critical of these studies. They argued that these drug-injected rats, although impaired, showed more learning than did lesioned rats; thus, drug injection and hippocampal lesions did not produce their effects by blocking the same learning process. It is difficult to judge just how severe a deficit drug injection should produce in learning relative to the deficit that hippocampal lesions produce. Some researchers have rejected the Keith and Rudy criticisms (e.g., Morris, 1990). This issue is significant because this research is an attempt to develop the necessary link between learning at the neuronal level and learning at the level of gross brain structures; in particular, it is crucial to judging whether LTP is responsible for the learning impaired by hippocampal lesions.

> *There is some evidence that drugs that prevent LTP produce learning deficits mimicking those produced by hippocampal lesions.*

Final Reflections on Conditioning

In both instrumental and classical conditioning experiments, animals and humans are capable of learning about their environments and responding adaptively. In classical conditioning they learn that one stimulus predicts another and they respond in anticipation of that fact. In instrumental conditioning they learn that a stimulus signals that a certain class of responses will lead to some outcome and they respond according to whether that outcome is reinforcing or not. This research fits the adaptive function of learning identified in the first chapter.

In keeping with the language of the field, this chapter has referred to organisms forming associations among stimuli and responses. However, the meaning of the term *association* does not capture all that is going on. The organisms are not just connecting these stimuli and responses; rather, they are learning that certain elements predict other elements. In the case of instrumental conditioning, they are learning about the causal structure of their environment—for instance, that a bar press causes food to be delivered. This learning need not involve an explicit causal model. This chapter showed how the Rescorla–Wagner theory is capable of implicitly encoding this causal structure in simple associations. We will return to the issue of causal inference in Chapter 10, "Inductive Learning," where we will learn about other mechanisms for inferring causal structure in humans.

In other paradigms, such as maze learning, organisms are learning something more specific than just what predicts what. They are learning about the spatial layout of their environment and what objects are located where. This cognitive map information can be used flexibly to achieve goals. The nature of spatial memory in the human case is further investigated in Chapter 6, "Acquisition of Memories."

A general characterization of conditioning is that it involves learning useful information that can be deployed in response to the reinforcement con-

tingencies of the experiment. The next chapter focuses on the role of reinforcement in conditioning.

---

*In a conditioning experiment, organisms are learning things
about their environment and using this information to achieve
their needs.*

Further Readings

The textbooks and journals cited at the end of Chapter 2 are also excellent
sources for research on instrumental conditioning. In addition, many research
articles on instrumental conditioning are found in *Learning and Motivation* and
Journal of the Experimental Analysis of Behavior. Balsam (1988) reviews the
research relevant to stimulus generalizations and discriminations. Staddon and
Ettinger's (1989) text on learning emphasizes its adaptive function. A number
of books focus on animal cognition, including those by Flaherty (1985) and
Roitblat (1987). A recent discussion of hippocampal function appeared in the
summer 1992 edition of the *Journal of Cognitive Neuroscience,* and Landfield
and Deadwyler (1988) edited a series of articles on LTP.

The Eight Levels of Citizenship

Clueless	Hasn't registered to vote
Hapless	Has registered, but doesn't vote
Reckless	Registered, votes, but has no idea who is running or what they are like
Puppets	Registered, votes, remembers to ask someone else who to vote for as they walk to the polling doors
Struggling	Registered, votes, reads the paper the week before and finds a reason for why they are going to vote the way they do
Conscious	Registered, votes, reads, watches the political process throughout the year and discusses issues
Empowered	Registered, votes, reads, watches, and donates money to candidates of their choice
Dedicated	Registered, votes, reads, watches, donates money, and works on campaigns to help elect good people to office

What do Candidates Need from Grassroots Activists?

Or

If this were a Perfect World

~ We would all be active in our local party

~ We would be active in our local community council

~ We would be active in our local PTA

~ We would know or be familiar with the people in the 50 houses around us

~ We would offer to TAKE A PUBLIC STAND and put up yard signs

~ We would take candidates we know to our neighbors and introduce them

~ We would volunteer on candidate's campaigns

In order for women to become more powerful, we need to participate in the system - we need to

WALK OUR TALK.

4

Reinforcement and Learning

Some Basic Concepts and Principles

The idea that organisms seek pleasure and avoid pain is as old as antiquity. Clearly, the reinforcement contingencies associated with a behavior have a lot to do with whether the organism actually performs the behavior. One long-standing question is what is the relationship of learning to reinforcement? Thorndike (see Chapter 1) proposed a particularly intimate relationship in his law of effect: learning would only occur if there was reinforcement. This idea was maintained by many of the behaviorists and proved a dividing issue between Hull and Tolman. Over time it has become apparent that too much learning takes place without any reinforcement for the law of effect to be viable. However, the question about the relationship of reinforcement to learning still stands. The answer was roughly outlined in Chapter 1—learning provides the knowledge, and reinforcers provide the goals to cause the organism to act on that knowledge. This chapter is concerned with how reinforcers provide those goals.

The basic thesis of this chapter is that organisms tend to behave rationally. Using the contingencies they have learned in the environment, they select the behavior that creates the best state of affairs for them. Suppose that four responses are available to an organism: R1, which increases the amount of food available; R2, which increases the rate at which the organism is shocked; R3, which decreases the rate at which it gets food; and R4, which decreases the rate at which it is shocked. The organism would not tend to produce R2 or R3, because nothing good comes of them; it would alternate between R1 and R4 as a function of how important getting food is relative to avoiding shock. This is rational behavior. This chapter further defines rational behavior and presents evidence relevant to assessing how rational organisms are. At the outset this chapter should state a disclaimer repeated elsewhere in the book: Apparent rational or optimal behavior need not imply conscious deliberation on the organism's part. Simple associative mechanisms often can produce highly adaptive behavior.

Although organisms tend to do the right thing, this chapter reviews situations in which they produce behavior that is far from optimal. This situation can be viewed as a glass half full or half empty. Historically, psychology has taken a half-empty perspective and emphasized deviations from optimality. More recently, psychologists have become impressed with how well even simple organisms do at behaving in near optimal ways. Cases of nonoptimality can often be understood as generally adaptive behavioral tendencies going astray in situations for which they did not evolve. For instance, human affection for sweet food reflects a tendency that selected food of high nutritional value at one time in our evolutionary history. However, in modern society with its capacity to create almost arbitrary food products, this tendency often selects the least nutritious of the food alternatives.

> *Learning provides knowledge of the reinforcement contingencies of actions, and organisms generally select the most beneficial action.*

Rational Behavior

It is worthwhile to address more precisely what is meant by rational behavior. Consider a situation that might be encountered by a rat in a laboratory experiment. Suppose that three significant actions are available to the rat: It can press a bar, play in an activity wheel, or do nothing (or, at least, do neither of the first two activities). Suppose that there are four possible consequences of its actions: it will receive food; it will be shocked; it will receive exercise; or nothing will happen.

The experimenter has arranged contingencies between each activity and each outcome, as shown in Table 4.1. If the rat presses the bar, there is a 67 percent chance of getting food and a 33 percent chance of being shocked. If it enters the activity wheel, there is a certainty of exercise. If it does nothing, there is a 90 percent chance of nothing happening, and a 10 percent chance of getting food. The rat has learned these behavioral contingencies from its exploration of the experimental situation. The knowledge in Table 4.1 reflects the product of its learning.

Simply knowing the behavioral contingencies in Table 4.1 does not tell us what is optimal behavior for the rat; we also need to know the value it places on various outcomes. Assume that the outcome of nothing has a value of 0, food has a large positive value of 10, shock has a large negative value of −25, and exercise has a mild positive value of 1. Now it is possible to predict what the rat will do if it is behaving rationally. Rational theory says that the rat should select the behavior with the highest **expected value**. The expected

Table 4.1 *Probabilities of Outcomes given Behaviors*

Outcomes	Behaviors		
	Press Bar	**Activity Wheel**	**Nothing**
Food	.67	.00	.10
Shock	.33	.00	.00
Exercise	.00	1.00	.00
Nothing	.00	.00	.90

value of an action is calculated by multiplying the probability of each possible outcome by its value and taking the sum of these products. This result reflects the average value that can be expected from that action. In the case of the bar press, there are two possible outcomes—food and shock. Performing this calculation for these two yields

Probability(food) × Value(food) + Probability(shock) × Value(shock)

$$= .67 \times 10.0 + .33 \times -25.0 = -1.55$$

In the case of entering the activity wheel there is only one possible outcome. Its value is calculated as

Probability(exercise) × Value(exercise) = 1 × 1.0 = 1.00

Finally, in the case of doing nothing there are two possible outcomes:

Probability(nothing) × Value(nothing) + Probability(food) × Value(food)

$$= .90 \times 0.0 + .10 \times 10.0 = 1.00$$

Thus the exercise wheel and doing nothing are of equal value, and the rat would be predicted to alternate between them. If the rat became satiated such that food lost its value, the rat would be predicted to select the exercise wheel exclusively. If the rat became hungrier and food increased its value, the rat would select nothing; if it became hungry enough (and food approached a value of 15 or more), the rat would select to press the bar despite the shocks.

If the hunger of the rat were manipulated, the rat would probably shift between the activity wheel, doing nothing, and pressing the bar as implied by this rational analysis. This behavior would not mean that the animal was explicitly representing probabilities, values, and calculating expected values, which is extremely implausible in the case of the rat. Rather, the rat would probably be doing something much simpler that allowed it to behave *as if* it were engaged in rational calculation. This chapter discusses several such simple mechanisms for behavior.

> *Rational behavior implies combining the probabilities of the outcomes of actions with their values and selecting the action with the highest expected value.*

Effects of Reward on Learning

Implicit in the analysis of Table 4.1 is that learning the contingencies or probabilities in the table does not depend on reinforcement. Reinforcement determines how the animal acts given knowledge of these probabilities. The claim that learning does not depend on reinforcement is quite remarkable. Certain things are more worthwhile to an organism, and thus it is to its advantage to learn these things rather than other things. The apparent adaptive advantage of making learning contingent on reward was part of the intuition of the early learning theorists, who made the connection between reinforcement and learning. However, maladaptive or not, it seems that there is not such a connection. Chapter 1 reviewed Tolman's research on latent learning in the rat, but some of the best research on the role of reinforcement in learning has been done on human subjects. This research not only indicates that learning does not depend on reward, but shows how reinforcement contingencies can nonetheless influence what is learned.

Numerous experiments involved telling subjects that they will be rewarded more for learning some items than for learning others. Such experiments frequently have subjects learn lists of words or other verbal stimuli. Subjects respond by learning the more valuable items more rapidly. On the other hand, if the manipulation is done between subjects so that some subjects are told that all items are worth more than other subjects are told, the reward has no effect (e.g., Harley, 1965). Thus, one line of research (when reward is manipulated within subjects) seems to indicate that learning depends on reinforcement, whereas the other line of research (when reward is manipulated between subjects) seems to indicate that it does not.

The explanation of these apparently contradictory results comes from studies of how subjects allocate their time as a function of reinforcement. A typical experiment is that of G. R. Loftus (1972). He presented subjects with pairs of naturalistic pictures to study for 3 sec. The left member of a pair was assigned 1, 5, or 9 points, and the right member of a pair was independently assigned 1, 5, or 9 points. Subjects were later asked to identify which pictures they had studied when these were mixed in with pictures they had not studied. Subjects were paid bonus points in proportion to the value of the pictures they could recognize. Figure 4.1a shows the probability of recognizing the target picture as a function of its value and the value of the picture with which it was paired. Subjects showed better recognition memory for a picture the more points assigned to it and the less points assigned to the other picture of the pair. This experiment is like the studies mentioned earlier that show the effects of reward when the reward varies within a set of items.

Loftus also monitored how often subjects fixated on each picture during the 3 sec of exposure. These data are presented in Figure 4.1*b*. Subjects fixated on the picture more if it was worth more and if the other picture was worth less. This result raises the question of whether memory performance is a function of the value of the picture or the number of fixations. Loftus did the relevant analysis in Figure 4.2, where memory performance is plotted as a function of the number of fixations for pictures of different values. As can be seen, memory performance was a function of how often subjects looked at a picture and not how much it was worth. As Figure 4.1 illustrates, subjects tend to look more at more valuable pictures and so show better memory for these pictures. However, as Figure 4.2 confirms, when Loftus controlled for the number of fixations received by a picture, value had no effect. These results reflect the general understanding of the influence of reward on memory. People (and presumably other animals) tend to spend more time attending to material that is worth more to them, but the reward does not affect how well they learn while attending to the material.

These results also explain the apparent contradiction in the earlier research. When different items in one list had more value, subjects tended to allocate more time to them and remember them better. When all the items in a list had the same value, subjects could not differentially allocate time to them as a function of reward. In this case, the value assigned to the items had no effect on learning.

FIGURE 4.1. (*a*) Probability of recognition and (*b*) mean number of fixations for pictures worth 1, 5, and 9 points. Separate curves are plotted for each of the three values of the paired-with picture. (From G. R. Loftus, 1972).

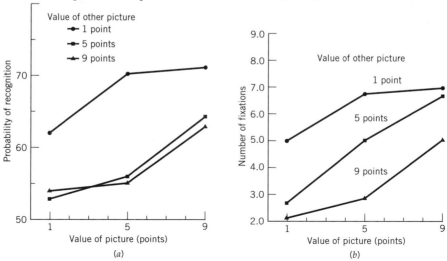

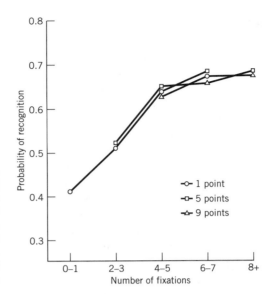

FIGURE 4.2. Probability of recognition as a function of number of fixations. A separate curve is plotted for pictures worth 1, 5, and 9 points. *Source:* From G. R. Loftus. *Cognitive Psychology, eye fixations and recognition memory for pictures.* Copyright © 1972 by Academic Press. Reprinted with permission.

Organisms pay more attention to material associated with greater reward but, controlling for attention, there is no effect of amount of reward on learning.

Reward and Punishment

Outcomes or stimuli that are made contingent on behavior can be desirable or aversive. When desirable, it is natural to refer to the stimuli as rewards, and when aversive, it is more natural to refer to the stimuli as punishments. When the organisms produces the response in question, the contingency can be one such that the stimulus is given or not. Table 4.2 illustrates the four logical possibilities obtained by crossing desirable or aversive stimuli with different contingencies between the stimulus and the response. In the first case reward is made contingent on a behavior. For instance, a child may be given a sum of money for mowing the lawn. This situation is referred to as **positive reinforcement** and should promote the behavior. In the second case a loss of a desirable stimulus is made contingent on the behavior. This is the favorite punishment of many parents for misbehavior—"You're grounded!" This situation is referred to as **omission training** and should decrease the behavior. The third possibility is for an aversive stimulus to be contingent on occurrence of a response. This is classical **punishment**, like a spanking, and again should decrease the behavior. The final possibility is for disappearance of an aversive stimulus to be contingent on the behavior. This situation is referred to as

Table 4.2 *Type of Stimulus and Contingency on Response*

	Stimulus if Behavior Is Performed	No Stimulus if Behavior Is Performed
Desirable Stimulus	Positive Reinforcement (reward training)	Omission Training
Aversive Stimulus	Punishment	Negative Reinforcement (escape or avoidance)

negative reinforcement, and it should produce the behavior, often called escape or avoidance behavior.

The fundamental assumption is that these contingencies control the behavior at hand. For a long time learning theorists were reluctant to accept such a proposal because it seemed to imply that something in the future (the reinforcement) was causing the response. It is generally accepted that causes only work forward in time, and so future reinforcement cannot cause present behavior. As Chapter 1 reviewed, Tolman was criticized on these grounds for his proposal that animals performed certain behaviors because they expected that these would lead to certain desired results. Chapter 1 also reviewed the major contribution of simulation models such as Newell and Simon's GPS, that showed how knowledge of contingencies, learned from experience, could result in goal-directed behavior. It is the knowledge or expectation of rein- forcement, based on past experience, that causes the animal to behave as if its actions are determined by the future. Not all organisms that display instru- mental learning function like GPS, but GPS demonstrates that there are mechanical ways in which knowledge of contingencies can control behavior. Many other mechanisms have since been proposed, some of which may be more plausible for lower organisms. In many cases the knowledge of contin-

A chimpanzee trained to exchange tokens for food.

gencies is not explicit or conscious, but rather is knowledge implicit in the processing of the organism.

Organisms behave in instrumental conditioning experiments in such a way as to obtain desirable stimuli and avoid aversive ones.

Aversive Control of Behavior

Tables 4.1 and 4.2 imply that aversive stimuli, such as shock, are effective in controlling behavior and that their effects are symmetrical with the effects of desirable stimuli, such as food. As Chapter 1 noted with respect to Thorndike's attitudes about punishment, there has been a long tradition in psychology of believing that punishment is not effective. In brief, these beliefs are wrong. This section reviews the evidence that aversive stimuli are quite effective and discusses how to maximize their effectiveness. Aversive stimuli can be used in punishment to decrease the rate of some response or in negative reinforcement to increase the rate of some response that serves to eliminate the aversive stimulus (see Table 4.2).

Punishment

Sometimes punishment can be so effective that a single learning experience eliminates a behavior. A child who touches a hot stove is unlikely to do so again. In one experimental paradigm (Jarvik & Essman, 1960), a rat is placed on a platform above a grid floor. When it steps off the platform it receives a painful shock. After a single experience, rats will not step down again. They learn to completely suppress a natural response in a single trial.

Several factors influence the effectiveness of punishment. One of the most important is the delay that exists between the response and the punishment (just as delay of positive reinforcement has a strong effect). In one experiment illustrating the effects of delay, Camp, Raymond, and Church (1967) contrasted several groups of rats. Each group was first trained to press a lever in response to a clicking sound; they were reinforced with food. After this training half the presses resulted in a shock at varying delays. For one group, the shock came immediately after pressing the lever, for other groups it came 7.5 or 30 sec after pressing the lever. A control group of rats received as many shocks, but the shocks were unrelated to when they pressed the lever. Figure 4.3 plots the percentage of clicks to which the rats pressed the bar. Note that the group with a 30-sec delay showed only a little more suppression of bar pressing than the control group for which there was no contingency (that is, shocks were delivered on a schedule completely unrelated to when the bar

---

124

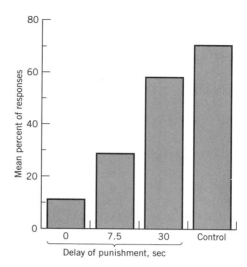

FIGURE 4.3. Mean percentage of responses as a function of sessions for groups with 0.0, 7.5, and 30.0-sec. delay of punishment and for a non-contingent-shock control group. (From Camp et al., 1967).

was pressed). Much more suppression of bar pressing occurred in the rats with immediate shock.

It is easy to extrapolate from such a result with rats to the conclusion that punishment should be immediate with humans, particularly with children. However, because children can be told the contingency that exists between the behavior and the punishment, the immediacy of punishment is probably not so critical.

The severity of the punishment can also have a strong influence on response suppression. Figure 4.4 displays data from Church (1969) on the amount of suppression (see the discussion of response suppression in CER with respect to Figure 2.9) in lever pressing for different levels of severity of shock (including no shock). There was only a little suppression with .15 mA (milliampere) of shock, a good deal more with .50 mA, and still more with 2.0 mA. Extrapolating this result to human beings raises some of the ethical issues in using punishment. Certain degrees of punishment are simply too extreme to be used.

For punishment to be effective, it should be used consistently and at as severe a level as acceptable. N. E. Miller (1960) found that if mild punishments were introduced and then increased in severity, the organism became less sensitive to punishment and the severest level of punishment was then not as effective as it would have been if introduced immediately. Azrin, Holz, and Hake (1963) found that the effectiveness of the punishment was reduced if only some responses were followed by punishment.

Church (1969) examined the effect of noncontingent punishment on later contingent punishment. Rats were given ten 30-min training sessions in which they learned to press a lever for food. In sessions 11 through 15 an experimental group received random 105-V shocks, independent of responses,

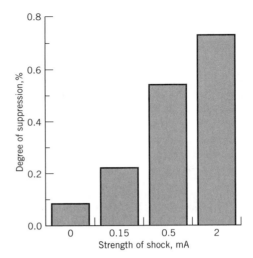

FIGURE 4.4. Median suppression ratio as a function of intensity of noncontingent shock. Lower values reflect increased suppression of responses. (From Church, 1969).

while a control group continued to receive just reinforcement during those sessions. Both groups were retrained without shock for sessions 16 through 20. Finally, during sessions 21 through 25, both groups received 145-V shocks contingent on pressing. Figure 4.5 shows the results in terms of rates of responding relative to the rates during the initial 10 sessions. During the initial noncontingent shock the experimental rats pressed somewhat less, showing a CER (see Chapters 1 and 2). They recovered during retraining and continued a high level of responding during the final phase, when the shock was contingent. In contrast, the control rats showed a nearly complete suppression in the

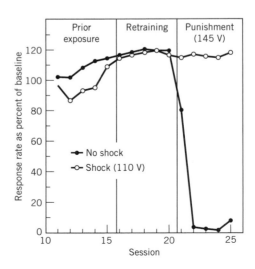

FIGURE 4.5. Median response rate to a punishment of 145 V as a function of prior exposure to noncontingent shock of 105 V. (From Church, 1969).

126

final phase, when shock was made contingent on their response. The implications of this experiment are clear: if punishment is to be used effectively it must be contingent on only the response it is intended to suppress. Gratuitous punishment may make its later use ineffective.

Punishment is much more effective if the organism is offered alternative responses. Often the behavior we want to eliminate is occurring because the organism finds it reinforcing in some way: If other responses that will deliver these reinforcers are made available to the organism, it will be easier to eliminate the undesirable behavior. For example, if people are able to work to earn money so that they do not have to steal, punishments for stealing (e.g., imprisonment) will be more effective in deterring the behavior.

An experiment by Azrin and Holz (1966) illustrates the importance of offering an alternative behavior if punishment is to be effective. Pigeons were first trained to peck at a key to receive food. Then they were shocked for pecking at the key. There were two conditions: in one there was another key that they could peck at, and in the other there was only the single key. Figure 4.6 shows response to the shocked key as a function of the intensity of the shock. Up to about 40 V, the shock intensity was not severe enough to affect responding to the key. However, at 50 V it was intense enough to produce a complete cessation of response and a shift to the alternative key in the condition that had an alternative key. In the condition without an alternative key, the pigeons persisted in pecking when the shock was much more intense.

FIGURE 4.6. The rate of punished responses as a function of the punishment intensity. (From Azrin & Holtz, unpublished data). *Source:* Figure 4.6 from N. H. Azrin and W. C. Holtz. *Punishment in Operant Behavior: Areas of Research and Application*, Honig ed., Copyright © 1966, p. 405. Reprinted by permission of Prentice-Hall, Englewood Cliffs, New Jersey.

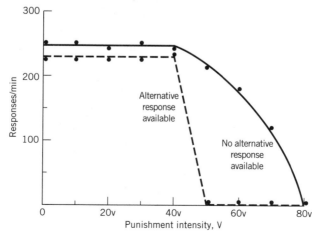

I would not want this review of punishment to be read as encouragement to use it as a major mechanism for controlling the behavior of children or others. Punishment can have a number of serious negative side effects. Azrin and Holz (1966) argued that punishment can lead to a general suppression of all behaviors, good and bad; it can lead to anger in the punished person and can motivate deception to avoid punishment. Children sometimes lie to their parents to get even for past punishment and to avoid future punishment. Also, there is evidence that punishment leads to more aggressive behavior in the punished (Ulrich & Azrin, 1962). Finally, children may inappropriately use punishment in interactions with their peers, modeling their parents' behavior toward them (Eron, Walder, Toigo, & Lefkowitz, 1963).

Punishment is effective to the degree that it is administered immediately, severely, and consistently and to the degree that the organism is offered alternative behaviors.

Negative Reinforcement

Just as behavior can be maintained because it achieves desirable stimuli, behavior can be maintained because it avoids aversive stimuli. Solomon and Wynne (1953) placed a dog in a compartment with a steel grid floor. At the beginning of a trial, the light went off; 10 sec later a severe shock was sent through the grid, causing the dog to run about trying to escape. The dog could leap over a barrier to escape the shock and eventually jumped over this barrier into another compartment that was shock free. Within a few trials the dog learned to jump the barrier on the signal and thus to avoid shock completely.

One of the curious features of such avoidance behavior is that it can be much more difficult to extinguish than behavior maintained by positive reinforcement. If food is no longer given conditional on some behavior, such as jumping over a barrier, in response to a stimulus, a dog soon stops the behavior. On the other hand, if the shock is removed, the dog will continue responding without any sign of extinction for 200 trials, escaping even faster (Solomon, Kamin, & Wynne, 1953). The dog's avoidance behavior denied it the opportunity to learn that the tone–shock contingency was no longer at work. There are two ways to extinguish an avoidance behavior. If the shock is administered even if the behavior occurs (Davenport & Olson, 1968), the animal learns that there is no contingency between behavior and avoiding shock. The avoidance behavior can also be extinguished by preventing the animal from executing it. Baum (1969), in a study of avoidance in rats, introduced a floor-to-ceiling barrier that prevented the rats from escaping. After about 5 min of forced exposure to the formerly aversive situation, the rats seemed to learn that there no longer was a contingency between the tone and the shock.

Preventing the avoidance behavior can be used in therapy to help patients get rid of phobias. For instance, an 11-year-old child who was terrified of loud noises was convinced to break a set of balloons (Yule, Sacks, & Hersov, 1974). After a few sessions of balloon breaking, the child lost the phobia and came to enjoy breaking balloons as most children do. This therapy worked, because the child had been made to realize that nothing terrible happens just because there is a loud noise.

An organism can also learn a behavior that delays an aversive event. This kind of avoidance behavior can be trained and is often studied in what is called a shock-postponement procedure (Sidman, 1966). For instance, by pressing a lever, an animal might be able to postpone shock for 30 sec. If it presses the lever in that 30-sec period, it gets another reprieve of 30 sec from the point of this new press. If the animal presses the lever at least once every 30 sec, it permanently avoids shock. Dogs master this task well, responding only a few times a minute and avoiding virtually all shock. Rats are less successful in that they respond more frequently, but they also get shocked more often because they suffer occasional lapses. Many human behaviors (e.g., brushing teeth) can be viewed as being maintained to permanently postpone aversive consequences.

Stable patterns of behavior can be maintained if they avoid aversive consequences.

The Nature of Reinforcement
Drive-Reduction Theory

What makes a reinforcer reinforcing? An obvious idea from biology is that positive reinforcers are good for the organism and negative reinforcers are bad, where "good" and "bad" are defined in evolutionary terms of survival of the organism and maximization of the number of its offspring. The problem with this view is that an organism does not really know what is good for it in such abstract terms. Therefore, various **drives** have been proposed—to consume food, drink water, have sex, and escape pain—which are usually correlated, although imperfectly, with these more long-term evolutionary goals. Behaviors that reduce or satisfy these drives are reinforcing for the organism. This view is known as the **drive-reduction theory** of reinforcement, and it has had a long history in psychology.

A drive is conceptualized as an aversive stimulus that can become more extreme as the organism continues to be deprived. For certain drives, such as hunger and thirst, this proposal is particularly intuitive. Almost all of us have felt hunger, found it aversive, and more so as deprivation continued.[1]

The major problem with the drive-reduction theory of reinforcement is that organisms can be reinforced by events that have no obvious biological value and for which it is peculiar to propose an increasingly aversive drive stimulus. For instance, Butler (1953) found that monkeys learn to perform a behavior just for the opportunity to look around the laboratory for a few moments. Rats learn to do behaviors for the opportunity to run in an exercise wheel. One could postulate curiosity drives and exercise drives (perhaps with boredom as the aversive state) and speculate about their potential biological value (for instance, the values of learning about the environment and keeping fit), but this has struck many people as creating a rather hollow theory. Any behavior could be explained by postulating a drive for it and proposing some fanciful biological function. Also, such hypothetical drives do not fit well with experiences of deprivation with more basic biological needs. Many people live a complete life without a strong desire to exercise similar to the desire they have to eat after a day without food.[2]

An even more serious problem for the theory is that behavior can be reinforced by things that leave drives unreduced or even increase them. For example, male rats ran a maze for the opportunity to copulate with a female rat even though they were not allowed to ejaculate (Sheffield, Wulff, & Backer, 1951). The male rats were being reinforced for a behavior that left them with increased drive. In a less extreme mode, humans find the company of attractive members of the opposite sex reinforcing even if it does not go beyond mere company. It seems that the behavior can be reinforcing, rather than the reduction of any biological drive.

Drive-reduction theory proposed that reinforcement consisted of reduction of various biological drives.

Premack's Theory of Reinforcement

Such difficulties led to an alternative conception developed by Premack (1959, 1965). The critical observation is that typical reinforcements, such as food, are reinforcing because they involve highly valued behavior, such as eating. Premack proposed that all behaviors have value to the organism and that a more valued behavior reinforces a less valued behavior. Thus, eating typically reinforces running in an activity wheel for a hungry rat because eating is more valued than running. There are several ways to determine the relative value of two activities. One method is to look at the frequency of each activity when

[1]However, there often seems to be a limit to the increase in aversiveness as the period of deprivation continues.

[2]Some athletes and other people do report such needs, however.

the organism has the opportunity to do both. A hungry rat spends more time eating than running in an activity wheel. Another method is to teach the animal a way to get either reinforcement—for instance, pressing one bar yields food and pressing another gives access to the activity wheel—the result chosen more often is the one that is preferred.

The basic predictions of Premack's theory have been well supported. For example, a thirsty rat can be shown to prefer drinking to running in an activity wheel, and it will increase its rate of running in an activity wheel if that behavior gets it access to water. On the other hand, a nonthirsty rat can be shown to prefer running in an activity wheel to drinking, and it will increase its drinking if that gets it access to an activity wheel (Premack, 1962). Premack (1959) found similar results with children. Some children preferred eating candy to playing a pinball machine. If access to candy was made contingent on playing the pinball machine, their rate of playing the pinball machine went up. However, if playing the pinball machine was made contingent on eating candy, their rate of eating candy did not change or it went down. The converse relationships were observed in those children who preferred playing the pinball machine to eating candy. According to Premack, punishment occurs when an organism is forced to engage in a less valued behavior as a consequence of engaging in the more valued behavior. Thus, forcing children who preferred candy to play the pinball machine if they ate candy would reduce their rate of eating candy.

Premack (1971) described an experiment by Weisman and Premack (1966) that illustrates the relativity in the concepts of reinforcement and punishment. They compared rats that were deprived of water and rats that were not deprived. When offered simultaneous access to an activity wheel and a drinking tube, deprived rats spent more time licking from the tube than running, whereas nondeprived rats spent more time running. Figure 4.7 shows the amount of time spent in the two activities in the two conditions when rats could choose to do either. Premack used such free-choice information to establish the relative value of the two activities. For the deprived rats drinking water was more valued, whereas for the nondeprived rats running the activity wheel was more valued.

Then Weisman and Premack introduced a contingency such that if a rat licked the tube 15 times it had to run for 5 sec and could run for no more than 5 sec. What should this contingency do to their licking? For the nondeprived rats, the activity wheel was more valued, and this contingency should reinforce licking. For the deprived rats, the wheel was less valued and so having to run in it should punish licking. Figure 4.8 compares the rates of licking before and after introduction of the contingency. As predicted, the contingency reinforced licking for the nondeprived rats and increased their rate of licking. On the other hand, it punished the licking for the deprived rats and decreased their rate.

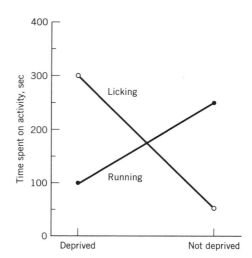

FIGURE 4.7. Comparison of base rates of running and licking for rats deprived of water and those not deprived of water.

Premack proposed that making behavior A contingent on behavior B would reinforce B if A was more valued and punish B if A was less valued.

Neural Basis for Reinforcement

Insight about the nature of reinforcement (and difficulties for both the drive-reduction theory and Premack's theory) can be obtained from studies of the brain mechanisms involved in reinforcement. Much of this research indicates that a particularly important structure for reinforcement is the hypothalamus, a subcortical brain structure (see Figure 1.15). The hypothalamus is phylogenetically a very old part of the brain. If different parts of the hypothalamus are removed, animals overeat, fail to eat or drink, or show loss of sexual behavior. Electrical stimulation of different regions can produce eating and sexual behavior (for a review see Stein, 1978).

Olds and Milner (1954) found that electrical stimulation of the hypothalamic area of the brains of rats could also serve as a reinforcer. Rats learned to press bars or perform other activities in order to receive such stimulation. In a few studies of human patients who had had such implants as part of treatment for severe neurological problems, such as epilepsy, the patients reported a number of feelings associated with self-stimulation, including feelings of being drunk and sexually aroused (e.g., Heath, 1963).

Stein (1978) argued that special neurotransmitters in these regions of the brain are biochemically distinct from other neurotransmitters. There is evidence that the effects of such drugs as opiates and cocaine take place in part on these neural areas, affecting the rate of synaptic transmission. The adminis-

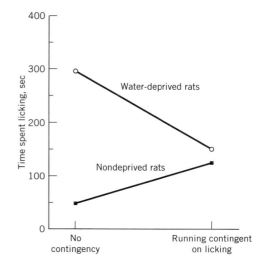

FIGURE 4.8. Impact of a contingency between licking and running on rate of licking for rats deprived of water and those not deprived.

tration of drugs that attenuate the effects of opiates and cocaine also attenuates the effects of brain stimulation (see Vaccarino, Schiff, & Glickman, 1989, for a review).

Brain stimulation and drugs are interesting categories of reinforcers because they have no obvious biological function, reduce no natural drive, and do not in any significant sense involve behaviors. Thus they contradict many theories of reinforcement, including drive reduction (they reduce no drive) and Premack's behavior theory (they involve no behaviors).

> *The hypothalamus seems intimately associated with reinforcement, and animals find pleasurable both electrical and pharmacological stimulation of the hypothalamus.*

Equilibrium Theory and Bliss Points

Although Premack's theory was a major conceptual advance, it had a number of difficulties. First, conceiving of reinforcement purely in terms of behaviors is too restrictive for some punishments and reinforcements. For instance, Staddon and Ettinger (1989) noted that shock is a punishment and electrical brain stimulation is a reward and neither can really be conceived of as a behavior. Thus it is not accurate to think of either responses or stimuli as rewards. Rather, we want to conceive of certain events more generally (activities or presentations of stimuli) as being preferred to other events.

A more fundamental problem is that one thing is not absolute in its ability to reinforce another thing. Allison and Timberlake (1974) found that rats, given the choice between two saccharin solutions, spent more time on the sweeter of the two when drinking freely. Premack would predict that drinking the sweeter solution would reinforce drinking the less sweet solution and not vice versa. A situation in which rats had to lick the less sweet solution once for every time they licked the sweeter solution (a 1-to-1 response ratio), would result in a confirmation of Premack's prediction. That is, rats would increase their rate of licking the less sweet solution to get access to the sweeter solution, but they would not increase their rate of licking the sweeter solution to get access to the less sweet solution. Allison and Timberlake did not use a 1-to-1 response ratio. In their study the rat had to lick the sweeter solution 10 times to get access to the less sweet solution. Since the 10-to-1 ratio was greater than the natural distribution between the solutions, if the rats licked the sweeter solution as much as they did in the free drinking situation, they would get less of the less sweet solution than in the free situation. In this experiment, the rats increased their rate of drinking the sweeter solution in order to gain more access to the less sweet solution. Opportunity to drink the less preferred solution had acquired the property to reinforce drinking of the sweeter solution.

To accommodate such results, Allison (1983) and Timberlake (1980) proposed a major elaboration of Premack's theory. They argued that organisms have a desired baseline rate for all sorts of events—that is, organisms have a certain desired frequency for drinking, eating, having sex, running, and so on—called the **bliss point** for that event. Organisms find anything that moves them in the direction of this baseline rewarding and anything that moves them away from the baseline punishing. This theory is called the **equilibrium theory**. In the experiment just described, the reinforcement schedule moved the rats from their bliss point for distributing their drinking over the two solutions. They increased their drinking of the sweeter solution over its base level to reduce the amount that their drinking of the less sweet solution was below its base level. They were trying to achieve a compromise that was as close as possible to their ideal bliss point.

Figure 4.9 illustrates Allison's (1989) general demonstration of the operation of bliss points. The figure represents the various amounts of activity that are possible for behaviors A and B. It shows the animal's bliss point for the optimal combination of these two behaviors. The animal might want to spend 150 min/day in activity A (perhaps eating) and 50 min/day in activity B (perhaps running in an exercise wheel). A schedule is introduced in which the animal must spend 1 min in activity A for each minute in activity B. The straight diagonal line reflects this schedule. The animal finds the point on this schedule closest to its bliss point—in this case the point at which it spends 100 min on each activity. In the example in which activity A is eating and activity B is running, food could be viewed as reinforcing running in the wheel because it increases running (alternatively, running in the wheel might be seen as punishing eating, because it decreases eating). Sup-

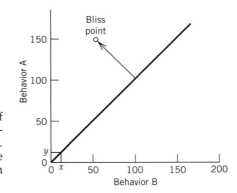

FIGURE 4.9. Behavior B as a function of Behavior A under a condition that constrains the two behaviors to be equal. The arrow points from the place on the curve closest to the bliss point. (From Allison, 1989).

pose that a schedule is created in which the animal must spend 10 min in activity A for each minute in activity B. Then the animal would increase activity A to get more B. In the example of food and exercise wheel, running would reinforce eating.

Konarski (1979) and Konarski, Johnson, Crowell, and Whitman (1980)—both reported in Timberlake (1980)—provide an interesting demonstration of the application of equilibrium theory to the education of children. Most young children can easily be made to do more math if an opportunity to color is made contingent on math. According to Timberlake, this happens because children normally have less opportunity than they want to color and more opportunity than they want to do math. However, if deprived of an opportunity to do math, children can be made to increase the amount of coloring over what they would normally do if this activity results in access to the opportunity to do math.

This more general view sees all creatures just as economists see humans—as desiring some overall mixture of goods and striving to get as close as possible to that bliss point within the constraints of the environment. This chapter later expands on this economic view of reinforcement.

Although experiments such as that just described are impressive demonstrations of the predictive power of equilibrium theory, the theory is still somewhat incomplete because it does not fully explain how the bliss points are determined. Equilibrium theory proposes that features such as the deprivation state of an organism and the quality of food in the feeder combine to determine the bliss point or optimal distribution of responses such as eating and exercising. Once that bliss point is known, the results of constraining these behaviors and making one behavior contingent on the other can be predicted. The theory does not provide an analysis of how this bliss point is set in the first place; ultimately, biological explanations for the setting of these bliss points are needed.

Organisms choose their behavior so as to move as close as possible to some overall bliss point of behaviors and experiences.

Studies of Choice Behavior

According to the current conception of reinforcement, an organism balances competing needs or goals in order to achieve the combination closest to its bliss point. Research on reinforcement seeks to determine how organisms make choices, given their experience with the constraints of their environment. Recent research has focused on choice behavior in animals. Before discussing this research, it is important to review some of the basic effects of different schedules of reinforcement, since many of these recent studies offer animals choices among schedules of reinforcement. It turns out that understanding behavior even under a single schedule also requires conceiving of the organism as making choices among alternative behaviors.

Schedules of Reinforcement

Chapter 3 described the remarkable partial reinforcement effect in extinction—organisms that are reinforced only occasionally are more resistant to extinction, and the more occasional the reinforcement, the greater the resistance. The publication of *Schedules of Reinforcement* by Ferster and Skinner (1957) marked a sharp increase in interest in the relationship between the schedule with which reinforcements are delivered and the resulting behavior. Four basic schedules have been studied, although there are many exotic variations. In the **fixed-ratio schedule (FR)** a reinforcement is given after every so many responses that the organism makes. A fixed-ratio schedule with a reinforcement after every 4 responses is denoted as a FR 4 schedule. In the **variable-ratio schedule (VR)** the number of responses for a reinforcement varies, but averages out to some value. A variable-ratio schedule in which an organism receives a reinforcement on average after every 10 responses is denoted as a VR 10 schedule. In a **fixed-interval schedule (FI)** the organism receives a reinforcement after a fixed amount of time has passed. For example, in a FI 15-sec schedule the organism receives a reinforcement for its next response after 15 sec has elapsed; the organism then waits another 15 sec before its next response produces a reinforcement and, so on. Finally, in a **variable-interval schedule (VI)** the time that must elapse between reinforcements varies, but it must average out to some value. For instance, in a VI 30-sec schedule the organism has to wait an average of 30 sec before a response produces a reinforcement.

It is important to appreciate a subtlety in the interval schedules. In a FI 15 schedule, for instance, the delay between reinforcements is not 15 sec; it is greater. Fifteen seconds must pass before a response from the organism produces the reward; the total time between rewards is 15 sec plus however long the organism then waits to respond.

Each schedule of reinforcement produces its own characteristic behavior. The behavior is typically measured in terms of cumulative response records, as discussed in Chapter 1 (see Figure 1.9), which are graphs of how the total number of responses so far increases with the passage of time. Figure 4.10 shows typical response records maintained under the different schedules. Variable schedules produce relatively fixed rates of responding, whereas fixed schedules produce variable rates. In the fixed-interval schedule, the organism appears to have come close to figuring out what the interval is and does its responding at about the end of that interval. In the fixed-ratio schedule, the organism pauses after each reinforcement, as if it is taking a rest before starting the next set of responses.

Response rates are generally higher in the ratio schedules than in interval schedules, an adaptive behavior, since the rate of reward in such schedules is directly related to the rate of response. Animals will respond to extreme ratios, as high as a 1000 responses to one reinforcement; however, they have to be shaped to do so, starting with much lower ratios and slowly working up. The rate of responding is little related to the reinforcement rate in a ratio

FIGURE 4.10. Stylized cumulative response records obtained under four common schedules of reinforcement. The ticks on the functions denote delivery of reinforcements.

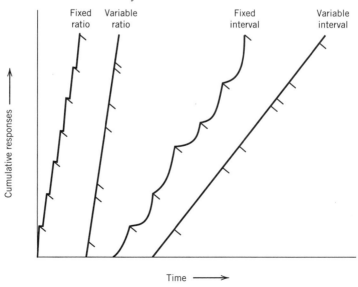

schedule. The major difference is that organisms show longer pauses after a reinforcement the higher the ratio of responses to reinforcers. There is a big burst of effort followed by a rest.

The pattern of behavior of organisms under these various schedules appears quite adaptive. It need not be the case, however, that they consciously know what the schedule is and respond accordingly. Rather, it is thought that the different schedules result in different patterns of behavior, which are adapted to the various schedules (Staddon & Ettinger, 1989). For instance, in a fixed-interval schedule, the animal is indirectly reinforced for interspersing other behaviors (such as grooming) between the bar presses, since such composite behavior produces the food plus other benefits (i.e., closer to bliss point). Animals can learn to respond according to what is called a differential low-rate schedule, in which they are reinforced only if they do not respond too rapidly. Under such a schedule intervening behaviors not only produce their own rewards but also serve a timing function to enable the animal to wait long enough to receive the primary reinforcement (Hemmes, Eckerman, & Rubinsky, 1979).

As a final comment, it is worth noting that the current conception sees the organism as making a choice among alternative behaviors when faced with a reinforcement schedule. One alternative is to press the bar, but there are other alternatives, such as engaging in grooming. The organism is conceived of as achieving an optimal division of behaviors in terms of approaching its bliss point. The next subsection considers an interesting example of this idea.

Organisms adaptively adjust their pattern of responding given various reinforcement schedules.

Ratio Schedules and the Labor Supply

Allison (1989) described an application of the bliss point construct to the rate of responding under variable-ratio schedules. Assume that a rat has a particular bliss point defined in terms of amount of bar pressing and amount of food consumption. Figure 4.11 illustrates that bliss point in a two-dimensional space. Not surprisingly, it is high on food and low on bar pressing. Different VR reinforcement schedules define *constraints* between different amounts of food and number of bar presses. The radiating lines in Figure 4.11 illustrate various such constraints, or VR schedules. The highest line describes a situation in which the rat averages two pellets per bar press, and the lowest line defines a schedule of one pellet for every four bar presses. The animal tries to find a point on each of these lines that is closest to the bliss point. In each case, the animal has to trade off some food to reduce the number of presses it makes. As shown, the amount of food consumed becomes less as the animal is put on schedules that require more responses per pellet (that is, the optimal

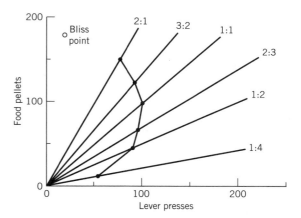

FIGURE 4.11. Food pellets as a function of lever presses under the constraint of six schedules (given as ratios of food pellets to bar presses). Each line represents a different schedule, and the dot on each line is the point closest to the bliss point.

points get lower and lower). For a while, the animal increases its number of presses to partially compensate for loss of food, but eventually it reaches the point at which the increase in presses is no longer worthwhile. The closest point to the animal's bliss point is one at which it presses little and eats little.

This animal behavior turns out to have an interesting human counterpart: the **labor supply curve**. As people are paid less and less for each unit of work, they increase the amount of work they do to partially compensate for the loss of wages—to a point. After they reach this point, it is no longer worthwhile and they begin to work less. In economics, this practice is often thought of as trading off leisure for money. The bliss point for money is high, corresponding to the large value for the number of pellets in Figure 4.11. The bliss point for labor is low (or the bliss point for leisure high), corresponding to the low value for number of presses. Up to a point, workers trade off leisure for money, but if the value of their work is cheapened too much they revert to mostly leisure. One economic goal might be to find the pay schedule that produces maximum productivity.

Animals and humans seek a combination of work and payment that is closest to their bliss point.

Variable-Interval Schedules and the Matching Law

In the situations presented thus far, the experimenter has offered the organism a single response–reinforcer contingency. However, organisms usually have a choice of a number of behaviors, as seen in Table 4.1. A great deal of research has been devoted to situations in which the experimenter provides multiple (usually two) responses with two different reinforcement contingencies. The most widely studied situation is one in which the two responses (typically two bars that can be pressed by rats or two keys that can be pecked by pigeons) are reinforced according to two different variable-interval schedules. Thus a pigeon may be presented with two keys, one of which is reinforced according to a VI 15-sec schedule and the other of which is reinforced according to a VI 30-sec schedule, so that a reinforcer is available on average every 15 sec or every 30 sec after a response. The time to the next reinforcer in either schedule only weakly depends on how often the animal pecks at the key.[3] Still, it is in the animal's best interest to peck at each key some of the time in order to obtain the reinforcers from both. The critical question is how it divides its pecking time between the two bars.

With practice the pigeon comes to respond in a reliable way. Let $B1$ be the number of pecks to key 1, and let $B2$ be the number of pecks to key 2. Let $R1$ be the rate at which the pigeon is reinforced for pecking at key 1, and let $R2$ be the rate at which it is reinforced for pecking at key 2. In the example given, the pigeon receives an average of four reinforcements per minute for pecking at key 1 and two reinforcements per minute for pecking at key 2. Thus $R1$ is 4 and $R2$ is 2. The animal divides its behavior between the two response alternatives in a proportion that matches the reinforcement proportion. That is,

$$\frac{B1}{B1 + B2} = \frac{R1}{R1 + R2}$$

If $R1 = 4$ and $R2 = 2$, $R1/(R1 + R2) = 2/3$; hence, $B1$ might be 10 and $B2$ might be 5 [or any other pair such that $B1/(B1 + B2) = 2/3$]. This equation is called the **matching law** because the behavioral proportion matches the reinforcement proportion. This law holds over a wide variety of situations, describing not only pigeons but also most other organisms, including humans. The law also holds true, at least approximately, if different magnitudes rather than different rates of reinforcement are used. For example, if one lever offers two pellets of food on a VI 30-sec schedule and the other lever offers one pellet of food on a VI 30-sec schedule, a rat spends twice as long pressing the lever that offers two pellets as pressing the one that offers one pellet.

Faced with two variable-interval schedules an organism divides its responses between them in proportion to their two rates of reinforcement.

---

[3]The weak dependence is produced because once the time for the reinforcer has come up, the food remains idle until the pigeon pecks. Only after the pigeon pecks does the timing begin for the next reinforcer.

Momentary Maximizing

It can be shown mathematically that for an organism to optimize its rate of reinforcement in a situation in which it is choosing between two VI schedules, its behavior should correspond closely to the matching law.[4] Thus the organism's behavior in matching can be nearly optimal. It could be argued that the organism is figuring out what pattern of behavior will achieve a global optimum, or *maximum*, in terms of overall intake of food. Such behavior is referred to as **global maximization**. It is unlikely, though, that the animal has consciously figured the contingencies and calculated the behavior that will result in optimal reward. Herrnstein and Vaughan proposed the **melioration theory** of choice, and others (Shimp, 1969; Silberberg, Hamilton, Ziriax, & Casey, 1978) have proposed the **momentary maximizing** theory of choice. Both theories seem to capture what animals are doing in that they both claim that animals tend to choose the response alternative that currently has the highest rate of reinforcement.[5]

Consider an application of melioration to the choice between a VI 1-min schedule and a VI 2-min schedule. Suppose that a pigeon makes some 3600 pecks in an hour (not an unusual number for a pigeon) and has to divide the pecks up between two keys. It starts out dividing equally, giving 1800 pecks to each key. Since it receives 60 reinforcers over the hour on the VI 1 schedule, the rate of reinforcement on the key is 60/1800 = $\frac{1}{30}$ of the pecks. Since it receives 30 reinforcements on the VI 2 key, its rate of reinforcement on that key is 30/1800 = $\frac{1}{60}$ of the pecks. According to meloriation, since the rate of reinforcement is greater for the VI 1 schedule, the pigeon should shift to giving more pecks to the key with the higher reinforcement rate, namely, the VI 1 key.

Suppose that the pigeon then shifts to 3000 pecks for VI 1 and 600 pecks for VI 2. Its reinforcement rate for VI 1 is 60/3000 = $\frac{1}{50}$, and its reinforcement rate for VI 2 is 30/600 = $\frac{1}{20}$. Now VI 2 has the higher rate, and the pigeon should shift to giving a greater proportion of its pecks to that key. The pigeon reaches a stable rate of responding when it gives twice as many pecks to VI 1. Assuming a total of 3600 pecks, VI 1 would receive 2400 and VI 2, 1200; the resulting rate of reinforcement on VI 1 is 60/2400 = $\frac{1}{40}$ and on VI 2 it is 30/1200 = $\frac{1}{40}$.

[4]Under these VI schedules, food becomes available but is not delivered until the next response. In order to minimize the time that the food is available but not delivered, the organism engages in behavior that results in matching. Such behavior maximizes total food by minimizing the time when food is waiting to be consumed and a VI schedule is not operative. There has been some dispute about whether matching produces the actual optimal rate of reinforcement or only a close approximation (e.g., Heyman & Luce, 1979).

[5]The two theories are subtly different. Momentary maximizing claims that the organism makes the best response now, whereas melioration claims that the response distribution shifts toward the current best. They differ in the time window over which the local optimization takes place.

As a contrast, consider the application of momentary maximizing to a variable-ratio schedule. Suppose that an animal is choosing between a VR 5 and a VR 10 schedule, which means that ⅕ of the responses are rewarded on average for the first key and ¹⁄₁₀ on average for the second key. No matter how often the first key is chosen, the reward for that key remains higher. In this situation momentary maximizing predicts that the animal will settle down to selecting the first key exclusively; this is, in fact, what happens (Staddon, 1983, chap. 8). This result is in sharp contrast with what happens with two VI schedules, when the animal divides its responses proportionately between the two keys.

Organisms choose the alternative that is currently offering the higher rate of return.

Momentary Maximization Versus Global Maximization

The momentary maximizing theory is an extremely simple theory of how to behave—always choose the alternative that is currently offering the best returns on effort. This theory usually leads to behavior that globally maximizes, or nearly so. However, under certain circumstances the theory leads to the opposite result, establishing that momentary maximizing is not equivalent to global maximizing. Consider a choice between two responses that are reinforced according to the following complex schedule:

> If the organism chooses response A less than ⅛ of the time, it receives three reinforcements for each minute it chooses A and one reinforcement for each minute it chooses response B.

> If the organism chooses response A between ⅛ and ¼ of the time, it receives three reinforcements per minute for either response A or response B.

> If the organism chooses response A between ¼ and ¾ of the time, it receives three reinforcements for each minute it chooses A and one reinforcement for each minute it chooses B.

> If the animal chooses response A between ¾ and ⅞ of the time, it receives reinforcements at the rate of one per minute for either response.

> If the animal chooses response A more than ⅞ of the time, it receives just one reinforcement for each minute it chooses A and three reinforcements for each minute it chooses B.

Unlike the standard two-choice situation with two VI schedules (which gave rise to the matching law), the timer for one response is not running while the animal is performing the other. The timer for a response is only running when the animal is making that response.

The optimal behavior for the organism is to choose A between ⅛ and ¼ of the time, as this results in a high rate of three reinforcements per minute all the time. The worst behavior is to choose A between ¾ and ⅞ of the time, as this results in just one reinforcement per minute. What does melioration predict? Suppose that the animal responds in the optimal range of ⅛ to ¼ and by chance deviates and starts responding more with A. Suddenly B yields a lot less reinforcement, and the animal chooses A more. A continues to offer more reinforcements until they reach the range of ¾ to ⅞, when A suddenly drops to B's level. The animal then stabilizes. If the animal were to slip down below the ¾ response to A, A would get a lot more reinforcement, the animal would choose A more often, and the animal would return to the stable region. If the animal started choosing A even more than ⅞ of the time, it would get more reinforcements for B and it would choose B more, thus returning to the stable region.

In this situation, melioration predicts that animals will choose the absolute worst behavior pattern, whereas global maximization predicts that they will choose the best. In fact, the animals stabilized at the worst rate of choosing A (Vaughan, 1981). Thus, by using a clever (but bizarre) set of reinforcement contingencies, this experiment showed that momentary maximization is a better description of what animals are doing than is global maximization. It usually makes sense to choose the behavior that is paying off more at the current moment, but experimental psychologists can be trusted to create a situation like that described here where this is not the case.

Organisms tend to choose the alternative that currently provides the best return even when this choice does not result in the best return in the long run.

Optimal Foraging Theory

The choice behavior of animals in the laboratory is not that different from such behavior in the wild, where animals must make choices about where and how to seek food. Biologists have developed a theory of how animals make their choices called **optimal foraging theory** (Stephens & Krebs, 1986). According to this theory, an animal's foraging behavior is sensitive to how much energy is being expended in foraging for food and how much energy is gained by the food obtained, and its foraging patterns are designed to maximize the expected net gain in energy. Suppose that an animal has a choice between two patches in which to seek food (e.g., a bird looking for food in one of two fields). The animal appears sensitive to the rate at which food is found in the patch, just as laboratory animals are sensitive to the momentary rate of reinforcement from two keys. The animal chooses the patch with the highest rate. Frequently, as it searches that patch, it depletes the patch. The animal chooses to move on to the other patch when the expected increase in food rate justifies the energy cost involved in making the journey. Fortunately for animals, nature does not tend to set up perverse schedules of reinforcement between the patches, such as those in the Vaughan experiment.

Some of the decisions that animals face when foraging in the wild have been investigated in the laboratory, for example, the effect of travel time between patches of food. In the studies of the matching law described so far, the animal faced no cost in shifting from one key (patch of food) to another key (another patch of food). However, in the wild it costs time to change patches of food. Thus animals should be more reluctant to leave an inferior patch when it takes a significant amount of time to get to another patch. This situation was investigated in the laboratory by introducing a delay when the animal switched keys, so that after switching from key 1 to key 2, both keys turned dark for a fixed interval, after which only key 2 functioned (Fantino & Abarca, 1985). In one experiment, Fantino and Abarca gave pigeons a choice between a VI 30-sec schedule and a VI 60-sec schedule. At any point in time, only one key was lit and could be pecked. If the pigeon started out on the VI 60 key it could switch to the superior VI 30 key by pecking a changeover key. However, a delay of 0, 4, or 16 sec was introduced before the other key became operative. Figure 4.12 shows the probability of switching keys as a function of the delay introduced. Pigeons showed an increased tendency to stay with the inferior key as the changeover delay (travel time) increased.

Humans can be similarly observed to forage and shift patches for foraging. The best analogy to foraging in the human case is working. People switch jobs if a new job offers a high enough increase in income. People are also sensitive to the travel time involved in making the switch. They are much more

A Bohemian Waxwing foraging for berries.

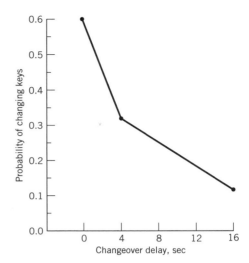

FIGURE 4.12. Probability of remaining in the presence of the stimulus leading to the less preferred outcome as a function of the duration of the changeover requirement (travel time). (From Fantino & Abarca, 1985).

willing to change jobs if the new job is in the same city and quite reluctant to change if it is in a different country. If the economic disparity is great enough, however, humans move great distances, as evidenced by the waves of immigration to the United States.

Another complication of foraging is that repeated foraging of some patches tends to deplete them. This situation was explored in the laboratory by giving blue jays a choice between a depleting and a nondepleting key (Kamil, Yoerg, & Clements, 1988). The probability of a peck being reinforced with a moth for the nondepleting key stayed constant at 25 percent. The probability of a peck being reinforced on the depleting key started at 50 percent, but only a fixed number of prey were available.[6] When the last prey was taken, the probability dropped from 50 percent to zero. Blue jays learned to be adaptive in their strategy, starting with the depleting key but switching over when that key began to reach depletion. Kamil et al. found that blue jays showed a strong tendency to switch over after experiencing a string of three failed pecks at the depleting key. After three such failed pecks, the odds were in fact fairly high that they had depleted the food source.

Animals choose among patches for foraging as a function of travel time to the patches and the current states of depletion of these patches.

---

[6]The blue jays were shown pictures of moths, but they were actually given pieces of mealworms.

Effects of Delay of Reinforcement

Problems that humans, particularly children, have with delayed gratification are well known. For example, my two boys had been campaigning for a puppy for months. We had finally agreed that we would get one when we returned from a vacation in Australia. However, while on vacation, we came upon a trashy (in my opinion) store, with a theme called "The Lost Forest," that sold stuffed animals. The boys were so enamored of those animals that they offered to give up their future prospect of a real puppy if they could have a few stuffed animals right away. They eventually prevailed upon us, and we made a decision that we all came to regret.

Lower organisms appear to be even more sensitive to delay of reward. Rachlin and Green (1972) showed that pigeons would peck at a red light that gave them an immediate reward of a small amount of food rather than at a green light that gave them a large reward at a 4-sec delay. It is difficult to know how to judge this issue. It could be argued that in the real world of pigeons things in the future are so uncertain that it makes sense for the pigeon to take what it can get right away.[7] The situation with our children turned out to illustrate the uncertainty of calculations about the future. Eventually, they were able to cajole their parents to get a puppy despite the bargain to the contrary. In this case a potential future loss (no puppy) turned out to be unreal.

Economists commonly deal with the phenomenon that the potential for gain or loss in the future is not worth the same as gain or loss right now, a phenomenon referred to as **discounting the future**. One analysis of discounting the future turns on the unpredictability of the future. Figure 4.13 illustrates the economic analysis and how it extends to experiments such as that of Rachlin and Green. The figure plots the **subjective value** of two rewards as a func-

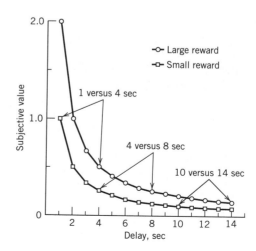

FIGURE 4.13. A hypothetical comparison of the value of different rewards at different delays.

[7]I could not resist making a pun about a bird in the hand being worth two in the bush.

tion of delay. The subjective value of an object is essentially how much the organism values it rather than its objective worth. At any delay, the large reward is worth twice the value of the small reward, but the subjective values drop off quite rapidly. Thus, when a small reward at 1 sec is compared with a large reward at 4 sec, the small reward has greater subjective value.

These curves decay in an interesting way. Suppose that a pigeon is offered a choice between a small reward at a 10-sec delay and a large reward at a 14-sec delay. The pigeon should choose the 14-sec delay, which is of greater value; Ainslie and Herrnstein (1981) confirmed this prediction. Figure 4.13 implies that pigeons should also be relatively indifferent to a choice between a small reward at 4 sec and a large reward at 8 sec; this prediction was also confirmed (Ainslie & Herrnstein, 1981; Rachlin & Green, 1972).

Rachlin and Green studied this issue in an interesting paradigm illustrated in Figure 4.14. At the beginning of a trial, pigeons pecked at either a right key or a left key. If the right key was chosen, after 10 sec of darkness they were exposed to a choice between a red key that gave the small reinforcement immediately or a green key that gave the large reinforcement after another 4-sec delay. They manifested an inability to delay gratification and almost always chose the red key. Thus if they chose the right key initially, they were effectively choosing a small reward at a 10-sec delay. If they chose the left key, 10 sec of blackout was followed by a green key that, if pecked, gave them a large reward in 4 sec. Thus if they chose the left key they were effectively choosing a large reward at 14 sec. Pigeons preferred the left key. They were making early on a choice that prevented them from later on making a choice for an immediate small reward. This phenomenon is called precommitment.

The notion of precommitment has been extended to human decision making. For instance, often dieters have trouble choosing a healthy, low-calo-

FIGURE 4.14. The procedure in the experiment by Rachlin and Green (1972).

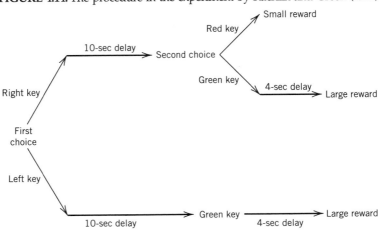

rie dish over a rich, high-calorie dish when both choices are presented to them. The immediate rewards of the high-calorie dish outweigh the long-term benefits of the healthy dish. However, if the dieters can order ahead, they choose the healthy dish. At a delay, the rich dish does not seem so tempting.

Organisms discount the future in such a way that they will prefer a small reward immediately to a large reward at a delay.

Mechanisms of Choice

Animals have thus far been described as being quite rational in their decision making. They strive to achieve the optimal trade-off among their competing needs, displaying rates of responding under different schedules that correspond to the prescriptions of economists for the labor supply curve. They make appropriate choices foraging in the wild (and between alternative schedules in the laboratory), behaving in a way that can be viewed as maximizing their net energy intake. Their discounting of time corresponds to economists' prescriptions for rational behavior. Along the way, peculiar laboratory situations have been noted in which animals perform nonoptimally, but these situations seem to say more about the laboratory experiments than about the animals' basic rationality.

This discussion raises the question of just how optimal animals are in their choices and how they achieve the high quality of their behavior. It is unlikely that they are engaging in anything like explicitly calculating the prescription for rational choice set forth at the beginning of the chapter. It also is implausible that they are always correct in the choices they make. Rather, animals can be viewed as being governed by what amounts to rules of thumb, which serve them relatively well in most situations. For instance, an animal could produce the matching law by always choosing the alternative with the higher momentary rate of reward. Similarly, the blue jays in the Kamil et al. (1988) experiment chose to leave a depleting patch after a string of three failures (which happened to be quite predictive of patch depletion). Animal behavior is probably controlled by such simple near-term rules that tend to approximate global optimal behavior.

Animals seem to make their choices by simple short-term rules of thumb that approximate global optimality.

Human Decision Making

Insight on animal decision making can be gained by looking at human decision making. Humans are presumably more deliberative and rational than other creatures and therefore should define the high point for rationality. It turns out, however, that humans tend to make their choices using such short-term rules of thumb also. Much research has involved making choices among sets of alternatives, such as the four apartments described in Table 4.3. One model for rational choice is to rate each apartment on each dimension, add up the ratings, and choose the apartment with the highest ratings. Table 4.3 illustrates a set of rated values for each attribute for each apartment. In terms of the bliss-point model of reinforcement the rated values in Table 4.3 could be viewed as reflecting how close each apartment is to the bliss point on each dimension (a high rating is closer to the bliss-point). At the bottom of the table, these numbers are summed to get the total overall value for the apartments, and the best choice is revealed to be B, which is cheap and scores reasonably on the other dimensions. All proposals for optimal behavior have the subject consider each apartment on each dimension and calculate some aggregate measure of goodness.

People have been observed to do many things in making decisions such as choosing among apartments, but seldom have they been observed to correspond to what could be recognized as such rational choice behavior. The following are two nonoptimal strategies that have been observed in human subjects.

Table 4.3 *Attributes of Various Apartments and Their Rated Values (in Parentheses)*

	Apartment A	Apartment B	Apartment C	Apartment D
Cost	$600 (−2)	$300 (10)	$325 (9)	$400 (6)
Number of Rooms	4 (8)	3 (4)	3 (4)	4 (8)
Distance from Work	2 miles (0)	1 mile (4)	½ mile (6)	½ mile (6)
Parking	Yes (3)	Yes (3)	No (0)	No (0)
Condition	Mint (8)	Good (5)	Good (5)	Fair (2)

Apartment A: $-2 + 8 + 0 + 3 + 8 = 17$

Apartment B: $10 + 4 + 4 + 3 + 5 = 26$

Apartment C: $9 + 4 + 6 + 0 + 5 = 24$

Apartment D: $6 + 8 + 6 + 0 + 2 = 22$

Elimination by aspects (Tversky, 1972). Focus on just the most important dimension first, for example, price. Eliminate from consideration any choices that are not close to the best on this dimension. Using Table 4.3, this practice might leave just B and C in the choice set. Then consider the next most important dimension. Continue until a single choice has been identified. The problem **elimination by aspects** is that it is possible, by focusing on the initial dimension, to eliminate a choice that might be so good on other dimensions as to be best overall.

Satisficing (Simon, 1955). Consider the alternatives one at a time in the order in which they occur. Set a cutoff for the value of an alternative of each dimension. Reject an alternative if any of its values are worse than the cutoff. Accept the first alternative whose values on all dimensions are above the threshold. Using Table 4.3, thresholds might be set on cost at $400, number of rooms at 3, distance at 1 mile, available parking, and good condition. Apartment A can be rejected immediately because it is too expensive; Apartment B is immediately accepted because it passes the threshold on all dimensions. C and D would not even be considered. Because it does not consider all the alternatives, **satisficing** may miss the best choice.

Although these strategies do not always yield the best results, they often yield the best result or a result close to the best and they produce results quickly because they allow the decision maker to focus on a subset of the information. Payne, Bettman, and Johnson (1988) showed that under time pressure, the elimination-by-aspects strategy more often yields the correct decision than the complete rational decision strategy. When the time is up, the rational decision strategy may not yet have considered the correct alternative, whereas the elimination-by-aspects strategy may have already identified the correct alternative. They also showed that subjects are sensitive to time pressure and tend to switch from an exhaustive strategy to an elimination-by-aspects strategy when time pressure increases.

Thus humans, like lower animals, use rules of thumb for making decisions, and these rules of thumb do not always yield the optimal choice. The Payne et al. study identified another important aspect of the process of making rational choice: different strategies take different amounts of time to execute. An individual cannot exhaustively consider all the apartments listed in a typical urban newspaper; nor can an animal in the wild, spend inordinate amounts of time making decisions. It might therefore be rational to use rules of thumb that only approximate the best decision but to do so quickly. Economists refer to this consideration as the cost of information. In judging what the best choice is, we need not only consider the value of the choice but also the cost of seeking the information that went into making that choice.

> *Humans often use rules of thumb to approximate best decisions, particularly when they are under time pressure.*

Final Reflections

This chapter concludes the discussions of research focused on animal learning, although later chapters will return many times to issues of animal cognition and memory. In general, animals learn the contingencies in the environment and behave in a way so as to nearly maximize what they desire. Issues of reinforcement necessarily play a major role in research on animal learning, because in order to determine what an animal has learned appropriate reinforcement conditions are needed to get the animal to display what it has learned. In contrast, humans can be directly queried, and experimenters can count on their general social cooperativeness to say what they have learned.

Much of human learning is available to consciousness, and humans often consciously decide what knowledge to display and how. For instance, students can tell what they know of a history lesson and why they chose to display this knowledge in a certain way in response to an essay question. However, as discussed in Chapters 8 and 9, not all human knowledge is available to consciousness and people are not always aware of the knowledge they are displaying. Few of us can tell what we know about riding a bike nor are we aware of how our knowledge comes into play in bike riding. The suspicion has always been that more (or all) of animal knowledge is of this unconscious, behavioral variety than is human knowledge.

Human behavior, which involves unconscious use of experience, can be as adaptive as behavior that involves deliberate choice based on consciously recalled experiences. The fact that animals tend to respond in near optimal ways to experience does not necessarily imply any conscious deliberation on their part.

> *Humans display what they have learned in both conscious and nonconscious ways. Both displays of learning can be equally adaptive.*

Further Readings

In addition to the sources suggested in Chapters 2 and 3, much of the research on schedules of reinforcement can be found in the *Journal of the Experimental Analysis of Behavior*. B. Williams (1988) provides an overview of research of choice behavior under different schedules. Herrnstein (1990) offers a readable discussion of the matching law and other issues about choice behavior. Staddon (1983) and Staddon and Ettinger (1989) present an adaptive analysis of behavior. The book edited by Klein and Mowrer (1989) contains a number of recent articles on the nature of reinforcement. The May 1993 edition of *Psychological Science* contains a series of articles on comparative cognition—relating animal cognition to human cognition.

5

Transient Memories

Conditioning Research
Versus Memory Research

This chapter marks a transition from research focused on animal conditioning to research focused on human memory. The critical distinction is not so much the species of the subject as it is the methodology used—the conditioning experiment versus the memory experiment. The typical conditioning experiment involves a rather complex situation from the point of view of the organism. The organism is put in a novel environment and is given some experiences that typically include strong manipulations of motivation. The experimenter is interested in the behavior that arises as a function of these experiences and motivational manipulations.

Figure 5.1 illustrates one way to conceive of what is happening in a conditioning experiment. The organism explicitly or implicitly has to figure out the structure of the environment, including reinforcement contingencies, from its experiences. The process by which it does so is sometimes called **induction**. The input to this process is its experience, possibly combined with biological predispositions and, in the case of humans, with some instructions. The result of this process is some knowledge of the environment, and this knowledge is deposited in memory. A process known as motivation then converts this knowledge into behavior. Figure 5.1 illustrates that this process of motivation is also affected by the organism's current goals. Memory is just one part of a larger system that is involved in a conditioning experiment; memory experiments try to focus on that one part.

Figure 5.1 also embodies the important discovery that learning processes are separate from motivational processes. Chapters 1 and 4 reviewed the evidence that motivation does not influence what is learned but how organisms display this learning. For instance, Tolman's rats learned about mazes in the absence of reinforcement, but only displayed that knowledge when food was

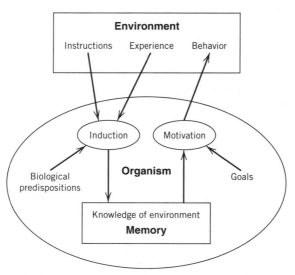

FIGURE 5.1. A conception of systems in a conditioning experiment.

put in the goal box. Thus Figure 5.1 illustrates that motivation does not control what goes into memory, but rather how memory maps onto behavior.

Figure 5.1 is a rational reconstruction of the factors that must be involved in a conditioning experiment. It is not meant to imply that there is always an induction stage, a memory stage, and a motivation stage. For instance, in *Aplysia* (Chapter 2) learning involved directly associating sensory neurons to motor neurons. This learning process implicitly induced the relationship between the CS and the US, resulted in a memory stored at the synapse, and produced an adaptive reflex, but there were not separate induction, memory, and motivation stages. As noted throughout this book, organisms can behave as if they went through a rational process without really doing so. The higher the organism is on the phylogenetic scale, the more likely that such rational processes actually occur at least in some cases. However, even in humans there is undoubtedly simpler "as if" learning as well.

A conditioning experiment requires that the organism induce the contingency, remember it, and use this knowledge to achieve its goals.

Animal Research Versus Human Research

With this picture in mind let us reflect again on the relative advantages of animal versus human experimentation, a topic mentioned in Chapter 1. Because of the greater complexity of human behavior, it is hard to study the full system shown in Figure 5.1 in one experiment, whereas a prototypical experiment with a rat in a Skinner box taps all aspects of the system. Animals are therefore often superior subjects for the study of the complete system. Animals are often superior subjects for the study of a single aspect of the system as well because there are fewer ethical constraints regarding their treatment. Many experiments on the motivation and physiology of learning involve extreme manipulations that can only be done with animals.

However, humans often offer advantages because they can be more carefully directed through instructions and experimenters can count on their social cooperativeness to obtain appropriate information. The advantage of human subjects is strongest in the behavioral study of the memory system. In the typical conditioning experiment, the memory system is only indirectly connected to the environment. The induction phase intervenes between the input from the environment and the memory system. The induction system figures out what goes with what and hence what should be stored in memory. Humans can be instructed as to what goes with what, and so researchers can effectively bypass the induction phase and study memory directly. Whereas a rat must figure out that pressing a lever causes food to be delivered, a human subject can simply be told. Because it is so easy to inform humans about what they should remember, experimenters typically have human subjects learn an amount of information that would be almost intractable in a conditioning experiment. A simple human memory experiment might require subjects to learn 20 stimulus–response paired associations, such as dog–6, where they must respond with the second term when shown the first. Twenty such pairs are a herculean number of stimulus–response associations to train in a conditioning experiment. With human subjects, researchers can focus on the storage of information in memory and not on how the organism figures out what should be stored in memory.

Just as induction causes difficulty on the input side in a conditioning experiment, motivational processes on the output side also create difficulty in making inferences about memory. With humans, experimenters do not usually have to worry about setting up complex contingencies to get the subjects to show what they have learned; the experimenters can simply ask and rely on social cooperativeness.

These experimental advantages have made humans the subjects of choice in behavioral studies of memory. These studies have yielded a great deal of knowledge, which is explored over the next four chapters. Researchers have also set up experimental paradigms to tap similar issues about memory in lower animals and have found that animal memory often appears to behave similarly to human memory. This comparative research is important both because it tells us about other animals and because lower organisms can provide an understanding of the physiological basis of memory.

Research on human memory has another advantage: it is more obviously relevant to us. Subsequent chapters frequently explore the implications of research for our own need to learn and remember information. This memory research is nowhere more relevant than in education. The typical memory experiment is often a miniature of the learning processes involved in mastery of a subject domain (such as the one you are studying in this text). The last chapter of this book is devoted to developing the implications of research on learning and memory for education.

Chapters 5 through 8 are the product of what is known as the **information-processing approach** in psychology. This cognitive approach views the nervous system abstractly as a system for processing information. The abstraction, which typifies this approach, shows most strongly in a relative lack of concern about the neural mechanisms underlying the information processing. This approach attempts to trace the course of information through the system, beginning as raw experience and being processed in ways that result in permanent changes called learning. The basic assumption is that records or memories must be formed to store these experiences. This chapter focuses on the transient ways in which the system can hold information for further processing. Chapters 6 through 8 consider the permanent memory system, which constitutes what we normally mean when we speak of memory.

> *Research on human memory allows experimenters to focus on a subset of the larger system that is involved in research on conditioning.*

Sensory Memory

How does information from the outside world get registered in some permanent memory? Perceptual systems, like our auditory and visual system, convert sensory energy arriving at our sensors (eyes, ears, etc.) into perceptual representations. It is necessary to hold this perceptual information in various sensory stores long enough so that we can identify what is actually being perceived and create a permanent representation of it. Much research has been devoted to the properties of the temporary stores that exist to hold visual and auditory information.

Visual Sensory Memory

One of the the temporary memories is **visual sensory memory,** which holds information perceived by the visual system. Let's consider one line of experiments that has been used to study visual sensory memory. Take a brief glance at Figure 5.2, turn your eyes away, and try to recall what letters were there. Most people, if they just have one brief look (less than 1 sec), report that they are able to recall only four or five letters. This procedure seems to tell us

FIGURE 5.2. Type				
of visual display	X	M	R	J
used in visual report	C	N	K	P
procedures.	V	F	L	B

about the capacity of visual sensory memory—that it can hold about four or five things. These informal observations have been confirmed by more careful laboratory studies in which subjects were given a very brief (e.g., 50 msec) exposure to an array of letters such as that shown in Figure 5.2. Such results might lead to the conclusion that only a few items can be stored in visual sensory memory.

However, many subjects indicated that it felt as if they actually saw more than the few letters that they reported, but that the other letters faded before they could report them. Perhaps you also had this experience. Sperling (1960) conducted a study that confirmed what the subjects were saying. As in the other experiments, he presented the visual array for a short period (50 msec). Rather than ask the subjects to report the whole visual array, he asked them to report one row from the array. Immediately after the array was removed, Sperling presented his subjects with a high tone, a middle tone, or a low tone. If the tone was high, subjects were supposed to report the top row; a middle tone corresponded to the middle row; and a low tone corresponded to the bottom row. This procedure is called the partial report procedure, in contrast to the whole report procedure, in which subjects must report everything. Sperling found that the subjects were able to recall a little over three of the four items that appeared in a row.[1]

Sperling concluded that immediately after the removal of the visual stimulus, the subjects' visual memories contained all the items in the array, but that the items rapidly faded from that memory. He studied the time course of the decay by delaying presentation of the tone after the removal of the array. Figure 5.3 shows how the number of letters that the subject could report decayed as the tone was delayed up to 1 sec: The number quickly dropped off. This result indicates that information in the visual sensory memory has a very short life. Probably much of what the subjects were able to recall after 1 sec reflected what they had identified in that second before they knew which row they would be asked to report.

Neisser (1967) called this short visual memory **iconic memory** and argued that it was critical in allowing us to recognize stimuli that are presented only for a brief duration. People need some system to hold the infor-

---

[1]The fact that their reports were not always perfect probably reflected difficulties in executing the reporting and the fact that some of that row might have faded before it could be reported.

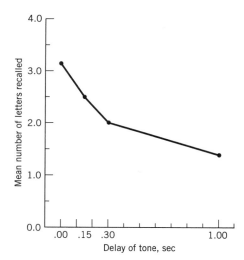

FIGURE 5.3. Results from Sperling's partial report procedure. As delay of signal is increased, number of items reported decreases.

mation until it is encoded into a more permanent form. **Encoding** information involves creating some long-term memory record for it.

Iconic memory appears to be sensory in character and may even reflect activation of the neural systems responsible for early visual processing. Sakitt (1976) argued that the icon is predominantly located in the photoreceptors of the retina. She showed that many of the timing and sensitivity properties of the iconic image mirror those of the rods, which are the photoreceptors in the eye responsible for night vision. According to this analysis the icon is very much like the afterimage of a bright light at night. Haber (1983) questioned the relevance of the icon for normal visual perception, because humans do not usually perceive the world in such brief flashes; he argued that the icon would only be relevant to reading in a lightning storm. Others have argued that the neural processes that underlie the icon go beyond the retina. Coltheart (1983) argued that icons are obtained when there are no rod-based afterimages and that these icons play an important role in everyday information processing.

The evidence is quite persuasive that visual information exists in the system at many levels after we see something. A great deal of information is maintained in such a form, but only briefly. However, there is not agreement as to the forms in which this information is maintained or how this information is used in higher-level cognition.

Sensory information is maintained in the visual system for brief periods of time.

Auditory Sensory Memory

Auditory information appears to be held in sensory memories just as visual information is temporarily stored in sensory memories. Early demonstrations of an **auditory sensory memory** were performed by Moray, Bates, and Barnett (1965) and Darwin, Turvey, and Crowder (1972). Darwin et al. presented subjects with simultaneous recordings of three lists of three items over two headphones. The items were letters and numbers; thus, one list might be 4 L 6. By stereophonic mixing of the signals from the two headphones it appeared that one list was coming from the subject's left, another list from the subject's right, and a third list from directly above the subject. As in the visual report procedures, subjects were not able to report all nine items (3 lists × 3 items) when asked to recall everything. However, the researchers also used a partial report condition similar to that used by Sperling. They asked the subjects to report just one of the three lists. They cued subjects as to which list to report by presenting a visual indicator on the right, middle, or left of a screen.

Subjects were able to report a higher percentage of the target set when they were cued than when they were told to recall the total list. Like Sperling, Darwin et al. interpreted this to mean that there were items in an auditory buffer that could not be recalled in the whole report procedure because they had faded from memory before the subject was able to report them. In the partial report procedure subjects had to report fewer items and so got to reporting the critical items sooner. Darwin et al. also showed that the amount that could be reported in the partial report procedure decreased as the delay between the end of the lists and the cue increased. After 4 sec there was very little advantage for the partial report procedure. As in the case of iconic memory, this result indicated that items were decaying and subjects were only able to remember something from the critical list if they encoded it before it had faded.

Neisser called the auditory sensory memory that held these items **echoic memory.** As in the case of iconic memory, he argued that people need some memory to hold the sensory experience so that it can be analyzed and encoded into a more permanent form.

Glucksberg and Cowan (1970) conducted a rather different experiment, which resulted in a similar estimate of the duration of the echoic store. They presented subjects with two spoken messages, one in each ear, and they required subjects to repeat the message that was being said in one ear. This task, called a shadowing task, is very demanding, and subjects typically remember nothing of what is said in the other ear. From time to time the experimenters said a digit to the ear that was not being shadowed. They stopped the subjects and asked whether a digit had occurred. They found that if they asked subjects right after the digit, subjects could still detect it with some success. This performance dropped off dramatically over the first 2 secs, and after 5 sec the subjects showed no ability to detect the digit. The researchers concluded that in less than 5 sec echoic memory was completely lost for the unattended digit.

Conrad (1960) and Crowder and Morton (1969) showed that information not only decays from echoic memory with the passage of time but that it can be interfered with by additional auditory information. Crowder and Morton presented the word *zero* just before asking subjects to recall a list of digits.

Subjects were told to ignore the last *zero* and to recall the preceding digits. This final digit seriously impaired memory for the list. This phenomenon is called the suffix effect, because an irrelevant suffix has been shown to impair memory. Impairment occurs because the *zero* enters auditory memory and interferes with the target list.

The interference associated with the suffix effect seems to be verbal in character. Crowder and Morton found that if they used a buzzer rather than a word as the suffix, there was no interference. Ayres, Jonides, Reitman, Egan, and Howard (1979) similarly contrasted speech syllables as suffixes with musical sounds. Again they found more interference with the speech sounds. Thus auditory memory appears to have a speechlike character.

Oral or spoken information is maintained in the auditory system for brief periods of time.

Conclusions About Sensory Memory

Sensory memory is capable of storing more or less complete records of what has been encountered for brief periods of time, during which people can note relationships among the elements and encode the elements in a more permanent memory. If the information in sensory memory is not encoded in the brief time before it decays, it is lost. What subjects encode depends on what they are paying attention to. The environment typically offers much more information at one time than we can attend to and encode. Therefore much of what enters our sensory system results in no permanent record. Similarly, instrumental conditioning research (see the discussion of dimensional learning in Chapter 3) has shown that animals often do not initially attend to certain aspects of the stimuli presented to them. Presumably, nonhumans are also overwhelmed by the richness of the stimuli they experience and can only pay attention to certain things.

Although the auditory and visual systems are perhaps the most important, they are not the only sensory systems that display transient memories for information. If someone steps on your foot, your tactile system remembers for a while which foot was stepped on. Athletes report motor memory for the recent performance of a skill. Information, as it is processed by many of our sensory systems, results in changes in the state of these sensory systems. In some circumstances we are able to use these state changes as transient records.

The remainder of the chapter is devoted to the properties of the system that initially holds the information after it is encoded into a more permanent form from the sensory stores. At one time it was thought that there was a sequence of memories, that information passed from sensory memory to short-term memory and then to long-term memory. The next section discusses the problems associated with the concept of an intermediate short-term memory. The new conception of memory that has come to replace this concept is then introduced.

Sensory systems can have transient records of the information they are processing and these can serve as temporary memories.

The Rise and Fall of the Theory of Short-Term Memory

The Atkinson and Shiffrin theory (see Figure 1.11 from Chapter 1) of memory proposed that there are separate short-term and long-term memories and that information is temporarily held in short-term memory by rehearsal. While it is in short-term memory, a permanent representation of the information can be built up in long-term memory. The classic example is a telephone number, silently repeated over and over again until it is memorized. The key feature of this theory is the proposal that short-term memory is a necessary halfway station between sensory memory and long-term memory. Many psychology texts still include this proposal of two separate memories, and it is worthwhile reviewing why this view was held. The distinction between short-term and long-term memory was predicated on a number of claims; particularly significant were the following three:

- Rehearsal of information in short-term memory builds up a representation of that information in long-term memory.
- The types of encodings are different in short-term and long-term memory.
- There is a dramatic difference in the durations of short-term and long-term memory.

Each of these claims was based on some empirical data. However, it has become apparent that all the data cannot be properly understood if there is assumed to be a short-term memory between sensory memory and long-term memory. This section considers each claim, the evidence for it, and the problems with it.

The theory of short-term memory was based on claims about the effects of rehearsal, coding differences, and retention of information.

Effects of Rehearsal

The experiment by Rundus (1971) showed that the longer information is rehearsed the better it is recalled. He asked subjects to rehearse out loud and counted the number of times they rehearsed each word. He found that the words that were rehearsed more often were better recalled (see Figure 1.12). This result was just as predicted by the Atkinson and Shiffrin theory, which proposed that information got into long-term memory by being rehearsed in short-term memory. Sometimes, however, rehearsal does little to improve long-term memory. Glenberg, Smith, and Green (1977) had subjects study a four-digit number for 2 sec, then rehearse a word for 2, 6, or 18 sec, and then recall the four digits. Subjects participated in 64 trials. Subjects thought that the experimenter's interest was in digit recall and that the words were only being used to fill up the retention interval. After the experiment, subjects were asked to recall the words they had been rehearsing. Their recall averaged an abysmal 11, 7, and 12 percent in the 2-, 6-, and 18-sec rehearsal intervals. Thus subjects showed little recall and no relationship between the amount of rehearsal and the amount of recall. Glenberg et al. also tried a recognition test for the words and found only a weak effect of amount of rehearsal on memory performance.

Craik and Watkins (1973) used another paradigm to show the lack of effect of passive rehearsal on memory. Their subjects heard a list of 21 words and were supposed to recall the last word that began with a certain letter. Thus if the critical letter was *G*, subjects might hear *daughter, rifle, garden, grain, table, football, anchor, giraffe, fish, tooth, book, heart, mouse, gold, can, ball, paper, fire, glass, house, shoe,* and should recall *glass.* When the subjects heard the first *G* word, they did not know whether it was the word they would have to recall and so they had to rehearse it until they heard the next *G*-word. Different words had to be rehearsed for different lengths of time. In the example given, *garden* would be rehearsed for zero words, *grain* three words, *giraffe* five words, *gold* four words, and *glass* two words. After studying 27 such lists subjects were given a surprise recall of all the words. Craik and Watkins found no relationship between how long the word was rehearsed and its final probability of recall.

Perhaps the most dramatic evidence for the lack of relationship between the amount of rehearsal and long-term recall is the report cited by Neisser (1982) of a Professor Sanford, who estimated that he had read the family prayers at meals some 5000 times over 25 years. Despite all this rehearsal, Professor Sanford found that when he tested his memory he had very little memory for the prayers. Sheer rehearsal is not enough to guarantee good long-term memory.

If it is not sheer repetition, what does determine how much we remember? Rundus found a relationship between number of rehearsals and recall but, unlike the experiments just cited, his subjects were actively processing the material with an eye to remembering it. In an influential article, Craik and

Lockhart (1972) argued that what was critical was the depth to which information was processed. According to this theory, called the **depth of processing theory**, rehearsal only improves memory if the material is rehearsed in a deep and meaningful way; passive rehearsal does not result in better memory. This point of view was nicely illustrated in a series of experiments by Craik and Tulving (1975). In one experiment they showed subjects a word, such as *table*, and asked them to make three types of judgments. The shallow-level judgment, about case, was whether the word was in capitals. The intermediate-level judgment was whether it rhymed with another word, for example, *cable*. The deep-level judgment was whether it fit in a sentence, for example, "He put the plate on the _____." They later asked subjects to recognize the words. Figure 5.4 shows the proportion of words recognized as a function of the type of processing of the words. The more deeply processed words were better remembered.

Craik and Lockhart argued that memory for material improves with more time for rehearsal only if the rehearsal creates a deeper encoding of the material. There was no improvement with rehearsal time in the Glenberg et al. or the Craik and Watkins studies because subjects continued to rehearse the words at a shallow level. The depth of processing explanation has been criticized because the concept of depth is somewhat vague (Nelson, 1977) and because, as reviewed in Chapter 8, there are interactions between the type of processing at study and at test. However, depth of processing experiments such as that reviewed here remain significant in that they show that mere rehearsal of material does not automatically result in better memory. This result was devastating for the original Atkinson and Shiffrin theory of short-term memory, which proposed that information was transferred to long-term memory as a function of verbal rehearsal.

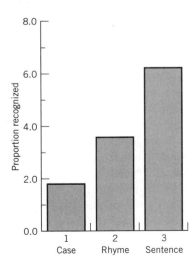

FIGURE 5.4. Proportion of words recognized as a function of type of initial processing. (From Craik & Tulving, 1975).

Passive rehearsal of material will not increase its recall, but deeper processing does.

Coding Differences

One of the arguments for a separate short-term memory was that information was coded differently in short-term memory and long-term memory. It seemed that the encodings in short-term memory were sensory in nature. People often rehearse material, such as word lists in experiments or telephone numbers in everyday life, by saying the items over and over again to themselves. This means that the information tends to have articulatory and acoustic features. It was thought that information in long-term memory was more concerned with representing the meaning of the items.

A classic experiment showing this distinction between short-term and long-term memory was performed by Kintsch and Buschke (1969). They had subjects study lists of 16 words presented visually at a rate of one word every 2 sec. They then provided subjects with one word from the list and asked them to recall the word that followed it in the list. It is worth reviewing how the Atkinson and Shiffrin theory is supposed to apply to memory for such a list of words (see the discussion surrounding Figure 1.12). The subject was assumed to be rehearsing in short-term memory the last few words read. Therefore, when asked to recall the words after study, the subject should display particularly good memory for the last few words in the list because these were rehearsed. This result did occur; the advantage for the last few words is referred to as the **recency effect.** Memory for the rest of the list depended on retrieving the words from long-term memory.

Kintsch and Bushke reasoned that if short-term memory was verbal in character, there would be a lot of acoustic interference if the words in the list sounded alike—for example, *see* and *sea*. If subjects were asked what followed *see* they might recall the word that followed *sea*. Such acoustical confusions would be a particular problem for words at the end of the list, which were supposed to be in short-term memory. On the other hand, words from the beginning of the list might produce semantic confusions if they were synonyms, such as *sea* and *ocean*, because these words were in long-term memory, where the coding was supposed to be semantic.

In three conditions, subjects saw words that were unrelated, synonyms (similar meaning), or homophones (similar sounding). Kintsch and Bushke found that recall for the last few words in the list was impaired if the words were homophones and that memory for the first words of the list was impaired if the words were synonyms. It seemed that short-term memory was acoustic (sound-oriented) and long-term memory was semantic (meaning-oriented), as hypothesized.

However, there are serious problems with trying to advance coding differences as a fundamental distinction between short-term memory and long-term memory. For instance, tasks that are supposed to rely on short-term memory also take advantage of meaningful codes. Bower and Springston (1970) showed that subjects had much larger memory spans for sequences of letters when they formed meaningful acronyms, as in,

IBM   FBI   ABC   USA

Memory for these letters was supported by semantic information which, according to the short-term memory theory, is a long-term memory coding. In addition, the fact that people can remember rhymes and sounds for long periods of time provides evidence of acoustic codings in long-term memory.

People can also make semantic confusions in a short-term memory task. Potter and Lombardi (1990) presented subjects with sentences such as

The knight rounded the palace searching for a place to enter.

Subjects then heard a list that included the word *castle*. After hearing the list, they were asked to recall the original sentence. About a quarter of the subjects recalled

The knight rounded the castle searching for a place to enter.

and thus intruded the semantically related word. This semantic confusion indicates that our immediate memory for a list of words (in this case a sentence) involves semantic information as well as acoustic information.

An alternative proposal, based on the concept of depth of processing (Craik & Lockhart, 1972; Wickelgren, 1974), proposes that different types of information are forgotten at different rates and that sensory information may be more shallowly processed and may be forgotten more rapidly. Memories initially may show a preponderance of sensory traces, but as time passes, semantic traces remain. (This issue of differential forgetting for different types of memory is addressed in more detail in Chapter 6.) Thus acoustic confusions predominate early in the Kintsch and Bushke experiment because the acoustic information has not been forgotten; as time passes the acoustic information is forgotten, leaving primarily semantic information, which was there all the time, and resulting in mainly semantic confusions.

Both acoustic and semantic information can serve as the basis of memory performance at short and long delays.

The Retention Function

Much of the belief about the dichotomy between short-term and long-term memory derives from the recency effect, which refers to the fact that the most recently encountered items are the best remembered. The ability to recall information decays rapidly in the short interval after it has been studied. According to the hypothesis of a separate short-term memory, the superior memory for recent material indicates that it is held in a special short-term memory store and the rapid decay reflects loss from short-term memory.

Several other paradigms have been used to show that there is an initial rapid loss of information. Brown (1958) and Peterson and Peterson (1959) traced the retention of simple nonsense trigrams, such as CHJ, over 18 sec. Subjects might not be expected to exhibit much forgetting of three letters over such a short period. However, the experimenters distracted subjects by having them count backwards by threes from a large number, such as 418. With this sort of distracting task there was rapid forgetting of the trigrams. Figure 5.5 shows the retention functions obtained. Note that retention decreased to about 20 percent, not to zero, supposedly reflecting what the subjects were able to store in long-term memory. Given longer initial study, subjects would have shown a higher level of performance after 18 sec, reflecting the transfer of more information to long-term memory.

There are several problems with such demonstrations. Such steeply decreasing retention functions are not obtained from subjects asked to recall their first nonsense trigram (Keppel & Underwood, 1962); in this case they show relatively little forgetting. Rapid forgetting only occurs after subjects have been in the experiment for many trials and have seen many trigrams. Thus an important contribution to this forgetting is interference from earlier trigrams that have been studied and are stored in long-term memory. Chapter 7 examines these studies and retention effects at greater length, but for now note that the forgetting in Figure 5.5 does not simply reflect a short-term

FIGURE 5.5. Decrease in recall as a function of duration of the distracting task. (From Murdock, 1961).

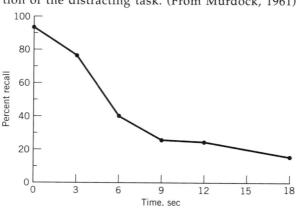

memory phenomenon, because it depends critically on what the subject has committed to long-term memory.

The retention curve in Figure 5.5 appears to show rapid initial forgetting followed by no further forgetting. This apparent discontinuity of the forgetting curve was used to argue for two stores (e.g., Waugh & Norman, 1965). The initial rapid drop-off was supposed to be due to loss from short-term memory, whereas the flat portion of the curve was supposed to represent what got into long-term memory. However, note that performance is still dropping off from 9 to 18 sec (and this curve would continue to drop off beyond 18 sec). Wickelgren pointed out that all retention curves for any period of time show **negative acceleration,** meaning that the rate of loss is initially large but decreases with time. Consider the retention study of Ebbinghaus (Figure 1.1 from Chapter 1). He looked at retention of material that was much better learned than that represented in Figure 5.5 over intervals of up to 30 days. Figure 1.2 shows a negatively accelerated retention curve with an apparent discontinuity at around 2 days, where the curve is flattening. Clearly, there is not a short-term memory of 2 days! The forms of retention curves are not evidence for a discontinuity between short-term and long-term memory; the curves are really continuous, and their apparent discontinuity is merely an artifact of the scales on which they are graphed. Chapter 7 discusses the nature of these retention functions more fully.

The shape of the early part of the retention function and the factors that influence it are the same as for the later part of the retention function.

Conclusions About Short-Term Memory

The two-memory proposal claimed that there are two separate memory stores with their own distinct characteristics and that information passes from the short-term store to the long-term store. The alternative proposal is that there is just one general memory system into which information from our sensory systems is encoded (e.g., Melton, 1963; Wickelgren, 1974). Different memories in that system can have different attributes. The way we process that information can influence how well we remember it. In particular, more deeply processed information tends to be forgotten less rapidly. There is no discontinuity in the retention functions for any kind of material. All forgetting functions are negatively accelerated through any retention interval.

The data on the effects of rehearsal, types of codes, and retention effects can be accommodated without postulating a short-term memory as a halfway station between sensory memory and long-term memory. However, people do engage in rehearsal processes, and these processes can affect memory performance. Baddeley (e.g., 1986) proposed a concept of slave **rehearsal systems** to help explain these effects. These rehearsal systems are considered next.

Rehearsal Systems

A previous section reviewed the evidence for the existence of sensory memories that maintain transient records of our experience. For instance, we have an acoustic memory that holds information for a few seconds. What happens if we say a set of numbers to ourselves? Presumably we are filling our echoic memory with a sensory record of our own speech. If we do this over and over again, we can keep a record of those digits in echoic memory. By rehearsal we are making our echoic memory a system for holding the digits. There are other ways in which we can use our bodies as systems for holding information. We can remember a digit by holding out the appropriate number of fingers; we can remember where something is in space by staring at that location; we can remember the width of a board by placing our two hands at its sides and then keeping our hands that far apart. People can be extremely imaginative in how they use their bodies as transient memories to hold information. The verbal system is particularly important, and a great deal of research has been devoted to how we use this system to hold information. Baddeley used the term **phonological loop** to refer to our use of the verbal system as a transient memory.

The Phonological Loop

According to Baddeley, the phonological loop is composed of two systems—a store capable of holding speech-based information and a system capable of subvocal speech (speaking to oneself). The phonological loop does not require speaking aloud. Since no auditory signal is needed, the phonological loop is not quite the same thing as the echoic store. Baddeley and Lewis (1981) referred to the system that holds speech-based information as the **inner ear** and the system for speaking to oneself as the **inner voice.** Although they are not the same, the inner ear and the inner voice are closely tied to the outer ear and the outer voice. Baddeley proposed that the phonological loop is capable of holding about 2-sec worth of information. Some of the best evidence for such a loop involves **memory-span tests** for various kinds of information that people tend to rehearse verbally. In a memory-span test the subjects hear a series of words and try to repeat them back perfectly. Baddeley, Thomson, and Buchanan (1975) had subjects try to repeat five words. They varied the number of syllables in the words from one syllable,

wit, sum, harm, bag, top

to five syllables,

university, opportunity, expository, participation, auditorium

Figure 5.6 shows the recall results. Recall decreased as the number of syllables increased, falling from about 4.5 words for the one-syllable words to 2.6 words for the five-syllable words. Figure 5.6 also plots the reading rate, the number of words of each syllable length that can be said in 1 sec. The reading rate also decreased as number of syllables increased. Dividing the number recalled by the reading rate produces a value of about 2 for all syllable lengths. For instance, subjects could recall about 3.5 of five three-syllable words and their reading rate was about 1.8 words/sec—giving 3.5/1.8, or approximately 2-sec worth of words. This result implies that subjects can recall what they can rehearse in 2 sec. What limits the capacity of the phonological loop is how far back the inner ear can remember hearing a word. The research of Darwin, Turvey, and Crowder (1972) and Glucksberg and Cowan (1970), reviewed earlier, indicated that echoic memory had a span of 4 or 5 sec. This span is a good bit longer than that estimated for Baddeley's phonological loop, but these studies involved rather different procedures and measures.

The crucial variable is spoken duration and not number of syllables. Words with long vowels, such as *Friday* and *harpoon,* show shorter spans than words with short vowels, such as *wicked* and *bishop* (Baddeley, 1990). There is an interesting relationship between speech rate and digit span. **Digit span** is a fairly standard test of memory that appears in intelligence tests. It involves seeing how many single-digit numbers a person can repeat back perfectly. Adult speakers of English have spans of about seven or eight digits. There is a correlation across languages between span and articulation length for digits. The articulation rate for Chinese is 265 msec/digit (Hoosain & Salili, 1988), compared with 321 msec/digit for English and 385 msec/digit for Welsh (Ellis & Hennelly, 1980). Correspondingly, spans are longest for Chinese (9.9), intermediate for English (6.6), and shortest for Welsh (5.8).

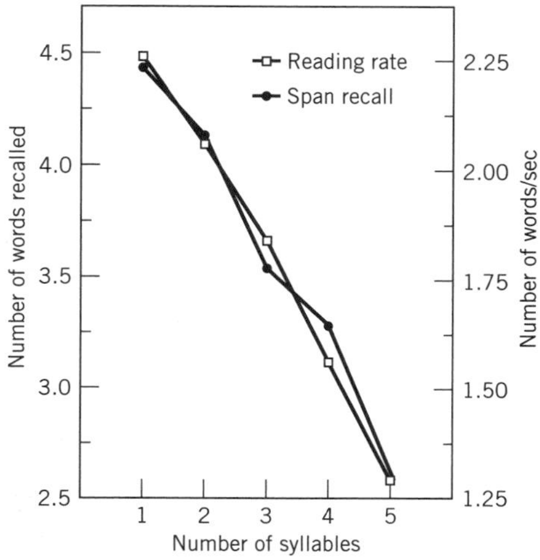

FIGURE 5.6. Number of words recalled (left-hand scale) and mean reading rate (right-hand scale) for sequences of five words as a function of the number of syllables in the words. (From Baddeley, 1986).

Trying to maintain information in the phonological loop is analogous to the circus act that involves spinning plates on reeds. The circus performer starts one plate spinning on a reed, then another on another reed, then another, and so on. The performer must return to the first before it slows down and falls off, respin it, and then respin the rest of the plates. There are only so many plates that the performer can keep spinning. Baddeley proposed the same situation with respect to working memory. If we try to keep too many items in working memory, by the time we get back to rehearse the first one, its representation is no longer available in the phonological store.

This phonological loop seems to involve speech. Conrad (1964) performed some of the original research establishing this point. He showed that when subjects misremembered something from a memory-span task, they tended to recall something that sounded similar. In his experiment, subjects were asked to recall a string of letters, such as HBKLMW. They were much more likely to misrecall *B* as its soundalike *V* than as an *S*, which does not sound similar. Conrad also found that subjects had a harder time recalling a string of letters that contained a high proportion of rhyming letters (such as BCTHVZ) than a string that did not (such as HBKLMW). He speculated that this problem arose because of confusion among the similar-sounding letters.

Further evidence that the phonological loop involves speech is provided by articulatory suppression techniques, which require the subject to say repeatedly an irrelevant word, such as *the* (Baddeley, Lewis, & Vallar, 1984). Subjects repeat the word while they listen to a list of words and while they try to write down the list in recall. Requiring the subject to say the word prevents the rehearsing of anything else in the phonological loop. Memory spans of subjects forced to engage in articulatory suppression are shorter than those of others. In contrast, concurrent nonspeech tasks, such as tapping, do not affect span. Articulatory suppression also reduces the phonological confusions among letters that Conrad found. When the original list is presented visually and the subject is engaged in articulatory suppression, the effect of phonological similarity is eliminated; it is reduced, but not eliminated, when the original presentation is auditory. With auditory presentation, the subject still has a phonological encoding of the original presentation, which can be confused on a phonological basis (Baddeley et al., 1984); with visual presentation, the subjects have neither the auditory presentation nor the results of their inner speech.

What is the difference between Baddeley's phonological loop and the short-term memory of Atkinson and Shiffrin? Although both are transient and rehearse verbal information, the phonological loop is not a halfway station to long-term memory. Information does not have to go through the loop to get into permanent memory, and while it is being rehearsed, no build up of its permanent representation must occur. There is as little relationship between the phonological loop and what happens to permanent memory as there is between a sheet of paper on which we take notes and permanent memory. Like the paper, the phonological loop can be a valuable system for storing information; unlike the paper, however, it is a transient representation and all records can be lost if rehearsal ceases.

The phonological loop can maintain about 2 seconds of speech by implicit verbal rehearsal.

The Visuo-spatial Sketch Pad

Among the other slave rehearsal systems proposed by Baddeley is the **visuo-spatial sketch pad,** a system for rehearsing visual or spatial information. He proposed that people can rehearse material by creating mental images that are in some ways like the sensory experiences they have when seeing. For instance, Baddeley (an Englishman) reported that he had difficulty following an American football game on the radio while driving. He had developed a complex image of the game, which was interfering with his ability to process the visual information required for driving. His imagery process was interfering with his visual process, suggesting that they are part of the same system.

Figure 5.7 illustrates some material that Baddeley adapted from Brooks (1967) to study the use of the visuo-spatial sketch pad to store visual information. In the spatial condition, subjects heard a series of sentences that they were to remember. To help them remember the sentences, they were

FIGURE 5.7. Example of material used by Baddeley in his study of the visuo-spatial sketch pad. *Source:* From A. D. Baddeley, S. Grant, E. Wight, and N. Thomson. *Attention and Performance V,* Volume 5. Imagery and Visual Working Memory. Copyright © 1975 by Academic Press. Reprinted by permission.

		3	4
	1	2	5
		7	6
		8	

Spatial material	Nonsense material
In the starting square put a 1.	In the starting square put a 1.
In the next square to the *right* put a 2.	In the next square to the *quick* put a 2.
In the next square *up* put a 3.	In the next square to the *good* put a 3.
In the next square to the *right* put a 4.	In the next square to the *quick* put a 4.
In the next square *down* put a 5.	In the next square to the *bad* put a 5.
In the next square *down* put a 6.	In the next square to the *bad* put a 6.
In the next square to the *left* put a 7.	In the next square to the *slow* put a 7.
In the next square *down* put an 8.	In the next square to the *bad* put an 8.

instructed to imagine placing the objects in a 4 × 4 matrix. Figure 5.7 illustrates how the matrix could code the information in the spatial sentences. In the nonsense condition, they heard sentences that were similar but that could not be coded in a matrix. Subjects were able to remember about eight of the spatial sentences and only five of the nonsense sentences, suggesting that they were able to use the image of the 4 × 4 matrix to supplement their memory for the sentences.

In an important elaboration on this basic study, Baddeley, Grant, Wight, and Thomson (1975) looked at the effect of a concurrent spatial tracking task on memory for the sentences. The concurrent tracking task involved keeping a stylus in contact with a spot of light that followed a circular track. Subjects had to remember eight spatial sentences or five nonsense sentences. Figure 5.8 shows the total number of errors made in remembering these sentences when the subjects were and were not simultaneously performing a spatial tracking task. The error rate was approximately the same for spatial and nonsense material without a spatial tracking task and was not impaired for nonsense sentences given a spatial tracking task. The error rate rose dramatically when subjects had to perform a spatial tracking task concurrently with memorizing the spatial sentences. This result indicates that the visuo-spatial sketch pad that supports the memory of the spatial sentences is tapping the same system that supports the representation of the tracking task.

The visuo-spatial sketch pad can maintain transient information in a spatial organization.

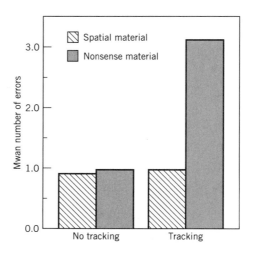

FIGURE 5.8. The influence of concurrent tracking on memory span for spatial and nonspatial sequences. (From Baddeley et al., 1974).

The Overall System and the Central Executive

Figure 5.9 illustrates Baddeley's overall conception of how these various slave systems interact. A **central executive** controls the use of various slave systems, like the visuo-spatial sketch pad and the phonological loop. The central executive can put information into any of these slave systems or retrieve information from the systems. It can also translate information from one system to the other. Baddeley claimed that the central executive needs its own transient store of information to make decisions about how to control the slave systems.

Consider the involvement of these systems in performing a mental multiplication task, such as 37 × 28. Try to figure out this product in your head and observe what you do. You might try to hold an image of the multiplication, which looks like

$$
\begin{array}{r}
37 \\
\times 28 \\
\hline
296 \\
740 \\
\hline
1036
\end{array}
$$

You might verbally rehearse information to help you retain it. Thus you might well use both your phonological loop and your visuo-spatial sketch pad to help you perform the task. But you need to access information that is in neither store. You have to remember that your task is multiplication; where you are in the multiplication; facts, such as 7 × 8 = 56; and temporary carries, such as 5 from 56. All this information is held by the central executive and used to determine the course of solving the problem and the use of the slave systems.

Some of the information required to perform a particular task is in the environment and can be stored by sensory systems. Other information may be held by slave rehearsal systems. Some information (such as 7 × 8 = 56) is in neither area. This latter type is the information that Baddeley conceived of as held by the central executive. A major issue in cognitive psychology is how to

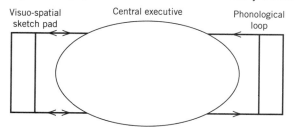

FIGURE 5.9. Baddeley's theory of working memory where a central executive coordinates a set of slave systems. *Source:* From A. D. Baddeley. *Working memory: Oxford psychology series* NO. 11. Copyright © 1986. Reprinted by permission of Oxford University Press.

Visuo-spatial sketch pad   Central executive   Phonological loop conceive of the information that is currently available but is not part of the slave systems or sensory stores. One view is that this information is part of the permanent store of knowledge, but is in a temporary transient state of high activation. **Activation** is an abstract concept used in cognitive psychology to refer to the availability of information. Cognitive psychologists often think of activation as neural activation, although they vary in how precise a connection they make with neural activation. The next section describes the general structure of permanent memory and how some parts of it can be transiently active.

A central executive coordinates the slave rehearsal systems and has its own transient memory store.

Activation in Permanent Memory

The Nature of Permanent Memory

Permanent memory can be conceived of as consisting of various **records** that have encoded in them the information we know and our various experiences. Figure 5.10 illustrates some memory records encoding some of the information an individual might know. These records include the arithmetical fact that $4 \times 7 = 28$, the note that the person is currently engaged in a mental multiplication, the location of the person's car in the parking lot, and the fact that cars have four wheels. The next chapter discusses more about how these records are represented in memory; for now let us conceive of them as little packages of information that store what we know.

These records have connections to various elements that a person might perceive in the environment or rehearse in a slave system. For instance, $4 \times 7 = 28$ is connected to 4, 28, and the word *multiplication* (it is also pre-

FIGURE 5.10. Memory records in permanent memory and their connections to various cues.

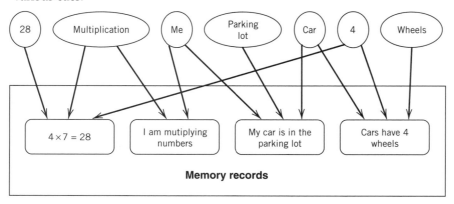

sumably connected to 7, but not all the connections are shown in Figure 5.10). Each element, which is connected to the memory records, is called a **cue.** When cues are attended to, either because they are in the environment or because they are rehearsed, they activate their associated records in permanent memory. A person has access to these memory records to the degree to which they are active. The state of being active or available is a transient property of memory records, so the currently active information in permanent memory is, in effect, another transient memory and an important part of the person's overall working memory. By focusing on different information in the environment or by rehearsing different information, a person can make different parts of permanent memory active. Thus, on hearing the word *mother*, information about a person's mother becomes active; similarly, on viewing a picture of the Eiffel Tower, information about Paris and France becomes active. In these examples, *mother* and the Eiffel Tower are the cues and the retrieved memories are the records.

A number of different theories in cognitive psychology embody this basic analysis of memory as records and cues, although they use different language to describe it. The language used in this chapter is similar to that of the **ACT** theory (J. R. Anderson, 1983a, 1993). Another well-known theory, **SAM** (Gillund & Shiffrin, 1984; Raaijmakers & Shiffrin, 1981), speaks of images (memory records) becoming more or less familiar (active) as a function of the cues in the context. Connectionist theories, reviewed in Chapter 2, are theories of neural information processing and have similar assumptions, except that the cues and records are referred to as neural units. Thus the system in Figure 5.10 reflects an emerging consensus in the field, although there is not yet consensus on the language that describes it. Much of the evidence for this system is presented in subsequent chapters. The following section reviews some of the data that indicate how the presentation of appropriate cues can facilitate access to memory records.

> *Permanent memory consists of a set of records that can be activated when their associated cues are in the environment or in rehearsal systems.*

Priming

A fundamental assumption of this model is that cues are connected strongly to only some memory records. For instance, the word *cow* is associated to memory records concerning *cow*-like things, such as giving *milk*. A fair amount of work has been done documenting the existence of such associations in what is called a lexical decision task. These are experiments in which subjects are given strings of letters, such as *milk* or *milc*, and have to decide which are words and which are not. The experiments manipulate whether subjects also see an associate of a target word, for example, *cow*. In the experimental condition subjects might first see *cow* and then have to judge whether *milk* is a word, whereas in the control condition they might first see *cot* and then *milk*. Using the analysis of record activation just given, the word *cow* might be expected to activate the representation of the memory record that encodes the spelling of *milk* (since *cow* is associated to *milk*), and so the lexical decision could be made faster in that case. In fact, this is what occurs. Balota and Lorch (1986) found that subjects took 583 msec to decide when the words were unrelated and 535 msec when they were related.[2]

This ability of a cue to make associated information more available is referred to as **priming.** The research of Balota and Lorch is just one example of the many lines of research showing that subjects' access to information is primed when associates of that information are present. A priming experiment of a very different scale was done by Kaplan (1989). He gave subjects a set of puzzles to take home and solve. One problem was

What goes up a chimney down but cannot go down a chimney up?

One of his subjects was stuck on this particular problem and could not solve it for days. Kaplan arranged to have the subject receive what appeared to be a mistaken phone call during which the caller asked if she had left her umbrella in the subject's office. Shortly after that, the subject reported the solution to this problem—umbrella—even though he was unaware that the telephone call was related to his finding the answer. Over a group of subjects and problems, Kaplan produced decisive evidence that placing relevant things in the environment primed them as solutions to problems, even though the subjects were not aware that priming was going on.

The things that we focus on in the environment make available information that we can access to solve our problems. Also, information that we rehearse in our slave systems can prime associated information in permanent memory. The next sections will present evidence that information is available to the degree that it is rehearsed.

Memory records become more available when associated information is in the environment or in one of the rehearsal systems.

---

[2]The 48-msec difference might seem small, but it reflects about a 10 percent difference, and these experiments achieve very accurate measurements.

The Sternberg Paradigm

Sternberg (1969) introduced a paradigm that became popular for studying immediate access to information in memory and is now referred to as the **Sternberg paradigm.** He gave subjects a set of digits to hold in memory, such as 4 1 8 5, and then asked them whether a particular probe digit was in the set. For this example a positive probe digit would be 8 and a negative probe would be 6. Sternberg was interested in the speed with which his subjects could make the judgment as a function of the size of the set they were holding in memory. Figure 5.11 shows his results. The straight line is the best fitting linear function relating judgment time to the size of the memory set. As the size of the memory set got larger, subjects took longer to make the judgment in the case of both positive probes and negative probes. He found that each digit added an extra 38 msec. to the judgment time. This 38 msec is the slope of the linear function in Figure 5.11.

Sternberg proposed an influential theory to account for these results: Subjects serially searched through the list of digits they held in memory. If they found the digit in the list they responded yes to the probe; otherwise, they responded no. The more digits in the list, the longer it took to search the list. The 38 msec measured the time to consider one item in the list. The positive probe might be expected to result in a shallower slope, because the subject could stop as soon as the target digit was encountered, whereas in the case of a negative probe the subject would have to exhaust the list. However,

FIGURE 5.11. Judgment time as a function of number of items in a memory set. (From Sternberg 1969). *Source:* From J. Antrobus. *Cognition and affect.* Copyright © 1970. Published by Little, Brown and Company. Reprinted by permission.

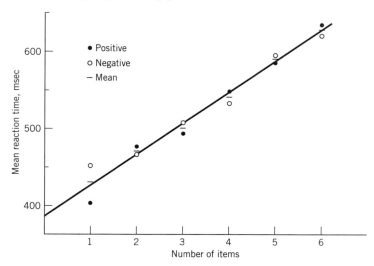

Sternberg proposed that even in the case of a positive probe subjects exhausted the list before responding. He argued that the scanning was taking place very rapidly and that checking whether to stop (because the probe had been found) would take longer than just going on to the end. Subjects certainly are not aware of doing any of this scanning; it is all happening too fast.

Many studies have involved variations of Sternberg's paradigm, and many alternative theories have been advanced for his data (see Glass, 1984, for a review). The functions are frequently not as linear as reported by Sternberg and have a decided curvilinear trend such that the rate of increase slows down for high memory set sizes. Even in Sternberg's data there is a hint of this trend, since the increase for positive probes is largest in going from memory set sizes of one to two.

Some researchers (e.g., J. A. Anderson, 1973) have argued that 38 msec is too rapid a comparison process to implement neurally and have argued for a parallel comparison process in which all the digits in the memory set are compared simultaneously against the probe. A single neural firing takes about 10 msec (see review in Chapter 1); thus, there can be a sequence of only about four neurons involved in checking an element for a match, which some people consider too few to perform a comparison. Parallel processing models have been proposed (e.g., Jones & Anderson, 1987) in which all the items in the memory set are processed at once, but the time to process the items is a function of how active they are. The more elements there are in this memory set, the less active any one item is, and the slower it will be processed.

In terms of Baddeley's theory, the digits are presumably being held in the phonological loop. Sternberg's results only hold for subspan strings of digits (less than the number that can be perfectly recalled). When the digits exceed what can be held in the loop, the results change dramatically, response times get much larger, and the effect of memory set size dramatically lessens (Atkinson & Juola, 1973). Thus it seems that Sternberg's results are related to the rehearsal process. Cavanagh (1972) looked at the relationship between memory span (the maximum number of elements that can be recalled perfectly) for various types of materials and the slope in a Sternberg task (e.g., the 38-msec increase shown in Figure 5.11). Figure 5.12 displays his results. Some of the material is verbal (nonsense syllables, words, letters, digits) and presumably is rehearsed in the phonological loop, whereas other information is visual (random forms, geometric shapes, colors) and presumably is rehearsed in the visuo-spatial sketch pad. The abscissa (memory span) in Figure 5.12 reveals a wide variation in how many items can be held in a span, and the ordinate (memory comparison time) reveals a wide variation in slope in a Sternberg task. The straight-line function in Figure 5.12 reveals that the two are closely related such that shorter spans are associated with larger slopes.

One explanation of the results of Cavanagh follows: As Baddeley argued (see the discussion relating to Figure 5.6), memory span for these items varies because they vary in the speed at which they can be rehearsed. Compare digits (memory span of eight) and words (memory span of five) and assume a

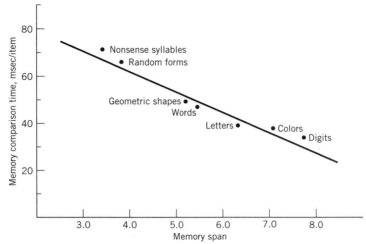

FIGURE 5.12. Memory comparison rate and memory span covary. (From Cavanagh 1972). *Source:* From J. P. Cavanagh. Relation between the immediate memory span and the memory search rate. *Psychological Review, Volume 79.* Copyright © 1981 by the American Psychological Association. Reprinted by permission.

phonological loop of 2.0 sec. The digits would be rehearsed at the rate of 2.0 ÷ 8 = 0.25 sec/digit, and the words would be rehearsed at the rate of 2.0 ÷ 5.00 = 0.40 sec/word. Suppose that the subject was trying to hold a four-item memory set in memory. In the case of digits, the subject would be able to rehearse the digits every .25 × 4 = 1 sec, but the words would be rehearsed every 0.40 × 4 = 1.6 sec. On average, the digits would have been rehearsed more recently and their permanent memory representations would be more active. If time to access these items is a function of how active they are in the rehearsal system, Cavanagh's function would be expected, because slower rehearsal would result in less active elements and in shorter memory spans.

> *As subjects have to hold more items in a rehearsal system their rate of access to any item decreases.*

Memory Span and Concurrent Processing

Starting with Baddeley and Hitch (1974), a number of experiments have looked at the effect of simultaneously maintaining a memory span while performing some other task. For instance, a subject might also be solving an algebraic problem like

$$3x + 6 = 9$$

In a typical experiment subjects might read a list of random letters, such as *c f r l*, solve the equation in their heads, and then recall the list of letters. This research was motivated by the view that memory span was maintained in the same common short-term memory system that was involved in solving the problem. Thus, both the rehearsal of the letters and the equation manipulation would be taking place in short-term memory. Therefore, as the subject was required to hold more items in the memory span, performance on the problem solving was expected to deteriorate substantially. However, the size of the concurrent span often only weakly affects performance of problem-solving tasks, such as this algebraic task (Halford, Bain, & Mayberry, 1983).

The prediction of an effect of memory span on a concurrent task reflects a carryover of the Atkinson and Shiffrin theory, which assumed that a single, common short-term memory must be used for all information processing. According to the more current view, no effect is expected, because the algebraic problem, $3x + 6 = 9$, is held in visual store while the phonological loop is being used to maintain the words of the memory span; the two are independent transient stores.

Anderson, Reder, and Lebiere (in preparation) did a study that demonstrated a large effect of a concurrent digit span on performing an algebraic task (see Carlson, Sullivan, & Schneider, 1989, for a similar demonstration). The procedure involved subjects first seeing a digit span, then solving an algebraic problem, and then recalling the digit span. The digit span involved two, four, or six digits. In the control condition, subjects solved an equation like that given earlier. In the experimental condition, they solved an equation of the form

$$ax + b = 9$$

where they were told that the value of *a* was the first digit in the digit span and the value of *b* was the second digit in the span. Thus if the digit span was 4 1 6 3, the equation would be $4x + 1 = 9$. The critical features of this condition were that the elements of the digit span were part of the equation and the level of rehearsal of the digits should have an impact on the subject's ability to solve the problem.

Figure 5.13 shows the results of this experiment in terms of how long it took subjects to solve the equations. In the control condition, when subjects did not have to make a substitution, the size of the memory set had only a weak effect. Subjects took longer when they had to perform the substitution, which is not surprising. The interesting result is that memory span had a large effect when subjects had to perform the substitution, indicating that the speed with which they performed the substitution was a function of the level of activation of the elements in the memory span. As in the Sternberg task (Figure 5.11), the more items in a memory span, the less active and less accessible is any one item.

As demonstrated by this experiment, information in a rehearsal system can affect the speed with which critical information can be retrieved to solve a

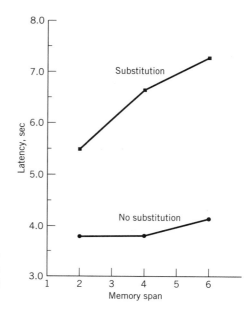

FIGURE 5.13. The effect of memory load on a task that is integrated with the memory and on one that is not integrated.

problem. When the activation of this information is lowered, retrieval time is increased and problem solving is slower.

The more pieces of information being rehearsed, the less available is any one piece for use in any task.

The Concept of a Working Memory

This chapter has discussed sensory stores, short-term memory, long-term memory, permanent memory, rehearsal systems, and states of activation. One additional term is frequently used in current discussions of memory—**working memory.** Although this term means different things to different theorists, here it is used to mean the information we currently have available in any of our memories for working on a problem. Working memory includes the information in the sensory buffers and the rehearsal loops and what is active in permanent memory. In solving an equation such as $3x + 6 = 15$, working memory includes the representation of the equation in iconic memory, partial results being rehearsed (such as $3x = 9$), and multiplication facts from permanent memory (such as $3 \times 3 = 9$).

Should the definition of working memory stop with the skin of the organism? When a person solves a complex mathematical problem on paper, the available information includes not only what the person currently registers from the page (sensory memory), but also information accessed by scanning to a point on the page where other equations are written. When a person is cooking, the current state of the kitchen and of the foods in preparation often remembers for the cook what to do next. When making scrambled eggs, if the pan is on the burner and the eggs are beaten, then the next step is to put them in the pan. These examples show that our immediate environment supports much information processing.

A current view is that cognitive psychology has erred in emphasizing the information that is inside the skin of the organism and not what is outside. An extreme version of this viewpoint, called situated cognition, has gone so far as to deny that there is any need to consider what is inside the organism (Agre & Chapman, 1987; Lave, 1988; and Suchman, 1987). This view flies in the face of an abundance of research that emphasizes the importance of the internal contribution of organisms. Rats have cognitive maps, and so do humans.

Some people extend the concept of working memory to the external environment. The problem with doing so is that it is unclear where to stop. If the information on a page of a text, on the computer screen, and on the kitchen counter is in working memory because it can be accessed with a change of glance, what about the information on the next page, or in a computer file, or in the kitchen cupboard, all of which can be accessed with only a little more effort? What about the information in the next room, in a library, or on a computer information retrieval system? Thus it seems reasonable to restrict working memory to information within the organism's skin.

Working memory includes records from permanent memory that are currently in a state of high activation. The distinction is slippery between which records are and are not part of working memory because activation is a continuous quantity and items can be active to various degrees The state of a record's activation is transient. When we attend to new aspects of our environment, some records will become more active and others will become less active.

Working memory refers to all transient information to which we currently have access.

Working Memory in Animals

Transient memories that serve as working memories are not unique to humans. Transient representations of information occur in all organisms, and there is evidence that they are used for many purposes. Chapter 3 discussed the evidence that the hippocampus serves as a working memory, particularly for spatial information in rats. It is worth noting some other evidence of transient memories in animals, both because it establishes the generality of the concept and because some of the results seem relevant to understanding transient memory in humans.

The Frontal Cortex and Primate Working Memory

The frontal cortex plays a major role in working memory, at least in primates. The frontal cortex shows a major enlargement from lower mammals, such as the rat, to the monkey, and it shows a proportionately greater development from the monkey to the human. The frontal cortex plays an important role in tasks that can be considered working memory tasks. The task that has been most studied in this respect is the **delayed match-to-sample task,** which is illustrated in Figure 5.14. A monkey is shown an item of food, which is placed in one of two identical wells (Figure 5.14*a*). Then the wells are covered, and the monkey is prevented from looking at the scene for a delay period, typically 10 sec (Figure 5.14*b*). Finally, the monkey is given an opportunity to retrieve the food, and must remember in which well it was hidden (Figure 5.14*c*). Monkeys with lesions to the frontal cortex are unable to perform this task (Jacobsen, 1935, 1936). Human infants are unable to perform successfully in similar tasks until their frontal cortices have matured at about 1 year of age (Diamond, in press).

A particular small area of the frontal cortex is involved when the monkey must remember where in space the object was placed (Goldman-Rakic, 1988). This area, called area 46, is found on the side of the frontal cortex (see Figure 5.15). Lesions to this specific area produce deficits in this task. It has been shown that neurons in this region fire only during the delay period of the task, as if they are keeping information active during that interval. They are inactive before and after the delay. Moreover, different neurons in that region seem tuned to remembering objects in different portions of the visual field (Funahashi, Bruce, & Goldman-Rakic, 1991). In humans, there is evidence of increased blood flow in the same region of the brain when retaining working memory information.[3]

Goldman-Rakic (1992) examined monkey performance on other tasks that require maintaining different types of information over the delay interval. For instance, in one task the monkey had to remember to select a red circle and not a green square after an interval. A different region of the prefrontal cortex appeared to be involved in this task. Different neurons in this area fired when the red circle was being remembered rather than the green square. Goldman-Rakic speculated that the prefrontal cortex is parceled into many small regions, each responsible for remembering a different kind of information.

[3]Jonathan Cohen at Carnegie Mellon University has been using MRI to visualize area 46 in humans; John Jonides and Ed Smith of the University of Michigan have been using PET (personal communications).

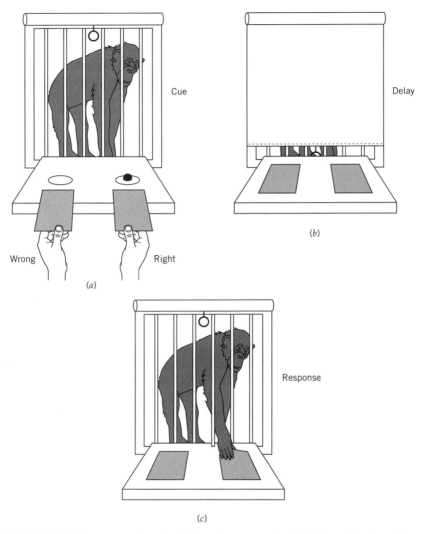

Cue

Delay

(*b*)

Wrong

Right

(*a*)

Response

(*c*)

FIGURE 5.14. An examples of a delayed memory task. (*a*) Food is placed in well on the right and covered; (*b*) curtain is drawn for delay period; and (*c*) curtain is lifted and monkey can lift cover from one of the wells. *Source:* From P. S. Goldman-Rakic. *Child Development,* Volume 58. Development of cortical circuitry and cognitive function. Copyright © 1987 by the Society for Research in Child Development. Reprinted by permission.

The prefrontal cortex has strong connections with the hippocampus, a subcortical structure that has a major role in learning (see Chapter 3). The different regions of the cortex have appropriate connections to other more sensory parts of the cortex. For instance, area 46, which serves as spatial working

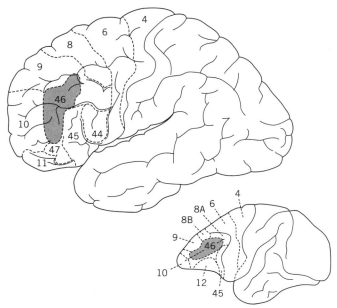

FIGURE 5.15. Lateral view of human and monkey cerebral cortex, with area 46 shaded *Source:* From P. S. Goldman-Rakic. *Handbook of physiology. the nervous system. higher functions of the brain.* Copyright © 1987 by the American Physiological Society. Reprinted by permission.

memory, has connections to the region of the parietal cortex that is responsible for processing spatial information in the world.

It is generally believed that both the hippocampus and the frontal cortex play critical roles in the formation and storage of permanent memories in primates. One hypothesis is that the hippocampus plays an important role in the creation of permanent memories, but that the memories reside in the frontal cortex (Squire, 1987). The role of the hippocampus in human memory is addressed in Chapter 8.

Goldman-Rakic has provided the most articulate description to date of the role of the frontal cortex in working memory. Still, it is unclear how to classify area 46 in terms of the various types of working memories that have been identified in behavioral studies of humans. It might represent the rehearsal system in Baddeley's visuo-spatial sketch pad, or, activation in area 46 might correspond to the activation that primes information in permanent memory. Perhaps it represents both.

The basis of working memory is probably different in species that do not have as developed frontal cortices. Chapter 3 mentioned that the hippocampus of a rat seems to serve as a working memory to represent where it is in space. This section has indicated that the frontal cortex, which is much more developed in primates, serves as a major source of primate working memory. The next section considers some evidence about the nature of working memory in pigeons. Although these animals are biologically different, they share the same need of primates to maintain information over periods of time.

In primates, different small regions of the frontal cortex serve as working memory for different types of information.

Delayed Matching to Sample in Pigeons

A variation of the delayed match-to-sample paradigm used with monkeys (Figure 5.14) has been developed for pigeons and has enabled exploration of their working memory (e.g., Grant, 1981; Honig, 1981; Maki, 1984). The typical trial might begin with a key lit red. After it has been lit for a period of time, say, 5 sec, the key is turned off, and the pigeon must wait for a period of time. After this retention interval, two keys are turned on—one red and one green. The pigeon must peck the key with the same color as the earlier lit key to obtain reinforcement. The initial key that the pigeon must match (the sample) varies from trial to trial. Pigeons are quite capable of solving this problem, but their accuracy in matching depends on the interval between the sample color and the test. Figure 5.16 presents some data from Grant (1976), showing how the probability of pecking the correct color falls off with delay. At all points performance is quite a bit better than chance performance, which would be 50 percent.

FIGURE 5.16. The percentage of correct choices (which key to peck) made by pigeons as a function of delay between the presentation of the information and opportunity to respond. *Source:* From D. S. Grant. *Learning and Motivation,* Volume 7. Copyright © 1976 by Academic Press. Reprinted by permission.

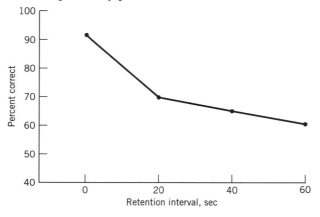

This retention curve is like the retention curves displayed by humans (e.g., Figure 5.5). Humans try to bridge these intervals by rehearsing the material to keep it active in working memory. There is evidence that pigeons also engage in rehearsal during this interval. For example, they show better retention when the factors that might distract them from rehearsing are reduced, such as when the lights are turned off during the retention interval (e.g., Grant & Roberts, 1976; Roberts & Grant, 1978). With the lights out, the pigeons can no longer look around the experimental chamber and process distracting stimuli.

One of the mechanisms that pigeons use to rehearse this information is body position; they remain oriented toward the critical key during the interval. This is a particularly clear case of how an organism can use its body as a transient memory for information. Postural rehearsal is not the only way in which pigeons can perform this task, however; they can also perform the task when the position of the colored key shifts from study to test and they must remember the color and not the location.

It further appears that pigeons can be instructed whether to rehearse the material or not (Maki & Hegvik, 1980). This phenomenon was demonstrated in experiments that were identical to match-to-sample experiments except that on some trials the pigeons did not get the opportunity to peck the key after the delay. They were given a cue to tell them whether or not they could peck. That is, after the pigeons had seen the original sample, a signal told them whether this was a trial in which they could peck or not. These cues are called remember cues and forget cues. For some pigeons turning the house light on served as the remember cue, and its absence as the forget cue; for others the cues were reversed. The pigeons remembered which key to peck quite well after a remember cue. Occasionally they were given a surprise test after a forget cue; on such surprise trials they were observed to show rapid forgetting in this situation.

These results are illustrated in Figure 5.17, which shows some data from Maki and Hegvik (1980). The percentage of recall in a delayed match-to-sample experiment is plotted for forget cues and remember cues at short delays (2 sec) and long delays (7 sec). Right after seeing the sample there was relatively little difference in performance with forget and remember cues. However, without the motivation to rehearse (forget cue), the ability to remember where to peck dropped off dramatically over the 7-sec retention interval. It appears that the ability of the pigeons to remember what to do was maintained by an active rehearsal process over the interval, and that they only engaged in this rehearsal process if they expected to be tested.

Pigeons are capable of rehearsing information about which key to peck over a retention interval.

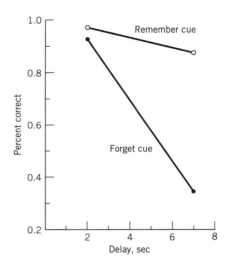

FIGURE 5.17. Retention in a delayed match-to-sample exeriment as a function of whether the pigeon anticipated being tested or not (From Maki & Hegvik, 1980).

Rehearsal and Classical Conditioning

Chapter 2 discussed Wagner's (1981) SOP theory of conditioning, which is concerned in part with the conditioning of opponent processes. However, other important aspects of the theory are concerned with how organisms process conditioning information. The theory claims that immediately after a conditioning event the organism is actively rehearsing the CS–US pairing and that the success of conditioning depends on this rehearsal successfully taking place. Evidence for this assertion was demonstrated in an experiment by Wagner, Rudy, and Whitlow (1973) on eyelid conditioning in rabbits. They followed a pairing of a CS and a puff of air by a surprising event (an unexpected pairing of two other stimuli). They predicted that this would cause the rabbit to cease rehearsing the CS–US pairing and start rehearsing the new event. Figure 5.18 displays the degree of conditioning as a function of the interval between the CS–US pairing and the surprising event. The longer the interval before the surprising event, the more time the rabbits should have to rehearse the CS–US pairing. As shown, conditioning did increase as the rabbits had longer to rehearse the pairing.

Wagner (1978) also suggested that such rehearsal processes might be part of the explanation of latent inhibition, which causes difficulty for the Rescorla–Wagner theory. This is the phenomenon that preexposure to a CS without a US makes it more difficult to later condition the CS to the US. Wagner suggested that the consequence of preexposure might be to make the CS so expected that the animal does not encode the CS when the animal is presented with a US. If it is not encoded it cannot be rehearsed, and if it is not rehearsed it cannot be conditioned.

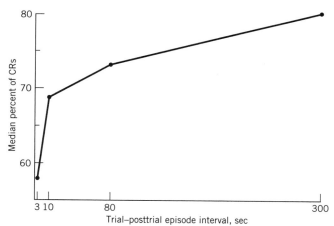

FIGURE 5.18. Amount of conditioning in four different groups of rabbits as a function of the interval between the conditioning trial and a surprising event. *Source:* From A. R. Wagner, et al. Rehearsal in animal conditioning. *Journal of Experimental Psychology. Volume 97.* Copyright © 1973 by the American Psychological Association. Reprinted by permission.

> *The degree of classical conditionning increases the longer the CS and US are rehearsed together.*

Final Reflections

This chapter has described some of the systems that we have for holding temporary information. It is remarkable how many there are. Sensory systems briefly hold the information they are receiving so that the organism has a chance to encode it into a permanent memory. Information can also be maintained in various sensory-like buffers by slave rehearsal processes. Information in these sensory systems or rehearsal systems can prime information in permanent memory and make that information temporarily available. The information in these various transient memories is what we use to guide our information processing. For this reason they can be collectively referred to as working memory.

It might seem a bit peculiar to speak of lower organisms, such as pigeons and rabbits, as having expectations and engaging in active rehearsal processes. However, it is to the advantage of lower organisms as well as humans to keep certain information available even when it is no longer present in the environment. Although nonverbal organisms do not have phonological loops for rehearsal, which seems the preferred means of rehearsal for humans, they probably do have other rehearsal systems for maintaining information in an active state when it is no longer present in the environment. For instance, pigeons orient to the key they will have to peck and maintain that orientation over a delay. In this case they are using their body posture as a slave system to rehearse the information they have to remember. Although these animals are rehearsing information, as do humans, this similarity with human behavior does not imply that they are acting in the same conscious way in which humans can act.

> *Organisms can maintain information in transient memories to guide their information processing.*

Further Readings

A number of textbooks are devoted to human memory, including those by Crowder (1976), Klatzky (1979), and Zechmeister and Nyberg (1982). Crowder (1982) discusses the demise of short-term memory. Baddeley's recent textbook (1990) on human memory provides a good exposition of his theory of working memory, and his research monograph (1986) also presents his theory. Journals devoted to human memory include the *Journal of Language and Memory* (formerly the *Journal of Verbal Learning and Verbal Behavior*), *Memory and Cognition*, and the *Journal of Experimental Psychology: Learning, Memory and Cognition*. The recent *Scientific American* article by Goldman-Rakic (1992) discusses the role of the prefrontal cortex in the working memory of primates. Roitblat, Bever, and Terrace (1984) review much of the research on animal memory. The January 1993 issue of the journal *Cognitive Science* is devoted to a discussion of situated cognition and its implications for such issues as working memory.

6

Acquisition of Memories

Stages of Memory

The previous chapter dealt with how information comes in and is maintained in an active state within working memory. These next three chapters discuss the subsequent course of information through memory. This chapter is concerned with **acquisition**—how a permanent representation of the information is encoded and how this record is strengthened. Chapter 7 focuses on **retention**—how this information is maintained in memory. Chapter 8 examines **retrieval**—how information is brought out of memory when needed. This organization follows Melton's (1963) classic analysis of memory into these three processes.

The material in these chapters is developed with respect to the cue-record structure illustrated in Figure 5.10. Figure 6.1 illustrates another such fragment of memory. This figure shows two memory records that you should encode as a function of reading this chapter. From what you have already studied, you should have created the record, "Memory involves acquisition, retention, and retrieval stages." You will soon read material from which you should encode the record, "Records acquire strength as a power function of

FIGURE 6.1. A representation of two memory records formed as a consequence of studying this text and their association to various cues. Compare with Figure 5.10.

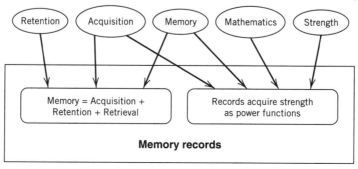

practice." Figure 6.1 shows these records and their association to such cues as *retention, acquisition, memory, mathematics,* and *strength.*

The three stages of memory can be conceived of in terms of the history of these records and their associations to cues. The acquisition process involves the initial creation of these records and their associations. The retention process is concerned with how these records decay over time and how various cues lose the ability to activate a memory record. The retrieval process is concerned with how current cues activate specific records.

It is not really possible to study just one of these processes alone. Any experiment involves initial acquisition of material, followed by some minimal retention interval, followed by a test that requires retrieval of information. Each chapter focuses on experiments that, assuming a framework similar to that shown in Figures 5.10 and 6.1, reflect mainly on one of the processes. However, as the chapters review, in some cases the interest is in the interaction between processes; for example, how the way in which we encode material at study determines the best retrieval conditions, how different types of memory records decay at different rates, how learning one type of material can cause us to forget another, how different retrieval conditions display different amounts of forgetting, and so on.

The memory process can be divided into an acquisition stage, a retention stage, and a retrieval stage.

Practice and Trace Strength

The classic proverb is practice makes perfect. Much research in psychology has been concerned with how memories improve with practice. Consider a simple paired-associate task. In one experiment (J. R. Anderson, 1981) subjects were presented with 20 paired associates, such as the pair *dog–3.* Subjects were asked to learn the pairs so that they could recall 3 when prompted with *dog.* They were given seven opportunities to study the list of paired associates. Figure 6.2*a* shows the decrease in the failure to recall as a function of the amount of practice. Subjects started out failing to recall about 47% of the items and ended up failing to recall about 5% of the items. Figure 6.2*b* shows the time it took subjects to recall the correct responses; speed of recall increased steadily with practice. Thus even after subjects had reached the point of recalling the paired associates successfully, further practice improved their memories for the paired associates as measured by retrieval speed.

There are other ways in which subjects show improved memory with further practice after they are able to recall the memory. As Chapter 1 discussed, Ebbinghaus and others found that practicing an item after it is learned results in improved performance on a retention test given later. Ebbinghaus used a savings measure, which involved looking at how much faster the list was

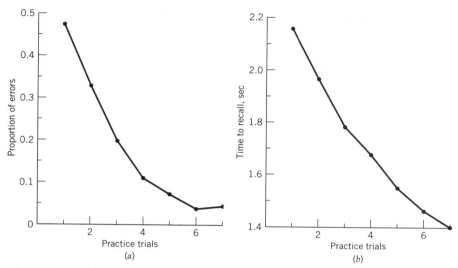

FIGURE 6.2. (*a*) Probability of recall and (*b*) time to recall paired associates as a function of amount of practice. (From Anderson, 1981).

relearned the next day after varying amounts of practice. As Figure 1.2 showed, Ebbinghaus was able to relearn the list faster and faster each subsequent day. Memory records are assumed to have a property called **strength,** which increases with repeated practice. Earlier chapters used a concept of strength in explaining conditioning phenomena. For instance, in the Rescorla–Wagner theory, strengths of CS–US associations increase with repetition. Those earlier chapters noted that researchers often thought of strength of conditioning in terms of the strength of synaptic connections. For instance, Chapter 2 discussed the delta learning rule, a neural embodiment of the Rescorla–Wagner theory. The concept of strength is often given similar interpretations in human memory; strength is viewed as indicating the degree to which cues can activate the memory record. As discussed in Chapter 5, the more the record can be activated the more available it will be. The amount of activation of a memory record is reflected in dependent measures in memory experiments, such as probability of recall, latency of recall, and savings in relearning.

A fair amount of research has studied how memory improves with massive amounts of practice. Since subjects quickly come to near-perfect levels of recall when measured by percentage of correct responses, time to retrieve the memory is usually used as the dependent measure because it is particularly sensitive to differences among high levels of strength. In one experiment (Pirolli & Anderson, 1985), subjects practiced memory for sentences for 25 days for 2 hr a day. During this time, they practiced just 15 sentences, such as

The doctor hated the lawyer.

The radical touched the debutant.

The sailor shot the barber.

A recognition memory test was used to test their memory for these sentences. After having memorized the sentences, subjects were required to discriminate them from sentences that they had not studied but that were made up of the same words. Examples of such foil sentences are

The doctor touched the barber.

The radical shot the lawyer.

Subjects had to press one button if a test sentence had been studied and another if it had not; the speed with which they were able to make this recognition judgment was measured. Subjects spent 25 days practicing these judgments and hence practicing the sentences. Figure 6.3*a* shows how recognition time decreased with the amount of practice. The improvement was rapid over the initial days, but the rate of improvement slowed down with the amount of practice.

Memories continue to improve with practice even after recall is perfect.

The Power Law of Learning

An interesting relationship appears if, rather than days of practice and time to respond, the logarithms of days and the logarithms of recognition time are

FIGURE 6.3. (*a*) Time to recognize sentences as a function of number of days of practice; (*b*) log–log transformation of data in (*a*) to reveal power function. (From Pirolli & Anderson, 1985).

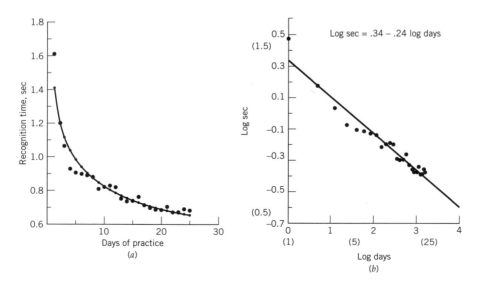

plotted. (Natural logarithms are used throughout this section, although other types of logarithms could be used just as well.) The logarithm compresses the differences among larger numbers. Some examples of log days for certain numbers of days are as follows:

DAYS	LOG DAYS
1	0.00
5	1.61
10	2.30
15	2.71
20	3.00
25	3.22

The difference between 25 days and 20 days is much smaller on the logarithmic scale than is the difference between 5 days and 1 day.

Figure 6.3*b* shows the data from Figure 6.3*a* replotted on a log–log scale. Consider how the data point for day 1 is plotted. The latency on day 1 is 1.61 sec. Log 1 = 0 and log 1.61 = .47. Therefore this point is plotted with coordinates of 0 and .47. Similarly, all the other points are replotted in Figure 6.3*b* on the transformed scale. Since the logarithm of a value less than 1 is negative, many of the log latencies are negative. The untransformed times and days that correspond to the transformed logarithm values are given in parentheses.

Figure 6.3*b* reveals a nearly linear relationship between log time and log practice. That is, the points fall very close to the straight line plotted in the figure. If T is used to denote the time in seconds and P the amount of practice in days, this linear relationship is described by the following function:

$$\log T = .34 - .24 \log P$$

The value .34 is where the function crosses the y-axis (i.e., when $\log P = 0$), and $-.24$ is the slope of the line. When this equation is transformed back into the original scales of time and practice, it becomes a power function,[1]

$$T = 1.40\ P^{-.24}$$

This is called a **power function** because the amount of practice (P) is being raised to a power. This function is the smooth curve drawn in Figure 6.3*a*. The power relationship between performance (measured in terms of response time and a number of other measures) and amount of practice is a ubiquitous phenomenon in learning. The straight-line function in the log–log scale of Figure 6.3*b* becomes a curvilinear function in the original scale of Figure 6.3*a*. This result implies that learning never stops, but that, as we practice, we get smaller and smaller benefits. The fact that almost all learning functions are power functions has been called the **power law of learning** (Newell & Rosenbloom, 1981).

---

[1]Taking the exponential of both sides of the equation yields

$$e^{\log T} = e^{.34 - .24 \log P} \quad \text{or} \quad T = e^{.34}\ P^{-.24} \quad \text{or} \quad T = 1.40\ P^{-.24}.$$

Newell and Rosenbloom (1981), following up on the work of Lewis (1978), brought this ubiquitous law of learning to the attention of the field. Whenever log performance time is plotted against log practice, the result is a linear function, which implies a power function relationship. Figure 6.4 shows some data from Blackburn (1936), who studied the effect of practicing addition problems for 10,000 trials. The results are plotted in log–log terms and show a linear relationship. On this graph and some others in this book, the original numbers (those given in parentheses in Figure 6.3*b*), rather than the logarithms of these numbers, are plotted on the logarithmic scale. (When original numbers are plotted on a log scale, it is so noted on the figure.) Blackburn's data show that the power law of learning extends to amounts of practice far beyond what was shown in Figure 6.3. Since its identification by Newell and Rosenbloom, the power law has attracted a great deal of attention in psychology, and researchers have tried to understand why learning should take the same form in all experiments (e.g., J. R. Anderson, 1982; Lewis, 1978; Logan, 1988; MacKay, 1982; Shrager, Hogg, & Huberman, 1988).

Figures 6.3 and 6.4 look at the decrease in time with practice. Error rates also often improve according to power functions. Figure 6.5 replots the data from Figure 6.2 in terms of log errors against log trials of practice. The approximately linear relationship implies that error rates decrease as a power function of time. Not all dependent measures show this power function relationship, but many, like performance time and error rate, do. Such power functions are distinguished by the property of **negative acceleration**; that is, each unit of practice produces a smaller and smaller improvement in performance. Thus the power law is a law of diminishing returns. If these measures

FIGURE 6.4. The improvement in adding two numbers as a function of practice. Data are plotted seperately for two subjects. (Plot by Crossman, 1959, using data from Blackburn, 1936). *Source:* Figure 6.4 from E. R. F. W. Crossman. *Ergonomics* Volume 2. A theory of the acquisition of speed-skill. Copyright © 1976 by Taylor & Francis Ltd. Reprinted by permission.

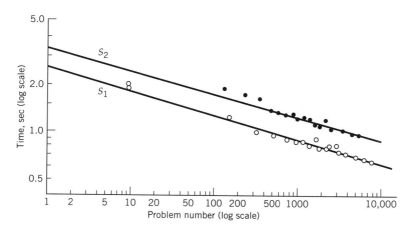

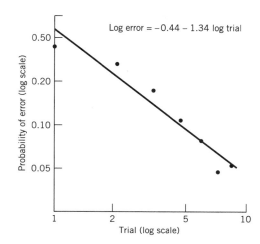

FIGURE 6.5. Data from Figure 6.2*a* replotted as log errors against log trials.

are interpreted to reflect the underlying strength of the record, then these power functions imply that practice will always increase the strength of the record, but in smaller and smaller amounts.

Memory strength increases as a power function of practice and is reflected in the dependent measures of recall time or error rates.

Repetition and Conditioning

What is the relationship between the practice curves in these human memory experiments and the conditioning curves given in earlier chapters? It is likely that practice in a conditioning experiment is controlling more than just the strength of a memory trace. That is, the more often the US follows the CS the more likely it is that they are causally related. Thus repetition of the CS and the US in conditioning trials also increases the evidence for the contingency between the events. Sometimes the conditioning curves have approximately the same shape as they do in human learning research. Figure 6.6 shows the time it took rats deprived of food for 2 or 22 hr to run a *T*-maze for food (Hillman, Hunter, & Kimble, 1953). Although the rats deprived for 22 hr ran the maze more rapidly, both groups showed improvements approximating a linear function on a log–log scale. Thus the speed of responding in rats is also approximately a power function of the amount of practice.

In other cases, the learning curves in the conditioning literature show a substantial difference from those of human memory functions. As discussed

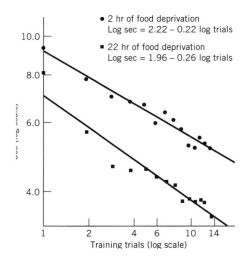

FIGURE 6.6. Time to run a maze as a function of the number of prior trials of training and the number of hours of water deprivation. (From Hillman et al., 1953).

earlier with respect to classical conditioning (see Figure 1.4), animals often show little increase in conditioning, then a large increase, and then little. Figure 6.7 plots an average learning function from Brogden (1949). He was concerned with the conditioning of an avoidance response in dogs. Figure 6.7 plots the percentage of avoidance in each unit of training. There was relatively little learning from the first unit to the second, then rapid learning, and then slower learning. These conditioning functions differ from human memory curves in this initial phase of slow learning. These functions are often referred

FIGURE 6.7. Acquisition of an avoidance response. *Source:* From W. J. Brogden. *Journal of Comparative and Physiological Psychology, Volume 42.* Copyright © 1949 in the Public Domain.

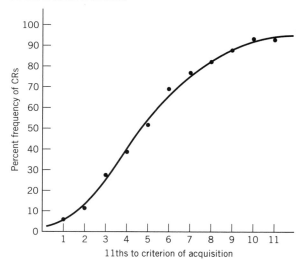

to as **S-shaped curves** (see Culler & Girden, 1951, for a review of such conditioning functions).

To understand why conditioning curves are different from learning curves, refer to Figure 5.1, which shows a schematic of a conditioning experiment. The conditioning experiment involves an additional induction phase in which the organism must figure out the causal relationship. The association cannot begin strengthening until it is identified. Conditioning curves for individual organisms often reveal some discrete point in time at which the organisms catch on. Figure 6.8 illustrates this situation with respect to the conditioning of four dogs in an experiment described by Culler and Girden (1951). Animals learned to retract their paws when they heard a sound that warned that a shock would come in 2 sec. The figure reveals that for long periods of time the individual animals did not recognize the connection. After some trial the response began to strengthen. Different animals began to show conditioning after different trials: in Figure 6.8*a* after trial 50, in Figures 6.8*b* and 6.8*c* after trial 100, and in Figure 6.8*d* after trial 75. Although the individual curves are quite variable after conditioning begins, at least some of them then show the property of power functions—rapid initial gains followed by slower gains.

Conditioning functions are often S-shaped, because conditioning requires an induction process before associative learning can begin.

Long-Term Potentiation and the Environment

Chapter 3 discussed long-term potentiation (LTP), which occurs in the hippocampus and cortical areas. LTP is a form of neural learning that seems related to behavioral measures of learning. When pathways are stimulated with high-frequency electrical current, the sensitivity of cells along that pathway to further stimulation is increased. Barnes (1979) studied this phenomenon in rats, measuring the percentage of increase in **excitatory postsynaptic potential (EPSP)** over its initial value.[2] She stimulated the hippocampus of the rats each day for 11 successive days and measured the growth in LTP in terms of the percentage of increase. Figure 6.9*a* displays the results, plotting percent of change against day of practice. There appears to be a diminishing increase with the amount of practice. To determine whether there is a power function, Figure 6.9*b* plots log percentage of change against log practice. The

---

[2]As discussed in Chapter 1, as the dendrite and cell body of a neuron become more excited, the difference in electric potential between the outside and the inside of the cell decreases. EPSPs refers to the size of this change.

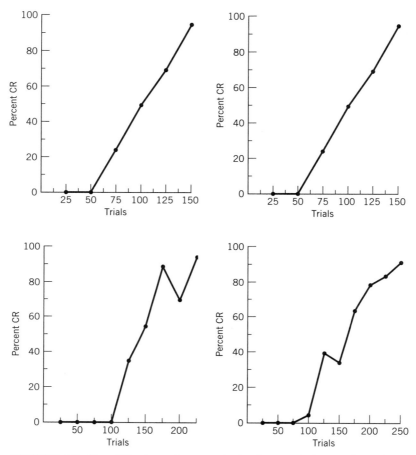

FIGURE 6.8. Conditioning of a sound–shock association in four dogs. (From Culler & Girden, 1953).

relationship appears approximately linear; thus it appears that neural activation changes with practice just as do behavioral measures.

Note that the activation measure in Figure 6.9a increases more and more slowly, whereas the performance measures, such as errors (Figure 6.2a) and time (Figure 6.2b) decrease more and more slowly. These performance measures are assumed to be inverse reflections of the growth in strength that is happening internally. As the strength of the record increases (reflected in Figure 6.9), the performance measures get better (which means shorter times and fewer errors).

It has been suggested (Anderson & Schooler, 1991) that memory (both its behavioral and its neural expressions) displays properties such as the power law of learning because these properties reflect an optimal response to the environment. A very general characterization of the learning functions reviewed in this chapter is that the more something is encountered, the more available it is in the future. A conjecture about the environment is that the more an organism has needed to remember something, the more likely it is that it will need to remember that thing again. Thus memory can be viewed as making more available information that is more likely to be needed.

This viewpoint raises the question of whether the power function displayed in the learning behavior of subjects mirrors a similar power function in the environment. Anderson and Schooler (1991) studied the patterns by which information tends to repeat in a number of different environments, including parental speech to children, electronic mail messages, and newspaper headlines. In the case of parental speech to children, the frequency of various words in parental utterances was examined. For example, if the word *ball* occurred 8 times in the last 100 utterances, what is the probability that it will occur on the 101st utterance? Figure 6.10 shows the relationship between the log frequency that a word has appeared in the last 100 utterances and the log probability that it will appear in the 101st utterance. The linear relationship is striking, implying a power function. The functional form of memory seems to mirror the functional form in the environment. Similar patterns were found in mail messages and newspaper articles. The more often one has had to retrieve the meaning of a word the more likely one will have to do so again.

In summary, three types of dependent measures change as power functions of practice: behavioral measures, such as error rate and latency; percentage of change in LTP; and probability of repetition in the environment. One proposal (J. R. Anderson, 1993) is that neural activation, which controls behavior, reflects the probability of an item occurring in the environment; thus the neural processes are designed to adapt behavior to the statistical properties of the environment.

FIGURE 6.9. Growth in LTP as a function of number of days of practice: (*a*) in normal scale; (*b*) in log–log scale. (From Barnes, 1979).

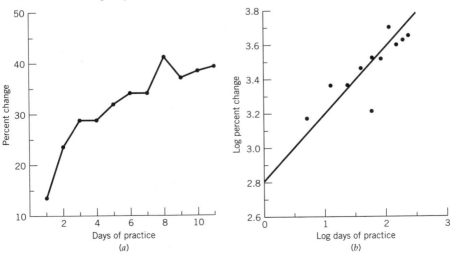

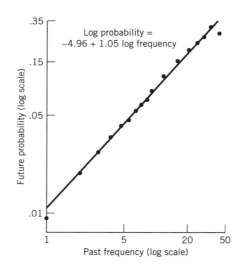

FIGURE 6.10. Relationship between log frequency with which a word has occurred in the last 100 utterances and log probability of it occurring in the 101st utterance. (From Anderson & Schooler, 1991).

Long-term potentiation and probability of repetition in the environment are both power functions of frequency of exposure.

Significance of a Power Function

What is the significance of the fact that the behavioral measures are power functions of practice? It could be that these power functions simply capture the natural result that learning is negatively accelerated and that each learning experience produces less of a benefit in terms of a performance measure. However, many potential mathematical functions have this property. The fact that learning is best captured by a power function is an important and hard-won generalization that emerged in psychology only after the extensive analysis of Newell and Rosenbloom.

The natural hypothesis that formerly dominated psychology was that performance was an **exponential function** of practice. If a time (*T*) were an exponential function of practice (*P*), it would take the form of a fraction raised to the amount of practice. For instance,

$$T = 10 \times .8^P$$

This exponential hypothesis was natural because it implied that with each trial, performance improved by a constant fraction. In the example given, each trial takes 80 percent, or .8, of the time of the previous trial. If the previous trial took 10 sec, a .8 reduction yields 8 sec, for a 2-sec gain for the current trial. When the time is 1 sec, a .8 reduction results in a .2-sec gain. Thus the reason that the function was negatively accelerated (showed less and less decrease) was that the base time (which was being reduced by .8 each trial) was going down.

Figure 6.11 compares an exponential function with a power function. Both functions are negatively accelerated, but the power function is much more so. Only after collection and analysis of a great deal of data was it conclusively established that learning functions are better described by power functions than by exponential functions (Newell & Rosenbloom, 1981). The rate of improvement with practice turns out to be even slower than formerly believed.

It is rather exciting to psychologists to be able to find simple functions, like the power function, that fit such a wide range of data. It is similar to discovering laws of the sort that physicists find (and psychologists have always had physics envy). However, the power function that describes the learning curve is not of the same status as the equations in physics books. The data from learning experiments are not perfectly accommodated by power functions, although they are accommodated much better by power functions than by some other forms, such as exponential functions. There are systematic deviations, and the nature of these deviations changes from experiment to experiment. The power function is only a good approximation to the learning functions.

Psychologists are not content with the discovery that the learning curves are power functions; they also try to understand why the data have this approximate form. As noted earlier, a number of theories of the mechanisms behind this power function have been proposed; frequently these theories predict only that the learning curve should be a good approximation to a power function. There has not been a resolution of these competing theories. My own view is that the explanation of the power function is to be found in the neural processes that underlie associative learning and that these neural learning processes have evolved to their current form because of the statistical properties of the environment. This phenomenon is just one token of the adaptiveness of learning.

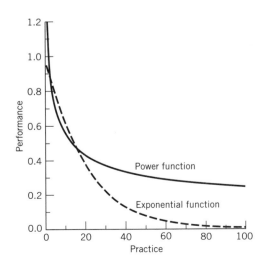

FIGURE 6.11. Comparison of exponential and power functions.

By way of summary, the following Strength Equation describes the strength of a memory record (see Figure 5.10) as a function of how frequently the memory record has been practiced.

$$\text{Strength} = \text{Practice}^b \qquad \text{(Strength Equation)}$$

where b is the exponent that controls how fast strength increases.[3] Chapter 7 elaborates on this strength equation with an additional factor to reflect forgetting.

The growth of strength with practice better approximates a power function than other common negatively accelerated functions.

Elaborateness of Processing

The preceding analysis implied that items accrue strength at a rate that depends only on how much the item has been studied. However, a great deal of evidence also indicates that how an item is studied can have an enormous impact on how much the subject remembers of the item. In some cases people can process items many times without much benefit. Chapter 5 discussed Neisser's description of Professor Sanford, who remembered little from thousands of repetitions of his prayers.

Bekerian and Baddeley (1980) reported a study of the efforts of BBC radio to get its listeners to learn the new wavelength at which it was going to broadcast. The BBC saturated the radio with announcements of the new wavelength. Bekerian and Baddeley tested subjects who had been exposed to the information for over 25 times a day for many weeks. Less than a quarter of the people they surveyed had learned the new wavelength. Sheer exposure to material is not enough to guarantee learning. Chapter 5 discussed Craik and Lockhart's (1972) depth of processing theory, which held that memory only improves if information is processed at a deep level. This chapter describes a variant of the depth of processing proposal, which emphasizes that what is important is how elaborately we process the to-be-remembered information.

Memory for material is improved the more elaborately it is processed.

---

[3]The exponent b is positive because strength is assumed to increase, producing decreases in measures of performance difficulty, such as time and errors.

The Generation Effect

Although the way in which information is processed is critical to what is recalled, there has been some question (including on the part of Craik) whether the concept of depth of processing totally captures this dependence. The concept of depth of processing is somewhat vague, but includes the idea that considering the meaning rather than the surface form of stimuli improves memory for the stimuli. For instance, if we think about what words rhyme with a to-be-remembered word, we recall less than if we think of what words are synonyms. The latter activity forces us to get at the meaning of the items. Although the depth of processing seems to have an effect, several studies have also shown that superior memory is achieved by actively processing material in a way that does not involve its meaning. Slamecka and Graf (1978) asked subjects in a generate condition to generate a synonym or rhyme of a target word that began with a target letter. For example, the subjects might have been asked to generate a synonym of *sea* that began with *o* (i.e., *ocean*) or a rhyme of *save* that began with *c* (i.e., *cave*). In the read condition, subjects read pairs of words that exemplified these relationships, for example, *sea–ocean* and *save–cave*. Then subjects were tested for their recognition of the second word in these pairs (e.g., *ocean* and *cave*). Figure 6.12 displays the results. Subjects showed an advantage with synonyms over rhymes. This effect is similar to other depth of processing effects in that it shows the advantage of semantic processing. However, an equally large advantage came from having to generate the items; rhymes that were generated were even slightly better recognized than synonyms that were read.[4] The term **generate effect** refers to the memory advantage of material that subjects generate for themselves.

Burns (1992) and Hirshman and Bjork (1988) have provided an explanation of the advantage of generative processing in experiments in which subjects must learn paired associates, such as the Slamecka and Graf experiment. According to these authors, generative processing enhances the encoding of features that connect the stimulus to the response. For instance, generating *cave* as a rhyme of *save* guarantees that subjects encode that both stimulus and response in the *save–cave* pair are in fact rhymes, whereas they might not attend to this common feature if they just read the pair of words. If the rhyme relationship is encoded at study, the subject can use it to retrieve the response at recall.

Bobrow and Bower (1969) reported another study that showed the advantages that accrue with self-generation. They looked at subjects' ability to remember simple paired associates, such as *dog–bike*. In one condition, sub-

---

[4]There has been a flurry of debate about whether the original Slamecka and Graf result was due to the fact that it involved a within-list design and subjects gave differential practice to the generate items. Slamecka and Katsaiti (1987) claimed it was an artifact, but others (e.g., Begg, Snider, Foley, & Goddard, 1989; Burns, 1992; Hirshman & Bjork, 1988; McDaniel, Waddill, & Einstein, 1988) have found effects in between-list designs.

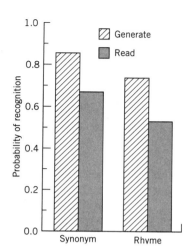

FIGURE 6.12. Probability of recognition as a function of type of elaboration and whether it was generated or read. (From Slamecka & Graf, 1978, experiment 2).

jects were shown sentences that linked the two words such as, "The dog chased the bike." Such subjects did better than subjects who just studied the paired associates. A third group of subjects, who had to generate such sentences, did even better.

Anderson and Reder (1979) suggested a general way of conceiving of the advantage of semantic processing and self-generation. These activities provide subjects with additional retrieval routes. With respect to the Bobrow and Bower experiment, if the subjects are given a cue of *dog* for recall and have studied the sentence, they can recall *bike* directly, but if this fails, they also can recall *chase* and use *chase* to recall *bike*. There is an additional retrieval route, which gives an advantage to the sentence elaboration condition.

What gives the added advantage when the subject has to generate the verb? The subject is likely to generate a verb that is easy for that subject to recall and from which it is easy for that subject to recall *bike*. When subjects can choose their own verbs, they generate items that make for particularly good retrieval routes. To summarize, elaborations help because they can provide additional retrieval routes. Generation helps further because the retrieval routes generated are particularly relevant to the subject. The Hirshman and Bjork explanation of the generation effect in the Slamecka and Graf paradigm similarly emphasizes facilitating the connection between stimulus and response.

Elaborative processing and self-generation improve memory through the enhancement of retrieval routes.

Differences Between Elaboration and Strength

In the context of this chapter, elaborative processing might be viewed as increasing the strength of the memory record, but this is not the best interpretation. When subjects elaborate, they create additional ways of recalling the memory that they are supposed to remember. If they cannot remember the original memory record, they may be able to use the other records to retrieve what they want. Thus, a subject trying to remember *dog–bike* without elaborations, is simply trying to remember the record of this paired associate. If that record cannot be retrieved, the subject is out of luck. However, if the subject has generated the elaboration, "The dog chased the boy on the bike," there is an additional route from which to retrieve *bike* given the cue of *dog*.

An experiment by Bradshaw and Anderson (1982) is consistent with this interpretation that elaborations serve to create additional ways to recall the target memory and do not increase the strength of a particular memory record. The experiment looked at subjects' ability to learn some little-known information about some famous people. In one condition subjects studied just a single fact:

Mozart made a long journey from Munich to Paris.

In another condition subjects learned two additional facts that were causally related to the target fact:

Mozart made a long journey from Munich to Paris.

plus

Mozart wanted to leave Munich to avoid a romantic entanglement.

Mozart was intrigued by musical developments coming out of Paris.

The additional sentences were experimenter-provided elaborations designed to boost memory for the target sentence.

Subjects were tested for their ability to remember the target facts at a week's delay. They were presented with names such as Mozart, and asked to recall the target sentence. The results are displayed in Table 6.1 in terms of percentage of recall of the target sentence and time to recognize the target sentence. The subjects' percentage of recall was higher for the target sentence when elaborating sentences were presented at study. However, when subjects were tested for their ability to recognize the target sentences, there was no latency advantage for the elaborated sentences. If anything, they were slower. This chapter noted earlier that retrieval time is a good measure of strength. The target sentences were not any stronger when studied with elaborations; however, these elaborations offered subjects another way to retrieve the target sentence if they were unable to recall the sentences directly. Strength and

Table 6.1 *Effect of Elaborating Sentences on Percentage of Recall Versus Recognition Time*

	Single Sentence Alone	Multiple Elaborating Sentences
Percentage of Recall	62%	73%
Recognition Time	1.81 sec	1.89 sec

elaboration are two different aspects of a memory, and they can both contribute to improved memory.

Strength involves the encoding of a specific memory record, whereas elaboration creates additional records to help retrieve the original record.

Incidental Versus Intentional Learning

One principle of memory implicit in the discussion to this point is that it does not really matter whether the person intends to learn the material or not. What is critical for memory is how the material is processed. This surprising truth about human memory has been demonstrated numerous times. For instance, Hyde and Jenkins (1973) looked at memory for individual words. Subjects performed one of two processing tasks: they rated the words for how pleasant they were or for whether they had an *e* or a *g*. The former task required the subject to think about the meaning of the words and should have led to more elaborative processing and better memory. Half the subjects in each processing condition were informed that they would be tested on their memory for the words; the other subjects were led to believe that the rating task was the primary purpose of the experiment. Thus for half the subjects, anything they learned would be incidental. All groups were asked to recall the list of 24 words. Table 6.2 displays the proportion recalled by the four groups of subjects. There is a large effect of how the subjects processed the material but essentially no effect of their intention to learn.

Another experiment that controlled processing and examined the effect of intention to learn was performed by Mandler (1967). He asked two groups of subjects to sort a set of words on cards (one word per card) into categories. One group of subjects was told that they would be tested later for their memory of the words; a second group was not so warned. When both groups were subsequently tested for their memory of the words, subjects who had been

208

Table 6.2 *Percent Recall as a Function of Orienting Task and Intention to Learn*

Learning-purpose Condition	Orienting Task	
	Rate Pleasantness	Check Letters
Incidental	68	39
Intentional	69	43

warned of the upcoming test recalled 31.4 words of 52, whereas those who had not been warned recalled 32.9—an insignificant difference. Both studies illustrate a general result: if subjects process material in the same way, they will recall the same amount whether they intend to learn or not. Frequently, subjects intending to learn are in fact able to recall more material, but only because they engage in processing more conducive to learning the material. For reviews of the lack of effect of intention to learn, see Nelson (1976) and Postman (1974).

These results add to the research reviewed in Chapter 4 that reinforcement contingencies do not affect what we remember from the material we process and further establish the separation between learning and motivation. The failure of motivation to affect learning can be seen from the viewpoint that people cannot learn what is important to them or from the viewpoint that they cannot avoid learning things that are unimportant. The latter interpretation seems more appropriate. People are best viewed as storing in memory everything they attend to, whether they want to remember it or not. To understand why there are memory failures, the next two chapters examine the processes of forgetting and retrieval.

Memory encodes a person's experiences whether there is any intention to learn or not.

Implications for Education

The educational implications of the research reviewed to this point in the chapter are both clear and important. The learning functions establish the obvious: practice makes perfect. The results on depth of processing, elaborative processing, and self-generation establish something that is not so obvious: how material is studied has important consequences for how much of the material is remembered.

These mode of processing results can be directly applied to trying to remember factual information, such as what is communicated in this textbook.

A number of successful study skill programs have been built on this insight, including the SQ3R method (Robinson, 1961) and the PQ4R method (Thomas & Robinson, 1972). PQ4R stands for preview, question, read, reflect, recite, and review. The reader is supposed to *preview* the text to be read (e.g., a chapter of a book) and identify the main sections, make up *questions* relevant to each section, and *read* the section trying to answer the questions and *reflect* on the text. After each section, the reader is supposed to *recite* the material from that section. At the end of the text, the reader should *review* the main points of the text. This method and methods like it require the reader to attack a text aggressively, making up questions about it and thinking about its implications. This is just the sort of elaborative and generative processing that has proved effective in the laboratory.

One experimental study (Frase, 1975) on the effectiveness of such processing techniques for study involved a collaborative learning technique. The text was divided into sections, and two people read it together. For each section, one person read with a mind to making up questions about that section and the other read and then had to answer those questions. Then roles were switched for each section. A control group of subjects who just read the material without doing anything special got 50 percent correct on the posttest. For the experimental subjects, the posttest questions could be divided roughly in half according to whether they were anticipated by the subjects' questions. The experimental subjects also got 50 percent correct of the unanticipated posttest questions, but got 69 percent correct of the anticipated posttest questions.

Chapter 11 further reviews research establishing the importance of such elaborative study skills. That chapter argues that this may be the most important educational application of research on human memory.

Question making and answering are effective ways to elaboratively process textbook material.

Representation of Knowledge

The previous sections reviewed the factors that influence our success in initially encoding material. This section addresses the issue of how the memory records are represented in memory. It turns out that the form in which information is represented can have substantial effects on later recall of the material.

Chunking

Research indicates that relatively little information can be stored in any one memory record, and therefore many records have to be used to store large amounts of information. People tend to store about three elements in any record. Much of the research has involved subjects trying to remember a series of letters, for example, DRQNSLWCF. Subjects break the series into a number of subsequences of letters. Miller (1956) coined the term **chunk** to describe these elements; chunks typically have about three elements. Subjects rehearse DRQ-pause-NSL-pause-WCF, with the pauses reflecting where they have broken up the series into chunks. When they recall the series later, they are observed to break it up into the same units.

The inference is that subjects store the letters in terms of these small chunks—*D*, *R*, and *Q* together; *N*, *S*, and *L* together; *W*, *C*, and *F* together. How can experimenters determine that these elements are actually stored together? Maybe subjects' rehearsal behavior just reflects habits of their speech and nothing about underlying memory representation. Johnson (1970) reported a series of experiments demonstrating that how subjects rehearsed these strings had strong effects on their memory for the strings. He presented his subjects with random strings of letters but encouraged them to use a particular chunk structure by placing spaces between the letters. So, he might have presented his subjects with

DY JHQ GW

Subjects' later recall of the string indicated that the elements within a chunk were stored together within memory. Subjects tended to recall a chunk, like JHQ, in an all-or-none manner. If subjects could recall *J*, there was only a 10 percent chance that they would fail to recall the subsequent *H*. In contrast, if the subjects recalled the *Y*, there was a 30 percent chance of failing to recall the *J* in the next chunk. Thus, recall of one item from a chunk was a better predictor of recall of other items from the same chunk than it was of items from some other chunk.

Such all-or-none performance would be expected if the letters were stored together in a memory record. If the record could be accessed, all the elements in the record could be retrieved. Thus, if the subject could retrieve one element from the record, the others should be retrievable. On the other hand, retrieving elements from one record implies nothing about whether elements from another record can be retrieved.

It seems that society implicitly recognizes this phenomenon about human chunking in how it breaks up numbers. In the United States, phone numbers are divided into an area code of three digits, followed by a prefix of three digits and a final group of four digits. Similarly, U.S. social security numbers are grouped into chunks of three digits, two digits, and four digits. Almost everywhere number strings are conventionally broken into chunk sizes of about three.

There is similar evidence that objects from a spatial array are remembered in terms of a set of records, each of which encodes the positions of a few objects. For instance, McNamara, Hardy, and Hirtle (1989) looked at memory for the 28 objects illustrated in Figure 6.13. Subjects saw these objects laid out in a 20 × 22 ft area. By looking at their patterns of recall, McNamara et al. found evidence that subjects organized these objects into groups. Specifically, subjects tended to recall certain groups of objects always together. Figure 6.13 illustrates the groups used by one subject. There are many different ways to chunk these objects, and different subjects came up with different organizations. Subjects gave evidence by other behavioral measures that elements from within a chunk were organized together in memory. For instance, McNamara et al. (1989) used a priming paradigm such as those discussed in the previous chapter. Subjects saw the name of one object (prime) from the array, followed 150 msec later by the name of another object (target). Subjects had to judge whether the second object was from the array. They compared target objects that either were or were not from the same chunk as the prime.

FIGURE 6.13. A layout used in the experiment by McNamara et al. (1989). The circles indicate hierarchical organization imposed by one subject on this array. Circles enclose objects in the same chunk or enclose chunks in the same higher order units. *Source:* From T. P. McNamara, J. K. Hardy, and S. C. Hirtle. *Journal of Experimental Psychology: Learning, Memory and Cognition, Volume 15.* Copyright © 1989 by the American Psychological Association. Reprinted by permission.

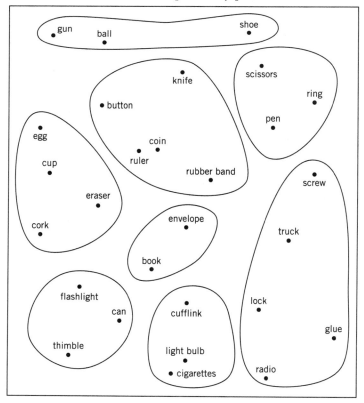

In both cases the targets were the same physical distance from the primes. Subjects took 797 msec to recognize the object when it was from the same chunk and 848 msec when it was not. This 50 msec advantage reflects the fact that elements from the same chunk tend to be retrieved together.

In addition to letter strings and scenes, similar effects have been demonstrated in memory for prose (e.g., Rumelhart, 1975; Thorndyke, 1977) and memory for chess positions (Chase & Simon, 1973). In all instances, a subject takes a complex stimulus and breaks it into a set of smaller units. Each unit has about three elements in it.

Memories are stored in records or chunks of a few elements.

Types of Codes

Although all types of memories seem to be organized into chunks, all memories are not encoded in the same way. We develop different **memory codes** for different types of material. A memory code refers to a distinctive way of encoding information into a record. One popular theory of memory is the **dual-code theory** (Bower, 1972; Paivio, 1971), which holds that we have separate codes for encoding verbal and visual material. Verbal information is stored as sequences of words, and visual information is stored in picturelike memory records. An experiment by Santa (1977) provides a nice illustration of the different properties of these two memory codes.

Subjects studied an array of three geometric figures. Then the subjects had to judge whether a test array contained the same elements as the original stimulus. Some of the possible test arrays are illustrated in Figure 6.14*a*. In many of the test arrays, the same elements were arranged in a different order from that of the study array. Subjects were to give affirmative responses to the array even though the order was different. Santa was interested in how long it took subjects to recognize that the arrays contained the same elements. The data are displayed in Figure 6.15. Perhaps not surprisingly, subjects were faster to recognize the same elements when they were in the original configuration than when they were arrayed linearly.

The stimuli in Figure 6.14*b* offer a striking contrast. These are the same stimuli as in Figure 6.14*a* except that the subjects studied words instead of geometric figures. Santa reasoned that subjects would encode these stimuli verbally rather than visually. In this case, subjects might actually do better when tested with the linear array because this encodes the items in the order in which they would occur if read left to right and top down, which is the standard reading order. As Figure 6.15 shows, Santa was right. When faced with a set of geometric stimuli, subjects encoded them spatially, but, when faced with a set of words, subjects encoded them linearly. These different encodings had significant consequences for how subjects could later access the information.

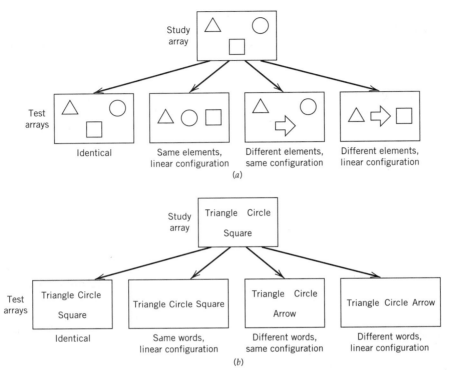

FIGURE 6.14. Procedure in Santa's experiment (1977): Subjects studied an array of elements and then had to judge whether a test array had the same elements. (*a*) Geometric condition; (*b*) verbal condition. *Source:* Figure 6.14 from J. R. Anderson. *The Architecture of cognition.* Copyright © 1983 by Harvard University Press. Reprinted by permission.

> *There is a spatial code for visual material and a linear code for verbal material.*

Memory for Visual Information

Different encodings of information appear to be remembered with different degrees of success. In particular, there is considerable evidence that visual material is particularly well remembered. Shephard (1967) compared recognition memory for magazine pictures with recognition memory for sentences. After studying a series of pictures or sentences, subjects were asked to identify the picture or sentence they had studied when it was presented with a distractor picture or sentence. Subjects misrecognized 1.5 percent of the pictures, compared with 11.8 percent of the sentences. In another experiment, Standing

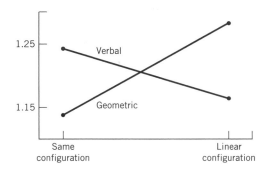

FIGURE 6.15. Time to judge an array in Santa's experiment as a function of type of material and the relationship between study array and test array. *Source:* Figure 6.15 from J. R. Anderson. *The Architecture of cognition.* Copyright © 1983 by Harvard University Press. Reprinted by permission.

(1973) presented subjects with some 10,000 pictures and found that they only misrecognized 17 percent!

However, it is not the case that people have photographic memories and can remember whatever they see. Goldstein and Chance (1970) studied memory for two types of visual material: faces and snowflakes. Figure 6.16 shows examples of the snowflakes. The individual snowflakes are quite distinct and seem at least as discriminable perceptually as individual faces. Subjects studied either 14 faces or 14 snowflakes and were tested for their recognition 48 hr later. Subjects were able to recognize 74 percent of the faces, but only 30 percent of the snowflakes. Thus good memory for pictorial material does not simply reflect how distinctive the stimuli are but also how well the subject can encode the material. Subjects are capable of attributing more significance to the features that separate faces than those that separate snowflakes.

Memory for pictorial information seems determined by the ability of subjects to place a meaningful interpretation on the picture. An amusing demonstration of this fact was performed by Bower, Karlin, and Dueck (1975). They had subjects study what are called droodles, such as those illustrated in Figure 6.17. One group of subjects saw just the droodles, without the explanatory labels. Another group of subjects saw the droodles and the explanatory labels. Subjects displayed better recognition memory for the pictures when they were accompanied by the labels, presumably because the labels enabled the subjects to elaborate the pictures.

FIGURE 6.16. Examples of the snow crystal photographs used as stimuli.

FIGURE 6.17. Droodles: A midget playing a trombone in a telephone booth. Panel b—An early bird who caught a very strong worm. *Source:* From G. H. Bower, M. B. Karlin, and A. Dueck. *Memory & Cognition,* Volume 3, pp. 216–220. Copyright © 1975. Reprinted by permission of Psychonomic Society, Inc.

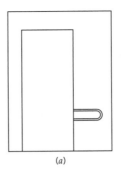

(a)   (b)

It seems that what subjects remember when they see a picture is a meaningful interpretation of the picture. Mandler and Ritchey (1977) performed an experiment in which subjects studied material such as that at the top of Figure 6.18. Their recognition memory for such pictures was tested by presenting them with the original pictures mixed in with distractors and requiring the subjects to identify which picture they had originally studied. The distractors could be either token distractors or type distractors. A token distractor changed some semantically irrelevant detail; for example, in Figure 6.18, the teacher's dress is changed. A type distractor changed a detail that might be relevant to an interpretation of the picture; in Figure 6.18, the material on the board is changed (from a geography lesson to perhaps an art lesson). Subjects falsely recognized 40 percent of the token distractors, whereas they falsely recognized only 6 percent of the type distractors. These results indicate that subjects remembered a meaningful interpretation of the picture rather than the physical details of the picture. When a distractor violated this interpretation, subjects had little difficulty in rejecting it as something not seen. When the distractor did not violate this interpretation, they had much more difficulty in identifying it as something not studied.

People have particularly good memory for their interpretations of pictorial material.

Effects of Imagery

Reflecting our high level of memory for visual material, we can improve memory for verbal material by constructing visual images of the material to be memorized. In one experiment, Bower (1972) had subjects try to commit to memory lists of 20 paired associates. In the experimental condition, subjects were instructed to develop a visual image of the pair interacting. Thus, if the pair was *dog–bicycle*, the subject might form an image of a dog riding a bicycle or of a dog chasing a child riding a bicycle. In the control condition, subjects

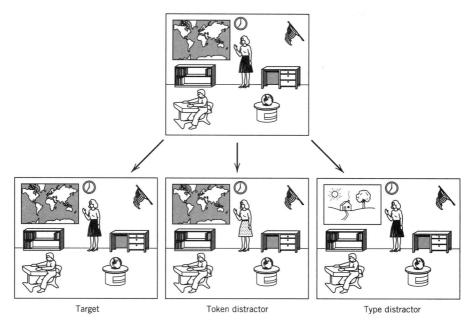

| Target | Token distractor | Type distractor |

FIGURE 6.18. Pictures used by Mandler and Ritchey (1977). *Source:* Figure 6.18 from J. M. Mandler and N. S. Johnson. *Journal of Experimental Psychology: Human Learning and Memory, Volume 2.* Copyright © 1976 by the American Psychological Association. Reprinted by permission.

were simply told to study the pairs. Subjects in the control condition recalled about 45 percent of the items, whereas subjects in the experimental condition, given the imagery instructions, recalled 75 percent.

As indicated in this example, the visual images can be bizarre (a dog riding a bicycle) or more common (a dog chasing a child on a bicycle). Another dimension of difference is that images can involve objects interacting (as is true of both the previous examples) or objects not interacting (e.g., a dog standing beside a bicycle). Wollen, Weber, and Lowry (1972) studied the relative contribution of bizarreness and interactive quality to memory. They gave their subjects pictures to help them learn paired associates, such as *piano–cigar*. Figure 6.19 illustrates the four kinds of pictures they used to realize the four possible combinations of bizarreness and interaction. Table 6.3 shows the levels of recall in the four conditions. There is a large effect of interaction but not of bizarreness; the effect of interaction is probably related to the effects of elaboration reviewed earlier. The interactive images promoted elaborative encoding that helped later recall.

There has been a history of varied results in studies of whether the bizarreness of the imagery improves memory. McDaniel and Einstein (1986) and Hirshman, Whelley, and Palu (1989) found cases where subjects displayed better memory for bizarre images. McDaniel and Einstein related this finding

FIGURE 6.19. Examples of pictures used to associate piano and cigar in the Wollen et al. (1972) study of image bizarreness. *Source:* From K. A. Wollen, A. Weber, and D. H. Lowry. *Cognitive Psychology, Volume 3.* Copyright © 1972 by Academic Press. Reprinted by permission.

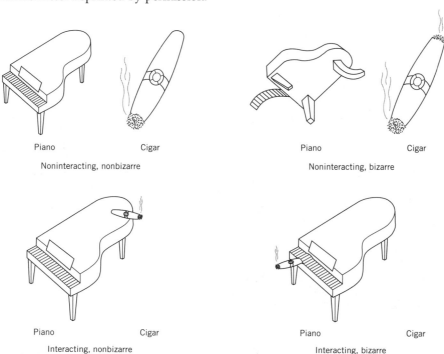

Noninteracting, nonbizarre   Noninteracting, bizarre

Interacting, nonbizarre   Interacting, bizarre

to whether a within-subject or between-subject design was used. The original Wollen et al. study used a between-subject design, in which some subjects studied all bizarre images and other subjects studied all nonbizarre images. In this kind of design, there is usually not an effect of bizarreness. In a within-subject design, half the items the subjects study involve bizarre images and half do not. In these designs bizarre images usually have advantages. McDaniel and Einstein argued that in a within-subject design the bizarre images stand out from the rest as the most distinctive. This distinctiveness gives them their advantage.

Table 6.3 *Mean Percentage of Recall in Wollen, Weber, and Lowry (1972)*

	Bizarre	Nonbizarre
Interacting	74%	73%
Noninteracting	34%	39%

Interactive images help memory, and sometimes bizarre images are more helpful because they are distinctive.

Meaningful Memory for Sentences

As reviewed earlier, when subjects remember a picture they tend to remember a meaningful interpretation of the picture. There is also evidence that when people hear a sentence, they tend to remember a meaningful interpretation of that sentence rather than the exact words. An experiment by J. R. Anderson (1974b) illustrates this abstract memory for sentences. Subjects were asked to remember sentences such as:

The missionary shot the painter.

This sentence is in the active voice. Other sentences were in the passive voice, for example:

The lawyer was kicked by the doctor.

Later, subjects were asked to recognize which sentences they had heard. If they had studied the first sentence in the example, they were tested with any of the following sentences:

1. The missionary shot the painter.
2. The painter was shot by the missionary.
3. The painter shot the missionary.
4. The missionary was shot by the painter.

Subjects had no difficulty in rejecting sentences such as 3 and 4 that had a different meaning. They had great difficulty in identifying whether they had studied sentence 1 or sentence 2. As in the case with pictorial material, subjects' memory for the material is highly interpreted.

Subjects appear to remember the meaning of their experiences rather than the exact details of the experiences. At a certain level this phenomenon seems to be highly adaptive. What we need to remember from a linguistic message (such as this textbook) is seldom the exact words, but rather the meaning of the text. Similarly, when we come upon a scene involving a set of people, it is much more likely that we will later need to know what they were doing rather than what they were wearing.

Subjects tend to remember the meaning of a text rather than its exact wording.

Differential Decay of Sensory and Semantic Information

There are, at least, two possible explanations for subjects' better ability to remember the semantic interpretation of an event rather than the sensory details. One explanation is that the semantic information is better encoded. The other is that the sensory information is forgotten more rapidly. The evidence seems to favor the latter explanation. Forgetting is discussed more thoroughly in the next chapter, but this section reviews two studies that show that different types of material have different rates of forgetting.

Gernsbacher (1985) had subjects study pictures such as those shown in Figure 6.20. Subjects studied one picture and then had to identify it when presented with a forced choice between that picture and the other. Because these pictures are mirror images of each other, this is an example of making a discrimination that is not critical to the meaning of the picture. At a 10-sec delay, subjects were 79 percent accurate in making this discrimination, but accuracy fell to only 57 percent at a 10-min delay (note that 50 percent would reflect chance guessing). Subjects remained at high levels of accuracy over a 10-min period when they had to discriminate the picture from one with a different meaning.

The experiment described in the preceding section (J. R. Anderson, 1974b), also looked at subjects' ability to remember which of the following two sentences they had studied:

1. The missionary shot the painter.
2. The missionary was shot by the painter.

These two sentences have different meanings. When tested immediately after hearing the sentences, subjects were 98 percent accurate; accuracy fell to 96 percent at a 2-min delay. Subjects' ability to discriminate between the following pair of sentences was also tested:

1. The missionary shot the painter.
2. The painter was shot by the missionary.

These two sentences have the same meaning but differ in wording. Subjects were 99 percent accurate in an immediate test and 56 percent accurate in a delay test (where 50 percent again reflects chance guessing). Subjects showed rapid forgetting of the nonmeaningful distinctions while retaining the meaningful distinctions.

Memory for semantic information is better retained than is memory for sensory information.

FIGURE 6.20. Pictures displayed in one orientation and the reverse. *Source:* From Gernsbacher, 1985.

Kintsch's Propositional Theory of Text Memory

This apparent abstraction from detail to meaning raises an interesting question. If the information is not represented in terms of the detail of the original sensory experience, what is the form of the more meaningful structure in which it is represented? Many researchers believe that memory for meaning is represented in what is called a propositional format.

Kintsch (1974) developed one propositional theory of memory for sentences. He proposed that meaningful material is stored in memory records, called **propositions.** A proposition is the smallest unit of knowledge that can stand as a separate assertion; that is, the smallest unit about which it makes sense to make a true or false judgment. Propositional analysis most clearly applies to linguistic information. Kintsch's work is particularly interesting because he has extended it to memory for large pieces of text (e.g., Kintsch & van Dijk, 1978). This application is important because it indicates that principles studied with simple laboratory materials may extend to the complex material we have to remember in our everyday lives.

Consider how a propositional analysis applies to the following sentence:

1. Lincoln, who was president during a bitter war, freed the slaves.

The information conveyed in this sentence can be communicated by the following simpler sentences.

2. Lincoln was president during a war.
3. The war was bitter.
4. Lincoln freed the slaves.

Each of these simpler sentences corresponds to a primitive proposition. This means that it is possible to judge whether each sentence is true or false and that it is not possible to decompose these sentences into simpler sentences about which such judgments can be made. If any of these smaller sentences were false, the larger sentence would be false. However, these sentences themselves are not propositions but rather they reflect the underlying propositional units. In essence, the proposition is the abstract idea behind each of these sentences. The reason for making this distinction between the sentence and the proposition is the evidence that subjects tend to remember the general meaning of even such simple sentences rather than the sentences themselves.

Kintsch (1974) advanced a proposal for how to represent the propositions that convey the meaning of these sentences. According to Kintsch, the propositions underlying sentences 2 through 4 are represented by the following list structures:

2a. (*president, Lincoln, war*)

3a. (*bitter, war*)

4a. (*free, Lincoln, slaves*)

Each of these lists begins with the **relation**—*president, bitter, free*—that organizes the proposition. The relation is followed by the other key terms from the proposition. These terms, which are typically nouns, are called **arguments.** Thus, the arguments for *president* are the president (*Lincoln*) and the time (*war*). The same propositional structure would be produced no matter how the sentence was stated. For instance, 2a could be the propositional representation for any of the following sentences as well as for 2:

> During the war, Lincoln was president.
>
> The president during the war was Lincoln.
>
> It was Lincoln who was president during the war.

What is critical in the Kintsch representation is what the relations are and what the arguments are. The list notation in 2a through 4a is only a convenient way of denoting that. The propositional lists in 2a through 4a can be thought of as the chunks or records in which the memory is stored.

One line of evidence for the propositional analysis comes from looking at patterns of recall for sentences. Anderson and Bower (1973) had subjects study sentences such as:

> The doctor who hated the lawyer liked the captain.

The two underlying propositions are:

> (*hate, doctor, lawyer*)
>
> (*like, doctor, captain*)

Subjects who could recall the noun *lawyer* were much more likely also to recall the verb *hated*, which appeared in the same proposition, than the verb *liked*, which did not. Thus they showed the same tendency for all-or-none recall for the propositions as Johnson's subjects showed for chunks of letters.

> *Kintsch proposed that semantic information is stored in propositional records.*

The Bransford and Franks Study

The fundamental claim of a propositional analysis is that when we hear a sentence, such as 1, the propositions, such as 2a through 4a, are an important part of what we commit to memory. Bransford and Franks (1971) performed an interesting demonstration of this fact. They had subjects study a set of sentences, including:

The ants ate the sweet jelly which was on the table.

The rock rolled down the mountain and crushed the tiny hut.

The ants in the kitchen ate the jelly.

The rock rolled down the mountain and crushed the hut beside the woods.

The ants in the kitchen ate the jelly which was on the table.

The tiny hut was beside the woods.

The jelly was sweet.

These sentences are all composed from two sets of four propositions. One set of four propositions can be represented as follows:

(eat, ants, jelly)

(sweet, jelly)

(on, jelly, table)

(in, ants, kitchen)

The other set of four propositions can be represented as follows:

(roll down, rock, mountain)

(crush, rock, hut)

(beside, hut, wood)

(tiny, hut)

Bransford and Franks then presented subjects with various sentences and asked them to judge whether that exact sentence had been studied. The following illustrates the three types of sentences they used:

223

OLD: The ants in the kitchen ate the jelly.

NEW: The ants ate the sweet jelly.

NONCASE: The ants ate the jelly beside the woods.

The first sentence has been studied, whereas the other two had not. The second sentence, however, was composed of the same propositions that the subject had studied. Subjects showed almost no ability to discriminate the NEW sentences from the OLD. These sentences seemed equally familiar and the subjects just could not remember which sentences they had studied. In contrast, subjects had no difficulty in recognizing that they had not studied the third, NONCASE sentence, which was composed of new propositions but the same words.

When the subjects heard the sentences, they abstracted the propositions and remembered them. They did not keep track of what propositions they had seen in what sentences. Indeed subjects were most likely to say they heard a sentence consisting of all four propositions, such as:

The ants in the kitchen ate the sweet jelly that was on the table.

even though they had not studied this sentence.

> *When we hear a complex linguistic communication, we tend to store it in terms of its primitive propositions.*

Distributed Versus Localist Representations

The type of memory representation (e.g., see Figures 5.10 and 6.1) assumed in most of this book is called a **localist representation**; that is, a unitary record encodes the memory. Interpreted literally, this view might seem to imply that there is a single neuron in the brain that corresponds to a specific memory. This interpretation does not seem particularly plausible. For instance, Lashley (1950) attempted to eliminate memory traces by removing specific regions of the brain and largely failed. However, such localist representations do not really require that a memory trace be stored in a specific location or in a specific neuron. The critical claim of localist representations is that memory records are organized according to elementary symbols, such as *Lincoln* and *freed*. These memory records can be encoded in many ways and can be duplicated throughout the brain. Consequently, Lashley's demonstrations and arguments are generally dismissed now as not persuasive arguments against localist representations. Nonetheless, some alternatives to localist representations do have interesting strengths and weaknesses. These are called distributed memory representations.

Distributed representations assume that a memory record does not reside in any single neural element but rather is represented by a pattern of activation over a set of neural elements. Suppose that a person wanted to learn a set of associations like the following three:

dog – 32

cat – 72

hat – 76

A distributed representation would try to encode the individual elements, such as *dog,* as patterns of activation over some neural elements. Assume that the stimuli and responses are represented as patterns of activation over four elements. (Four is used for simplicity of exposition; more realistic proposals might involve hundreds of elements.) If elements are simply active or inactive (ignoring intermediate values), the following might be the distributed representation for the elements:

dog = on, on, off, off

cat = on, on, off, on

hat = off, off, on, off

32 = off, on, off, off

72 = off, off, on, on

77 = on, off, on, on

Note that the representations of *dog* and *cat* are similar (only differing in the fourth element) and so are the representations of 72 and 77 (only differing in the first element). This situation reflects the semantic similarity of the elements. The ability to represent semantic similarity in this way is one of the virtues of a distributed representation and leads to a number of successful applications. This example illustrates the fundamental distinction between localist and distributed representations. Distributed representations can be analyzed into components and the components can overlap in ways that reflect similarity among memory records.

Learning these paired associates involves setting up some network of connections among the neural elements such that if the pattern corresponding to a stimulus occurs in one set of elements the pattern corresponding to the response appears in another set of elements. Figure 6.21 shows one such network. There are excitatory (+) and inhibitory (-) associations among the elements. Consider how this network would respond if dog were input. The top two elements for the stimuli would be turned on to represent the pattern for dog. They would send positive and negative input to the third element of the response set. These inputs would cancel out. Only a positive signal would be sent to the second response element from the second stimulus element. Thus the second response element would be the only one turned on. This result would correspond to the pattern for 32, which is the correct response. If the pattern for either of the other two stimuli were input, the output pattern for the corresponding response would result. Thus this network successfully associates these stimuli and responses. Figure 6.21 represents just one way of encoding associations in a distributed network. A number of other schemes have been considered (e.g., Rumelhart & McClelland, 1986). All these schemes have the property that the memories are really stored in the connections among the elements.

There remains the learning problem. Figure 6.21 shows a set of connections that successfully reproduce the stimulus–response pairs. How they are to be learned in the first place? A number of neural net learning rules, such as the delta rule (discussed in Chapter 2), have been proposed for learning such associative connections. These learning algorithms have had some major successes. Chapter 10 describes a successful application to learning the English past-tense system. However, there have been serious problems in applying such learning rules to human memory experiments. One major problem is called catastrophic interference. It turns out that learning new elements often overwrites and destroys the connections that encoded older elements (McCloskey & Cohen, 1989; Ratcliff, 1990). Chapter 7 presents some evidence for interference, but nothing on the scale that is found with these learning algorithms. An important current research topic is how to deal with such catastrophic interference, and a number of solutions have been suggested (e.g., Lewandowsky, 1991; McRae & Hetherington, 1993; Sloman & Rumelhart, 1992). Localist representations do not have the same degree of problems with catastrophic interference because each memory is represented separately and one cannot overwrite another.

Much of what is described in these chapters on memory is neutral to the issue of distributed versus localist representations. However, the distinction

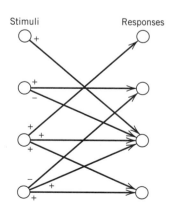

FIGURE 6.21. A set of associations connecting distributed representations of stimuli to distributed representations of responses.

can be important when dealing with effects of similarity, since distributed representations lead to predictions of generalizations and confusions among similar memory records. The distinction will become increasingly important as the field tries to understand the neural basis of memory records.

There are two proposals for memory records: unanalyzed localist representations and distributed representations that assume a pattern of activation over neural elements.

Memory Representation in Other Species

To what extent are these representational phenomena unique to humans and to what extent do they generalize to other species? There is evidence that other animals encode information into serial and spatial patterns (e.g., Roberts, 1984; Terrace, 1984). Pigeons are capable of learning specific sequences of pecks just as humans can remember sequences of letters (Terrace, 1984), and, as reviewed in Chapter 3, rats can learn the location of objects in space as well as humans can (Roberts, 1984). In addition, there is evidence that animals are capable of identifying the meaning of pictures independently of the exact physical details. For instance, Chapter 3 reviewed the evidence that pigeons can identify instances of natural categories, such as "tree."

Sequential Memory of Pigeons

A number of paradigms have been used to study memory for serial order in pigeons. One paradigm involves teaching pigeons to discriminate certain orders of stimuli from others. For instance, Weisman, Wasserman, Dodd, and Lunew (1980) trained pigeons that two sequences of visual stimuli signaled that a peck would be reinforced with food. These two sequences might be a green color, followed by a red, followed by a horizontal bar and the sequence red–green–vertical. Any other combination of colors and bars indicated a peck would not be reinforced. The pigeons learned to peck only at the correct sequences, indicating that they had discriminated these from all others.

Another paradigm requires the birds to reliably produce a particular sequence of responses (e.g., Straub, Seidenberg, Bever, & Terrace, 1979). They might be shown a set of four keys (e.g., red, white, blue, green) and be reinforced for pecking in a particular sequence of colors no matter what the spatial arrangement of the keys. Again, pigeons can reach quite high levels of performance in the task.

Both of these paradigms require the pigeon to learn just one or two sequences. More impressive are the experiments that require the pigeons to learn a different sequence each trial. For instance, Shimp (1976) presented a sequence of X-shaped forms occurring either to the left or to the right of the pigeon. The first form might be presented to the left of the pigeon and the next two to the right. The pigeon was then presented with a color. Red signaled that the pigeon would be reinforced for pecking where the first form occurred (in the example given this would be pecking left), a blue indicated to peck where the second form appeared (right in the example), and a white signaled to peck where the third form appeared (right in the example). Pigeons learned to perform this task with considerable accuracy.

Although humans and pigeons both show an ability to remember serial order, it does not follow that they remember it in the same way. For one thing, much of human sequential memory is verbally mediated, for example, through rehearsing a sequence of letters. Even human memory for nonverbal stimuli, such as movement, shows properties not true of pigeon memory. Humans show an accuracy gradient in reproducing a sequence of three elements such that they are most accurate for the first, next most accurate for the last, and least accurate for the middle. In contrast, in all the pigeon paradigms reviewed, pigeons are most accurate for the last element of the sequence and show equal accuracy among the remaining elements.

Pigeons as well as humans must be able to encode the sequential structure of the environment in order to adapt to it. Therefore, it should come as no surprise that pigeons can perform well at these tasks. However, pigeon brains are different from human brains, and hence it is also not surprising that the sequential structure is encoded somewhat differently.

Pigeons can remember the sequential structure of events and act on those memories.

Primates and Propositional Representations

Several experiments have involved teaching chimpanzees to use language (e.g., Gardner & Gardner, 1969; Premack, 1976; Terrace, Pettito, Sanders, & Bever, 1979). Chapter 10 discusses these experiments in detail. This section examines one of the consequences of such language training for representational capacity. Premack (1976) taught chimpanzees to order plastic shapes on a magnetic board. The shapes were to be treated as words that constituted sentences. Chimpanzees were taught to follow complex instructions, such as, "Put the banana in the pail and the apple in the dish," which were communicated by a sequence of plastic shapes that stood for the individual words.

Premack and Premack (1983) discovered that some of their language-trained chimpanzees were capable of engaging in behaviors that implied a capacity for propositional representation. Figure 6.22 shows some of the test material

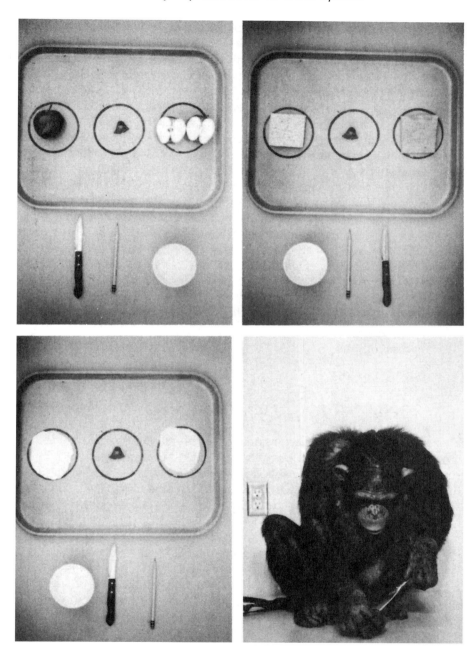

FIGURE 6.22. The tests are for cutting, wetting, and marking, respectively. The missing item is the instrument. In the lower right is the chimpanzee Elizabeth enthusiastically cutting an apple.

used with the chimps. The animals were to choose the instrument that transformed the first object into the second. So, in the first case shown in Figure 6.22, a knife transforms a whole apple into pieces of an apple. In the second case, water converts a dry sponge into a wet sponge. Premack and Premack found that some of their chimpanzees were able to solve these problems. To do so requires abstractly encoding the significance of events, such as a knife cutting an apple, and abstractly mapping this code onto the current situation. There is no common element to the answers to these problems at a superficial level. The common relationship of instrumentality must be abstracted. This kind of relational abstraction is characteristic of propositional representations. Premack and Premack noted that only language-trained chimpanzees were able to solve such problems. This observation raises an interesting question about the role of language in enabling propositional representations. Perhaps it is the use of language that induces propositional representations in humans as well. On the other hand, maybe the language-trained chimpanzees had simply become more facile in responding to the experimenters' contingencies.

Chimpanzees trained with an artificial language are capable of responding to abstract relationships typical of propositional representations.

Final Reflections

This chapter has addressed acquisition, how information is stored in memory. One view of memory is that everything we attend to is organized in terms of small, chunk-like records and stored away in memory. It does not matter what the memory is about or whether we want to remember it at all; we are always storing away the things we attend to. The animal learning literature often creates a picture of rather little learned, but this is because it is so difficult to get nonhumans to display what they have learned. With human subjects, there is evidence of relatively rapid rates of learning. It has been estimated that people learn a new record every 10 sec (Newell & Simon, 1972), and this is probably a gross underestimate of the speed of learning. Still, people clearly fail to recall much of what they experience. Such failures of memory can be attributed to forgetting and failures at retrieval, the topics of the following two chapters.

Whether it is because of differential success at initial encoding or differential success at retention and retrieval, what we do at the time of study can have a large impact on how much we remember. This chapter reviewed three classes of encoding factors: *amount of study*, which results in differential strength of the memory records; *elaboration*, which results in additional retrieval routes; and *type of trace*, which results in differential forgetting rates. There is something generally adaptive in how memory responds. We are more likely to need to remember things the more frequently we encounter them and the more elaborately we process them. We are more likely to need to remember the gist of our experiences than the details. It might even be argued that we are more likely to need to recall visual experiences than verbal ones, since visual information necessarily comes from our direct experience whereas linguistic information can communicate experiences we may never encounter.

We may store everything we attend to, and memory failure may be due to forgetting and retrieval factors rather than to acquisition factors.

Further Readings

In addition to the sources mentioned in the previous chapter, several works present the topics of this chapter in greater detail. The power law of learning is examined by Anderson and Schooler (1991) and Newell and Rosenbloom (1981). The book edited by Cermak and Craik (1978) presents a number of discussions on depth and elaborativeness of encoding. My cognitive psychology text (J. R. Anderson, 1990) discusses the issue of knowledge representation at greater length. Kintsch's (1974) book is a good source for his propositional encoding. Roitblatt (1987) presents extensive discussion of knowledge representation in nonhuman animals. Premack and Premack (1983) offer an interesting description of the cognitive capabilities of chimpanzees.

7

Retention of Memories

Overview

I don't know how many times I have had the same conversation with people on planes, on ski slopes, at baseball games, and wherever strangers meet. The conversation always follows the same script with slight variations:

> STRANGER: What do you do?
> ME: I am a psychologist.
> STRANGER: What do you study?
> Me: Human memory.
> STRANGER: I have a terrible memory. I am always forgetting things. What can I do about that?

This dialogue reflects the fact that many people's most salient experience of their memories is that they are aware of having known many things that they can no longer remember. This chapter is concerned with what underlies forgetting. Along the way the chapter notes two possibilities that might surprise people:

1. Forgetting may not be such a bad thing.
2. People may not really forget anything.

However, there is some territory to cover before expanding on these two curiosities.

There are three basic hypotheses about what causes forgetting. The **decay hypothesis** asserts that memories simply weaken as a function of time and therefore are harder to retrieve. The **interference hypothesis** claims that competition from other memories blocks retrieval of a target memory. The **retrieval-cue hypothesis** asserts that at the time of retrieval we lose access to the cues that would serve to retrieve the memories. Traditionally, research on forgetting has tried to distinguish among these theories, but each factor contributes to the overall forgetting process. This chapter examines the first two hypotheses in some detail, postponing full discussion of the third hypothesis until Chapter 8.

The Retention Function

Memories seem to fade with the passage of time. Many experiments have studied memory loss as a function of time. Chapter 1 discussed some of the earliest studies of memory by Ebbinghaus on the **retention function.** The retention function demonstrates how memory performance deteriorates with the passage of time. Figure 7.1a reproduces Ebbinghaus's retention function. He used a savings measure of memory, which reflects how much easier it is to relearn a list than it is to learn the list originally. Ebbinghaus's data show rapid initial forgetting followed by much slower forgetting.

All retention functions show this same basic form. Initially, forgetting is rapid, but memories continue to worsen nearly forever. Retention functions differ with respect to the scales on which they display these basic phenomena. Other measures, in addition to Ebbinghaus's savings measure, include probability of recall or time to recall memories that can be recalled. These measures show rapid initial deterioration, followed by continued, ever-slowing deterioration. Retention functions also vary in the time spans over which they occur. Ebbinghaus's functions are over 30 days. Figure 5.5 displayed similar forgetting over 18 sec. The period of time over which forgetting is manifested is a func-

FIGURE 7.1. Ebbinghaus's classic retention data (*a*) showing percentage of savings as a function of retention interval; (*b*) with both scales log transformed to reveal a power relationship.

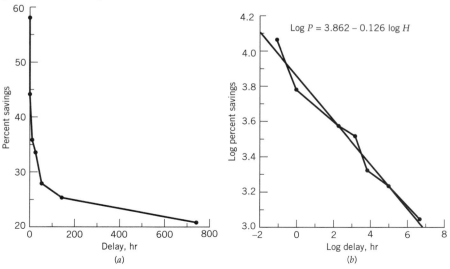

tion of the strength of the memory record and the sensitivity of the memory measure. The weaker the memory or the more sensitive the measure, the more rapid forgetting is.

Retention functions show rapid initial forgetting followed by ever-slower forgetting.

Decay: The Power Law of Forgetting

The last chapter described the learning function, which is negatively accelerated as is the forgetting function. In the case of the learning function more and more practice produces smaller and smaller gains, whereas in the case of the forgetting function more and more delay produces smaller and smaller losses. As discussed in the preceding chapter, taking the logarithm of both the performance measure and the practice measure reveals a regularity with respect to the learning function. Figure 7.1*b* shows the regularity that is revealed by taking logarithms of the performance scale and the time scale for retention functions. Again, there is a linear relationship between the two logarithmic scales. For Ebbinghaus's data, this function is

$$\text{Log savings} = 3.86 - .126 \text{ Log delay}$$

where 3.86 is the intercept of the line in Figure 7.1*b* and $-.126$ is the slope. As discussed in the previous chapter, such a linear relationship between log performance and log time implies that performance is a power function of time. For the Ebbinghaus data that power function is

$$\text{Savings} = 47.5 \text{ Delay}^{-.126}$$

This function implies that performance at a delay of 1 hr is a 47.5 percent savings and that as delay increases this savings is multiplied by a decreasing fraction (delay$^{-.126}$), which is less than one.

As noted in Chapter 6, a critical feature of such power functions is their negative acceleration. Also as noted, power functions are not the only negatively accelerated functions that could be fitted to the data. The more obvious negatively accelerated functions are exponential functions, which have been particularly popular for theories of forgetting because they describe many decay processes in nature, including radioactive decay. Only recently (Wixted & Ebbesen, 1991) has it been established that the forgetting functions are power functions. This generalization is referred to as the **power law of forgetting.** Power functions differ from exponential functions in that they are even more negatively accelerated, implying that the rate of forgetting becomes very slow indeed.

Although Ebbinghaus used percentage of savings, the more common measure for memory performance is probability of recall and retrieval time.

234

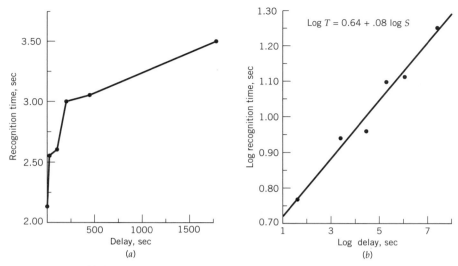

FIGURE 7.2. (*a*) Success at sentence recognition as measured by reaction time as a function of delay; (*b*) replotted as a log–log plot. (Adapted from Anderson & Paulson, 1977).

Retrieval time measures typically show a power relationship. Figure 7.2 shows some data (Anderson & Paulson, 1977) obtained from looking at the speed of recognizing a sentence for delays ranging from 5 sec to 30 min. As shown in Figure 7.2*a*, increased delays caused slower retrieval times, but the rate of slowing decreased with time. Figure 7.2*b* displays this data with both scale log transformed; the functions in the log–log scales are approximately linear, implying a power function. Note that the functions in 7.2 are increasing whereas those in Figure 7.1 are decreasing, since longer latency reflects worse performance (Figure 7.2) and lesser savings reflect worse performance (Figure 7.1).

Similar power law curves are obtained when the dependent measure is probability of recall. Krueger (1929) looked at retention of paired associates. Figure 7.3*a* shows the number of paired associates that subjects recalled (out of 12) at various delays from 1 to 28 days. Again, the classic, negatively accelerated retention function is obtained. Figure 7.3*b* reveals an approximately linear function when log number recall is plotted against log time, implying a power function in the original scales.

Squire (1989) documented such retention functions on a very different time scale. He looked at people's ability to recognize the name of a TV show for varying numbers of years after it had been canceled. Figure 7.4*a* shows percentage of recognition as a function of number of years since the show last aired. Recognition dropped more rapidly initially and then slowed down. Figure 7.4*b* regraphs this data on log–log coordinates, revealing a linear relationship indicative of a power function in the original scale.

How should this systematic decrease in performance with time be interpreted? Wickelgren (1971) argued that the strength of a memory record sys-

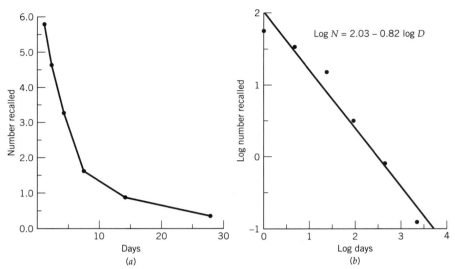

FIGURE 7.3. (*a*) Krueger's (1929) data showing number of paired associates recalled as a function of retention interval; (*b*) log transformation of the data.

tematically decays over time. Such a decay theory of forgetting is obvious and has been around since the beginning of psychology. People with no background in psychology often believe that memories spontaneously decay with time. Despite its obviousness, decay theory has had a controversial history in psychology, which will be described after the discussion of interference. To

FIGURE 7.4. (*a*) Probability of recognizing a TV show as a function of time since cancellation; (*b*) the same data on a log–log scale. (From Squire, 1989).

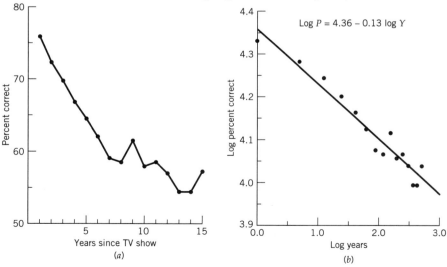

foreshadow the conclusion, however: there is more to forgetting than decay, but decay is part of the story.

Memories decay as a power function of the time over which the memories are being retained.

Degree of Learning and Forgetting

How does amount of practice affect the retention curve? Can forgetting be prevented by initially practicing the material enough? This question has been investigated in a number of experiments, and a systematic relationship has emerged between the degree of practice and the retention function over a wide variety of material. Figure 7.5a shows data from Slamecka and McElree (1983) looking at retention of sentences over intervals up to 5 days. Figure 7.5b shows data from Wixted and Ebbesen (1991) looking at retention of words at delays of up to 40 sec. In both cases subjects received more or less study of the material. The figures plot the data in log–log form. Increased practice resulted in increased retention, but performance fell off linearly in the log–log scale for all degrees of practice.

In both cases the underlying functions are not only approximately linear, they are approximately parallel, indicating that materials at different degrees of learning were being forgotten at the same rate. Functions can be fit to the data

FIGURE 7.5. (*a*) Data from Slamecka and McElree (1983) showing the effect of an extra trial practice in the retention function. (*b*) Data from Wixted and Ebbesen (1991) showing the effect of 1 versus 5 sec of study in the retention function.

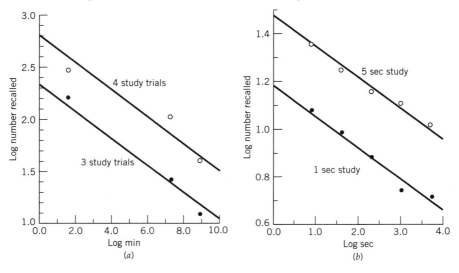

predicting recall from amount of practice and delay. For instance, the function that fits the Wixted and Ebbesen data is

$$\text{Log recall} = 1.17 + .19 \text{ Log practice} - .13 \text{ Log delay}$$

and if one converts this back to power functions[1] this becomes

$$\text{Recall} = 3.2 \text{ Practice}^{.19} \text{ Delay}^{-.13}$$

This function combines the power law of practice with the power law of retention. In this equation 3.2 reflects the average number of words that would be recalled after 1 sec delay with 1 sec of learning. This amount is multiplied by the amount of practice (measured in seconds) raised to the power of .19. This step reflects the power law of practice. The result is multiplied by delay (measured in seconds) raised to a negative power of –.13. This step reflects the power law of retention. Thus the power function of practice multiplies the power function of the retention interval. Similar functions can fit the data from Slamecka and McElree.

More generally the following equation captures the relationship between practice and delay:

$$\text{Strength} = A \times \text{Practice}^{b} \times \text{Delay}^{-c} \qquad \text{(Strength Equation)}$$

This is a rather important equation in that it shows how memory varies with two of the most important factors—practice and delay—that affect memory performance.

If the straight lines in Figure 7.5 perfectly predicted the data, all the points would be on the lines; however, the points deviate from the lines to varying degrees. There are two reasons for such deviations. First, psychological data are inherently variable. If these experiments were repeated they would yield somewhat different numbers. Because of this variability (sometimes called noise) the points would not be expected to fall exactly on the true curve. However, there is another reason for such deviations. These power function characterizations of forgetting are only approximate, although they are better than other functions, such as the exponential function. To reiterate the point of the previous chapter, the strength equation is not intended as an exact function to describe memory—it only captures the major trends in the data.

This general trend implied by the strength equation not only applies to human memory, but also applies to animal memory. Chapter 5 described the matching-to-sample paradigm used to study pigeon memory (see Figure 5.16). Pigeons are shown a color and must remember it for some period of time so that they can later peck a key of that color. Grant (1976) exposed his pigeons to the sample light for 1, 4, 8, or 14 sec and then tested their memory for the color at delays up to 60 sec. Figure 7.6 shows their performance as a function of both the amount of practice and the retention interval. There are different

---

[1] A multiplicative relation in normal scale becomes an additive relation in a log scale and vice versa.

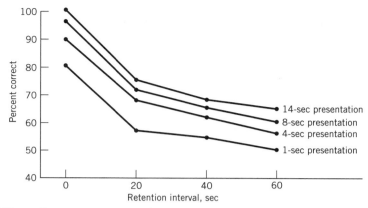

FIGURE 7.6. Pigeon's accuracy of matching as a function of retention interval and time of exposure to the sample. *Source:* From D. S. Grant. *Learning and motivation, Volume 7.* Copyright © 1976 by Academic Press. Reprinted by permission.

retention curves for different amounts of practice. There are technical problems[2] with determining whether these curves really correspond to power functions, as the strength equation would predict, but at a qualitative level the retention curves are much like those from human data.

The effect of practice on the retention function is to shift it up by a multiplicative factor.

Environmental and Neural Bases for the Strength Equation

The strength equation appears to describe human memory performance in a wide variety of situations using all sorts of measures. Why should there be this apparently universal property of memory? Chapter 6 noted that more frequent things are more likely to repeat and that this situation may underlie the power law of learning. Anderson and Schooler (1991) argued that the strength equation reflects an attempt of memory to adapt to the statistical structure of the environment.

To appreciate this analysis, it is necessary to realize that things repeat with different patterns in the environment. Think about the need to know information about various countries. Westerners typically need to recall infor-

---

[2]It is necessary to estimate the true delay in Grant's zero-delay condition and to correct for chance performance, which is 50 percent. Also as Anderson & Schooler (1991) argued, the function should fit odds of recall.

mation about Great Britain (e.g., who is its current leader?) more often than corresponding information about Angola. Therefore, their memories would be more adaptive if information about Great Britain were more available. What factors could memory use to determine the probability that a particular piece of knowledge would be used? Relevant factors would be the recency and frequency with which that knowledge has been used in the past.

Anderson and Schooler investigated the relationship between recency and frequency of past usage and probability of current usage in a variety of domains, including the pattern with which various topics appeared in *New York Times* headlines. What is the relationship between the frequency and recency with which *Libya* has appeared in the past and the probability that it will appear in the current day's headlines? They calculated how often various words appeared in the last 100 days and how recent the last occurrence was.

Figure 7.7 shows the probability that a word will appear on the current day as a function of the recency of its last occurrence and how many times it occurred in the last 100 days. These data are plotted on a log–log plot for comparison with the forgetting functions in Figures 7.1 through 7.5. As shown, these data from the environment mirror data from human memory. In particular, the log probability of reappearing decreases linearly with long delay, implying a power function. Moreover, the functions for different frequencies define approximately parallel lines. Anderson and Schooler showed that the functions that fit the *New York Times* data hold up in several domains, such as electronic mail messages and parental speech to children. They argued that memory uses statistics about frequency and recency of memories to judge which memories to make available. Memories ubiquitously correspond to the strength equation because in doing so they adapt to the statistical structure of the environment. The memory system makes most available the memories that are most likely to be needed.

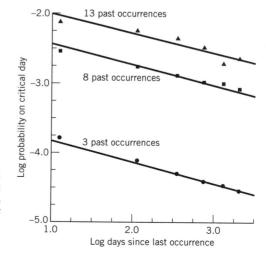

FIGURE 7.7. Log probability of a word occurring in a *New York Times* headline as a function of time since last occurence for three levels of frequency of past occurrence. (From Anderson & Schooler, 1991).

Chapter 6 also showed that the power law increase in behavioral measures with practice was mirrored by a power law increase in long-term potentiation (LTP) with practice. Does this measure of neural learning similarly mirror the behavioral retention function? Figure 7.8 presents some data from Barnes (1979), who examined how LTP in the hippocampus decreased with time. Recall that the LTP procedure involves administering a high-frequency stimulation to a neural path. Afterward this path shows increased response to further stimulation. As discussed with respect to Figure 6.9, LTP is frequently measured in terms of how much more responsive the neural pathway is to stimulation over its baseline responsiveness.

Barnes investigated the decrease in LTP for periods from 2 min up to 14 days. She also looked at retention after one or four high-frequency stimulations. Figure 6.9 showed LTP increases with frequency of stimulation. Figure 7.8 plots log percentage above baseline against log delay. Individual data points are somewhat noisy, but Figure 7.8 shows the best-fitting linear functions for one and four stimulations. The rates of decay are approximately linear and parallel. Thus the behavioral retention functions shown in Figures 7.1 through 7.5 may reflect changes in the strength of neural association. To reiterate a theme from the previous chapter, the neural learning function may have this form because it mirrors the structure of the environment (Figure 7.7).

The strength equation approximately characterizes changes in LTP and approximately mirrors the statistical structure of the environment.

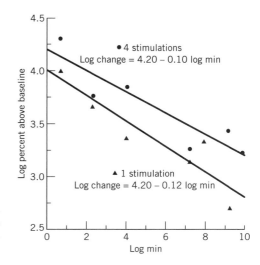

FIGURE 7.8. Percentage of LTP as a function of log delay for two levels of practice. (Data from Barnes, 1979).

Spacing Effects

Scientists love parsimonious theories of empirical phenomena. From a scientist's perspective, it would be nice if memory were as simple as the strength equation implies. However, things are a good bit more complicated in many ways. Chapter 6 discussed the complications created by elaborative processing. Another complication concerns the spacing between the times when an item is studied. An elegant demonstration of these effects is found in the research of Glenberg (1976), who used a continuous paired-associate procedure. Subjects saw a long sequence of 500 study and test events; that is, some of the events were paired associates to study, and others were stimuli to which the subjects were to recall the response. Part of such a sequence might be:

bank–tail

fish–home

fish–??

bank–tail

pail–nose

frog–girl

pail–??

snow–ball

bank–??

Subjects had two opportunities to study each critical paired associate. The *bank–tail* pair in the example is such a critical paired associate that is studied twice and then tested. Glenberg manipulated both the interval between the two opportunities to study each paired associate and the delay from the second study until subjects were tested for memory of the paired associate. These delays were defined in terms of how many trials (study or test) were between the two events. In the *bank–tail* example there are two events between the two studies and four events from the second study to the test. Glenberg used delays of 2, 8, 32, or 64 trials between the two presentations and delays of 0, 1, 4, 20, or 40 trials between the second presentation and the test.

The results are displayed in Figure 7.9. There are four curves, one for each retention interval. The curves for longer retention intervals are lower, reflecting a simple forgetting. However, the effect of the study interval between the two presentations changed with the test interval. At long test intervals, there was an increasing effect of study interval, whereas the trend at short intervals was more curvilinear. The study interval that gave the best performance for each test interval is starred in Figure 7.9. The data can be approximately characterized as showing the best performance for a particular retention interval when the study interval matches it.

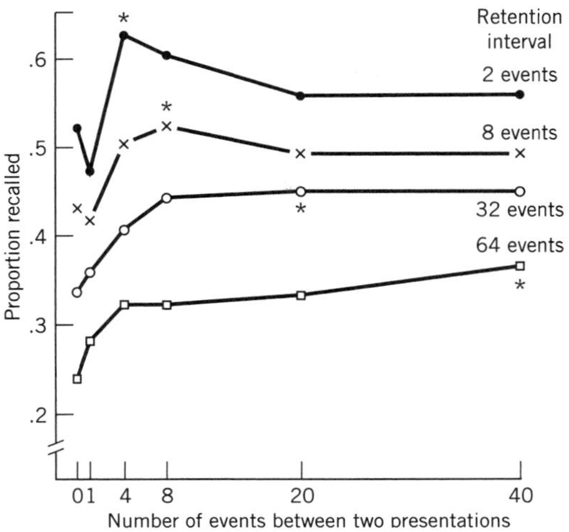

Spacing Effects

FIGURE 7.9. Results from Glenberg (1976). The effect of different spacings between two studies at different retention intervals. *Source:* Figure 7.9 from A. M. Glenberg. *Journal of Verbal Learning and Verbal Behavior, Volume 15.* Copyright © 1976 by Academic Press. Reprinted by permission.

There are other demonstrations of the effect of study spacing. For instance, Table 7.1 shows some data from Bahrick (1984), who was interested in the effect of spacing on the learning of 50 Spanish–English vocabulary items. He used three conditions in which he varied the spacing among the studies. In the zero-delay condition, subjects did all their studying in a single day. They studied the 50 items and underwent a series of five test–study cycles. In each cycle they were first tested for the Spanish equivalent of the vocabulary item and, if they answered incorrectly, they were told what it was so that they could study it. In the zero-delay condition there was no delay between these cycles. In the 1-day delay condition, each test–study cycle occurred at a day's delay from the previous cycle. That is, each day subjects were tested for the 50 vocabulary items and then had an opportunity to study them. In the 30-day delay condition, there was a 30-day delay between each test–study cycle. The groups with the shorter intervals between cycles did better initially, reflecting a standard retention effect. However, all groups were administered one final test at a 30-day delay from their last test–study cycle. In this case the order of the results

Table 7.1 *Percentage of Recall of Spanish Vocabulary Items for Various Delays Between Studies*

Intersession Interval (days)	Test					Final 30-Day Test
	1	2	3	4	5	
0	82	92	96	96	98	68
1	53	86	94	96	98	86
30	21	51	72	79	82	95

Source: Data from Bahrick, 1984.

was reversed; the group that did the best was the group with 30-day intervals between studies. Thus, the best performance is obtained when the delays between successive studies match the delay until test.

This dependency of retention on the spacing of successive studies is referred to as the **spacing effect.** The implications of the spacing effect for study habits are both clear and important. In order to remember material for long periods of time, it is important to study the material at widely spaced intervals; the study intervals are then more like the retention interval. On the other hand, in order to do well on a specific test, studying should be done just before the test; the best performance is achieved when the retention interval is short and the study intervals are similarly short. This effect is one of the great tragedies of modern education, for it implies that the study behavior that is optimal for test performance (cramming) is the worst for long-term retention.

Memory is best when the study intervals match the retention interval.

Spacings Effects on the Retention Function

The spacing of study appears to affect the retention function. Keppel (1964) looked at the effect of distribution of practice on retention of paired associates. Subjects studied the paired associates either eight times on 1 day or two times for each of 4 days. Figure 7.10 shows the retention curves. Subjects were somewhat better in the massed practice condition, when given a retention test immediately after learning. However, the massed practice subjects forgot more rapidly.

If forgetting is more rapid in the massed learning condition, why is massed learning superior at short retention intervals? When the retention interval is short and all the study is massed, the delay from all the presenta-

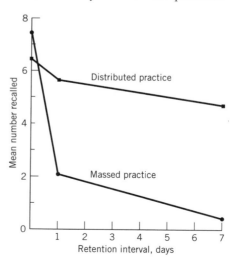

FIGURE 7.10. Retention following learning by distributed versus massed practice. (From Keppel, 1964, by permission).

tions to test is short and the subject enjoys the benefit of the sum of many short retention intervals. At a short retention interval, it does not matter that forgetting is rapid with massed presentation because there is little delay over which forgetting can take place. In contrast, if the study is spaced and the test interval is short, the retention interval for the final presentation is short, but the retention intervals for the earlier presentations are long and there is some forgetting. Each presentation has its own retention function and performance is a function of the sum of the individual retention functions. At long retention intervals, memory is best when it is the sum of a number of slowly decaying retention functions, which is the case in spaced practice. At short retention intervals, performance is best when memory is a sum of retention functions that have not had long to decay, which is the case when all the practices are massed close to the retention test.

An item that is studied twice close together is forgotten more rapidly than if the two studies are far apart. This phenomenon raises the question whether both presentations are being forgotten more rapidly, or just one, and if one, which one. Hintzman, Block, and Summers (1973) conducted a study relevant to this issue. They presented subjects with some words once and some words twice, varying the spacing among the words presented twice. Sometimes words were presented in the visual modality and sometimes in the auditory. When words were presented twice, sometimes both presentations were in the same modality and sometimes they were in different modalities. Subjects were asked to recall the words, say whether they had been studied once or twice, and recall the modalities in which they had been studied. The critical conditions were when the words were presented twice in different modalities. For instance, consider a word that is first presented visually and then auditorily (presentations were counterbalanced; this discussion refers to one specific case). If the subject remembers only one presentation, will it be the auditory or visual presentation? At short delays between the presentations, subjects tended to remember only the first presentation, suggesting that the second presentation was being forgotten. It appears that massed presentation increases the rate of forgetting of later presentations.

If an item is presented for study at a short lag after a previous study, the effect of the second presentation decays more rapidly.

Spacing Effects in the Environment

Data from Anderson and Schooler presented earlier in this chapter (Figure 7.5) suggested that the retention function for memory mirrors a retention function in the environment. Do retention functions in the environment show effects of spacing similar to those of memory retention functions? Figure 7.11 presents some data from the *New York Times* data base of Anderson and Schooler. Looking at items that appeared just twice in the previous 100 days, separate retention functions are plotted for those words that occurred close together (9 or fewer days apart) and those that occurred farther apart (10 or more days apart). The retention function in the environment is steeper for items that occurred relatively close together. Items that occurred twice close together had a higher probability of occurring again after a short interval than did items that occurred twice far apart. However, this trend reversed at longer delays. The spacing effect in human memory does appear to mirror a spacing effect in the environment. Memory identifies massed items and makes them unavailable when they are no longer likely to reappear.

Both Figures 7.7 and 7.11 show that there is a relationship between the pattern with which an item has appeared in the past and the probability with which it will appear now. Memory seems adapted to these patterns and adjusts the strengths of records accordingly. The strongest memory records are the most likely to be needed. Recall from Chapters 2 and 3 that animal conditioning appears to reflect near optimal statistical inference about the causal structure of the environment. Human memory appears to be another system producing near optimal statistical inferences. In both cases the apparent optimality of these basic phenomena has come as something of a surprise to psychologists. However, the caveat from previous chapters needs to be repeated: the apparent optimality does not imply that the system is engaged in explicit statistical inference. Simple associative learning processes can display these properties of statistical optimality.

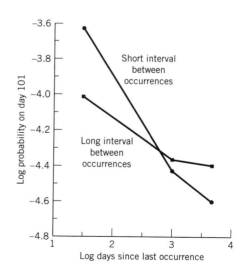

FIGURE 7.11. Probability that a word that has appeared twice in the *New York Times* will appear again. The curves are a function of the amount of time since the last occurrence. The two curves reflect cases when the two presentations were either close together or far apart. (From Anderson & Schooler, 1991).

Memory uses the pattern of past occurrences to infer which items are most likely to be useful now.

Interference

Thus far this chapter has described forgetting as if it were just a function of time. However, the amount and rate of forgetting can vary dramatically with what is learned before and after the critical material. Consider again the Brown–Peterson paradigm (Figure 5.5), which showed substantial forgetting over 18 sec. Data in those figures were averaged over many trials. Keppel and Underwood (1962) were interested in what happened on the very first trial of such an experiment. Figure 7.12 shows the retention functions for the first, second, and third trials of such an experiment. There does not appear to be any forgetting on the first trial; forgetting seems to appear gradually with subsequent trials. Other research (e.g., Houston, 1965; Noyd, 1965; see Crowder, 1989, for a review) has been inconsistent on the issue of whether there is forgetting on the first trial. Thus the amount of forgetting is a function of the amount of material that has been previously learned. Earlier material interferes with retention of later material. A great deal of research has studied such interference effects.

Interference refers to a negative relationship between the learning of two sets of material. Such negative relationships can be manifested in three ways. The learning of the first material can impede the learning of the second material; this situation is referred to as **negative transfer.** The learning of the first material can accelerate the forgetting of the second material; this situation is known as **proactive interference** and is illustrated in the analysis of the Brown and Peterson paradigm in Figure 7.12. The distinction between proac-

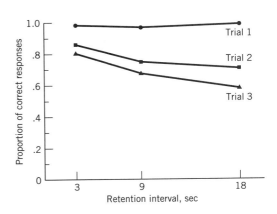

FIGURE 7.12. Retention as a function of length of interval and number of prior syllables. Compare with Figure 5.5. *Source:* From G. Keppel and B. J. Underwood. *Journal of Verbal Learning and Verbal Behavior, Volume 1.* Copyright © 1962 by Academic Press. Reprinted by permission.

tive interference and negative transfer is subtle, and sometimes the terms are used interchangeably. For example, is the poorer performance with successive syllables in Figure 7.12 the result of poorer initial learning of the later lists or of greater forgetting? Poorer performance on an immediate test would indicate negative transfer. If memory was equivalent initially but separated with time, it would be proactive inference. Since Figure 7.12 does not have a retention test at zero delay, whether it is negative transfer or proactive interference cannot be determined.[3]

The third possibility is that the learning of the second material can accelerate the forgetting of the first material; this situation is referred to as **retroactive interference**.[4] Retroactive interference is an obvious candidate for a cause of the forgetting functions documented earlier (see Figures 7.1–7.5). As more time passes since original learning, there is more opportunity to learn new material, which will interfere with retention of old material. It could be argued that the forgetting seen in these earlier figures is entirely a function of such retroactive interference. However, there has to be more to forgetting than just retroactive interference. For instance, the forgetting shown in Figure 7.12 is affected by proactive interference, not by retroactive interference.

The learning of one set of material often interferes with the learning and retention of another set of material.

Item-Based Interference

Insight into the nature of interference comes from research that shows that the relationship among the two sets of materials determines how much interference is displayed. In particular, interference is high among associations that overlap in the items they involve. This phenomenon has traditionally been studied in a paired-associate paradigm in which subjects learn to respond with one item to another. For instance, subjects learn to say a response, for example, *dog*, to a stimulus, such as *vanilla*.

Table 7.2 illustrates some of the interference paradigms for paired associates (for reviews of research using such paradigms see Postman, 1971, and Wickelgren, 1976). The experimenter can focus either on the effect of an ear-

[3]Other methods have been used to show that the poorer performance in the Brown and Peterson task is due to proactive interference and not to negative transfer (Loftus & Patterson, 1975; Watkins & Watkins, 1975).

[4]There is a fourth logical possibility that the learning of the second material can impede the learning of the first material, but this situation would be a scientific contradiction as it would require causality to work back in time such that a later event would affect an earlier event.

Table 7.2 *Interference Paradigm for Paired Associates*

(a) Proactive Paradigm

	A–B, A–D Experimental	C–B, A–D Experimental	Rest, A–D Control
Manipulation	Learn A–B	Learn C–B	Rest
Target List	Learn A–D (worse)	Learn A–D (better)	Learn A–D
Retention	Test A–D (worse)	Test A–D (worse)	Test A–D

(b) Retroactive Paradigm

	A–B, A–D Experimental	A–B, C–D Experimental	A–B, Rest Control
Target List	Learn A–B	Learn A–B	Learn A–B
Manipulation	Learn A–D	Learn C–D	Rest
Retention	Test A–B (much worse)	Test A–B (worse)	Test A–B

lier experience on a later list or on the effect of a later experience on retention of an earlier list. The first is a proactive paradigm, and the latter is a retroactive paradigm. In the proactive paradigm in Table 7.2, the experimenter is interested in the learning and retention of the second list, which is designated A–D. A stands for the stimuli, and D for the responses. An A stimulus might be *frog*, and a D response *tire*. That is, the subject has to learn to say *tire* to *frog*. Before learning the A–D list, the subject may learn another list or be in a rest condition. If there is a preceding list, it can share the same stimuli or not. The A–B condition reflects shared stimuli (A) with different responses (B). Thus the subject might learn *frog–door*. The C–B condition denotes new stimuli (C) as well as new responses (B). Thus a subject might learn *coat–ball*.

Part (a) of Table 7.2 also includes information about whether learning and retention are better or worse than the rest control. In the proactive paradigm, learning of the second A–D list is slower in the A–B, A–D condition than in the rest control condition, reflecting negative transfer. On the other hand, the C–B, A–D condition actually displays faster learning of A–D than the rest, A–D condition. This occurrence is typically thought to reflect a learning-to-learn phenomenon. Subjects have learned techniques for learning paired associates as a function of their experience with the first list (perhaps they have learned to use the elaborative techniques discussed in the previous chapter). This learning-to-learn must also be occurring in the A–B, A–D condition, so the net negative transfer in that condition is all the more remarkable.

In the typical experiment, the A–D lists are brought to the same level of learning in all three conditions by giving more learning trials in the A–B,

A–D condition and fewer learning trials in the C–B, A–D condition. All groups are then given a retention test for A–D. At this point both groups who learned prior lists are worse than the rest condition, even though they were brought to the same level of learning. This result is said to reflect proactive interference.

Part (b) of Table 7.2 displays the retroactive paradigm. Interest is in the retention of an original A–B list as a function of whether there is an interpolated list with the same stimuli (A–D), a list with different stimuli (C–D), or a rest period. The standard result is worst retention in the A–B, A–D condition and best retention in the A–B, rest condition, with the A–B, C–D condition falling in the middle. Thus a subsequent paired-associate list can interfere considerably with the retention of the first list, particularly when the two lists share the same stimuli.

As a general summary of these results, additional material tends to impede the learning and particularly the retention of other material. The interference is especially strong when the items share common stimuli. It should be emphasized that such interference is specific to using the common A items as stimuli. For instance, in an A–B, A–D retroactive paradigm, although subjects show interference in trying to recall the B responses to the A stimuli, they show little interference when the test is turned around and they are asked to recall the A stimuli to the B responses.

Similar effects of inference can be shown on retrieval time. J. R. Anderson (1981) looked at time to retrieve the responses in the second list of paired-associate paradigms, such as those described in Table 7.2. Not only were subjects unable to recall as many responses in the retention test for the interference condition, they were also much slower when they could recall the responses. In the A–B, A–D retroactive paradigm, for example, it took 2.0 sec to recall the A-B associate after learning A–D, but it took only 1.4 sec in the control condition.

One of the dramatic examples of item-based interference is the difficulty children have learning the addition and multiplication tables. Only about 100 facts have to be learned of the form 2 + 3 = 5, 4 + 3 = 7, and 7 × 3 = 21, but children spend years of intensive practice trying to master them. In the meantime they are learning dozens of other facts each day (such as the names of the newest cartoon characters). Why are the arithmetic facts so hard to learn? The answer is in part that the arithmetic facts define a huge interference experiment. The same numbers (such as 3) appear in many different arithmetic facts and interfere with each others' learning and retention.

There is a great deal of interference when we try to maintain multiple associates to the same items.

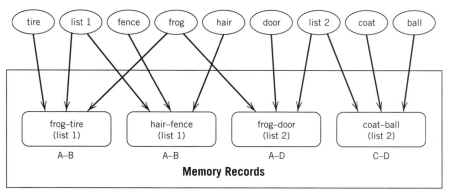

FIGURE 7.13. A representation of the associations to memory records in an A–B, A–D paradigm (*frog–tire, frog–door*) and in an A–B, C–D paradigm (*hair–fence, coat–ball*).

A Theory of Associative Interference

One explanation for item-based interference has proved to be the basis for an understanding of many memory phenomena. It is the same basic explanation found in the ACT theory (J. R. Anderson, 1983a, 1993) and in the SAM theory (Gillund & Shiffrin, 1984; Raaijmakers & Shiffrin, 1981); the core idea is that when an item is presented, such as the stimulus of a paired associate, it proves to be the source for activation of the memory record that encodes that paired associate. Both ACT and SAM offer more complex mathematical developments than are presented here, but the following discussion captures their gist.

Figure 7.13 illustrates the underlying concept in the case of the A–B, A–D interference paradigm versus an A–B, C–D condition. From list 1 the subject learns the associations *frog–tire* and *hair–fence*; then the subject learns the associations *frog–door* and *coat–ball* from list 2. The *frog–tire* and *frog–door* combinations define an A–B, A–D condition, and the *hair–fence* and *coat–ball* combinations define an A–B, C–D condition. These are stored as memory records along with information about the relevant list. Figure 7.13 shows the stimuli, responses, and lists as different elements that can serve to activate the target memory.[5]

The assumption is that any item (like the stimulus *frog*) has a fixed capacity for activating memories. Thus, if an item is part of two memories, it cannot activate either as well as it could if it were only associated with one. It takes longer to learn a new response to the same stimulus because the new

[5]Figure 7.13 has compressed the A–B, A–D and A–B, C–D paradigms together, whereas more typically they are between subjects; thus it illustrates a mixed-list design.

response must compete with the other record for activation, producing negative transfer. Once the new response has been learned, the existence of this new association takes activation away from the old response, producing retroactive interference.

The basic theory can be described with the following two equations. The first equation asserts that the activation of a memory record by a stimulus is a function of the record's strength and the strength of the association from the stimulus:

Record activation = Record strength + Association strength

(Activation Equation)

The strength of a record is governed by the strength equation given earlier in this chapter. A further assumption is that there is an upper bound λ on the total strength of associations to a stimulus; that is, if there are n associations to a stimulus, each has a fraction $1/n$ of the total strength λ:

Association strength = λ/n

(Association Equation)

Thus there is a fixed capacity for sending activation from any stimulus, and the association between that stimulus and any particular record must compete with all other associations from the stimulus.

Table 7.3 illustrates how these equations apply to the retroactive paradigm illustrated in Figure 7.13. The top of the table represents the learning history of *frog–tire* and *frog–door*, which are in an interference relationship, and the bottom represents the learning history of *hair–fence* and *coat–ball*, which are not. For illustration purposes it is assumed that the records gather a strength of 1.0 in the learning of list 1. Similarly, it is assumed that λ, the sum of all association strengths from a cue, is 1.0. Since there is only one association for either *frog* or *hair* after the first list, that association gets all of this associative strength. The activation of the record is the sum of these two strengths, or 2.0, in both the experimental and the control conditions.

Consider what happens when the same number of trials are given to the learning of the list 2 paired associates in the interference and control conditions: the *frog–door* record and the *coat–ball* record reach a strength of 1.0. However, the *frog–door* association in the interference condition must now be shared with *frog–tire*. Assuming an equal division, both get 0.5. Thus in the interference condition both records have a total activation of 1.5. In contrast, the *coat–ball* association does not need to be shared, and so it has a 1.0 associative strength. Adding this to the record strength yields a total activation of 2.0. Thus, in list 2, *coat–ball* has an advantage over *frog–door*. To raise list 2 performance in the experimental condition to the level of the control condition, additional trials must be given to the *frog–door* pair to increase its record strength to 1.5. The need for these extra trials reflects negative transfer. Negative transfer occurs because *frog–door* from list 2 shares the same stimulus with *frog–tire* from list 1.

Table 7.3 *Analysis of the Memory Records and Associations from Figure 7.13 in a Retroactive Paradigm*

Experimental (A–B, A–D)

	Frog–Tire			Frog–Door		
	Record Strength	+ Associative Strength	= Record Activation	Record Strength	+ Associative Strength	= Record Activation
Learn List 1	1.0 +	1.0	= 2.0	—	—	—
Learn List 2 Original Trials	1.0 +	0.5	= 1.5	1.0 +	0.5	= 1.5
Learn List 2 Extra Trials	1.0 +	0.5	= 1.5	1.5 +	0.5	= 2.0

Control (A–B, A–D)

	Hair–Fence			Coat–Ball		
	Record Strength	+ Associative Strength	= Record Activation	Record Strength	+ Associative Strength	= Record Activation
Learn List 1	1.0 +	1.0	= 2.0	—	—	—
Learn List 2 Original Trials	1.0 +	1.0	= 2.0	1.0 +	1.0	= 2.0

Now consider what happens in a final retention test for *frog–tire* versus *hair–fence*. The strength of association for *frog–tire* has been reduced to 0.5, and so its total activation is 1.5. In contrast, the *hair–fence* pair has been unaffected by list 2 learning and so retains its activation of 2.0. This difference results in the differential retention and the retroactive interference for the *frog–tire* pair. Again, this retroactive interference is a consequence of shared stimuli across the two lists.

> *According to the theory of associative interference, item-based interference occurs because the record gets less activation from its association to the item.*

Relationship to the Rescorla–Wagner Theory

The association equation has an interesting relationship to the Rescorla–Wagner learning theory described in Chapters 2 and 3. Recall from Chapter 3 that, in applying the Rescorla–Wagner theory to instrumental conditioning, the strength of association between the stimulus and the response changes according to the following equation:

$$\Delta V = \alpha(\lambda - \Sigma V)$$

where α is the learning rate; λ is the maximum strength of association; and ΣV is the sum of the existing associative strengths from the stimuli present on that trial. This relationship is known as a competitive learning rule, because various stimuli compete for association to the response. The association equation for memory implies that various responses compete for association to the stimulus. This relationship would seem to imply that the Rescorla–Wagner theory and the Association Equation are diametrically opposed in terms of where the competition lies. However, upon closer inspection it turns out that the two rules are consistent and, in fact, that the Rescorla–Wagner theory provides a mechanism for implementing the Association Equation.

The Rescorla–Wagner theory describes competition among simultaneously present stimuli, whereas the Association Equation describes competition among different responses associated with the same stimulus at different times. Consider the implications of the Rescorla–Wagner rule for the learning of the paired associates shown in Figure 7.13. Since the stimulus *frog* is associated to two different responses (*tire* and *door*) in two different lists, each response is being reinforced only some of the time. On trials in which *tire* occurs as a response, the strengthening rule according to Rescorla–Wagner is

$$\Delta V = \alpha(\lambda - V)$$

where V is the current strength of association between *frog* and *tire*. On trials in which *tire* does not occur (and *door* does) the strengthening rule for *frog–tire* is

$$\Delta V = \alpha(0 - V)$$

where 0 is the strength of association that can be maintained when the response does not occur. An equal mixture of list 1 and list 2 practice results in an asymptotic value of $V = \lambda/2$. More generally, if there are n responses equally practiced to a stimulus, the resulting strength of association is be λ/n. This result is exactly the Association Equation, which asserts that there is a fixed value for the sum of associative strengths to one stimulus.

The Rescorla–Wagner theory produces the associative interference because interference manipulations result in less reinforcement of any one response.

Recognition Memory and Multiple Cues

Thus far in this chapter interference has been considered with respect to recall memory. What happens in tests of recognition memory? That is, what happens if, rather than presenting a word and asking subjects to recall the associated memory, the experimenter presents subjects with what they studied and asks them whether they recognize it. Consider the following experiment with sentence recognition (J. R. Anderson, 1974a). Subjects memorized facts of the form *A person is in the location*. Examples of the material subjects studied are

(1-1)   A doctor is in the bank.
(1-2)   A firefighter is in the park.
(2-1)   A lawyer is in the church.
(2-2)   A lawyer is in the park.

As can be seen, the same profession could occur in multiple sentences and the same location could occur in multiple sentences. The sentences here are prefixed by two digits. The first digit indicates how many sentences the profession occurs in and the second how many sentences the location occurs in. In the experiment, some professions and locations occurred in three sentences as well as the one and two sentence cases shown here. Figure 7.14 illustrates the memory records that are being created and their associations. Note that terms such as *park* and *lawyer* are associated with multiple records and so should be less able to activate any particular record than cues like *doctor* and *bank*, which are associated with single records.

Subjects practiced this material until they could recall all the material correctly. Then they were asked to perform a fact-recognition task. They were supposed to recognize sentences they had seen when those sentences were mixed in with combinations of professions and locations that they had not seen, for example, "The doctor is in the park." Table 7.4 displays the speed with which subjects made these judgments as a function of the number of facts they had studied about the person and the location of the sentence. Subjects were slower to recognize the sentence when they had studied additional facts about the person or the location; that is, the recognition of any one fact was interfered with by additional facts studied about the person or location.

FIGURE 7.14. Memory records being created in an experiment by J. R. Anderson (1974a).

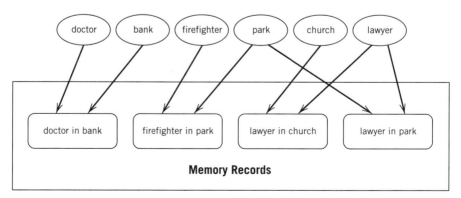

Table 7.4 *Mean Times to Recognize Sentences in Person–Location Experiment*

		Number of Sentences Per Profession		
		1	2	3
Number of Sentences per Location	1	1.11 sec (1 + 1 + 1=3.00)	1.17 sec (1 + 1 + 1/2 = 2.50)	1.22 sec (1 + 1 + 1/3 = 2.33)
	2	1.17 sec (1 + 1 + 1/2 = 2.50)	1.20 sec (1 + 1/2 + 1/2 = 2.00)	1.22 sec (1 +1/2 +1/3= 1.83)
	3	1.15 sec (1 + 1 + 1/3 = 2.33)	1.23 sec (1 + 1/2 + 1/3 = 1.83)	1.36 sec (1 + 1/3 + 1/3 = 1.67)

Note: hypothetical activation values in parentheses.

This experiment differs in some important ways from the interference paradigms previously considered. First, this is a recognition memory test and not a recall test. Second, there is no control group, just one group of subjects. Some of the material the subjects learn is being interfered with and other material is not. Demonstration of interference in such a paradigm is particularly important theoretically because it rules out certain explanations of interference effects. One explanation of the interference effects in the standard paired-associate paradigm (Table 7.2) is that, when subjects try to recall the responses from one list, the items learned from the other list intrude and block recall of the target responses (e.g., Postman, Stark, & Fraser, 1968). For instance, when subjects try to recall *door* to *frog* in list 1, *tire* from list 2 intrudes (see Figure 7.13) As a consequence, subjects learn to repress all the items from the interfering list. However, in this experiment there are no competing lists of responses nor do subjects have to recall responses.

This experiment shows that interference is not all or none—there is more interference when subjects have to learn three sentences associated with a term than two, and more interference with two than one. The mathematical theory presented earlier can be extended to apply to this experiment with one further assumption: the record receives activation from all the items in the memory probe, and its total activation is the sum of the activation from all these sources. In the experiment detailed in Table 7.4, the memory probes are the sentences to be recognized, such as "The doctor is in the bank," and this assumption means that the memory record is activated by *doctor* and *bank*.[6] Thus, our activation equation becomes

$$\text{Record activation} = \text{Record strength} + \Sigma \text{ Association strengths}$$
$$\text{(Activation Equation)}$$

where the summation (denoted by Σ) is over the associations to all the terms (*doctor, bank* in this example) in the probe.

[6]The word *in* should also be considered an activation source, but it is being ignored here for simplicity of exposition.

Consider how these ideas apply to the data in Table 7.4. Suppose that the strength of each record is set at 1 and total association strength, λ, is set at 1. Table 7.4 reproduces the expected activation values under this assumption. When one sentence (record) is associated with the profession and two are associated with the location, the total activation is 1 (strength of record) + 1 (association to profession) + 1/2 (association to location) = 2.50. The recognition times generally increase as the activation values decrease.

This theory also explains why performance is usually better on recognition memory tests than on recall memory tests. A recognition probe typically provides more stimuli from which to probe memory. For instance, the recognition question, "True or False: Harding was the president after Wilson" provides one more item to probe memory than the recall question, "Who was the president after Wilson?" This extra item is the term *Harding*. The association equation implies that activation sums from this additional cue and increases the availability of this memory record. Chapter 8 expands on the difference between recall and recognition.

Activation sums from the various terms in a memory probe in inverse proportion to their number of associations.

Item Strength and Interference

This analysis implies that the strength of a memory record and the strengths of associations sum to produce an overall activation. Thus even the activations of very strong records are less in conditions of more interference where there is less associative support. Consider the experiment described in Chapter 6, in which subjects practiced the recognition of sentences such as "The doctor hated the lawyer" for 25 days. Figure 6.3 shows data for sentences in which each concept occurred uniquely. However, there was also an interference condition, in which each of the main words (*doctor, hated,* and *lawyer*) occurred in two sentences. Figure 7.15 compares the data for the interference and the noninterference conditions of this experiment. The speedup in both conditions follows a power law improvement fairly closely. The lines are the best-fitting power functions. Even after 25 days there is a substantial disadvantage for the interference material. Thus interference does not disappear with practice, in contrast to certain speculations (e.g. Hayes-Roth, 1977).

Note, however, that the reaction time disadvantage of the interference condition decreases with practice. On day 1, it is more than .4 sec, but by day 25 it is less than .2 sec. This occurs because the judgment times are getting closer to zero and so differences among conditions are being compressed. In psychology such compression of data is often referred to as a floor effect.

FIGURE 7.15. Recognition times for interference and noninterference sentences as a function of practice. The solid lines represent the predictions of the best-fitting power functions. (From Pirolli & Anderson, 1985). *Source:* Figure 7.15 from J. R. Anderson. *The architecture of cognition.* Copyright © 1983 by Harvard University Press. Reprinted by permission

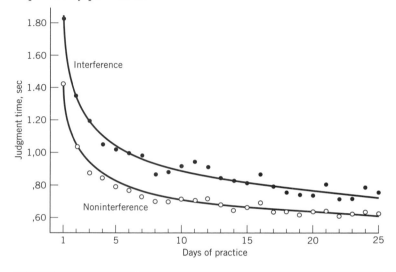

Even strongly encoded records show interference when measured by recognition time.

Interference with Preexperimental Memories

This discussion has been assuming that the only memories associated with a term like *doctor* are those learned in the experiment. However, subjects have learned many prior associations. Suppose that a subject has m prior associations and learns n new associations in the experiment. Then the amount of activation to an experimental fact from a term, such as *doctor,* should be approximately $\lambda/(m + n)$. One of the interesting implications of this analysis is that learning information in the laboratory should interfere with memories subjects had before the experiment. These memories may be so strong that there is no effect on the probability of recalling them, but an effect should still be detectable with latency measures.

Peterson and Potts (1982; see also Lewis & Anderson, 1976) performed an experiment to determine whether there was interference for material known before the experiment. Table 7.5 shows the material they used. Subjects studied one or four facts that they did not previously know about famous historical figures, such as Julius Caesar and Beethoven. They were then tested on memory for facts they did know before the experiment, for facts they had

Table 7.5 *Examples from the Peterson and Potts Materials*

Examples of Learned Facts

1 fact studied	Julius Caesar was left-handed.
4 facts studied	Beethoven never married.
	Beethoven suffered from syphilis.
	Beethoven was a very poor student.
	Beethoven died of pneumonia.

Examples of Test Items

Known facts

0 facts studied	Thomas Edison was an inventor.
1 fact studied	Julius Caesar was murdered.
4 facts studied	Beethoven was a musician.

Learned facts

1 fact studied	Julius Caesar was left-handed.
4 facts studied	Beethoven never married.

False facts

0 facts studied	Thomas Edison was a congressman.
1 fact studied	Julius Caesar was a printer.
4 facts studied	Beethoven was an exceptional athlete.

learned as part of the experiment, and for false facts. They had to recognize as true the first two categories of facts and reject as false the third category of facts. Subjects were tested 2 weeks later about people for whom they had not learned any experimental facts, about people for whom they had learned one fact, and about people for whom they had learned four facts. The speed with which they could judge the known facts and the studied facts is shown in Figure 7.16 at the 2-week delay (similar results were found in the immediate test). Since subjects knew the studied facts less well than the known facts, they recognized them less well. However, recognition memory for both studied and known facts was influenced by the number of experimental facts

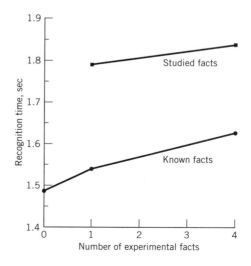

FIGURE 7.16. Reaction times from Peterson and Potts (1982). The task was to recognize known and experimentally learned facts about public figures. Data shown are a function of number of experimental facts learned and delay for testing.

learned. These interference effects were weak—in no case much more than 0.1 sec. A careful experimental design is required to detect such weak effects. It is particularly interesting that these interfering influences remained 2 weeks after the initial learning.

This last result brings up what has been called the paradox of the expert (Smith, Adams, & Schorr, 1978). The results thus far indicate that, the more a person knows about any particular topic, such as Julius Caesar, the harder it is to remember anything more about that topic. This implication paints a pretty dismal picture of memory in everyday life. The paradox of the expert is so called because it implies that the more expert a person is on a topic and the more that is known about the topic, the greater the interference and the poorer memory will be for that material. However, even though there are times when new information is hard to retain, such as when children try to remember all their addition and multiplication facts, most of the time people do not feel hard-pressed to learn new material.

There is a boundary condition on these interference effects, which means that they do not apply in many situations: interference only occurs when the memories people are trying to associate to a term are unrelated. When the memories are related, memory does not worsen, and often improves as additional facts are learned. For example, Chapter 6 described an experiment by Bradshaw and Anderson (1982) in which subjects learned some little-known information about famous people. In one condition, subjects studied just a single fact:

Mozart made a long journey from Munich to Paris.

In another condition, subjects learned two additional facts that were causally related to the target fact:

Mozart made a long journey from Munich to Paris.

plus

Mozart wanted to leave Munich to avoid a romantic entanglement.

Mozart was intrigued by musical developments coming out of Paris.

The additional sentences were experimenter-provided elaborations designed to boost memory of the target sentence. As reviewed in Chapter 6, subjects' memory for the target sentence was improved by having to learn these redundant sentences. The experiment also examined subjects' memory when they studied additional sentences unrelated to the target sentences:

Mozart made a long journey from Munich to Paris

plus

Mozart wrote an important composition when he was 14 years old.

Mozart's father was critical of his marriage.

Subjects who learned two such unrelated facts showed worse memory for the target facts than subjects who studied just the target fact. This experiment shows that whether additional facts are facilitating or interfering depends on whether they are consistent with the target material.

Subjects' memory for prior knowledge can be interfered with by unrelated material learned in the laboratory.

Context-Based Interference

The previous sections documented that item-based interference is a robust phenomenon happening for all sorts of materials in all sorts of conditions. However, interference can be obtained among materials that do not explicitly overlap in any component items. For instance, in an A–B, C–D condition, there is interference in retention of the A–B items even though their stimuli do not overlap with the C–D items.

On deeper analysis it turns out that the lists A–B and C–D may overlap in items that might cue their memory. For instance, they are learned in the same laboratory. Rather than committing to memory "B is the response for A," the subject must actually commit to memory something like, "B is the response for A in the laboratory." Then *laboratory* becomes an element that could cue the recall of the paired associate. This is an example of a **context cue**. Context cues are elements of the general learning situation that can become associated to the memory record. There are many potential context cues, including things like the temperature of the room or the sound of a bird chirping outside. Context cues also include internal items, such as the subject's mood and hunger pangs. The basic idea is that the external and internal environment of the subject provides items that might become associated to the memory record. In the A–B, C–D paradigm, memory records from both lists are likely to be associated to some of the same contextual cues and so interfere with each other for association to these cues. The interference in such a paradigm may be a case of item-based interference, where the items are parts of the context.

J. R. Anderson (1983b) performed an experiment that found evidence for interference as a result of shared context. The experiment contrasted two groups of subjects who learned three lists of paired associates on three successive days. Two experimental contexts were used. In one context, subjects learned the lists from a computer in a windowless cubicle. In the other context, they learned the lists from a human experimenter in a windowed seminar room. They learned a list on one day and were retested on the next day. There were two conditions for learning lists 2 and 3; they could be learned in the same context as the previous lists or in a different context (the assignment of context to conditions was counterbalanced over subjects). Figure 7.17 plots

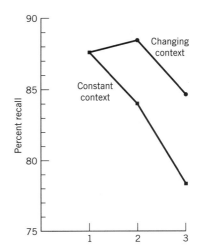

FIGURE 7.17. Percent retention of successive lists as a function of whether the context in which they were learned changed or not. (From J. R. Anderson, 1983b).

retention performance of subjects with the changing context versus those with the nonchanging context. The subjects with the constant context showed less retention of each successive list, displaying cumulative proactive interference. Subjects with a changing context showed little loss in their retention. Thus, contextual interference may be one cause of memory loss in conditions where material does not explicitly overlap in the items being memorized. Even though the items do not overlap, the contextual cues do and the memory records are interfering with each other's association to the cues.

As described, memory can be impaired when the physical contexts for two sets of memories overlap, producing interference. Memory can also be impaired if the context changes over time, since the context cues at test may not be the cues associated to the memories at study. Certainly a person's internal state (mood, boredom, hunger) changes over time. In addition, what a person encodes from the external context may change over time. For instance, a subject may focus initially on the experimenter, encode his or her features, and later attend to features in the room. The elements that serve as context gradually drift. Many theorists (Estes, 1955; Gillund & Shiffrin, 1984; Landauer, 1975) have speculated that this drift may be the true source of the gradual decay in the forgetting curves. As time passes, the overlap between the context cues at study and those at test gradually decreases. For example, the material that students learn in a classroom is associated to that classroom, their mood at the time, the people with whom they associate, the season of the year, and so on. As time passes, these context cues tend to change and access to these memories is lost. Chapter 8 reviews evidence that memory is impaired when the context changes from study to test.

Memory can be impaired when there is interference with associations to context cues or when the context cues shift.

Is All Forgetting a Matter of Interference?

There is evidence that prior learning can have a massive effect in producing forgetting. Keppel, Postman, and Zavortnik (1968) had five subjects study some 36 lists of paired associates. The lists, consisting of 10 pairs of common words, were learned at 2-day intervals. Just before learning a new list, subjects were tested on the previous list. Figure 7.18 plots performance on the retest averaged across successive sets of three lists. Subjects averaged more than 50 percent on the first three lists, but by the last lists they averaged less than 10 percent. Thus subjects showed massive cumulative proactive interference. This deterioration in performance is an extended version of the phenomenon displayed in Figure 7.17 and may be similarly due to contextual inference.

Results like these show that interference can produce a great deal of forgetting and so encourage the hypothesis that all forgetting might be a function of interference from prior material or subsequent material. In addition, decay, the alternative forgetting mechanism, has been questioned as a respectable scientific hypothesis. In an influential paper, McGeoch (1932) argued that time per se is an unsatisfactory theoretical variable because it cannot cause forgetting; rather, some process, such as interference, which is correlated with time, must be the cause. That is, the more time that has passed, the more opportunity there is for material to retroactively interfere with the memory. Although it is true that time per se cannot cause forgetting, it is possible that some neural change may occur, similar to the atrophy of muscles with disuse, and that this change may not be affected by material learned earlier or later. Decay theory is best understood as the proposal that forgetting is produced by neural

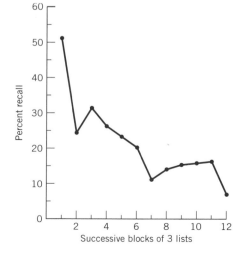

FIGURE 7.18. Mean percent recall after 48 hr, as a function of lists and successive blocks of three lists. (From Keppel et al., 1968).

263

processes that progress at a steady rate independent of what other material has been learned. As such it is a perfectly respectable scientific theory, but not necessarily a correct theory.[7]

The interference results reviewed in this section make the case that decay cannot be the only cause of forgetting, since different amounts of forgetting occur over the same delay depending on interference conditions. The question is whether any forgetting can be attributed to decay. The ideal way to see if there is any forgetting due to decay would be to eliminate all interference by preventing the subject from learning any new material over the retention interval. While this is impossible, there have been efforts to minimize the amount of other material that is learned between study of the critical material and the retention test. Such experiments thus try to eliminate retroactive interference but do nothing about proactive interference. One manipulation has been to have subjects sleep or not during the retention interval. As early as 1924, Jenkins and Dallenbach conducted this type of study. Subjects learned a list of 10 nonsense syllables and were tested after 1, 2, 4, or 8 hr, during which they were awake or asleep. Much less forgetting occurred during sleep, during which there should be less interference. Ekstrand (1972) reviewed a great deal of research consistent with the conclusion that less is forgotten during the period of sleep.

Unfortunately, these results are not conclusive evidence against the decay theory. Decay theorists (Wickelgren, 1977) have argued that the rate of decay is slower during sleep. Particularly compelling for this point of view is the study of Hockey, Davies, and Gray (1972). They observed that sleep studies compared retention during the night (sleep condition) with retention during the day (waking condition). When they kept subjects awake during the night and had them sleep during the day, they found that night versus day, and not sleep was the critical factor. This result suggests that forgetting may vary with the daily rhythms of the body. This chapter further discusses the effect of time of day on retention in a later section.

Although the sleep studies do not support the interference hypothesis, it is nonetheless possible that forgetting is entirely a function of interference. Sleep studies test only the hypothesis that forgetting is due to retroactive interference, that is, that forgetting is influenced by other materials learned in the retention interval. As can be seen in Figures 7.12 or 7.18, a more potent factor might be proactive interference, that is, influence of material prior to retention. There is not a good theoretical understanding of proactive interference. Proactive interference, when it is properly demonstrated by experiments such as that of Keppel et al. (1968), involves accelerated loss of material that was brought to

---

[7]McGeoch (1942) considered the possibility that decay should be given a neural interpretation but believed such a view was unsupported by neural evidence. As he wrote, "No one has ever published experimental evidence that synaptic junctions decrease in intimacy, or in anything else, when one forgets" (p. 24). On this score the experimental evidence has changed dramatically in the last 50 years (e.g., Figure 7.8).

the same level of initial learning. It is extremely difficult to explain why materials brought to the same level of learning then display different forgetting functions over intervals in which the subjects' activities are identical.[8]

How much of forgetting can be attributed to interference remains very much an open issue.

Retention of Emotionally Charged Material

Before concluding the topic of retention, it is worth considering whether the retention of materials might be affected by their emotional content. As it turns out, there does appear to be an effect, but it is rather different from what most scholars initially expected.

Freud's Repression Hypothesis

An influential hypothesis about forgetting, advanced by Freud (1901), is that people actively repress unpleasant memories. There is little doubt that terrible experiences can produce disturbances of memory, although by their very nature they defy careful experimental analysis. People who have experienced traumatic events, such as the murder of a loved one, are often unable to recall many details and sometimes go into what are called fugue states, in which they temporarily lose all or most of their memories.

Freud thought that repression was much more common and did not require such extreme negative situations. In his view, **repression** was a major factor in promoting forgetting. Several laboratory studies have attempted to determine whether negative memories are repressed. Loftus and Burns (1982) looked at how well bank employees remembered a training film about a holdup in which a boy was brutally murdered. Memory for detail in the film was poorer than memory for a comparable film that did not involve the murder. Peters (1988) asked subjects to try to recognize a nurse who had given them an inoculation. Memory for the nurse was poorer than memory for a neutral helper. One problem with these studies is that subjects' encoding of the events may change as a function of the negative experience; for instance, subjects may choose not to look at the nurse's face. Thus the results may reflect poorer encoding rather than more rapid forgetting.

To show accelerated forgetting, the retention curve must be traced out. Meltzer (1930) had college students describe their experiences over the

---

[8]For an attempt at an explanation, see J. R. Anderson, 1983.

Table 7.6 *Mean Number of Associations Recalled out of 30 as a Function of Retention Interval and Emotionality.*

Immediate Recall		Delayed Recall	
Emotional	Neutral	Emotional	Neutral
24.1	27.6	21.1	18.3

December break immediately after returning to school from the holidays. Six weeks later he asked them to recall their experiences again. He found that more of the unpleasant memories had been forgotten in the interval. Such an experiment is open to other interpretations besides Freud's repression hypothesis. For instance, it is possible that the subjects chose not to rehearse the unpleasant memories.

Parkin, Lewinsohn, and Folkard (1982), in an extension of an experiment by Levinger and Clark (1961), looked at retention of associations to negative-charged words, such as *quarrel*, *angry*, and *fear*, in contrast to neutral words, such as *window*, *cow*, and *tree*. They looked at the number of associations recalled in the two categories immediately and at a 7-day delay. Table 7.6 shows their results. Consistent with Loftus and Burns and Peters, they found superior memory for the neutral words in an immediate test. However, at a delay the results were reversed and memory was better for the emotional words. These results are the opposite of what Freud's repression hypothesis would have predicted.

Although subjects may show worse encoding of negative memories, there is not a well-established relationship between valence of memory and its retention.

Arousal and Retention

The critical variable for retention may not be the negative emotions associated with the material but the arousal that the material produces in the subject. Kleinsmith and Kaplan (1963) had subjects learn neutral paired associations and monitored the subjects' galvanic skin response (GSR)[9] to identify the level of arousal while they were learning each paired associate. For each subject, Kleinsmith and Kaplan classified half the paired associates as learned with relatively high arousal and the other half as learned with low arousal. They then looked at retention of these paired associates at 2 min, 20 min, and 1 week. Figure 7.19 shows the results. Subjects displayed better memory for the low

[9]GSR measures the capacity of the skin to conduct electrical current by passing a small electrical current through the skin. Because one component of arousal is perspiration, this measure of skin conductance increases at points of arousal.

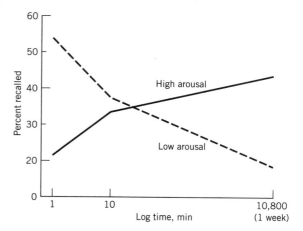

FIGURE 7.19. Differential recall of paired associates as a function of arousal level. *Source:* From L. J. Kleinsmith and S. Kaplan. Interaction of arousal and recall interval in nonsense syllable paired-associate learning. *Journal of Experimental Psychology, Volume 67.* Copyright © 1964 by the American Psychological Association. Reprinted by permission.

arousal items initially, but this result reversed at a delay, showing **reminiscence** (improvement with time) in the high arousal condition. Although the general interaction reported by Kleinsmith and Kaplan has been replicated, reminiscence in the high arousal condition is unusual. There is usually less forgetting of high arousal items rather than actual improvement. Levonian (1972) reviewed a series of studies that showed greater retention but often worse initial performance for high arousal items. One reason for the initially poor performance is that subjects may encode less of what they are presented in a high arousal state; however, they retain more of what they do encode.

The effect of arousal on memory appears to go beyond specific items. Memory performance is enhanced when learning takes place after administration of drugs that are stimulants, such as amphetamines, caffeine, nicotine, picrotoxin, and strychnine (McGaugh & Dawson, 1971), and memory performance decreases after administration of depressants such as alcohol, marijuana, chlorpromazine, ether, or nitrous oxide (e.g., Steinberg & Summerfield, 1957). Learning tends to be best at times of day associated with highest arousal in the daily cycle (Eysenck, 1982). Exactly why there is this relationship between learning and arousal is something of a mystery. However, it seems basically adaptive to remember better material acquired in high arousal states since high arousal is evidence that the material is important to remember.

Folkard, Monk, Bradbury, and Rosenthal (1977) reported a demonstration of the effects of time of day. The average young person is at the highest level of arousal somewhere between noon and 8 P.M., depending on the measure of arousal (Folkard, 1983). In this study 13-year-olds memorized a story at either 9:00 in the morning or 3:00 in the afternoon. Folkard et al. looked at recall on an immediate test or a test at a 1-week delay. Figure 7.20 shows the results. Immediately, students showed better memory when they had studied at 9:00 in the morning, a time of relatively low arousal. In the retention test a week later, performance was better when children had studied at 3:00 in the afternoon, a time of relatively higher arousal.

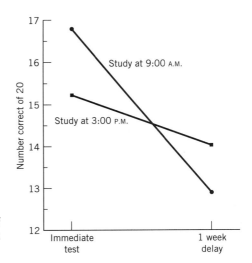

FIGURE 7.20. Effect of time of day of learning on retention of a story. (From Folkard et al., 1977).

Retention is better for material learned in high arousal states.

Eyewitness Memory and Flashbulb Memories

The preceding results have some interesting implications for eyewitness testimony. A witness who sees a crime is given very high weighting in the deliberations of a jury. If the Freudian hypothesis had any validity, eyewitness reports might be suspect at least in cases of awful crimes. The results reviewed on arousal might lead to just the opposite conjecture. Apparently lawyers have conflicting views as to whether high arousal leads to accurate testimony. Most defense lawyers think high arousal impairs face recognition, whereas most prosecutors do not (Brigham, 1981). Perhaps their beliefs just reflect what is best for the positions they argue in court.

In fact, eyewitness testimony is often quite inaccurate. People who swear earnestly and honestly that they saw a person at a crime are often wrong. One of the more peculiar cases (described in Baddeley, 1990) involved a psychologist, Donald Thompson, who had appeared on a television program discussing eyewitness testimony. A few weeks later he was picked up and identified by a woman as having raped her at the exact time he was on television. The woman had indeed been raped at that time, but the television had been on while she was being raped so she had confused his face with that of the rapist.

Easterbrook (1959) wrote an analysis of the effects of high levels of arousal on eyewitness testimony. He reviewed some of the research on arousal in animals that showed that arousal resulted in narrower attention. For example, E. E. Johnson (1952) had found that water-deprived animals displayed less latent learning of a maze, and Bruner, Matter, and Papanek (1955) had found

Mistaken identity: The men on the left and right were arrested for the crimes performed by the man in the middle.

that food-deprived animals learned less about various features in maze running. On the basis of these studies, Easterbrook hypothesized that humans in conditions of extreme arousal tend to focus on just a few details and do not encode the entire situation. This view has been called the weapon focus hypothesis, because victims of violent crimes may zoom in on the weapon and not even encode the criminal's face. The research on extreme arousal in humans does indicate generally poorer memory (see Deffenbacher, 1983, for a review), which may be because of poorer initial encoding. What is actually encoded may be retained better, reflecting the advantage of high arousal.

A general theory in psychology known as the **Yerkes–Dodson law** (Yerkes & Dodson, 1908) claims that there is an optimal level of arousal for performance on any task and that performance is poor at low or high levels of arousal and best at intermediate levels of arousal. This general law may apply to memory. Higher degrees of arousal lead to better retention. On the other hand, as arousal increases a person becomes more narrowly focused and only encodes a smaller amount of the available information. Thus intermediate levels of arousal might be best because a person can encode most of the material (arousal not too high) and show good retention (arousal high enough). The Yerkes–Dodson law has interesting implications for test anxiety: a little test anxiety may improve performance on a test, but too much is detrimental.

A related phenomenon concerns what are called **flashbulb memories** (Brown & Kulik, 1977)—memories for sudden, significant events that people feel have been burned into their minds forever. Many people report flashbulb memories for where they were when they learned of or saw the *Challenger* explosion in 1986. People of my generation have this feeling about when they learned of the Kennedy assassination in 1963, and people of an earlier generation have the same feeling about hearing of the bombing of Pearl Harbor in 1941. These memories are extremely emotionally-charged, and people can vividly recollect years later many details of their receipt of the news. Partly because of the high emotional overtones, there is an impression of great accuracy in these details. It has been proposed that some special memory mechanism may be responsible for the extreme vividness of these memories. Whether these memories are particularly accurate is unclear (Neisser, 1982). McCloskey, Wible, and Cohen (1988) interviewed 29 subjects 1 week after the *Challenger* accident and again 9 months later. They found that, although subjects still reported vivid memories 9 months later, they had forgotten and distorted information. Somewhat different results were obtained in a more recent study of subjects' memories of the 1989 San Francisco earthquake (Palmer, Schreiber, & Fox, 1991). People who experienced the earthquake firsthand showed enhanced retention of many details of their experience, whereas subjects who only watched it on TV did not. The critical factor may have been the firsthand nature of the earthquake experience. Flashbulb memories may simply be a special case of the generally better retention of material learned in a high arousal state.

People may encode less of what they experience in a high arousal state, but they may better retain what they do encode.

Final Reflections

Lay people typically view forgetting as one of the most frustrating aspects of their minds. However, numerous memory theorists have pointed out that forgetting can be quite adaptive. Maintaining a memory has costs, both because of the physical cost of storing it and because it can intrude when it is not wanted. Every other system that stores records (e.g., libraries, computer file systems, personal records of bills and payments) eventually reaches its capacity for storage and must throw something out. It is in the interest of our memories, too, to forget (throw out) those things that are not useful.

The factors that influence retention can be seen as examples of memory throwing out the less useful information. The retention and spacing functions in memory mirror similar functions in the environment. These environmental functions measure how likely the information is to be useful. Item-based interference can be understood in terms of a similar tendency to favor likely memories. When an item like *frog* appears, it is likely that we will need to retrieve some memory involving it. As an item is associated with more memories, any particular memory is less likely to be the one that is needed when the item appears.

An interesting question, considered in detail in Chapter 8, is whether forgetting amounts to the actual loss of the information from memory or whether we just no longer can retrieve the information. Often, retrieval failure is the better interpretation of forgetting. Less useful memories may not be truly lost, they may just become less accessible. There are many analogies in information storage systems. Less useful books in libraries are often moved to auxiliary storage buildings where they are not so readily accessible. Data not currently used in computer systems are stored on tapes, which can be a bother to retrieve and read.

Nelson (1971, 1978) conducted a series of experiments to show that material that subjects can no longer recall or recognize is still there. Subjects learned paired associates and were then retested at delays varying from 2 to 4 weeks. Nelson identified items that subjects could no longer recall or recognize in the retention test. A subject may have learned a pair like *43–dog* but could no longer recall or recognize it. Subjects then learned a new list that involved either the old paired associate, *43–dog*, or a repairing, such as *43–house*. He found that subjects were able to better learn the unchanged *43–dog* even though they could not recall or recognize having seen it from their earlier learning experiences. They showed savings in relearning for old material. Although this result does not establish that everything that has been forgotten is still there, it does show that there are some remnants of some memories that we no longer retrieve. It may make more sense to think of

People with first-hand experiences have flashbulb memories of the San Francisco earthquake.

forgetting as resulting in memories becoming less and less available rather than being deleted.

The memory system makes more available those memories that are more likely to be useful.

Further Readings

Two reviews of the classic research on retention are found in works by Postman (1971) and Wickelgren (1977). There has been a recent revival of interest in the shape of the retention functions, as indicated by articles such as that written by Wixted and Ebbesen (1991). Bahrick (1984) presents some data on retention functions over 50 years, in which he characterizes their asymptotic levels as being in a "perma store." J. R. Anderson (1983c) reviews research on interference using the more sensitive latency measure. Neisser (1982) presents a series of articles concerned with the relationship between memory and everyday life. Loftus (1979) discusses research relevant to eyewitness testimony.

8

Retrieval of Memories

Overview

This chapter considers issues about the retrieval of information from memory. The retrieval process logically follows the acquisition and retention processes addressed in the two previous chapters. Retrieval is perhaps the most critical process in that often information can be in memory and yet not retrieved. Chapter 7 ended with the research of Nelson which demonstrated that subjects enjoyed savings in relearning for memories they could no longer recall or recognize. That research raised the tantalizing possibility that people may never truly forget memories, but rather just lose access to them. Unfortunately, there is no resolution as to whether this haunting possibility is really true, but it is possible to come to some understanding of how memories can be unavailable for recall in one situation and yet show their influences in another situation. This chapter reviews the three main approaches to this issue.

1. *The Relationship between Various Explicit Measures of Recall.* Everyone has had the experience of being unable to recall something on one occasion but able to recall the same thing on some other occasion. Although memory is inherently variable, some ways of testing memory are more sensitive than others. The most common example of this situation is the different performance people display on recognition versus recall tests. For instance, students almost always claim that multiple-choice questions are easier than fill-in-the-blank questions.

2. *Interactions between Study and Test.* How well people perform on a test of memory depends not only on the conditions of test but also on the relationship of these conditions to the conditions of learning. Many of us have had the experience of returning to a place we have not been to for years and being flooded with memories that we had "forgotten" we had. Or, we have gone to see a movie that we seem to have forgotten and find ourselves remembering everything once we begin to watch. Apparently, being placed back in the context in which these memories were learned makes them available again. A great deal of research has been done on such effects. Such interactions may underlie some of forgetting, in that with the passage of time people may lose access to cues that had allowed them to recall their memories.

3. *Implicit Measures of Memory.* People know many things of which they are quite unaware. If explicitly asked about these things they may draw a blank, but in an appropriate circumstance they give evidence of what they know. For instance, students often claim that they have completely forgotten what they have learned in abstract mathematics courses, but they are nonetheless able to relearn the material faster (just as Nelson's subjects were able to relearn the paired associates faster). This chapter reviews some of the many ways in which people give evidence of things that they cannot consciously remember.

These three topics reflect the shift of interests in the psychology of memory. Research on the relationship between explicit measures of memory was an important topic in the 1960s and 1970s. Research on interactions between study and test was an important topic in the 1970s and 1980s. Research on implicit memories has been an important topic in the 1980s and 1990s. As some understanding of one topic was reached, attention shifted to the next topic.

People's memory performance depends on the type of memory test and its relationship to the conditions at study.

The Relationship Between Various Explicit Measures of Memory

There is ample evidence that information can be stored away in our long-term memory and yet cannot be retrieved in some circumstances. As already noted, the most common demonstration of this phenomenon involves contrasts of recognition memory tests and recall tests. People typically do better on recognition tests (although cases in which this outcome is reversed will be discussed). Using a history test as an example, a student who is unable to recall which U.S. president followed Wilson, might well be able to recognize that Harding was that president. How much we can remember is in part a function of the conditions under which we have to retrieve information from memory.

Chapter 7 discussed why recognition memory might be superior to recall memory. The Association Equation assumed that the activation of a memory record increased with the number of associated cues in the environment. Thus a recall question, such as, "Who was the president after Wilson?" presents one relevant cue, namely, *Wilson*. A recognition question, such as, "Was Harding the president after Wilson?" presents two relevant cues, namely, *Harding* and *Wilson*. With two cues, the memory record is more active and more likely to be recalled.[1]

---

[1]Actually, *president* could also be counted as a cue, in which case the comparison would be of two versus three cues.

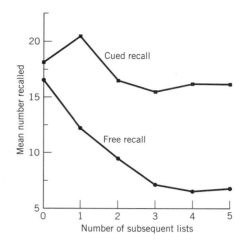

FIGURE 8.1. Number of words recalled as a function of number of subsequent lists studied. (From Tulving & Psotka, 1971).

How well we can remember something depends in part on how well we can regenerate the cues to which the memory is associated. An experiment by Tulving and Psotka (1971) showed that what might appear to be recall failure may really be loss of access to appropriate retrieval cues. Subjects saw up to six lists of 24 words. Each list consisted of four members of each of six categories, for example, *dog, cat, horse*, and *cow* from the mammal category. After they had studied all the lists, subjects were tested for their memory of the first list under two conditions:

1. *Free recall.* They were to recall the words from the list in any order.
2. *Cued recall.* They were shown the six category names and asked to recall the words in any order.

Figure 8.1 shows the number of words successfully recalled from list 1 as a function of the number of subsequent lists learned. The free recall data show a standard result of retroactive interference in that recall goes down as a function of the number of subsequent lists. When subjects were given the category labels as cues, there was relatively little forgetting. Tulving and Psotka argued that forgetting is largely loss of access to retrieval cues, such as category labels.

Much of memory failure can be attributed to loss of access to appropriate retrieval cues.

Recognition Versus Recall of Word Lists

Experimental psychologists have studied extensively the relationship between recognition and recall. Reviewing this research offers an opportunity to test whether the difference between the two memory measures is simply that recognition provides more retrieval cues. Much of this research has been concerned with understanding memory for a list of words. In a typical experiment, subjects might be shown 30 words at the rate of one every 2 sec and then are asked to recall as many of the words as they can in any order (a free recall test) or to recognize the 30 words when they are mixed in with 30 distractors. Such experiments often show that subjects have near perfect recognition memory for the 30 words, but may be able to recall fewer than 10 words.

The issue of the difference between recall and recognition is much larger than the issue of how people recall versus recognize such lists of words. Much more complex memories can be tapped by recall or recognition tests, as any student can testify on the basis of exam experiences. Still, learning lists of words has been the focus of much of the research, and this section concentrates on this paradigm.

As discussed in the previous chapter, subjects appear to be learning associations between items they have to remember and the experimental context, which includes information about the external environment and the subject's internal state. List learning can be viewed as paired-associate learning in which subjects form associations between words and some representation of the experimental context. This representation of the list is sometimes referred to as the **list context**. Figure 8.2 shows a representation of the memory records that might be formed. A separate record encodes the appearance of each word in the list context. The list context is associated to all these records. Each word is also associated to the record encoding that it occurred in the list context.

In a recall task, subjects are informed of the list they are to recall and must retrieve the words. Thus they are given the list context as the cue and must retrieve memories of words seen in that context. Because the list con-

FIGURE 8.2. Memory records encoding some of the words in a list and their connections with the list context.

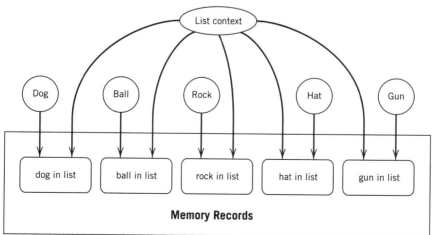

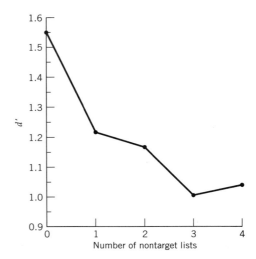

FIGURE 8.3. Recognition memory for words as a function of the number of nontarget lists in which they appeared. (From Anderson & Bower, 1974).

text is associated to all the records, this is a massive interference paradigm; it is not surprising that performance is usually poor in a recall test. In contrast, subjects in a recognition test are given basically two cues to memory—the list context and the word to be recognized. The word is a much better cue than the list context because there is no experimental interference involving the word. It is not surprising, then, that recognition memory is much better.

Anderson and Bower (1974) did an experiment in which subjects studied a number of lists of words, with certain words reappearing in varying numbers of lists. They found that as the same word appeared in other lists, recognition memory for whether the word appeared in a target list deteriorated. Figure 8.3 shows how recognition performance, measured by a *d*-prime (*d'*) measure,[2] declined with the greater number of additional lists, just as predicted from this associative analysis. There would be a different list context element for each list. Thus not only would there be multiple associations to the list context, as seen in Figure 8.2, there would also be multiple associations to the words. As a word appears in more lists, it acquires more associations to other list contexts, which interfere with one another.

In list memory, a recognition test involves retrieving from both the word and the list context, whereas a free recall test involves retrieving from just the list context.

---

[2]Later this section discusses the d-prime measure, which has been advanced as a superior measure of recognition memory.

Retrieval Strategies and Free Recall

In free recall situations, many subjects take special actions to help themselves remember the words, such as forming special associations among the words. One subject (J. R. Anderson, 1972) on the second study of a list of words generated a narrative to connect the words as follows (the number beside each word indicates where it occurred in a list of 40; capitalized words indicate words the subject was supposed to recall):

1. garrison—GARRISON, LIEUTENANT, DIGNITARY.

3. vulture—VULTURE . . . bird, there was a bird PRESENT . . . VULTURE, bird . . . GARRISON.

13. lieutenant—LIEUTENANT is in the GARRISON . . . and he is being attacked by a VULTURE that came through the window.

21. scorpion—SCORPION, remember VULTURE with SCORPION, the GARRISON is loaded with kooky animals.

28. mercenary —the LIEUTENANT was the MERCENARY, right.

31. officer—the LIEUTENANT is an OFFICER in the . . . oh . . . he didn't obey the duties.

32. destroyer—the LIEUTENANT is an OFFICER, DESTROYER, MERCENARY . . . the LIEUTENANT is too much . . . he's a DESTROYER.

37. sideburns—SIDEBURNS, the LIEUTENANT has SIDEBURNS, the DIGNITARY has a BEARD.

The subject was building up a set of associations among the words. Then at time of recall the subject used these interword associations as an aid to recalling the words:

> The LIEUTENANT . . . lieu-ten-ant . . . is a MERCENARY with SIDE-BURNS . . . DESTROYER . . . OFFICER . . . who's in the GARRISON . . . and is being attacked by VULTURES and SCORPIONS . . . and a . . .

As the subject said each capitalized word she wrote it down as part of the recall. Subjects often use interword associations to avoid having to cue all their recall from just the list context. If they can retrieve one word, they can use it to cue recall of associated words, and these to cue recall of associated words, and so on.

Much of the behavior of subjects in a free recall experiment can be understood in terms of their attempts to come up with additional retrieval cues to help recall. The subject just quoted was spontaneously using a story-making strategy to help retrieve the words. Bower and Clark (1969) performed an experiment that looked explicitly at the effect of story making on memory for a list of words. They told their subjects to commit to memory lists of 10 unrelated nouns by making up a story involving the words. One subject made up the following story:

A LUMBERJACK DARTed out of a forest, SKATEd around a HEDGE past a COLONY of DUCKS. He tripped on some FURNITURE, tearing his STOCKING, while hastening toward the PILLOW where his MISTRESS lay.

The control group was given equal time to just study the words. Subjects in the two groups studied 12 lists of 10 words. At the end of the experiment they were asked to recall all 120 words. The experimental group was able to recall 94 percent of the words, whereas the control group could only recall 14 percent. This dramatic difference is testimony to the importance of retrieval strategies for cuing memory in a free recall experiment.

Story making is just one of the many ways in which memory can be improved in a free recall experiment. Another method is to organize the words to help the formation of associations among them. Consider the following list: *Dog, cat, mouse, chair, sofa, table, milk, eggs, butter.* The list is organized into categories—three animals, three pieces of furniture, and three food items. If subjects detect such a categorical organization, they take advantage of it to improve their recall. They can recall many more words when a list is explicitly organized into categories, as in this example, than when the same words are randomly spread throughout the list (Dallett, 1964). If subjects recall one word from a category, they tend to recall the rest, and then move on to the next category. Their memories are further improved if at the time of test they are cued with the category names, for example, *animal* and *food* (Tulving & Ostler, 1968; Tulving & Pearlstone, 1966). Even though such words do not appear in the list, subjects can use them to organize recall by generating various members of the category and then trying to recognize which ones they saw in the list.

One theory of how subjects recall items in a free recall test is that they have some strategy for generating words that might be in the list. They may consider words that pop into their minds, recall stories they made up, think of instances of categories they noticed. Whenever they think of a word, they engage in a recognition judgment to see if it is a word they studied. They recall the word if they can recognize it. This theory of recall is called the **generate-recognize theory** (Anderson & Bower, 1972; Kintsch, 1970b) because it assumes that subjects first generate candidate words and then try to recognize them.

The generate-recognize theory of free recall assumes that subjects use various strategies for generating words and then try to recognize words that they generate.

Mnemonic Strategies for Recall

Everyday life presents situations similar to the free recall situation. We might want to make a series of points in a speech that has to be delivered without notes, or we remember a grocery list without writing it down. Waiters are often expected to take orders without notes. Memory can be greatly enhanced in such situations by the use of some method to systematically cue memories for the information to be recalled. There are several such **mnemonic techniques**. This section describes two of the more famous techniques, the pegword method and the method of loci, and shows how their effectiveness can be understood in terms of the generate-recognize theory.

Pegword Method. The pegword method involves learning a set of associations between numbers and words, as in the following well-known set:

One is a bun

Two is a shoe

Three is a tree

Four is a door

Five is a hive

Six is sticks

Seven is heaven

Eight is a gate

Nine is wine

Ten is a hen

Suppose you want to remember the following grocery list: milk, hot dogs, dog food, tomatoes, bananas, and bread. You would take the first item and try to associate it to the element that corresponds to one—bun. Perhaps you would develop an image of a bun floating in milk. Similarly, you would develop images for the rest of the list: hot dogs sticking out of a shoe like toes, a tree bearing cans of dog food as fruit, a door with a tomato for a handle, a hive with bananas flying in and out of it, and sticks that when broken turn out to be bread (i.e. breadsticks). These images are bizarre, but as reviewed in Chapter 6, they are effective ways of associating items. When you wanted to recall the list you could retrieve the word that corresponded to one, namely, *bun*, and then retrieve the item associated with it, namely, *milk*, and then continue through the rest of the list. The pegwords, such as *bun*, can be used over and over again to learn new lists (Bower & Reitman, 1972).

This technique is very successful and confers on the user near perfect memory for the items to be remembered. The basic technique capitalizes on two things. First, memorizing a sequence of items, such as *bun, shoe, tree*, ahead of time provides an orderly way of going through the material to prompt recall of each item. Second, the concrete pegwords provide excellent cues to memory when combined with learning by imagery. Both these advantages have their effect by helping the person generate items for recognition.

The Method of Loci. Another classic mnemonic technique, the method of loci, also has its effect by promoting good organization in recall situations. This method involves using some familiar path in life and associating to-be-remembered items to locations on that path. For instance, you might know a path that goes from a service station past a police station, a department store, a movie theater, and a restaurant, to a beach. Suppose you want to use this path to memorize the same list of six items: milk, hot dogs, dog food, tomatoes, bananas, and bread. You would mentally walk along the path forming visual images that link the locations and the items. Thus you might imagine the service station attendant pumping milk from the gas pump, a police officer at the station smoking a hot dog, a mannequin holding dog food in the department store window, a movie theater advertising *The Attack of the Killer Tomatoes*, the restaurant's menu written on a banana, and loaves of bread washed ashore by waves at the beach. To recall these items at a later date, you would walk down this path in your mind, reviving the images associated with each location. Like the pegword method, this method has proved an effective way for learning multiple lists (Christen & Bjork, 1976; Ross & Lawrence, 1968).

Both the method of loci and the pegword method combine the same two principles to achieve high levels of recall. They start with a fixed sequence of elements that the memorizer already knows. Then they use vivid visual images to assure that the new items get associated to these elements. Their effectiveness can be understood in terms of the generate-recognize theory. They are designed to try to guarantee success in the difficult generation phase. The assumption is that once the items are generated, memory will be able to recognize them. The next section considers situations (different from those created by these mnemonic techniques) in which that assumption is not valid.

The pegword method and the method of loci facilitate recall by helping to generate candidates for recognition.

Evaluation of the Generate-Recognize Theory

Much evidence suggests that in many situations subjects try to recall by generating possible candidates and seeing which they can recognize. As in the example given earlier, subjects can sometimes be observed to do this. Manipulations that affect the organization of lists (like story telling, categorization, or mnemonic strategy) have much stronger effects on recall than on recognition (Kintsch, 1970b; Mandler, 1967). This result makes sense because organization should help subjects generate items for recognition but should do little to help them recognize the words. Subjects who are instructed that there will be a memory test do better than incidental learning subjects on a free recall test but not on a recognition test (Eagle & Leiter, 1964). This result makes sense because the intentional learning subjects would know to engage in appropriate organizational strategies.

The generate-recognize theory seems to imply that recognition memory would always be better than recall memory, because recall involves both generating the words and recognizing them. This assumption came in for some critical evaluation in a series of experimental investigations reported by Tulving and Thomson (1973) and Watkins and Tulving (1975). Subjects studied pairs of words, such as *train–black*, and were told they would be tested on their memory for the second word (e.g., *black*). The pairs of words were chosen because they were weak associates; that is, people will occasionally generate *black* as an associate to *train* in a free association test.

Subjects were tested in two critical conditions:

Recall condition. Subjects were presented with cues, such as *train*, and were asked to recall the target words, here *black*. Note that this is not the free recall condition for which the generate-recognize theory was developed; this condition provides a much better cue for recall (namely, *train*) than does the typical free recall experiment in which the subject only has the list context.

Recognition condition. Subjects were presented with a high associate of the target word, for example, *white* (people frequently generate *black* as an associate of *white*), and asked to generate four free associates to the word. Typically, one of these free associates was the target word, *black*. The subjects were asked to judge if any of the words generated was the target word. Thus the subjects were put in a situation in which they would have a high probability of generating the word, and their only difficulty should be recognizing the word.

The results from such an experiment can be classified according to whether a word is recalled and, independent of recall, whether the word can be recognized. Table 8.1 shows some data from Tulving and Wiseman (1975) classified according to these factors. The table reports the proportion of words in each of the four states obtained by crossing these factors. Two results from this paradigm are thought to challenge seriously the generate-recognize theory. One is that memory performance is sometimes higher in the recall condition than in the recognize condition. Table 8.1 shows that subjects can display a higher probability of recalling *black* to *train* (60%) than of recognizing *black* (40%) when they generate it as an associate to *white*. This result is surprising because it seems to violate the common wisdom that recognition is easier than recall.

The second result involves a comparison of the conditional probability of recognition of a word, given that it is recalled, with the unconditional probability of recognition of the word. The unconditional probability of recognition

Table 8.1 *Proportion of Words in Various Conditions of Tulving and Wiseman (1975)*

	Recognized	Not Recognized	Totals
Recalled	.30	.30	.60
Not Recalled	.10	.30	.40
Totals	.40	.60	1.00

is calculated by dividing the number of words recognized by the number tested. The unconditional probability is 40 percent in Table 8.1. The conditional probability is the number of recalled and recognized words divided by the total number recalled. The conditional probability might be expected to be much higher than the unconditional probability and close to 1.0 on the view that any word that can be recalled should be able to pass the easier recognition test. In fact, the conditional probability is only slightly higher than the unconditional probability. In Table 8.1, it is 30/60 = 50 percent, which is only slightly higher than 40 percent, the unconditional probability. Many words can be recalled but not recognized when they are generated in the free association test. Failure to recognize recallable words is called **recognition failure**. Although these results do not directly address the question of what is happening in a free-recall experiment, they do call into question the view that recognition is easier than recall—one of the basic assumptions of the generate-recognize theory of free recall.

On careful analysis both results turn out to be much less surprising than they seem at first. Consider the cues made available for the subjects to access their memory in the two cases. In the recall case the cue was *train*; in the recognition case it was *black*. In each case there was just one cue. In cases in which recognition is superior to recall, the recognition test has provided more cues to memory. Given that the subjects were told that they were supposed to remember *black* and this is what they were shown in a recognition test, *black* might seem to be the better cue than *train*. However, it is conceivable that *train* is a better cue for the memory record than *black*. These words were not chosen randomly—*train* was chosen because it has a low but nonzero probability of evoking *black* in a free association test, not vice versa. Subjects were also instructed to study the words so that they could recall *black* given *train*. Rabinowitz, Mandler, and Barsalou (1977) turned the typical experiment around. They looked at the relationship between recognition of *black* (as before) and recall of *train* given *black* as a prompt (turned around). They found that recall was much poorer in the reverse direction (*black* as a prompt for *train*), confirming that target words (*black*) are poorer cues to memory than cue words (*train*). Moreover, recognition failure was much lower when conditional on recall in the reverse direction. That is, the probability was very high that the subject could recognize *black* in a recognition test conditional on being able to recall *train*. Tulving and his associates were able to get recall to be better than recognition because they created a situation in which the recall test provided better cues for memory than did the recognition test.

Recall tests can produce better memory performance than recognition tests when they provide better cues for retrieval.

Measuring Recognition Memory: The High-Threshold Model

This discussion of recognition memory has ignored the issue of just how to conceive of and measure recognition memory. Suppose that a subject recognizes all 30 words in a list. That might seem to be good memory, but what if the subject also claims to recognize all 30 distractors? Then the subject is obviously guessing and should not be given credit for high-recognition memory. Of course, subjects do not typically behave in this way. Typical subjects might say that they recognize 25 of the words they saw and that they fail to recognize 5. They might also say that they recognize 5 of the distractors and correctly reject the other 25. Such a false acceptance is often called a **false alarm**. How can psychologists assign a measure to how good the memory of a subject is? They need some way of combining the probability of accepting a target—$P(\text{YES}|\text{Target}) = 25/30 = 5/6$—and the probability of accepting a distractor—$P(\text{YES}|\text{Distractor}) = 5/30 = 1/6$—to get a single measure of recognition memory.

One model for measuring recognition memory, the high-threshold model (Murdock, 1974), views false acceptances by subjects as reflecting guesses. In this example, with 5 false acceptances, the subject is guessing 1/6 of the time. The high-threshold model assumes that the subject says that the item is a target if it is actually recognized or if it is not actually recognized and the subject guesses. Thus, if p is the probability of actually recognizing the item, and g is the probability of guessing, the probability of say yes to target is

$$P(\text{YES}|\text{Target}) = p + (1 - p)\,g$$

A little algebra reveals the following correction for guessing to obtain the true probability:

$$p = \frac{P(\text{YES}|\text{Target}) - P(\text{YES}|\text{Distractor})}{1 - P(\text{YES}|\text{Distractor})}$$

substituting $P(\text{YES}|\text{Distractor})$ for g. In the example, where $P(\text{YES}|\text{Target}) = 5/6$ and $P(\text{YES}|\text{Distractor}) = 1/6$, the actual probability, p, of recognizing a target, can be estimated to be $p = .8$.

In measuring recognition memory it is necessary to correct for the subject's tendency to false alarm to items not studied.

Signal Detectability Theory

Psychology has developed a more sophisticated and useful way of measuring recognition memory than this simple correction for guessing, which turns on a deeper understanding of what is happening when the subject commits a false alarm. Sometimes a false alarm reflects a wild guess on the subject's part (as is assumed in the analysis of the preceding section), but other times it reflects a deeply held belief. For instance, subjects can be asked to assign confidences to their recognition judgments, for example, on a 1 to 7 scale, with 1 indicating a guess and 7 indicating high confidence. Subjects identify some of their false alarms (and some of their correct recognitions) as guesses, but assign considerable confidence to others. More than once I have had heated arguments with subjects who insisted that I was wrong when I informed them that a word did not occur on a list.

How can a subject hallucinate that a word occurred on the list? It is important to appreciate what a recognition experiment is from a subject's perspective. A distractor word has occurred in many contexts, and the subject may confuse some other context with the list context. Anderson and Bower (1974; see Figure 8.3) presented words in multiple lists. Subjects frequently thought a word occurred in a target list if it occurred in the preceding list, consistent with the notion that subjects were somewhat confused about just what context defined the list context. Subjects decided that a word was studied if it occurred in a context similar to the study context.

Researchers have suggested other bases for deciding whether a word has occurred in a target list. As discussed later, a common idea is that subjects use the raw sense of familiarity that they have about the word; a word that occurred in the most recent list might seem particularly familiar, and subjects use this feeling of familiarity to infer they have seen the word. Words not in the target list might be familiar for other reasons and so might be the source of false alarms.

There are probably other bases for making recognition judgments besides similarity of context and familiarity. Abstracting over these various possible bases, a word can be considered as offering some evidence for being in the target list. A word that is in the target list usually offers greater evidence than a word that is not, but sometimes a word not in the list offers more evidence than a word in the list.

A methodology called **signal detectability theory** has been developed to help psychologists model how subjects make decisions when faced with the need to discriminate between two stimuli of this kind. In the case of recognition memory, the assumption is that there is a distribution of evidence for list

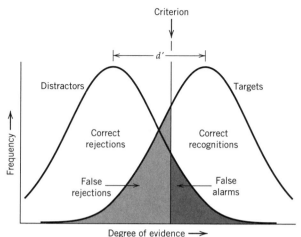

FIGURE 8.4. Distribution of evidence for targets and distractors (foils) in a recognition memory experiment.

membership for those words that are in the list and another distribution of list membership for distractor words. Figure 8.4 illustrates these two distributions as normal distributions, which is what they are usually assumed to be. These distributions reflect the probability that a particular word has a particular degree of evidence. As shown, most target words have higher evidence than most distractor words, but there is some overlap in the distributions, and some distractor words show more evidence than some target words.

What subjects do is to select some criterion of evidence such that if the word is above this criterion they accept it and if it is below this criterion they reject it. The target words above the criterion point correspond to those words that are correctly recognized. The distractor words above the criterion point correspond to the false alarms. The proportions of these two types of words can be used to estimate how far apart the two distributions are in terms of distance from the center of the target distribution to the center of the distractor distribution. This distance is measured in terms of standard deviations, often referred to as a **d' (*d*-prime) measure.**[3]

Signal detectability theory is not an esoteric model that applies only to deciding whether a word has been seen in a list memory experiment. Judgments of this sort are constantly involved in memory decision judgments. When we decide whether we have met someone before, we are judging some sense of familiarity in the person's face and trying to decide whether it is the kind of familiarity we would associate with a face we have seen before or whether it reflects the familiarity associated with a novel face. When we try to remember whether we have been in a particular location, we are judging how similar that location is to other locations we have been. Signal detectability

[3]Massaro (1989) is one source for the details of how to compute these quantities.

theory provides a helpful way to model these decisions. It has also been used to describe sensory judgments, such as whether a faint tone is heard. Indeed, the signal detectability methodology was originally developed to describe sensory judgments.

This analysis of recognition memory implies that a subject's performance on a recognition memory test is a function of how difficult it is to discriminate distractors from targets. Presumably, if the targets were words and the distractors were numbers, subjects would display very good recognition memory. In this case, the two distributions would be very far apart in terms of degree of evidence. If the distractors were very similar, recognition memory would be poor. For instance, subjects fare worse in recognition memory tests in which the distractors are semantically similar to the targets (Underwood & Freund, 1968).

Signal detectability theory measures recognition memory in terms of how far the average evidence for targets is from the average evidence for distractors.

Conclusions About Recognition Versus Recall

This section started with the general observation that recognition is better than recall. Although this phenomenon could be attributed to the more cues a recognition memory test usually provides, there are complications. For instance, subjects can use mnemonic strategies to generate additional cues and so improve their performance in free recall. Just how well a subject does on a recognition test depends on the context (cues) in which the test is given and the difficulty of the distractors. Thus the exact level of performance in recall and recognition tests can depend on many factors.

Interactions Between Study and Test

The preceding section treated recognition and recall as measures that generally differ in their sensitivity to memory. However, sometimes one testing procedure does not uniformly reveal more memory than another; rather, different test procedures are more appropriate for material learned in different ways. The next section considers manipulations of context at study and at test.

Context Dependency of Memory

Chapter 7 introduced the idea of **context-dependent memory**, that is, memories get associated to the context in which they are studied. The preceding section discussed the idea that items get associated to some representation of the

---

list context. A person's ability to recall an item depends on the person's ability to reproduce the list context. This ability might well be a function of the similarity between the context at study and the context at test. There is evidence that subjects have difficulty recalling items when the context changes between study and test. Perhaps the most dramatic demonstration of this fact was provided by Godden and Baddeley (1975). They had divers learn a list of 40 words either on land or underwater, and they had the divers recall the words either on land or underwater. Figure 8.5 displays the results of this experiment. Subjects displayed much better memory when the context of the recall test matched the context in which the list was studied. The interpretation is that some of the cues that the divers had associated with the words were the contextual elements of water or land, and it was difficult to retrieve these items in the other context. This outcome portends a serious problem for diver education since much of it occurs on dry land but must be retrieved underwater.

The effect displayed in the Godden and Baddeley study is much larger than most other context effects reported (e.g., Smith, Glenberg, & Bjork, 1978), which have used less substantial manipulations of context. Several researchers have failed to find context effects at all (e.g., Fernandez & Glenberg, 1985; Saufley, Otaka, & Bavaresco, 1985). Eich (1985) argued that the magnitude of these effects depends on the degree to which the context is integrated into the memories. He contrasted two conditions in which subjects learned a list of nouns by means of imagery. In one condition subjects were to imagine the nouns alone, and in the other case they were to imagine the nouns integrated into the context. Eich found larger effects of context variation when subjects imagined the words integrated with the context. In terms of the cue-record representation (e.g., Figure 8.2), such integration manipulations can be thought of as affecting whether contextual elements, such as the experimental room, get associated as cues to the memory record.

FIGURE 8.5. Mean number of words recalled as a function of study and test environments. (From Godden & Baddeley, 1975).

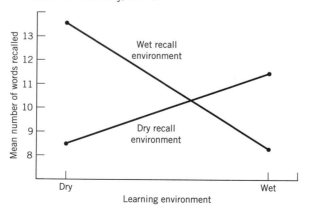

Context-dependency effects have interesting implications with respect to tasks such as exam taking. They suggest that people will do best on an exam if they study in the same context in which they will take the exam, and that test performance will be further enhanced if students try to integrate what they are studying with the test context. Unfortunately, it is not always easy to gain access to a test room or to get a match on many of the internal components of context.

When people integrate the context with their memories, they show enhanced recall if they are put back in that context.

State-Dependent Memory

The concept of context can be extended to the internal state of the subject, which can vary depending on whether the subject is happy or sad, hungry or not, excited or calm, and so on. In some cases subjects show better recall when their state at test matches their state at learning. This phenomenon is referred to as **state-dependent memory**. One dimension of state dependency on which there has been considerable research involves various drug-induced states. With drugs like alcohol and marijuana, there is some evidence that subjects show better recall if they study and are tested while sober or if they study and are tested while intoxicated than if they study in one state and are tested in another state (Eich, Weingartner, Stillman, & Gillin, 1975; Goodwin, Powell, Bremer, Hoine, & Stern, 1969). A representative experiment (Goodwin et al., 1969) from this area, illustrated in Figure 8.6, looked at the effect of being tested while sober or intoxicated with alcohol after studying while sober or intoxicated. Subjects on the first day (learning) were asked to make up eight

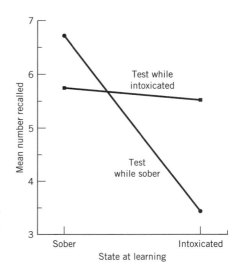

FIGURE 8.6. Mean number of errors of associative recall as a function of study and test states. (From Goodwin et al., 1969).

paired associates, and then on the second day (recall) to recall them. Subjects were able to recall more when their state at recall matched their state during study. Figure 8.6 also reflects another effect frequently found in this research: subjects performed worse when they studied while intoxicated. This result is particularly evident in the poor performance of subjects who studied while intoxicated and were tested while sober. Depressant drugs, such as alcohol, tend to lower the amount learned, and this effect often overwhelms any effects of state dependency. Subjects tend to show poor memory for material they learned while in an intoxicated state, independent of how they are tested. This outcome may in part reflect the effect of lack of arousal on retention. As reviewed in Chapter 7, there is better retention for material learned in a high arousal state.

Subjects can show better memory when their mental states at study and at test match.

Mood-Dependency and Mood-Congruence Effects

Similar state-dependent effects occur when internal state is defined in terms of mood. Figure 8.7 shows data from Eich and Metcalfe (1989) on the interaction between mood at study and at test. Subjects studied and recalled in happy or sad moods induced by listening to happy or sad music. Subjects learned words in a generate condition or a read condition, similar to the experiment of Slamecka and Graf (1978) described in Chapter 6; that is, subjects either read a to-be-remembered word (*vanilla*) or generated it to a cue that had very high probability of evoking it (e.g., *milkshake flavors: chocolate–*). Three effects are apparent in these data:

1. Replicating Slamecka and Graf, there was much higher recall when subjects generated the words.
2. There was a state-dependent effect, with better recall when the test mood matched the study mood.
3. The state dependency was much greater in the generate condition.

There have been frequent findings of weak or no state-dependent effects of mood. This is basically the result found in the read condition shown in Figure 8.7. As with the effects of external context, state-dependent effects are larger when the mood is integrated into the memories. The generate condition of Eich and Metcalfe can be viewed as achieving an integration of study mood with memory record. Study mood influences retrieval only if it is associated to the memory record.

Mood-congruency is a different but apparently stronger mood-dependent effect that may actually be the cause of the state-dependent effect. Mood

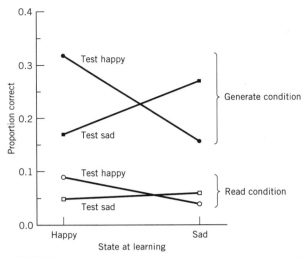

FIGURE 8.7. Mean proportion of generate and read items recalled as a function of encoding and retrieval moods. (From Eich and Metcalfe, 1989, Experiment 1).

congruency refers to the fact that people find it easier to remember happy memories when happy and sad memories when sad. It is important to understand the difference between state dependency and mood congruency. The state-dependent effect concerns the effect of the mood the subject was in during study on memory for all elements, including emotionally neutral items. The mood-congruent effect concerns memory for happy or sad material even if acquired in an emotionally neutral state. Both cases involve a match to test mood, but in one case the match is with the emotional state at learning and in the other case it is with the emotional content of the memory.

Blaney (1986) reported a review of such research. A typical study was conducted by Teasdale and Russell (1983). They had subjects learn a word list containing neutral, negative, or positive trait words. Before recall, an elated or depressed mood state was induced. Figure 8.8 shows the result of mood induction on mean recall of trait words. Subjects recalled many more words that matched their mood at test. In another study, Laird, Wagner, Halal, and Szegda (1982) looked at memory for anger-provoking editorials or humorous Woody Allen stories. Mood at test was induced by asking subjects either to frown or to smile. Smiling subjects recalled more of the Woody Allen material, whereas frowning subjects recalled more of the editorial material.

The results of mood-congruence effects can snowball for depressed patients. Once depressed, patients tend to remember unhappy events, which increases the depression, which increases the retrieval of unhappy events, and so on. At high levels of depression there is also an overall decrement in memory performance, not just for pleasant memories. Depressed subjects show lower memory performance on standard memory tests (e.g., Watts, Morris,

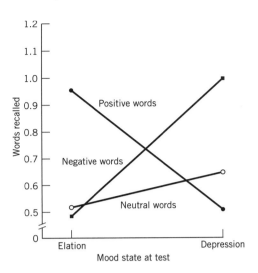

FIGURE 8.8. Recall of positive, negative and neutral trait words in elated and depressed mood states. *Source:* From J. D. Teasdale and M. L. Russel. Differential Effects of Induced Mood on the Recall of Positive, Negative, and Neutral Words. *British Journal of Clinical Psychology, Volume 22*, p. 163–171, Figure 1. Copyright © 1983 by the British Psychological Society. Reprinted by permission.

& MacLeod, 1987; Watts & Sharrock, 1987). Baddeley (1990) argued that depressed people put less effort into elaborative learning strategies. Watts, MacLeod, and Morris (1988) found that depressed patients show improved memory performance if they are encouraged to use memory strategies, such as interactive mental imagery.

Although mood-congruence and state-dependent mood effects differ in the experimental conditions that produce them, they probably reflect the same underlying mechanism. The mood the subject is in at test serves as one element to help cue memory. As a consequence, the subject shows better memory for things associated with that mood element. Mood congruence is produced because happy and sad memories are associated to the corresponding mood elements. State-dependent mood effects occur because in elaborating at study the subject associates these mood elements as cues to the memory records. In both cases, the effect is produced by overlap between the mood at test and the elements associated to the memory.

Subjects show better memory when their mood at test matches the mood elements they have integrated into their memories.

Encoding-Specificity Principle and Transfer-Appropriate Processing

This chapter has reviewed some special cases of context-dependent learning that manipulate the match between the cues at study and test. Tulving (1975) articulated a general principle of memory that captures such interactions. This **encoding-specificity principle** says that memory performance is best when the cues present at test match those that were encoded with the memory at study. A good illustration of the encoding-specificity principle is the difficulty people have recognizing someone they normally see dressed informally when they encounter that person dressed formally (or vice versa). Part of our recognition of such individuals is tied to the clothes they wear.

Bransford articulated a variant of this principle, known as **transfer-appropriate processing**. This principle focuses on the processes (rather than the cues) involved in the original encoding and at test. Bransford's principle claims that memory is best when subjects process the memory probe at test in the same way in which they process the material at study. A representative experiment showing such effects was performed by Morris, Bransford, and Franks (1977). Subjects processed words with reference to either their semantic properties or their phonetic properties. For example, for the word *hail*, semantic processing was induced by having the subject study the word with the associate *snow*, whereas phonetic processing was induced by having the subject study the word with the rhyme *pail*. At test subjects were cued for their recall of the words by being tested with either a different associate (e.g., *sleet*) or a different rhyme (e.g., *bail*).

Figure 8.9 illustrates two basic results from the Morris et al. study. First, replicating the results about depth of processing, semantic processing at encoding produced higher levels of recall. However, there was also an interaction such that a semantic associate was a better cue if the processing at encoding was semantic, whereas a rhyme was a better cue if the processing at encoding was phonetic. Since the cues were always changed from study to test, the results are not a matter of simple overlap in the cues. What is critical is the processing that these cues induced. Transfer-appropriate processing is further discussed in the section on implicit memory.

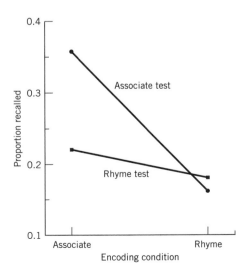

FIGURE 8.9. The interaction between the encoding condition and the recall condition(From Morris et al., 1977).

Memory is better when the cue at test is processed in the same way in which the memory was processed at study.

Reconstructive and Inferential Memory

One type of semantic processing that has frequently been investigated is inferential, or reconstructive, processing at test. People often cannot retrieve the memory they have studied, but can retrieve other memories that allow them to reconstruct or infer what the target memory must have been. A good deal of everyday recall depends on reconstructive memory. For example, if you saw the *Star Wars* trilogy some time ago, try to recall the plot. You will quickly find that you cannot remember many of the events and are inferring what happened. You will also find yourself unsure of whether you are actually remembering things or just inferring that they must have happened. Similar inferential processes can be shown in response to more direct questions. Try to answer the question, "Was Princess Lea related to Darth Vader?" You may not remember whether this relationship was ever directly asserted, but you may recall that Luke Skywalker was Princess Lea's brother and Darth Vader's son. Combining these two facts, you might infer that Princess Lea and Darth Vader were related. Or consider the question, "Was Darth Vader evil?" Again, you might not remember whether this trait was ever asserted in the movie series, but you can recall various events that allow you to answer this question in the affirmative. Thus people can use memories that they can retrieve to infer what must be true. This ability to extend our knowledge inferentially is an important additional attribute of our memory system.

The British psychologist F. C. Bartlett wrote an important treatise on memory in 1932 and is famous for emphasizing the reconstructive character of human memory. Neisser, the American psychologist, reemphasized the reconstructive character of memory in the 1960s. He described the process of reconstructing a memory from what could be retrieved as similar to the process a paleontologist follows to reconstruct a dinosaur from bone chips:

> The traces are not simply "revived" or "reactivated" in recall; instead, the stored fragments are used as information to support a new construction. It is as if the bone fragments used by the paleontologist did not appear in the model he builds at all—as indeed they need not, if it is to represent a fully fleshed-out, skin-covered dinosaur. The bones can be thought of, somewhat loosely, as remnants of the structure which created and supported the original dinosaur, and thus as sources of information about how to reconstruct it. (Neisser, 1967, pp. 285–286)

The basic idea is that people retrieve whatever they can from memory and then infer what the experiences must have been that gave rise to these memory fragments. **Reconstructive memory** is the term used to refer to the processes by which people try to inferentially recreate their memories from what they can recall.

How would a psychologist go about documenting that people actually engage in such inferential processes when trying to recall information? One way is to contrast conditions that facilitate or inhibit such inferences. Bransford and Johnson (1972) looked at the effect of either enabling inferential elaborations or not. They had two groups of subjects study the following passage, which you should try to read and then recall:

> The procedure is actually quite simple. First arrange items into different groups. Of course one pile may be sufficient depending on how much there is to do. If you have to go somewhere else due to lack of facilities that is the next step; otherwise, you are pretty well set. It is important not to overdo things. That is, it is better to do too few things at once than too many. In the short run this may not seem important but complications can easily arise. A mistake can be expensive as well. At first, the whole procedure will seem complicated. Soon, however, it will become just another facet of life. It is difficult to foresee any end to necessity for this task in the immediate future, but then, one never can tell. After the procedure is completed one arranges the material into different groups again. Then they can be put into their appropriate places. Eventually they will be used once more and the whole cycle will then have to be repeated. However, that is part of life. (P. 322)

Before reading this passage, some subjects were told that the passage involved washing clothes. Given this information, they found (and presumably you would, too) that it was easier to elaborate on this material with inferences. For instance, the beginning of the passage could be elaborated with information about sorting clothes by colors; the middle of the passage, with information about costly mistakes in washing clothes. Subjects who were told that the passage was about doing laundry before they read it were able to recall more of the story than were two control groups. One control group was not given this information at all. The other control group was given this information only after reading the story. So, knowing that the passage was about doing laundry only at test was not adequate; the material had to be encoded in this way at study. This experiment provides a nice example of Bransford's transfer-appropriate processing. By studying the story with the knowledge that it involved washing clothes, subjects enabled themselves to take advantage of that information at recall.

Chapter 6 discussed how memory for information is better if it is processed more elaborately at study. One explanation is that this practice allows for reconstructive retrieval at the time of recall. The elaborations generated at study can be used at test to infer what the actual studied material was.

There can be a beneficial interaction between elaborative processing at study and test, as in the Bransford and Johnson experiment. These findings have implications for reading a text such as this: by placing as much meaning as possible on the text while studying it, the reader is optimally positioned for meaningful reconstruction later.

People's ability to reconstruct what they have studied is facilitated if they have processed the material in an appropriate, meaningful way.

Inferential Intrusions in Recall

Another way to show inferential processing in recall is to demonstrate that subjects recall things they did not study but that follow inferentially from what they did study. For instance, Sulin and Dooling (1974) had subjects study the following passage:

Carol Harris's Need for Professional Help

Carol Harris was a problem child from birth. She was wild, stubborn, and violent. By the time Carol turned eight, she was still unmanageable. Her parents were very concerned about her mental health. There was no good institution for her problem in her state. Her parents finally decided to take some action. They hired a private teacher for Carol. (P. 256)

One group of subjects studied this paragraph, but another group of subjects read a paragraph that substituted "Helen Keller" for "Carol Harris."[4] Later, subjects were asked whether they had read the following sentence:

She was deaf, dumb, and blind.

Subjects are much more likely to think that they had studied this sentence if they had read the Helen Keller passage than if they had read the Carol Harris passage. From the point of view of a laboratory memory experiment, such a recognition is often classified as an error. However, from the point of view of adapting to the world at large, such inferences can be seen as quite appropriate. For instance, in taking an exam, a student is expected to include plausible inferences from the study materials as part of the answer to a question.

Researchers have been interested in how subjects come to recall such sentences that are not part of the original passage. One possibility is that sub-

[4]Helen Keller is famous to most Americans as someone who overcame being both blind and deaf.

jects make the inference while reading the passage, and the other possibility is that they make the inference only at the time of recall. Dooling and Christiansen (1977) tested these possibilities by having subjects study the Carol Harris passage and then presenting them, just before test, with the information that Carol Harris was really Helen Keller. Subjects were much more inclined to believe they had studied the "deaf, dumb, and blind" sentence when informed about the identity of Helen Keller just before test than when not informed at all. Since they could not have made the inference when they studied the paragraph, they must have made the inference when tested with the sentence.

An experiment by Owens, Bower, and Black (1979) showed that when subjects engaged in inferential processing, not only was there an increase in their ability to retrieve the information that they had read, but there was also an increase in their intrusion of information that they had not read. They had subjects read a story about a typical day in the life of a college student. Included in the story was the following paragraph:

Nancy went to see the doctor. She arrived at the office and checked in with the receptionist. She went to see the nurse, who went through the usual procedures. Then Nancy stepped on the scale and the nurse recorded her weight. The doctor entered the room and examined the results. He smiled at Nancy and said, "Well, it seems my expectations have been confirmed." When the examination was finished, Nancy left the office. (P. 186)

Two groups of subjects studied the story. The only difference between the groups was that the theme group had read the following information before reading any of the story:

Nancy woke up feeling sick again and she wondered if she really were pregnant. How would she tell the professor she had been seeing? And the money was another problem. (P. 185)

Much like telling subjects that Carol Harris was Helen Keller, this additional information made the passage much more interesting and enabled the subjects to make many inferences that they might not otherwise have been able to make. Owens et al. asked subjects to recall the story 24 hr later. They looked at facts recalled from the story that were either actually stated in the story or could be inferred from the story, for example, "The doctor told Nancy she was pregnant." Table 8.2 displays the number of facts of each kind that were recalled as a function of whether subjects were given the additional thematic passage or not. Given the thematic passage, subjects recalled many additional facts that were studied as well as many that were inferred. By increasing the subjects' ability to make inferences, the experimenters enabled them to remember a much richer version of the story.

Table 8.2 *Number of Facts Recalled in Theme Versus Neutral Condition*

	Theme Condition	Neutral Condition
Studied facts	29.2	20.2
Inferred facts	15.2	3.7

Source: Adapted from Owens et al., 1979.

As part of memory reconstruction, subjects infer and recall information that was not actually studied.

Conclusions About Study–Test Interactions

Many of the results about study–test interactions are captured by Tulving's encoding-specificity theory and Bransford's transfer-appropriate processing theory. The encoding-specificity theory emphasizes the overlap among the elements at study and at test. Transfer-appropriate processing emphasizes the overlap in processes. An additional dimension of complexity concerns semantic processing. Generally, focusing on meaningful elements or meaningful processing produces more potent results, partly because subjects can better reconstruct their memories at test from meaningfully elaborated memory fragments.

Explicit Versus Implicit Memories[5]

The discussion in the past three chapters has focused on **explicit memories**, memories that subjects are consciously aware of when they retrieve them. Much recent research has been concerned with displaying that subjects can show evidence of memories for experiences that they cannot consciously retrieve. Such memories are called **implicit memories**, in contrast with the explicit memories of which people are conscious.

Feeling of Knowing

Sometimes memories can be just on the verge of consciousness. When people can almost recall an item but not quite, they are said to be in a tip-of-the-tongue state. An example is almost remembering someone's name but not quite being able to recall it. This phenomenon was investigated experimentally

[5]I would like to thank Lynne Reder for her assistance in pointing out the studies reviewed in this section.

by Brown and McNeill (1966), who presented subjects with dictionary defini-tions, for example, "an instrument used by navigators to measure the angle between a heavenly body and a horizon" or "a flat-bottomed Chinese boat usually propelled by two oars."[6] Often the subjects were able to recall the word being defined or could confidently report that they had no idea of what the word was. Occasionally subjects reported that they felt the word was on the tip of their tongues. If the target word was *sampan* and the subjects were not quite able to recall the word, they reported that it sounded like *saipan, Siam, Cheyenne,* and *sarong.* For words that subjects identified as being in tip-of-the-tongue states, Brown and McNeill asked subjects questions like, "What is the first letter?" "How many syllables does it have?" and "Can you tell me what the word sounds like?" Subjects were able to answer such questions quite accurately.

Subjects are fairly accurate in judging whether they know something. In one of the original studies of the feeling of knowing, Hart (1967) presented subjects with questions like, "Who wrote The Tempest?" and "What is the capital of Colombia?" If subjects were unable to recall the answer, they were asked to rate whether they would be able to recognize the answer. Subjects were able to predict quite well whether they would be able to recognize the answer. Other research has demonstrated the accuracy of such feeling-of-knowing judgments in other ways. Freedman and Landauer (1966) and Gruneberg and Monks (1974) showed that subjects who thought they knew the answer were better able to recall the answer when cued with the first let-ter. Nelson, Gerber, and Narens (1984) showed that subjects who reported high feelings of knowing were better able to perceive the answer when it was presented in a brief visual flash. All these experiments converge in demon-strating that subjects can quite accurately judge that they know facts that they cannot consciously recall.

A related phenomenon is the quick judgment of knowing that we see played out in game shows. The announcer may begin to ask a question of a contestant, and before the question is finished the contestant presses a buzzer and claims to know the answer to the question. Reder's research (1987) demonstrated that subjects can judge they know an answer to a question before they have retrieved the answer. She asked subjects to judge as quickly as possible whether they could answer questions like "Where did the Greek gods live?" by pressing a button. She found that subjects could judge that they knew the answer (Mount Olympus) much faster than they could recall the answer. Subjects averaged 2.5 sec to begin recalling the answer, but only 1.7 sec to judge that they knew the answer. Their judgments of knowing were also quite accurate. Ninety percent of the time when they said they knew the answer they could in fact recall the answer.

---

[6]sextant, sampan.

These are all examples of subjects being aware that they know something without being aware (yet) of what it is they know. Subjects' implicit knowledge is manifested in the accuracy of their answers to such questions as how many syllables the item has or whether they will be able to recall the answer later. The next section considers situations in which subjects are aware that they have some familiarity with the material but do not really know the basis for that familiarity.

People can be aware that they know something without being able to recall what they know.

Familiarity

The earlier discussion of recognition memory spoke of subjects judging whether they had seen an item in terms of the degree of evidence they had for its list membership. Two types of evidence were suggested: an explicit memory that the word was seen in the list context, and a sense that the word just seemed more familiar. Subjects sometimes are not sure why the word is familiar, but judge that they have seen the word because of its familiarity.

Evidence for this distinction came from an experiment of Atkinson and Juola (1974), who had subjects study a list of words and then looked at subjects' recognition for these words when they were mixed in with distractor words. Subjects underwent a series of four tests in which they had to discriminate the targets from the distractors. Atkinson and Juola were interested in the speed with which subjects could make these recognition judgments. Figure 8.10 shows that the speed of these recognition judgments varied with the

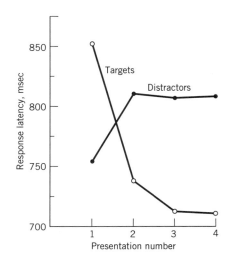

FIGURE 8.10. Time to recognize targets and distractors as a function of the number of times they were presented in the recognition test. (From Atkinson & Juola, 1974).

number of times subjects had been tested on the target or distractor. With repeated testing, subjects got faster on the targets but slower on the distractors. Atkinson and Juola argued that in the first test subjects could reject the distractors quickly because they were unfamiliar, but with repeated testing the distractors became more familiar and subjects had to consciously decide whether they occurred in the list. The targets, with repeated testing, became so familiar that subjects could quickly recognize them.

Jacoby (1991) used a paradigm in which subjects read a list of 15 words and then heard a list of 15 different words. Then subjects were presented with a recognition test in which they saw these 30 words plus 15 more new ones. Subjects were instructed to recognize only the last 15 words they had heard and not the earlier ones they had seen. They were tested under two conditions. In a divided-attention condition subjects had to monitor a sequence of digits spoken on a tape recorder, looking for a sequence of three odd digits in a row (e.g., 9, 3, 7); in the full-attention condition they could devote their full attention to the primary task. Figure 8.11 shows the results. First, subjects falsely recognized many of the words they had seen. Thus having read the words created a sense of familiarity, which led them to believe that they had heard the words. Second, this tendency was enhanced under conditions of divided attention. Subjects were less able to engage in a process of conscious recollection and so had to count more on their sense of familiarity.

Reder (Reder & Gordon, in press; Reder, Nelson, & Stroffolino, in preparation) developed a theory that explains this result plus a great many other phenomena in implicit memory. She proposed that in judging the familiarity of items subjects may be responding to simply the strength of the memory records that underlie these items. Subjects can more rapidly and more easily judge how strong a memory record is than what its actual contents are. Thus, strength serves as a basis for rapid judgments of familiarity in the Atkinson and Juola experiment or as a basis for judgment under divided attention in experiments like that of Jacoby.

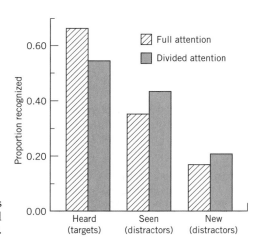

FIGURE 8.11. Proportion of words recognized as heard under full and divided attention. (From Jacoby, 1991).

301

Jacoby, Woloshyn, and Kelley (1989) showed that the sense of familiarity can lead subjects to make a number of memory misattributions. They had subjects first read a series of names, for example, Sebastian Weisdorf. Subjects studied this material in a divided-attention condition or in a full-attention condition. Then subjects were presented with these names mixed in with names of famous people, such as Wayne Gretzky, as well as names of other nonfamous people. Subjects were to judge who was famous and who was nonfamous. An important aspect of this experiment was that subjects were told explicitly if they remembered the name from the earlier study phase it was not famous. Figure 8.12 shows the results. Subjects who were in the full-attention condition were better able to reject studied names than other new names as nonfamous. They were able to use their explicit recall of studying these names in the experimental context as a basis for rejecting them. On the other hand, subjects in the divided-attention condition tended to false alarm to names they had studied. Reder has explained this result by assuming that when subjects studied the names under divided attention, they increased the strength of the memory records encoding these names but did not explicitly associate the experimental content with the names.

Note that the experiment depicted in Figure 8.11 manipulated attention at test, whereas the experiment depicted in Figure 8.12 manipulated attention at study. Divided attention at test produces greater reliance on record strength because the subject cannot process the test material so carefully. Divided attention at study makes it harder for the subject to encode the source of strength and so makes it harder to filter out records that are strong for spurious reasons.

Arkes, Hackett, and Boehm (1989) and Hasher, Goldstein, and Toppino (1977) showed that this sort of familiarity can lead subjects to come to believe various assertions. They had subjects study sentences such as, "The largest dam in the world is in Pakistan" and then asked them whether they believed these assertions when mixed in with others. The previously studied sentences

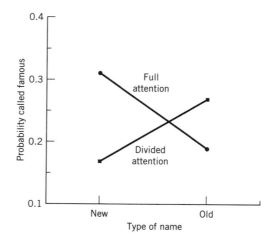

FIGURE 8.12. Probability of judging a nonfamous name famous after reading a list on which the name appeared. *Source:* From L. L. Jacoby and C. M. Kelly. Current Directions in Psychological Science, Volume 1. Copyright © 1992 by the American Psychological Society. Reprinted by permission of Cambridge University Press.

received increased credibility. This is a potentially frightening result in that it implies that propaganda does work. Merely exposing people to assertions increases the credibility of these assertions.

People sometimes respond to the raw familiarity of an item without determining the source of that familiarity.

Priming Effects

People can also show implicit memory for material by showing facilitation in their processing of material as a function of exposure to the material. They can sometimes show improved processing of material when they do not even remember the material. Jacoby, Toth, and Yonelinas (1993) had subjects study words under full- or divided-attention conditions as in the earlier Jacoby studies (Figures 8.11 and 8.12). They then tested the subjects in a stem-completion task in which subjects were given a word stem and asked to complete it. For example, the word might be *motel* and the stem, *mot—*. Some of the subjects were explicitly instructed not to complete the stem with a word that they had studied, whereas others were told that they could complete the stem with any word that came to mind. Figure 8.13 shows the results in terms of how frequently subjects completed the stem with the target (i.e., *motel* in this example). When subjects studied the target and were told they could give it as a response they generated it much more frequently than when they did not have prior exposure (inclusion instructions versus no prior exposure). Thus they were facilitated in their retrieval of the target. This facilitation is referred to as a **priming effect**.[7] The more interesting contrast involves subjects' performance under exclusion instructions. Particularly when they had studied the words under divided attention, they were more likely to recall the target word, even though they had been explicitly instructed not to do so. The word was more available because of its prior exposure, but they did not remember having experienced it. As in the case of the familiarity effects, Reder et al. (in preparation) argues that the word's increased availability was due to the strengthening of its representation.

Jacoby argued that the bases for implicit and explicit memory are independent. Implicit memory is relatively unaffected by divided attention, whereas explicit memory is seriously impaired. In the experiment depicted in Figure 8.13, Jacoby argued that only implicit memories were formed when subjects studied under divided attention. Since no explicit memories were

---

[7]Chapter 5 discussed associative priming effects, where presenting associated material made target material more available. Here priming refers to the effect of prior exposure of the target material.

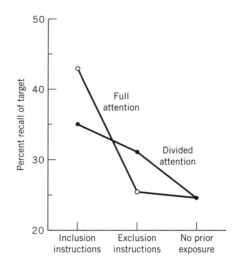

FIGURE 8.13. Probability of generating a word in a stem-completion task with full and divided attention.

formed, subjects did not have the advantage of them to boost recall in the inclusion condition or to filter recall in the exclusion condition.

Access to infomation can be primed by experiences that do not result in explicit memories.

Interactions with Study Conditions

How subjects study the material appears to have different effects on implicit versus explicit memory. For example, in another experiment Jacoby (1983) had subjects study information about a word in one of three conditions. Using the word *woman* as the example:

1. **No context.** Subjects just studied *woman* alone.
2. **Context.** Subjects studied the word in the presence of an opposite, *man–woman.*
3. **Generate.** Subjects saw the word *man* and had to generate the opposite, *woman.*

These three conditions manipulate the degree to which the subject engaged in elaborative processing of the material. As indicated in Chapter 6, more elaborative processing results in better memory in a standard memory test. Jacoby then tested his subjects' memories in one of two ways:

1. **Explicit.** Subjects were given a standard recognition test—they saw a list of words and had to recognize which they had studied.

2. ***Implicit.*** Subjects were presented with the word for a brief period of time (40 msec) and had to simply say what the word was. This was a test of their ability to perceive the word when presented briefly.

The results from these two tests are displayed in Figure 8.14. The explicit condition showed the classic generation effect, with best memory in the condition that involved the greatest semantic engagement by the subject. The results were just the opposite in the implicit condition. Identifications were best in the No Context condition that involved the least semantic processing. In all study conditions word identification was better than in a condition of no prior exposure. In this control condition subjects were able to perceive only 60 percent of the words. Jacoby interpreted these results in terms of the match between the processing required at study and at test. In the no-context condition, when subjects originally encountered the word they had to rely mostly on perceptual processing to identify it, whereas in the generate condition there was not even a word to read. The result that perceptual identification is better in the no-context condition than the generate condition has not always been found (e.g., Masson & MacLeod, 1992); in some experiments there is no difference. However, there is always the interaction between type of processing and type of test.

Schacter, Cooper, Delaney, Peterson, and Tharan (1991) demonstrated another example of perceptual priming. They presented their subjects with drawings similar to those in Figure 8.15. Some were possible figures and some were impossible figures. Subjects were asked to judge whether these objects faced primarily to the left or to the right. Some subjects were also asked to make a conceptual decision—whether the object best fit the category type of furniture, household object, or type of building. Thus Schacter et al. manipulated the depth at which their subjects processed the material, with the perceptual judgment being shallow and the conceptual judgment deep. At test

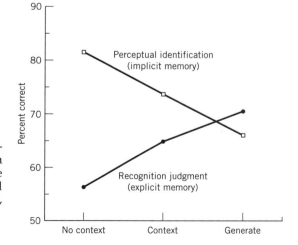

FIGURE 8.14. Ability to recognize a word increases with depth of processing while ability to perceive the word decreases. (From Jacoby, 1983).

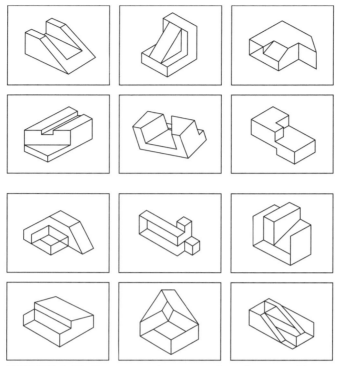

FIGURE 8.15. Representative examples of target objects. The figures in the upper two rows depict possible objects, and the figures in the lower two rows depict impossible objects. *Source:* From D. L. Schacter, L. A. Cooper, S. M. Delaney, M. A. Peterson, and M. Tharan. *Journal of Experimental Psychology: Learning, Memory, and Cognition, Volume 17.* Copyright © 1991 by the American Psychological Association. Reprinted by permission.

the subjects were presented with figures they had studied and figures they had not studied and asked to make one of two decisions about these objects:

1. **Perceptual decision.** The object appeared for just 100 msec and the subject had to decide whether it was a possible object or not. This is an implicit memory test in which the experimenters were interested in how much better subjects judged studied versus nonstudied objects.

2. **Object recognition.** Subjects were given unlimited time to view the objects and had to decide whether the were objects that had been studied. This is an explicit memory test.

The results are displayed in Figure 8.16. Typical of other explicit memory tasks, subjects showed a large advantage of a conceptual or semantic processing. In sharp contrast, there was no significant effect in the implicit object-decision task.

Both the Jacoby and the Schacter et al. studies involved an interaction between the mode of processing at study and the type of test. Elaborative or conceptual processing led to enhanced performance on a test of subjects' ability to consciously recognize what they had studied. Subjects showed no advantage of such processing in a task that only implicitly tapped their memory for such a task. Roediger and Blaxton (1987) interpreted such results in terms of Bransford's notion of transfer-appropriate processing, discussed earlier in this chapter. They argued that tests of implicit memory, such as stem completion, word identification, or object recognition, involve perceptual processes, whereas tasks such as explicit recall and recognition memory are more conceptual in nature. Therefore, only the explicit memory tests should be facilitated by study tasks that involve conceptual processing. They argued that high performance is obtained when the type of test matches the type of processing at study.

Elaborative processing facilitates explicit memory but not implicit memory.

Procedural Memory

In many ways people can be affected by experiences but unable to recall the experiences. One way is that memory records for elements, such as words, involved in the experiences can be strengthened. A second is that the perceptual processing of these elements can be facilitated in the case of word-identification and object-identification tests. Another kind of knowledge that can be

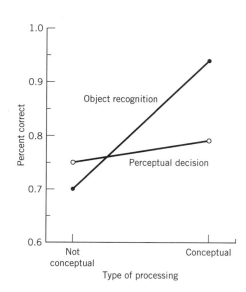

FIGURE 8.16. Performance on perceptual-decision and object-recognition tasks as a function of type of processing at study. (From Schacter et al., 1991).

facilitated is knowledge about how to perform tasks. Often people become quite facile at doing a task without any ability to explicitly say what they have learned. A classic example is learning to ride a bike, a skill many people acquire without having any idea of what it is they do.

This type of knowledge has been studied in a serial reaction time task (Curran & Keele, 1993; Lewicki, Hill, & Bizot, 1988; Nissen & Bullemer, 1987). Subjects press a set of keys according to a computer-generated sequence. A computer monitor might display an X over the key to be pressed and wait until it is pressed. For example, there might be four keys, and the computer might indicate to press the sequence third, second, fourth, third, and so on. A sequence or pattern of key presses is repeated over and over again, but the subjects are not explicitly told that this is the case. For some subjects, for example, in the Curran and Keele experiment the key sequence 1-2-3-2-4-3 was repeated over and over again. In this type of task, subjects get faster at the repeated pattern compared to random patterns, but they frequently have little ability to articulate what the sequence is. In some sense, their fingers know the sequence but they do not.

The experiment by Berry and Broadbent (1984) involved a rather different situation in which procedural knowledge was dissociated from explicit knowledge. They had subjects try to control the output of a hypothetical sugar factory (simulated by a computer program) by manipulating the size of the work force. Subjects saw the month's output of the sugar factory in thousands of tons (e.g., 6000 tons) and then had to choose the next month's work force in hundreds of workers (e.g., 700). They would then see the next month's output of sugar (e.g., 8000 tons) and have to pick the work force for the following month. Table 8.3 shows a series of interactions with the hypothetical sugar factory. The subject's goal was to keep sugar production within the range of 8000 to 10,000 tons.

If one tries to infer the rule relating sugar output to labor force in Table 8.3, one finds that it is not particularly obvious. Sugar output in thousands (S) was related to the work force in hundreds (W) and the previous month's sugar output in thousands ($S1$) by the following formula: $S = 2 \times W - S1$. (A random fluctuation of 1000 tons of sugar was sometimes added.) Oxford undergraduates were given 60 trials at trying to control the factory. During the course of the 60 trials, they became very good at controlling the output of the factory. However, they were unable to state the rule and claimed that they made their responses on the basis of some sort of intuition or because a response felt right. Thus subjects were able to acquire implicit knowledge of how to operate such a factory without corresponding explicit knowledge.

A distinction frequently made in psychology is that between declarative and procedural knowledge (e.g., J. R. Anderson, 1976; Cohen & Squire, 1980; Schacter, 1987). **Declarative knowledge** is explicit knowledge that we can report and of which we are consciously aware. **Procedural knowledge** is knowledge of how to do things, and it is often implicit. Much of the last four

Table 8.3 *An Illustrative Series of Inputs and Outputs for Sugar Production in the Berry and Broadbent Experiment (1984)*

Workforce (input)	Sugar Output (tons)
	6,000
700	
	8,000
900	
	10,000
800	
	7,000
1,000	
	12,000
900	
	6,000
1,000	
	13,000
1,000	
	8,000

chapters has been about declarative knowledge. The next chapter is devoted to skill learning, and so has a good deal more to say about procedural knowledge.

People can learn to perform skills without being able to say what they have learned.

Amnesia in Humans

The distinction between implicit and explicit memory is important in understanding the data on amnesia in humans. **Amnesia** refers to the loss of memory. It can be caused by many insults to the brain, such as a blow to the head; brain infections, such as encephalitis; a stroke; aging phenomena, such as senile dementia; chronic alcoholism; or surgical removal of part of the brain. Two types of amnesia have been observed—**retrograde amnesia**, which refers to loss of memory for items and experiences that occured before the brain insult, and **anterograde amnesia**, which refers to loss of ability to remember things that occured after the injury. Damage to the hippocampus is particularly important in producing anterograde amnesia. Chapter 3 reviewed the evidence that the hippocampus plays an important role in the memories of lower organisms, such as rats. This section reviews some evidence about its role in human and primate memory (see Squire, 1987, 1992, for a more elaborate discussion).

The most famous amnesic patient is H.M., from whom large parts of the temporal lobes and related subcortical areas were removed to relieve intractable epilepsy. Included in the subcortical areas removed was the hippocampus. H.M. has poor memory for events just before his surgery but apparently no loss of memories from his early childhood. Most dramatically, he appears to have lost all ability to learn new information. He immediately forgets people he has met and has virtually no memory for what has happened in the 40 years since his surgery. A number of other patients with hippocampal damage show severe memory loss, although usually not as complete as that of H.M.

There are also patients who suffered severe damages to the hippocampal area because of a history of severe alcoholism coupled with nutritional deficits. They show memory loss, known as **Korsakoff's syndrome**, with a pattern similar to that of patients like H.M. Such patients have approximately normal immediate memory for information but show severe deficits in tests of long-term retention of material acquired after developing their symptoms. Korsakoff's patients and other patients suffering hippocampal damage show only mild loss of memories acquired before the onset of their condition. Nonhuman primates also show relatively preserved memory for information learned prior to hippocampal damage.

In the case of humans and primates, the hippocampus cannot be the site of permanent memory storage, or there would be greater loss of memories acquired before the injury. Rather, it seems that the hippocampus must be critical in the creation of permanent memories, which are stored elsewhere, probably in the cortex.

Humans and other primates show an inability to acquire new long-term memories after hippocampal damage but experience relatively little loss of memories acquired before hippocampal damage.

Selective Amnesia

As noted in Chapter 3, lower organisms do not show complete loss of ability to learn after removal of the hippocampus; however, there is some controversy about how to characterize their selective learning difficulty. Such selective loss also occurs in humans, and the amnesia appears to be restricted to explicit, declarative memories. Graf, Squire, and Mandler (1984) performed an experiment that illustrates one of the ways in which amnesiacs have preserved memory. Subjects were shown a list of common words, such as *cheese*, and then later tested for their memory of these words in one of three conditions:

1. ***Free recall.*** They were simply asked to recall all the words they had studied.

2. ***Cued recall.*** They were shown the three-letter stem of the word (e.g., *che* for *cheese*) and asked to recall the word they had studied that began with that stem.

3. ***Completion.*** They were shown the stem and asked to say any word (not necessarily from the list) that began with that stem.

Figure 8.17 compares the performance of normal and amnesic subjects in these three conditions. Normal subjects did better in the free recall condition. This advantage was much reduced in the cued recall condition and was actually reversed for the completion task. In the completion task, the baseline probability of completing the stem with the target word was 9 percent when the target word had not been studied. Both normal and amnesic subjects showed large effects of their exposure to the words, but amnesiacs were only able to make this information available when they were not explicitly trying to recall it. This experiment is an instance of a priming paradigm. Amnesiacs show normal levels of priming in most paradigms.

Priming is only one of the paradigms in which amnesiacs show preserved learning. Amnesiacs also show preserved procedural learning relative to their declarative learning. They have been shown capable of learning many skills, such as rotary pursuit tasks, mirror reading, or finger maze tasks. They show normal learning curves on such tasks even though they claim on the next day of training not to have seen the task. Phelps (1989) argued that amnesic subjects are capable of learning any skill that does not require explicitly retrieving information from long-term memory. Under appropriate circum-

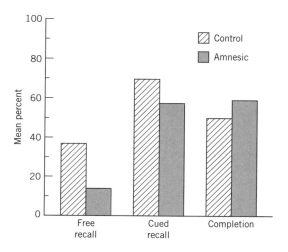

FIGURE 8.17. Memory for words displayed by amnesic and normal subjects in three kinds of tests. *Source:* From P. Graf, L. R. Squire, and G. Mandler. *Journal of Experimental Psychology: Learning, Memory and Cognition, Volume 10.* Copyright © 1984 by the American Psychological Association. Reprint-ed by permission.

stances patients even appear capable of learning a new language (Hirst, Phelps, Johnson, & Volpe, 1988) or a new mathematical algorithm (Milberg, Alexander, Charness, McGlinchey-Berroth, & Barrett, 1988). The patient H.M. (Cohen, Eichenbaum, Deacedo, & Corkin, 1985) has been shown capable of learning a complex problem-solving skill over days, even though each day when he is shown the task he protests that he has never seen it before. Thus skill learning or procedural learning is another major type of learning left intact in such patients.

It appears that it is a very select kind of knowledge that cannot be remembered by amnesiacs with hippocampal damage: they seem unable to create new declarative memory records. They can strengthen existing memory records and thus show priming, and they can learn new procedures. Chapter 3, in discussing the effects of hippocampal damage in rats, reviewed the theory that the effect of hippocampal lesions was to prevent learning of configural associations. Configural associations link a number of elements together in a conditioning experiment. A memory record is essentially a configuration of several cues. For instance, memory for the chunk RXL involves associating *R*, *X*, and *L* together in one configuration. Since humans with hippocampal lesions have difficulty with just such tasks, it may be that the nature of the deficit is similar in humans and in rats.

Humans with hippocampal lesions have selective deficits in learning new declarative information.

Final Reflections

One way to review the research presented in this chapter is to consider its implications for good memory performance. Suppose you are trying to remember some past memories. Given that they are in the past, there is nothing you can do to better encode these memories or retain them—the topics of the previous two chapters. Worrying about these factors would be worrying about spilled milk. What can you do to help retrieve those old memories?

This chapter demonstrated that people enjoy better memory if they can recreate the elements that were associated with the memory. If you are trying to retrieve a former acquaintance's name, it might help to recreate in your mind past experiences and contexts in which you used that name. For example, you might think of names of people associated with the person whose name you are trying to recall. It would also help if you could convert the task to a recognition task, such as going through an old class list.

The chapter also reviewed the importance of inferential memory for reconstructing what can no longer be recalled. Suppose that you are trying to remember where you placed an object. You might go through the process of trying to reconstruct where you might have put it, perhaps retracing your steps, and so on.

The last part of the chapter was devoted to the notion that people have implicit memories of which they are not consciously aware. This implies that we should try to engage in some task that might involve the information and see if our task performance does not have the critical knowledge embedded in it. A classic example is knowledge of the positions of the keys on a standard typewriter keyboard. Many people are not able to recall this information, but are nonetheless successful touch typists. They can remember where a letter is by imagining themselves typing a word that involves the letter and seeing where their finger goes.

It is sometimes possible to recall additional information by utilizing knowledge about different conditions of retrieval.

Further Readings

Massaro (1989) provides a review of the high-threshold and signal detectability theories of recognition memory. Tulving's (1983) book is an extensive development of his theory of memory. Hintzman (1992) and Tulving and Flexser (1992) engaged in an exchange on recognition failure. Squire (1987) reviews the physiology of memory, including a thorough discussion of amnesic dissociations. Schacter (1987) provides a classic article reviewing the research on implicit memory. Squire (1992) reviews the research on the role of the hippocampus in human memory. Roediger (1990) also provides a review of the distinction between implicit and explicit memory and discusses this distinction in terms of the concept of transfer-appropriate processing. Reder and Gordon (in press) and Reder, Nelson and Stroffolino (in preparation) describes Reder's theory of implicit memory.

9

Skill Acquisition

Overview

The past four chapters primarily addressed the acquisition of declarative knowledge. Chapter 8 concluded by contrasting the acquisition of declarative knowledge and the acquisition of procedural knowledge. Chapter 8 reviewed the evidence that people have knowledge of which they are not conscious but that can be effectively deployed to perform tasks. Such procedural knowledge is often referred to as **skill**. This chapter reviews what is known about the acquisition of skills and their relationship to declarative knowledge.

We all acquire many skills to varying degrees of proficiency. Each of us learns a few skills to a high degree of proficiency. For most of us, these high-proficiency skills include speaking our native language, reading, basic mathematical skills, interacting with other people, and driving a car. As we specialize, we tend to develop our own unique skills. Some of us become excellent chess players, tennis players, physicists, computer programmers, Nintendo players, carpenters, pianists, teachers, and so on. The amount of time it takes to become highly proficient at a skill is great, often measured in the hundreds and sometimes thousands of hours. Over that period of practice, the nature of the skill may change dramatically.

Skills such as those mentioned here have much greater complexity than the behavior that is typically studied in a conditioning experiment or a memory experiment. One of the major issues this chapter addresses is how people cope with such complexity. One dimension of learning is the acquisition of better and better strategies for dealing with complexity. One way of coping with complexity is to automate more and more of the skill. When part of a skill is automated, it no longer requires cognitive involvement, which frees the cognitive systems to focus on the most problematic aspects of the skill.

An example of a fairly complex skill is editing text on a word processor. When people are first introduced to such a system, they use it in a painfully

→ *not only will the unit nodes in these traces*

accrue strength with days of practice, but also the element nodes will accrue strength. As will be seen, this power function prediction corresponds to the data about practice. A set of experiments was conducted to test the prediction about a *the* power-law increase in strength with extensive practice. In one experiment subject studied subject-verb-object sentences of the form (The~~e~~ lawyer hated the doctor). After studying ~~fur-~~
, *these sentences they were transferred to a*
~~thermore, the thought prevents the study~~ sentence recognition paradigm in which they had to discriminate these sentences from foil by the mind sentences made of the same words as the illustrates sentence but in new combinations. There were 25 days of tests and hence practice. Each day subjects were tested on each sentence 12 times (in one group) or 24 times in the other group. There was no difference

FIGURE 9.1. Sample page of corrections. *Source:* From M. K. Singley and J. R. Anderson. *The Transfer of cognitive skill.* Copyright © 1989 by Harvard University Press. Reprinted by permission.

slow and self-conscious way. With time, the situation changes dramatically. My secretary is quite capable of carrying on a telephone conversation while whipping through edits on a manuscript such as this. This chapter traces how such a skill develops from its initial awkward performance to a state of high automatization.

A good deal of research has focused on the development of text-editing skill. In one experiment, Singley and Anderson (1989) studied the beginning stages of the acquisition of text-editing skills. The subjects were secretarial students who were proficient as typists but had not yet used word processors. Over 6 days they were given practice at text editing 3 hr/day. They received a page of a manuscript marked with six changes to be made (Figure 9.1). This page appeared on their computer screens, and they had to make changes to reflect the edits.

Figure 9.2 shows how the time to make the edits to each page decreased as a function of the number of days of practice. Subjects took an average of almost 8 min per page on the first day, which became about 2 min per page by the sixth day. This total time was divided into two categories. There were periods of time during which the subjects were not typing; any period of time when more than 2 sec elapsed between keystrokes was classified as *thinking time.* The remaining time, when keystrokes were produced at a rate of more than one

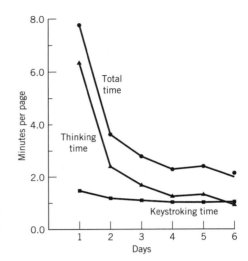

FIGURE 9.2. Improvement in text-editing skill over six consecutive days of practice. (From Singley & Anderson, 1989).

every 2 sec, was classified as *keystroking time*. Most of the reduction in time resulted from a reduction in thinking time. Keystroking time was somewhat reduced, but not as a result of an improved rate of typing; rather, the subjects were making fewer errors and more efficient edits, so they were producing fewer keystrokes. The subjects' rates of keystroking remained constant throughout the experiment at about two and a half keystrokes per second.

Figure 9.2 reflects the basic characteristics of many examples of skill acquisition. Skill acquisition starts out with a large cognitive component. With practice, that cognitive component decreases. By day 6 shown in Figure 9.2, the thinking component was reduced to taking the same amount of time as a motor component (keystroking). As this chapter documents, with continued practice the thinking component continues to decrease. Eventually all cognitive involvement is squeezed out and there is only an automated motor routine.

As a skill becomes more practiced, the skill undergoes dramatic changes, including great reductions in its cognitive involvement.

Power Law Learning

The learning function shown in Figure 9.2 is best fit by a power function, like the functions of Chapter 6 that describe simple associative learning. In general, power-law learning curves fit skill-acquisition functions well. Figure 9.3 presents data collected by Neves and Anderson (1981), who looked at improvement in doing proofs in a logic system. Figure 9.3a displays the data on the original scales and 9.3b presents the data on log–log scales, showing power functions as linear functions. Figure 9.4 presents some of the most famous skill-learning data in the literature (Crossman, 1959), obtained from monitoring a factory worker's improvement in making cigars over a 10-year period. The rate of improvement followed a power function until the worker reached the *cycle time* of the equipment she was using. This situation is generally true of skill learning—the only limitation on improvement is the cycle time of the equipment being used. The "equipment" in this statement includes the physical structure of the person—it takes a certain amount of time for nerve impulses to reach the brain from receptors, such as the eye, and

FIGURE 9.3. Time to generate proofs in a geometry-like proof system as a function of the number of proofs already done. (*a*) Function on a normal scale; (*b*) function on a log–log scale. (From Neves & Anderson, 1981). *Source:* Figure 9.3 from *Cognitive psychology and its implications* by John R. Anderson. Copyright © 1990 by W. H. Freeman. Reprinted with permission.

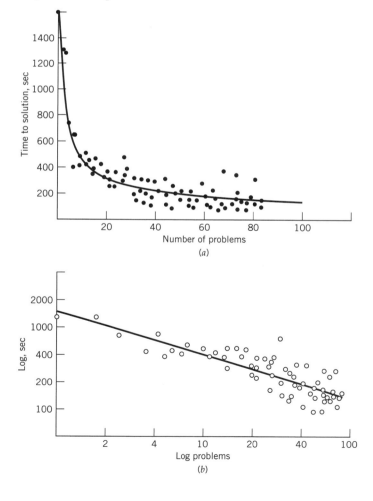

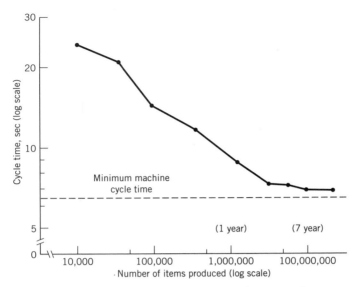

FIGURE 9.4. Time to produce a cigar as a function of amount of experience. (From Crossman, 1959).

to go from the brain to effectors, such as the hand; in addition, the hand can only move through space so fast. Skilled performance continues to speed up until it reaches the minimum time implied by these physical limitations.

The fact that skill learning tends to display this continuous power law learning may seem surprising. Over the course of many years of practice making cigars, the skill itself undergoes rather dramatic shifts in the nature of its performance, which might be expected to be mirrored by shifts in the learning function. J.R. Anderson (1982) argued that the reason for the uniformity in the learning function is that all the changes, including the qualitative changes, depend on simple associative learning, which obeys a power law, as discussed in Chapter 6. The complex skill obeys a power law because each of its components does.

An interesting case study of skill acquisition was reported by Ohlsson (1992), who looked at the development of Isaac Asimov's writing skill. Asimov was one of the most prolific authors of our time, writing approximately 500 books in a career that spanned 40 years. He sat down at his keyboard every day at 7:30 A.M. and wrote until 10:00 P.M. Figure 9.5 shows the average number of months he took to write a book as a function of practice on a log–log scale. It corresponds closely to a power function.

The speed of performing a complex skill improves according to a power function.

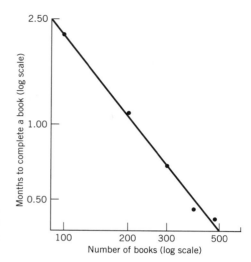

FIGURE 9.5. Time to complete a book as a function of practice, plotted with logarithmic coordinates on both axes. (From Ohlsson, 1992).

Stages of Skill Acquisition

Fitts (1964) and J.R. Anderson (1982) proposed that skills go through three characteristic stages as they develop. The following sections consider each of these stages. Fitts called the first stage the **cognitive stage**. In this stage, the learner often works from instructions or an example of how the task is to be performed. For example, when I learned how to shift gears with a standard transmission I was both told the principles and my teacher demonstrated how to shift the gears. Whether example or instruction, the information a person learns from initially is represented declaratively and must be interpreted in a way to yield appropriate behavior. The learner can often be observed to rehearse the instructions in this phase—"Second is directly below first," I would say to myself.

The second stage is called the **associative stage**. In this stage the skill makes a transition from a declarative representation to a procedural representation. It becomes a lot more fluid and error free. For instance, I slowly learned to coordinate releasing the clutch in first gear with applying the gas so as not to kill the engine. Verbalization of the skill drops out in this phase. I no longer rehearsed where second was, and I went to it much more rapidly.

The third stage is the **autonomous stage**. The skill becomes continuously more automated and rapid, and cognitive involvement is gradually eliminated. Sometimes a person even loses the ability to verbally describe the skill. In such a case, the skill becomes totally a matter of implicit memory (see Chapter 8). An interesting example involves my wife, who was teaching me how to shift gears. She had completely forgotten whether the gas should be released when engaging the clutch; that is, she could not say what she did, though her foot knew perfectly well what to do. When she wanted to find out what to tell me, she had to assume the driver's seat and see what she did.

This chapter is organized according to these three stages. These are not discrete stages, but they characterize approximate points in the qualitative evolution of a skill. The continuous nature of the power law improvement reviewed in the previous section seems somewhat at odds with the fact that a skill undergoes what amounts to a dramatic qualitative evolution. The apparent power law improvement is probably only approximate; it is as good an approximation as it is because associative learning (which also approximates a power function) governs the qualitative changes.

A skill develops from the cognitive stage to the associative stage and then to the autonomous stage.

The Cognitive Stage

Most people might not realize the intimate relationship that skill acquisition has to problem solving. When we think of a skill we tend to think of a smooth behavioral performance. When we think of problem solving, we tend to think of something that is performed in fits and starts as a person works out a solution. However, every smooth, skilled performance has its origins as a solution to a novel problem. For instance, the secretarial students in the Singley and Anderson experiment were faced with making edits in a novel word-processing system—something they had never done before. They eventually became facile at this task, but they started out with all the awkwardness associated with novel problem solving. The first thing a learner must do when faced with a new task is to organize some solution to this problem. The learner starts with some declarative information about the problem. The secretarial students, for instance, were told about the basic commands of the word processor and given examples of each command. The cognitive stage of skill acquisition involves these initial problem-solving efforts. The field of problem-solving research is concerned with how people go from some initial declarative knowledge about a problem domain, such as text editing, to their first solutions of problems in that domain.

The Structure of Problem Solving

Research on problem solving has been strongly influenced by developments in artificial intelligence, a branch of computer science concerned with creating intelligent computers. As reviewed in Chapter 1, Newell and Simon (1972) synthesized ideas from artificial intelligence and experimental research on human problem solving to produce an extremely influential framework for understanding human problem solving. Their framework is defined in terms of the following key concepts:

1. States. At any point in solving a problem, the problem can be conceived of as being in some current state. In the case of text editing the current state is the representation of the manuscript in the computer. In repairing an appliance, the current state is the condition (possibly half-dismantled) of the appliance. In solving an algebraic equation, the current state is the current form of the equation. Future hypothetical states can also be described such as an equation with all the variable terms on one side. A state is a characterization of a situation, current or hypothetical, in terms relevant to the problem solving.

2. Goals. A goal is a state that a person is trying to achieve. In the case of text editing, the goal is a corrected manuscript as specified on the marked-up page (e.g., Figure 9.1); in the case of the appliance, the goal is a functioning appliance; in the case of the equation, the goal is an equation of the form Variable-to-be-solved-for = Number (e.g., $x = 4$).

3. Operators. Operators are steps that can be taken to change the current state into another state closer to the goal. In the case of text editing, they are the various text-editing commands; in the case of the appliance, they are the various actions involved in taking apart and putting back together the appliance; in the case of the equation, they are the various transformations that preserve the equality. Any operator can be characterized by what preconditions have to be met by the current state for it to apply and what changes it causes in the state. To delete a word using a text editor, the precondition is to move the cursor to the word before the delete command can be executed. In algebra, all terms have to be at the same level in the equation and they are replaced by one term as in the following algebraic transformation:

$$3x + 7x = 10 \longrightarrow 10x = 10$$

where $3x$ and $7x$ have been collected to become $10x$.

4. Search. Some problems can be solved by applying a single operator, but the solution of complex problems requires the application of a sequence of operators. For text editing, there is a sequence of actions in the word processor; for the appliance there is a sequence of taking it apart, finding the broken piece, replacing it, and putting the appliance back together; algebraic problems can require a sequence of transformations like the one illustrated above. The fundamental *problem* in problem solving is finding some sequence of operators that will transform the current state into the goal state. This problem is called the search problem, because there are many possible sequences of actions and only a few will result in the goal state. The problem solver must explicitly or implicitly search among the possible sequences to find a successful one.

Problem-solving activity can be characterized as a search for a sequence of operators that will transform the current state into the goal state.

Operator Acquisition and Selection

The two essential issues involved in problem solving are discovering what operators can be used and then guiding their application to achieve the goal. When faced with a new domain, neither the operators nor how to use them is obvious. This is part of what has to be learned.

Operator acquisition is essentially what was studied in the conditioning and memory chapters. When a rat learns to press a bar, it is learning an operator that can get it food. When human subjects learn a paired associate, such as *dog–vanilla*, they are learning an operator, "respond with *vanilla* to *dog*," that will earn the experimenter's approval. Corresponding to the memory and conditioning experiments, there are two ways for humans to acquire operators: they can be told what they are or they have to discover what they are. In education, students are often simply told what the operators are. In algebra class, for example, students are shown the various operations that can be used to transform equations. Learning these operators is fundamentally no different from learning any other fact presented in a memory experiment. On other occasions, the operators have to be discovered. Discovery may be straightforward, such as discovering which button turns a TV on, or it may be quite challenging, as in the case of an animal discovering what factors determine the delivery of food in a Skinner box. Much of human discovery learning involves an important modeling component. For instance, a young child may observe how an older sibling uses a remote control to turn on the TV and then may do the same. Not only humans, but primates in general, are noted for such imitative learning.

It is reasonable to infer that, however an operator is acquired, the principles of memory (as reviewed in earlier chapters) describe how the operator is encoded in memory, retained, and retrieved. However, skill acquisition involves more than just learning the operators; it often involves executing a complex sequence of many operators. How to convert operator knowledge into successful behavior is not always apparent. For instance, knowing what constitutes a legal chess move does not mean knowing how to play a successful game of chess. The issue of converting learning into performance has been a constant theme in this book since the discussion of Tolman in Chapter 1. There are two principal mechanisms by which people select operators to perform tasks:

1. **Difference reduction.** People select operators that will eliminate differences between their current states and their goals. A simple case is when a single operator transforms the current state into the goal state, such as a bar press delivering food. Often the problem solver must settle for an operator that removes a single difference between the current state and the goal state. For instance, a subject in the text-editing experiment, faced with the marked-up page shown in Figure 9.1, might choose to

delete "illustrates," because this action would move the page one step closer to the target state but leave more changes to be performed.

2. ***Operator subgoaling.*** In the process of trying to achieve a goal, people set subgoals when operators do not work because some precondition is not satisfied. For example, the subject may want to delete a word but first must find where that word is in the manuscript. Locating the word in the manuscript file becomes a subgoal to deleting it. A **subgoal** is a goal pursued in service of a higher goal. This is the means–ends step in the Newell and Simon theory of problem solving, which was discussed in Chapter 1.

The next sections describe difference reduction and operator subgoaling in human problem solving.

Difference reduction and operator subgoaling are two mechanisms for guiding the selection of problem-solving operators.

Difference Reduction

Difference reduction is apparent as a guiding force in many domains. When people try to get from one location to another, they choose moves that reduce their distance from the goal. When I need to tidy up my office, I choose to tidy up part of it at a time, confident that by eliminating differences one at a time between the current office and a tidy office I will finally arrive at a tidy office.[1] More often than not, problem solving that focuses on difference reduction is successful because it is usually possible to get from where we are to where we want to be by reducing the differences. However, puzzles can be created that violate this general rule of thumb. Sometimes the only way to solve a problem is to temporarily increase the differences between the current state and the goal. Some of the best evidence that distance reduction is important in human problem solving comes from the difficulty subjects have in solving such puzzles. A good example is the hobbits and orcs problem:

> On one side of a river are three hobbits and three orcs. There is a rowboat on their side, but only two creatures can row across at a time. All of them want to get to the other side of the river. At no point can orcs outnumber hobbits on either side of the river (or the orcs would eat the outnumbered hobbits). The problem, then, is for the creatures to find a method of rowing back and forth in the boat such that they all eventually get across and the hobbits are never outnumbered by the orcs.

[1]Actually, as my secretary points out, this leaves a somewhat exaggerated impression of how much I am responsible for tidying my office. It appears that little elves do a lot of work while I am on business trips.

Figure 9.6 illustrates a solution to this problem. It represents where the hobbits (H) are, where the orcs (O) are, and where the boat (b) is relative to the river, which is the line. The transition between state 6 and state 7 is critical. On the far side of the river in state 6 there are two hobbits and two orcs, whereas in state 7 there is only one hobbit and one orc. This transition goes against the grain of difference reduction, but it is absolutely critical to solving the problem. Subjects have particular difficulty with this move and often give up finding a solution at this point (e.g., see Greeno, 1974, and Jeffries, Polson, Razran, & Atwood, 1977). Frequently what makes a puzzle a puzzle is that it requires the problem solver to temporarily abandon difference reduction.

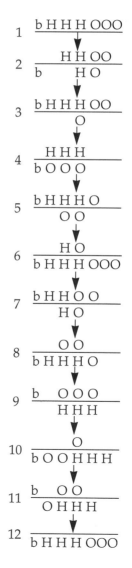

FIGURE 9.6. A diagram of the successive states in a solution to the hobbits and orcs problem. *Source:* From *Cognitive psychology and its implications* by John R. Anderson. Copyright © 1990 by W. H. Freeman. Reprinted with permission.

Difference reduction describes the approach to solving problems used by almost all species. Even the simplest organisms have tropisms, which are tendencies to approach various desired states. For instance, the wood louse (Gunn, 1937) continuously moves in the direction of moister areas because it will dehydrate if the air is too dry, and cockroaches flee light as a general defense mechanism. Organisms generally behave in a way that reduces the difference between their current state and their goal state (bliss point in the language of Chapter 4). To reiterate the theme from that earlier chapter, this tendency does not mean that organisms consciously choose such operators, only that they act *as if* they are choosing them.

Humans and other primates are capable of organizing their behavior in ways that are more complex than difference reduction. This more complex behavior is produced by operator subgoaling, the topic of the next section.

Organisms have a strong tendency to behave in a way that reduces the differences between the current state and the goal state.

Operator Subgoaling

When humans set an operator subgoal, they suspend the attempt to achieve their main goal and pursue the subgoal, which has no intrinsic value; its pursuit is justified by the belief that it will help achieve the main goal. Most of the goals people try to achieve, for example, good grades, are really subgoals in service of higher goals, such as graduation with honors or admission to graduate school, which in turn are in service of yet higher goals. Tool building, a trait associated primarily with humans and to a much lesser degree with higher primates, such as chimpanzees, is an exercise in subgoaling. Creating a tool means creating an object whose justification is the higher goals it helps achieve.

Tool building is almost unique to the human species. The only other species that have been observed to engage in novel tool building to any significant extent are the apes, particularly the chimpanzees. Chimpanzees have been observed to make novel objects to serve as weapons, to shelter them from rain, and to reach food (B.B. Beck, 1980). A clever episode (Köhler, 1927) concerned a chimpanzee who was trying to reach food outside its cage with two poles, each of which was too short. The chimp fitted one pole inside the other and so made a composite pole long enough to reach the food. Figure 9.7 shows the chimpanzee at the critical moment in the solution.

It is significant that only the species closest to humans have been observed to engage in novel tool building. This fact indicates that the capacity to learn to handle goals and subgoals is a relatively species-specific skill, unlike many of the learning phenomena reviewed in this book. Despite the

FIGURE 9.7. Köhler's chimpanzee solving the two-stick problem.

accomplishments of chimpanzees and other apes, humans far exceed them in the ability to manage goal structures. It has been speculated that the process of handling goals is performed by the frontal cortex of the brain (J.R. Anderson, 1993), a structure that is much expanded in primates over most mammals, and much expanded in humans over primates. Chapter 5 discussed the evidence for the critical role of the frontal cortex in working memory. Memory for goals is a special kind of working memory.

A fair amount of research on the moment-to-moment dynamics of human subgoal creation has been conducted using the Tower of Hanoi problem. A simple version of this problem is illustrated in Figure 9.8. There are three pegs and four disks of differing sizes. The disks have holes in them, so they can be stacked on the pegs. The disks can be moved from any peg to any other peg. Only the top disk on a peg can be moved, and it can never be placed on a smaller disk. The disks all start out on peg A, but the goal is to move them all to peg C, one disk at a time, by means of transferring disks among pegs.

It is possible to mimic this problem with paper and coins. Draw three circles in a row on a sheet of paper and place four coins (a quarter, a nickel, a penny, and a dime) in order of size in one circle. Your task is to move all of the coins to another circle one at a time. The constraint is that you can never place a larger coin on a smaller coin. This is an analogue of the Tower of Hanoi

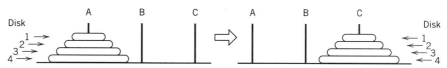

FIGURE 9.8. The four-disk version of the Tower of Hanoi problem.

problem in which the circles are the pegs and the coins are the disks. Try to solve this problem.

Table 9.1 attempts to illustrate the goals that have to be created to solve the Tower of Hanoi problem using a subgoaling approach. At the beginning the focus is on the biggest difference, which is to move disk 4 from peg A to peg C. Disk 4 is blocked by disk 3, which is on top of it. A subgoal is created to move disk 3 out of the way to peg B. But movement of disk 3 is blocked by disk 2, and a subgoal is created to move it out of the way to peg C. To move disk 2, a subgoal is created to move disk 1 out of the way to peg B. This goal can be achieved directly by a move, and this is the first move made in Table 9.1. Before this move could be made, four subgoals had to be created. Next to each move in Table 9.1 the number of goals necessary before that move could occur is given in parentheses.

Subjects are often quite explicit about their subgoaling. Consider the following protocol of a subject (Neves, 1977) who was faced with the Tower of Hanoi problem shown in Figure 9.9. This is the problem in an intermediate state, with disks 1 and 2 moved off peg 1. The subject chose to move disk 1 to peg 3, but before doing so gave the following justification of the choice[2]:

> The 4 has to go to the 3. But the 3 is in the way. So you have to move the 3 to the 2 post. The 1 is in the way there. So you move the 1 to the 3.

The subject began by setting the subgoal to remove the largest difference between the goal and the current state—"The 4 has to go to the 3." The operator to move this disk was blocked by the precondition that there could be nothing on disk 4. The subject then sees a subgoal of getting disk 3 out of the way. This was the second subgoal. To achieve this subgoal, the subject had to set a third subgoal, to get disk 1 off peg 2. This third subgoal was actually governing the move that the subject made. The second and third subgoals were operator subgoals that would enable moves; in contrast, the first goal was a difference reduction goal designed to get a disk to the target peg.

Although Neves's experiment gave verbal evidence that one subject might have used subgoaling once, it did not address the issue of how prevalent this strategy is in solving the Tower of Hanoi problem. Anderson, Kushmerick, and Lebiere (1993) examined the problem solving of a large number of subjects and determined how many subgoals subjects had to set before each move if

---

[2]In this protocol the subject is using digits to refer to pegs as well as disks; see Figure 9.9.

they were engaged in operator subgoaling. This number was inferred by assuming that the subjects were using an optimal subgoaling strategy to solve the problem. Fifteen moves were required to solve the problem. For each move the number of subgoals was determined from Table 9.1 and the average amount of time the subject took to make the move was calculated. Figure 9.10 shows the relationship between these two measures. The time to make a move strongly mirrored the number of subgoals that had to be set. It appears that goal setting is a major determinant of problem-solving time.

Table 9.1 *Goals, Subgoals, and Moves in Solving the Tower of Hanoi Problem*

	Difference Reduction Goal: Move disk 4 to Peg C
	Operator Subgoal: Move disk 3 out of the way to Peg B
	Operator Subgoal: Move disk 2 out of the way to Peg C
	Operator Subgoal: Move disk 1 out of the way to Peg B
1.	**Move disk 1 to Peg B (4 goals)**
2.	**Move disk 2 to Peg C (0 goals)**
	Operator Subgoal: Move disk 1 out of the way to Peg C
3.	**Move disk 1 to Peg C (1 goal)**
4.	**Move disk 3 to Peg B (0 goals)**
	Operator Subgoal: Move disk 2 out of the way to Peg B
	Operator Subgoal: Move disk 1 out of the way to Peg A
5.	**Move disk 1 to Peg A (2 goals)**
6.	**Move disk 2 to Peg B (0 goals)**
	Operator Subgoal: Move disk 1 out of the way to Peg B
7.	**Move disk 1 to Peg B (1 goal)**
8.	**Move disk 4 to Peg C (0 goals)**
	Difference Reduction Goal: Move disk 3 to Peg C
	Operator Subgoal: Move disk 2 out of the way to Peg A
	Operator Subgoal: Move disk 1 out of the way to Peg C
9.	**Move disk 1 to Peg C (3 goals)**
10.	**Move disk 2 to Peg A (0 goals)**
	Operator Subgoal: Move disk 1 out of the way to Peg A
11.	**Move disk 1 to Peg A (1 goal)**
12.	**Move disk 3 to Peg C (0 goals)**
	Difference Reduction Goal: Move disk 2 to Peg C
	Operator Subgoal: Move disk 1 out of the way to Peg B
13.	**Move disk 1 to Peg B (2 goals)**
14.	**Move disk 2 to Peg C (0 goals)**
	Difference Reduction Goal: Move disk 1 to Peg C
15.	**Move disk 1 to Peg C (0 goals)**

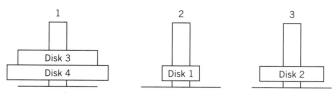

FIGURE 9.9. The state of the Tower of Hanoi problem facing the subject whose protocol was reported in Neves (1977).

Subjects set subgoals to enable them to apply operators that will achieve the main goal.

Conclusions About the Cognitive Stage

There are two requirements for solving a novel problem: acquiring the appropriate operators and deploying them. The principles of conditioning and memory seem to describe operator acquisition. New complexities arise in operator deployment. Most species, including humans, show a strong tendency to approach goals directly by eliminating differences between the current state and the goals. Humans show an additional problem-solving facility to organize their solution hierarchically by means of operator subgoaling. This method allows humans to postpone directly approaching the goal by setting subgoals to achieve along the way to achieving the main goal.

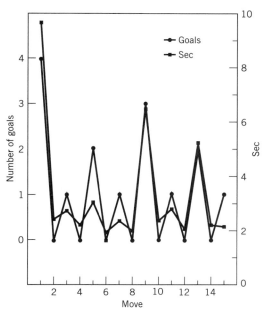

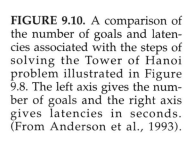

FIGURE 9.10. A comparison of the number of goals and latencies associated with the steps of solving the Tower of Hanoi problem illustrated in Figure 9.8. The left axis gives the number of goals and the right axis gives latencies in seconds. (From Anderson et al., 1993).

The Associative Stage

The second stage of skill acquisition is the associative stage, in which people stop using general problem-solving methods and start using methods specific to the problem domain. Essentially, they convert their declarative knowledge of the domain into procedural knowledge. The learning of domain-specific procedures is referred to as **proceduralization**. The changes in problem solving as learners move from declarative knowledge to procedural knowledge can be quite dramatic. Neves and Anderson (J. R. Anderson, 1982) looked at the changes in application of knowledge of geometry, such as that involved in the side-angle-side postulate. This postulate states that if two sides and the included angle of one triangle are congruent to the corresponding parts of another triangle, the triangles are congruent. Figure 9.11 illustrates the first problem one student had to solve using this postulate. Below is the protocol of that student as he reasoned through how to apply the postulate.

> If you looked at the side-angle-side postulate (long pause) well RK and RJ could almost be (long pause) what the missing (long pause) the missing side. I think somehow the side-angle-side postulate works its way into here (long pause). Let's see what it says: "Two sides and the included angle." What would I have to have to have two sides. JS and KS are one of them. Then you could go back to RS = RS. So that would bring up the side-angle-side postulate (long pause). But where would Angle 1 and Angle 2 are right angles fit in (long pause) wait I see how they work (long pause). JS is congruent to KS (long pause) and with Angle 1 and Angle 2 are right angles that's a little problem (long pause). OK, what does it say—check it one more time: "If two sides and the included angle of one triangle are congruent to the corresponding parts." So I have got to find the two sides and the included angle. With the included angle you get Angle 1 and Angle 2. I suppose (long pause) they are both right angles, which means they are congruent to each other. My first side is JS is to KS.

FIGURE 9.11. The first geometry proof problem that a student encounters that requires the side-angle-side postulate. (From J. R. Anderson, 1982).

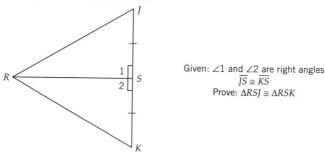

Given: ∠1 and ∠2 are right angles
$\overline{JS} \cong \overline{KS}$
Prove: $\triangle RSJ \cong \triangle RSK$

And the next one is RS to RS. So these are the two sides. Yes, I think it is the side-angle-side postulate. (J. R. Anderson, 1982, pp. 381–382)

After solving two more problems by means of side-angle-side (and two by side-side-side), the student faced the more difficult problem illustrated in Figure 9.12. The method-recognition portion of the protocol follows:

Right off the top of my head I am going to take a guess at what I am supposed to do: Angle DCK is congruent to Angle ABK. There is only one of two and the side-angle-side postulate is what they are getting to. (J. R. Anderson, 1982, p. 382)

The contrast between these protocols is striking. The student no longer had to verbally rehearse the postulate and search for correspondence between it and specific pieces of the problem. Rather, the student simply recognized the applicability of the rule. Because the application of the protocol switched to a pattern recognition, there was no longer a need to hold information in a rehearsal buffer, and so there were not the frequent failures of working memory when the student lost track of what he was trying to do. This is part of what is involved in the reduction of the cognitive component in a skill. Much of the effort that went into recognizing an appropriate problem-solving operator (in this case side-angle-side) has disappeared.

As students become more practiced in a skill, they come to recognize directly what they formerly had to think through.

Production Rules

Skill learning or procedural learning involves acquisition of a pattern-recognition basis for performing the skill. Numerous researchers (e.g., J. R. Anderson,

FIGURE 9.12. The sixth geometry proof problem encountered after studying the side-side-side and side-angle-side postulates. (From J. R. Anderson, 1982).

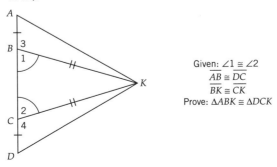

Given: $\angle 1 \cong \angle 2$
$\overline{AB} \cong \overline{DC}$
$\overline{BK} \cong \overline{CK}$
Prove: $\triangle ABK \cong \triangle DCK$

1983a; Bovair, Kieras, & Polson, 1990; Newell, 1991) have postulated that procedural knowledge takes the form of what are called **production rules**. The following production rule corresponds to the recognition of the applicability of the side-angle-side postulate.

> IF the goal is to prove that triangle 1 is congruent to triangle 2,
>   and triangle 1 has two sides and an included angle
>   that appear congruent to the two sides and included angle of
>   triangle 2
> THEN set as subgoals to prove that the corresponding sides and angles
>   are congruent
>   and then to use the side-angle-side postulate to prove that
>   triangle 1 is congruent to triangle 2.

A production rule contains a condition in its IF part, which specifies when the rule is to apply. In its THEN part is an action, which specifies what to do in that situation. Rules like this correspond to the basic steps of solving a problem, and a complex cognitive skill involves many of these rules. As described in Chapter 11, the competence needed to do proofs in high school geometry involves many hundreds of such rules.

One of the consequences of transforming knowledge into production rules is that the use of the knowledge becomes asymmetrical. Singley and Anderson (1989) studied the development of asymmetry in rule application by looking at the relationship between differentiation and integration in calculus. Although the procedures can be a bit more complex, the experiment involved simple calculus rules, such as the rule for powers:

$$y = ax^n <\!\!-\!\!> \frac{dy}{dx} = anx^{n-1}$$

In differentiation, an equation such as that on the left-hand side is transformed into an equation such as that on the right-hand side; integration moves from the right-hand side to the left-hand side. Initially subjects were equally facile in either direction. However, they were given practice in going in just one direction and so created production rules to perform that transformation. This practice improved the subjects' performance in the practiced direction but did not affect their performance in the unpracticed dimensions. Subjects had acquired one-direction rules, such as:

> IF the goal is to differentiate $y = ax^n$
> THEN write $dy/dx = anx^{n-1}$

which could not be reversed.

Another case of learning production rules involves the formation of new rules to capture repeated sequences of steps in the performance of a skill. For instance, whenever I use the bank machine, I put in my card, type in my code, hit *Enter*, and then hit *Withdrawal*. At one point these were four separate steps, but they have collapsed into a production rule of the form:

IF the goal is to get money from the bank machine
and I have put in my card
THEN type the code, hit *Enter,* and hit *Withdrawal.*

---

*Production rules are condition–action pairs that are postulated
to represent procedural knowledge.*

Development of Expert Rules

New, more powerful production rules are acquired as a person becomes more expert in a domain. Larkin (1981) showed that there are differences in the way in which physics students approach problems, such as that shown in Figure 9.13, as they gain experience. Novices begin with some physics principles that involve the quantity they are looking for and reason backward. For the problem in Figure 9.13, to find velocity students might use the equation:

$$v = at$$

(velocity equals acceleration times time) and then set as subgoals finding the values of the terms in this equation, for example, the acceleration, a. Essentially, they reason backward from their goal (e.q., v) to the givens in the problem. In contrast, experts reason forward from the givens of the problem. An expert might first calculate the forces acting on the object even though these forces have no immediate connection to the goal. Continuing the process of elaborating physics problems in this way eventually yields the answer. This forward elaboration strategy avoids having to maintain in memory complex sequences of subgoals.

Larkin showed that the differences between novices and experts could be captured in their having different production rules. She built a computer simulation to model novices and experts. Novice students are simulated by means–ends productions, such as:

FIGURE 9.13. A sketch of a sample physics problem. A block is sliding down an inclined plane of length l, where θ is the angle between the plane and the horizontal. The coefficient of the friction is μ. Find the velocity of the block when it reaches the bottom of the plane. The answer is $v = \sqrt{2\,lg\,(\sin\theta - \mu\cos\theta)}$. (From Larkin, 1981).*Source:* Figure 9.13 from J. H. Larkin. In J. R. Anderson (Ed). *Cognitive skills and their acquisition.* Copyright © 1981 by Lawrence Erlbaum Associates, Inc. Reprinted by permission.

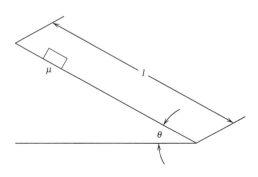

IF the goal is to calculate quantity v
THEN try to use the principle $v = at$
    and set as subgoals to find a and t.

Expert students are modeled with production rules such as:

IF the quantities a and t are known
THEN calculate v according to the formula $v = at$.

The novice production rule responds to the goal of finding the velocity and proposes a candidate equation. This is a working-backward production rule. The expert production rule responds to the fact that acceleration and time are known, which enables velocity to be calculated. This is a working-forward production rule. With experience in physics the problem solver learns more effective ways to approach the problem. Changes in the structure of skill have been reported in many domains. As a very different example, fighter pilots report that, with experience, they no longer approach the task of combat engagement from the perspective of being in the cockpit, but take a God's-eye view of their plane and others in space—that is, they feel that they are looking down on their plane and others in space. Various domains induce different skill reorganizations, but these reorganizations always reflect attempts to adapt to the structure of the problem domain.

As people become more expert in a domain, they may learn new production rules, which reorganize how they solve problems.

The Knowledge-Intensive Nature of Skill

Underlying a complex skill are hundreds or thousands or even tens of thousands of such rules. Simon and Gilmartin (1973) estimated that chess masters have acquired on the order of 50,000 rules for playing chess. It has been estimated that students who successfully master high school mathematics material have to acquire somewhere between 1000 and 10,000 rules (J. R. Anderson, 1992). It takes a great deal of time to achieve expertise in demanding domains. J. R. Hayes (1985) studied geniuses in fields varying from music to science. He found that no one produced work reflecting genius until after 10 years of work in a particular field.[3] Contrary to popular opinion, genius is 90 percent perspiration and 10 percent inspiration. A great deal of knowledge has to be mas-

---

[3]Frequently cited as an exception to this generalization is Mozart, who wrote his first symphony when he was 8 years old. However, his early works are not of genius caliber and are largely of historical value only. Schonberg (1970) claimed that Mozart's great works were produced after the 20th year of his career.

tered to display genius-level work, and mastering that knowledge takes a great deal of time.

Ericsson, Krampe, and Tesch-Römer(1993) have taken an extreme position and argued that there is nearly no contribution of innate talent to expert performance and that expert performance is almost entirely a matter of practice. They quoted studies (Bloom, 1985a, 1985b) of the histories of people who eventually became great in such fields as swimming and music. Bloom found that at some point in childhood the parents of these experts and geniuses decided that their children had special talents, even though objective evidence would suggest that this was just wishful thinking on the parents' parts. The parents then expended enormous resources in time and money on their children's training. It is this effort in training that produced the results, Ericsson and Krampe argued, not any initial talent.

Ericsson and Krampe studied violinists at the Music Academy of West Berlin. They found that what determined the relative rankings of these violinists was the amount of practice in their past. They also found that the best violinists were characterized by high-quality practice, such as practicing when they were well rested. Ericsson and Krampe's research does not really establish the case that a great deal of practice is sufficient for great talent. It seems more accurate to claim that extensive practice is a necessary but not a sufficient condition for developing a great ability. There probably is an innate contribution as well.

One of the interesting differences between experts and novices in a domain is their ability to remember information about problems they solve in that domain. De Groot (1965) found few differences between grand masters and other chess players besides the quality of their game. Grand masters are not more generally intelligent by conventional measures of intelligence, do not consider more moves, and do not appear to see further ahead in the game. The one difference he did find concerned their ability to reproduce a chessboard after a single glance. Grand masters are able to reconstruct more than 20 pieces from a chessboard after viewing it for only 5 seconds, whereas novices can only reconstruct 4 or 5 pieces. This result only holds when experts are shown actual board positions from chess games. If they are shown random configurations of pieces, their ability to reconstruct the board is no better than that of novices. Similar abilities of experts to remember meaningful problem situations have been shown in a large number of domains, including the game of Go (Reitman, 1976), electronic circuit diagrams (Egan & Schwartz, 1979), bridge hands (Charness, 1979; Engle & Bukstel, 1978), and computer programming (McKeithen, Reitman, Rueter, & Hirtle, 1981; Schneiderman, 1976).

It is speculated that the high memory performance of experts reflects the acquisition of relevant patterns that they have encountered during their prolonged efforts in the domain. Chase and Simon (1973) showed that subjects represented a chessboard in terms of game-relevant configurations, such as pawn chains. Newell and Simon (1972) speculated that these patterns are effectively the condition sides (the IF part) of productions. Experts recognize certain patterns in a problem and have rules for responding to these patterns. In essence, the good memory for problem states is reflecting the many production rules that experts have acquired for behaving in these domains.

A similar conclusion was reached in efforts to develop artificial intelligence programs to reproduce various types of human expertise. Computer systems can perform medical diagnosis, decide where to drill oil wells, and configure computers (Hayes-Roth, Waterman, & Lenat, 1983). These systems perform their specialized tasks with the facility of the best practitioners in the fields. In each case, a great deal of knowledge was learned from human experts and coded into the computer systems to match human performance. Still, these systems only match human performance in a narrow domain. To create a computer system as widely intelligent as a human seems a truly overwhelming task. Millions of facts and rules would have to be identified and coded into the computer.

People who develop a great talent have to invest an enormous amount of time to acquire and perfect a great number of rules.

Learning Histories of Individual Rules

The argument in this section is that the development of a skill can be identified with the acquisition of production rules. This argument raises the question of what the learning history of individual rules is like. Anderson, Conrad, and Corbett (1989) explored this question within the domain of the complex skill of computer programming.

They were interested in identifying the knowledge base that allows beginning computer programmers to write programs after a semester's course in computer programming. It was estimated that students needed to learn on the order of about 500 rules of programming. Students typically put a minimum of 100 hr into mastering such a course, which amounts to learning about five rules an hour. By means of a computer-based system for instructing computer programming (presented in Chapter 11), the learning of individual rules was monitored. Figure 9.14 gives two curves that display the average learning of these rules, measured either in errors per rule (Figure 9.14*a*) or in time to write the code corresponding to a rule (Figure 9.14*b*—only when correct). Log performance measures are plotted against log number of opportunities to practice the rule to see whether the relationship is linear, implying a power function. There is basically a linear relationship between the performance measures and the practice measures except for the transition from the first to the second opportunity, which is associated with creating the underlying rule. After the second opportunity the graph shows the kind of gradual improvement associated with the strengthening of knowledge.

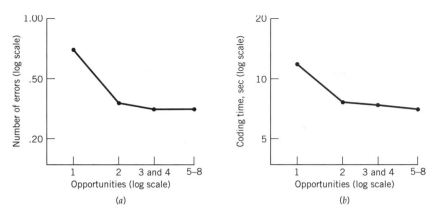

FIGURE 9.14. Learning data from a programming tutor: (*a*) number of errors per production (*b*) time to correctly code a production. (From Anderson et al., 1989).

This research indicates that the learning of a complex skill, such as computer programming, can be understood as the combination of 500 such learning processes for the 500 individual rules. This is an important conclusion, because it indicates that the principles of memory studied in the previous chapters apply to the learning of the pieces of a complex skill. The complexity of the skill acquisition comes from the overall organization of the skill, not the learning of the individual pieces.

The learning of a complex skill can be decomposed into the learning of the component rules.

Summary

To summarize the discussion to date, acquiring a complex skill involves

1. Acquiring the operators of the domain. This acquisition process is described by the principles of conditioning and memory.
2. Organizing these operators by means of problem-solving principles, such as difference reduction and operator subgoaling. The complexities of the skill are tackled in this process.
3. Converting the knowledge of how to solve the problems into production rules. This step marks the transition to the procedural form.
4. Strengthening the production rules. This process is described by the principles of memory, and in particular, seems to be a case of power law learning. (See the discussion of Figure 9.14.)

The Autonomous Stage

As subjects continue to practice a skill, its nature changes beyond the addition of new rules and the strengthening of existing ones. These further changes belong to the autonomous stage of skill acquisition, so named because the skill becomes more automatic, requiring less attention and interfering less with other ongoing tasks. When people learn to drive, initially they need to pay all their attention to driving and they are unable to maintain a conversation. As they become more practiced they are able to maintain a conversation while driving. The driving skill becomes so automatic that it seems to require no attention at all, at least when driving conditions are not demanding. People report driving miles on a highway without recalling anything of what they did.

Spelke, Hirst, and Neisser (1976) reported an interesting experimental demonstration of the growth of automaticity. Their subjects performed an odd pair of tasks simultaneously. The first task was to read a text for comprehension. The second was to transcribe (without looking at what they were writing) material that was being spoken. At first, subjects found this a difficult combination of tasks. Their comprehension of the text suffered dramatically. The rate at which they read also slowed down dramatically. Over a 6-week period they gradually improved their speed of reading until they were reading at preexperimental speeds without any loss of comprehension. However, they showed almost no ability to remember what they were transcribing, just as someone loses memory for what happens on the road if engrossed in conversation. Spelke et al. were able to show that, with even further practice, subjects could also remember what they were transcribing.

There are two key features of a skill when it becomes totally automatized: it can be performed without engaging the cognitive system, freeing the person to pursue other cognitive goals in a dual-task situation; and it becomes less interruptible. When learning to shift gears, for instance, a driver can choose to stop at any point in the process, but once the driver is proficient, the shifts are produced in one fluid motion and it is difficult to stop at a particular point. Skills develop these two features because more and more of the skill becomes implemented as a motor program and less and less is performed at a cognitive level. The next section discusses motor programs.

As a skill develops in the autonomous stage, it requires less attention but is harder to interrupt.

The Motor Program

A **motor program** is a prepackaged sequence of actions. Good examples are a person's signing his or her own name or a skilled typist's typing of "the." A novice typing "the," will be observed to find the *t*, strike it, check that the correct result was produced, find the h, strike, check, and then do the same for the e. None of this sequentiality is observed in the skilled typist. While the left index figure is going to the t, the right index finger is already going to the h. The execution of one keystroke is not waiting for feedback on the completion of the execution of the other keystroke. If the execution of the t is blocked by a stuck key, the h follows without alteration.

A distinction is made within the motor performance literature between **open-loop performance** and **closed-loop performance**. A closed-loop system waits for feedback from one action before taking the next action. A thermostat that controls a furnace is an example. After turning the furnace on, it waits until the temperature reaches the target level before turning the furnace off. An open-loop system executes a fixed sequence of actions without checking to see that the earlier actions achieved their intended effects. Old-fashioned copiers worked this way; they continued to feed paper after a jam had occurred. Modern copiers are closed loop and sense whether there is a paper jam.

Motor programs are open-loop segments of behavior. They are typically embedded in a larger, closed-loop structure, as in the case of a typist who may encode a familiar sequence of letters, type them in a closed-loop fashion, check, encode, execute, and so on. Also, what might be open-loop at a higher neural level is often closed-loop at a lower neural level. For instance, this section reviews the evidence that the cortex issues open-loop instructions to the effect that a hand should push and does not provide further monitoring. Closed-loop circuits at the level of the spinal cord monitor the execution of these commands.

Schmidt (1988b) cited three lines of evidence for the existence of open-loop motor programs. One is the slowness of closed-loop behavior. It takes about 200 msec for information to be perceived from the environment and registered in the cortex and for an appropriate reaction to be taken. (This estimate comes from the fact that the shortest simple reaction time is about 200 msec.) People are capable of executing actions much faster. Skilled pianists can perform as many as 16 finger movements per sec. There is not time for the person to sense the result of one movement before executing the next.

The second argument offered by Schmidt is that movements appear to be planned in advance. As the complexity of the movement increases, it takes longer to initiate the movement. If a typist is shown a single word and has to type it, the time from the presentation of the word to the first keystroke increases with the length of the word (Salthouse, 1985, 1986). The delay that increases with program complexity reflects the time needed to prepare the open-loop program.

The third argument comes from the results of deafferentation studies of monkeys (e.g., Taub & Berman, 1968). The deafferentation procedure eliminates sensory input by cutting through the dorsal roots of the spinal cords. It does not affect motor signals to the effectors. This procedure creates an organism that can move its limbs but has lost all sensory feedback from them. Such animals are still capable of learning to perform complex actions and then performing them in the dark (lights out) so that they cannot receive any visual input to guide the limbs. These animals receive no sensory feedback, and yet their limbs execute learned sequences, such as moving a hand to a lever.

There is evidence that at a certain point the instructions in the motor program are sent to the effectors (muscles) and the response cannot be stopped. Skilled typists type the next few characters after being told to stop (Salthouse, 1985, 1986). In a study by Slater-Hammel (1960), subjects watched the hand of a sweep timer that made one revolution per second. They were supposed to stop the movement by lifting a finger from a key when the hand reached a certain position. To do this successfully, they had to send a signal to their hand in anticipation of it reaching the target location. Occasionally, the timer hand stopped before it reached the target position and the subjects were to inhibit lifting their fingers. If the timer hand stopped at least 250 msec before reaching the target position, the subjects were able to stop their movement, but when it stopped less that 150 msec before the target, the subjects were unable to stop lifting their fingers. Subjects reported that they saw the clock stop and their hands responded anyway, as if they had no control over their hands.

Global control of behavior is a closed-loop routine that calls many open-loop motor programs. A tennis player responds to where the ball is by positioning the body and choosing the tennis stroke. Once the stroke begins its execution it largely runs in an open loop. A person composing at a typewriter may deliberately choose a word and then type it in an open-loop manner. The closed-loop phase involves the more deliberative processes of the cognitive and associative stages. What has been totally routinized gets packaged into open-loop motor programs. Successful performance depends on being able to assign much of the behavior to these open-loop segments that do not require cognitive monitoring. For instance, successful tennis is very much a game of strategy in terms of positioning on the court and choosing where to place the shots. Professional players can focus on this strategy because the actual process of executing a tennis shot has been automated.

Motor programs are open-loop segments of behavior that are performed without cognitive control.

Noncognitive Control

There can be nonconscious control over the execution of a behavior. As a skill develops, more and more of the control shifts to this nonconscious level. A good fraction (but hardly all) of this nonconscious control is performed by neural structures that are below the cortex. In one experiment Dewhurst (1967) had subjects hold a light weight at a particular angle. When the weight was suddenly changed, compensating activity could be recorded in the muscles just 30 msec after the change. This activity was initiated in the spinal cord where the sensory neurons synapse onto the motor neurons. The spinal cord knew that the arm was intended to be held in a certain position and began to take compensatory action as soon as a change occurred.

Other motor control takes place above the spinal cord but still at a subconscious level. This control occurs in both the cortex and the cerebellum. The cerebellum in the brain stem is particularly important in motor control (see Figure 1.15). The Dewhurst study demonstrated another compensating reflex to pressure changes that took about 80 msec. Unlike the spinal reflex, this reflex was to some degree instructable. If the person was told to let go when there was increased pressure, there was no compensatory response at 80 msec, but the spinal 30 msec reflex still occurred. This 80 msec is still much quicker than the 200 msec for conscious reaction time.

Schmidt called the 80-msec response the long-loop response. It is responsible for performing much of the microstructure of intentional action. As an interesting example, some objects, such as wine glasses, tend to slip through the hand and require compensatory increases of pressure to hold them in place. Johansson and Westling (1984) showed that when an object began to slip, there was a compensating increase in pressure 80 msec later. Subjects were quite unaware of the fact that their hands were making these adjustments.

Subcortical mechanisms control many complex aspects of behavior. This control has been displayed in research (Shik, Severin, & Orlovskii, 1966) on cats whose midbrains were severed such that the cerebellum was still connected to the spinal cord. Although the cats could no longer exercise cortical control (since the cortex was severed from the spinal cord) over their behavior, they were nonetheless capable of displaying coordinated walking patterns on a treadmill. As the treadmill sped up, they shifted their pattern from a walk to a trot to a gallop. These cats also shook a paw violently to get rid of a piece of tape placed on it. If placed on the treadmill with tape on a paw, they displayed a coordinated sequence of shaking the paw and walking. These experiments show that complex and coordinated pieces of behavior can be performed without any cortical involvement.

The detailed execution of motor programs can be guided by short-latency control processes in the spinal cord and cerebellum and by nonconscious cortical structures.

Generality of Motor Programs

Schmidt also argued that motor programs are general, not specific, sequences of behavior. Consider the writing examples in Figure 9.15 from Raibert (1977).

In the first case, the writing is normal with the right hand; in the second case, with the wrist immobilized; in the third case, with the left hand; in the fourth case, with the pen gripped in the teeth; and in the last case, with the pen taped to the foot. Not only was Raibert able to write in each case, but the writing preserves certain invariant features of Raibert's style, such as the curl on the top of the capital *E*. It appears that the same motor program is being executed in each case.

Schmidt suggested that the general program can be executed by different effectors (e.g., hands, mouth, feet) and with different parameters. Among the critical parameters that can be varied are the force and timing of the behavior. A person can write in large strokes by increasing the force of the movements and a person can slow down the rate of writing. Schmidt noted that these changes tend to be proportionate: if writing a signature is slowed by 50 percent, all components of the signature are slowed by about the same amount; if the force is increased, all letters show the same magnification.

Rosenbaum, Inhoff, and Gordon (1984) reported an interesting example of the generality of motor programs. College students were asked to perform a finger-tapping sequence. For instance, subjects might have to tap twice the

FIGURE 9.15. Raibert's attempts at writing: (A) with right hand; (B) with wrist immobilized; (C) with left hand; (D) with teeth; (E) with foot. *Source:* From Motor Control and Learning by the State-Space Model by M.H. Raibert, 1977, Technical Report, Artificial Intelligence Laboratory, MIT, (AI-TR-439), p. 50. Copyright © 1977 by M.H. Raibert. Reprinted by permission.

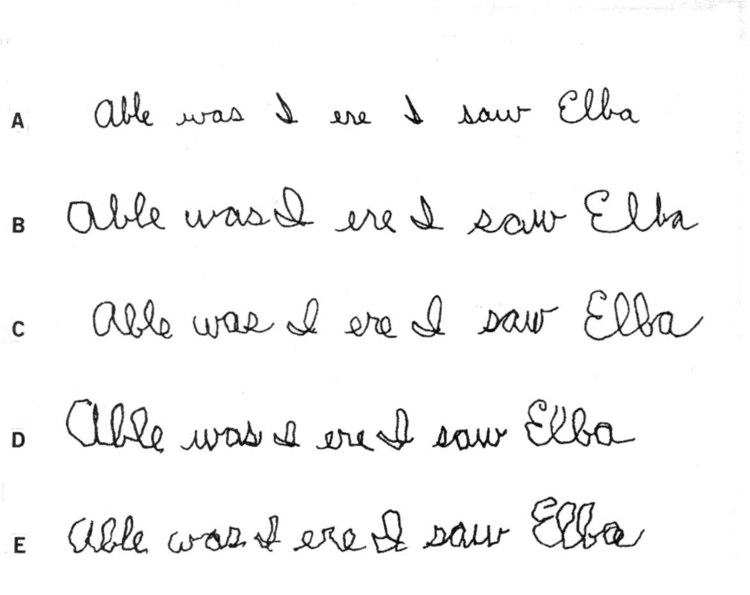

index finger on their left hand and then their left middle finger. They were responsible for two sequences—one for the left hand and one for the right hand. They were faster if both sequences involved the corresponding fingers on both hands—for example, they were faster if they had to tap *index, index, middle* on both hands than if they had to tap *index, index, middle* on the left and *index, middle, index* on the right. If both sequences were alike, the students had to hold in mind only one motor program, which they could send to either hand. This result illustrates how different effectors (in this case, the two hands) can execute the same motor program.

A motor program has certain parameters associated with it that allow it to be executed with different speed, with different force, and by different effectors.

Learning of Motor Programs: The Schema Theory

How are such motor programs acquired? Keele (discussed in Schmidt, 1988b) suggested that new motor programs are generated by stringing together smaller units of behavior. Figure 9.16 illustrates his proposal for the development of the skill of shifting gears. The process starts out as individual actions, such as lifting the foot, which the person presumably already knows. Eventually these become packaged into an overall behavior, which is shifting gears.

FIGURE 9.16. Keele's proposal for the process by which individual components of the gearshift change become composed into a single production. (From Schmidt, 1988). *Source: From Motor control and learning: a behavioral emphasis, Second Edition, (p. 477) by R. A. Schmidt, Champaign, IL: Human Kinetics Publishers. Copyright © 1988 by Richard A. Schmidt. Reprinted by permission.*

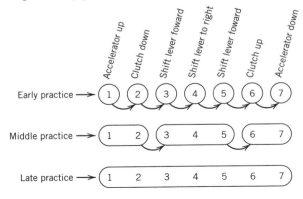

A critical issue in developing a motor program is learning to properly tune it. How do we learn just the right force and angle to use in making a basketball shot? How can we generalize that knowledge to different locations on the basketball court? J. A. Adams (1971) developed a theory of such learning, which was elaborated by Schmidt (1988b) in his **schema theory**. Schmidt holds that the learner develops two representations of the skill. One, called the recall memory, is the motor program itself—a prepackaged sequence of actions. The second, called the recognition memory, is a representation of the desired outcome of the action in terms of both the response-produced feedback and the external sensory consequences. A player taking a basketball shot can compare the outcome with the ideal (recognition memory) and adjust the motor program (recall memory) appropriately.

Schmidt emphasizes that neither the recall memory nor the recognition memory are for a specific action but rather are for a class of actions. Different actions can be achieved from the same motor program by evoking it with different parameters. A person can throw a ball a novel distance, having been trained on specific distances, by extrapolating the forces used for the training distances to the force needed for the new distance. In numerous studies subjects have been trained to perform a skill that involves different positions or to react to objects at different speeds (see Shapiro & Schmidt, 1982, for a review). People show considerably greater success in extrapolating to new values if they have practiced with a variety of values.

In a study on variability of practice, Catalano and Kleiner (1984) had subjects press a button when a moving target reached a certain point. The moving object could be traveling at one of a number of speeds (5, 7, 9, or 11 mph). The constant group was trained on just one of these speeds (different subjects, different speeds), and the variable group had practiced on all four speeds. Then subjects were transferred to novel speeds outside the previous range (1, 3, 13, or 15 mph). During original training, subjects were less accurate in the variable training condition (38 vs 52 msec error) but in the transfer task they were more accurate (60 vs 49 msec error). The constant training conditioning was easier because it involved adapting to only one value, but it did not prepare subjects as well for dealing with novel values. As Schmidt and Bjork (1992) noted, these results generalize to verbal tasks. For instance, it is easier to learn the meaning of a new word if it is used in a number of contexts.

Koh and Meyer (1991) did one study of how subjects extrapolate response values. At the beginning of each trial, subjects saw two vertical bars separated by various distances. Subjects were to make two taps separated by a pause the duration of which was determined by the distance. Figure 9.17 illustrates the true function that Koh and Meyer wanted subjects to learn. Subjects were tested with 12 different stimulus distances, but they received information on the correct duration for only the outer 8 stimuli. It was up to the subjects to assign durations to the middle four distances; they did not receive feedback as to what durations were correct. Subjects were given five 1-hr training sessions. Figure 9.17 presents data from the first and fifth sessions, including subjects'

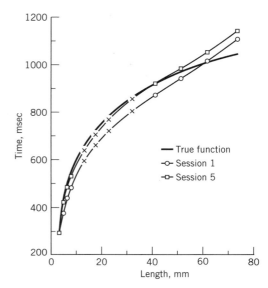

FIGURE 9.17. Duration of responses to stimuli in session 1 and session 5 of the experiment. The solid line represents the true function. The *x*'s denote values for which subjects received no feedback. (Data from Koh & Meyer, 1991).

responses for the middle four values, on which they received no feedback. Subjects were somewhat more accurate in the fifth session than in the first, but in all sessions they were fairly accurate at extrapolating responses to the untrained values.

Schmidt's theory holds that the recall memory is improved by comparing the action produced with an internal standard in the recognition memory of what the action should be like. This position implies that subjects should be capable of detecting errors in their actions without any external feedback. This situation occurs for actions that are rapidly produced and that the subject does not have the opportunity to correct. For instance, Schmidt and White (1972) looked at a ballistic timing task in which subjects were to move a slide 23 cm, taking as close to 150 msec as possible. After each movement and before being told what their actual error was, subjects were asked to estimate how far off the timing of the move was. Subjects' estimates were quite accurate. The correlations between the actual errors and the estimated errors approached 1 (perfect) after 2 days of practice.

We learn what the appropriate execution of a motor program is like and use this knowledge to correct the program.

The Role of Feedback

A critical issue is how the learner takes advantage of feedback to tune the motor programs. Some feedback is necessary for learning, but is more feedback always better? Detailed and immediate feedback after every attempt might be expected to produce the best learning results, but the research indicates otherwise. Bilodeau and Bilodeau (1958) looked at subjects learning to turn a knob to a target position. They varied the probability that a trial would be followed by feedback on error from 10 percent to 100 percent. There was no difference in amount learned as a function of percentage of feedback in training. Other studies (e.g., Ho & Shea, 1978; Schmidt & Shapiro, 1986) have looked at what happens when subjects are retested at a delay with no knowledge of results. The group that received the lowest frequency feedback often performed best at a delay. Salmoni, Schmidt, and Walter (1984) speculated that this result occurrs because subjects with constant feedback come to rely too much on it and cannot perform without the feedback. Also, processing the feedback may disrupt learning.

Schmidt, Shapiro, Winstein, Young, and Swinnen (1987) looked at a task that involved intercepting a pattern of moving lights by an arm movement (something like hitting a ball with a bat). They gave subjects feedback about the error in their movement after every trial, or information about average error after 5, 10, or 15 trials. Subjects who received constant feedback did best during the training. When tested in a situation with no feedback, subjects who had received summaries after every five trials did best. Intermittent feedback proved better than continuous feedback.

According to Schmidt, learning a skill does not depend on correcting the motor program with some external result. Rather, the motor program must be corrected with respect to an internal representation of the skill—Schmidt's recognition memory. Whether there is external feedback or not, there is always an internal representation, and the motor program is corrected after each trial. It is not necessary to have feedback after every trial to build up this internal representation of what the skill is like; occasional information about how the performance is progressing is sufficient to update the representation of the desired behavior.

Is it better to give only intermittent feedback for other learning tasks besides motor skills? What about academic learning tasks? As Schmidt and Bjork (1992) lamented, there has not been a great deal of research on this topic. Schooler and Anderson (1990) did one study of the acquisition of computer programming skill, which showed that at least sometimes feedback disrupts the learning. While students try to understand the feedback, they lose track of where they are in the problem.

Wulf, Schmidt, and Deubel (in press) pointed out that there really are two components to learning a motor program: learning the general structure of the program and learning how to parameterize the program. They looked at subjects making the sinusoidal movements illustrated in Figure 9.18. All the movements in Figure 9.18*a* illustrate the same general program. The only difference is the timing of the up and down movements. Similarly, all the movements in Figure 9.18*b* reflect the same program and vary only in the force with which the up and down movements are made. Wulf et al. con-

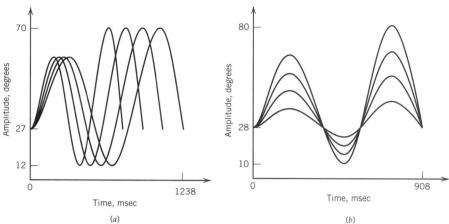

(a) (b)

FIGURE 9.18. (*a*) A set of actions reflecting the same motor routine but varying in timing; (*b*) A set of actions reflecting the same motor routine but varying in force. *Source:* From G. Wulf, R. A. Schmidt, and H. Deubel. Reduced feedback frequency enhances generalized motor program learning but not parameterization learning. *Journal of Experimental Psychology: Learning, Memory, and Cognition, Volume 19.* Copyright © 1993 by the American Psychological Association. Reprinted by permission.

A subject tracking a signal like that in Figure 9.18.

trasted intermittent feedback (63% of the time) with constant feedback (100% of the time). They developed separate measures of whether the subjects had learned the general pattern of the movement and whether they had learned the precise timing and force of one of these movements. They found that learning the general movement was better with intermittent feedback. However, learning the timing and the force was as good, and even a little better, with constant feedback.

> *Only occasional feedback is sufficient to tune the internal representation of the skill, and too frequent feedback can be disruptive.*

Final Reflections

This chapter has followed the process of skill learning from its initial organization in the first performances to the point at which the detail of the performance of a task is lost to cognition and becomes embedded in motor programs. Declarative memory plays a significant role initially, but is quickly replaced by a procedural memory in the form of production rules. The production rule is the key construct unifying the course of skill acquisition. Production rules embody the organization placed on the cognitive skills by the problem-solving processes during the cognitive stage. The development of the skill in the associative stage can be decomposed into the learning histories of the many component production rules. A motor program is essentially the action (or THEN) part of a production rule, and its learning in the autonomous stage amounts to the fine-tuning of a production rule.

Several studies of transfer among skills indicate that the degree of transfer is a function of the overlap between the skills in terms of production rules. As a person becomes more advanced in a domain, the person acquires additional production rules that take advantage of the special characteristics of that domain. One consequence of this specialization of skills is that there is less and less transfer among skills as the skills become more advanced (Henry, 1968).

The picture of learning from the skill-acquisition literature is much more complex than the picture painted in the early chapters of animal learning and human memory. Skill acquisition is concerned with behaviors of true significance that develop over scales of time more typical of learning outside the laboratory. Problem-solving organization has a role in human (and probably primate) skill aquisition that was not apparent in the simpler laboratory studies of learning. However, the processes of learning and strengthening apply to the component production rules much as they apply to the learning seen in the simpler laboratory studies.

> *The course of skill acquisition is determined by the learning history of the individual productions that make up the skill.*

Further Readings

The book by Newell and Simon (1972) remains a classic on problem solving. The artificial intelligence perspective on problem solving can be found in the texts by Rich (1983) and Winston (1984). Research on cognitive skill acquisition is reviewed in J. R. Anderson (1990) and Van Lehn (1989). Singley and Anderson (1989) review production rule theories of skill acquisition and transfer with a particular discussion of text editing. Klahr, Langley, and Neches (1987) review production system theories of skill acquisition. Newell (1991) describes his SOAR theory, and the ACT theory is described in J. R. Anderson (1983a, 1993). Rosenbaum (1991) and Schmidt (1988b, 1991) discuss motor performance and motor learning and Schmidt includes an exposition of his schema theory. Gentner (1987) provides a review critical of the idea that there is a proportionate timing parameter for motor programs. A recent comparison of motor learning and verbal learning is found in the work of Schmidt and Bjork (1992). The second half of the book edited by Osherson, Kosslyn, and Hollerbach (1990) consists of a series of review chapters on motor behavior and motor programs.

10

Inductive Learning

Overview

Most laboratory research on human learning has studied learning in a setting that is much like a traditional classroom. Subjects are supposed to learn basic facts or skills and are trained until these facts or skills are mastered. This sort of paradigm is useful for understanding the principles of memory, but it ignores a critical component of learning—determining just what it is that should be learned. This component loomed large in the conditioning experiments where the organism had to determine what controlled the appearance of a reinforcer. Figure 5.1 introduced the concept of an inductive component in explaining the relationship between a typical conditioning experiment and a typical memory experiment. Induction refers to the process by which the system makes probable inferences about the environment on the basis of experience. For instance, in a typical conditioning experiment the inductive component figured out what was related to what. In contrast, the need for this process was bypassed by the use of instructions in a memory experiment.

Much of human learning avoids the need for induction because much of our environment is understood and we can be directly instructed on it. Still, a significant fraction of human learning involves induction. We have to figure out what things annoy or please an acquaintance. We have to figure out how to operate many appliances without direct instruction. Children manage a great deal of learning without instruction. For instance, they figure out which animals are dogs and which are cats without being told what makes an animal a dog or a cat. Perhaps most impressive, they learn to speak their first language without direct instruction.

Learning the structure and rules of a particular domain without direct instruction is referred to as **inductive learning**. Inductive learning involves uncertain inferences from experience. Suppose that you come upon a microwave oven and press 1 followed by *start* on its button panel. You observe that the oven runs for exactly 60 sec. You might make the inference that pressing the 1 caused it to run for 1 min and that pressing the 2 would cause it to run for 2 min. This conclusion is an **inductive inference**. It may not be correct—the 1 may control the power level at which the oven operates—but suppose it is correct. Now you want to run the oven for 10 min, but there are only buttons with the digits 0 through 9. What do you do? You might infer that pressing a 1 followed by a 0 would achieve the goal. This is another inductive inference. What if you want the device to operate for only 30 sec? You might notice a button labeled *seconds* and infer that pressing *seconds* before pressing 3 and 0 would yield the desired effect. What if you want to have it run 2 min and 20 sec? What if you want it to run at half intensity? By a process of hypothesis and test, you would probably come to an understanding of how the device functions. The total episode is an example of inductive learning.

Philosophers make a contrast between induction and deduction. In deduction, inferences are logically certain, whereas in induction they are not. If told that an animal is a poodle, a person can infer with certainty that the animal is a dog. This type of inference is a **deductive inference** because all poodles are dogs. If an animal is heard barking, a person might also infer that the animal is a dog. This is an inductive inference, because it is conceivable that some other animal might bark. As this example makes clear, inductive inference really adds something to knowledge and so counts as a kind of learning. In contrast, there is a sense in which deductive inference adds nothing but only makes explicit what is already known.

An element of inductive learning is involved in nearly every learning situation—even direct instruction. A tennis coach illustrates how to hold the racket for a two-handed backhand, but leaves the player to figure out which aspects of the demonstration are the critical aspects. A geometry teacher works through the steps of a proof and usually does not tell the students why an inference is made at one point rather than another—the student must figure it out. In English class a teacher marks a sentence as awkward—but what aspect of the sentence is awkward?

Much of what the earlier chapters reviewed about conditioning was concerned with inductive learning. This chapter reflects a return to these earlier issues, but focuses more on human inductive learning. The chapter addresses the topics of concept formation, causal inference, and language acquisition, three types of human inductive learning that have received much research. It reveals that the inductive learning required of people can be very tricky indeed. This chapter also reviews the argument that it would be impossible for children to learn a language unless they were born knowing a great deal about language already and that language acquisition is a uniquely human ability.

Inductive learning involves making uncertain inferences that go beyond our direct experience.

Concept Acquisition

Concept acquisition research is concerned with how we learn natural categories, such as "dog," "chair," "car," and "tree." It is not particularly obvious how children learn what separates a dog from a cat or a chair from a table. Adults have difficulty articulating the difference between these concepts—how do children figure it out? The mystery of this learning process is intensified by the fact that most of it happens in childhood when the learners are not particularly articulate. However, concept learning does extend to adulthood. When I visited Australia, I learned new animal concepts, such as "echidna" and "kookaburra," and I learned to recognize a number of categories of birds for which I never did learn the verbal labels. It is no more clear to me how I learned to recognize these animals than it is to a child how he or she comes to recognize a dog. However, researchers have used a number of different approaches to shed light on what is involved in learning a new concept. Much of this research has been done with adult subjects.

A major issue in this research has been to what degree concept acquisition is like the associative learning characteristic of conditioning experiments. An early experiment by Hull (1920) suggested that concept learning is like conditioning. His subjects learned to categorize different Chinese alphabet characters, such as those shown in Figure 10.1; each row reflects a different concept defined by the presence of a Chinese radical. Subjects were not informed about the critical feature. Gradually they learned how to classify the stimuli, but they

FIGURE 10.1. Example of stimulus material used by Hull (1920). Each row represents a category defined by the presence of the Chinese radical. *Source:* From C. L. Hull. Quantitative aspects of the evolution of concepts: An experimental study. Copyright © 1920 in the Public Domain.

were quite incapable of saying what they did to classify these stimuli. Hull concluded that concepts are learned by simple associative learning.

Since Hull's research, the field has vacillated in terms of how to think about the nature of human concept learning, moving full circle from Hull's position to regarding human concept learning, as dramatically opposed to associative learning, back to seeing much in common between the two types of learning.

A key issue has been whether human concept learning can be understood in terms of simple associative learning.

Concept-Identification Studies

A new view about human concept learning began with a classic series of experiments by Bruner, Goodnow, and Austin (1956). Figure 10.2 illustrates the kind of material they used. Eighty-one stimuli varied along four possible dimensions: number of objects (one, two, or three); number of borders (one, two, or three); shape of objects (cross, circle, or square); and color of objects (green, black, or red). There were three possible values on each of the four dimensions and thus $3 \times 3 \times 3 \times 3 = 81$ possible objects. Subjects were told that there was some concept that referred to a specific subset of the objects,

FIGURE 10.2. Material used by Bruner et al. (1956) to study concept identification. *Source:* From J. S. Bruner, J. J. Goodnow, and G. A. Austin. *A study of thinking.* Copyright © 1956 by J. S. Bruner.

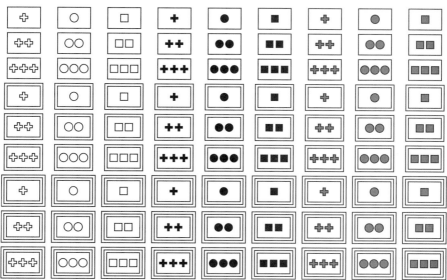

for instance, all green squares. Subjects were instructed to discover the concept and were shown various stimuli identified as members of the concept or not. When they thought they knew what the concept was, they could announce the concept.

Given the research of Hull and others, psychologists had thought of concept learning as involving the simple associative learning processes discussed in the conditioning chapters. Thus for the concept of "green squares," "green" and "square" would gradually get associated to the category. Bruner et al. and subsequent researchers found evidence that subjects engaged in conscious hypothesis testing. This research helped fuel the cognitive revolution against the prevailing behaviorist paradigm. Before describing the results of this research, it is important to identify its methodological features.

The Bruner et al. paradigm is somewhat different from concept learning in real life, that is, people normally do not suddenly announce that they have a new concept. A person displays knowledge of the concept "dog" by successfully classifying new instances as dogs. Research subsequent to that of Bruner et al. has used successful classification behavior as evidence for knowing the concept; that is, if the subjects could correctly categorize new instances they were credited with having the concept.

Another dimension of the experimental design is whether subjects select instances to get information about or whether they receive a series of instances classified for them. The former paradigm is called the selection paradigm, and the latter the reception paradigm. Subjects in a selection paradigm can behave more like a scientist and select instances to test their current hypothesis about what the concept is. Learning in the reception paradigm is more like learning concepts in the real world, where we encounter instances and noninstances of categories with little control over which instances we encounter. Although Bruner et al. studied both paradigms, subsequent research has tended to focus on the reception paradigm.

Figure 10.3 contains three examples of what subjects might see. Each column contains a sequence of objects associated with a different category. A plus sign (+) beside the object means it is a member of the category and a minus sign (−) means it is not. Subjects are presented with these instances one at a time. You should try to figure out the category represented by each column.

The category for the first column is "two crosses," for the second column, "two borders or circles," and for the third column, "number of borders equals number of objects." The first category probably seems the most natural. It is referred to as a conjunctive concept because it requires that all of a set of features be present. The second is called a disjunctive concept because it only requires that at least one member of a set of features be present. The third is called a relational concept because it involves a relationship among the dimensions. Subjects find conjunctive concepts much easier than disjunctive or relational concepts and learn them after seeing fewer instances (Bourne, 1974; Bourne, Ekstrand, & Dominowski, 1971).

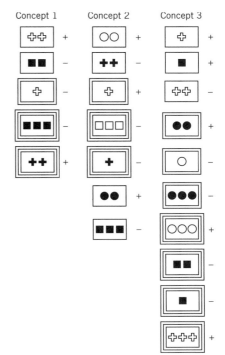

FIGURE 10.3. Examples of sequences of instances from which a subject is to identify concepts. Each column gives a sequence of instances and noninstances for a different concept: A plus (+) signals a positive instance and a minus (−) a noninstance. *Source:* From *Cognitive psychology and its implications* by John R. Anderson. Copyright © 1990 by W. H. Freeman. Reprinted with permission.

Concept formation has been studied in paradigms in which subjects see instances identified as members or nonmembers of a concept they are supposed to identify.

Hypothesis Testing

These tasks are not all that different from conditioning experiments (Chapters 2 through 4) in which the organisms must figure out what features in the environment are controlling reinforcement. The earlier chapters reviewed the evidence that organisms tend to strengthen associations between various features in the environment and responses. One feature of their learning is that it is gradual. In contrast, human learning in these experiments seems to be anything but gradual. Bruner et al. characterized their subjects as engaging in **hypothesis testing**. Subjects have specific hypotheses, such as, "I think it is three crosses," and they may completely change their hypothesis from one trial to the next. Bruner et al. characterized hypothesis testing as following roughly these steps:

1. Pick some hypothesis consistent with the instances that have been encountered. (In some experiments the instances are arrayed in front of the subjects, whereas in other experiments subjects must try to remember the instances.)
2. Classify new instances according to this hypothesis.
3. If the classification of new instances is correct, stick with the hypothesis.
4. If the classification is wrong, go back to step 1.

This procedure, which is dramatically different from associative learning, produces discontinuities in performance such that subjects behaving according to one hypothesis will change their behavior to conform to a new hypothesis given a single disconfirming episode in step 4.

As an example of hypothesis-testing behavior, suppose that a subject is entertaining the hypothesis that the concept is simply "black objects." The subject sees three black squares in two borders and identifies it as an instance of the concept. Suppose this identification is correct. Next the subject sees three white squares in three borders and identifies it as not an instance of the concept. If the subject is told that this is wrong, the subject abandons completely the old hypothesis of "black" and may then entertain the hypothesis that the concept is "square objects." This one-trial switch from "black" to "squares" is quite unlike associative learning about the relevant features of a stimulus, in which organisms gradually strengthen or weaken associations to features such as squareness.

If subjects are asked to say what concept they are considering, such one-trial switches can be seen directly. More typically, researchers simply observe which instances subjects classify as members of the category and which they do not. Researchers infer from this classification data what concept a subject is entertaining.

Some early research on human concept formation that used this methodology yielded data that seemed to favor the gradual learning rather than the all-or-none-learning assumption of hypothesis-testing models. In the typical paradigm, during one trial a subject is shown a stimulus, is asked to indicate if it is in the category, and is then given feedback as to whether the classification is correct. Such trials are repeated over and over again. Figure 10.4 shows a typical plot of probability of a correct response as a function of trial number. The percentage of correct classifications is averaged over all the subjects in the experiment. The figure shows a continuous approach to perfect performance, suggesting that subjects gradually develop associations to the correct stimulus features. The apparent gradualness of Figure 10.4 seems to contradict the hypothesis-testing explanation, which claims that subjects identify the correct hypothesis or concept on a single trial. According to that view, subjects would perform at a chance level (50%) for a while and then abruptly jump to 100 percent on the trial when they identified the correct hypothesis.

Bower and Trabasso (1964) wondered whether the apparent gradualness of concept discovery might be the result of averaging over subjects. They

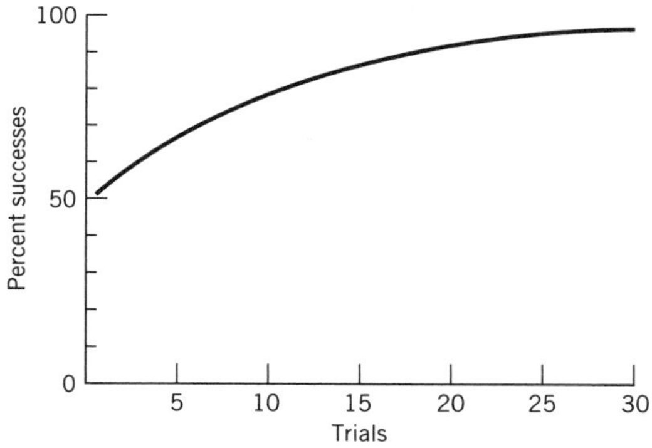

FIGURE 10.4. Probability of classifying an instance as a function of trial in the typical concept-identification experiment. The probabilities in this hypothetical curve have been averaged over subjects.

thought that one subject might have selected the correct concept after an error on trial 10 and shown an abrupt jump to perfect categorization, another subject might have selected the correct concept on trial 6, and still another on trial 20, and so on. Averaging different subjects together would give the illusion of gradual improvement as more and more subjects identified the correct concept. The increase in average probability of correct classification would just reflect the growing percentage of subjects who had identified the concept and who were responding perfectly. To test for this possibility, Bower and Trabasso developed a new method for plotting the data. They identified the last trial on which each subject made an error and then plotted probability of correct categorization back from that trial. Figure 10.5 shows those data. Suppose the last error one subject made was on trial 9. For this subject, trial 1 in Figure 10.5 would come from trial 8, trial 2 would come from trial 7, and so on; finally, trial 8 would come from trial 1. For another subject whose last error was on trial 21, trial 1 in Figure 10.5 would come from trial 20, trial 2 would come from trial 19, and so on; finally, trial 20 would come from trial 1.[1] Thus, trial 1 is the trial just before the last error for all subjects, trial 2 is the second trial before the last error for all subjects, and so on. The curve illustrated in Figure 10.5 is called a **backwards learning curve**.

If each subject had been gradually learning the concept, there would be a gradual improvement in this backwards learning curve as it approached trial 1 (the trial before the last error for all subjects). However, probability correct hovers around the chance level of 50 percent right up to the trial just before the last error (trial 1 in Figure 10.5). These data are good evidence for **all-or-none learning**. That is, on the last error subjects made a complete switch from a wrong hypothesis, which was yielding chance performance, to the correct one, which yielded perfect performance. This analysis contains a significant lesson: an average learning curve (Figure 10.4) that apparently displays gradual learning can actually be hiding all-or-none learning, which can be uncovered by a backwards learning curve (Figure 10.5).

[1]One consequence of this process is that fewer and fewer subjects contribute to trials that are more and more removed from the trial of last error.

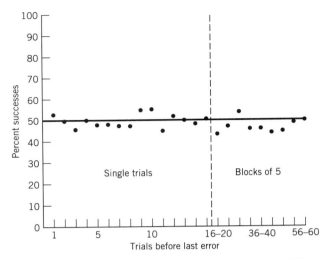

FIGURE 10.5. A backwards learning curve: Probability of correctly classifying an instance as a function of number of trials before last error. (From Bower & Trabasso, 1964). *Source:* Figure 10.5 from R. C. Atkinson, Ed. *Studies in mathematical psychology.* Copyright © 1964 by Stanford University Press. Reprinted by permission.

Figure 6.8 analyzed some individual-animal conditioning curves. Each animal appeared to begin conditioning on a certain trial, but it took many more trials to perfect the conditioning. It was argued that conditioning consisted of an all-or-none induction phase followed by a gradual strengthening phase. The concept-learning experiments discussed here focus only on that all-or-none induction phase.

Concept learning can involve abrupt changes in hypotheses when the current hypothesis is disconfirmed.

Natural Concepts

There has been increased questioning of what these laboratory experiments on concept acquisition reveal about human learning of **natural categories**, such as "dog" or "tree." Subjects approach such experiments with a problem-solving orientation, which does not seem to be how natural categories are learned. This approach certainly appears too sophisticated and conscious for children learning in a natural environment. Moreover, it has been argued (Rosch, 1973, 1975, 1977) that natural categories are not the sorts of things that have the all-or-none logical structure of these laboratory categories. One of the major characteristics of natural categories is that they are not defined by the presence of a few features. Rather, many features tend to be associated with the category, and an instance is a member of a category to the degree that it possesses these characteristic features. For example, birds are characteristically of a certain size and can fly. However, an ostrich, which cannot fly and is very large, is recognized as a bird because it has other birdlike features, such as feathers, wings, and a beak. Even though an ostrich can be so recognized, a person seeing one for the first time might certainly hesitate in making the classification.

Rosch performed several experiments examining the structure of natural categories. In one experiment (1973), subjects were asked to rate how typical various members of categories were on a 1 to 7 scale, where 1 meant very typical and 7 meant very atypical. Table 10.1 reproduces some of the ratings obtained. Different members of a category received rather different ratings as to how typical they were. Rosch argued that various instances are members of a category to the degree that they are typical of that category. In another experiment Rosch (1975) had subjects categorize pictures of animals and plants, such as robins and chickens (both birds) and apples and watermelons (both fruits). She found that subjects were more rapid at identifying the category membership of the pictures of the more typical objects. For instance, they more quickly recognized a robin as a bird than an ostrich as a bird and they more quickly recognized an apple as a fruit than a watermelon as a fruit. Rosch argued that instances are members of a category to the degree to which they possess features that are associated with that category. Thus the reason that robins are seen as more typical of birds than are ostriches is that they can fly and their size and shape are more commonly associated with birds.

McCloskey and Glucksberg (1978) provided one of the more convincing demonstrations of the fact that natural categories do not have fixed boundaries. They found that there were various items about which subjects could not agree as to category membership. For instance, is stroke a disease? Sixteen of 30 subjects thought so, whereas the other 14 disagreed. Is a leech an insect? Thirteen subjects said yes and 17 said no. Is a pumpkin a fruit? Sixteen sub-

Table 10.1 *Ratings of Category Goodness*

Fruit			Vehicle		
	Apple	1.3		Car	1.0
	Strawberry	2.3		Boat	2.7
	Fig	4.7		Tricycle	3.5
Sport			Crime		
	Football	1.2		Murder	1.0
	Hockey	1.8		Embezzling	1.8
	Wrestling	3.0		Vagrancy	5.3
Bird			Vegetable		
	Robin	1.1		Carrot	1.1
	Wren	1.4		Onion	2.7
	Ostrich	3.3		Parsley	3.8

Source: From Rosch, 1973.

jects said yes and 14 said no. In a retest a month later, 11 subjects reversed themselves on stroke, 3 reversed themselves on leech, and 8 reversed themselves on pumpkin. Not only do subjects disagree among themselves as to category membership, but individual subjects are inconsistent in assignment to category.

A basic feature of natural categories is that they have these vague boundaries; as a consequence, instances are members of the categories to the degree to which they are typical. The hypothesis-testing behavior reviewed earlier seems only appropriate for learning categories with crisp, discrete boundaries. A number of experiments have studied the acquisition of artificial concepts that have a structure more like that of natural categories. A simple example of such an experiment was performed by Medin and Schaffer (1978). They had subjects study the six items in Table 10.2. In category A the majority of the stimuli are one object, large, red, and triangular, whereas in category B the majority of the stimuli are two objects, small, blue, and circular. There are exceptions, and no feature is sufficient for category membership, nor is there any apparent rule for classification. After studying these items, subjects were asked to rate how typical various stimuli were of their category. Medin and Schaffer found that stimuli were judged typical to the extent that they had the features that were associated with that category. In Table 10.2 stimulus 1 was judged most typical of category A and stimulus 4 was judged most typical of category B.

Two types of theories based on such experiments have been advanced to account for how people learn the structure of natural categories. **Schema theories** hold that people form associations between various features and categories to the degree to which category members tend to display these features. In effect, subjects develop a schema, or a prototype, of what a typical member of the category is like. A test stimulus is assigned to the category that has the strongest associations to the features of that test stimulus. **Exemplar theories** hold that people classify instances as members of a category to the extent to which they are similar to other instances of a category. This theory holds that we do not really create categories but rather judge category membership on the basis of similarity to specific instances. The next two sections describe examples of these two kinds of theories.

Table 10.2 *An Example of the Experimental Material Used in Medin and Schaffer (1978)*

1. One large red triangle is in category A.
2. Two small red triangles is in category A.
3. One large blue circle is in category A.
4. Two small blue circles is in category B.
5. One large red circle is in category B.
6. Two small blue triangles is in category B.

Natural concepts have vague boundaries in which items are members of the category to varying degrees.

A Schema Theory: Gluck and Bower

Chapter 2 described Gluck and Bower's (1988) application of the Rescorla–Wagner theory to describe the learning of two disease categories. Their model is an example of a current successful schema theory. It has attracted particular attention because it has been presented as a connectionist model related to other data on neural learning (Gluck & Thompson, 1987). Gluck and Bower's model assumes that strengths of association are formed between stimulus features and categories according to the Rescorla–Wagner rule. (The stimulus features are treated as CSs and the category is treated as the US.) Suppose that a stimulus consisting of two small red triangles is presented and is said to be in category A. Then the strengths of association from the stimulus features two objects, small, red, and triangular to category A are changed according to the rule:

$$\Delta V = \alpha (\lambda_A - \Sigma V_A)$$

where ΔV is the amount of change; α is the learning rate; λ_A is the strength of association that category A can support; and ΣV_A is the total strength of the existing associations of these features to category A. If there is an alternative category B, strengths of association from these features to that category are decreased according to the rule:

$$\Delta V = \alpha (0 - \Sigma V_B)$$

where ΣV_B is the sum of the strengths of existing associations to B. As discussed in the conditioning chapters, the strengths of association among individual stimulus features and a category are set according to how well these stimulus features predict that category. With respect to the example in Table 10.2, these equations imply that the features associated with category A (one object, large, red, triangular) eventually acquire strengths of association to category A of .22 λ_A, and the other features have strengths of association of zero. With respect to category B, these other features acquire strengths of .22 λ_B, whereas the A features have no association. The Gluck and Bower theory nicely accounts for the fact that instances are seen as members of categories to the extent that they display features associated with the category. Another advantage of the Gluck and Bower theory is that it accurately predicts the learning curves that describe how subjects gradually develop their ability to categorize with exposure to more and more instances (as reviewed in the next section).

Consider how the Gluck and Bower model would apply to the stimuli in Table 10.2. It would predict that the features one object, large, red, and triangular would be associated with category A, and the features two objects, small, blue, and circular would be associated with category B. Consider how it would respond to the stimuli:

1. One large red triangle (in category A):   4 A features, 0 B features
2. Two small red triangles (in category A):   2 A features, 2 B features
3. One large blue circle (in category A):   2 A features, 2 B features
4. Two small blue circles (in category B):   0 A features, 4 B features
5. One large red circle (in category B):   3 A features, 1 B feature
6. Two small blue circles (in category B):   1 A feature, 3 B features

If the subjects adopted the rule to classify in category A all stimuli with two or more A features, they would correctly classify all but stimulus 5. The Rescorla–Wagner rule cannot correctly categorize stimulus 5 because it contains more A features than B features. To deal with such problems, Gluck and Bower proposed that subjects use configural stimuli. For instance, subjects might associate red circles with category B. Chapter 2 discussed how it was necessary to augment the Rescorla–Wagner theory with configural stimuli to account for results in the conditioning literature. The same history of theories that appeared in the conditioning literature is being played out in this categorization research.

The Gluck and Bower theory illustrates the apparent cyclic character of theories in psychology. Psychologists such as Hull originally proposed using strength-of-association theories to account for human concept formation. Subsequent research on hypothesis testing in concept formation indicated that categories were learned in a more all-or-none manner than envisioned in those theories. Later researchers questioned whether the concepts learned in the experiments were like natural concepts. When the learning of natural concepts was studied, the process of learning appeared to be much more similar to that proposed by Hull.

Gluck and Bower proposed that strengths of association between features and concepts are strengthened according to the Rescorla–Wagner learning rule.

An Exemplar Theory: Medin and Schaffer

The other kind of theory, the exemplar theory, proposes that the subject forms no categories at all; rather, the subject simply remembers some or all the instances of various categories. When asked to categorize an instance, the subject determines what past instance is similar to this test instance and infers that the test instance is in the same category as the past instance. A particularly successful version of this kind of theory is the exemplar theory of Medin and Schaffer (1978; see also Nosofsky, 1988).

To formally develop the Medin and Schaffer theory, it is necessary to specify the probability of retrieving a past study instance given a particular test instance. This is a function of the similarity of the study instance to the test instance relative to the similarity of other studied instances to the test instance. The similarity between a study instance and a test instance is calculated in terms of the similarity of their component features. Thus, a study stimulus of two large blue triangles is similar to a test stimulus of one large blue circle to the extent that *one* and *two* are similar, *large* and *large* are similar, *blue* and *blue* are similar, and *triangle* and *circle* are similar. Medin and Schaffer proposed to measure the features on a 0-to-1 scale with 0 meaning totally dissimilar and 1 meaning identical. They proposed that the similarity of the two stimuli was a product of the similarities of the component features. In one of their applications, they proposed the similarity would be 1 if two features matched and .2 if the features mismatched. In the example given here, where there are two matches and two mismatches, the overall similarity is $1 \times 1 \times .2 \times .2 = .04$.

As a full illustration of the Medin and Schaffer theory, suppose that the subject has studied the six stimuli in Table 10.2 and must classify the test stimulus *one large blue triangle*. To apply the theory it is necessary to calculate the similarity of this test stimulus to each study stimulus in Table 10.2. These calculations are performed in Table 10.3.

Table 10.3 *Calculation of the Similarity of* One Large, Blue Triangle *to Each Study Stimulus in Table 10.2*

	Number		Size		Color		Shape		Similarity
Category A Study Item 1	1	×	1	×	.2	×	1	=	.200
Category A Study Item 2	.2	×	.2	×	.2	×	1	=	.008
Category A Study Item 3	1	×	1	×	1	×	.2	=	.200
Category B Study Item 4	.2	×	.2	×	1	×	.2	=	.008
Category B Study Item 5	1	×	1	×	.2	×	.2	=	.040
Category B Study Item 6	.2	×	.2	×	1	×	1	=	.040

The probability of categorizing the test stimulus in category A is its total similarity to the category A stimuli (first three in the table) relative to its similarity to all stimuli:

$$\frac{.200 + .008 + .200}{.200 + .008 + .200 + .008 + .040 + .040} = .822$$

Thus the chances are high that the subject would place this particular stimulus in category A.

The exemplar theory is able to predict certain results that simple versions of schema theory cannot. Consider classification of the problematical item 5, *one large red circle*, given the items in Table 10.2. Since the features *one, large,* and *red* are all associated with category A, the schema theory would predict that the item would be classified in that category. To account for the correct classification of this item, Gluck and Bower assumed that subjects responded to configural cues, which are combinations of features. The Medin and Schaffer theory has no problems accounting for the successful classification of this item. Since it was studied as being in category B and it is maximally similar to itself, subjects are likely to retrieve it and use it for its own classification. Put another way, the Medin and Schaffer theory proposes that subjects classify this item by remembering it specifically and the category it came from.

Estes, Campbell, Hatsopoulos, and Hurwitz (1989) compared the Gluck and Bower network model with the Medin and Schaffer model. Their experiment involved subjects categorizing patients' symptoms into a rare versus a common disease (the same sort of experiment as described with respect to Figure 2.15). Subjects practiced categorizing the symptoms of 240 patients. Various symptom combinations occurred with various probabilities with the two diseases. Figure 10.6 compares the subjects' success in predicting blocks of 10 patients with the success of the two models. Since symptom combinations occurred with the diseases with only certain probabilities, subjects could not be perfect. The fluctuations in Figure 10.6 from block to block reflect how difficult each block was. Subjects showed some tendency to improve (chance is 50%). What is remarkable is how well the two theories do at predicting the ups and downs in subject accuracy. Both theories seem to do a good job in predicting all the ups and downs in the data. The Gluck and Bower model does a little better, but the real message of this figure is that two very different theories can yield such similar predictions.

Exemplar theories claim that subjects classify a test instance by retrieving a similar study instance and using its category.

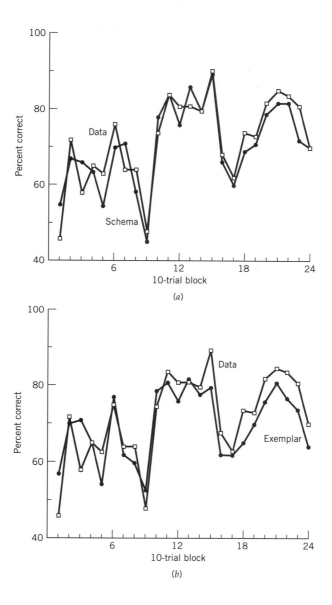

FIGURE 10.6. Comparison of schema and exemplar models in accounting for block-by-block learning data. *Source:* From W. K. Estes, J. A. Campbell, N. Hatsopoulos, and J. Hurwitz. *Journal of Experimental Psychology: Learning, Memory and Cognition, Volume 4.* Copyright © 1989 by American Psychological Association. Reprinted with permission.

Conclusions About Concept Acquisition

Categories are powerful mental constructs because they allow us to make a lot of sense out of the world. Knowing that an object is a dog allows us to predict how it will react to a thrown ball; knowing that an object is a stove allows us to cook a meal. There has been a long history of concern in psychology with how people form categories. Research has progressed as if all categories were learned a single way, but in retrospect this seems unlikely. Some categories are probably learned by direct instruction, as you, the reader of this book, learned about the category of classical conditioning experiments. Other categories, if defined by rigid rules, may be learned by explicit hypothesis testing. For instance, an observer of baseball for the first time might use this method to determine what defines a hit. Categories that have less rigid definitions may be learned by simple associative learning (such as in the Gluck and Bower theory) if they have a core set of features. If members of the category are more scattered, as is the case for the items in Table 10.2, an exemplar theory, like that of Medin and Schaffer, may be appropriate. There is probably not one correct theory of category learning. It is more likely that the different theories reviewed in this section are correct in different situations.

Causal Inference

Another critical kind of inductive learning involves figuring out what causes what in our environment. People frequently engage in such causal inference. Every time we come across a new device, we have to figure out how it works. A person entering a new room may need to determine what causes a light to go on. Children try to figure out what gets their parents angry, and parents try to figure out what gets their children to obey. Police try to find out who committed crimes, and physicians try to identify the causes of symptoms. It is important to understand the causal structure of our environment, because knowing that allows us to use it to achieve our purposes. Indeed, as suggested in Chapters 2 and 3, much of animal conditioning was really concerned with how animals, in effect, inferred the causal structure of their environments. Research with humans sheds further light on causal inference.

It is useful to appreciate how both categorization and causal attribution are instances of inductive inference but also how they are different. Categorical inference involves noting that a set of features cluster together. In forming the category of "bird," a person is responding to the fact that the same kinds of animals tend to have feathers, to have beaks, and to lay eggs. Causal inference involves noting that one set of events tends to predict another. For instance, a person may determine that flipping a switch causes the light to come on or that pressing a bar causes food to appear. In both cases, the person infers a predictive relationship in the world—in one case among features of an object and in the other case among events. Causal inference is inherently directional. If a bar is pressed, food is expected to appear in the feeder, but if food is put in the feeder, the bar is not expected to depress. Categorical inference is symmetrical. An animal that has feathers is expected to have a beak and an animal that has a beak to have feathers.

The general approach to understanding human causal inference has been to study how people use various cues to causality (e.g., Einhorn & Hogarth, 1986). When two events (such as flipping a switch and turning a light on) are in a cause-and-effect relationship, there are certain telltale cues as to that relationship. The following sections review some of the cues people use to determine causality.

Statistical Cues

Perhaps the most obvious cue is that of statistical **contingency**. Recall from the discussion of conditioning that contingency refers to whether one event predicts another. If whenever event A occurs, event B follows, and B never occurs unless A has occurred, then there is strong evidence for the proposition that A causes B. However, things are often not that certain. Consider the proposal that smoking causes heart disease. Suppose that we observe some people who smoke and others who do not. Some people who smoke will develop heart disease, some who smoke will not develop heart disease, some who do not smoke will develop heart disease, and yet others who do not smoke will not develop heart disease. The data can be organized according to a 2 × 2 table, like Table 10.4, which gives the number of observations of the four kinds.

The data in Table 10.4 (totally hypothetical) appear to provide evidence for a causal relationship: a person who smokes has a 75 percent chance of developing heart disease, and a person who does not smoke has only a 40 percent chance. Table 10.4 uses the variables a to d to stand for the frequencies in various cells. The greater a (co-occurrence of cause and effect) and d (occurrence of neither) are, the stronger evidence there is for an effect. The greater b

Table 10.4 *Hypothetical Relationship Between Cholesterol and Heart Disease*

Number of Patients in Each Cell		
	Effect Present: Heart Disease	*Effect Absent: No Heart Disease*
Cause Present: Smoking	$a = 75$	$b = 25$
Cause Absent: No smoking	$c = 40$	$d = 60$

(occurrence of cause but not effect) and *c* (no occurrence of cause but effect) are, the less evidence there is for a relationship. Researchers have studied how sensitive subjects are to variations in these four quantities—*a, b, c,* and *d*. The animal research considered earlier (e.g., Figures 2.9 and 3.12) indicated a general sensitivity to these factors. The human research (e.g., Crocker, 1981; Jenkins & Ward, 1965; Schustack & Sternberg, 1981; Shaklee & Tucker, 1980) has been specifically concerned with how people respond to variations in the four individual quantities. In general, people behave in a rational way by increasing their belief in a causal relationship as *a* or *d* increases and decreasing their belief as *b* or *c* increases. Subjects appear to be most sensitive to changes in *a*, about equally sensitive to changes in *b* or *c*, and least sensitive to changes in *d*.

In a typical experiment performed by Anderson and Sheu (1994), subjects tried to judge whether a drug had a side effect or not. Three of the variables *a* through *d* were held constant, and the remaining variable was manipulated from values of 1 to 15. Subjects had to judge on a scale from 0 to 100 how likely it was that the drug caused the side effect. Figure 10.7 shows how these judgments varied with changes in these variables. Changing *a* (cause and effect present) from 1 to 15 increased judged causal effectiveness by 40 points; changing *b* (cause but not effect) decreased judged effectiveness by 30 points; changing *c* (no cause and effect) decreased judged effectiveness by 20 points; and changing *d* (neither cause nor effect) increased judged effectiveness by only 5 points. Subjects were sensitive to all variables but certainly differed in how sensitive they were.

In considering the application of the Rescorla–Wagner theory to these causal inferences (see the discussion pertaining to Figure 3.14), Chapter 3 noted that the Rescorla–Wagner theory learns strengths of association between cause and effect that are proportional to the differences in probabili-

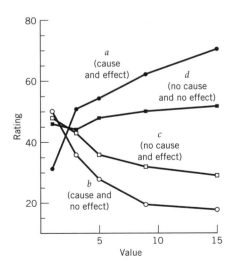

FIGURE 10.7. Effects of variables *a* through *d* on causal inference. From Anderson & Sheu (1994).

ties between the effect in the presence of the purported cause and not. That is, the strength of association between possible cause C and effect E is proportional to $P(E|C) - P(E|-C)$ where[2]

$$P(E|C) = \frac{a}{a + b}$$

$$P(E|-C) = \frac{c}{c + d}$$

This model predicts a general sensitivity to the variables a through d. One problem with this model is that it predicts that subjects should be as sensitive to a change in a or b affecting $P(E|C)$ as they are to a change in c or d affecting $P(E|-C)$. However, Figure 10.7 shows that subjects are not equally sensitive.[3]

It seems unlikely that human subjects are simply forming strengths of association as the Rescorla–Wagner theory suggests. When queried by Anderson and Sheu, the majority of subjects reported that they were explicitly trying to calculate $P(E|C)$ and $P(E|-C)$ and compare them. A minority of subjects reported calculating only $P(E|C)$ and basing their judgments on this. The majority showed relatively equal effects of a through d, whereas the minority showed only effects of a and b. It seems that subjects followed conscious strategies of probability estimation and that the variables had different-sized effects because some subjects ignored some of the information. Subjects behaved in a rather conscious hypothesis-testing manner, which happened to be mimicked by the Rescorla–Wagner theory. It is quite plausible that lower organisms are incapable of such conscious calculations, but do behave in accord with the Rescorla–Wagner theory. This is another instance of rather different mechanisms producing similar results.

Subjects base their causal attributions on the probability of the effect in the presence versus absence of the cause.

Cues of Spatial and Temporal Contiguity

The British philosopher David Hume noted that when one event occurs just before a second event and close in space to the second event, the first appears to be the cause of the second. Thus if lightning is followed immediately by thunder, we tend to think of the lightning as causing the thunder. The earlier

[2]P(E|C) is to be read as probability of effect given cause and P(E|-C) is to be read as probability of effect given absence of cause.

[3]Wasserman et al. (1993) showed that having different learning rates for the four cases can yield different effects of a through d.

chapters reviewed the evidence that animals are also more likely to display conditioning when two events to be conditioned are close together in time. Proximity in space is important, too—if I find spilled milk near one of my children and not the other I am liable to attribute the spill to the child it is close to. Researchers have studied how people combine spatial and temporal contiguity to make attributions of causality.

Figure 10.8 shows the device used by Bullock, Gelman, and Baillargeon (1982) in a study of causal attribution. Subjects saw two balls drop into tubes at the end of a box. Then a jack-in-the-box appeared in the center of the box. There were four conditions, depending on the temporal proximity and spatial proximity of the dropping of the two balls. In condition 1, the two balls were equally distant from the jack-in-the-box but one was dropped before the other. In this condition, 65 percent of the subjects attributed the appearance of the jack-in-the-box to the dropping of the second ball, which was closer in time. In condition 2, the two balls were dropped at the same time but one was closer to where the jack-in-the-box appeared. In this circumstance, 100 percent of the subjects attributed the cause to the closer ball. In a third condition, one ball was close in both time and space to the appearance of the jack-in-the-box. In this condition, 100 percent of the subjects also chose the closer ball. The fourth condition involved a conflict: one ball was closer in time but the other was closer in space. In this condition, 70 percent of the subjects chose the ball that was closer in space.

Subjects in the Bullock et al. experiment tended to prefer the cue that was closer in space over the cue that was closer in time. Other researchers (e.g., Shultz, Fischer, Pratt, & Rulf, 1986) found that subjects preferred as a cause what was closer in time. Thus one cue is not always dominant. Both cues are effective, and which is dominant depends on the particular situation.

Figure 10.9*a* shows a computer display used to study the role of temporal and spatial contiguity in causal attribution (J. R. Anderson, 1991). In this experiment, a hand dropped a weight on a beam and a trapdoor opened up, releasing a ball. Subjects were asked to rate how compelling was the perception of a causal relationship between the dropping of the weight and the popping out of the ball. The distance was varied between the weight and the door, and the delay was varied between the dropping of the weight and the opening of the

FIGURE 10.8. The apparatus used by Bullock et al. (1982). *Source:* From M. Bullock, R. Gelman, and R. Baillargeon in W. J. Friedman, Ed. *The developmental psychology of time.* Copyright © 1982 by Academic Press. Reprinted by permission.

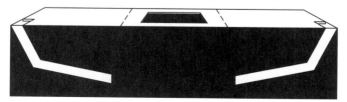

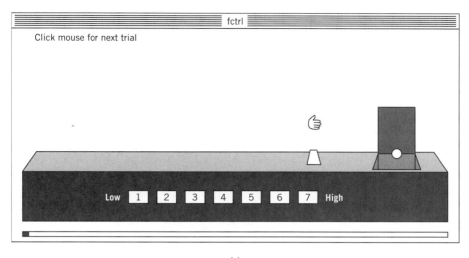

(a)

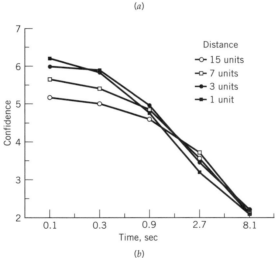

(b)

FIGURE 10.9. The vibratory wave model: (*a*) the computer display; (*b*) strength of causal perception as a function of distance in space and time. *Source:* From J. R. Anderson. Is Human Cognition Adaptive? *Behavioral and Brain Sciences, Volume 14.* Copyright © 1991. Reprinted by permission of Cambridge University Press.

door. Subjects rated the causal link between the two events on a 1 to 7 scale, where 7 meant definitely causally related and 1 meant no causal relationship. Figure 10.9*b* shows how the strength of causal attribution varied with these two factors. In this experiment, time was the dominant variable and distance only entered into strength of attributions when the delay was short.

Researchers (e.g., Shultz, 1982) have argued that subjects do not blindly use spatial and temporal contiguity to infer a causal relationship but that they show some appreciation of the possible underlying mechanisms. Figure 10.9*a* can be interpreted in these terms. The probable causal mechanism is one in which the dropping of the weight on the beam sets up a vibratory wave, which propagates down the beam and releases some mechanism (e.g., a catch). Such mechanical waves should propagate down the beam almost instantaneously, and so any significant delay between the dropping of the weight and the opening of the door would appear causally inconsistent. The closer the weight to the door, the more force the wave has, and so the more likely it is that the wave will jar loose the mechanism. At short delays, subjects should prefer the cause when it is closer, which is just what is shown in Figure 10.9b.

Figure 10.10*a* shows an interesting contrast condition (J. R. Anderson, 1991) to the one in Figure 10.9*a*. A hand dropped a ball into a hole in the beam. Sometime later a trapdoor opened and a ball appeared, just as in Figure 10.9*a*. As with Figure 10.9*a*, the distances in time and space between the first event and the second were manipulated. Figure 10.10*b* shows how subjects' causal attributions varied in this condition. The results are in considerable contrast to the data in Figure 10.9b. In Figure 10.10b there is no favored time or distance. Rather, as the distance increased, subjects favored longer and longer times. Subjects reported looking for a match between distance and time. Their model was one in which the ball traveled through the beam to appear at the trapdoor, and they were looking for a situation where the time was appropriate (not too long or too short) for the distance traveled.

Human subjects are quite sophisticated in their interpretation of temporal and spatial contiguity. Earlier chapters reviewed the evidence for a similar degree of sophistication in animals in how much they rely on temporal contiguity. For instance, rats connect taste with poisoning after much longer delays than usually work in conditioning. A possible reason is that poisoning is the kind of effect that often appears at a considerable delay after ingestion. It seems unlikely, however, that rats behave with as explicit and conscious a model as human subjects sometimes do.

Humans use temporal and spatial cues to judge causality in accord with how well these cues fit a prior causal model.

Kinematic Cues

Subjects often display great sophistication in their interpretation of kinematic cues. Kinematic cues refer to properties that would be expected of events causally related according to the laws of physics. When the conditions are right, kinematic cues can give rise to extraordinarily compelling perceptions of causality. Some of the original research on this topic was performed by Michotte (1946). Subjects observed a black circle move across a screen and touch a second circle; then the second circle moved off. When the second

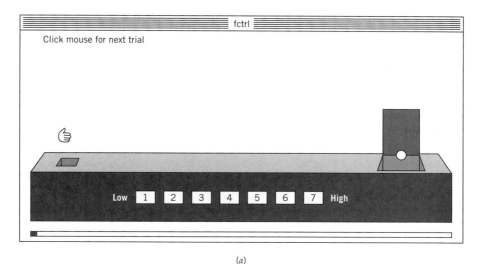

(a)

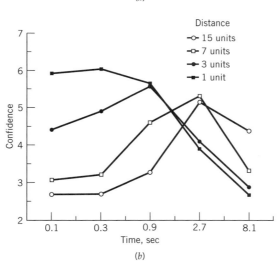

(b)

FIGURE 10.10. The ball and projectile model: (*a*) the computer display; (*b*) strength of causal perception as a function of distance in space and time. *Source:* Figure 10.10 from J. R. Anderson. Is Human Cognition Adaptive? *Behavioral and Brain Sciences, Volume 14.* Copyright © 1991. Reprinted by permission of Cambridge University Press.

circle moved immediately after it was touched, subjects had a compelling impression of a collision in which the first object set the second in motion, as when one billiard ball hits another. When there was any delay between the two events, the perception of a causal connection dissolved.

In variations on Michotte's experiment, Kaiser and Proffitt (1984) manipulated the velocity and angle at which the two objects parted after the collision. Subjects' perceptions of causality were sensitive to the laws of physics governing such collisions, and they judged as causally anomalous collisions that involved impossible angles or rates of acceleration. Subjects could also judge the relative mass of the two objects from the velocity and angle at which the objects separated.

In some situations subjects' judgments are not so in tune with the correct scientific model. Consider the situation in which an object moves off a surface, such as when a ball rolls off a table. The correct scientific model is one in which the trajectory of the object after it leaves the table is a curve reflecting a combination of the original horizontal velocity and the downward negative force caused by gravity. Some people believe that the object will go directly down, and others predict an L-shaped trajectory in which the object goes straight forward for a while and then falls down. Judgments in this domain show a definite developmental trend, with older subjects showing fewer misconceptions. Apparently people come to tune their models with experience and education (Kaiser, Proffitt, & McCloskey, 1985).

Even more curious are judgments about the trajectory of an object after it leaves a curve-shaped tube, such as the one in Figure 10.11 (Kaiser, McCloskey, & Proffitt, 1986; McCloskey, 1983). A common misconception is that it will show a curved trajectory rather than a straight one. This belief shows a U-shaped developmental trend, with children around the sixth grade showing the most misconceptions and preschoolers and college students about equivalent and somewhat better.

People possess models for how physical events should take place and use these to make judgments of causality. Sometimes their physical models are correct and sometimes they are not. People are referred to as having naive physics models that are partially correct. One goal in modern physics education is to better train these naive physics models (e.g., Champagne, Gunstone, & Klopfer, 1985).

People have naive physics models, which they use to judge causality from kinematic cues.

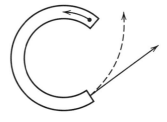

FIGURE 10.11. C-shaped tube problem used by Kaiser, McCloskey, and Proffitt (1986). *Source:* From M. K. Kaiser, M. McCloskey, and D. R. Profitt. *Developmental Psychology, Volume 22.* Copyright © 1986 by the American Psychological Association. Reprinted by permission.

Understanding Complex Devices

An interesting series of studies was performed by Shrager, Klahr and Dunbar. In the original experiment by Shrager (1985), subjects were shown a toy tank with a keypad similar to that shown in Figure 10.12 and were told to figure out how the machine worked. The tank could be instructed to go forward or backward for a number of feet, to rotate for a number of clock ticks (minutes on a clock), to pause for various amounts of time, and to fire its gun. Given the command sequence:

↑ 5,

← 7,

↑ 3,

➡ 15,

HOLD 5,

FIRE 2,

↓ 8

the tank would move forward 5 ft, rotate counterclockwise 7 clock ticks, move forward 3 ft, rotate clockwise 15 ticks, pause 5 sec, fire twice, and move back 8 ft. Most of Shrager's subjects, who were undergraduates, were able to figure out within an hour how to program the tank by simply experimenting with various key combinations. This result is testimony to the sophistication of our ability to do inductive learning in the modern technological world.

Klahr and Dunbar (1988) studied in detail how subjects learned about one aspect of the device—the RPT key. When this key is followed by a number, it repeats that number of previous moves. For example, RPT 3 repeats the last three moves. However, subjects had many different ideas about what the key did. A favorite hypothesis was that RPT 3 would repeat the whole sequence of actions 3 times. Klahr and Dunbar found that subjects

FIGURE 10.12. Key pad for programming a toy tank. *Source:* From J. C. Shrager. Instructionless Learning: Discovery of the mental model of a complex device. Copyright © 1985 by Jeffrey C. Shrager. Reprinted by permission.

behaved basically like scientists in determining what the key did, designing experiments and formulating hypotheses on the basis of the results, and then designing new experiments to test these hypotheses. Human adults take a much more sophisticated approach to understanding the causal structure of a device than did Thorndike's cats in trying to understand their puzzle boxes.

Dunbar and Klahr (1989) compared the behavior of children (third to sixth graders) and adults and found several differences. First, children had less complete hypotheses, often conjecturing that RPT repeated part of the program without identifying what part. Second, children were more reluctant to abandon a hypothesis in the face of disconfirming evidence. Third, children sometimes did not check whether a new hypothesis was consistent with previous data. Children were poorer scientists, but still tended to take a scientific approach to understanding how the device worked.

People adopt a scientific approach in learning how devices work.

Conclusions About Causal Inference

As discussed in the early chapters on animal conditioning, causal inference is particularly important to adapting to the environment. Knowing what causes what enables an organism to achieve its goals. Humans are often quite sophisticated and deliberate in how they go about inducing the causal structure of their environment. They entertain sophisticated hypotheses for what mechanisms might produce the effects in their environment and test these hypotheses against the available data. This chapter has noted throughout that simpler associative learning mechanisms often mimic the results of humans' more conscious hypothesis-testing approach. Why is it, then, that humans engage in this more sophisticated approach when simpler methods yield the same results? Simple associative learning only works in simple situations. The advantages of the more deliberate approach become apparent when looking at learning about complex devices, such as the toy tank shown in Figure 10.12. It may be the propensity to use tools that has moved the causal learning mechanisms of humans in the direction of conscious hypothesis testing. Hypothesis testing may well be overlaid on more automatic inductive learning mechanisms, such as that captured by the Rescorla–Wagner theory.

Conscious hypothesis testing is more successful than simple associative learning when the situation is complex.

Language Acquisition

Some people believe that acquisition of a natural language is the most impressive inductive learning feat of the human species. Many argue that only humans can learn a language and that our language facility reflects something unique about the human mind (e.g., Chomsky, 1965, 1975). In a few short years young children figure out what generations of Ph.D. linguists have not— the rules of language. This contrast needs to be emphasized—scientists have not been able to characterize what the rules of language are and yet children figure it out with relative ease. Of course, children cannot say what the rules are that they have learned. In the terms of Chapter 8, this is an instance of implicit learning. The fact that people are so successful in such implicit learning of a first language has been used to argue that we must have special innate and unconscious knowledge as to the structure of language.

It is important to recognize what makes language learning such a difficult task. Most people are quite aware that language contains many words— tens of thousands in fact. Studies of young children have suggested that they learn more than five new words each day (Carey, 1978; Clark, 1983). Learning the meanings of all of these words defines an enormous concept-acquisition task. Unlike learning a second language, a person learning a first language cannot rely on the assistance of definitions stated in another language.

Although vocabulary is the most obvious aspect of language learning, it is generally not considered the most daunting aspect. Learning the morphophonology and syntax of language is more demanding. Morphophonology refers to how the sound system determines meaning, for example, adding an *s* in English to indicate possession (Fred's sister), and syntax is concerned with how word order determines meaning (for example, "sister of Fred"). Languages may possess tens of thousands of such rules, many of which are rather subtle. Long after second-language learners have mastered the vocabulary of the language, they continue to make errors in pronunciation and grammar.

Not only are there many phonological and syntactic rules to be learned, but the conditions in which children learn them seem far from ideal. No one explicitly instructs children as to what the rules of language are. Children have to induce these rules by hearing language spoken to them. Any particular sentence involves many rules acting together to determine the sentence. The many components of the sentence must be unraveled. Parents and other care givers might be thought to teach children by explicitly correcting their speech. However, many children learn a language just fine without receiving such correction, and the available evidence suggests that such correction does not help those children who receive it (e.g., Braine, 1971, McNeill, 1966; for a recent discussion see MacWhinney, 1993). McNeill (1966) cited a famous example of how impervious children can be to correction:

> CHILD: Nobody don't like me.
> MOTHER: No, say, "Nobody likes me."

CHILD: Nobody don't like me.
[dialogue repeated eight times]
 MOTHER: Now listen carefully, say, "Nobody likes me."
 CHILD: Oh! Nobody don't likes me.

Children accomplish an enormous task in acquiring language, and they put a lot of time into it. Children do not master the subtleties of language until age 10. By that time, they have put thousands of days and presumably tens of thousands of hours into language acquisition. Recall from the previous chapter the evidence that mastery of any complex skill involves an enormous investment of time in which the various rules of that skill are mastered one by one. Language is no exception to this principle. It may, however, be the most complex rule system that people have to learn.

Natural languages are very complex rule systems that only humans are capable of mastering.

Character of Language Acquisition

It is interesting to review some of the basic features of language acquisition by children. Children show a characteristic way of approximating adult speech (for more detail, see Pinker, 1989). It takes a long time before they speak in what adults recognize as sentences. Almost all children, starting at about 1 year of age, go through a one-word utterance stage in which all their utterances are single words, such as "Mommy," "jump," and "bird." Starting at about 18 months, children tend to go through a distinct two-word stage, in which their utterances are either single words or pairs of words, such as "doggie bark," "shoe off," or "there cow." These two-word utterances appear to be communicating meanings that adults would communicate in more complete sentences.

Even when children graduate from the two-word stage and start speaking in longer utterances, their utterances preserve what might be regarded as a telegraphic property, in that they tend to omit some of the less important words. Table 10.5 shows some examples of such multiword utterances. Gradually the utterances begin to fill out, so that by the age of about 4 children speak essentially in sentences. The sentences may be simple and limited by adult standards and still contain grammatical errors, but they are recognizable as sentences.

This developmental sequence is unique to children. Adults learning a second language try to speak in more complete sentences right from the beginning—even if their sentences are limited and often not grammatical. It has been conjectured that limited memory capacity may be a reason for the

Table 10.5 *Multiword Utterances*

Put truck window	My balloon pop
Want more grape juice	Doggie bit me mine boot
Sit Adam chair	That Mommy nose right there
Mommy put sock	She's wear that hat
No I see truck	I like pick dirt up fire truck
Adam fall toy	No pictures in there

Source: From Brown, 1973.

shortness of children's utterances (J. R. Anderson, 1983a). Young children are not able to keep in mind and plan longer utterances. It has been shown, for instance, that children have severe limitations in their ability to repeat longer utterances (Brown & Fraser, 1963). Chapter 5 noted that memory span is related to speed of articulation. Since young children are still learning to speak, their articulatory rate is much slower (Gathercole & Hitch, 1993), and so they are able to encode less of the sentences spoken to them and can only plan shorter utterances.

Another feature of language is that it contains many rules that often apply to only some of the words in the language, for example, rules for past-tense in English. Most verbs are made into the past tense by adding *ed* or one of its phonological variants. There are, however, clusters of exceptions—*ring–rang, sing–sang,* and so on. Some words follow their own unique rules, such as *eat–ate.* As children learn the complex rules and exceptions of past tense, they go through a series of stages. First, they do not try to indicate past tense; then, they overgeneralize the dominant rules (e.g., *singed*); finally, they achieve basic mastery. Children (and adults) are capable of applying such rules to novel words. So, for instance, on being told that there is a verb *gring* (meaning, perhaps, "to splash in the waves"), children spontaneously use either *gringed* or *grang* as the past tense.

Children start speaking in short nonsentences and gradually increase their length and approximation to grammatical sentences.

Theories of Past-Tense Acquisition

In the domains of both categorization and causal inference there have been contests between the simple associative explanations of inductive learning and the more rule-based, hypothesis-testing explanations. The same debate has taken place in the case of language acquisition. This debate has been particularly detailed concerning the acquisition of past tense in English. The prevailing rule-based viewpoint had assumed that children learn the basic rules and the exceptions. Learning may not involve conscious hypothesis testing and rule formation on the children's part, but the rule-based account claimed that unconsciously children speak according to rules, such as "add *-ed*" or "change *-ing* in the verb to an *-ang.*"

Rumelhart and McClelland (1986) offered a major challenge to this prevailing viewpoint and argued that past-tense generation could be explained by a connectionist net, such as that illustrated in Figure 10.13. The root form of the word (e.g., *kick, sing*) enters the input nodes and, after passing through a couple of layers of network, the past-tense form (e.g., *kicked, sang*) comes forth. The system must learn associations between the features of roots and the features of past tenses. These associations are learned according to a variant of the Rescorla–Wagner associative rule introduced in Chapter 2 (Figures 2.14 and 2.15).

A computer simulation of their model was trained on 420 root–past-tense pairs. It successfully learned to generate past tenses for roots on which it was trained; moreover, it was able after learning to generate past tenses for roots on which it had not been trained. It also mirrored a particular sequence of generalization stages noted of children. Initially it tended to produce the irregular past tenses, like *came* for *come*, then it generated overregularized forms (*comed* for *come*), and finally returned to the original, correct irregular forms. Children appear to have just this pattern of development. Rumelhart and McClelland proclaimed:

> We have, we believe, provided a distinct alternative to the view that children learn the rules of English past-tense formation in any explicit sense. We have shown that a reasonable account of the acquisition of past

FIGURE 10.13. A network for past tense. The phonological representation of the root is converted into a distributed feature representation. This is converted into the distributed feature representation of the past tense which is then mapped onto a phonological representation of the past tense. *Source:* From J. L. McClelland and D. E. Rumelhart. *Parallel distributed processing: explorations in the microstructure of cognition.* Copyright © 1986 by the MIT PRESS. Reprinted by permission.

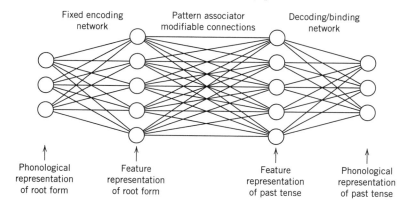

tense can be provided without recourse to the notion of a "rule" as anything more than a *description* of the language. We have shown that, for this case, there is no *induction problem*. The child need not figure out what the rules are, nor even that there are rules. (P. 267)

Their challenge has not gone unanswered. Pinker and Prince (1988) published an extensive criticism of the Rumelhart and McClelland study. Many of their issues had to do with the details of the model. They pointed out that the ability to account for the generalization stages depended on initially presenting the network with many irregular verbs, whereas children do not encounter a special abundance of irregular verbs early on. Pinker and Prince also pointed out that some of the errors made by the model were quite unlike errors made by children. For instance, the model generated *membled* as the past tense of *mail*.

Pinker and Prince argued that the English past-tense system is more rule-governed than can be accounted for by a simple associative network. They used the example that the same root word can have different past-tense realizations depending on context. The word *ring* has two realizations as a verb—to make a sound or to encircle. Although the root is the same, the past tense for the former meaning is *rang*, and for the latter meaning is *ringed*, as in:

He rang the bell.
They ringed the fort with soldiers.

Without further elaboration, it is impossible for the Rumelhart and McClelland network to capture this subtlety of the language.

A substantial debate has gone on in psychology about whether the deficits in the Rumelhart and McClelland model reflect fundamental flaws in the associative network approach or not. More adequate connectionist models have subsequently appeared (e.g., Daugherty, MacDonald, Petersen, & Seidenberg, 1993; MacWhinney & Leinbach, 1991). It is fair to say the issue is far from resolved. The debate once again illustrates the tension between associative models of inductive learning and rule-based, hypothesis-testing approaches.

Connectionist models have been proposed that claim that English-past tense formations can be accounted for by simple associative learning.

A Critical Period for Language Acquisition

One of the curious features of language acquisition in children is that there appears to be a critical period during which children are best able to learn at least some of the features of language. An analogy can be made to critical periods for learning in other species. For instance, some songbirds (Nottebohm, 1970) can only learn the song for their species if they are exposed to it at a certain critical period in their development. For humans, the critical period appears to stop at puberty, or about age 12. It seems much easier for a child to learn a first or second language before that period (Lenneberg, 1967). From a certain perspective, this is a rather amazing claim, since older children are generally able to learn most subjects faster than their younger siblings—presumably reflecting the advantage of their greater intelligence.

There are two main sources of data supporting the claim of a critical period. One source is the ability to reacquire language after a severe brain injury has resulted in **aphasia** (loss of language function). Lenneberg (1967) reported that all children who suffered such an injury before the age of 10 or so were able to recover full language function, whereas at best 60 percent of those sustaining such injuries after the age of 12 were able to recover language function.

The other source of evidence is observations of children when they move into a new linguistic community, as in the case of immigrants to the United States or children whose parents move to a new country in response to a corporate assignment. It is often claimed that younger children learn the language faster than older children or their parents. Such observations are terribly confounded with factors such as motivation and opportunity. For instance, children are often forced to become immersed in the other linguistic community at school, are less self-conscious about trying to learn, and are less resistant to changing their primary language. Younger children's utterances are also simpler and judged by a more lenient standard. In more controlled studies it appears that older children are able to learn the same aspects of the language more quickly than their younger siblings (Ervin-Tripp, 1974).

Although older children are able to learn more rapidly initially, they tend never to master certain fine points of the language as well as do their younger siblings (Lieberman, 1984; Newport, 1986). One of the most characteristic fine points is the ability to speak a second language without an accent, which is difficult if the language is learned after about age 12.

Newport (1990) reported a rare study on the effect of age of acquisition on first language learning. She studied deaf children of speaking parents who often did not learn sign language until quite late in their development and did not speak any language during their early years. She found a strong relationship between the age at which these deaf people started to learn sign language and their eventual level of mastery of sign language in adulthood. There appeared to be a particularly large deficit if their learning was postponed until after the age of 12. The existence of a critical period for language acquisition has been used to argue for the special character of human language learning. This topic is addressed in the next section.

It is hard to come to full mastery of a language if it is learned after the age of about 12.

Innate Language-Learning Abilities?

Several researchers have proposed that children are born with special innate abilities to learn a natural language, but that these abilities atrophy at about the age of 12. This position is consistent with the data on a critical period for language acquisition. It has also been argued that learning a language is so difficult that it would be impossible unless children were born with special knowledge of what a natural language might be like (Chomsky, 1965, 1986). This position sees human language learning as a species-specific ability similar to the species-specific learning tendencies reviewed in Chapters 2 and 3.

The linguist Chomsky (1965) proposed that children are born knowing **language universals**, which are features that are true of all languages. Children do not have to learn these facts; they know them from birth. Chapter 1 argued that it is more adaptive to code innately into the organism things that do not vary and that learning should be reserved for things that vary. The natural languages of the world certainly vary enormously in vocabulary, phonology, and syntax. However, Chomsky and others have argued that they all have in common some deep properties that do not need to be learned.

Mathematical analyses show that in some sense Chomsky is right—children could not learn every possible language; therefore they must come into the world biased to learn certain languages, and these languages are the natural languages (Pinker, 1989). There is a great deal of controversy over the significance of this argument. Humans similarly enter the world only able to use certain kinds of vehicles (e.g., they could not use a vehicle that required three hands), but no one would want to claim that humans have innate vehicle-acquisition devices. The question is whether the constraints on language reflect anything more than the general cognitive and physical constraints that are part of being a human. These constraints may have shaped the form of languages invented by humans, but they are in no sense special to language.

Chomsky and others have argued that there is something special about the innate contribution to human language acquisition, that it involves some specialized linguistic knowledge about things like the syntax of natural language. For instance, there is a correlation across languages between what is called pronoun dropping and the existence of expletive pronouns. Some languages, such as Spanish, allow for optional dropping of pronouns. Whereas English speakers say "I go to the cinema tonight" with an obligatory "I," Spanish speakers can say "Voy al cine esta noche" without a first-person pronoun. Certain languages, such as English, have expletive pronouns, for example, *it* and *there* in the sentences "It is raining" and "There is no money." It is a universal of natural languages that any language that has optional pronoun dropping does not have expletive pronouns. Hyams (1986) argued children are born knowing this rule, and if they notice that pronouns are being dropped they know they do not have to learn expletive pronouns. Language induction would be easier if humans were born knowing these many details of language rather than having to figure them out.

There is a second sense in which Chomsky and others have argued that innate linguistic abilities are special and specific to the human species. No other organism has innate knowledge about natural languages, and therefore no other organism can learn the kinds of languages that humans can learn. The argument is sometimes made that it is linguistic ability more than anything else that distinguishes humans intellectually as a species.

It is argued that only humans have special innate knowledge about natural languages.

Animal Language Learning

One way to address the question of whether there is something special about how humans learn language is to see if other animals can learn a language. The natural targets for these experiments are the higher apes, which are quite intelligent and phylogenetically most similar to humans. Several early attempts to teach chimpanzees to speak failed completely (C. Hayes, 1951; Kellogg & Kellogg, 1933). It is now clear (Lenneberg, 1967) that the human's vocal apparatus is specially designed to permit speech, whereas the ape's is not.

Although the vocal ability of apes is limited, their manual dexterity is considerable. Several attempts have been made to teach apes languages using a manual system. Some studies have used American Sign Language (Ameslan), which is used by many deaf people. If apes could become proficient in Ameslan, their capacity for acquiring a language would be firmly established. One of the best-known research efforts was started by the Gardners in 1966 on a 1-year-old female chimpanzee named Washoe (Gardner & Gardner, 1969). Washoe was raised like a human child, following regimens of play, bathing, eating, and toilet training, all of which provided ample opportunities for sign learning. After 4 years, she had a vocabulary of 132 signs and was able to sign utterances up to five words in length. Washoe showed some mastery of word order, using utterances such as "You tickle me" and "I tickle you" to distinguish subject from object. This was the first study of many that established that apes have more linguistic capability than was previously thought.

One of the more impressive demonstrations of ape linguistic capacity was performed by Premack (1971, 1976; Premack & Premack, 1983). He developed an artificial language in which the words were colored plastic shapes that could be attached to a magnetic board. A chimp named Sarah, raised in a laboratory

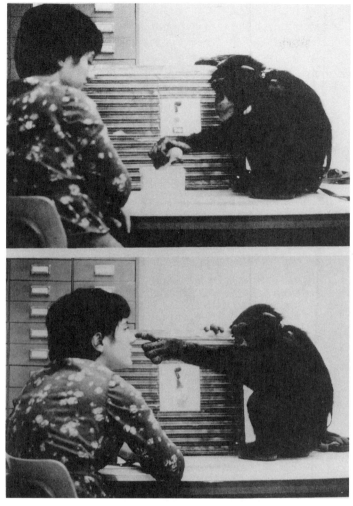

Peony, another of Premack's chimpanzees, interpreting plastic instructions on the board.

situation, was trained to use the symbols to make up sentences. Sarah showed considerable mastery of a number of aspects of language: yes–no interrogatives; negatives; class concepts of color, size, and shape; compound and coordinate sentences; quantifiers (all, none, one, several); logical connectives (if . . . then); linking verbs (is); metalinguistic utterances (e.g., name of); and who interrogatives (what, where, when, etc.). Chapter 6 discussed Premack's conjecture that linguistic training, such as that given to Sarah, enabled chimps to develop more complex propositional representations.

Despite such successes, the general conclusion seems to be that chimpanzees cannot approach the proficiency in language that humans can. A particularly negative report in this regard was published by Terrace et al. (1979), who taught American Sign Language to a chimpanzee named Nim. They noted that there were substantial differences between the utterances of their subject and those of children. Nim's utterances tended to be more repetitive, more imitative, and more stereotypical.

It is hard to know what to make of the part success and part failure of the attempts to teach apes languages. It is not really a matter of their being inferior to humans. They are different in many ways that have nothing to do with linguistic ability. Therefore, one should not expect their linguistic learning (or, indeed, any other learning) to be identical to human learning. One lesson from the early chapters on animal learning is that learning manifests itself according to the unique characteristics of each species.

Chimpanzees and other apes can learn languages that are more limited than human languages.

Final Reflections

Induction is the process by which we make inferences that go beyond our experiences to make predictions about new situations—about whether a creature we encounter is a dog and whether it is likely to bite, about whether having a high-cholesterol diet will cause a patient to suffer heart disease, or about whether a new linguistic utterance will be deemed grammatical. It is a critical aspect to learning, since the function of learning is to allow us to use our experiences in the past to adapt to the future.

Essentially any situation in which we manifest learned behavior involves an inductive component. It is easy to overlook this inductive component in many human situations. When children spell words as they have been taught, they are making the inference that what has been accepted in the past will continue to be accepted in the future. We depend on an implicit social contract in our lives that the rules will not change. Indeed, much of human society can be seen as organized to diminish the inductive component in learning (to take the guesswork out of learning). Scientists study the world and codify its principles, and educational institutions communicate this knowledge to the next generation. Products, such as appliances, are made with an eye to quality so that they will behave reliably and as expected. They come with manuals that try with varying degrees of success to make explicit their principles of operation. Chapter 11 is concerned with what the research on learning has to say about how to facilitate the process of explicit instruction.

> *Modern society is structured to reduce the inductive component in learning.*

Further Readings

Levine (1975) presents several reports on the hypothesis-testing approach to concept learning. Smith (1989) provides a survey of research on induction and concept learning. Schultz (1982) offers an overview of causal learning, and Wasserman (1990) is particularly interested in the connections between causal inference and animal conditioning. Klahr, Fay, and Dunbar (1993) report a recent assessment of children's skills at scientific experimentation. Pinker (1989) provides a review of research on language acquisition. Holland, Holyoak, Nisbett, and Thagard (1986) present an influential monograph on the many varieties of inductive learning.

11

Applications to Education

The Goals of Education

An underlying message in the previous chapters was that learning is an adaptation of the organism to its environment. To understand an organism's learning, it is necessary to understand the learning tasks that the organism faces in its environment. Chapters 2 and 3 reviewed how animals show species-specific associative biases, for instance, the bias of pigeons to peck at objects to receive food and to flap their wings to escape harm. Chapters 6 and 7 reviewed how human memory is tuned to the statistical patterns by which things reappear in the environment.

When it comes to understanding the situation in which human learning takes place, it is important to recognize that a major portion of human learning takes place in situations in which there is some explicit effort at instruction. The process of teaching the young is hardly unique to the human species, but it takes on a uniquely large scale with humans. One of the ways in which humans differ from other species is in the length of childhood—both in absolute years and as a proportion of total life span. It has been argued (de Beer, 1959) that the reason for prolonged childhood is so that the task of education can be completed. This argument suggests that to fully understand human learning it is important to understand its relationship to education.

Although heavy investment in the education of youth has been found in all cultures throughout the history of the human species, the prominence of formal educational institutions is a relatively recent phenomenon. The invention of writing systems a few thousand years ago was the precipitating event for many changes in human society, including the advent of formal education. A writing system created the need to learn demanding new skills—reading and writing—and allowed for the accumulation of a great repository of knowledge, some of which was deemed worthy of communicating to the next generation. The beginnings of modern Western schooling can perhaps be traced to early schools in Greece (sixth century B.C.) that taught music, reading, and gymnastics (Boyd & King, 1975).

At least since ancient Greek times, some privileged children have received formal education, but the concept of public education has only taken shape over the last few hundred years. The current system of public elementary schools, high schools, and universities in the United States was established in the nineteenth century (Good, 1962). The goal of universal education through high school was articulated in the United States between the two world wars and in many other modern countries only after World War II. The current curriculum that occupies public education has been in place for less than 100 years.

Higher education has always carried with it a sense of class privilege. Much of education in previous centuries, such as training in the classics, was conceived of as placing on students the mark of the upper class—that is, teaching students to be "gentlemen." Only in the last 100 years has education for all been justified in terms of its utilitarian content—that is, teaching students things that are useful to being good citizens (e.g., being able to read and judge an article about public policy in a magazine) and productive workers (e.g., being able to run an accounting system for a company). Even today there are serious questions about how much of public education really is useful and how much of it is actually devoted to establishing tokens of class privilege (e.g., Lave, 1988). This chapter discusses some of these current criticisms in the section on mathematics education.

There is much debate over the success of the educational system, particularly in the United States. At one level it is a resounding success: almost all the citizenry achieves at least a modest level of literacy. The United States has a technologically sophisticated society that simply would not be possible without modern education. On the other hand, the U. S. educational system is succeeding much less well than the nation's citizens would like. As Resnick and Resnick (1977) documented with respect to literacy, this lack of success results largely because people have ever higher aspirations as to what the educational system should achieve. Although there has always been a very literate elite, in this century Americans have demanded that more and more citizens be able to read more and more difficult material. The interesting question is whether these expectations are realistic or not. One way to answer this question is to compare the achievement of American children with that of children in other educational systems. If other countries are able to produce higher achievement, the U.S. system should be able to also. This chapter focuses on what psychology has to say about teaching (or learning) reading and mathematics, two of the core skills targeted by modern education. It is worthwhile considering the relative international standing of American students with respect to these two topics.

Formal education has evolved to teach useful knowledge.

Reading

It is particularly difficult to compare the reading achievement levels of American students to those of students of other nations because different nations have different languages and orthographies. Differences in societies also pose a problem in judging international performance. The United States aspires to keep all students in school for 12 years and succeeds with over 80 percent (McKnight, Crosswhite, Dossey, Kifer, Swafford, Travers, & Cooney, 1990). In other nations many students leave the school system earlier. It would not be fair to compare the top 20 percent of one nation with the greater mix represented by the 80 percent of graduating American students. Societies also vary in terms of their cultural and economic heterogeneity; the United States has a culturally diverse society and increasing disparity in the economic standings of its citizenry. Educational goals are generally easier to achieve in a culturally homogeneous society, where education can be tailored to the specifics of the one group, than in a diverse society, where different cultural groups may require different educational situations to optimize their learning. There is also a very strong correlation between economic status and educational achievement (California Assessment Program, 1980; Gamoran, 1981). This correlation suggests that the growing underclass in the United States is going to be an increasing source of educational underachievement.

Despite these problems, there is reason to believe that U. S. schools succeed relatively well at teaching reading. In most international comparisons, American students do as well as students of most other countries (Stevenson & Stigler, 1992). When the reading achievements of non-Hispanic, white, middle-class Americans are compared with those of the ethnically dominant, middle-class children of other societies, Americans often outperform the other children. This result suggests that a major mechanism for improving the reading scores of American children as a group would be to improve the economic standing of the underclass and to learn how to tailor reading education to minority ethnic groups. In summary, the U.S. educational establishment does a relatively good job at teaching reading; the problems that exist are as much societal as educational.

Figure 11.1 compares American and Chinese students and is representative of the international comparisons. It shows the number of students graduating from the first grade with reading scores at various grade levels (1:1 stands for the first half of first grade and 1:2 for the second half). Note that a significant number of first graders in the United States read one and two grade levels above their age and a few read at even higher grade levels, whereas very few Chinese students read above their grade level. On the other hand, almost 40 percent of American first graders have not even mastered the lowest level of first-grade reading, whereas almost all Chinese students have. This chart illustrates the great disparity among reading performances within the United States. The students with very low reading scores come disproportionately from economically disadvantaged families.

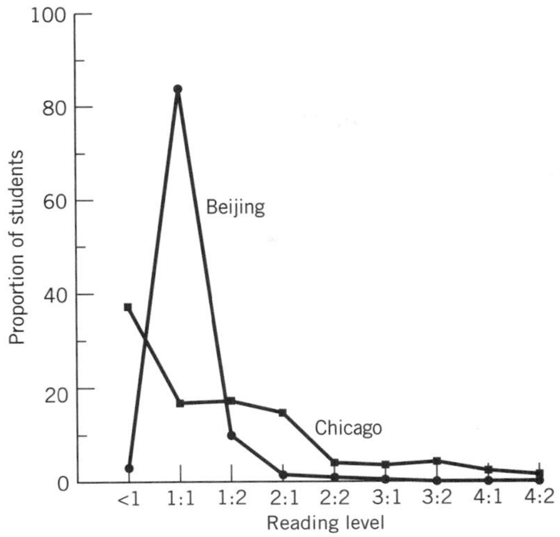

FIGURE 11.1. Histogram showing relative proportion of Chinese students (from Beijing) and American students (from Chicago) at various reading levels. (From Stevenson & Stigler, 1992).

There is a wide range in reading achievement in the United States, with the better students doing at least as well as the top students of most nations.

Mathematics

The international standing of U. S. students in terms of mathematics achievement is much worse. In international comparisons, American children enter the first grade knowing a comparable amount of mathematics (Stevenson & Stigler, 1992), but steadily fall behind until they are one of the poorest-achieving groups of students (McKnight et al., 1990). Figure 11.2 compares the performance of U.S. 12th graders with respect to algebra, geometry, and calculus with the performance of students at comparable levels in other countries. For each topic, the Americans are near the bottom of all countries surveyed and Japan and Hong Kong hold the top two positions. Unlike some of the other countries, Japan aspires to give all its citizens 12 years of education and succeeds with more than 90 percent. So this comparison is not an artifact of a relatively select Japanese student population. Also, Japan and the United States are not very different in the level of reading achievement found in their schools. Several comparisons of Japanese and U.S. mathematics education have tried to identify the cause of the difference in mathematics achievement. In one careful comparison of fifth graders in Minneapolis and Sendai, Japan, two comparable cities, it was found that no school in Minneapolis had an average mathematics score higher than any school in Sendai (Stevenson & Stigler, 1992). This sample included rich, suburban Minneapolis schools, indi-

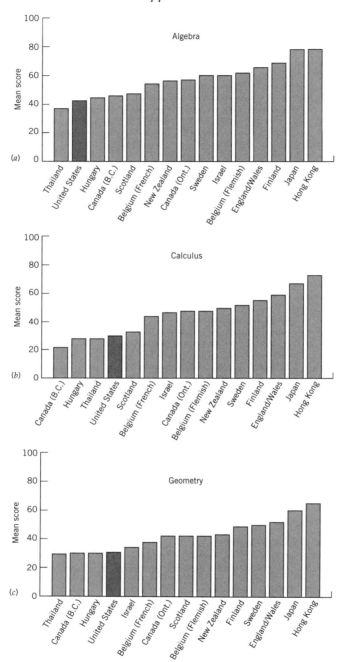

FIGURE 11.2. International comparison of 12th grade achievement scores in (a) algebra, (b) calculus, and (c) geometry. *Source:* From C. C. McKnight, F. J. Cross-white, J. A. Dossey, E. Kifer, J. O. Swafford, K. J. Travers, and T. J. Cooney. *The underachieveing curriculum: assessing U. S. School Mathematics from an international perspective.* Copyright © 1987 by Stipes Publishing Company. Reprinted by permission.

cating that the problems with mathematics achievement in the United States are not restricted to culturally or economically disadvantaged children.

McKnight et al. (1990) reviewed a number of popular explanations of the difference in learning achievement in mathematics. One explanation involves classroom size, but Japanese classrooms average 41 students and U.S. classrooms average only 26. A second explanation is the quality of the teachers. Teachers in the two countries have relatively comparable training and backgrounds, but Japanese teachers have more time for class preparation and do less teaching (an average 23 class hours in the United States versus 17 in Japan). They also receive more mentoring and more state direction and guidance on how to prepare their class presentations. American teachers often complain that the curriculum is constantly changing, so that they never can develop expertise in teaching it. Later this chapter explores the reasons for frequent changes in the U.S. mathematics curriculum.

Probably the major reason for the differences in achievement is the amount of time actually spent on mathematics education. Large differences exist at almost all grade levels. In Japan, elementary students spend twice as much class time on mathematics as do elementary students in the United States (White, 1987). Time is also used much more efficiently in the Japanese classroom, and there are fewer distractions (such as announcements, special class elections, or outings; Stevenson & Stigler, 1992). Most of the Japanese students go to after-school Juku classes in which mathematics is the prime subject, especially in the later grades. Juku classes (White, 1987) are special classes to help students improve their performance in school and prepare for national exams. It is estimated that the average Japanese parent spends $2000 per year on Juku.[1]

Societal attitudes probably magnify the basic differences (Stevenson & Stigler, 1992). Japanese parents and children tend to believe that mathematics achievement is primarily a result of effort, whereas American parents and children tend to believe it is a talent that a person either has or does not have. American parents, although they may deplore their nation's achievement in mathematics, tend to be satisfied with the achievement levels of their own children. In contrast, Japanese parents, who may be proud of their nation's achievement, tend to think that their own children could do better (Stevenson & Stigler, 1992). Japanese parents are inclined to help their children with mathematics at home, whereas American parents think that such help is the province of the school system.

There is always a suspicion that the differences in mathematics achievement between the United States and Asian countries may reflect some innate racial differences. Although it cannot be proved conclusively that this is not

---

[1]"More than 50% of the 5 million lower secondary (7th to 9th grades) school students attend a juku. In the last seven years, for instance, the amount spent by Japanese parents on cram-schools and tutoring has doubled to $10.9 Billion ($109 oku)." From "For Japanese, Cramming for Exams Starts Where the Cradle Leaves Off," *International Herald Tribune*, April 28, 1992, p. 1.

the case, there is good evidence that it is not a major factor. Stevenson and Stigler (1992) reported no differences in general intelligence scores of the population. The best American students typically do very well in international Math Olympiad competitions. Invariably, such students are the few American children who have devoted themselves to mathematics achievement and received extensive support outside the classroom. Although there may well be innate mathematical talent, the more critical variable is effort, as discussed in Chapter 9.

It surely should come as no surprise in the context of this book that time spent learning has a major impact on learning outcome. In this regard, it should also be noted that the amount of time spent on reading education is much more comparable between Japan and the United States, and the outcomes are correspondingly more comparable (Stevenson & Stigler, 1992; White, 1987). However, although time spent learning has an important impact on learning outcome, most of this book has been devoted to secondary variables, which have an impact on how effective learning time is. This chapter focuses on how learning time can be made more effective.

There is a wide range of mathematics achievement in the United States, but all but the very best students do worse than students of most nations.

Psychology and Education

The psychology of learning can suggest ways to make the instructional process more effective. Corresponding to the two themes in the research on learning, two approaches to education can be identified: a behaviorist approach and a cognitive approach.

The Behaviorist Program

Starting with the attempts of Thorndike and Skinner to apply their work to education, there has been a considerable tradition of behaviorist applications to education. Despite its acknowledged weaknesses, the behaviorist approach remains the most coherent and influential psychology-based approach to education. Probably the major contribution of the approach has been **task analysis**. Just as a Skinnerian might decompose a conditioning task into a set of subtasks, so task analysis takes a complex skill, such as multicolumn subtraction, and decomposes it into a set of what are called **behavioral objectives**. Consider what is involved in solving a subtraction problem, such as:

$$4203$$
$$-\ 728$$

Behavioral objectives include knowing simple subtraction facts ($13 - 8 = 5$), borrowing, the special case of borrowing across zero, and subtracting when there is only a top number. Each of these behavioral objectives is taught separately. Gagné (1962) succinctly described what is involved in task analysis:

> The basic principles of training design consist of: (a) identifying the component tasks of a final performance; (b) insuring that each of these component tasks is fully achieved; and (c) arranging the total learning situation in a sequence that will insure optimal mediational effects from one component to another. (1962, p. 88)

Each of the components identified by Gagné is essential to the success of the behaviorist program in education:

a. The emphasis on task analysis is absolutely critical. If teachers know what they want to teach, they are in a much better position to achieve that goal. The problem with the behaviorist approach, as this chapter discusses, is that it sometimes does a poor job of analyzing the components of a complex cognitive skill.

b. The behaviorist methodology is associated with the concept of **mastery learning**—ensuring that each component is brought to a level of achievement. This concept is probably the most profound and controversial aspect of the behaviorist program. The next section discusses mastery learning in detail.

c. Gagné is best known for his behavioral learning hierarchies—the idea that some skills are prerequisite to others. For instance, Gagné would argue that basic arithmetic skills need to be mastered before a student can progress to algebra. Many algebra teachers can attest to the difficulty students have who do not know their fractional arithmetic. However, recent technological changes are beginning to challenge this wisdom (Anderson, Corbett, Koedinger, & Pelletier, in press). Students can now use hand-held calculators to do the fractional arithmetic.

Gagné's statement contains no reference to principles of reinforcement. Although these principles are emphasized in Skinner's and Thorndike's original educational proposals and are frequently referenced in behaviorist writings on education, such references are primarily lip service. As discussed in Chapters 4 and 6, learning is largely independent of the reinforcement contingencies, provided that the student processes the material appropriately.

A way of designing and delivering instruction, often called instructional technology, has been built around these ideas. Sometimes each student is individually taught by computer, an approach frequently referred to as programmed instruction or computer-assisted instruction. Many textbooks for a wide variety of subjects have been written according to the principles of programmed instruction, and mastery learning principles have been articulated in ways to manage whole classes so that every student reaches mastery. The key idea unifying these various approaches is that a task can be broken down into a set of behavioral objectives each of which can be taught individually.

Some large gains have been reported for these efforts. One spelling program got students to mastery in one-third of the time required by conventional instruction (Porter, 1961). On average the level of gain associated with behaviorist programs is probably much less than behaviorist theories would suggest. For tasks such as geometry, application of the program might actually lead to lower achievement. A behaviorist program applied to geometry tends to emphasize instructional objectives, such as knowing the reflexive law, whereas a cognitive analysis reveals the many different rules that underlie the use of this law (see the later section on geometry). Behaviorist analyses have these shortcomings because they ignore the covert problem-solving steps involved in some problems, and so the units they identify for instruction only correlate somewhat with the targets of instruction. To the extent that the correlation is poor, the instruction is less effective than might be hoped.

Modern educational writing frequently assumes that the behaviorist approach to education has been a failure, although little hard evidence has been cited. Recent writings have tended to generalize the perceived failures of the behaviorist program to the conclusion that any program that attempts to analyze a skill into components will fail. In a gross misreading of the cognitive psychology literature, it has been claimed that modern cognitive research has proved that such componential analysis is in error (e.g., Shepard, 1991). However, modern cognitive psychology only quarrels with what the units of analysis are. Given the correct units, there is every reason to believe that Gagné's basic program for designing instruction would be successful.

Behaviorists have developed a powerful approach to education but have applied it to a weak analysis of the knowledge to be taught.

Mastery Learning

One of the most significant outcomes of the behaviorist tradition is a set of instructional strategies generally called mastery learning. Mastery learning is based on two assumptions:

1. Almost all students should be able to learn almost all the material in a standard school curriculum.
2. If students have not learned material early in a curriculum, they will have more difficulty with material later in the curriculum.

With mastery learning techniques, students are given as much time as they need to master early material before moving on to later material. This approach guarantees learning and makes the learning of later material easier. There are two types of mastery curricula. One (Glaser, 1972; Keller, 1968; Suppes, 1964) involves having each student follow an individual course of learning. The second, associated with Bloom (1968, 1976), is more appropriate to standard schoolroom classes and gets the whole class to mastery of a topic before the students move on. The latter approach is much easier to manage than the individualized method, which requires tracking each student separately. The individualized method has been used primarily with college or adult populations, where individual students are more mature and more capable of managing their own learning. Many psychology departments (including my own at Carnegie Mellon) have self-paced introductory courses in which students have to achieve a particular grade level on a chapter before they can go on to the next. It is up to the student how to study and when to schedule the tests. These often are lectureless courses.

In general mastery programs lead to higher achievement (Guskey & Gates, 1986; Kulik, Kulik, & Bangert-Downs, 1986). However, it has also been claimed that mastery programs result in reduced individual differences, since all students master the prerequisite material (Bloom, 1976). That is, since all students master the same material in the earlier units, they should take about the same time to master the material in the later units that depend on these earlier units. The evidence for this claim is weaker than for the claim of higher achievement (Resnick, 1977), and large individual differences remain in the time to learn material to reach the mastery level. The failure of mastery learning to eliminate individual differences should not obscure the fact that it results in higher educational achievement for all students. Despite the positive evidence, the educational establishment tends to view these efforts as failures. This is one of many examples of how the educational establishment ignores empirical evidence in its desire to follow fashion.

Many mastery programs introduced in schools have been dropped. Maintaining a successful mastery program requires a lot of teacher commitment and energy. The standard classroom is much easier to manage—this issue of ease of classroom management is a significant issue that has caused many efforts at educational reform to fail (Grittner, 1975).

Significant instructional gains can be achieved by ensuring that students have mastered earlier material before progressing to later material.

The Cognitive Approach

The field of cognitive psychology has not produced anything as well organized or coherent as the instructional design approach of behavioral psychology.

Which principles reviewed in the previous chapters form a basis for ideas to make instruction more effective? A great deal of psychological research has focused on human memory for declarative facts, which seems a logical starting point. Perhaps the most powerful idea in this area for education is the importance of elaborative strategies and organizational strategies for good memory. Chapter 6 reviewed some of the educational programs based on these strategies, for example, the PQ4R method, and this chapter reviews some elaborations of these ideas under the topic of reading. Such techniques are important for learning declarative information, such as that presented in this book, and certainly much of modern education involves trying to communicate such facts. These study techniques are important skills, and they need to be taught every bit as much as the more basic skills involved in the three Rs (reading, writing, and arithmetic).

The research on skill acquisition reviewed in Chapter 9 provides ideas for instruction on skills like reading and mathematics. Chapter 9 discussed how complex skills can be decomposed into a large number of production rules and how the learning of the skills can be analyzed as the learning of the component rules. This approach implies that the key step in teaching a particular skill is a cognitive analysis into the component rules and that a Gagné-like program should be applied to the instruction of these target rules. **Componential analysis** is the term used for the analysis of instructional material into its underlying components, which are the basic facts and rules. There is some controversy in the field of education about what the components are, but when the skills are agreed upon, there can be good success in instructing them.

Analysis of instructional material into its cognitive components enables more effective instruction.

Reading Instruction

Compared to the situation in mathematics, there is relative agreement about what the target of reading instruction should be. Society wants its citizens to be able to read at a level that will allow them to process policy information so that they can vote intelligently, to process information about commodities so that they can be good consumers, to process technical information so that they can be good workers, and in other ways to take in written information so that they can be effective citizens. As already noted, the educational establishment can claim some success at achieving this, at least for those who are not socially disadvantaged.

However, there has been one major controversy in the teaching of reading. This is the conflict between the **phonics method** and the **whole-word**

method of instruction. The phonics method emphasizes training children how to go from letters and letter combinations to sound, and from sound to the words and their meanings. The whole-word method emphasizes direct recognition of words and phrases and going directly from words to meaning.

In the United States there have been swings of fashion in reading instruction. Until the 1800s, the principal emphasis was on the phonics method. With the appearance of the McGaffey readers in the 1800s, emphasis switched to the whole-word method. Emphasis has fluctuated back and forth since then. Children learn to read under both methods, although studies tend to find that the phonics approach is somewhat superior (M. J. Adams, 1990; I. L. Beck, 1981; Chall, 1967; Johnson & Baumann, 1984). J. P. Williams (1979) and Perfetti (1985) pondered why there is not greater use of phonics-based instruction given the positive evidence. As Williams lamented,

> Today as in the past, data do not carry a great deal of weight in determining educational practice. (P. 921)

Both Williams and Perfetti concluded that the whole-word approach, with its emphasis on meaning, is more appealing in that it appears superficially to be in keeping with cognitive trends in psychology, to be more fun, and to be a higher-status skill to teach than low-level phonetic decoding skills.

The popular press has given a great deal of attention to **dyslexia**, which is best defined as underachievement in reading performance. The most common definition of a dyslexic is a person of normal or high IQ who reads at least two grade levels below the expected reading level. In a review of dyslexia, Just and Carpenter (1987) noted that in the United States and Great Britain .5 percent of girls and 3 percent of boys could be classified by this criterion as dyslexic. The general public tends to believe that dyslexia is a visual problem involving confusion of letters, but as Just and Carpenter noted, the major source of the deficit is in making correspondences from symbols to sounds. The phonics method, which focuses on this aspect of reading, may be particularly appropriate for dealing with the problems of the dyslexic population (Lundberg, 1985; Perfetti, 1985).

There is somewhat greater success in teaching reading according to the phonics method than according to the whole-word method.

Nature of the Adult Skill

To determine what children should learn, it is useful to look at successful adult readers and determine what it is they do. Some people believe that reading is the process of moving the eyes smoothly across the page, but this is not so.

Readers engage in a large number of jumps of eye fixation, called saccades. Most saccades last about a quarter of a second. Figure 11.3 illustrates the eye movements of one college student while reading a text. Readers tend to make one fixation on each word, sometimes skipping less important words and sometimes making more than one fixation on long or difficult words. When a reader fixates on a word, that word is centered so that its image falls on the fovea, which is the most sensitive part of the retina of the eye. People normally only detect successfully letters that are close to the fovea and perceive no more than 10 characters to the left or right of the fovea (McConkie & Rayner, 1974). Thus people can read at most a few words in a particular fixation.

As the difficulty of the text increases, the length of fixations, number of fixations per line, and number of regressions also increase. A regression is returning to a previously read word. One minor regression is illustrated in Figure 11.3. The average adult can read material of average difficulty at a rate between 200 and 400 words per minute; more adults read near the 200 word rate than near the 400 word rate. The reading rate for adults is not limited by perceptual or orthographic skills, but by comprehension skills. Adults also cannot follow spoken text at much faster than 200 to 400 words per minute. For adults, individual differences in the comprehension of spoken material are the best predictors of individual differences in the comprehension of written materials (Jackson & McClelland, 1979; Sticht, 1972).

There are three logical steps to reading skill. One step is the perceptual skill of identifying the individual graphemes (letters). For a language with an alphabet, this skill is relatively easy; for example, English has only 26 graphemes that need to be recognized. For a language with thousands of characters, such as Japanese or Chinese, this identification is much more challenging, and children spend many years mastering it. The second step of reading is the orthographic step. Orthography is concerned with going from symbol combinations

FIGURE 11.3. Eye fixation while reading a passage about flywheels. Reading is left-to-right except for the one regression indicated with the arrows. The fixation times in msec are given in circles. (Adapted from Just & Carpenter, 1980). *Source:* From M. A. Just and P. A. Carpenter. *A theory of reading: from eye fixations to comprehension.* Copyright © 1980 by the American Psychological Association. Reprinted by permission.

Flywheels are one of the oldest mechanical devices known to man. Every

internal-combustion engine contains a small flywheel that converts the jerky

motion of the piston into the smooth flow of energy that powers the drive shaft.

to sound, whereas the perceptual component is concerned with identifying the individual symbols. Orthography is the major component of reading skill in English and involves a great many complicated rules and special cases, as all of us can attest who have been frustrated in attempts at spelling. It is a relatively smaller component in languages such as Chinese or Japanese, where symbols can map onto whole words. The task in these languages is more perceptual and less orthographic. The two reading systems can be viewed as involving different design decisions about how to divide up the task between perceptual work and orthographic work. The third stage of reading involves going from the words to the meaning. This component is not unique to reading, but is also a part of listening to language. These steps may not always be discrete. In particular, skilled readers may go directly from perceptual patterns to meaning, bypassing the need for an orthographic stage.

The whole-word method of teaching reading is an attempt to minimize the intermediate orthographic stage. It is a step in the direction of treating English like a nonalphabetic system. The fact that people learn to read quite well in languages without alphabetic orthographies should be proof that the whole-word method can succeed. However, the method does not appear to do as well for English, which may indicate that it is more efficient to learn to read English by including an intermediate letter-to-sound stage. M. J. Adams (1990) argued that high-frequency words in English may be processed by the whole-word method but that most lower frequency words are better dealt with by the phonics method, because low-frequency words do not receive enough practice to become automatically recognized at the whole-word level.

English uses a large number of patterns and rules. Only 26 letters in just a few renditions (uppercase, lowercase, printed, cursive) and between 41 to 45 sounds (depending on how they are counted) need to be recognized. However, many orthographic rules for going from letters to sounds and linguistic rules for going from words to meaning must be learned. Venezky (1970) in his analysis of English orthography listed hundreds of rules and exceptions for translating written to spoken English. Typical estimates of the number of rules in English grammar (words to meaning) are in the many thousands. An average successful adult reader has put an enormous amount of time into mastering this skill—students may have spent 10,000 hr reading by the time they reach college. The effort put into reading is commensurate with the complexity of the skill. In addition, as noted in Chapter 10, adults have put tens of thousands of hours into processing spoken English and the comprehension skills it shares with reading.

There is a pattern of skill development such that measures of letter recognition best predict reading skill in the first grade, measures of orthographic knowledge best predict reading performance in the later elementary grades (Lesgold, Resnick, & Hammond, 1985), and measures of comprehension of spoken text best predict reading skill in adults (Sticht & James, 1984). This situation suggests that, as children grow up, perceptual and then orthographic components become less important, leaving the most difficult comprehension skills as the critical factor. Even in adulthood phonetic decoding skills contribute to the prediction of reading level, although general language comprehension skills contribute more (Jackson & McClelland, 1979). Some adults appear to have reading difficulties at the orthographic level. As noted, dyslexia is a condition associated with impaired ability to perform the character-to-speech transition, although dyslexics form only a small fraction of the overall population.

This pattern of development would be predicted from a componential analysis of reading—letter recognition must be mastered before sound can be assigned to letter combinations, and assigning sound to letter combinations must be mastered before the words can be comprehended. The next sections focus on phonetic decoding skills and language comprehension skills, which are the two critical components of reading English.

Reading English involves letter recognition, letter-to-sound conversion, and language comprehension.

Phonetic Decoding Skills

The study by Ehri and Wilce (1983) is typical of research illustrating the importance of orthographic or phonetic decoding skills in the early grades. They measured how fast children in the first through fourth grades could read common words, like *hat* and *boy*. They looked at reading speed separately for skilled readers and unskilled readers. The results are shown in Figure 11.4. In the first grade the gap between the ability of skilled and unskilled readers to perform such simple word identifications was wider, but the differences almost completely disappeared by the fourth grade. This research implies that, at least in the early grades, reading ability is strongly related to the speed with which simple decoding can be performed.

Other, more subtle measures indicate that differences remain between good and poor readers into the later grades. Frederiksen (1981) looked at the speed with which high school students could identify pronounceable nonsense words, such as *noke* or *pight*. Figure 11.5 shows the results as a function of the reading level: students with higher reading abilities were faster at identifying the nonsense words.

Results such as those shown in Figures 11.4 and 11.5 only indicate a correlation between phonetic decoding skills and reading ability; they do not actually establish that the reading differences are caused by these phonetic skill differences. It could be the other way around; that is, better readers may read more and so develop their decoding skills further. Lesgold et al. (1985) showed that a student's phonetic decoding skills in the previous grade predict current reading comprehension better than reading comprehension ability in

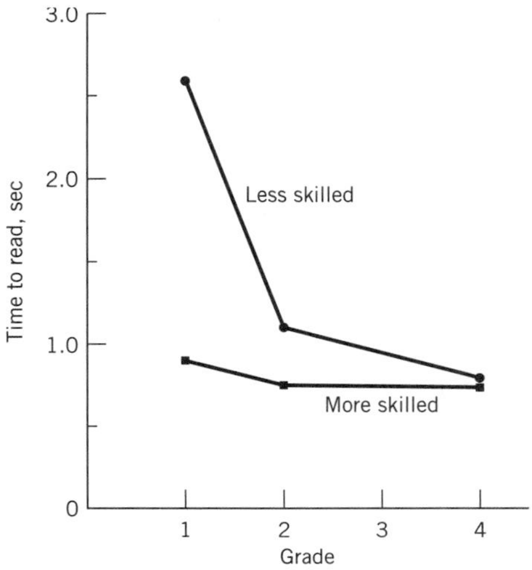

FIGURE 11.4. Time to read a word as a function of grade level. (From Ehri & Wilce, 1983). *Source:* Figure 11.4 from D. A. Hinsley, J. R. Hayes, and H. A. Simon in M. A. Just and P. A. Carpenter, Eds. *Cognitive processes in comprehension.* Copyright © 1977 by Lawrence Erlbaum Associates, Inc. Reprinted by permission.

the previous grade predicts current decoding skills. This study implies that the decoding skills developed in one year lay the groundwork for reading gains in the next year.

To strongly establish the direction of causality, it must be shown that improving phonetic decoding skills directly improves reading skills. The frequent success of phonics-based reading programs (M. J. Adams, 1990; I. L. Beck, 1981; Chall, 1967; Johnson & Baumann, 1984) is one piece of evidence. More focused studies show that orthographic training does help reading skills, at least at the early grades. A study by Lundberg, Frost, and Petersen (1988) looked at the effect of teaching Danish kindergarten children phonological skills to identify the sounds that make words such as *tom*. This sound training

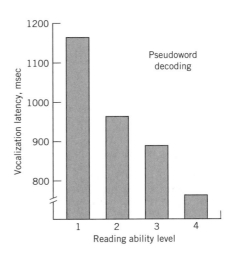

FIGURE 11.5. Mean speed to read a pronounceable nonsense word as a function of reading level. Source: From J. R. Fredriksen in A. M. Lesgold and C. A. Perfetti, Eds. *Interactive Processes in Reading.* Copyright © 1981 by Lawrence Erlbaum Associates, Inc. Reprinted by permission.

involved no practice reading. Children were trained to identify beginning sounds, end sounds, vowels, and the like. The training proved useful when the children entered a regular reading program in the first grade. They were able to read more words correctly, and they maintained this advantage into the second grade. Another study, by Ehri and Wilce (1987), looked at the effect of spelling training on reading. Spelling is a major exercise in understanding the orthography of the language. Kindergarten children who were given spelling training showed better ability to read new words.

M. J. Adams (1990) argued that successful reading depends on practicing these phonetic decoding skills to the point at which they become automatic. Recall from the discussion of automaticity in Chapter 9 that people are better able to concentrate on high-level skills when the low-level components are automated. In the case of reading, people can concentrate on comprehending the text when they no longer have to worry about decoding the words.

Improving phonetic decoding skills in the early grades will improve later reading performance.

Comprehension Skills

Comprehension skills play an increasingly important role in the later grades. These skills can be analyzed and trained. One of the more successful training programs was Palincsar and Brown's (1984) reciprocal teaching program. They identified four basic strategies that foster comprehension: summarizing, clarification of difficulties, asking a question that could appear on a test, and making a prediction about upcoming content. They worked on a one-on-one basis with seventh-grade students who were performing at the 20th percentile of their class in reading scores. The researchers modeled how to perform these activities and slowly encouraged the students to do the same. Table 11.1 illustrates the modeling with one seventh grader of question-asking skills over a 15-day period. After this training program the students were scoring at the 56th percentile, and they maintained their improved achievement 2 months later.

The Palinscar and Brown method is just a more extensive version of the kinds of study-skill programs discussed in Chapter 6, which work by creating more elaborative representations of the text. Palinscar and Brown's effort was more successful than most programs because it involved 15 days of training, which is a good deal more than in most experimental studies. Their research emphasizes two critical points about reading comprehension. First, an important measure of reading comprehension is memory, and successful readers are those who can remember more from what they read. Second, the kinds of skills that go into achieving good memory performance are hardly automatic and require extensive training, as does any other kind of skill.

Table 11.1 *The Acquisition of Question Asking Skill*
(*Note: T = teacher; S = student*)

Day 1:

TEXT: The water moccasin, somewhat longer than the copperhead, is found in the southeastern states. It lives in swampy regions. It belongs, as do also the copperhead and the rattlesnakes, to a group of poisonous snakes called pit vipers. They have pits between their eyes and their nostrils which, because they are sensitive to heat, help the snakes tell when they are near a warm-blooded animal. Another name for the water moccasin is "cottonmouth." This name comes from the white lining of the snake's mouth.

1. S: What is found in the southeastern snakes, also the copperhead, rattlesnakes, vipers—they have. I'm not doing this right.
2. T: All right. Do you want to know about the pit vipers?
3. S: Yeah.
4. T: What would be a good question about the pit vipers that starts with the word "why?"
5. S: (No response)
6. T: How about, "Why are the snakes called pit vipers?"
7. S: Why do they want to know that they are called pit vipers?
8. T: Try it again.
9. S: Why do they, pit vipers in a pit?
10. T: How about, "Why do they call the snakes pit vipers?"
11. S: Why do they call the snakes pit vipers?
12. T: There you go! Good for you.

Day 7:

TEXT: Perhaps you are wondering where the lava and other volcanic products come from. Deep within our earth there are pockets of molten rock called *magma*. Forced upward in part by gas pressure, this molten rock continually tries to reach the surface. Eventually—by means of cracks in the crustal rocks or some similar zone of weakness—the magma may break out of the ground. It then flows from the vent as lava, or spews skyward as dense clouds of lava particles.

22. S: How does the pressure from below push the mass of hot rock against the opening? Is that it?
23. T: Not quite. Start your question with, "What happens when?"
24. S: What happens when the pressure from below pushes the mass of hot rock against the opening?
25. T: Good for you! Good job.

Day 15:

TEXT: Scientists also come to the South Pole to study the strange lights that glow overhead during the Antarctic night. (It's a cold and lonely world for the few hardy people who "winter over" the polar night.) These "southern lights" are caused by the Earth acting like a magnet on electrical particles in the air. They are clues that may help us understand the Earth's core and the upper edges of its blanket of air.

28. S: Why do scientists come to the South Pole to study?
29. T: Excellent question! That is what this paragraph is all about.

Source: From A. S. Palinscar and A. L. Brown, *Cognition and instruction.* Copyright © 1984 by Lawrence Erlbaum Associates, Inc. Reprinted by permission.

It is important when reading to be able to appreciate the main points of paragraphs and how other points relate to the main points. So, for instance, the points in this paragraph are all organized as evidence for the main point in the preceding sentence (and what was that point?). Meyer, Brandt, and Bluth (1978) found that many ninth graders were poor at recognizing the relationship of various points in a paragraph to one another. Poorer readers tended to be poorer at identifying the main points of a piece of text. In a companion study, B. J. Bartlett (1978) found that a program to train students to identify the main points of paragraphs and their relationships more than doubled their recall performance. Once the main points were identified, the students could organize the rest of the text with respect to these points.

Dansereau and his colleagues (Dansereau, 1978; Dansereau, Collins, McDonald, Holley, Garland, Diekhoff, & Evans, 1979; Holley, Dansereau, McDonald, Garland, & Collins, 1979) taught a networking strategy for identifying the main points of a passage. This strategy involved identifying all the ideas in a text and the relationships among them and then drawing a network showing the relationships. The types of relationships included part of, type of, leads to (causal), and characteristic of. Figure 11.6 shows a network representation of a passage on wounds from a nursing textbook. The strategy led to about a 50 percent improvement in the recall of low-GPA students, but did not benefit high-GPA students. Apparently, high-GPA students already had effective strategies for organizing text material.

The studies reviewed here were concerned with reading to extract factual information from a text. Such a reading strategy is appropriate to texts such as this, but extracting such information is just one purpose of reading. The purpose of reading a mathematics or physics text can be different; for example, the goal might be to extract information about problem-solving procedures. Chi, Bassock, Lewis, Riemann, and Glaser (1989) showed that successful readers of such texts spend a great deal of time trying to understand examples of problem-solving procedures. When reading these examples, they try to imagine themselves going through the steps of the problem and compare what they do with the example.

Reading comprehension can be improved by programs that try to analyze and teach reading comprehension skills.

Conclusions About Reading Instruction

Although most students seem to learn to read in most reading programs, the more successful reading programs are those that identify the critical components of reading skill and try to find ways to train these components. Under any teaching method, reading skill requires learning and automating a lot of specific orthographic knowledge, which requires a great deal of time. In addi-

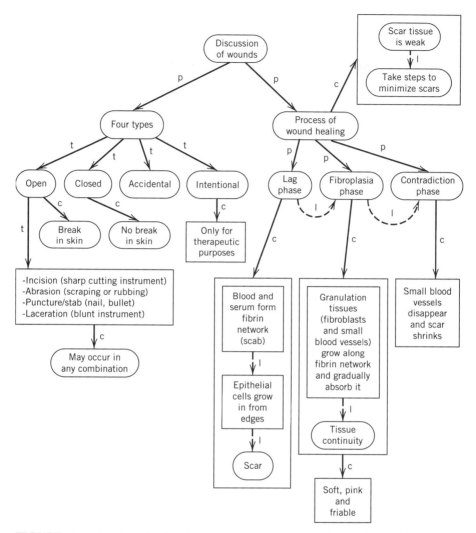

FIGURE 11.6. A network of a chapter from a nursing textbook, from Holley et al., 1979). Note that p = part of, t = type of, l = leads to, and c = characteristic of. *Source:* From C. D. Holley, D. F. Dansereau, B. A. McDonald, J. C. Garland, and K. W. Collins. *Contemporary Educational Psychology, Volume 4.* Evaluation of a Hierarchical Mapping Technique as an Aid to Prose Processing. Copyright © 1976 by Academic Press. Reprinted by permission.

tion, a major part of adult reading skill overlaps with adult listening skills; by practicing listening to complex communications, people are also practicing skills relevant to reading.

Not everything relevant to reading is being taught. The large effects produced by the training programs of Palinscar and Brown and of Bartlett are evidence that schools are not doing everything they can to instruct reading. In particular, it seems that the goal of schools is to create students who have mastered the orthographic component of reading. More research needs to be done on reading for special purposes, such as retention of concepts and facts and acquisition of problem-solving procedures, and more effort needs to be given to training the cognitive components involved in reading for these special purposes. Perhaps the lack of adequate training of reading skills for particular purposes comes from an unfortunate tendency to align reading instruction with literature instruction. The goal in reading a poem or a novel is literary appreciation. Although undoubtedly an important ability, this is only one of the reasons for reading. A major flaw in most educational programs is the belief that reading for literary appreciation prepares a student to read for other purposes. This belief reflects a lack of task analysis, which would readily reveal the different goals of different reading activities.

Reading ability can be improved by teaching how to read for particular purposes.

Mathematics Instruction

Controversy surrounds the subject of what the target of mathematics instruction should be, and this controversy is reflected in the waves of curriculum reform that have occurred in U.S. mathematics education. In the 1960s the new math movement attempted to conform to modern conceptions of mathematics and to develop mathematics in school as a mathematician would. This movement was followed by the back-to-basics movement in the 1970s and 1980s, which emphasized developing perfection of traditional mathematical skills, such as addition facts or the solution of linear equations. This approach has now largely been replaced by what is termed the constructivist movement, which focuses on having children discover mathematics for themselves and relate mathematics to their experiences in everyday life. This newest movement is motivated in part by the observation that many students do not value mathematics and do not see it as having any practical role in their lives. Each of these movements has some intrinsic merit. However, there was nothing about society in the 1960s that made formal mathematics more essential then, or about the 1980s that especially required basic skills, or about today that especially requires making mathematics practical and relevant. The goals of formal appreciation, proficiency, and practicality are always desirable. Each has its constituency, and the different fashions reflect which constituency momentarily has the attention of mathematics education. As noted earlier, the result for teachers is disaster. Teachers no sooner learn how to teach to one goal than they find that the curriculum goals have changed. Few nations undergo such rapid changes in the goals of their mathematics curriculum.

There are reasons for curriculum change, besides fad. The nature of mathematics is changing. Mathematics is a developing subject, and there are new domains that may be important to teach to children. The computer revolution is requiring a major rethinking of what sorts of skills should be expected of children. As much as a year of a child's mathematics education may be spent learning the long-division algorithm. This seems rather wasteful in the era of calculators. Schools should probably abandon teaching the long-division algorithm just as they long ago gave up teaching children the algorithm for calculating square roots. Algebraic skills that were formerly the domain of high school mathematics classes and college calculus classes can also be embedded in a hand-held calculator. Everywhere educators must ask themselves what is still important to teach. Calculators are available that can solve an equation with the push of a button, differentiate it, or integrate it. The practical needs of the nation are also changing. There is relatively little need to perform routine arithmetic calculations and greater need to be able to use mathematically based computer software, such as spreadsheets. The need for computer literacy has increased the need for students to understand discrete mathematics. Developments in mathematics and the social sciences require a citizenry much more sophisticated in statistics. Almost everyday the news contains some claim about the effectiveness of a social program, which cannot be evaluated without a considerable understanding of the statistical basis for that claim.

Another problem in achieving consensus with respect to mathematics education lies in the different conceptions of the nature of mathematical talent. As mentioned earlier, Americans hold an unhealthy belief that mathematical talent is a gift and not something developed through extensive practice. It is part of the general Western illusion that genius is something that should come effortlessly and in great flashes of insight. Since mathematical talent is so much tied to the Western conception of intelligence, it bears an unfortunately heavy load of this misconception about the nature of talent. The worst part of this misconception is a resistance to believing that mathematical talent can be analyzed into its component skills and that these skills can be taught.

This section considers several mathematical skills that have been successfully analyzed into their components, including knowledge of basic arithmetic facts, multicolumn subtraction skills, solution of algebraic word problems, and proof skills in geometry. This section ends with a review of the debate about the value of these traditional mathematical skills.

Mathematics instruction has been hampered by the rapidly changing goals for the mathematics curriculum.

Basic Arithmetic Facts

Strange as it may sound, there are not that many basic arithmetic facts to be learned in a base-10 number system. Exactly how many there are depends on just how they are counted. Is $3 + 4 = 7$ separate from $4 + 3 = 7$? Is the addition fact $3 + 4 = 7$ separate from the subtraction fact $7 - 4 = 3$? The same questions can be asked about multiplication and division. Is $3 \times 4 = 12$ different from $4 \times 3 = 12$ and $12 \div 4 = 3$? By any way of counting, there are not that many facts—not more than 500 and perhaps as few as 100. Still, learning these facts poses a considerable challenge for children. As discussed in Chapter 7, these facts define a horrendous interference paradigm in which a number, for example, 3, is being associated with a large number of interfering facts: $4 \times 3 = 12$; $7 - 4 = 3$; $3 + 3 = 6$; $3 \times 3 = 9$; $6 - 3 = 3$; and so on.

Siegler (Siegler, 1988; Siegler & Shrager, 1984) completed a successful analysis of how these facts are learned, focusing on the more basic addition and multiplication facts. He noted that most children know a backup strategy for solving these problems, which they can use if they cannot remember the facts. In the case of addition, this backup strategy is counting. Thus, to add 4 and 3, some children can be observed to count out 4 fingers, then count 3 more, and then count that they now have 7 fingers. Other children count silently to themselves. There are a number of variations on this counting strategy, and some are more efficient than others. The strategies are all sound mathematically, although young children often make slips in trying to execute the counting strategies and come up with wrong answers. The backup strategy for multiplication is repeated addition. To multiply 3×4, the child just adds 4 three times. If addition has been mastered, this backup strategy for multiplication is also a mathematically sound strategy, but one in which the students make frequent errors, such as $6 \times 4 = 18$ (forgetting to add one 6).

While they are using these backup strategies, children try to memorize the facts, since recall is a much faster and ultimately less error-prone way of solving these problems. Once they can automatically recall the facts, they free up working-memory capacity for higher-order problem solving. As a simple example, it is very difficult for children to execute the repeated addition algorithm for multiplication if they also have to execute the counting algorithm for addition. The degree of learning of specific facts is a function of how often a particular fact is encountered. Children learn simple facts, such as $2 + 2 = 4$, faster than facts such as $4 + 7 = 11$, because they encounter them more often—another testimony to the effects of practice reviewed in Chapter 6. A major complication is that the errors children make in their backup computations create false facts, which can interfere with memory. Occasionally children display evidence of these interference problems; given a problem such as $3 \times 4 = ?$, they recall answers such as 15 (giving a different answer from the multiplication table) or 7 (confusing multiplication and addition). Siegler showed that children are sensitive to their state of knowledge of specific facts and only begin to recall them when they are fairly sure of producing a correct recall.

Siegler's analysis is a triumph of the componential approach. Children's ability to reproduce the addition and multiplication facts rests on mastering specific strategies and memorizing specific facts, one at a time. Final mastery is achieved when the child has built up enough strength for each correct fact to overcome the interference inherent in the addition and multiplication tables. Further practice brings automaticity, which facilitates using this knowledge in more complex algorithms.

There are relatively few arithmetic facts to be learned, but they suffer from high interference.

Multicolumn Subtraction

Multicolumn subtraction involves solving problems, such as:

$$\begin{array}{r} 3206 \\ -1147 \\ \hline \end{array}$$

Production rule theories, such as those considered in Chapter 9, can be used to model such skills (Van Lehn, 1990; Young & O'Shea, 1981). Much of subtraction skill can be modeled by the seven rules given in Table 11.2. Van Lehn (1990) studied typical mathematics texts and found that there is a tendency for each lesson to introduce one new rule. Children at different levels of competence can be modeled as knowing different numbers of these rules.

What do children do when they come upon a problem that has a step that they cannot perform? Often they do not just fail to do the problem, but try to invent some answer to fill the gap in their knowledge. Sometimes they come to believe their inventions and display what Brown and Van Lehn (1980) called bugs. A bug is a wrong rule that leads the child to make systematic errors. Burton and Brown tabulated over 100 such bugs. Table 11.3 displays some of the most common. The most common error is to always subtract the smaller number from the larger to avoid the need for borrowing. Many of the errors involve inventions to deal with the problem of borrowing across zero.

Burton (1982) developed a diagnostic program called BUGGY, which can take a student's performance on subtraction test problems and automatically identify the student's bugs. In one experiment, BUGGY processed the solutions of 1300 students and found that 40 percent had systematic bugs. The program has also been used to help train teachers to diagnose various bugs.

Students' subtraction errors can be explained by what correct production rules they are missing and what incorrect rules they have.

Table 11.2 *Production Rules for Multicolumn Subtraction*

IF the goal is to solve a subtraction problem
THEN make the subgoal to process the right-most
  column

IF there is an answer in the current column
  and there is a column to the left
THEN make the subgoal to process the column to the
  left

IF the goal is to process a column
  and there is no bottom digit
THEN write the top digit as the answer

IF the goal is to process a column
  and the top digit is not smaller than the
  bottom digit
THEN write the difference between the digits as the answer

IF the goal is to process a column
  and the top digit is smaller than the
  bottom digit
THEN add 10 to the top digit
  and set as a subgoal to borrow from the
  column to the left

IF the goal is to borrow from a column
  and the top digit in that column is not zero
THEN decrease the digit by 1

IF the goal is to borrow from a column
  and the top digit in that column is zero
THEN replace the zero by 9
  and set as a subgoal to borrow from the
  column to the left

Algebraic Word Problems

Children's ability to perform the algorithmic mathematical skills taught in school is often divorced from their ability to use these skills in solving real-world problems. Carraher, Carraher, and Schliemann (1985) reported a study of Brazilian schoolchildren who also worked as street vendors. These children were capable of solving addition and subtraction problems in the marketplace (What is the cost of five lemons at 35 cruzeros a piece?) when they could not solve the equivalent classroom problem ($5 \times 35 = ?$). Perhaps more disturbing to mathematics educators is evidence of children who can solve the formal mathematics problems but who cannot apply mathematics outside the classroom. This issue has been studied using algebraic word problems, where students must use knowledge of algebra to solve problems stated verbally.

Table 11.3 *Some of the More Common Bugs in Subtraction*

1. Smaller-from-larger. The student subtracts the smaller digit in a column from the larger digit regardless of which one is on top.

$$\begin{array}{r} 326 \\ -117 \\ \hline 211 \end{array} \qquad \begin{array}{r} 542 \\ -389 \\ \hline 247 \end{array}$$

2. Borrow-from-zero. When borrowing from a column whose top digit is 0, the student writes 9 but does not continue borrowing from the column to the left of the 0.

$$\begin{array}{r} 6\overset{9}{\cancel{0}}{}_{\!1}2 \\ -437 \\ \hline 265 \end{array} \qquad \begin{array}{r} 8\overset{9}{\cancel{0}}{}_{\!1}2 \\ -396 \\ \hline 506 \end{array}$$

3. Borrow-across-zero. When the student needs to borrow from a column whose top digit is 0, he or she skips that column and borrows from the next one.

$$\begin{array}{r} {}^{5}\!\cancel{6}02 \\ -327 \\ \hline 225 \end{array} \qquad \begin{array}{r} {}^{7}\!\cancel{8}0{}_{\!1}4 \\ -456 \\ \hline 308 \end{array}$$

4. Stop-borrow-at-zero. The student fails to decrement 0, although he or she adds 10 correctly to the top digit of the active column.

$$\begin{array}{r} 70{}_{\!1}3 \\ -678 \\ \hline 175 \end{array} \qquad \begin{array}{r} 60{}_{\!1}4 \\ -387 \\ \hline 307 \end{array}$$

5. Don't decrement-zero. When borrowing from a column in which the top digit is 0, the student rewrites the 0 as 10 but does not change the 10 to 9 when incrementing the active column.

$$\begin{array}{r} {}^{6}\!\cancel{7}{}_{\!1}0{}_{\!1}2 \\ -368 \\ \hline 344 \end{array} \qquad \begin{array}{r} {}^{1}\!\cancel{1}{}_{\!1}0{}_{\!1}5 \\ 9 \\ \hline 1106 \end{array}$$

6. Zero-instead-of-borrow. The student writes 0 as the answer in any column in which the bottom digit is larger than the top

$$\begin{array}{r} 326 \\ -117 \\ \hline 210 \end{array} \qquad \begin{array}{r} 542 \\ -389 \\ \hline 200 \end{array}$$

7. Borrow-from-bottom-instead-of-zero. If the top digit in the column being borrowed from is 0, the student borrows from the bottom digit instead.

$$\begin{array}{r} 70{}_{\!1}2 \\ -3\overset{5}{\cancel{6}}8 \\ \hline 454 \end{array} \qquad \begin{array}{r} 50{}_{\!1}8 \\ -4\overset{7}{\cancel{8}}9 \\ \hline 109 \end{array}$$

Source: From L. Resnick in T. P. Carpenter, J. M. Moser, and T. A. Romberg, Eds. *Addition and subtraction: a cognitive perspective*. Copyright © 1982 by Lawrence Erlbaum Associates, Inc. Reprinted by permission.

Table 11.4 gives some of the examples of the algebraic word problems frequently used in high school geometry texts. Many students who have mastered the mechanics of algebra find such problems difficult. Mayer (1987) and Singley, Anderson, Givens, and Hoffman (1989) conducted task analyses of

Table 11.4 *Examples of Algebra Problem Types*

Category	Example
Triangle	Maria walks one block east along a vacant lot and then two blocks north to a friend's house. Phil starts at the same point and walks diagonally through the vacant lot coming out at the same point as Maria. If Maria walked 217 feet east and 400 feet north, how far did Phil walk?
Distance-rate-time	In a sports-car race, a Panther starts the course at 9:00 A.M. and averages 75 miles per hour. A Mallotti starts 4 minutes later and averages 85 miles per hour. If a lap is 15 miles, on which lap will the Panther be overtaken?
Interest	A certain savings bank pays 3% interest compounded semiannually. How much will $2500 amount to if left on deposit for 20 years?
Area	A box containing 180 cubic inches is constructed by cutting from each corner of a cardboard square a small square with sides of 5 inches and then turning up the sides. Find the area of the original piece of cardboard.
River current	A river steamer travels 36 miles downstream in the same time that it travels 24 miles upstream. The steamer's engines drive in still water at a rate that is 12 miles an hour more than the rate of the current. Find the rate of the current.
Number	The units digit is 1 more than 3 times the tens digit. The number represented when the digits are interchanged is 8 times the sum of the digits.
Work	Mr. Russo takes 3 minutes less than Ms. Lloyd to pack a case when each works alone. One day, after Mr. Russo spent 6 minutes packing a case, the boss called him away, and Ms. Lloyd finished packing in 4 more minutes. How many minutes does it take Mr. Russo alone to pack a case?

Source: D.A. Hinsley, J. R. Hayes, and H.A. Simon (1977). From words to equations: Meaning and representations in algebra word problems. In M. A. Just and P.A. Carpenter (Eds.) *Cognitive processes in comprehension.* Pages 93–94. Reprinted by permission.

what is involved in solving such problems. These analyses identified four major stages: comprehension, equation embellishment, combination of information, and algebraic symbol manipulation.

1. Comprehension. Although their language comprehension abilities are generally adequate, many high school students lack the ability to process appropriately the kinds of linguistic expressions that are used to communicate mathematical relationships. A particularly notorious example was studied by Soloway, Lochhead, and Clement (1982), who asked subjects to translate the following assertion: "There are six times as many students as professors at this university." Many students translated this as $6S = P$ rather than $6P = S$.

The output of this comprehension phase should be a set of equations that summarize the information in the problem. Consider the following problem:

A picture frame measures 20 cm by 14 cm; 160 square cm of the picture shows. What is the width of the frame around the picture?

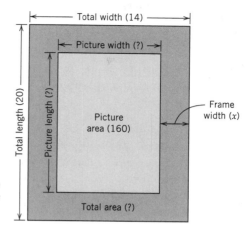

FIGURE 11.7: A diagrammatic representation of the situation described by the word problem.

The reader might be helped by Figure 11.7, but such aids are typically not given to the student. The output of comprehending this problem should include assignments, such as:

a. Total length = 20
b. Total width = 14
c. Picture area = 160

This list represents some of the equations required to solve the problem, but, as shown in the next stage, it does not include all the equations.

2. *Equation embellishment.* Problems like this picture-frame problem require recognizing the type of situation and stating a set of equations to describe that situation. For this problem, the additional equations include:[2]

d. Total area = Picture area + Frame area
e. Total area = Total width × Total length
f. Picture area = Picture width × Picture length
g. Total length = Picture length + 2 × Frame width
h. Total width = Picture width + 2 × Frame width

This information is not contained in the problem statement, so students must embellish the problem with an appropriate mathematical model, as shown. Students often find it easier to come up with these relationships if they draw a diagram such as that shown in Figure 11.7. The example given is a case of the picture-frame problem, but there are many other types of problems, and students appear to master each separately. Table 11.4 includes some of the other types. Mayer (1987) found approximately 100 problem types in typical algebra texts.

[2]All these equations are not required to solve this problem, but they do come up in other picture-frame problems.

3. *Combination of information.* The information has to be combined to find the desired quantity. If x is the width of the picture frame, these steps of combination might be

i. 20 = Picture length + 2x (combining a and g)
j. 14 = Picture width + 2x (combining b and h)
k. 160 = (20 − 2x)(14 − 2x)   (combining c, i, and j)

Students have great difficulty in seeing the appropriate combinations of equations to achieve the quantity they want.

4. *Algebraic symbol manipulation.* Finally, various symbol manipulation skills are needed to solve the equations. In this case, the student has to do some algebraic rearrangement and then solve a quadratic equation. Thus equation k becomes

$$4x^2 - 68x + 120 = 0$$

which can be simplified to

$$x^2 - 17x + 30 = 0$$

which can be factored into

$$(x - 15)(x - 2) = 0$$

which shows that the one acceptable solution is $x = 2$. Some students have difficulty with this stage, but, as noted, others have difficulties with the other components.

Singley et al. (1989) showed that one of the reasons that students have great difficulty with these problems is that not all of these steps are explained to them. The components of algebraic symbol manipulation are sometimes well taught, but the other components of solving word problems are not explicitly taught. Singley et al. were able to substantially enhance students' performance by explicitly teaching these steps.

Solving algebraic word problems involves four stages, and students do not receive instruction on all these stages.

Geometric Proof Skills

A traditional geometry course with a focus on doing formal proofs in a Euclidean system is a frustrating course for most high school students. Students often rate it as their least favorite course (Hoffer, 1981). A typical geometry class is characterized by low class morale and low levels of achievement. In an investigation of what is involved in the skill of doing proofs in geometry, Anderson, Bellezza, and Boyle (1993) discovered that much of what is involved in the skill of proof construction is not being taught to students. First, the typ-

(*a*)

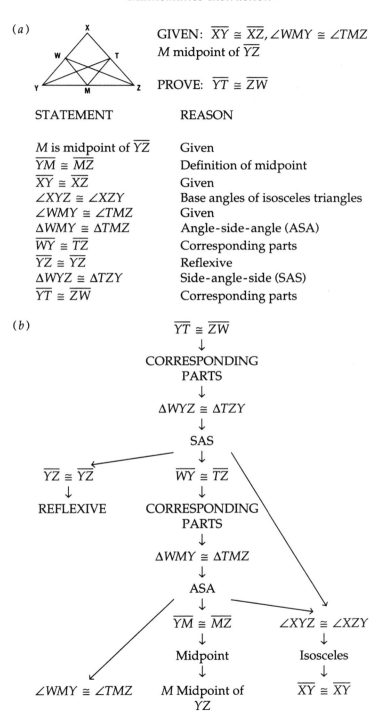

GIVEN: $\overline{XY} \cong \overline{XZ}$, $\angle WMY \cong \angle TMZ$
M midpoint of $\overline{YZ}$

PROVE: $\overline{YT} \cong \overline{ZW}$

STATEMENT	REASON
M is midpoint of $\overline{YZ}$	Given
$\overline{YM} \cong \overline{MZ}$	Definition of midpoint
$\overline{XY} \cong \overline{XZ}$	Given
$\angle XYZ \cong \angle XZY$	Base angles of isosceles triangles
$\angle WMY \cong \angle TMZ$	Given
$\triangle WMY \cong \triangle TMZ$	Angle-side-angle (ASA)
$\overline{WY} \cong \overline{TZ}$	Corresponding parts
$\overline{YZ} \cong \overline{YZ}$	Reflexive
$\triangle WYZ \cong \triangle TZY$	Side-angle-side (SAS)
$\overline{YT} \cong \overline{ZW}$	Corresponding parts

(*b*)

$\overline{YT} \cong \overline{ZW}$
↓
CORRESPONDING
PARTS
↓
$\triangle WYZ \cong \triangle TZY$
↓
SAS

$\overline{YZ} \cong \overline{YZ}$ $\overline{WY} \cong \overline{TZ}$
↓   ↓
REFLEXIVE   CORRESPONDING
PARTS
↓
$\triangle WMY \cong \triangle TMZ$
↓
ASA
↓
$\overline{YM} \cong \overline{MZ}$ $\angle XYZ \cong \angle XZY$
↓   ↓
Midpoint   Isosceles
↓   ↓
$\angle WMY \cong \angle TMZ$ M Midpoint of $\overline{XY} \cong \overline{XY}$
YZ

FIGURE 11.8. (*a*) A proof problem; (*b*) a representation of the logical structure of inferential support.

ical two-column proof format hides from students the overall structure of a proof problem. Therefore, a tree structure was introduced to illustrate the proof. Figure 11.8 shows the contrast between the typical, linear, two-column proof structure and the graphic, or flow proof. The flow proof connects the statements below that support a conclusion above.

Second, to create a proof in geometry students need to know a lot of strategic information about when to make various rules of inference. For instance, geometry has the reflexive rule, which states that any segment is congruent to itself. This is usually a rather useless rule of inference, but on some occasions it is critical to a proof. One such occasion is when a student needs to prove that two triangles are congruent and the two triangles share a side. In this instance it is useful to establish that the two triangles have one pair of congruent sides, because the shared side is congruent to itself. This rule is used in this way in Figure 11.8, where the inference is made that $\overline{YZ}$ is congruent to $\overline{YZ}$ so that ΔWYZ can be proved congruent to ΔTZY. The researchers found that much of geometry competence could be modeled by means of special production rules that contained such strategic information, for instance:

> IF the goal is to prove ΔABC congruent to ΔDBC
> THEN conclude that $\overline{BC}$ is congruent to $\overline{BC}$ by the reflexive rule.[3]

Anderson et al. developed an intelligent tutoring system (such systems are described in the next section) for instructing such geometry skills, which resulted in a large improvement in the achievement level of students. Moreover, as Schofield and Evans-Rhodes (1989) described in their studies of these geometry classrooms, there was a dramatic change in the attitude and motivation of the students. Able to succeed at the task, they found geometry fun.

Geometric proof skills are better learned when a student is given more direct instruction on the underlying components.

Intelligent Tutoring Systems

The major lessons in each of the case studies just reviewed are that mathematical competence can be decomposed into a number of underlying rules or facts and that the course of mathematical learning is the course of acquisition of these individual components. The Advanced Computer Tutoring Project at Carnegie Mellon University (Anderson et al., in press) has developed an approach to instruction based on such a componential analysis. It involves having a computer deliver instruction with the goal of providing individualized

---

[3]Where the letters A, B, C, and D are variables that can match to any letters in the problem.

instruction for each student and optimizing that student's learning of the component rules. The approach is an attempt to take the instructional design approach of the behaviorist program and apply it to a more accurate model of the underlying cognitive skills to be taught. These systems are often called **intelligent tutoring systems** (Polson & Richardson, 1988; Wenger, 1987) because they combine cognitive models with techniques from artificial intelligence to achieve computer-based instructional interactions with students.

The first step in creating such a tutor is to work with educators to develop a computer interface for the instruction of the skill. This interface will be a powerful system for doing mathematical problem solving. Figure 11.9 illustrates a system for solving problems in algebra. It consists of a spreadsheet, a graphing facility, and a symbol manipulation facility. The tutor teaches students to use these three types of mathematics software to solve real-world problems, such as the one illustrated in Figure 11.9.

After designing the interface, the next step is to develop a cognitive model of the knowledge that students must have to solve the problems posed in that interface. Such a model is created as a production system and is quite capable of solving the problems given to students. This model serves two major instructional goals. First, the production rules are the instructional objectives. Second, because the model is created as a working program, it can run along with the student to help the computer tutor understand what the student is doing to solve the problem.

Student working with a computer tutor.

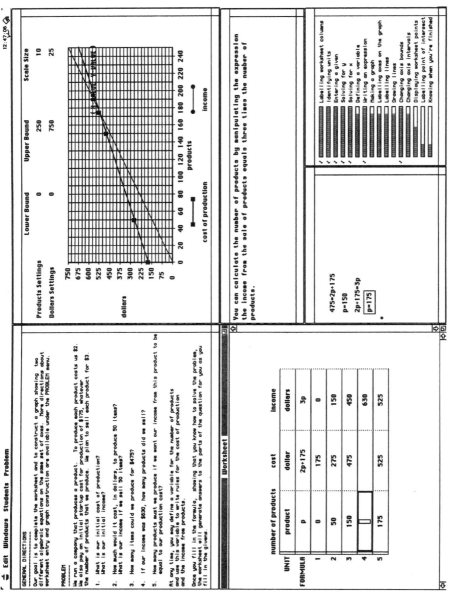

FIGURE 11.9. Example of the algebra word problem tutor.

Table 11.5 *The LISP Tutor Interacting with a Student*

The student is working on writing a piece of code to satisfy the problem description below. Before each point where the tutor and student interact, the partial code that the student has written is printed out.

The Problem Description

Define a function called ctof that takes a degree reading in Celsius degrees and converts it to Fahrenheit degrees. First, you need to change the scale by multiplying the argument by 1.8. Then you need to translate the scale by adding 32, since 0 Celsius = 32 Fahrenheit. For example, (ctof 20) returns 68.

Code: *(defun ctof (cdeg) (*))*

Tutor: Yes, you will need to call "*" to get the degree on the enlarged scale, but you are ultimately trying to get the Fahrenheit equivalent of the Celsius degree. So you need to code a different function here that takes a call to "*" as an argument.

Code: *(defun ftoc (cdeg) (+ <NUM> <NUM2>))*

Student: Help

Tutor: You need to multiply together the Celsius degree reading and the size of Fahrenheit degrees using the function *. When you multiply these numbers you will get the degree on the enlarged scale, which is 36 in our example.

Code: *(defun ctof (cdeg) (+ (* 1.8 cdge) <NUM2>)))*

Tutor: Did you mean cdeg?

Student: Yes

Code: *(defun ctof (cdeg) (+ (* 1.8 cdeg) 32)))*

Tutor: You are done. Type next to go on after testing the function you have defined.

Then the instructional component is prepared. This includes instruction on the individual productions and a system of hints and corrections that the computer tutor can provide during the problem solving. The latter, dynamic instruction is more useful; the tutor is able to point out to students where they are making errors and steer them in the correct direction, avoiding much of the confusion and wasted time that normally occurs as students practice a problem-solving skill.

Finally, a curriculum plan and a set of mastery criteria are prepared. These are used to guide the students through the material in a way that ensures that they reach mastery on the underlying production rules. Figure 11.9 shows a window that displays for students how well they are doing on the component skills (production rules). There are skills associated with identifying the units of measurement, determining appropriate bounds for the graph, and identifying the points of intersection.

Table 11.5 presents a short interaction with the LISP tutor, which has been teaching a course in LISP at Carnegie Mellon University since 1984. LISP is the main programming language of artificial intelligence. The student in this example is writing a function to convert temperature from Celsius to Fahrenheit. The table shows the tutor and the student interacting in a series of cycles in which the student types some code, the tutor responds with a comment, and the student writes some more code. Note that the tutor can monitor what the student is doing on a symbol-by-symbol basis, judging each symbol as it comes in. It can provide such articulate instruction because, behind the scenes, it is solving the problem in a symbol-by-symbol basis just as the student is. The tutor can provide cogent help and correction as needed. Students working with the LISP tutor are able to reach the same level of achievement as students in a conventional classroom in one-third the time (Corbett & Anderson, 1990).

A number of tutors, such as those for algebra and geometry, have achieved similar successes in instruction. In each case the success depends on a careful analysis that identifies the cognitive components (production rules) underlying successful performance. With these components identified, the tutor is then able to provide intelligent instruction directed to the underlying skill. As Table 11.5 illustrates, this instruction can be tailored to the particular student. The success of the tutors is evidence that learning a complex skill is the learning processes reviewed in this book taking place on the individual components of the skill. As seen in Chapter 9, the individual production rules in these tutors show rather standard learning curves (Figure 9.14).

The approach taken by the tutors has a lot in common with the mastery learning approaches reviewed earlier. Although the tutors typically result in somewhat higher achievement gains, other mastery approaches also result in achievement gains. Nonetheless, traditional mastery classrooms have been disappearing in part because such classrooms are somewhat difficult to manage. In this case the tutoring approach has an advantage. Each computer tutor is in effect a teaching assistant to the teacher, helping the teacher manage the learning of a particular student.

Teachers in tutored classrooms report that their experiences are fulfilling (e.g., Wertheimer, 1990). When students are learning with these tutors, the teachers circulate around the class providing instruction to the students for whom the tutor's explanations are not adequate. Teachers are the ultimate domain experts, focusing on the difficult learning problems and leaving the simple learning problems to the computer.

Intelligent tutoring systems can be built around a production-rule analysis of the components of the skill to be learned.

The Role of Mathematics in Life

Discussion has proceeded on the assumption that the mathematics that should be taught in U.S. schools is more or less the mathematics that has been taught in the schools of the United States and the rest of the world during this century and that the only issue is how to achieve competence in this mathematics. However, as intimated, there are some real controversies as to what should be taught as well as how it should be taught, and it is only honest to expose some of this discussion here. Much of the controversy surrounds the purpose for mathematics education. Three general purposes for mathematics education have been cited:

1. Students should learn to do mathematics because it makes them much better thinkers generally. There is virtually no evidence for such general transfer, and much of this book suggests that this is an unlikely possibility. Transfer depends on two tasks having specific rules and facts in common.

2. Students should learn mathematics to appreciate the intellectual beauty of that discipline. The public has extremely varied opinions on the worth of mathematics appreciation, and few students achieve deep mathematics appreciation.

3. Students should learn mathematics to make them better citizens and better workers. This is undoubtedly the major reason for public support of mathematics education and the major reason for the crisis attitude about the poor mathematical achievement of American students.

Unfortunately, people have a poor understanding of how mathematics is used in everyday life. Employers are forever complaining about the mathematical preparation of American workers, but when asked what they are looking for, they report a need either for the basic computational skills that are taught in the early grades or for skills so specific to the particular job that it would be unreasonable to expect a general education to teach them (Secretary's Commission on Achieving Necessary Skills, 1991). There is little mention of the academic mathematics that occupies high school or college. This mathematics undoubtedly plays a major foundational role in many engineering applications, but computer software can now perform many of the mathematical calculations that engineers once had to perform by hand. At the high technology end employers are looking more for workers who can use this software intelligently and creatively rather than for workers who really appreciate the underlying mathematics. Scientists and mathematicians still need to practice academic mathematics, and such people play a key role in society. However, it is unclear whether all students should be taught academic mathematics to prepare such a select minority of society.

Again, there are serious questions about the relationship between school-taught mathematics and the mathematics used in everyday life, as illustrated by the example of the Brazilian children who could perform mathematics in the marketplace but not in school. As another example, Lave (1988) reported a study of Orange County, California, shoppers making best-buy calculations. Some of the problems were rather simple, such as, "What is the better buy, an 8-oz yogurt at 35 cents or a 6-oz yogurt at 43 cents?" Others were more difficult, for example, "What is the better buy, a 20.5-oz can of refried beans at 57 cents or a 17-oz can of refried beans at 49 cents?" The more difficult problems required some form of fractional arithmetic. Lave found that these experienced shoppers were able to make 98 percent of their choices correctly. In contrast, in a study of their ability to solve standard mathematics problems, such as ⅖ × .75, they only averaged 70 percent correct.

Lave found an interesting relationship among various measures of individual differences. She found a strong correlation between the income of her subjects, their performance on academic mathematics, and their schooling, but none of these measures was related to how well they did at best-buy calculations. From this Lave drew a powerful conclusion: standard academic mathematics is used to help define the class structure in our society (and hence the correlation with income), but it is in fact as arbitrary as Latin and Greek were in past generations (hence the lack of relationship to best-buy calculations).

Lave went far beyond the evidence, although there may be some truth to her conclusions. Since all her participants were expert at best-buy calculations there was no room for a relationship to be found between that skill and anything else. All people do not perform all real-world tasks at uniformly high levels of excellence. As any employer can testify, different workers vary widely in the quality of their job performance. Moreover, measures of academic achievement do predict future job performance (Hunter & Hunter, 1984). This does not establish, however, that academic achievement is necessary for good job performance. It may be that whatever distinguishes people who do well at academic tasks also makes for people who learn to do their jobs well. Measures of intellectual ability tend to predict job performance better than measures of academic achievement (Hunter & Hunter, 1984). Intellectual ability may be the critical factor determining both academic performance and job performance.

Whatever the final verdict on Lave's arguments, they highlight the difficult issues that society faces about the role of mathematics in everyday life and the role it should have in the classroom. The lack of answers and consensus is part of what fuels the never-ending reforms of the mathematics curriculum. As noted earlier, the consequence of the reform-crazy movement in the United States is that mathematics educators never settle on a curriculum long enough to teach it well.

There are serious questions about whether academic mathematics helps in the performance of real-world tasks.

Final Reflections

The news media in the United States is full of proclamations of the failure of the educational system. As discussed previously, these claims of failure are a bit overstated. Part of the failure to reach levels of high achievement in the United States reflects the lack of economic equity in the society. It is a serious mistake to burden the school systems with trying to patch up a problem whose source is elsewhere. Even with its diverse population, the United States does reasonably well in the instruction of reading but is failing dismally in international comparisons of achievement in mathematics. The explanation for the disparity in reading and mathematics achievement is largely in the amount of time spent in mathematics instruction and in the pernicious belief in the United States that mathematics achievement is a matter of talent rather than effort. Poor achievement is further exacerbated by the failure of the mathematics education community to stay committed to a specific curriculum.

Success in learning a subject, such as mathematics, is not just a function of the amount of time spent in the classroom and doing homework. As this book has shown in many ways, how the time is spent is critical. Some ways of representing the skill are more effective than others. In the case of reading instruction, for example, although students can learn to read by both the phonics method and the whole-word method, the phonics method appears to be more successful, probably because it teaches a more efficient method for reading English.

Frequently, however, the problem is not that there are competing ways of teaching a skill, but that there is no way of teaching the skill. With respect to many skills of reading comprehension and such topics in mathematics as algebraic word problems and geometric proof skills, the usual problem is that students are not told how to perform the task and instead are left to find some method for themselves.

Cognitive task analysis is the critical prerequisite to effective instruction. It identifies precisely the skills to be taught and allows effective programs of instruction to be pursued. In particular, it serves as the foundation for a computer-based method of individualized instruction that can speed up the rate of learning by as much as a factor of three.

This is the appropriate topic on which to end a book on learning and memory. Education is the obvious application for the research reviewed in the book, and education is sorely in need of a science to understand how educational manipulations map onto outcomes. In the future, as psychology generates more and better analyses of educationally relevant outcomes and as education becomes more knowledgeable about these analyses, education, like other applied fields, can be expected to have a more scientific basis for its applications. It would be a sign that both fields have finally matured if the psychology of learning and cognition could play a cogent role in educational applications.

Instruction can be improved by a cognitive task analysis that identifies the components to be learned.

Further Readings

Several texts describe the application of the psychology of learning and cognition to instruction, including those by Farnham-Diggory (1992), Gagné, Yekovich, and Yekovich (1993), and Mayer (1987). Stevenson and Stigler

(1992) wrote a popular and psychologically informed comparison of educational achievement in Japan and the United States. Gagné, Briggs, and Wager (1988) present a series of recent papers on instructional technology. Just and Carpenter (1987) provide a thorough analysis of the reading process and apply that analysis to educational issues. M. J. Adams (1990) offers an up-to-date discussion of reading and the phonics method. Anderson, Corbett, Koedinger, and Pelletier (in press) describe their intelligent tutoring work and its application to mathematics education. Westbury (1992) and Baker (1993) engage in an informed debate about the significance of the differences in mathematical achievement between Japan and the United States.

Glossary

acquisition: The process by which new memories are encoded into long-term memory.

ACT: J. R. Anderson's theory of how declarative and procedural representations underlie human information processing.

action potential: The sudden change in electrical potential that travels down the axon of a neuron.

activation: An abstract concept in cognitive psychology used to refer to the availability of information; sometimes thought of in terms of neural excitation.

activation equation: The equation stating that the activation of a memory record is the sum of the record strength plus its strengths of association to the cues in the memory probe.

all-or-none learning: Learning that takes place in a single trial rather than gradually.

amnesia: Loss of memory, frequently occuring as a result of brain injury.

anterograde amnesia: Inability to remember new information after a brain insult.

aphasia: Loss of language function resulting from brain injury.

Aplysia: A sea slug with a simple nervous system that has been extensively studied.

arguments: The elements of a propositional representation that are organized by the relation; frequently they are nouns.

artificial intelligence: A field of computer science that tries to get computers to behave intelligently.

association equation: The equation stating that the strength of association between a cue and a memory record decreases with the number of records associated to that cue.

associative bias: The predisposition to associate certain stimuli to certain other stimuli or responses.

associative stage: The second stage in Fitts' stages of skill acquisition which involves developing production rules to perform the skill.

auditory sensory memory: A system that holds about the last 4 seconds of auditory information.

autonomous stage: The third stage in Fitts's stages of skill acquisition in which performance of the skill becomes automatic.

autoshaping: The experimental phenomenon that animals spontaneously produce species-specific consummatory responses to stimuli that precede reinforcers.

axoaxonic synapse: A synapse of an axon onto another axon.

axon: The portion of a neuron that carries information from one region of the brain to another.

backwards learning curve: A curve in which the probability of an error is plotted backward from the trial of the last error.

behavioral objectives: A set of goals for instruction derived from a behavioral task analysis.

behaviorism: An approach to psychology that emphasizes casting theories in terms of external behavior rather than discussing the internal mechanisms responsible for the behavior.

bliss point: The organism's ideal distribution of time spent on various events.

blocking: The tendency for one stimulus to overshadow another in conditioning.

causal inference: Induction of what causes what in our environment.

central executive: The part of Baddeley's working memory that controls the various slave rehearsal systems.

CER: An abbreviation of **conditioned emotional response**.

cerebellum: The subcortical structure involved in motor coordination.

cerebral cortex: The highest area of the brain. In the human it is a sheet of neural tissue about 1 meter square folded around various subcortical areas.

chunk: A term coined by G. A. Miller (1956) to refer to the units or memory records that encode a small number of elements.

classical conditioning: The procedure in which an organism comes to display a conditioned response (CR) to a neutral conditioned stimulus (CS) that has been paired with a biologically significant unconditioned stimulus (US) that evoked an unconditioned response (UR).

closed-loop performance: A sequence of actions in which execution of later actions waits for feedback from the results of earlier actions.

codes: See **memory codes**.

cognitive map: A mental representation of the layout of objects and routes in space that an organism can use to guide its locomotion.

cognitive stage: The first stage in Fitts's stages of skill acquisition, which involves working from a declarative representation of the skill.

cognitivism: An approach to psychology that involves abstract descriptions of the information-processing mechanisms responsible for behavior.

competitive learning: The proposal in such theories as the Rescorla–Wagner theory that a US can support only so much associative strength and that the CSs compete for their share of this maximum possible strength.

componential analysis: The analysis of instructional material into its underlying cognitive components.

computer simulation: A methodology for deriving predictions from a complex theory by simulating on a computer the processes assumed by the theory.

concept acquisition: The learning of categories, such as "dog" and "chair."

conditioned emotional response: A characteristic response pattern emitted by an organism in anticipation of an aversive stimulus, such as a shock.

conditioned inhibition: The expectation conditioned to a CS that it is associated with the absence of the US.

conditioned reinforcer: See **secondary reinforcer**.

conditioned response: The response that the organism learns to make in a classical or instrumental conditioning paradigm.

conditioned stimulus: The stimulus that signals the unconditioned stimulus in a classical conditioning paradigm.

conditioning curve: The function showing the increase in the conditioned response as a function of the number of conditioning trials.

configural cues: Stimulus combinations that become associated as single elements to stimuli and responses.

connectionism: The attempt to account for behavior by the computations of large numbers of neural elements connected to one another.

context cue: An element in the experiment context that can serve as a cue for a memory record.

context-dependent memory: The phenomenon that memory performance is often better when the context of test matches the context of study.

contiguity: The occurrence of two items close together in time and space, which some theories claim is sufficient to condition an association.

contingency: The occurrence of one item increases the probability that another item will occur—some theories claim that this is sufficient to form an association.

counter conditioning: A method of getting rid of an unwanted response to a stimulus by conditioning an antagonistic response.

CR: An abbreviation of **conditioned response**.

CS: An abbreviation of **conditioned stimulus.**

cue: An element that is associated to a memory record and that can help retrieve it.

cumulative response record: A record of the total number of responses emitted as a function of time.

decay hypothesis: The theory of forgetting that asserts that memories weaken with the passage of time.

declarative knowledge: Knowledge of factual information.

deductive inference: An inference that definitely follows from what is known about the world.

delayed match-to-sample task: A paradigm in which the organism is shown a correct response alternative and must remember that response over a delay period.

delta rule: An application of the Rescorla–Wagner theory to learning in neural networks.

dendrites: The branching portion of a neuron that receives synapses from the axons of other neurons.

depth of processing theory: The theory that memory for information is a function of the depth to which it is processed.

desensitization: A technique for treating phobias by having the patient learn to relax in situations that gradually approximate the fear-evoking situation.

devaluation paradigm: A paradigm in which a US or a reinforcer is devalued and the consequence for the conditioning that involved that stimulus is observed.

difference reduction: Selecting problem-solving operators to reduce the difference between the current state and the goal state.

digit span: A memory-span test in which subjects must reproduce a series of digits.

discounting the future: Valuing a future gain or loss less than a current gain or loss.

discrimination: Differential responding to stimuli.

discrimination learning: The process by which an organism learns which stimuli are associated with the experimental contingency.

distributed representations: A representation that assumes that a memory record is encoded as a pattern over a set of neural elements.

d-prime measure: Measure of the distance between the signal and distractor distributions of evidence in signal detectability theory.

drive-reduction theory: The theory that reinforcement depends on the reduction of biological drives.

drives: States of deprivation which supposedly energize behavior in an organism.

dual-code theory: The theory of Paivio that information is stored in long-term memory in terms of verbal and visual representations.

dyslexia: A condition whereby children or adults of normal or above-normal intelligence are substantially subnormal in their reading ability.

echoic memory: Neisser's term for auditory sensory memory.

elimination by aspects: A theory proposed by Tversky according to which people make choices among alternatives by first focusing on the most important aspects of the alternatives.

encoding: The process of creating a long-term memory record to store an experience.

encoding-specificity principle: The idea that memory performance is better when tested in the presence of the same cues that were present when the memory was formed.

EPSP: An abbreviation of **excitatory post-synaptic potential**.

errorless discrimination learning: A procedure of gradually fading in a discrimination in a way that avoids errors.

equilibrium theory: The theory that an organism finds reinforcing anything that moves it toward its bliss point and punishing anything that moves it away from that point.

excitatory postsynaptic potential: A measure of the decrease in the difference in electrical potential between the outside and inside of the neuron; used as a measure in studies of long-term potentiation.

excitatory synapses: Synapses where the neurotransmitters decrease the potential difference across the membrane of a neuron.

exemplar theories: Theories that hold that subjects categorize a test stimulus according to past stimuli that are similar to the test stimulus.

expected value: The sum of the values of the consequences of an action weighted by the probabilities of these consequences.

explicit memories: Memories of which a person is consciously aware during retrieval.

exponential function: A mathematical function of the form $y = ab^x$, where the independent variable, x, is in the exponent.

extinction: The procedure in a conditioning experiment where the unconditioned stimulus or the reinforcer is no longer presented.

extinction function: The reduction in the conditioned response as a function of the number of extinction trials.

false alarm: The tendency for subjects to say that they have studied an item that they have not studied.

FI: An abbreviation of **fixed-interval schedule**.

fixed-interval schedule: An organism is given a reinforcement for the first response after a fixed interval.

fixed-ratio schedule: An organism is given a reinforcement after a fixed number of responses.

flashbulb memories: Memories for extremely significant and emotion-laden events; such memories often seem particularly vivid and detailed.

forgetting function: See **retention function**.

FR: An abbreviation of **fixed-ratio schedule**.

free recall: A memory paradigm in which items are presented one at a time and then subjects can recall them in any order.

frontal cortex: The region at the front of the cerebral cortex that includes the motor cortex and the prefrontal cortex.

generalization: When a behavior is evoked by a stimulus other that the one it was conditoned to.

generalization gradient: Representation of the tendency of various stimuli to evoke a cĬonditioned response.

generate-recognize theory: A theory of free recall that claims that subjects generate candidate items and then recognize which ones they have studied.

generation effect: People tend to display better memory for material they generate for themselves.

global maximization: The theory that an organism will choose a pattern of responding that will lead to optimal outcome overall.

goal: The desired state in solving a problem.

hippocampus: The subcortical area that plays a critical role in the formation of permanent memories.

hypothalamus: The subcortical area that regulates expression of basic drives and is involved in motivation.

hypothesis testing: A deliberate approach to inductive learning in which particular hypotheses are consciously considered and tested against the data.

iconic memory: Neisser's term for **visual sensory memory**.

implicit memories: Memories that a person is not consciously aware of retrieving.

induction: The process by which a system makes inferences about the structure of the environment from its experience with that environment.

inductive inference: An uncertain inference about the state of the world based on experience with that world.

inductive learning: Learning by means of inductive inferences.

information-processing approach: An approach in cognitive psychology that theorizes about information in the abstract and how it progresses through the cognitive system.

inhibition: A response suppression caused by factors such as fatigue and extinction.

inhibitory synapses: Synapses where the neurotransmitters decrease the potential difference across the membrane of a neuron.

inner ear: The part of Baddeley's phonological loop responsible for perceiving inner speech.

inner voice: The part of Baddeley's phonological loop responsible for generating inner speech.

instinctive drift: The tendency for animals to revert to innate, species-specific response patterns in a learning experiment.

instrumental conditioning: The procedure in which a reinforcement is made conditional on emitting a response in a particular stimulus situation.

intelligent tutoring systems: Computer systems that combine cognitive models with techniques from artificial intelligence to create instructional interactions with students.

interference: A negative relationship between the learning of two sets of material.

interference hypothesis: The theory of forgetting that asserts that competing memories block retrieval of the target memory.

Korsakoff's syndrome: Anterograde amnesia that occurs after a long history of alcoholism coupled with nutritional deficits.

labor-supply curve: The curvilinear relationship that exists between amount of pay per unit of work and the amount of work a laborer will do.

language universals: Features that are true of all natural languages.

latent inhibition: If a stimulus is given pre-exposures before conditioning, the rate of conditioning to the stimulus is slowed.

latent learning: Learning that takes place in the absence of any reinforcer and is only manifest when a reinforcement is introduced into the situation.

law of effect: The claim that reinforcement is necessary for learning.

learned helplessness: When an aversive stimulus, such as shock, is given independent of an organism's behavior, the organism comes to behave as if it believed that it has no control over the environment.

learning: The process by which relatively permanent changes occur in behavioral potential as a result of experience.

learning curve: A function showing the increase in learning as a function of the amount of practice.

list context: Representation of the list to which items are associated in a list learning experiment.

localist representation: A representation that assumes that a memory record is encoded into a single, unanalyzable symbol.

long-term memory: A rather permanent memory system that stores most of our knowledge about the world.

long-term potentiation: When brief, high-frequency electrical stimulation is administered to some areas of the brain, including the hippocampus, there is a long-term increase in the magnitude of the response of the cells to further stimulation.

LTP: An abbreviation of **long-term potentiation**.

mastery learning: An instructional strategy in which earlier material is brought to mastery before instruction begins on later material.

matching law: Given the choice between two variable-interval schedules, organisms distribute their responses between the two schedules in proportion to the rates of reinforcement from the two schedules.

means–ends analysis: A method of problem solving that sets subgoals as the means to obtaining some larger goal.

melioration theory: The theory that an organism will shift its behavior toward the alternative that is currently offering the highest rate of return.

memory: The relatively permanent trace of the experience that underlies learning.

memory codes: Distinctive ways of encoding information in a memory record. Memory codes include verbal, spatial, and propositional.

memory-span test: A task in which subjects are presented with a series of items and must reproduce them, usually immediately.

mnemonic techniques: Techniques for enhancing memory performance.

momentary maximizing: The theory that at any point in time an organism will choose the response alternative that is currently offering the highest rate of return.

mood congruency: The phenomenon that recall of material may be higher if the subject's mood at recall matches the emotional tone of the material the subject is trying to recall.

motor program: A prepackaged sequence of actions that can be executed according to different parameters without central control.

natural categories: Categories of objects that are found in the real world, such as "dog" or "tree."

negative acceleration: A property of functions, such as learning curves or retention curves, whereby the rate of change becomes smaller and smaller.

negative reinforcement: An instrumental conditioning procedure in which an aversive stimulus is made contingent on omission of a response.

negative transfer: The phenomenon that learning of earlier material impairs the learning of later material.

nerve impulse: Action potentials that move down axons.

neurons: The cells in the brain that are most directly responsible for neural information processing.

neurotransmitters: Chemicals that cross the synapse from the axon of one neuron to alter the electrical potential of the membrane of another neuron.

occipital lobe: The region at the back of the cerebral cortex that is mainly devoted to vision.

omission training: An instrumental conditioning procedure in which a desirable stimulus is made contingent on omission of a response.

open-loop performance: A sequence of actions performed without waiting for feedback from the results of earlier actions before performing later actions.

operant: A term Skinner used to describe an action, such as a lever press, that produced some change in the environment.

operant conditioning: Learning that changes the frequency of a response type in the environment.

operator: An action that transforms one problem-solving state into another problem-solving state.

operator subgoaling: If an operator cannot be applied to achieve a goal, the problem solver sets a subgoal to transform the state so that the operator can be applied.

opponent process: A mechanism that is evoked when a stimulus evokes a strong response in one direction; this mechanism produces a compensatory response in the opposite direction.

optimal-foraging theory: The theory that organisms forage for food so as to maximize their net energy gain (food intake minus energy spent foraging).

paired-associate learning: A memory procedure in which the subject learns to give a response when presented with a stimulus.

parietal lobe: The region at the top of the cerebral cortex that is involved in higher level sensory functions.

partial-reinforcement extinction effect: The phenomenon that animals show greater resistance to extinction when trained under a partial reinforcement schedule.

partial-reinforcement schedule: A reinforcement schedule that reinforces only some of the organism's responses.

peak shift: The phenomenon in discrimination learning that maximal response is gotten to stimuli shifted away from the positive stimulus in a direction that is also away from the negative stimulus.

phonics method: A method of reading instruction that emphasizes going from letter combinations to sound.

phonological loop: The system proposed by Baddeley for rehearsing verbal information by silently saying it over and over again.

positive reinforcement: An instrumental conditioning procedure in which a desirable stimulus is made contingent on a response.

power function: A mathematical function of the form $y = ax^b$, where the independent variable, x, is raised to a power to get the dependent variable, y.

power law of forgetting: The observation that memory performance decreases as a power function of the delay since training.

power law of learning: The observation that performance increases as a power function of the amount of practice.

prefrontal cortex: The region at the front of the frontal cortex that is involved in planning and other higher-level cognition.

presynaptic facilitation: An enhancement of a synaptic connection by increasing the neurotransmitter release from the axon.

primacy effect: The phenomenon that the early items in a list are better remembered.

priming: The process by which the appearance of an item in the environment can make available associated memories for use in a wide variety of tasks.

priming: The process by which a prior exposure makes a memory more available or facilitates the perceptual processing of an item.

proactive interference: The phenomenon that learning of earlier material accelerates the forgetting of later material.

proceduralization: The process of converting declarative knowledge about a domain into domain-specific procedures.

procedural knowledge: Knowledge of how to perform various tasks.

production rules: Condition–action pairs that are postulated to represent procedural knowledge.

proposition: A type of code in memory in which the record abstractly represents the smallest meaningful unit of information. Kintsch proposed a propositional representation in which relations organized arguments.

punishment: An instrumental conditioning procedure in which an aversive stimulus is made contingent on a response.

rate of firing: The rate at which nerve impulses are generated along axons.

recency effect: The phenomenon that the last items in a list are better remembered.

recognition failure: Failure to recognize items in one context when these items can be recalled in another context.

reconstructive memory: The phenomenon that people will try to inferentially recreate their memories from what they can recall.

record: Abstract conception of the unit in which memories are encoded.

rehearsal: The process of repeating information to oneself to help remember the information.

rehearsal systems: Systems for maintaining transient sensory records of information.

reinforcer: A stimulus that changes the probability of a response in an instrumental conditioning paradigm.

relation: The element in a propositional representation that organizes the arguments.

reminiscence: The occasional result that memories improve with time.

repression: A forgetting mechanism proposed by Freud that actively represses unpleasant memories.

Rescorla–Wagner theory: Theory that the rate of growth of the strength between a CS and a US is proportional to the difference between the sum of current associative strengths and the maximum associative strength that the US permits.

response-prevention paradigm: A paradigm in classical conditioning where the organism is prevented from emitting the UR.

retention: The maintenance of memories after their initial encoding.

retention curve: Function showing amount remembered as a function of time.

retrieval: The process of getting access to memories.

retrieval-cue hypothesis: The theory of forgetting that asserts that people lose access to memories because they lose access to the cues that can retrieve them.

retroactive interference: The phenomenon that the learning of later material causes the forgetting of earlier material.

retrograde amnesia: Inability to remember information from before a brain insult.

SAM: Shiffrin's theory of memory, which holds that memories are retrieved as a function of their strengths of association to cues.

satisficing: A theory proposed by Simon that people make choices among alternatives by selecting the first item that meets a certain threshold of acceptability.

scalloped function: Functions, such as some cumulative response records, which display cycles of rapid increases followed by slow rates of increase.

schema theories: Theories according to which subjects categorize a test stimulus into the category that shares the most features in common with the test stimulus.

schema theory: Schmidt's theory of motor learning, which holds that people learn a representation of the desired outcome of an action which they use to tune the motor program.

search: The process of finding some sequence of operators that will transform the current state into the goal state.

secondary reinforcer: A neutral stimulus that has become associated with reinforcement. Money is sometimes thought of as a secondary reinforcer.

second-order conditioning paradigm: A classical conditioning paradigm in which an association is first learned from a neutral CS1 to a US, and then an association is learned from a neutral CS2 to CS1.

sensory preconditioning paradigm: A classical conditioning paradigm in which an association is first learned from a neutral CS2 to a neutral CS1, and then an association is learned from CS1 to a US.

serial position curve: A function showing probability of recall of an item as a function of its position in the input order.

short-term memory: A purported storage system in human memory capable of holding a small amount of information for a short period of time.

signal detectability theory: The theory that subjects judge whether they have seen an item according to how much evidence there is for having seen an item. It is assumed that this evidence continuously varies and that subjects must set some threshold for recognition.

skill: Procedural knowledge of how to perform a task.

Skinner box: An apparatus for studying instrumental conditioning containing a lever that the animal can press for reinforcement.

SOP: Stands for "sometimes opponent processes," which is Wagner's theory of the conditioning of opponent processes; also sometimes stands for "standard operating procedure."

spacing effect: Performance on a retention test is usually best when the spacing of the studies of the material matches the retention interval.

species-specific defense reactions: Innate behaviors that are evoked in different species when they are in danger.

spontaneous recovery: The recovery of a conditioned response after a period of time has intervened since an extinction procedure.

S–R association: An association between a stimulus and a response, a hypothetical CS–CR association in classical conditioning.

S–S association: An association between two stimuli, a hypothetical CS–US association in classical conditioning.

S-shaped curves: Functions, such as the conditioning function, that begin with little change, then show rapid change, and then have little change again.

state: A situation relevant to solving a problem.

state-dependent memory: The phenomenon that memory performance is often better when the subject's internal state at test matches the internal state at study.

Sternberg paradigm: A procedure for studying retrieval from memory in which subjects are given a small set of items and then asked whether a probe item occurred in that set.

stimulus-response bonds: Direct associations between stimuli and responses that many behaviorists believed underlie all behavior.

strength: An attribute of memory records and their associations that determines how active they can become.

strength equation: The equation stating that the strength of a memory record varies as a product of the power functions of learning and forgetting.

subgoal: A goal pursued in service of a higher goal.

subgoaling: The process in problem solving by which one goal is created as a subgoal in service of another.

subjective value: The value that an organism places on an alternative.

superstitious learning: The observation that animals will spontaneously produce behaviors even when there is no contingency between that behavior and reinforcement. Skinner described the animals as developing the "superstition" that the behavior was instrumental in getting the reinforcement.

synapse: The location at which the axon of one neuron almost makes contact with another neuron.

task analysis: An attempt to identify the components of a task that need to be taught.

temporal lobe: The region at the side of the cerebral cortex that has the primary auditory areas and is involved in the recognition of objects.

trace: The record that encodes a memory experience.

transfer-appropriate processing: The idea that memory performance is better when the subject processes the probe at test in the same way in which the material was processed at study.

unconditioned response: The response that the unconditioned stimulus naturally evokes.

unconditioned stimulus: The biologically significant stimulus that follows a conditioned stimulus in a classical conditioning paradigm.

UR: An abbreviation of **unconditioned response**.

US: An abbreviation of **unconditioned stimulus**.

variable-interval schedule: An organism is given a reinforcement for the first response after a variable interval. The intervals average to a certain specified length.

variable-ratio schedule: An organism is given a reinforcement after a variable number of responses. The number of responses average to certain specified value.

VI: An abbreviation for **variable-interval schedule**.

visual sensory memory: A system that holds the last 1 or 2 seconds of visual information.

visuo-spatial sketch pad: Baddeley's system for rehearsing visual or spatial information.

VR: An abbreviation for **variable-ratio schedule**.

whole-word method: A method of reading instruction that emphasizes direct recognition of words and phrases.

working memory: The information that is currently available in memory for working on a problem.

Yerkes–Dodson law: The proposal that performance is optimal at intermediate levels of arousal.

Bibliography

Adams, J. A. (1971). A closed-loop theory of motor learning. *Journal of Motor Behavior, 3*, 111–150.

Adams, M. J. (1990). *Beginning to read: Thinking and learning about print.* Cambridge, MA: MIT Press.

Agre, P. E., & Chapman, D. (1987). Pengi: An implementation of a theory of activity. *Proceedings of the Sixth National Conference on Artificial Intelligence*, (pp. 268–272). Menlo Park, CA: American Association for Artificial Intelligence.

Ainslie, G., & Herrnstein, R. J. (1981). Preference reversal and delayed reinforcement. *Animal Learning and Behavior, 9*, 476–482.

Alkon, D. L. (1984). Calcium–mediated reduction of ionic currents: A biophysical memory trace. *Science, 226*, 1037–1045.

Allison, J. (1983). *Behavioral economics.* New York: Praeger.

Allison, J. (1989). The nature of reinforcement. In S. B. Klein & R. R. Mowrer (Eds.), *Contemporary learning theories: Instrumental conditioning and the impact of biological constraints on learning* (pp. 13–39). Hillsdale, NJ: Erlbaum.

Allison, J., & Timberlake, W. (1974). Instrumental and contingent saccharin-licking in rats: Response deprivation and reinforcement. *Learning and Motivation, 5*, 231–247.

Amiro, T. W., & Bitterman, M. E. (1980). Second-order appetitive conditioning in goldfish. *Journal of Experimental Psychology: Animal Behavior Processes, 6*, 41–48.

Amsel, A. (1967). Partial reinforcement effects on vigor and persistence. In K. W. Spence & J. T. Spence (Eds.), *The psychology of learning and motivation* (Vol. 1). New York: Academic Press.

Anderson, J. A. (1973). A theory for the recognition of items from short memorized lists. *Psychological Review, 80*, 417–438.

Anderson, J. R. (1972) FRAN: A simulation model of free recall. In G. H. Bower (Ed.), *The psychology of learning and motivation* (Vol. 5). New York: Academic Press.

Anderson, J. R. (1974a). Retrieval of propositional information from long-term memory. *Cognitive Psychology, 6*, 451–474.

Anderson, J. R. (1974b). Verbatim and propositional representation of sentences in immediate and long-term memory. *Journal of Verbal Learning and Verbal Behavior, 13*, 149–162.

Anderson, J. R. (1976). *Language, memory, and thought.* Hillsdale, NJ: Erlbaum.

Bibliography

Anderson, J. R. (1981). Interference: The relationship between response latency and response accuracy. *Journal of Experimental Psychology: Human Learning and Memory, 7,* 311–325.

Anderson, J. R. (1982). Acquisition of cognitive skill. *Psychological Review, 89,* 369–406.

Anderson, J. R. (1983a). *The architecture of cognition.* Cambridge, MA: Harvard University Press.

Anderson, J. R. (1983b). Retrieval of information from long-term memory. *Science, 220,* 25–30.

Anderson, J. R. (1983c). A spreading activation theory of memory. *Journal of Verbal Learning and Verbal Behavior, 22,* 261–295.

Anderson, J. R. (1990). *Cognitive psychology and its implications* (3rd ed.). New York: W. H. Freeman.

Anderson, J. R. (1991). Is human cognition adaptive? *Behavioral and Brain Sciences, 14,* 471–484.

Anderson, J. R. (1992). Intelligent tutoring and high school mathematics. *Proceedings of the Second International Conference on Intelligent Tutoring Systems.* Montreal.

Anderson, J. R. (1993). *Rules of the mind.* Hillsdale, NJ: Erlbaum.

Anderson, J. R., Bellezza, F. S., & Boyle, C. F. (1993). The geometry tutor and skill acquisition. In J. R. Anderson (Ed.), *Rules of the Mind.* Hillsdale, NJ: Erlbaum.

Anderson, J. R., & Bower, G. H. (1972a). Configural properties in sentence memory. *Journal of Verbal Learning and Verbal Behavior, 11,* 594–605.

Anderson, J. R., & Bower, G. H. (1972b). Recognition and retrieval processes in free recall. *Psychological Review, 79,* 97–123.

Anderson, J. R., & Bower, G. H. (1973). *Human associative memory.* Washington, DC: Winston.

Anderson, J. R., & Bower, G. H. (1974). A propositional theory of recognition memory. *Memory and Cognition, 2,* 406–412.

Anderson, J. R., Conrad, F. G., & Corbett, A. T. (1989). Skill acquisition and the LISP Tutor. *Cognitive Science, 13,* 467–506.

Anderson, J. R., Corbett, A. T., Koedinger, K., & Pelletier, R. (in press) Cognitive tutors: Lessons learned. *The Journal of Learning Sciences.*

Anderson, J. R., Kushmerick, N., & Lebiere, C. (1993). The Tower of Hanoi and goal structures. In J. R. Anderson (Ed.), *Rules of the mind.* Hillsdale, NJ: Erlbaum.

Anderson, J. R., & Paulson, R. (1977). Representation and retention of verbatim information. *Journal of Verbal Learning and Verbal Behavior, 16,* 439–451.

Anderson, J. R., & Reder, L. M. (1979). An elaborative processing explanation of depth of processing. In L. S. Cermak and F. I. M. Craik (Eds.), *Levels of processing in human memory.* Hillsdale, NJ: Erlbaum.

Anderson, J. R., & Reder, L. M., & Lebiere, C. (in preparation). Working memory and the ACT theory.

Anderson, J. R., & Schooler, L. J. (1991). Reflections of the environment in memory. *Psychological Science, 2,* 396–408.

Anderson, J. R., & Sheu, C. F. (1994). Causal inferences based on contingency information.

Arkes, H. R., Hackett, C., & Boehm, L. (1989). The generality of the relation between familiarity and judged validity. *Journal of Behavioral Decision Making, 2,* 81–94.

Atkinson, R. C., Bower, G. H., & Crothers, E. J. (1965). *Introduction to mathematical learning theory.* New York: Wiley.

Atkinson, R. C., & Juola, J. F. (1973). Factors influencing speed and accuracy of word recognition. In S. Kornblum (Ed.), *Attention and performance IV* (pp. 583–612). New York: Academic Press.

Atkinson, R. C., & Juola, J. F. (1974). Search and decision processes in recognition memory. In D. H. Krantz, R. C. Atkinson, R. D. Luce, & P. Suppes (Eds.), *Contemporary developments in mathematical psychology* (Vol. 1, pp. 242–293). San Francisco: W. H. Freeman.

Atkinson, R. C., & Shiffrin, R. M. (1968). Human memory: A proposed system and its control processes. In K. W. Spence & J. T. Spence (Eds.), *The psychology of learning and motivation* (Vol. 2). New York: Academic Press.

Atkinson, R. L., Atkinson, R. C., & Hilgard, E. R. (1983). *Introduction to psychology* (8th ed.). San Diego: Harcourt Brace Jovanovich.

Ayres, T. J., Jonides, J., Reitman, J. S., Egan, J. C., & Howard, D. A. (1979). Differing suffix effects for the same physical suffix. *Journal of Experimental Psychology: Human Learning and Memory, 5,* 315–321.

Azrin, N. H., & Holz, W. C. (1966). Punishment. In W. K. Honig (Ed.), *Operant behavior: Areas of research and application.* New York: Appleton-Century-Crofts.

Azrin, N. H., Holz, W. C., & Hake, D. F. (1963). Fixed-ratio punishment. *Journal of the Experimental Analysis of Behavior, 6,* 141–148.

Baddeley, A. D. (1986). *Working memory.* Oxford: Oxford University Press.

Baddeley, A. D. (1990). *Human memory: Theory and practice.* Boston: Allyn & Bacon.

Baddeley, A. D., Grant, S., Wight, E., & Thomson, N. (1975). Imagery and visual working memory. In P. M. A. Rabbit & S. Dornic (Eds.), *Attention and performance V* (pp. 205–217). London: Academic Press.

Baddeley, A. D., & Hitch, G. J. (1974). Working memory. In G. H. Bower (Ed.), *Recent advances in learning and motivation* (Vol. 8). New York: Academic Press.

Baddeley, A. D., & Lewis, V. J. (1981). Inner active processes in reading: The inner voice, the inner ear, and the inner eye. In A. M. Lesgold and C. A. Perfetti (Eds.), *Interactive processes in reading* (pp. 107–129). Hillsdale, NJ: Erlbaum.

Baddeley, A. D., Lewis, V. J., & Vallar, G. (1984). Exploring the articulatory loop. *Quarterly Journal of Experimental Psychology, 36,* 233–252.

Baddeley, A. D., Thomson, N., & Buchanan, M. (1975). Word length and the structure of short-term memory. *Journal of Verbal Learning and Verbal Behavior, 14,* 575–589.

Bahrick, H. P. (1979). Maintenance of knowledge: Questions about memory we forget to ask. *Journal of Experimental Psychology: General, 108,* 296–308.

Bahrick. H. P. (1984). Semantic memory content in permastore: Fifty years of memory for Spanish learned in school. *Journal of Experimental Psychology: General, 113,* 1–24.

Bailey, C. H., & Chen, M. (1983). Morphological basis of long-term habituation and sensitization in *Aplysia. Science, 220,* 91–93.

Baker, D. P. (1993). Compared to Japan, the U. S. is a low achiever . . . Really: New evidence and comment on Westbury. *Educational Researcher, 22,* 18–21.

Balota, D., & Lorch, R. (1986). Depth of automatic spreading activation: Mediated priming effects in pronunciation but not in lexical decision. *Journal of Experimental Psychology: Learning, Memory, and Cognition, 12,* 336–345.

Balsam, P. D. (1988). Selection, representation and equivalence of controlling stimuli. In R. C. Atkinson, R. J. Herrnstein, G. Lindzey, and R. D. Luce (Eds.), *Stevens' handbook of experimental psychology* (Vol. 2, 2nd ed., pp. 111–166). New York: Wiley.

Barnes, C. A. (1979). Memory deficits associated with senescence: A neurophysiological and behavioral study in the rat. *Journal of Comparative Physiology, 43,* 74–104.

Bibliography

Bartlett, B. J. (1978). *Top-level structure as an organizational strategy for recall of classroom text.* Unpublished doctoral dissertation, Arizona State University.

Bartlett, F. C. (1932). *Remembering.* Cambridge: Cambridge University Press.

Baum, W. M. (1969). Extinction of avoidance response following response prevention: Some parametric investigations. *Canadian Journal of Psychology, 23,* 1–10.

Beck, B. B. (1980). *Animal tool behavior: The use and manufacture of tools by animals.* New York: Garland STPM Press.

Beck, I. L. (1981). Reading problems and instructional practices. In T. S. Waller & G. E. MacKinnon (Eds.), *Reading research: Advances in theory and practice* (Vol. 2). New York: Academic Press.

Bedford, J., & Anger, D. (1968). *Flight as an avoidance response in pigeons.* Paper presented to the Psychonomic Society, St. Louis.

Begg, I., Snider, A., Foley, F., & Goddard, R. (1989). The generation effect is no artifact: Generation makes words distinctive. *Journal of Experimental Psychology: Learning, Memory, and Cognition, 15,* 977–989.

Bekerian, D. A., & Baddeley, A. D. (1980). Saturation advertising and the repetition effect. *Journal of Verbal Learning and Verbal Behavior, 19,* 17–25.

Bernstein, I. L., & Borson, S. (1986). Learned food aversion: A component of anorexia syndromes. *Psychological Review, 93,* 462–472.

Bernstein, I. L., Webster, M. M., & Bernstein, I. D. (1982). Food aversions in children receiving chemotherapy for cancer. *Cancer, 50,* 2961–2963.

Berry, D. C., & Broadbent, D. E. (1984). On the relationship between task performance and associated verbalizable knowledge. *Quarterly Journal of Experimental Psychology, 36A,* 209–231.

Berry, D. C., & Broadbent, D. E. (1987). The combination of explicit and implicit learning processes in task control. *Psychological Research, 49,* 7–15.

Berry, D. C., & Broadbent, D. E. (1988). Interactive tasks and the implicit–explicit distinction. *British Journal of Psychology, 79,* 251–272.

Bilodeau, E. A., & Bilodeau, I. M. (1958). Variable frequency knowledge of results and the learning of simple skill. *Journal of Experimental Psychology, 55,* 379–383.

Blackburn, J. M. (1936). *Acquisition of skill: An analysis of learning curves* (IHRB Report No. 73).

Blaney, P. H. (1986). Affect and memory: A review. *Psychological Bulletin, 99,* 229–246.

Bliss, T. V. P., & Lomo, T. (1973). Long–lasting potentiation of synaptic transmission in the dentate area of the anesthetized rabbit following stimulation of the preforant path. *Journal of Physiology, 232,* 331–356.

Bliss, T. V. P., & Lynch, M. A. (1988). Long-term potentiation of synaptic transmission in the hippocampus: Properties and mechanisms. In P. W. Landfield and S. A. Deadwyler (Eds.), *Neurology and Neurobiology: Vol. 35. Long-term potentiation: From biophysics to behavior.* New York: Alan R. Liss, Inc.

Bloom, B. S. (1968). Learning for mastery. *Evaluation Comment, 1,* 2.

Bloom, B. S. (1976). *Human characteristics and school learning.* New York: McGraw-Hill.

Bloom, B. S. (Ed.). (1985a). *Developing talent in young people.* New York: Ballantine Books.

Bloom, B. S. (1985b). Generalizations about talent development. In B. S. Bloom (Ed.), *Developing talent in young people,* (pp. 507–549). New York: Ballantine Books.

Blough, D. S. (1959). Delayed matching in the pigeon. *Journal of the Experimental Analysis of Behavior, 2,* 151–160.

Blough, D. S. (1975). Steady state data and a quantitative model of operant generalization and discrimination. *Journal of Experimental Psychology: Animal Behavior Processes, 1,* 3–21.

Bobrow, D. G., & Bower, G. H. (1969). Comprehension and recall of sentences. *Journal of Experimental Psychology, 80,* 455–461.

Bolles, R. C. (1970). Species-specific defense reactions and avoidance learning. *Psychological Review, 77,* 32–48.

Boring, E. G. (1950). *A history of experimental psychology.* New York: Appleton-Century.

Boring, E. G. (1953). A history of introspection. *Psychological Bulletin, 50,* 169–189.

Bourne, L. E., Jr. (1974). An inference model of conceptual rule learning. In R. Solso (Ed.), *Theories in cognitive psychology.* Washington, DC: Erlbaum.

Bourne, L. E., Ekstrand, B. R., & Dominowski, R. L. (1971). *The psychology of thinking.* Englewood Cliffs, NJ: Prentice-Hall.

Bovair, S., Kieras, D. E., & Polson, P. G. (1990). The acquisition and performance of text-editing skill: A cognitive complexity analysis. *Human Computer Interaction, 5,* 1–48.

Bower, G. H. (1972). Mental imagery and associative learning. In L. Gregg (Ed.), *Cognition in learning and memory.* New York: Wiley.

Bower, G. H., & Clark, M. C. (1969). Narrative stories as mediators for serial learning. *Psychonomic Science, 14,* 181–182.

Bower, G. H., & Hilgard, E. R. (1981). *Theories of learning* (5th ed.). Englewood Cliffs, NJ: Prentice-Hall.

Bower, G. H., Karlin, M. B., & Dueck, A. (1975). Comprehension and memory for pictures. *Memory and Cognition, 3,* 216–220.

Bower, G. H., & Reitman, J. S. (1972). Mnemonic elaboration in multilist learning. *Journal of Learning and Verbal Behavior, 11,* 478–485.

Bower, G. H., & Springston, F. (1970). Pauses as recoding points in letter series. *Journal of Experimental Psychology, 83,* 421–430.

Bower, G. H., & Trabasso, T. R. (1963). Reversals prior to solution in concept identification. *Journal of Experimental Psychology, 66,* 409–418.

Boyd, W., & King, E. J. (1975). *The history of western education* (11th ed.). Totowa, NJ: Barnes & Noble Books.

Bradshaw, G. L., & Anderson, J. R. (1982). Elaborative encoding as an explanation of levels of processing. *Journal of Verbal Learning and Verbal Behavior, 21,* 165–174.

Braine, M. D. S. (1971). On two types of models of the internalization of grammars. In D. I. Slobin (Ed.), *The ontogenesis of grammar: A theoretical symposium.* New York: Academic Press.

Bransford, J. D., & Franks, J. J. (1971). The abstraction of linguistic ideas. *Cognitive Psychology, 2,* 331–380.

Bransford, J. D., Franks, J. J., Morris, C. D., & Stein, B. S. (1979). Some general constraints on learning and memory research. In L. S. Cermak & F. I. M. Craik (Eds.), *Levels of processing in human memory* (pp. 331–354). Hillsdale, NJ: Erlbaum.

Bransford, J. D., & Johnson, M. K. (1972). Contextual prerequisites for understanding: Some investigations of comprehension and recall. *Journal of Verbal Learning and Verbal Behavior, 11,* 717–726.

Breland, K., & Breland, M. (1951). A field of applied animal psychology. *American Psychologist, 6,* 202–204.

Breland, K., & Breland, M. (1961). The misbehavior of organisms. *American Psychologist, 16,* 681–684.

Bibliography

Brigham, J. C. (1981, November). The accuracy of eyewitness evidence: How do attorneys see it? *The Florida Bar Journal*, pp. 714–721.

Broadbent, D. E. (1957). A mechanical model for human attention and immediate memory. *Psychological Review, 64*, 205–215.

Brodgen, W. J. (1949). Acquisition and extinction of a conditioned avoidance response in dogs. *Journal of Comparative Physiological Psychology, 42*, 296–302.

Brooks, L. R. (1967). The suppression of visualization by reading. *Quarterly Journal of Experimental Psychology, 19*, 289–299.

Brown, J. (1958). Some tests of decay theory of immediate memory. *Quarterly Journal of Experimental Psychology, 10*, 12–21.

Brown, J. S., & Van Lehn, K. (1980). Repair theory: A generative theory of bugs in procedural skills. *Cognitive Science, 4*, 397–426.

Brown, P. L., & Jenkins, H. M. (1968). Auto-shaping of the pigeon's key-peck. *Journal of the Experimental Analysis of Behavior, 11*, 1–8.

Brown, R. (1973). *A first language*. Cambridge, MA: Harvard University Press.

Brown, R., & Fraser, C. (1963). The acquisition of syntax. In C. N. Cofer and B. Musgrave (Eds.), *Verbal behavior and learning: Problems and processes* (pp. 158–201). New York: McGraw-Hill.

Brown, R., & Kulik, J. (1977). Flashbulb memories. *Cognition, 5*, 73–99.

Brown, R., & McNeill, D. (1966). The "tip of the tongue" phenomenon. *Journal of Verbal Learning and Verbal Behavior, 5*, 325–337.

Bruner, J. S., Goodnow, J. J., & Austin, G. A. (1956). *A study of thinking*. New York: Wiley.

Bruner, J. S. Matter, J., & Papanek, M. L. (1955). Breadth of learning as a function of drive level and mechanization. *Psychological Review, 62*, 1–10.

Bullock, M., Gelman, R., & Baillargeon, R. (1982). The development of causal reasoning. In W. Friedman (Ed.), *The developmental psychology of time* (pp. 209–254). New York: Academic Press.

Burns, D. J. (1990). The generation effect: A test between single- and multifactor theories. *Journal of Experimental Psychology: Learning, Memory, and Cognition, 16*, 1060–1067.

Burns, D. J. (1992). The consequences of generation. *Journal of Memory and Language, 31*, 615–633.

Burton, R. R. (1982). Diagnosing bugs in a simple procedural skill. In D. Sleeman & J. S. Brown (Eds.), *Intelligent tutoring systems*. New York: Academic Press.

Butler, R. A. (1953). Discrimination learning by rhesus monkeys to visual-exploration motivation. *Journal of Comparative and Physiological Psychology, 46*, 95–98.

California Assessment Program. (1980). *Student achievement in California schools: 1979–80 annual report*. Sacramento: California State Department of Education.

Camp, D. S., Raymond, G. A., & Church, R. M. (1967). Temporal relationship between response and punishment. *Journal of Experimental Psychology, 74*, 114–123.

Capaldi, E. J. (1967). A sequential hypothesis of instrumental learning. In K. W. Spence & J. T. Spence (Eds.), *The psychology of learning and motivation* (Vol. 1). New York: Academic Press.

Carew, T. J., Hawkins, R. D., & Kandel, E. R. (1983). Differential classical conditioning of a defensive withdrawal reflex in *Aplysia californica. Science, 219*, 397–400.

Carey, S. (1978). The child as word learner. In M. Halle, J. Bresnan, & G. Miller (Eds.), *Linguistic theory and psychological reality*. Cambridge, MA: MIT Press.

Bibliography

Carlson, R. A., Sullivan, M. A., & Schneider, W. (1989). Practice and working memory effects in building procedural skill. *Journal of Experimental Psychology, 15,* 517–526.

Carraher, T. N., Carraher, D. W., & Schliemann, A. D. (1985). Mathematics in the streets and in the schools. *British Journal of Developmental Psychology, 3,* 21–29.

Catalano, J. F., & Kleiner, B. M.(1984). Distant transfer and practice variability. *Perceptual and Motor Skills, 58,* 851–856.

Catania, A. C. (1992). *Learning* (3rd ed.). Englewood Cliffs, NJ: Prentice–Hall.

Cavanagh, J. P. (1972). Relation between the immediate memory span and the memory search rate. *Psychological Review, 79,* 525–530.

Cermak, L. S., & Craik, F. I. M. (Eds.). (1978). *Levels of processing in human memory.* Hillsdale, NJ: Erlbaum.

Chall, J. S. (1967). *Learning to read: The great debate.* New York: McGraw-Hill.

Champagne, A. B., Gunstone, R. F., & Klopfer, L. E. (1985). Effecting changes in cognitive structures among physics students. In H. T. West & A. L. Pines (Eds.), *Cognitive structure and conceptual change.* Orlando, FL: Academic Press.

Chapman, G. B., & Robbins, S. J. (1990). Cue interaction in human contingency judgment. *Memory and Cognition, 18,* 537–545.

Charness, N. (1979). Components of skill in bridge. *Canadian Journal of Psychology, 33,* 1–16.

Chase, W. G., & Simon, H. A. (1973). The mind's eye in chess. In W. G. Chase (Ed.), *Visual information processing.* New York: Academic Press.

Chi, M. T. H., Bassock, M., Lewis, M., Reimann, P., & Glaser, R. (1989). Self-explanations: How students study and use examples in learning to solve problems. *Cognitive Science, 13,* 145–182.

Chomsky, N. (1959). Review of Skinner's *Verbal Behavior. Language, 35,* 26–58.

Chomsky, N. (1965). *Aspects of the theory of syntax.* Cambridge, MA: MIT Press.

Chomsky, N. (1975). *Reflections on language.* New York: Random House.

Chomsky, N. (1986). *Knowledge of language.* New York: Fontana.

Christen, F., & Bjork, R. A. (1976). *On updating the loci in the method of loci.* Paper presented at the seventeenth annual meeting of the Psychonomic Society, St. Louis.

Church, R. M. (1969). Response suppression. In B. A. Campbell & R. M. Church (Eds.), *Punishment and aversive behavior.* New York: Appleton-Century-Crofts.

Clark, E. V. (1983). Meanings and concepts. In P. H. Mussen (Ed.), *Handbook of child psychology.* New York: Wiley.

Cohen, N. J., Eichenbaum, H., Deacedo, B. S., & Corkin, S. (1985). Different memory systems underlying acquisition of procedural and declarative knowledge. In D. S. Olton, E. Gamzu, & S. Corkin (Eds.), *Memory dysfunctions: An integration of animal and human research from preclinical and clinical perspectives. Annals New York Academy of Sciences, 444,* 54–71.

Cohen, N. J., & Squire, L. R. (1980). Preserved learning and retention of pattern analyzing skills in amnesia: Dissociation of knowing how and knowing that. *Science, 210,* 207–210.

Coltheart, M. (1983). Iconic memory. *Philosophical Transactions of the Royal Society, London B, 302,* 283–294.

Conrad, R. (1960). Very brief delay of immediate recall. *Quarterly Journal of Experimental Psychology, 12,* 45–47.

Conrad, R. (1964). Acoustic confusion in immediate memory. *British Journal of Psychology, 55,* 75–84.

Corbett, A. T., & Anderson, J. R. (1990). The effect of feedback control on learning to program with the LISP tutor. *Proceedings of the 12th Annual Conference of the Cognitive Science Society* (pp. 796–803).

Colwill, R. M., & Rescorla, R. A. (1985a). Instrumental responding remains sensitive to reinforcer devaluation after extensive training. *Journal of Experimental Psychology: Animal Behavior Processes, 11,* 520–536.

Colwill, R. M., & Rescorla, R. A. (1985b). Postconditioning devaluation of a reinforcer affects instrumental responding. *Journal of Experimental Psychology: Animal Behavior Processes, 11,* 120–132.

Colwill, R. M., & Rescorla, R. A. (1986). Associative structure in instrumental learning. In G. H. Bower (Ed.), *The psychology of learning and motivation* (Vol. 20). New York: Academic Press.

Colwill, R. M., & Rescorla, R. A. (1988). Associations between the discriminative stimulus and the reinforcer in instrumental learning. *Journal of Experimental Psychology: Animal Behavior Processes, 14,* 155–164.

Cowles, J. T. (1937). Food-tokens as incentive for learning by chimpanzees. *Comparative Psychology Monographs, 14* (No. 5).

Craik, F. I. M., & Lockhart, R. S. (1972). Levels of processing: A framework for memory research. *Journal of Verbal Learning and Verbal Behavior, 11,* 671–684.

Craik, F. I. M., & Tulving, E. (1975). Depth of processing and the retention of words in episodic memory. *Journal of Experimental Psychology: General, 104,* 268–294.

Craik, F. I. M., & Watkins, M. J. (1973). The role of rehearsal in short-term memory. *Journal of Verbal Learning and Verbal Behavior, 12,* 599–607.

Crocker, J. (1981). Judgment of covariation by social perceivers. *Psychological Bulletin, 90,* 272–292.

Crossman, E. R. F. W. (1959). A theory of the acquisition of speed skill. *Ergonomics, 2,* 153–166.

Crowder, R. G. (1976). *Principles of learning and memory.* Hillsdale, NJ: Erlbaum.

Crowder, R. G. (1982). The demise of short-term memory. *Acta Pychologica, 50,* 291–323.

Crowder, R. G. (1989). Modularity and dissociations in memory systems. In H. L. Roediger, & F. I. M. Craik (Eds.), *Varieties of memory and consciousness: Essays in honour of Endel Tulving.* Hillsdale, NJ: Erlbaum.

Crowder, R. G., & Morton, J. (1969). Precategorical acoustic storage (PAS). *Perception and Psychophysics, 5,* 365–373.

Culler, E., & Girden, E. (1951). The learning curve in relation to other psychometric functions. *American Journal of Psychology, 64,* 327–349.

Curran, T., & Keele, S. W. (1993). Attentional and nonattentional forms of sequence learning. *Journal of Experimental Psychology: Learning, Memory, and Cognition, 19,* 189–202.

Dallett, K. M. (1964). Number of categories and category information in free recall. *Journal of Experimental Psychology, 68,* 1–12.

Dansereau, D. F. (1978). The development of a learning strategies curriculum. In H. F. O'Neill, Jr. (Ed.), *Learning strategies.* New York: Academic Press.

Dansereau, D. F., Collins, K. W., McDonald, B. A., Holley, C. D., Garland, J. C., Diekhoff, G., & Evans, S. H. (1979). Development and evaluation of an effective learning strategy program. *Journal of Educational Psychology, 71,* 64–73.

Darwin, C. (1975). *The origin of the species* (P. Appleman, Ed.). New York: W. W. Norton (original work published 1859).

Darwin, C. J., Turvey, M. T., & Crowder, R. G. (1972). The auditory analogue of the Sperling partial report procedure: Evidence for brief auditory storage. *Cognitive Psychology, 3*, 255–267.

Daugherty, K. G., MacDonald, M. C., Petersen, A. S., & Seidenberg, M. S. (1993). Why no mere mortal has ever flown out to center field but people often say they do. *Proceedings of the 15th Annual Conference of the Cognitive Science Society* (pp. 383–388).

Davenport, D. G., & Olson, R. D. (1968). A reinterpretation of extinction in discriminated avoidance. *Psychonomic Science, 13*, 5–6.

de Beer, G. R. (1959). *Paedomorphesis. Proceedings of the 15th International Congress of Zoology* (pp. 927–930).

Deffenbacher, K. A. (1983). The influence of arousal on reliability of testimony. In S. M. A. Loyd-Bostock & B. R. Clifford (Eds.), *Evaluating witness evidence* (pp. 235–254). Chichester, England: Wiley.

de Groot, A. D. (1965). *Thought and choice in chess.* The Hague, Netherlands: Mouton.

Dewhurst, D. J. (1967). Neuromuscular control system. *IEEE Transactions on Biomedical Engineering, 14*, 167–171.

Diamond, A. (in press). Frontal lobe involvement in cognitive changes during the first year of life. In K. Gibson, M. Konner, & A. Petersen (Eds.), *Brain and behavioral development.* New York: Aldine Press.

Domjan, M. (1993). *The principles of learning and behavior* (3rd ed.). Pacific Grove, CA: Brooks/Cole.

Dooling, D. J., & Christiansen, R. E. (1977). Episodic and semantic aspects of memory for prose. *Journal of Experimental Psychology: Human Learning and Memory, 3*, 428–436.

Dunbar, K., & Klahr, D. (1989). Developmental differences in scientific discovery processes. In D. Klahr & K. Kotovsky (Eds.), *Complex information processing: The impact of Herbert A. Simon* (pp. 109–143). 21st Carnegie Mellon Symposium on Cognition, Pittsburgh, PA.

Eagle, M., & Leiter, E. (1964). Recall and recognition in intentional and incidental learning. *Journal of Experimental Psychology, 68*, 58–63.

Easterbrook, J. A. (1959). The effect of emotion on cue utilization and the organization of behavior. *Psychological Review, 66*, 183–201.

Ebbinghaus, H. (1913). Memory: A contribution to experimental psychology (H. A. Ruger & C. E. Bussenues, Trans.). New York: Teachers College, Columbia University. (Original work published 1885)

Egan, D. E., & Schwartz, B. J. (1979). Chunking in recall of symbolic drawings. *Memory and Cognition, 7*, 149–158.

Ehri, L. C., & Wilce, L. C. (1983). Development of word identification speed in skilled and less skilled beginning readers. *Journal of Educational Psychology, 75*, 3–18.

Ehri, L. C., & Wilce, L. C. (1987, winter). Does learning to spell help beginners learn to read words? *Reading Research Quarterly, 22.*

Eich, E. (1985). Context, memory, and integrated item/context imagery. *Journal of Experimental Psychology: Learning, Memory, and Cognition, 11*, 764–770.

Eich, E., & Metcalfe, J. (1989). Mood dependent memory for internal versus external events. *Journal of Experimental Psychology: Learning, Memory, and Cognition, 15*, 443–455.

Eich, J. E., Weingartner, H., Stillman, R. C., & Gillin, J. C. (1975). State-dependent accessibility of retrieval cues in the retention of a categorized list. *Journal of Verbal Learning and Verbal Behavior, 14*, 408–417.

Einhorn, H. J., & Hogarth, R. M. (1986). Judging probable cause. *Psychological Bulletin, 99*, 3–19.

Ekstrand, B. R. (1972). To sleep, perchance to dream. In C. P. Duncan, L. Sechrest, & A. W. Melton (Eds.), *Human memory: Festschrift in honor of Benton J. Underwood* (pp. 59–82). New York: Appleton-Century-Crofts.

Ellis, N. C., & Hennelly, R. A. (1980). A bilingual word-length effect: Implications for intelligence testing and the relative ease of mental calculation in Welsh and English. *British Journal of Psychology, 71*, 43–52.

Engle, R. W., & Bukstel, L. (1978). Memory processes among bridge players of differing expertise. *American Journal of Psychology, 91*, 673–689.

Epstein, S. (1967). Toward a unified theory of anxiety. In B. A. Maher (Ed.), *Progress in experimental personality research* (Vol. 4). New York: Academic Press.

Ericsson, K. A., Krampe, R. T., & Tesch-Römer, C. (1993). The role of deliberate practice in the acquisition of expert performance. *Psychological Review, 100*, 363–406.

Eron, L. D., Walder, L. O., Toigo, R., & Lefkowitz, M. M. (1963). Social class, parental punishment for aggression, and child aggression. *Child Development, 34*, 849–867.

Ervin-Tripp, S. M. (1974). Is second language learning like the first? *TESOL Quarterly, 8*, 111–127.

Estes, W. K. (1955). Statistical theory of spontaneous recovery and regression. *Psychological Review, 62*, 145–154.

Estes, W. K., Campbell, J. A., Hatsopoulos, N., & Hurwitz, J. B. (1989). Base-rate effects in category learning: A comparison of parallel network and memory storage-retrieval models. *Journal of Experimental Psychology: Learning, Memory, and Cognition, 15*, 556–571.

Etscorn, F., & Stephens, R. (1973). Establishment of conditioned taste aversions with a 24-hour CS–US interval. *Physiological Psychology, 1*, 251–253.

Eysenck, M. W. (1982). *Attention and arousal: Cognition and performance.* Berlin: Springer-Verlag.

Fantino, E., & Abarca, N. (1985). Choice, optimal foraging, and the delay-reduction hypothesis. *Behavioral and Brain Sciences, 8*, 315–330.

Farnham-Diggory, S. (1992). *Cognitive processes in education* (2nd ed.). New York: Harper Collins.

Fernandez, A., & Glenberg, A. M. (1985). Changing environmental context does not reliably affect memory. *Memory and Cognition, 13*, 333–345.

Ferster, C. S., & Skinner, B. F. (1957). *Schedules of reinforcement.* New York: Appleton-Century-Crofts.

Fitts, P. M. (1964). Perceptual-motor skill learning. In A. W. Melton (Ed.), *Categories of human learning.* New York: Academic Press.

Fitzgerald, R. D., Martin, G. K., & O'Brien, J. H. (1973). Influence of vagal activity on classically conditioned heart rate in rats. *Journal of Comparative Physiological Psychology, 83*, 485–491.

Flaherty, C. F. (1985). *Animal learning and cognition.* New York: McGraw-Hill.

Folkard, S. (1983). Diurnal variation. In G. R. J. Hockey (Ed.), *Stress and fatigue in human performance* (chap. 9, pp. 245–272). New York: Wiley.

Folkard, S., Monk, T. H., Bradbury, R., & Rosenthal, J. (1977). Time of day effects in schoolchildren's immediate and delayed recall of meaningful material. *British Journal of Psychology, 68*, 45–50.

Frase, L. T. (1975). Prose processing. In G. H. Bower (Ed.), *The psychology of learning and motivation* (Vol. 9). New York: Academic Press.

Frederiksen, J. R. (1981). Sources of process interactions in reading. In A. M. Lesgold & C. A. Perfetti (Eds.), *Interactive processes in reading.* Hillsdale, NJ: Erlbaum.

Freedman, J. L., & Landauer, T. K. (1966). Retrieval of long-term memory: "Tip-of-the-tongue" phenomenon. *Psychonomic Science, 4*, 309–310.

Freud, S. (1971). *The psychopathology of everyday life*. (A. Tyson, Trans.). New York: W. W. Norton. (Original work published in 1901)

Funahashi, S., Bruce, C. J., & Goldman-Rakic, P. S. (1991). Neural activity related to saccadic eye movements in the monkey's dorsolateral prefrontal cortex. *Journal of Neurophysiology, 65*, 1464–1483.

Gagné, E., Yekovich, C. W., & Yekovich, F. R. (1993). *The cognitive psychology of school learning*. New York: Harper Collins.

Gagné, R. (1962). The acquisition of knowledge. *Psychological Review, 69*, 355–365.

Gagné, R., Briggs, L. J., & Wager, W. W. (1989). *Principles of instructional design*. New York: Holt, Rinehart, & Winston.

Gamoran, A. (1987). The stratification of high school learning opportunities. *Sociology of Education, 60*, 135–155.

Garcia, J., & Koelling, R. A. (1966). Relation of cue to consequence in avoidance learning. *Psychonomic Science, 4*, 123–124.

Gardner, R. A., & Gardner, B. T. (1969). Teaching sign language to a chimpanzee. *Science, 165*, 664–672.

Gathercole, S. E., & Hitch, G. J. (1993). Developmental changes in short-term memory: A revised working memory perspective. In A. F. Collins, S. E. Gathercole, M. A. Conway, & P. Morris (Eds.), *Theories of memory*. Hillsdale, NJ: Erlbaum.

Gentner, D. R. (1987). Timing of skilled motor performance: Tests of the proportional duration model. *Psychological Review, 94*, 255–276.

Gernsbacher, M. A. (1985). Surface information loss in comprehension. *Cognitive Psychology, 17*, 324–363.

Gillund, G., & Shiffrin, R. M. (1984). A retrieval model for both recognition and recall. *Psychological Review, 91*, 1–67.

Glaser, R. (1972). Individuals and learning: The new aptitudes. *Educational Researcher, 1*, 5–13.

Glass, A. L. (1984). Effect of memory set on reaction time. In J. R. Anderson & S. M. Kosslyn (Eds.), *Tutorials in learning and memory* (pp. 119–136). New York: W. H. Freeman.

Glenberg, A. M. (1976). Monotonic and nonmonotonic lag effects in paired-associate and recognition memory paradigms. *Journal of Verbal Learning and Verbal Behavior, 15*, 1–16.

Glenberg, A. M., Smith, S. M., & Green, C. (1977). Type I rehearsal: Maintenance and more. *Journal of Verbal Learning and Verbal Behavior, 16*, 339–352.

Gluck, M. A., & Bower, G. H. (1988). From conditioning to category learning: An adaptive network model. *Journal of Experimental Psychology: General, 8*, 37–50.

Gluck, M. A., & Thompson, R. F. (1987). Modeling the neural substrates of associative learning and memory: A computational approach. *Psychological Review, 94*, 176–191.

Glucksberg, S., & Cowan, G. N., Jr. (1970). Memory for nonattended auditory material. *Cognitive Psychology, 1*, 149–156.

Godden, D. R., & Baddeley, A. D. (1975). Context-dependent memory in two natural environments: On land and under water. *British Journal of Psychology, 66*, 325–331.

Goldman-Rakic, P. S. (1987). Circuitry of primate prefrontal cortex and regulation of behavior by representational memory. In *Handbook of physiology. The nervous system. Higher functions of the brain* (Vol. 5, pp. 373–417). Bethesda, MD: American Physiology Society.

Bibliography

Goldman-Rakic, P. S. (1988). Topography of cognition: Parallel distributed networks in primate association cortex. *Annual Review of Neuroscience, 11*, 137–156.

Goldman-Rakic, P. S. (1992). Working memory and mind. *Scientific American, 267*, 111–117.

Goldstein, A. G., & Chance, J. E. (1970). Visual recognition memory for complex configurations. *Perception and Psychophysics, 9*, 237–241.

Good, H. G. (1962). *A history of American education.* New York: Macmillan.

Goodwin, D. W., Powell, B., Bremer, D., Hoine, H., & Stern, J. (1969). Alcohol and recall: State-dependent effects in man. *Science, 163*, 1358–1360.

Gordon, W. C. (1989). *Learning and memory.* Pacific Grove, CA: Brooks/Cole.

Gormezano, I. (1965). Yoked comparisons of classical and instrumental conditioning of the eyelid response; and an addendum on "Voluntary Responders." In W. F. Prokasy (Ed.), *Classical conditioning* (pp. 48–70). New York: Appleton-Century-Crofts.

Gormezano, I., Kehoe, E. J., & Marshall, B. S. (1983). Twenty years of classical conditioning research with the rabbit. In J. M. Prague & A. N. Epstein (Eds.), *Progress in psychobiology and physiological psychology* (Vol 10). New York: Academic Press.

Gormezano, I., Prokasy, W. F., & Thompson, R. F. (Eds.). (1987). *Classical conditioning* (3rd ed.). Hillsdale, NJ: Erlbaum.

Graf, P., Squire, L. R., & Mandler, G. (1984). The information that amnesic patients do not forget. *Journal of Experimental Psychology: Learning, Memory, and Cognition, 10*, 164–178.

Grant, D. A. (1973). Cognitive factors in eyelid conditioning. *Psychophysiology, 10*, 75–81.

Grant, D. S. (1976). Effect of sample presentation time on long delay matching in the pigeon. *Learning and Motivation, 7*, 580–590.

Grant, D. S. (1981). Short-term memory in the pigeon. In N. E. Spear & R. Miller (Eds.), *Information processing in animals: Memory mechanisms* (pp. 227–256). Hillsdale, NJ: Erlbaum.

Grant, D. S., & Roberts, W. A. (1976). Sources of retroactive inhibition in pigeon short-term memory. *Journal of Experimental Psychology: Animal Behavior Processes, 2*, 1–16.

Greeno, J. G. (1974). Hobbits and orcs: Acquisition of a sequential concept. *Cognitive Psychology, 6*, 270–292.

Grittner, F. M. (1975). Individualized instruction: An historical perspective. *The Modern Language Journal*, 323–333.

Gruneberg, M. M., & Monks, J. (1974). Feeling of knowing and cued recall. *Acta Psychologica, 38*, 257–265.

Gunn, D. L. (1937). The humidity reactions of the wood louse, *Porcellio scaber* (Latreille). *Journal of Experimental Biology, 14*, 178–186.

Guskey, T. R., & Gates, S. (1986). Synthesis of research on the effects of mastery learning in elementary and secondary classrooms. *Educational Leadership, 43*, 73–80.

Guthrie, E. R. (1952). *The psychology of learning* (rev. ed.) New York: Harper & Row.

Guttman, N., & Kalish, H. I. (1956). Discriminability and stimulus generalization. *Journal of Experimental Psychology, 51*, 79–88.

Gynther, M. D. (1957). Differential eyelid conditioning as a function of stimulus similarity and strength of response to the CS. *Journal of Experimental Psychology, 53*, 408–416.

Haber, R. N. (1983). The impending demise of the icon: A critique of the concept of iconic storage in visual information processing. *Behavioral and Brain Sciences, 6*, 1–11.

Haig, K. A., Rawlins, J. N. P., Olton, D. S., Mead, A., & Taylor, B. (1983). Food searching strategies of rats: Variables affecting the relative strength of stay and shift strategies. *Journal of Experimental Psychology: Animal Behavior Processes, 9,* 337–348.

Halford, G. S., Bain, J. D., & Maybery, M. T. (1984) Does concurrent memory load interfere with reasoning? *Current Psychological Research and Reviews, 3,* 14–23.

Hammond, L. J. (1980). The effect contingency upon the appetitive conditioning of free operant behavior. *Journal of the Experimental Analysis of Behavior, 34,* 297–304.

Harley, W. F., Jr. (1965). The effect of monetary incentive in paired-associate learning using a differential method. *Psychonomic Science, 2,* 377–378.

Hasher, L., Goldstein, D., & Toppino, T. (1977). Frequency and the conference of referential validity. *Journal of Verbal Learning and Verbal Behavior, 16,* 107–112.

Hart, J. T. (1967). Memory and the memory-monitoring process. *Journal of Verbal Learning and Verbal Behavior, 6,* 685–691.

Hawkins, R. D., Abrams, T. W., Carew, T. J., & Kandel, E. R. (1983). A cellular mechanism of classical conditioning in *Aplysia*: Activity-dependent amplification of presynaptic facilitation. *Science, 219,* 400–404.

Hawkins, R. D., & Bower, G. H. (Eds.). (1989). *The Psychology of Learning and Motivation:Vol. 23. Computational models of learning in simple neural systems.* San Diego: Academic Press.

Hayes, C. (1951). *The ape in our house.* New York: Harper.

Hayes, J. R. (1985). Three problems in teaching general skills. In J. Segal, S. Chipman, & R. Glaser (Eds.), *Thinking and learning* (Vol. 2). Hillsdale, NJ: Erlbaum.

Hayes-Roth, B. (1977). Evolution of cognitive structures and processes. *Psychological Review, 84,* 260–278.

Hayes-Roth, F., Waterman, D. A., & Lenat, D. B. (1983). *Building expert systems.* Reading, MA: Addison-Wesley.

Hearst, E. (1988). Fundamentals of learning and conditioning. In R. C. Atkinson, R. J. Herrnstein, G. Lindzey, and R. D. Luce (Eds.), *Stevens' handbook of experimental psychology: Vol. 2. Learning and cognition* (pp. 3–110). New York: Wiley.

Heath, R. G. (1963). Electrical self-stimultion of the brain in man. *American Journal of Psychitry, 120, 571-577.*

Hemmes, N. S., Eckerman, D. A., & Rubinsky, H. J. (1979). A functional analysis of collateral behavior under differential-reinforcement-of-low-rate schedules. *Journal of Animal Learning and Behavior, 7,* 328–332.

Henry, F. M. (1968). Specificity vs. generality in learning motor skill. In R. C. Brown & G. S. Kenyon (Eds.), *Classical studies on physical activity* (pp. 331–340). Englewood Cliffs, NJ: Prentice-Hall. (Original work published 1958)

Herrnstein, R. J. (1990). Rational choice theory. *American Psychologist, 45,* 356–367.

Herrnstein, R. J., Loveland, D. H., & Cable, C. (1976). Natural concepts in pigeons. *Journal of Experimental Psychology: Animal Behavior Processes, 2,* 285–302.

Herrnstein, R. J., & Vaughan, W. (1980). Melioration and behavioral allocation. In J. E. R. Staddon (Ed.), *Limits to action: The allocation of individual behavior.* New York: Academic Press.

Heyman, G. M., & Luce, R. D. (1979). Operant matching is not a logical consequence of maximizing reinforcement rate. *Animal Learning & Behavior, 7,* 133–140.

Hillman, B., Hunter, W. S., & Kimble, G. A. (1953). The effect of drive level on the maze performance of the white rat. *Journal of Comparative Physiological Psychology, 46,* 87–89.

Hineline, P. N., & Rachlin, H. (1969). Escape and avoidance of shock by pigeons pecking a key. *Journal of the Experimental Analysis of Behavior, 12,* 533–538.

Hinton, G. E. (1992) How neural networks learn from experience. *Scientific American, 267*, 145–151.

Hintzman, D. L. (1992). Mathematical constraints and the Tulving-Wiseman law. *Psychological Review, 99*, 536–542.

Hintzman, D. L., Block, R. A., & Summers, J. J. (1973). Modality tags and memory for repetitions: Locus of the spacing effect. *Journal of Verbal Learning and Verbal Behavior, 12*, 229–238.

Hiroto, D. S., & Seligman, M. E. P. (1975). Generality of learned helplessness in man. *Journal of Personality and Social Psychology, 31*, 311–327.

Hirshman, E., & Bjork, R. A. (1988). The generation effect: Support for a two-factor theory. *Journal of Experimental Psychology: Learning, Memory, and Cognition, 14*, 484–494.

Hirshman, E., Whelley, M. M., & Palu, M. (1989). An investigation of paradoxical memory effects. *Journal of Memory and Language, 28*, 594–609.

Hirst, W., Phelps, E. A., Johnson, M. K., & Volpe, B. T. (1988). Amnesia and second language learning. *Brain and Cognition, 8*, 105–116.

Ho, L., & Shea, J. B. (1978). Effects of relative frequency of knowledge of results on retention of a motor skill. *Perceptual and Motor Skills, 46*, 859–866.

Hockey, G. R. J., Davies, S., & Gray, M. M. (1972). Forgetting a function of sleep at different times of day. *Experimental Psychology, 24*, 386–393.

Hoffer, A. (1981). Geometry is more than proof. *Mathematics Teacher*, 11–18.

Holland, J. H. Holyoak, K., Nisbett, R. E., & Thagard, P. R. (1986). *Induction: Processes of inference, learning, and discovery.* Cambridge, MA: MIT Press.

Holland, P. C. (1985a). Element pretraining influences the content of appetitive serial compound conditioning in rats. *Journal of Experimental Psychology: Animal Learning and Behavior, 14*, 111–120.

Holland, P. C. (1985b). The nature of conditioned inhibition in serial and simultaneous feature negative discriminations. In R. R. Miller & N. E. Spear (Eds.), *Information processing in animals: Conditioned inhibition* (pp. 267–297). Hillsdale, NJ: Erlbaum.

Holland, P. C., & Rescorla, R. A. (1975). The effects of two ways of devaluing the unconditioned stimulus after first- and second-order appetitive conditioning. *Journal of Experimental Psychology: Animal Behavior Processes, 1*, 355–363.

Holley, C. D., Dansereau, D. F., McDonald, B. A., Garland, J. C., & Collins, K. W. (1979). Evaluation of hierarchical mapping technique as an aid to prose processing. *Contemporary Educational Psychology, 4*, 227–237.

Holyoak, K. J., Koh, K., & Nisbett, R. E. (1989). A theory of conditioning: Inductive learning within rule-based default hierarchies. *Psychological Review, 96*, 315–340.

Honig, W. K. (1981). Working memory and the temporal map. In N. E. Spear & R. Miller (Eds.), *Information processing in animals: Memory mechanisms* (pp. 167–197). Hillsdale, NJ: Erlbaum.

Hoosain, R., & Salili, F. (1988). Language differences, working memory, and mathematical ability. In M. M. Gruneberg, P. E. Morris, & R. N. Sykes (Eds.), *Practical aspects of memory: Current research and issues: Vol. 2. Clinical and educational implications* (pp. 512–517). Chichester, England: Wiley.

Houston, J. P. (1965). Short-term retention of verbal units with equated degrees of learning. *Journal of Experimental Psychology, 70*, 75–78.

Houston, J. P. (1991). *Fundamentals of learning and memory* (4th ed.). Orlando, FL: Harcourt Brace Jovanovich.

Hull, C. L. (1920). Quantitative aspects of the evolution of concepts. *Psychological Monographs* (Whole No. 123).

Hull, C. L. (1952a). Autobiography. In C. A. Murchinson (Ed.), *A history of psychology in autobiography* (Vol. 4). New York: Russell & Russell Press.

Hull, C. L. (1952b). *A behavior system: An introduction to behavior theory concerning the individual organism*. New Haven, CT: Yale University Press.

Hunter, J. E., & Hunter, R. F. (1984). Validity and utility of alternative predictors of job performance. *Psychological Bulletin, 96*, 72–98.

Hyams, N. M. (1986). *Language acquisition and the theory of parameters*. Dordrecht, Netherlands: D. Reidel.

Hyde, T. S. , & Jenkins, J. J. (1973). Recall for words as a function of semantic, graphic, and syntactic orienting tasks. *Journal of Verbal Learning and Verbal Behavior, 12*, 471–480.

Jackson, M. D., & McClelland, J. L. (1979). Processing determinants of reading speed. *Journal of Experimental Psychology: General, 108*, 151–181.

Jacobsen, C. F. (1935). Functions of frontal association areas in primates. *Archives of Neurology and Psychiatry, 33*, 558–560.

Jacobsen, C. F. (1936). Studies of cerebral functions in primates: I. The function of the frontal association areas in monkeys. *Comparative Psychology Monographs, 13*, 1–60.

Jacoby, L. L. (1983). Remembering the data: Analyzing interactive processes in reading. *Journal of Verbal Learning and Verbal Behavior, 22*, 485–508.

Jacoby, L. L. (1991). A process dissociation framework: Separating automatic from intentional uses of memory. *Journal of Memory and Language, 30*, 513–541.

Jacoby, L. L., Toth, J. P., & Yonelinas, A. (1993). Separating conscious and unconscious influences of memory: Measuring recollection. *Journal of Experimental Psychology: General, 122*, 139–154.

Jacoby, L. L., Woloshyn, V., & Kelley, C. (1989). Becoming famous without being recognized: Unconscious influences of memory produced by dividing attention. *Journal of Experimental Psychology: General, 118*, 115–125.

Jarvik, M. E., & Essman, W. B. (1960). A simple one-trial learning situation for mice. *Psychological Reports, 6*, 290.

Jeffries, R. P., Polson, P. G., Razran, L., & Atwood, M. (1977). A process model for missionaries–cannibals and other river-crossing problems. *Cognitive Psychology, 9*, 412–440.

Jenkins, H. M., & Harrison, R. H. (1960). Effects of discrimination training on auditory generalization. *Journal of Experimental Psychology, 59*, 246–253.

Jenkins, H. M., & Harrison, R. H. (1962). Generalization gradients of inhibition following auditory discrimination learning. *Journal of the Experimental Analysis of Behavior, 5*, 435–441.

Jenkins, H. M., & Moore, B. R. (1973). The form of the auto-shaped response with food or water reinforcers. *Journal of the Experimental Analysis of Behavior, 5*, 435–441.

Jenkins, H. M., & Ward, W. C. (1965). Judgment of contingency between responses and outcomes. *Psychological Monographs: General and Applied, 79* (1, Whole No. 594), 1–17.

Jenkins, J. G., & Dallenbach, K. M. (1924). Oblivisence during sleep and waking. *American Journal of Psychology, 35*, 605–612.

Johansson, R. S., & Westling, G. (1984). Roles of glabrous skin receptors and sensorimotor memory in automatic control of precision grip when lifting rougher or more slippery objects. *Experimental Brain Research, 56*, 560–564.

Johnson, D. D., & Baumann, J. F. (1984). Word identification. In P. D. Pearson, R. Barr, M. Kamil, & P. Mosenthal (Eds.), *Handbook of reading research*. New York: Longman.

Bibliography

Johnson, D. M. (1972). *A systematic introduction to the psychology of thinking*. New York: Harper & Row.

Johnson, E. E. (1952). The role of motivational strength in latent learning. *Journal of Comparative Physiological Psychology, 45*, 526–530.

Johnson, N. F. (1970). The role of chunking and organization in process recall. In G. H. Bower (Ed.), *Psychology of language and motivation*, Vol. 4. New York: Academic Press.

Jones, W. P., & Anderson, J. R. (1987). Short- and long-term memory retrieval: A comparison of the effects of information load and relatedness. *Journal of Experimental Psychology: General, 116*, 137–153.

Just, M. A., & Carpenter, P. A. (1987). *The psychology of reading and language comprehension*. Newton, MA: Allyn & Bacon.

Kaiser, M. K, McCloskey, M., & Proffitt, D. R. (1986). Development of intuitive theories of motion: Curvilinear motion in the absence of external forces. *Developmental Psychology, 22*, 67–71.

Kaiser, M. K., & Proffitt, D. R. (1984). The development of sensitivity to causally relevant dynamic information. *Child Development, 55*, 1614–1624.

Kaiser, M. K., Proffitt, D. R., & McCloskey, M. (1985). The development of beliefs about falling objects. *Perception and Psychophysics, 38*, 533–539.

Kamil, A. C. (1978). Systematic foraging by a nectar-feeding bird, the Amakihi (*Loxops virens*). *Journal of Comparative Physiological Psychology, 92*, 388–396.

Kamil, A. C., Yoerg, S. I., & Clements, K. C. (1988). Rules to leave by: Patch departure in foraging blue jays. *Animal Behavior, 36*, 843–853.

Kamin, L. J. (1968). "Attention-like" processes in classical conditioning. In M. R. Jones (Ed.), *Miami Symposium on the Prediction of Behavior: Aversive stimulation* (pp. 9–31). Miami, FL: University of Miami Press.

Kamin, L. J. (1969). Predictability, surprise, attention, and conditioning. In B. A. Campbell & R. M Church (Eds.), *Punishment and aversive behavior* (pp. 279–296). New York: Appleton-Century-Crofts.

Kandel, E. R. (1976). *Cellular basis of behavior: An introduction to behavioral neurobiology*. New York: Freeman.

Kandel, E. R., & Hawkins, R. D. (1992). The biological basis of learning and individuality. *Scientific American, 267*, 78–87.

Kandel, E. R., & Schwartz, J. H. (Eds.). (1985). *Principles of neural science* (2nd ed.). New York: Elsevier.

Kandel, E. R., Schwartz, J. H., & Jessell, T. M. (Eds.). (1991). *Principles of neural science*. New York: Elsevier.

Kaplan, C. A. (1989). *Hatching a theory of incubation: Does putting a problem aside really help? If so, why?* Unpublished doctoral dissertation, Carnegie Mellon University. Pittsburgh, PA.

Katz, B. (1952). The nerve impulse. *Scientific American, 187*, 55–64.

Keele, S. W. (1987). Sequencing and timing in skilled perception and action: An overview. In A. Allport, D. G. McKay, & W. Prinz (Eds.), *Language perception and production: Relationships between listening, speaking, reading, and writing* (pp. 463–487). London: Academic Press.

Keeton, W. T. (1980). *Biological science*. New York: W. W. Norton.

Kehoe, E. J., & Gormezano, I. (1980). Configuration and combination laws in conditioning with compound stimuli. *Psychological Bulletin, 87*, 351–387.

Keith, J. R., & Rudy, J. W. (1990). Why NMDA-receptor-dependent long-term potentiation may not be a mechanism of learning and memory: Reappraisal of the NMDA-receptor blockade strategy. *Psychobiology, 18*, 251–257.

Keller, F. S. (1968). "Good-bye teacher. . . ." *Journal of Applied Behavior Analysis, 1,* 78–89.

Kellogg, W. N., & Kellogg, L. A. (1933). *The ape and the child.* New York: McGraw-Hill.

Keppel, G. (1964). Facilitation in short- and long-term retention of paired associates following distributed practice in learning. *Journal of Verbal Learning and Verbal Behavior, 3,* 91–111.

Keppel, G., Postman, L., & Zavortnik, B. (1968). Studies of learning to learn: VIII. The influence of massive amounts of training upon the learning and retention of paired-associate lists. *Journal of Verbal Learning and Verbal Behavior, 7,* 790–796.

Keppel, G., & Underwood, B. J. (1962). Proactive inhibition in short-term retention of single items. *Journal of Verbal Learning and Verbal Behavior, 1,* 153–161.

Kimble, G. A. (1961). *Conditioning and learning* (2nd ed.). New York: Appleton-Century-Crofts.

Kintsch, W. (1970a). *Learning, memory, and conceptual processes.* New York: Wiley.

Kintsch, W. (1970b). Models for free recall and recognition. In D. A. Norman (Ed.), *Models of human memory.* New York: Academic Press.

Kintsch, W. (1974). *The representation of meaning in memory.* Hillsdale, NJ: Erlbaum.

Kintsch, W., & Buschke, H. (1969). Homophones and synonyms in short-term memory. *Journal of Experimental Psychology, 80,* 403–407.

Kintsch, W., & van Dijk, T. A. (1978). Toward a model of text comprehension and reproduction. *Psychological Review, 85,* 363–394.

Klahr, D., & Dunbar, K. (1988). Dual space search during scientific reasoning. *Cognitive Science, 12,* 1–55.

Klahr, D., Fay, A. L., & Dunbar, K. (1993). Heuristics for scientific experimentation: A developmental study. *Cognitive Psychology, 25,* 111–146.

Klahr, D., Langley, P., & Neches, R. (Eds.). (1987). *Production system models of learning and development.* Cambridge, MA: MIT Press.

Klatzky, R. L. (1979). *Human memory.* New York: W. H. Freeman.

Klein, S. B., & Mowrer, R. R. (Eds.). (1989). *Contemporary learning theories: Instrumental conditioning theory and the impact of biological constraints on learning.* Hillsdale, NJ: Erlbaum.

Kleinsmith, L. J., & Kaplan, S. (1963). Paired associate learning as a function of arousal and interpolated interval. *Journal of Experimental Psychology, 65,* 190–193.

Koh, K., & Meyer, D. E. (1991). Function learning: Induction of continuous stimulus–response relations. *Journal of Experimental Psychology: Learning, Memory, and Cognition, 17,* 811–836.

Köhler, W. (1927). *The mentality of apes.* New York: Harcourt, Brace.

Köhler, W. (1955). Simple structural functions in the chimpanzee and in the chicken. In W. D. Ellis (Ed.), *A source book on Gestalt psychology.* London: Routledge & Kegan Paul.

Konarski, E. A., Jr. (1979). *The necessary and sufficient conditions for increasing instrumental responding in the classroom: Response deprivation vs. probability differential.* Unpublished doctoral dissertation, University of Notre Dame, Notre Dame, IN.

Konarski, E. A., Jr., Johnson, M. R., Crowell, C., & Whitman, T. L. (1980). *Response deprivation, reinforcement, and instrumental academic performance in an EMR classroom.* Paper presented at the 13th annual Gatlinburg Conference on Research in Mental Retardation and Developmental Disabilities, Gatlinburg, TN.

Krueger, W. C. F. (1929). The effects of overlearning on retention. *Journal of Experimental Psychology, 12,* 71–78.

Bibliography

Kulik, C., Kulik, J., & Bangert-Downs, R. (1986). *Effects of testing for mastery on student learning*. Paper presented at the annual meeting of the American Educational Research Association, San Francisco.

Laird, J. D., Wagner, J. J., Halal, M., & Szegda, M. (1982). Remembering what you feel: Effects of emotion on memory. *Journal of Personality of Social Psychology, 42,* 646–657.

Landauer, T. K. (1975). Memory without organization: Properties of a model with random storage and undirected retrieval. *Cognitive Psychology, 7,* 495–531.

Landfield, P. W., & Deadwyler, S. A. (Eds.). (1988). *Neurology and neurobiology: Vol. 35. Long-term potentiation: From biophysics to behavior.* New York: Alan R. Liss, Inc.

Larkin, J. (1981). Enriching formal knowledge: A model for learning to solve textbook physics problems. In J. R. Anderson (Ed.), *Cognitive skills and their acquisition.* Hillsdale, NJ: Erlbaum.

Lashley, K. S. (1924). Studies of cerebral function in learning: V. The retention of motor habit after destruction of the so-called motor area in primates. *Arch, neuro. Psychiatry, 12,* 249-276.

Lashley, K. S. (1950). In search of the engram. *Symposia of the Society for Experimental Biology, 4: Physiological mechanisms in animal behavior.* New York: Academic Press.

Lave, J. (1988). *Cognition in practice: Mind, mathematics, and culture in everyday life.* New York: Cambridge University Press.

Lawrence, D. H., & DeRivera, J. (1954). Evidence for relational transposition. *Journal of Comparative and Physiological Psychology, 47,* 465–471.

Leaf, R. C. (1964). Avoidance response evocation as a function of prior discriminative fear conditioning under curare. *Journal of Comparative Physiological Psychology, 58,* 446–449.

Leahey, T. H. (1992). *A history of psychology.* Englewood Cliffs, NJ: Prentice-Hall.

Lennenberg, E. H. (1967). *Biological foundations of language.* New York: Wiley.

Lesgold, A. M., Resnick, L. B., & Hammond, K. (1985). Learning to read: A longitudinal study of work skill development in two curricula. In G. Waller & E. MacKinnon (Eds.), *Reading research: Advances in theory and practice* (Vol. 4). New York: Academic Press.

Levine, M. (1975). *A cognitive theory of learning.* Hillsdale, NJ: Erlbaum.

Levinger, G., & Clark, J. (1961). Emotional factors in the forgetting of word associations. *Journal of Abnormal and Social Psychology, 62,* 99–105.

Levonian, E. (1972). Retention over time in relation to arousal during learning: An explanation of discrepant results. *Acta Psychologica, 36,* 290–321.

Lewandowsky, S. (1991). Gradual unlearning and catastrophic interference: A comparison of distributed architectures. In W. E. Hockley & S. Lewandowsky (Eds.), *Relating theory and data: Essays on human memory in honor of Bennet B. Murdock.* Hillsdale, NJ: Erlbaum.

Lewicki, P., Hill, T., & Bizot, E. (1988). Acquisition of procedural knowledge about a pattern of stimuli that cannot be articulated. *Cognitive Psychology, 20,* 24–37.

Lewis, C. H. (1978). *Production system models of practice effects.* Unpublished doctoral dissertation, University of Michigan, Ann Arbor.

Lewis, C. H., & Anderson, J. R. (1976). Interference with real world knowledge. *Cognitive Psychology, 7,* 311–335.

Lieberman, P. (1984). *The biology and evolution of language.* Cambridge, MA: Harvard University Press.

Bibliography

Light, J. S., & Gantt, W. H. (1936). Essential part of reflex are for establishment of conditioned reflex. Formation of conditioned reflex after exclusion of motor peripheral end. *Journal of Comparative Psychology, 21*, 19–36.

Loftus, E. F. (1979). *Eyewitness testimony*. Cambridge, MA: Harvard University Press.

Loftus, E. F., & Burns, T. E. (1982). Mental shock can produce retrograde amnesia. *Memory and Cognition, 10*, 318–323.

Loftus, G. R. (1972). Eye fixations and recognition memory for pictures. *Cognitive Psychology, 3*, 525–551.

Loftus, G. R., & Patterson, K. K. (1975). Components of short-term proactive interference. *Journal of Verbal Learning and Verbal Behavior, 14*, 105–121.

Logan, G. D. (1988). Toward an instance theory of automatization. *Psychological Review, 96*, 492–527.

Lundberg, I. (1985). Longitudinal studies of reading and reading difficulties in Sweden. In G. E. MacKinnon & T. G. Waller (Eds.), *Reading research: Advances in theory and practice* (Vol. 4, pp. 65–105). Orlando, FL: Academic Press.

Lundberg, I., Frost, J., & Petersen, O. P. (1988). Effects of an extensive program for stimulating phonological awareness in preschool children. *Reading Research Quarterly, 23*, 263–284.

MacCorquodale, K. O. (1970). On Chomsky's review of Skinner's *Verbal Behavior*. *Journal of the Experimental Analysis of Behavior, 13*, 83–99.

Macfarlane, D. A. (1930). The role of kinesthesis in maze learning. *California University Publication Psychology, 4*, 277–305.

MacKay, D. G. (1982). The problem of flexibility, fluency, and speed-accuracy trade-off in skilled behavior. *Psychological Review, 89*, 483–506.

Mackintosh, N. J. (1974). *The psychology of animal learning*. New York: Academic Press.

Mackintosh, N. J. (1975). A theory of attention: Variations in the associability of stimuli with reinforcement. *Psychological Review, 82*, 276–298.

Mackintosh, N. J., & Little, L. (1969). Intradimensional and extradimensional shift learning by pigeons. *Psychonomic Science, 14*, 5–6.

MacPhail, E. M. (1968). Avoidance responding in pigeons. *Journal of the Experimental Analysis of Behavior, 11*, 625–632.

MacWhinney, B. (1993). The (il)logical problem of language acquisition. *Proceedings of the 15th Annual Conference of the Cognitive Science Society* (pp. 61–70). University of Boulder, CO. Hillsdale, NJ: Erlbaum.

MacWhinney, B., & Leinbach, J. (1991). Implementations are not conceptualizations: Revising the verb learning model. *Cognition, 29*, 121–157.

Maier, S. F., Jackson, R. L., & Tomie, A. (1987). Potentiation, overshadowing, and prior exposure to inescapable shock. *Journal of Experimental Psychology: Animal Behavior Processes, 13*, 260–270.

Maki, W. S. (1984). Some problems for a theory of working memory. In H. L. Roitblat, T. G. Bever, & H. S. Terrace (Eds.), *Animal cognition* (pp. 117–133). Hillsdale, NJ: Erlbaum.

Maki, W. S., & Hegvik, D. K. (1980). Directed forgetting in pigeons. *Animal Learning and Behavior, 8*, 567–574.

Mandler, G. (1967). Organization and memory. In K. W. Spence & J. T. Spence (Eds.), *The psychology of learning and motivation* (Vol. 1, pp. 327–372). New York: Academic Press.

Mandler, J. M., & Ritchey, G. H. (1977). Long-term memory for pictures. *Journal of Experimental Psychology: Human Learning and Memory, 3*, 386–396.

Massaro, D. W. (1989). *Experimental psychology: An information processing approach*. San Diego: Harcourt Brace Jovanovich.

Masson, M. E. J., & MacLeod, C. M. (1992). Reenacting the route to interpretation: Enhanced identification without prior perception. *Journal of Experimental Psychology: General, 121*, 145–176.

Mayer, R. E. (1987). *Educational psychology: A cognitive approach*. Boston: Little, Brown.

Mazur, J. E. (1990). *Learning and behavior* (2nd ed.). Englewood Cliffs, NJ: Prentice-Hall.

Mazur, J. E. (1994) *Learning and behavior* (3rd ed.). Englewood Cliffs, NJ: Prentice-Hall.

McAllister, W. R. (1953). Eyelid conditioning as a function of the CS–UCS interval. *Journal of Experimental Psychology, 45*, 417–422.

McCoskey, M. (1983). Intuitive physics. *Scientific American, 248*, 122–130.

McCloskey, M., & Cohen, N. J. (1989). Catastrophic interference in connectionist networks: The sequential learning problem. In G. H. Bower (Ed.), *The psychology of learning and motivation, 24*, 109–164. New York: Academic Press.

McCloskey, M. E., & Glucksberg, S. (1978). Natural categories. Well-defined or fuzzy sets? *Memory and Cognition, 6*, 462–472.

McCloskey, M., Wible, C. G., & Cohen, N. J. (1988). Is there a special flashbulb-memory mechanism? *Journal of Experimental Psychology: General, 117*, 171–181.

McConkie, G. W., & Rayner, K. (1974). *Identifying the span of the effective stimulus in reading*. (Final Report OEG 2-71-0531). U. S. Office of Education.

McDaniel, M. A., & Einstein, G. O. (1986). Bizarre imagery as an effective memory aid: The importance of distinctiveness. *Journal of Experimental Psychology: Learning, Memory, and Cognition, 12*, 54–65.

McDaniel, M. A., Waddill, P. J., & Einstein, G. O. (1988). A contextual account of the generation effect: A three factor theory. *Journal of Memory and Language, 27*, 521–536.

McGaugh, J. L., & Dawson, R. G. (1971). Modification of memory storage processes. *Behavioral Science, 16*, 45–63.

McGeoch, J. A. (1932). Forgetting and the law of disuse. *Psychological Review, 39*, 352–370.

McGeoch, J. A. (1942). *The psychology of human learning*. New York: Longmans, Green.

McKeithen, K. B., Reitman, J. S., Rueter, H. H., & Hirtle, S. C. (1981). Knowledge organization and skill differences in computer programmers. *Cognitive Psychology, 13*, 307–325.

McKnight, C. C., Crosswhite, F. J., Dossey, J. A., Kifer, E., Swafford, J.O., Travers, K. J., & Cooney, T. J. (1990). *The underachieving curriculum: Assessing U. S. school mathematics from an international perspective*. Champaign, IL: Stipes Publishing Company.

McNamara, T. P., Hardy, J. K., & Hirtle, S. C. (1989). Subjective hierarchies in spatial memory. *Journal of Experimental Psychology: Learning, Memory, and Cognition, 15*, 211–227.

McNeill, D. (1966). Developmental psycholinguistics. In F. Smith & G. A. Miller (Eds.), *The genesis of language: A psycholinguistic approach*. Cambridge, MA: MIT Press.

McRae, K., & Hetherington, P. A. (1993). Catastrophic interference is eliminated in pretrained networks. *Proceedings of the 15th Annual Conference of the Cognitive Science Society* (pp. 723–728).

Medin, D. L., & Schaffer, M. M. (1978). Context theory of classification learning. *Psychological Review, 85*, 207–238.

Bibliography

Melton, A. W. (1963). Implications of short-term memory for a general theory of memory. *Journal of Verbal Learning and Verbal Behavior, 2,* 1–21.

Meltzer, H. (1930). Individual differences in forgetting pleasant and unpleasant experiences. *Journal of Educational Psychology, 21,* 399–409.

Meyer, G. J. F., Brandt, D. M., & Bluth, G. J. (1978). *Use of author's textual schema: Key for ninth-grader's comprehension.* Paper presented at the annual conference of the American Educational Research Association, Toronto.

Michotte, A. (1946). *La perception de la causalité.* Paris: Vrin.

Milberg, W., Alexander, M. P., Charness, N., McGlinchey-Berroth, R., & Barrett, A. (1988). Complex arithmetic skill in amnesia: Evidence for a dissociation between compilation and production. *Brain and Cognition, 8,* 77–90.

Miller, G. A. (1956). The magical number seven plus or minus two: Some limits on our capacity for processing information. *Psychological Review, 63,* 81–97.

Miller, N. E. (1960). The value of behavioral research on animals. *American Psychologist, 40,* 423–440.

Miller, R. R., & Spear, N. E. (1985). *Information processing in animals: Conditioned inhibition.* Hillsdale, NJ: Erlbaum.

Moore, J. W., & Gormezano, I. (1961). Yoked comparisons of instrumental and classical eyelid conditioning. *Journal of Experimental Psychology, 62,* 552–559.

Moray, N., Bates, A., & Barnett, T. (1965). Experiments on the four-eared man. *Journal of the Acoustical Society of America, 38,* 196–201.

Morris, C. D., Bransford, J. D., & Franks, J. J. (1977). Levels of processing versus transfer appropriate processing. *Journal of Verbal Learning and Verbal Behavior, 16,* 519–533.

Morris, R. G. M. (1981). Spatial localization does not require the presence of local cues. *Learning and Motivation, 12,* 239–260.

Morris, R. G. M. (1990). It's heads they win, tails I lose. *Psychobiology, 18,* 261–266.

Morris, R. G. M., Anderson, E., Lynch, G. S., & Baudry, M. (1986). Selective impairment of learning and blockade of long-term potentiation by an N-methyl-D-aspartate receptor antagonist, AP5. *Nature, 319,* 774–776.

Morris, R. G. M., Garrud, P., Rawlins, J. N. P., & O'Keefe, W. (1982). Place navigation is impaired in animals with hippocampal lesions. *Nature (London), 297,* 681–683.

Muenzinger, K. F. (1928). Plasticity and mechanization of the problem box habit in guinea pigs. *Journal of Comparative Psychology, 8,* 45–69.

Murdock, B. B., Jr. (1961). The retention of individual items. *Journal of Experimental Psychology, 62,* 618-625.

Murdock, B. B., Jr. (1974). *Human memory: Theory and data.* Hillsdale, NJ: Erlbaum.

Nathan, P. E. (1976). Alcoholism. In H. Leitenberg (Ed.), *Handbook of behavior modification and behavior therapy.* Englewood Cliffs, NJ: Prentice-Hall.

Neisser, U. (1967). *Cognitive psychology.* New York: Appleton.

Neisser, U. (1982). *Memory observed.* San Francisco: W. H. Freeman.

Nelson, T. O. (1971). Savings and forgetting from long-term memory. *Journal of Verbal Learning and Verbal Behavior, 10,* 568–576.

Nelson, T. O. (1976). Reinforcement and human memory. In W. K. Estes (Ed.), *Handbook of learning and cognitive processes* (Vol. 3). Hillsdale, NJ: Erlbaum.

Nelson, T. O. (1977). Repetition and depth of processing. *Journal of Verbal Learning and Verbal Behavior, 16,* 151–172.

Nelson, T. O. (1978). Detecting small amounts of information in memory: Savings for nonrecognized items. *Journal of Experimental Psychology: Human Learning and Memory, 4,* 453–468.

Nelson, T. O., Gerber, D., & Narens, L. (1984). Accuracy of feeling-of-knowing judgments for predicting perceptual identification and relearning. *Journal of Experimental Psychology: General, 113,* 282–300.

Neves, D. M. (1977). *An experimental analysis of strategies of the Tower of Hanoi puzzle* (C.I.P. Working Paper No. 362). Pittsburgh, PA: Carnegie Mellon University.

Neves, D. M., & Anderson, J. R. (1981). Knowledge compilation: Mechanisms for the automatization of cognitive skills. In J. R. Anderson (Ed.), *Cognitive skills and their acquisition.* Hillsdale, NJ: Erlbaum.

Newell, A. (1991). *Unified theories of cognition.* Cambridge, MA: Harvard University Press.

Newell, A., & Rosenbloom, P. S. (1981). Mechanisms of skill acquisition and the law of practice. In J. R. Anderson (Ed.), *Cognitive skills and their acquisition.* Hillsdale, NJ: Erlbaum.

Newell, A., & Simon, H. A. (1961). GPS, a program that simulates human thought. In H. Billing (Ed.), *Lernende Automaten* (pp. 109–124). Munich: R. Oldenbourg.

Newell, A., & Simon, H. A. (1972). *Human problem solving.* Englewood Cliffs, NJ: Prentice-Hall.

Newport, E. L. (1986, October 17–19). *The effect of maturational state on the acquisition of language.* Paper presented at the 11th Annual Boston University Conference on Language Development.

Newport, E. L. (1990). Maturational constraints on language learning. *Cognitive Science, 14,* 11–28.

Nissen, M. J., & Bullemer, P. (1987). Attentional requirements of learning: Evidence from performance measures. *Cognitive Psychology, 19,* 1–32.

Nosofsky, R. (1988). Similarity, frequency, and category representation. *Journal of Experimental Psychology: Learning, Memory, and Cognition, 10,* 104–114.

Nottebohm, F. (1970). The ontogeny of birdsong. *Science, 167,* 950–956.

Noyd, D. E. (1965). *Proactive and intra-stimulus interference in short-term memory for two-, three- and five-word stimuli.* Paper presented at the meeting of the Western Psychological Association, Honolulu, HI.

Obrist, P. A., Sutterer, J. R., & Howard, J. L. (1972). Preparatory cardiac changes: A psychobiological approach. In A. H. Black & W. F. Prokasy (Eds.), *Classical conditioning II.* New York: Appleton-Century-Crofts.

Ohlsson, S. (1992). The learning curve for writing books: Evidence from Professor Asimov. *Psychological Science, 3,* 380–382.

O'Keefe, J., & Nadel, L. (1978). *The hippocampus as a cognitive map.* Oxford: Clarendon Press.

Olds, J., & Milner, P. (1954). Positive reinforcement produced by electrical stimulation of septal area and other regions of rat brain. *Journal of Comparative Physiology and Psychology, 47,* 419–427.

Olton, D. S. (1978). Characteristics of spatial memory. In S. H. Hulse, H. Fowler, & W. K. Honig (Eds.), *Cognitive processes in animal behavior.* Hillsdale, NJ: Erlbaum.

Olton, D. S., Becker, J. T., & Handelmann, G. E. (1979). Hippocampus, space and memory. *Behavioral and Brain Sciences, 2,* 313–365.

Olton, D. S., & Samuelson, R. J. (1976). Remembrance of places passed: Spatial memory in rats. *Journal of Experimental Psychology: Animal Behavior Processes, 2,* 97–116.

Osherson, D. N., Kosslyn, S. M., & Hollerbach, J. M. (Eds.). (1990). *Visual cognition and action: An invitation to cognitive science* (Vol. 2). Cambridge, MA: MIT Press.

Owens, J., Bower, G. H., & Black, J. B. (1979). The "soap opera" effect in story recall. *Memory and Cognition, 7,* 185–191.

Bibliography

Paivio, A. (1971). *Imagery and verbal processes*. New York: Holt, Rinehart, & Winston.

Palinscar, A. S., & Brown, A. L. (1984). Reciprocal teaching of comprehension-fostering and comprehension-monitoring activities. *Cognition and Instruction, 1,* 117–175.

Palmer, S., Schreiber, G., & Fox, C. (1991, November 22–24). *Remembering the earthquake: "Flashbulb" memory of experienced versus reported events*. Paper presented at the 32nd annual meeting of the Psychonomic Society, San Francisco.

Parkin, A. J., Lewinsohn, J., & Folkard, S. (1982). The influence of emotion on immediate and delayed retention: Levinger and Clark reconsidered. *British Journal of Psychology, 73,* 389–393.

Pavlov, I. P. (1927). *Conditoned reflexes*. Oxford: Oxford University Press.

Payne, J. W., Bettman, J. R., & Johnson, E. J. (1988). Adaptive strategy selection in decision making. *Journal of Experimental Psychology: Learning, Memory, and Cognition, 14,* 534–552.

Pearce, J. M., & Hall, G. (1980). A model for Pavlovian learning: Variations in the effectiveness of conditioned but not unconditioned stimuli. *Psychological Review, 87,* 532–552.

Perfetti, C. A. (1985). *Reading ability*. New York: Oxford University Press.

Peters, D. P. (1988). Eyewitness memory and arousal in a natural setting. In M. M. Gruneberg, P. E. Morris, & R. N. Sykes (Eds.), *Practical aspects of memory: Current research and issues: Vol. 1. Memory in everyday life* (pp. 89–94). Chichester, England: Wiley.

Peterson, L. R., & Peterson, M. (1959). Short-term retention of individual items. *Journal of Experimental Psychology, 58,* 193–198.

Peterson, S. B., & Potts, G. R. (1982). Global and specific components of information integration. *Journal of Verbal Learning and Verbal Behavior, 21,* 403–420.

Phelps, E. A. (1989). *Cognitive skill learning in amnesics*. Unpublished doctoral dissertation, Princeton University, Princeton, NJ.

Pinker, S. (1989). Language acquisition. In M. I. Posner (Ed.), *Foundations of cognitive science*. Cambridge, MA: MIT Press.

Pinker, S., & Prince, A. (1988). On language and connectionism: Analysis of a parallel distributed processing model of language acquisition. *Cognition, 28,* 73–193.

Pirolli, P. L., & Anderson, J. R. (1985). The role of practice in fact retrieval. *Journal of Experimental Psychology: Learning, Memory, and Cognition, 11,* 136–153.

Polson, M., & Richardson, J. (Eds.). (1988). *Handbook of intelligent training systems*. Hillsdale, NJ: Erlbaum

Porter, D. (1961). *An application of reinforcement principles to classroom teaching*. Cambridge, MA: Harvard University, Graduate School of Education, Laboratory for Research in Instruction.

Postman, L. (1964). Short-term memory and incidental learning. In A. W. Melton (Ed.), *Categories of human learning*. New York: Academic Press.

Postman, L. (1974). Transfer, interference, and forgetting. In L. W. Kling & L. A. Riggs (Eds.), *Experimental psychology*. New York: Holt, Rinehart, & Winston.

Postman, L., Stark, K., & Fraser, J. (1968). Temporal changes in interference. *Journal of Verbal Learning and Verbal Behavior, 7,* 672–694.

Potter, M. C., & Lombardi, L. (1990). Regeneration in the short-term recall of sentences. *Journal of Memory and Language, 29,* 633–654.

Premack, D. (1959). Toward empirical behavioral laws: I. Positive reinforcement. *Psychological Review, 66,* 219–233.

Premack, D. (1962). Reversibility of the reinforcement relation. *Science, 136,* 235–237.

Premack, D. (1965). Reinforcement theory. In D. Levine (Ed.), *Nebraska Symposium on Motivation*. Lincoln: University of Nebraska Press.

Premack, D. (1971). Catching up with common sense or two sides of a generalization: Reinforcement and punishment. In R. Glaser (Ed.), *The nature of reinforcement*. New York: Academic Press.

Premack, D. (1976). *Intelligence in ape and man*. Hillsdale, NJ: Erlbaum.

Premack, D., & Premack, A. J. (1983). *The mind of an ape*. New York: W. W. Norton.

Prokasy, W. F. (Ed.). (1965). *Classical conditioning: A symposium*. New York: Appleton-Century-Crofts.

Prokasy, W. F., Grant, D. A., & Myers, N. A. (1958). Eyelid conditioning as a function of UCS intensity and intertrial interval. *Journal of Experimental Psychology, 55*, 242–246.

Raaijmakers, J. G. W., & Shiffrin, R. M. (1981). Search of associative memory. *Psychological Review, 88*, 93–134.

Rabinowitz, J. C., Mandler, G., & Barsalou, L. W. (1977). Recognition failure: Another case of retrieval failure. *Journal of Verbal Learning and Verbal Behavior, 16*, 639–663.

Rachlin, H. C., & Green, L. (1972). Commitment, choice, and self-control. *Journal of the Experimental Analysis of Behavior, 17*, 15–22.

Raibert, M. H. (1977). *Motor control and learning by the state-space model* (Tech. Rep. No. AI-TR-439). Cambridge, MA: MIT, AI Laboratory.

Rashotte, M. E., Griffin, R. W., & Sisk, C. L. (1977). Second-order conditioning of the pigeon's keypeck. *Animal Learning and Behavior, 5*, 25–38.

Ratcliff, R. (1990). Connectionist models of recognition memory: Constraints imposed by learning and forgetting functions. *Psychological Review, 97*, 285–308.

Raymond, M. J. (1964). The treatment of addiction by aversion conditioning with apomorphine. *Behavior Research and Therapy, 1*, 287–291.

Razran, G. (1971). *Mind in evolution: An East/West synthesis of learned behavior and cognition*. Boston: Houghton Mifflin.

Reder, L. M. (1987). Strategy selection in question answering. *Cognitive Psychology, 19*, 90–138.

Reder, L. M., & Gordon, J.S. (in press). Subliminal perception: Nothing special cognitively speaking. To appear in: Cohen, J. and Schooler, J. (Eds.) *Cognitive and neuropsychological approaches to the study of consciousness*. Hillsdale, NJ: Erlbaum.

Reder, L. M., Nelson, S., & Stroffolino, P. (In preparation). Understanding cognitive illusions: The role of activation in misattributions in memory.

Reiss, S., & Wagner, A. R. (1972). CS habituation produces a "latent inhibition" effect but no active conditioned inhibition. *Learning and Motivation, 3*, 237–245.

Reitman, J. (1976). Skilled perception in GO: Deducing memory structures from interresponse times. *Cognitive Psychology, 8*, 336–356.

Reitman, W. (1965). *Cognition and thought*. New York: Wiley.

Rescorla, R. A. (1968a). Pavlovian conditioned fear in Sidman avoidance learning. *Journal of Comparative and Physiological Psychology, 65*, 55–60.

Rescorla, R. A. (1968b). Probability of shock in the presence and absence of CS in fear conditioning. *Journal of Comparative and Physiological Psychology, 66*, 1–5.

Rescorla, R. A. (1973). Effect of US habituation following conditioning. *Journal of Comparative Physiological Psychology, 82*, 137–143.

Rescorla, R. A. (1988a). Facilitation based on inhibition. *Animal Learning and Behavior, 16*, 169–176.

Rescorla, R. A. (1988b). Pavlovian conditioning: It's not what you think it is. *American Psychologist, 43*, 151–160.

Rescorla, R. A., & Wagner, A. R. (1972). A theory of Pavlovian conditioning: Variations on the effectiveness of reinforcement and nonreinforcement. In A. H. Black & W. F. Prokasy (Eds.), *Classical conditioning: II. Current research and theory* (pp. 64–99). New York: Appleton-Century-Crofts.

Resnick, D. P., & Resnick, L. B. (1977). The nature of literacy: An historical exploration. *Harvard Educational Review, 47*, 370–385.

Resnick, L. B. (1977). Assuming that everyone can learn everything, will some learn less? *School Review, 85*, 445-452.

Restle, F. (1957). Discrimination of cues in mazes: A resolution of the "place-vs.-response" question. *Psychology Review, 64*, 217–228.

Rich, E. (1983). *Artificial intelligence*. New York: McGraw-Hill.

Rilling, M. (1977). Stimulus control and inhibitory processes. In W. K. Honig & J. E. R. Staddon (Eds.), *Handbook of operant behavior*. Englewood Cliffs, NJ: Prentice-Hall.

Rizley, R. C., & Rescorla, R. A. (1972). Associations in higher order conditioning and sensory preconditioning. *Journal of Comparative Physiological Psychology, 81*, 1–11.

Roberts, W. A. (1984). Some issues in animal spatial memory. In H. L. Roitblat, T. G. Bever, & H. S. Terrace (Eds.), *Animal cognition* (pp. 425–443). Hillsdale, NJ: Erlbaum.

Roberts, W. A., & Grant, D. S. (1978). An analysis of light-induced retroactive inhibition in pigeon short-term memory. *Journal of Experimental Psychology: Animal Behavior Processes, 4*, 219–236.

Robinson, F. P. (1961). *Effective study*. New York: Harper & Row.

Robinson, G. S., Jr., Crooks, G. B., Jr., Stinkman, P. G., & Gallagher, M. (1989). Behavioral effects of MK-901 mimic deficits associated with hippocampal damage. *Psychobiology, 17*, 156–164.

Roediger, H. L. (1990). Implicit memory: Retention without remembering. *American Psychologist, 45*, 1043–1056.

Roediger, H. L., & Blaxton, T. A. (1987). Retrieval modes produce dissociations in memory for surface information. In D. Gorfein & R. R. Hoffman (Eds.), *Memory and cognitive processes: The Ebbinghaus Centennial Conference* (pp. 349–379). Hillsdale, NJ: Erlbaum.

Roitblat, H. L. (1987). *Introduction to comparative cognition*. New York: W. H. Freeman.

Roitblat, H. L., Bever, T. G., & Terrace, H. S. (1984). *Animal cognition*. Hillsdale, NJ: Erlbaum.

Rosch, E. (1973). On the internal structure of perceptual and semantic categories. In T. E. Moore (Ed.), *Cognitive development and the acquisition of language*. New York: Academic Press.

Rosch, E. (1975). Cognitive representations of semantic categories. *Journal of Experimental Psychology: General, 104*, 192–223.

Rosch, E. (1977). Human categorization. In N. Warren (Ed.), *Advances in cross-cultural Psychology* (Vol. 1). London: Academic Press.

Rosenbaum, D. A. (1991). *Human motor control*. San Diego: Academic Press.

Rosenbaum, D. A., Inhoff, A. W., & Gordon, A. M. (1984). Choosing between movement sequences: A hierarchical editor model. *Journal of Experimental Psychology: General, 113*, 372–393.

Ross, J., & Lawrence, K. A. (1968). Some observations on memory artifice. *Psychonomic Science, 13*, 107–108.

Ross, L. E. (1965). Eyelid conditioning as a tool in psychological research: Some problems and prospects. In W. F. Prokasy (Ed.), *Classical conditioning* (pp. 249–268). New York: Appleton-Century-Crofts.

Rumelhart, D. E. (1975). Notes on a schema for stories. In D. G. Bobrow & A. M. Collins (Eds.), *Representation and understanding.* New York: Academic Press.

Rumelhart, D. E., & McClelland, J. L. (1986). *Parallel distributed processing: Explorations in the microstructure of cognition* (Vol. 1). Cambridge, MA: MIT Press/Bradford Books.

Rundus, D. J. (1971). Analysis of rehearsal processes in free recall. *Journal of Experimental Psychology, 89,* 63–77.

St. Claire-Smith, R., & MacLaren, D. (1983). Response preconditioning effects. *Journal of Experimental Psychology, 1,* 41–48.

Sakitt, B. (1976). Iconic memory. *Psychological Review, 83,* 257–276.

Salmoni, A. W., Schmidt, R. A., & Walter, C. B. (1984). Knowledge of results and motor learning: A review and critical reappraisal. *Psychological Bulletin, 95,* 355–386.

Salthouse, T. A. (1985). Anticipatory processes in transcription typing. *Journal of Applied Psychology, 70,* 264–271.

Salthouse, T. A. (1986). Perceptual, cognitive, and motoric aspects of transcription typing. *Psychological Bulletin, 99,* 303–319.

Saltzman, I. J. (1949). Maze learning in the absence of primary reinforcement: A study of secondary reinforcement. *Journal of Comparative and Physiological Psychology, 42,* 161–173.

Santa, J. L. (1977). Spatial transformations of words and pictures. *Journal of Experimental Psychology: Human Learning and Memory, 3,* 418–427.

Saufley, W. H., Otaka, S. R., & Bavaresco, J. L. (1985). Context effects: Classroom tests and context independence. *Memory and Cognition, 13,* 522–528.

Schacter, D. L. (1987). Implicit memory: History and current status. *Journal of Experimental Psychology: Learning, Memory, and Cognition, 13,* 501–518.

Schacter, D. L., Cooper, L. A., Delaney, S. M., Peterson, M. A., & Tharan, M. (1991). Implicit memory for possible and impossible objects: Constraints on the construction of structural descriptions. *Journal of Experimental Psychology: Learning, Memory, and Cognition, 17,* 3–19.

Schmidt, R. A. (1988a). Motor and action perspectives on motor behavior. In O. G. Meijer & K. Rother (Eds.), *Complex movement behavior: The motor–action controversy* (pp. 3–44). Amsterdam: Elsevier.

Schmidt, R. A. (1988b). *Motor control and learning: A behavioral emphasis.* Champaign, IL: Human Kinetics Publishers.

Schmidt, R. A. (1991). Motor skills acquisition. In R. Dulbecco (Ed.), *Encyclopedia of human biology* (Vol. 5, pp. 121–129). Orlando, FL: Academic Press.

Schmidt, R. A., & Bjork, R. A. (1992). New conceptualizations of practice: Common principles in three paradigms suggest new concepts for training. *Psychological Research, 3,* 207–217.

Schmidt, R. A., & Shapiro, D. C. (1986). *Optimizing feedback utilization in motor skill training* (Tech. Rep. No. 1/86). Motor Control Laboratory, UCLA. (ARI Contract No. MDA-903-85-K-0225).

Schmidt, R. A., Shapiro, D. C., Winstein, C. J., Young, D. E., & Swinnen, S. (1987). *Feedback and motor skill training: Relative frequency of KR and summary KR* (Tech. Rep. No 1/87). Motor Control Laboratory, UCLA. (ARI Contract No. MDA903-85-K-0225).

Schmidt, R. A., & White, J. L. (1972). Evidence for an error detection mechanism in motor skills: A test of Adams' closed-loop theory. *Journal of Motor Behavior, 4,* 143–154.

Schneiderman, B. (1976). Exploratory experiments in programmer behavior. *International Journal of Computer and Information Sciences, 5,* 123–143.

Bibliography

Schneiderman, N. (1973). *Classical (Pavlovian) conditioning*. Morristown, NJ: General Learning Press.

Schofield, J. W., & Evans-Rhodes, D. (1989). Artificial intelligence in the classroom: The impact of a computer-based tutor on teachers and students. *Proceedings of the Fourth International Conference on AI and Education* (pp. 238–243). Amsterdam.

Schonberg, H. C. (1970). *The lives of great composers*. New York: W. W. Norton.

Schooler, L. J., & Anderson, J. R. (1990). The disruptive potential of immediate feedback. *Proceedings of the 12th Annual Conference of the Cognitive Science Society* (pp. 702–708). Cambridge, MA.

Schustack, M. W., & Sternberg, R. J. (1981). Evaluation of evidence in causal inference. *Journal of Experimental Psychology: General, 110*, 101–120.

Schwartz, B. (1973). Maintenance of keypecking in pigeons by a food avoidance but not a shock avoidance contingency. *Animal Learning and Behavior, 1*, 164–165.

Schwartz, B. (1989). *Psychology of learning and behavior* (3rd ed.). New York: W. W. Norton.

Secretary's Commission on Achieving Necessary Skills. (1991, November). *Scales for competencies and foundation skills* (Draft). Washington, DC: United States Department of Labor.

Seligman, M. E. P. (1975). *Helplessness: On depression, development and death*. San Francisco: W. H. Freeman.

Seligman, M. E. P., & Maier, S. F. (1967). Failure to escape traumatic shock. *Journal of Experimental Psychology, 74*, 1–9.

Shaklee, H., & Tucker, D. (1980). A rule analysis of judgments of covariation between events. *Memory and Cognition, 8*, 459–467.

Shapiro, D. C., & Schmidt, R. A. (1982). The schema theory: Recent evidence and developmental implications. In J. A. S. Kelso & J. E. Clark (Eds.), *The development of movement control and coordination* (pp. 113–150). New York: Wiley.

Sheffield, F. D., Wulff, J. J., & Backer, R. (1951). Reward value of copulation without sex drive reduction. *Journal of Comparative and Physiological Psychology, 44*, 3–8.

Shepard, L. A. (1991). Psychometricians' beliefs about learning. *Educational Researcher, 20*, 2–16.

Shephard, R. N. (1967). Recognition memory for words, sentence, and pictures. *Journal of Verbal Learning and Verbal Behavior, 6*, 156–163.

Shettleworth, S. J. (1975). Reinforcement and the organization of behavior in golden hamsters: Hunger, environment, and food reinforcement. *Journal of Experimental Psychology: Animal Behavior Processes, 104*, 56–87.

Shik, M. L., Severin, F. V., & Orlovskii, G. N. (1966). Control of walking and running by means of electrical stimulation of the mid-brain. *Biophysics, 11*, 756–765.

Shimp, C. P. (1969). Optimal behavior in free-operant experiments. *Psychological Review, 19*, 311–330.

Shimp, C. P. (1976). Short-term memory in the pigeon: Relative recency. *Journal of the Experimental Analysis of Behavior, 25*, 55–61.

Shrager, J. (1985). *Instructionless learning: Discovery of the mental model of a complex device*. Unpublished doctoral dissertation, Carnegie Mellon University, Pittsburgh, PA.

Shrager, J. C., Hogg, T., & Huberman, B. A. (1988). A dynamical theory of the power-law learning in problem-solving. *Proceedings of the 10th Annual Conference of the Cognitive Science Society* (pp. 468–474). Hillsdale, NJ: Cognitive Science Society.

Shultz, T. R. (1982). Rules for causal attribution. *Monographs of the Society for Research in Child Development, 47* (1, Serial No. 194).

Shultz, T. R., Fischer, G. W., Pratt, C. C., & Rulf, S. (1986). Selection of causal rules. *Child Development, 57,* 143–152.

Sidman, M. (1966). Two temporal parameters of the maintenance of avoidance behavior in the white rat. *Journal of Comparative and Physiological Psychology, 46,* 253–261.

Siegel, S. (1983). Classical conditioning, drug tolerance, and drug dependence. In Y. Israel, F. B. Glaser, H. Kalant, R. E. Popham, W. Schmidt, & R. G. Smart (Eds.), *Research advances in alcohol and drug problems* (Vol. 7). New York: Plenum.

Siegel, S., Hearst, E., George, N., & O'Neil, E. (1968). Generalization gradients obtained from individual subjects following classical conditioning. *Journal of Experimental Psychology, 78,* 171–174.

Siegler, R. S. (1988). Strategy choice procedures and the development of multiplication skill. *Journal of Experimental Psychology: General, 117,* 258–275.

Siegler, R. S., & Shrager, J. C. (1984). A model of strategy choice. In C. Sophian (Ed.), *Origin of cognitive skills* (pp. 229–293). Hillsdale, NJ: Erlbaum.

Silberberg, A., Hamilton, B., Ziriax, J. M., & Casey, J. (1978). The structure of choice. *Journal of Experimental Psychology: Animal Behavior Processes, 4,* 368–398.

Simon, H. A. (1955). A behavior model of rational choice. *Quarterly Journal of Economics, 69,* 99–118.

Simon, H. A., & Gilmartin, K. (1973). A simulation of memory for chess positions. *Cognitive Psychology, 5,* 29–46.

Singley, M. K., & Anderson, J. R. (1989). *The transfer of cognitive skill.* Cambridge, MA: Harvard University Press.

Singley, M. K., Anderson, J. R., Givens, J. S., & Hoffman, D. (1989). The algebra word problem tutor. *Artificial Intelligence and Education,* 267–275.

Skinner, B. F. (1938). *The behavior of organisms.* New York: Appleton-Century-Crofts.

Skinner, B. F. (1948). *Walden two.* New York: Macmillan.

Skinner, B. F. (1957). *Verbal behavior.* Englewood Cliffs, NJ: Prentice-Hall.

Skinner, B. F. (1971). *Beyond freedom and dignity.* New York: Knopf.

Slamecka, N. J., & Graf, P. (1978). The generation effect: Delineation of a phenomenon. *Journal of Experimental Psychology: Learning, Memory, and Cognition, 4,* 592–604.

Slamecka, N. J. & Katsaiti, L. T. (1987). The generation effect as an artifact of selective displaced rehearsal. *Journal of Memory and Language, 26,* 589–607.

Slamecka, N. J., & McElree, B. (1983). Normal forgetting of verbal lists as a function of their degree of learning. *Journal of Experimental Psychology: Learning, Memory, and Cognition, 9,* 384–397.

Slater-Hammel, A. T. (1960). Reliability, accuracy and refractoriness of a transit reaction. *Research Quarterly, 31,* 217–228.

Sloman, S. A., & Rumelhart, D. E. (1992). Reducing interference in distributed memory through episodic gating. In A. F. Healey, S. M. Kosslyn, & R. M. Shiffrin (Eds.), *From learning theory to cognitive processes: Essays in honor of William K. Estes.* Hillsdale, NJ: Erlbaum.

Smith, E. E. (1989). Concepts and induction. In M. I. Posner (Ed.), *Foundations of cognitive science* (pp. 501–526). Cambridge, MA: MIT Press.

Smith, E. E., Adams, N., & Schorr, D. (1978). Fact retrieval and the paradox of interference. *Cognitive Psychology, 10,* 438–464.

Smith, S. M., Glenberg, A., & Bjork, R. A. (1978). Environmental context and human memory. *Memory and Cognition, 6,* 342–353.

Solomon, R. L., & Corbit, J. D. (1974). An opponent-process theory of motivation: I. The temporal dynamics of affect. *Psychological Review, 81,* 119–145.

Solomon, R. L., Kamin, L. J., & Wynne, L. C. (1953). Traumatic avoidance learning: The outcomes of several extinction procedures with dogs. *Journal of Abnormal and Social Psychology, 48,* 291–302.

Solomon, R. L., & Wynne, L. C. (1953). Traumatic avoidance learning: Acquisition in normal dogs. *Psychological Monographs, 67* (Whole No. 354).

Soloway, E., Lochhead, J., & Clement, J. (1982). Does computer programming enhance problem solving ability? Some positive evidence on algebra word problems. In J. Seidel, R. E. Anderson, & B. Hunter (Eds.), *Computer literacy.* New York: Academic Press.

Spear, N. E., & Miller, R. R. (1981). *Information processing in animals: Memory mechanisms.* Hillsdale, NJ: Erlbaum.

Spelke, E., Hirst, W., & Neisser, U. (1976). Skills of divided attention. *Cognition, 4,* 215–230.

Spence, K. W. (1937). The differential response in animals to stimuli varying within a single dimension. *Psychological Review, 44,* 430–444.

Spence, K. W. (1952). The nature of the response in discrimination learning. *Psychological Review, 59,* 89–93.

Spence, K. W., & Ross, L. E. (1959). A methodological study of the form and latency of eyelid responses in conditioning. *Journal of Experimental Psychology, 58,* 376–381.

Sperling, G. A. (1960). The information available in brief visual presentation. *Psychological Monographs, 74* (Whole No. 498).

Squire, L. R. (1987). *Memory and brain.* New York: Oxford University Press.

Squire, L. R. (1989). On the course of forgetting in very long-term memory. *Journal of Experimental Psychology: Learning, Memory and Cognition, 15,* 241–245.

Squire, L. R. (1992). Memory and the hippocampus: A synthesis from findings with rats, monkeys, and humans. *Psychological Review, 99,* 195–232.

Staddon, J. E. R. (1983) *Adaptive behavior and learning.* Cambridge: Cambridge University Press.

Staddon, J. E. R., & Ettinger, R. H. (1989). *Learning: An introduction to the principles of adaptive behavior.* San Diego: Harcourt Brace Jovanovich.

Staddon, J. E. R., & Simmelhag, V. L. (1971). The "superstition" experiment: A reexamination of its implications for the principles of adaptive behavior. *Psychological Review, 78,* 3–43.

Standing, L. (1973). Learning 10,000 pictures. *Quarterly Journal of Experimental Psychology, 25,* 207–222.

Staubli, U., Thibault, O., DiLorenzo, M., & Lynch, G. (1989). Antagonism of NMDA receptors impairs acquisition but not retention of olfactory memory. *Behavioral Neuroscience, 103,* 54–60.

Stein, L. (1978). Reward transmitters: Catecholamines and opioid peptides. In M. A. Lipton, A. DiMascio, & K. F. Killam, (Eds.), *Psychopharmacology: A generation of progress* (pp. 569–581). New York: Raven Press.

Steinberg, H., & Summerfield, A. (1957). Influence of a depressant drug on acquisition in rote learning. Quarterly *Journal of Experimental Psychology, 9,* 138–145.

Stephens, D. W., & Krebs, J. R. (1986). *Foraging theory.* Princeton, NJ: Princeton University Press.

Sternberg, S. (1969). Memory scanning: Mental processes revealed by reaction time experiments. *American Scientist, 57,* 421–457.

Stevenson, H. W., & Stigler, J. W. (1992). *The learning gap: Why our schools are failing and what we can learn from Japanese and Chinese education.* New York: Summit Books.

Sticht, T. G. (1972). Learning by listening. In R. O. Freedle & J. B. Carroll (Eds.), *Language comprehension and the acquisition of knowledge*. Washington, DC: Winston.

Sticht, T. G., & James, J. H. (1984). Listening and reading. In P. D. Pearson, R. Barr, M. L. Kamil, & P. Mosenthal (Eds.), *Handbook of reading research*. New York: Longman.

Straub, R. O., Seidenberg, M. S., Bever, T. G., & Terrace, H. S. (1979). Serial learning in the pigeon. *Journal of the Experimental Analysis of Behavior, 32*, 137–148.

Suchman, L. A. (1987). *Plans and situated action: The problem of human–machine communication*. New York: Cambridge University Press.

Sulin, R. A., & Dooling, D. J. (1974). Intrusion of a thematic idea in retention of prose. *Journal of Experimental Psychology, 103*, 255–262.

Suppes, P. (1964). Modern learning theory and the elementary school curriculum. *American Educational Research Journal, 2*, 79–93.

Sutherland, R. J., & Rudy, J. W. (1991). Configural association theory: The role of the hippocampal formation in learning, memory, and amnesia. *Psychobiology, 17*, 129–144.

Swanson, L. W., Teyler, T. J., & Thompson, R. F. (Eds.). (1982). *Mechanisms and functional implications of hippocampal LTP* (Neurosciences Research Program 20). Boston: MIT Press.

Taub, E., & Berman, A. J. (1968). Movement and learning in the absence of sensory feedback. In S. J. Freedman (Ed.), *The neuropsychology of spatially oriented behavior*. Homewood, IL: Dorsey Press.

Teasdale, J. D., & Russell, M. L. (1983). Differential effects of induced mood on the recall of positive, negative and neutral words. *British Journal of Clinical Psychology, 22*, 163–171.

Terrace, H. S. (1963). Errorless transfer of a discrimination across two continua. *Journal of Experimental Analysis of Behavior, 6*, 223–232.

Terrace, H. S. (1972). By-products of discrimination learning. In G. H. Bower (Ed.), *The psychology of learning and motivation* (Vol. 5). New York: Academic Press.

Terrace, H. S. (1984). Animal cognition. In H. L. Roitblat, T. G. Bever, & H. S. Terrace (Eds.), *Animal cognition*. Hillsdale, NJ: Erlbaum.

Terrace, H. S., Pettito, L. A., Sanders, R. J., & Bever, T. G. (1979). Can an ape create a sentence? *Science, 206*, 891–902.

Thomas, E. L., & Robinson, H. A. (1972). *Improving reading in every class: A sourcebook for teachers*. Boston: Allyn & Bacon.

Thompson, R. F. (1986). The neurobiology of learning and memory. *Science, 233*, 941–947.

Thompson, R. F., Donegon, N. H., & Lavond, D. G. (1988). The psychobiology of learning and memory. In R. C. Atkinson, R. J. Herrnstein, G. Lindzey, and R. D. Luce (Eds.), *Stevens' handbook of experimental psychology: Vol. 2. Learning and cognition* (pp. 245–350). New York: Wiley.

Thorndike, E. L. (1898). Animal intelligence: An experimental study of the associative processes in animals. *Psychological Monographs, 2* (Whole No. 8).

Thorndyke, P. W. (1977). Cognitive structures in comprehension and memory in narrative discourse. *Cognitive Psychology, 9*, 77–110.

Timberlake, W. (1980). A molar equilibrium theory of learned performance. In G. H. Bower (Ed.), *The psychology of learning and motivation* (Vol. 14). New York: Academic Press.

Timberlake, W. (1983). Rats' responses to a moving object related to food or water: A behavior-systems analysis. *Animal Learning and Behavior, 11*, 309–320.

Timberlake, W. (1984). Behavior regulation and learned performance: Some misapprehensions and disagreements. *Journal of the Experimental Analysis of Behavior, 41,* 355–375.

Timberlake, W., & Grant, D. S. (1975). Auto-shaping in rats to the presentation of another rat predicting food. *Science, 190,* 690–692.

Tinklepaugh, O. L. (1928). An experimental study of representative factors in monkeys. *Journal of Comparative Psychology, 8,* 197–236.

Tolman, E. C., & Honzik, C. H. (1930a). "Insight" in rats. *University of California Publ. Psychology, 4,* 215–232.

Tolman, E. C., & Honzik, C. H. (1930b). Introduction and removal of reward, and maze performance in rats. *University of California Publ. Psychology, 36,* 221–229.

Tolman, E. C., Ritchie, B. F., & Kalish, D. (1946). Studies in spatial learning: II. Place learning versus response learning. *Journal of Experimental Psychology, 36,* 221–229.

Tolman, E. C., Ritchie, B. F., & Kalish, D. (1947). Studies in spatial learning: V Response learning vs. place learning by the non-correction method. *Journal of Experimental Psychology, 37,* 285–292.

Trowbridge, M. H., & Cason, H. (1932). An experimental study of Thorndike's theory of learning. *Journal of General Psychology, 7,* 245–258.

Tulving, E. (1975). Ecphoric processing in recall and recognition. In J. Brown (Ed.), *Recall and recognition.* London: Wiley.

Tulving, E. (1983). *Elements of episodic memory.* Oxford: Oxford University Press.

Tulving, E., & Flexser, A. J. (1992). On the nature of the Tulving-Wiseman function. *Psychological Review, 99,* 543–546.

Tulving, E., & Osler, S. (1968). Effectiveness of retrieval cues in memory for words. *Journal of Experimental Psychology, 77,* 593–601.

Tulving, E., & Pearlstone, Z. (1966). Availability versus accessibility of information in memory for words. *Journal of Verbal Learning and Verbal Behavior, 5,* 381–391.

Tulving, E., & Psotka, J. (1971). Retroactive inhibition in free-recall: Inaccessibility of information available in the memory store. *Journal of Experimental Psychology, 87,* 1–8.

Tulving, E., & Thomson, D. M. (1973). Encoding specificity and retrieval processes in episodic memory. *Psychological Review, 80,* 352–373.

Tulving, E., & Wiseman, S. (1975). Relation between recognition and recognition failure of recallable words. *Bulletin of the Psychonomic Society, 6,* 79–82.

Tversky, A. (1972). Elimination by aspects: A theory of choice. *Psychological Review, 79,* 281–299.

Ulrich, R. E., & Azrin, N. H. (1962). Reflexive fighting in response to aversive stimulation. *Journal of the Experimental Analysis of Behavior, 5,* 511–520.

Underwood, B. J., & Freund, J. S. (1968). Errors in recognition learning and retention. *Journal of Experimental Psychology, 78,* 55–63.

Underwood, B. J., & Freund, J. S. (1970). Relative frequency judgments and verbal discrimination learning. *Journal of Experimental Psychology, 83,* 279–285.

Vaccarino, F. J., Schiff, B. B., & Glickman, S. E. (1989). Biological view of reinforcement. In S. B. Klein & R. R. Mowrer (Eds.), *Contemporary learning theories: Instrumental conditioning and the impact of biological constraints on learning* (pp. 111–142). Hillsdale, NJ: Erlbaum.

Van Lehn, K. (1989). Problem-solving and cognitive skill acquisition. In M. Posner (Ed.), *Foundations of cognitive science.* Cambridge, MA: MIT Press.

Van Lehn, K. (1990). *Mind bugs: The origins of procedural misconceptions.* Cambridge, MA: MIT Press.

Vaughan, W., Jr. (1981). Melioration, matching, and maximizing. *Journal of the Experimental Analysis of Behavior, 36*, 141–149.

Venezky, R. L. (1970). *The structure of English orthography.* The Hague, Netherlands: Mouton.

Wagner, A. R. (1969). Stimulus validity and stimulus selection in associative learning. In N. J. Mackintosh & W. K. Honig (Eds.), *Fundamental issues in associative learning* (pp. 90–122). Halifax, Nova Scotia, Canada: Dalhousie University Press.

Wagner, A. R. (1978). Expectancies and the priming of STM. In S. H. Hulse, H. Fowler, & W. K. Honig (Eds.), *Cognitive aspects of animal behavior.* Hillsdale, NJ: Erlbaum.

Wagner, A. R. (1981). SOP: A model of automatic memory processing in animal behavior. In N. E. Spear & R. R. Miller (Eds.), *Information processing in animals: Memory mechanisms* (pp. 5–47). Hillsdale, NJ: Erlbaum.

Wagner, A. R., Rudy, J. W., & Whitlow, J. W. (1973). Rehearsal in animal conditioning. *Journal of Experimental Psychology, 97*, 407–426.

Wasserman, E. A. (1990a). Attribution of causality to common and distinctive elements of compound stimuli. *Psychological Science, 1*, 298–302.

Wasserman, E. A. (1990b). Detecting response–outcome relations: Toward an understanding of the causal texture of the environment. In G. H. Bower (Ed.), *The psychology of learning and motivation* (Vol. 26, pp. 27–82). San Diego: Academic Press.

Wasserman, E. A., Elek, S. M., Chatlosh, D. C., & Baker, A. G. (1993). Rating causal relations: Role of probability in judgments of response–outcome contingency. *Journal of Experimental Psychology: Learning Memory, and Cognition, 19*, 174–188.

Wasserman, E. A., Franklin, S. R., & Hearst, E. (1974). Pavlovian appetitive contingencies and approach versus withdrawal to conditioned stimuli in pigeons. *Journal of Comparative and Physiological Psychology, 86*, 616–627.

Wasserman, E. A., Kiedinger, R. E., & Bhatt, R. S. (1988). Conceptual behavior in pigeons: Categories, subcategories, and pseudocategories. *Journal of Experimental Psychology: Animal Behavior Processes, 14*, 235–246.

Watkins, M. J., & Tulving, E. (1975). Episodic memory: When recognition fails. *Journal of Experimental Psychology, General , 1*, 5–29.

Watkins, O. C., & Watkins, M. J. (1975). Build-up of proactive inhibition as a cue-overload effect. *Journal of Experimental Psychology: Human Learning and Memory, 104*, 442–452.

Watts, F. N., MacLeod, A., & Morris, L. (1988). A remedial strategy for memory and concentration problems in depressed patients. *Cognitive Therapy and Research, 12*, 185–193.

Watts, F. N., Morris, L., & MacLeod, A. (1987). Recognition memory in depression. *Journal of Abnormal Psychology, 96*, 273–275.

Watts, F. N., & Sharrock, R. (1987). Cued recall in depression. *British Journal of Clinical Psychology, 61*, 1–12.

Waugh, N. C., & Norman, D. A. (1965). Primary memory. *Psychological Review, 72*, 89–104.

Weisberg, P., & Waldrop, P. B. (1972). Fixed-interval work habits of congress. *Journal of Applied Behavior Analysis, 5*, 93–97.

Weisman, R. G., & Premack, D. (1966). *Reinforcement and punishment produced by the same response depending upon the probability relation between the instrumental and contingent responses.* Paper presented at the Psychonomic Society Meeting, St. Louis.

Weisman, R. G., Wasserman, E. A., Dodd, P. W., & Lunew, M. B. (1980). Representation and retention of two-event sequences in pigeons. *Journal of Experimental Psychology: Animal Behavior Processes, 6,* 312–325.

Wenger, E. (1987). *Artificial intelligence and tutoring systems: Computational and cognitive approaches to the communication of knowledge.* Los Altos, CA: Morgan Kaufmann.

Wertheimer, M. (1979). *A brief history of psychology* (2nd ed.). New York: Holt, Rinehart, & Winston.

Wertheimer, R. (1990). The Geometry Proof Tutor: An "Intelligent" Computer-based tutor in the classroom. *Mathematics Teacher,* 308–313.

Westbury, I. (1992). Comparing American and Japanese achievement: Is the United States really a low achiever? *Educational Researcher, 21,* 18–24.

Westbury, I. (1993). American and Japanese achievement . . . again: A response to Baker. *Educational Researcher, 22,* 21–25.

White, M. (1987). *The Japanese education challenge: A commitment to children.* New York: Free Press.

Wickelgren, W. A. (1974). *How to solve problems.* New York: W. H. Freeman.

Wickelgren, W. A. (1976). Memory storage dynamics. In W. K. Estes (Ed.), *Handbook of learning and cognitive processes* (Vol. 4). Hillsdale, NJ: Erlbaum.

Wickelgren, W. A. (1977). *Learning and memory.* Englewood Cliffs, NJ: Prentice-Hall.

Wilcoxon, H. C., Dragoin, W. B., & Kral, P. A. (1971). Illness-induced aversions in rat and quail: Relative salience of visual and gustatory cues. *Science, 171,* 826–828.

Williams, B. (1988). Reinforcement, choice, and response strength. In R. C. Atkinson, R. J. Herrnstein, G. Lindzey, and R. D. Luce (Eds.), *Stevens' handbook of experimental psychology: Vol. 2. Learning and cognition* (pp. 167–244). New York: Wiley.

Williams, J. P. (1979). Reading instruction today. *American Psychologist, 34,* 917–922.

Winston, P. H. (1984). *Artificial intelligence.* Reading, MA: Addison-Wesley.

Wixted, J. T., & Ebbesen, E. B. (1991). On the form of forgetting. *Psychological Science, 2,* 409–415.

Wolfe, J. B. (1936). Effectiveness of token-rewards for chimpanzees. *Comparative Psychology Monographs, 12* (5, Serial No. 60).

Wollen, K. A., Weber, A., & Lowry, D. H. (1972). Bizarreness versus interaction of images as determinants of learning. *Cognitive Psychology, 3,* 518–523.

Wolpe, J. (1958). *Psychotherapy by reciprocal inhibition.* Stanford, CA: Stanford University Press.

Wolpe, J. (1982). *The practice of behavior therapy* (3rd ed.). New York: Pergamon.

Wulf, G., Schmidt, R. A., & Deubel, H. (1993). Reduced feedback frequency enhances generalized motor program learning but not parameterization learning. *Journal of Experimental Psychology: Learning, Memory, and Cognition, 19,* 1134–1150.

Yerkes, R. M., & Dodson, J. D. (1908). The relation of strength of stimulus to rapidity of habit formation. *Journal of Comparative Neural Psychology, 18,* 459–482.

Young, R., & O'Shea, T. (1981). Errors in children's subtraction. *Cognitive Science, 5,* 153–177.

Yule, W., Sacks, B., & Hersov, L. (1974). Successful flooding treatment of a noise phobia in an eleven-year-old. *Journal of Behavior Therapy and Experimental Psychiatry, 5,* 209–211.

Zechmeister, E. B. & Nyberg, S. E. (1982). *Human memory: An introduction to research and theory.* Monterey, CA: Brooks/Cole Publishing Co.

Zimmer-Hart, C. L., & Rescorla, R. A. (1974). Extinction of Pavlovian conditioned inhibition. *Journal of Comparative and Physiological Psychology, 86,* 837–845.

Photo Credits

Chapter 1   Page 9: Sovfoto/eastfoto. Figure 1.5: From *Human Memory: Theory and Practice*, Allan Baddeley, Allyn and Bacon Publishing. Page 21: (left) Courtesy Pfizer, Inc.; (right) Courtesy B. F. Skinner. Figure 1.13: From *Comparitive Psychology: A Modern Survey*, McGraw Hill, Inc.,1973.

Chapter 3   Figure 3.9: From R. J. Herrnstein, D. H. Loveland, and C. Cable. Natural concepts in pigeons, *Journal of Experimental Psychology: Animal Behavior Processes*, Vol. 2., No. 4 (1976). Reprinted with permission. Page 99: From Jenkins, H. M. and Moore, B. R., *The Form of the Auto-Shaped Response with Food or Water Reinforcers*, photo courtesy of The Society for the Experimental Analysis of Behavior, Inc.

Chapter 4   Page 123: Courtesy Yerkes Regional Primate Research Center, Emory University. Page 144: Thomas D. Mangelsen.

Chapter 6   Figure 6.16: From A.G. Goldstein and J.E. Chance, *Perception & Psychophysics*, Volume 9, p. 237–24, copyright ©1970. Reprinted with permission of Psychonomic Society, Inc. Figure 6.22: From Premack and Premack, *The Mind of An Ape*, W. W. Norton & Co., 1983.

Chapter 7   Page 269: AP/Wide World Photos. Page 271: Borden/Sygma.

Chapter 9   Figure 9.7: From *The Mentality of Apes*, plate III, p. 128, Routeledge & Kegan Paul, Ltd., 1925. Page 347: Courtesy Dr. Gabriele Wulf and Dr. R. A. Schmidt.

Chapter 10   Page 385: From Premack and Premack, *The Mind of An Ape*, W. W. Norton & Co., 1983.

Chapter 11   Page 419: John Heller.

Author Index

Subject Index